I AM! I CAN!

The Daycare Handbook

By Grace L. Mitchell and Harriet Chmela

GREYLOCK PUBLISHERS
Stamford, Connecticut

Printed in the United States of America
Library of Congress Catalog Card Number: 77-80654
ISBN: 0-89223-039-8 (hard cover)

Produced by Immediate Press Inc., Stamford, Conn.
Illustrations by Ted Dewan
Photography by Anthony Lupo
Rudolf Mitchell
Peter Simmons

CONTENTS

Acknowledgements

We wish to express our deepest appreciation to the officers and board of the Living and Learning Schools and Green Acres Day School for cooperating with us over the past six years as we developed this book, never forgetting that while they gave freely of classroom "laboratory" space, ideas and criticisms from teachers, children and parents, that "I AM! I CAN!" was ours to use as we wished.

Over the years *hundreds* of teachers at Green Acres and Living & Learning Schools have contributed descriptions of successful teaching experiences.

Special thanks is due to Dorothea Gledhill who shared a wealth of art ideas and to Lois Marsh Carol for her inventive musical experiences.

Child care experts June McClure, Mary Winsky, Alice Herrmann, Margaret Sanstad and Betty Caldwell were generous as they gave several hours each in reading the lengthy manuscript and offered many constructive suggestions. Long before the final copy was ready, Glorene Edwards read and evaluated the work and it was her contribution which gave us the extra boost to see the project through, and to Chris Jennison who gave us the second nudge.

Deborah Mitchell Haney was truly "our girl Monday through Friday" during the first typing of the manuscript, but Debby was far more than a typist and the book reflects much of her very own creative energy.

Margo Childs, who typed the second draft, has been an invaluable aide in editing and helping to check and clarify details, details and more details... .

We are grateful also to James Hymes, Margaret Connett, Helen Buckley, Carol Glavin, Helen Campbell, Connie Greenman, Norma Cushman, and Barbara Delinsky for use of their original material in the book.

The authors individually wish to thank the following people:

Harriet has been rewarded with a wealth of creative ideas as she worked as a volunteer parent with her own children, Carl, Amy and Clea, and their colleagues and teachers at Franklin Elementary, Clarke Junior High and Lexington High Schools. "The process of teachers and children reflecting the enthusiasm and creative *vigor* of childhood back to me inspires me to continue helping children to achieve the best which life has in store for them. Undergirding all my endeavors was the philosophy given by Howard Thurman that "The growing edge" is ever present and awaiting nourishment. My own personal times to be creative and strive for musical excellence were constantly enriched by the inspiration and *drive* of Allen Lannom. And, of course, my husband, Albert, who daily assures me that "YOU CAN!"

Grace's philosophy of early childhood education grew out of her experiences at the Nursery Training School of Boston under the tutelage of Abigail Eliot, Ruth Taylor Stone,

Elizabeth Laurie, Martha Chandler, Beatrice Spaulding and Theresa Dowd. The writings of James Hymes and Katherine Read Baker reinforced and extended that philosophy. Sylvia Feinburg patiently and persistently helped me through the transition from rigidity to creativity. Beatrice Spaulding succeeded in convinving me that music is an *inherent right,* not a special talent—one which all teachers possess and can share with children!

An observer once said, "Watching Dolly Bailey work with children is almost a spiritual experience." She has provided us with a role model which has kept our standards high.

My dear friend, Helen Peterson, never wavered in her stanch support of my efforts.

No creative effort is ever possible without making demands on Donald, my understanding and sympathetic husband.

Finally, we would be remiss in not acknowledging our appreciation to one another! This was truly a cooperative effort; what one of us lacked the other seemed to possess. When one was "down" the other was "up." It would be difficult to point out "that was your idea" or "you wrote that" as every part of the book seems to reflect something of each of us. One seemed to pick up where the other left off over and over again. Most important of all, neither of us can recall a time when we were let down, discouraged, disappointed, hurt, upset or *uninspired* by the other. Writing "I AM! I CAN!" has been a good experience from start to finish. Finish?...we sincerely hope that this will become the *beginning* of many new ideas for all who use the book for the ultimate benefit of children!

Grace Mitchell and Harriet Chmela

FOREWARD

In 1970 I met George Naddaff, a busy executive who was searching for a nursery school for his young son. When he learned that there was a great shortage of such services in our area, he began to talk about starting a group of child care centers. I was, at that time, *totally involved* at Green Acres Day School and had no need for added work! But George was very persuasive. He soon convinced me that many children were deprived of the chance to grow and develop surrounded by other children in the care of professionals dedicated to bringing them the best that early childhood education could offer. He convinced me that together we could build a system of child care centers which would benefit from his talents as a businessman and my experience as an educator.

The Living and Learning Schools began the *adventure* and in five years they had grown to nearly thirty centers scattered throughout Massachusetts and Connecticut. It was George Naddaff's task to find these locations and oversee the construction, maintenance, equipping and staffing of the schools and to run them in an efficient, business-like manner.

My task was to create within those buildings a healthy environment for the growth and development of young children as well as to oversee the training of the staff responsible for such guidance. This meant that I would have to find the method which would successfully reach out with my philosophy to over two thousand children and several hundred adults. In my thirty years as director of Green Acres Day School I had built upon a philosophy of education which, as practiced and developed there, had nurtured growth not only in young children but in staff as well. My philosophy had stood the test of experience in a single school under my close supervision. But could it be translated successfully into writing, and be made to work in schools scattered many miles apart and each with its own particular problems and makeup?

At one time the word "curriculum" was offensive to many professionals in the field of early childhood education, myself included. It suggested structure, rigidity, and adherence to daily lesson plans, all of which contradicted the successful training of the very young. Now I was faced with the task of preparing a "curriculum" or worse still, a "manual" to help me with my task as the educational director of thirty schools.

The writing of *I Am! I Can!* began gradually as we collected ideas, tried them in classrooms, used them in training sessions, and revised them from many errors. The directors and staffs of those first laboratories proved to be an invaluable resource as they patiently guided each other through the tasks of day by day living with young children. We all worked together, teachers, directors, drivers, cooks, secretaries, parents, specialists, financial advisors and business people. It soon became apparent that all were vital to the success of each aspect of every school.

As the centers grew, the children and the staff grew, and the book began to grow and became a unifying resource of practical ideas; an overall "Curriculum Guide and Manual" which those involved in every aspect of child care could use as a tool and point of reference.

I was also aware that unless such a guide was *practical* and *readable* it would not be of use to those busy people who are totally involved in the care of young children. The style of writing had to be informal and rich with anecdotes of actual experiences to appeal to a teacher looking for still another way to enlighten a child. This task came easily to Harriet Chmela, a parent of three youngsters. Her introduction to early childhood education began with their days at Green Acres. Her enthusiasm as a parent volunteer combined with a special talent for writing brought us together as co-authors. She gained also from her experiences as a classroom teacher both at Green Acres and later in the first Living and Learning School. She enriched her background through courses in child growth and development. Harriet's ability to bring sparkle, humor and creativity to my thoughts makes *I Am! I Can!* the kind of practical handbook necessary for those who work with the very young.

This book *grew out of a real need* and we believe its success will be reflected in many future child care centers and teacher training programs. But in the words of the adage: "The proof of the pudding is in the eating." We invite our readers to visit any of the Living and Learning Centers and Green Acres Day School in Waltham, Massachusetts to witness the results of our efforts. We offer a generous share of what we have learned in the hope that more and more children (and adults!) will be rewarded with a healthy *I Am! I Can!*

Grace L. Mitchell

PHILOSOPHY
I AM! I CAN!

"I AM! I CAN!," a philosophy of education stated in four short words. Its goal—to help children develop into confident competent human beings, endowed with a zest for life and an appetite for all that life offers. In sharp contrast to, "sit still," "keep still," "do as you are told," "I AM! I CAN!" invites and encourages children to think creatively, to use all of their senses, to become *involved* in every facet of learning.

To have a strong "I AM," every individual must accept his 'self,' *his* weakness, *his* strengths. Above all, he must take pride in his uniqueness. When the "I AM" is secured, the "I CAN" within surfaces and sparks the discovery of each individual's full potential for living and learning.

Growth is a continuous process from the moment of birth until the final breath is drawn. While growth patterns may reach plateaus, seeming to stop for a rest, they inevitably move, upward or downward. These patterns are sharper, more distinct during the early childhood years. *At birth*, an infant is barely aware of himself as a human being, yet before he reaches the age of five, he has become a contributing member of a socially organized society! Conception and birth are but glorious beginnings in the continually unfolding miracles of life. The rapid intellectual, physical, social and emotional *realization* during the first five years of human life is a significant, and indeed, miraculous fact, as expressed in this poem by Mamie Cole...

> "I come into your world
> about which I know nothing,
> How I came I know not,
> Why I came I know not,
> I am curious,
> I am interested,
> I am the child."

A *tiny baby* has only one means of expressing his feelings—he cries! When he is uncomfortable and his needs are met for food, warmth, LOVE, he develops into a being who trusts in the world and what it does for and to him. On the other hand, if his world treats him harshly, if his needs are too often denied or unfulfilled, he acquires a fearful, angry, or suspicious nature. His "I AM" experiences its first major setback.

By the time a child reaches nursery school, his personality traits are well on the way to being established. He is a person—a 'self'. Whether or not he has learned to *like*, to be *comfortable* with, to TRUST that *'self'*, will greatly influence his ability to adjust to a larger society. As the product of his environment, his attitudes will reflect the relationships of his experiences. the child's growth *output* will be in direct relationship to this past *intake*, whether trusting and secure, or fearful and cautious.

INTELLECTUAL

I AM!

PHYSICAL

EMOTIONAL

I CAN!

SOCIAL

This diagram depicts a frame for the "I AM! I CAN!" philosophy, expressed through this manual. The four sides of the square represent the four areas of human growth and development.

A child grows in all four of the areas shown on the square, but growth will not be balanced or equal in all areas at all times. At times, physical growth is rapid, at others the child is bursting with ideas and creative energy. There come times when the need for the companionship of his peers is uppermost in his mind. He will work hard to master the techniques of human relationships. Emotional growth will reach highs and lows. Parents and teachers must constantly recognize and *accept* these highs and lows. A sudden spurt in one direction will often be followed by a plateau—a quiet time when the growing individual seems to be absorbing and *assimilating* what he has experienced.

The weavers of oriental rugs deliberately alter their patterns so that designs are not perfectly balanced nor evenly matched, believing it presumptuous for man to attempt to create a *perfect* object—a right reserved for the Deity. Human beings also fall short of perfection, never becoming totally 'normal', 'well adjusted', 'emotionally stable', 'socially well integrated', 'intellectual geniuses'. The circle within the square, representing the 'well-rounded' personality is as mythical as the perfect human being. Indeed, a world full of smooth, round pegs fitting neatly into smooth, round holes, would be dull. In a world abounding in variety and differences, there is a place for everyone. Each must seek *his* particular place in life which will allow him to use *his* individual skills, talents, interests... .

The human personality in the developing process might be compared to the human figure in the growing process, bulging in one spot today, sticking out in another next week, or being completely lopsided for an extended period. The I AM! I CAN! philosophy does not seek to create perfect patterns of the square and circle, but uses the image symbolically to define a basic philosophy of education.

Teachers have a responsibility to *constantly* evaluate *total* development, to be aware of the progress of each child in each area of growth at *all* times. They observe* children with this pattern in mind never "losing a child in the crowd," never seeing him solely as a part of a "class" rather than as an individual.

There will always be children who capture attention because they are at one end or the other of the continuum, either bright attractive children who make teaching a joy or those who because of their behavior, appearance, or personalities are hard to love. In between these two extremes are the "deprived" children, neither "good" nor "bad" enough to capture attention. They go through life unnoticed, never receiving the extra attention which might develop the potential which might alter their "middle group" status. The true TEACHER sees and appreciates each and every child for his own "SELF." Each child deserves and should receive his *full share* of time and attention. The teacher recognizes, however, that it is never possible or necessary to give each an *equal share,* since needs vary, both within groups as well as within individuals at any given time. The child who is suddenly spurting with creative energy after a month of easy social growth needs to be stimulated and encouraged as he explores this new growing edge. The teacher who has kept lap and arms ready for the shy and insecure child, intuitively senses when to pull back and let him go at that moment when he begins to pull away. He may even need a gentle nudge of encouragement to realize his freedom.

A teacher will know which child can climb the ladder to the tree house, which one is poorly coordinated; which one is trying to find a friend, cautiously working his way into becoming a social being. It is important also to recognize the not so cautious biting, kicking and grabbing behavior of a child as another form of social awakening. When this aggressive child is helped to discover that there are better ways to get a bike than by pushing another child off, one of the sharp corners of his developing square will be chipped away. A teacher can "read" the frustration of a child through his behavior. As the child, guided by the teacher, accepts the fact that life is not always exactly as he wants it to be, another sharp corner of the developmental square will be rounded. Teachers need to help children recognize that they can *change their position* on the developmental ladder, that there is always another rung, and that they can become strong enough to climb higher.

An imaginative teacher, who always found a use for everything, took the outside casing off a hand drier and used it for painting. By placing a paper plate holding globs of paint on the center post of the motor children were able to spin beautiful designs. Each child who tried it expressed joy, wonder and delight. Thinking of the plate as the child, the teacher as the pivot and the paint as the various aspects of the daily program, the emerging beautiful designs of human personality can be observed.

What happens to the child who is constantly put down, denied inherent rights to physical and psychological protection, thwarted, discouraged, labeled by society as a misfit or a dropout? This continual assault on his "I AM!" will make it impossible for him to become a competent, confident, contributing member of society. The lack of decent self image has cheated them out of their "I AM!" and they have long since lost the desire for the "I CAN!" They may, in fact, go into reverse and use the "I CAN!" in negative ways in an attempt to "pay back" the society which has mistreated and cheated them.

"I AM!" "I CAN!" — A child who knows this takes a giant step toward creating a better world. Seeding the "I AM!" through a child's whole being and spirit when he is young is the very essence of "becoming." "I AM!" comes through development of a healthy ego, through accepting oneself as a worthwhile human being—needed, wanted, liked, LOVED—and at all times, in all things—BEING ACCEPTED AS IS. This means that differences are not only taken for granted, they are recognized and appreciated. They are also nurtured through program; through helping parents to accept differences; through jealously guarding the rights of each child to be respected for himself.

The "I CAN" begins to develop only when the "I AM" is established. Every teacher thrills to see that glow on the face of a child when he succeeds and strives to create opportunities for each child to succeed in some way—EVERY DAY!

The growing edge of the young child is tender, it can be fed from many springs, it can stretch out and reach up. The blights and droughts of bad experience have not yet damaged its roots and they are strong and eager to branch out in every direction, into every crevice seeking nourishment. Rachel Carson says in "A Sense of Wonder," "The years of early childhood are the time to prepare the soil." This is the task of those who work with young children. Everything written in the pages which follow is intended as a guide to stimulate healthy growth in all areas of development, enabling each child to say—"I AM! I CAN!"

* See Observation and Recording.

DEDICATED TO
LOUISE BARNICLE

We learned through her that fun and adventure happen in every place where children are... *we* must look and listen for it to see it. Louise represented the child in all of us—she had fun! She took time to *listen* to the children.

Illustrator—Ted Dewan, a sixteen-year-old, Lexington, Massachusetts high school student, has had a strong interest in drawing since 1967. As a fourth grader in 1971, Ted began to depict life through his comic strip character *HAROLD*® , who appears occasionally in *I AM! I CAN!* Ted has won prizes in the Regional Scholastic Art Awards sponsored by the *Boston Globe* and has earned two gold keys as well as a blue ribbon in the 1976 National Student Art Awards. He submitted the winning layout for the "Our Town" poster competition at Lexington High School in conjunction with the production of the Thornton Wilder play by the Lexington Theater Company.

Part I

Chapter 1

Who Are The People?

THE YOUNG CHILD

The young child comes to the teacher as a puzzle, holding the promise of a beautiful picture when "completed." At times the teacher will feel the frustration of solution, unable to find a missing piece, always careful not to make assumptions when an important bit of information, a piece of the puzzle, seems to be a perfect fit but will not fall smoothly into place. The child, unlike the puzzle, will never be seen in totality by his teachers. The separate bits of information or pieces of the puzzle will only aid in the solution, perhaps completing the outer borders into which his life-long growth will blend the final picture.

Who is He?

The early years of childhood are a time of sorting out the *many* pieces of this human being puzzle. The wobbly edges of social awakening, the rounded shapes of physical progress, the straight edges of intellectual growth, the bright and subtle shades of emotional color.

Teachers of the very young are among the first *important* outside influences who will begin to work on this puzzle. How? Where are the clues? One of the most significant and valuable tools will be *observation,* sometimes by standing off to gain an impression of the total developing picture, this growing child; at other times, by careful and close scrutiny of a single facet, a tiny puzzle piece. First, the teacher must understand the full scope of the developmental patterns of the growing child. How he grows? Why? When? Where? The following section, Ages and Stages, describes these patterns in greater detail, giving the over-all panorama of early childhood. The individual child must be placed against this background and accepted as HE is. Facts, beginning with his name, age, phycial make-up, family setting, experiences, cultural heritage, neighborhood, have all contributed to his "I AM." A teacher learns as much as possible before he comes into the classroom and can sometimes determine that this child came from a world he has learned to trust; another from an environment which has taught him to be wary and suspicious.

What are the *facts*?
Dick is the youngest of five children.
Frances is an only child.

Mary's mother is pregnant.

José speaks Spanish, very little English.

Bill has had one year in a highly structured nursery school.

Steve recently moved from far away.

David was recently in a car accident and is still having nightmares.

Peter's mother is dead and he has had to adjust to the requirements imposed by a succession of housekeepers, while coping with his loss.

Kathie is confused by the impending divorce of her parents and the relationship of her mother and a new boyfriend.

What does the teacher *see*?

A physical being—short, tall, fat, agile, clumsy, pale, ruddy, freckle-faced, blue-eyed, elfin brunette, pixie blond.

An emotional being—screaming, stamping a foot in anger, dictating demands to a mother, whining, silent, cowering, whimpering.

A social being—darting from people to things, sampling all with enthusiasm and interest; a shy, scared child, clinging to a mother.

An intellectual being—unusual vocabulary, book reader, questions and answers about classroom materials, recognition and writing of letters and numerals, response to directions.

This background information is merely the outer frame for the puzzle, much more is needed. The teacher will never know all of the facts and must be cautious not to jump to conclusions, based on circumstantial evidence. At first it is enough just to be THERE, comforting, caring, keeping the child close for as long as the security of this presence is needed. But the teacher is also in a position to contribute to change by constantly seeking to understand behavior, needs and growth patterns through careful observations. (See Observations—records and discussions with staff members and parents.)

Ages and Stages   We speak of a developmental approach to early childhood education. What specifically does this mean?

First—it acknowledges that there are certain behavior changes which go along with physical change. The poor muscular coordination of the two year old must certainly have some bearing on the developing "I AM! I CAN!," as does the acquisition of new skills at age five.

Second, we recognize the individual growth patterns of each child. Thus we refrain from saying to Jim, "Sammy can do it and he is six, why can't you?"

Third, we recognize that the environment in which the child is growing will have a direct effect on his development.

Since individuals are as different as their fingerprints we will not find a single child who is exactly on target in all four areas of development at a given point. The "norms" which have been developed as a result of research can be compared to the inch marks on the ruler. They give us a measuring stick, which we must constantly remind ourselves is to be used only as a guide to understanding behavior.

The inquisitive teacher might ask "Who said so? Who determined that it is "normal" for a four year old to use so much silly talk?"

A simplified answer is that observations of 100 children, identical in chronological age, will show that a given behavior will be common to about 50%, twenty-five percent will not have reached that level, and another 25% will have gone past it. Thus, the behavior of the middle group will be described as typical for that particular age.

There is some danger in attempting to allocate certain characteristics to age levels.

"The book says a child SHOULD be able to... by the 38th month." And so his parents either push him to make sure he doesn't fail the test when the fateful date arrives or they worry because he didn't even seem interested in that particular performance. Either way the child is vaguely aware of pressure, that he is not quite measuring up to the expectations of the adult he wants to please—be it parent or teacher, and his "I AM" suffers.

An observer in a school with chronological age groupings will see the same basic pieces of equipment in each class, i.e., blocks, paint and clay, water and sand tables, housekeeping and library corners. If each of these teaching tools is being used in the same way at each age level, something is wrong. But when the classroom observer can see a growth progression in the use of a toy such as the "stacking up/knocking down" block play of the twos to the sophisticated block village of fives then "growth and development" becomes more than educational jargon. Developing children use the same materials in different ways at different age levels.

It would be well for the teacher of young children to keep in mind the word "kindergarten"—thinking of the classroom as a "childgarden." The gardener does not try to pattern his plants, he accepts their differences in growth and design. He protects them, nurtures them, but lets them do their OWN growing. He does not poke at the seed to make it sprout more quickly, or try to pull open the first buds. Sometimes it seems as if parents and teachers are using hedge clippers in an attempt to make a smooth, even "look alike" product—a "group" that merges into a solid blob. In a child care center we will see as many varieties of children as there are flowers, each one interesting and beautiful in its own right.

It is important for a child care worker to know that growth is not always vertical. There are distinct swings in the stage of development, described by Pitcher and Ames* as periods of *equilibrium* and *disequilibrium,* and by Piaget as *stability* and *change.* Advance knowledge of these reversals in behavior will enable the adult to accept it with some degree of equanimity, to see it as a normal phase of growth rather than discouraging regression.

Teachers need to know what they may expect of a child in physical development, in social skills, in ability to cope with emotional frustrations and in cognitive development. They need a nodding acquaintance, at least, with more than one theory of learning. They need to analyze the similarities and differences, and to measure them against their own observations. They need to THINK about children, understand them and to constantly seek the perfect match, offering enough challenge to keep the child involved, but never so much as to discourage him; enough stimulation to help him reach higher, but avoiding the blanket of discouragement which falls when the standards are set too high. Teachers need to recognize that when a child has ample opportunity to creep before he walks, when his experimentation with sounds is recognized as a pre-requisite for speech, and when his scribbles and blobs are appreciated as a stage in development leading towards representation—the fruition of these graduated experiences will be rich and satisfying. When teachers push, prod and accelerate this natural development they diminish the child's "I AM!" and stifle his "I CAN!".

The following descriptions of and suggestions for each age are intentionally simplified. They will serve to give the beginning child care worker a minimal understanding of reasonable norms. There are many books and pamphlets listed in the bibliography which are recommended for additional reading. Consulting more than one is advisable, observing that descriptions and opinions will vary. The beginning teacher will gain more from reading material when it is combined with frequent consultations with experienced staff members.

TWOS—A two-year-old may be compared to an adult with his first powerful, shiny, new car, who is anxious to get out into the country and test it, who wants to be strong, to have power, and who wants everything NOW—twos cannot wait. He is inclined to be inflexible, rebelling against any changes in routines. This is not the best time to attempt to introduce new foods or new rules. The two-year-old has a basic need for repetition and will want the SAME story, the same fingerplay.

The two-year-old will frequently say "NO," and has a real need to bump against adult reactions to find the limits within which he can safely operate.

Twos are negative but once their "I AM" begins to take root and emerge, this negativism starts to subside, a healthy and welcome sign to frustrated parents and teachers.

"Do it myself" is a common response, and adults should provide clothing, toys, challenges which enable him to satisfy this urge and develop the "I CAN."

In planning an environment for twos we recognize their need for gross motor activity. Indoors they need toys to push, pull and roll; a small climbing apparatus, some steps, places to crawl through, and climb over, safe high places to let them feel big and places to crawl in and feel small and cozy. *Twos are still nesting.*

We set the stage for later learning when we give these young children toys that enable them to "do"; to act on the environment rather than placidly observing it. Children who, at an early age, gain satisfaction from success in manipulating objects, are less likely later on to be content to sit before the TV set. They are too busy, too involved.

Playgrounds for twos should, if possible, be separated from those of threes, fours and fives. They should be fenced and not too large! Older children can be invited to visit the little ones in their play yard, helping or just playing with them. At the right time, and with plenty of supervision, twos may venture into the larger areas for brief periods, and it will be an adventure. The needs for pushing and pulling are met outdoors with carts and wheelbarrows. Properly scaled climbing apparatus will develop large muscles.

Emotionally twos need the lulling effects of swinging and rocking, which we wean older children away from just as we gradually take the pacifier away from the baby. Rocking horses or boats or chairs are safe places from which to watch and relax before venturing forth into active participation. Indoors water play, clay and fingerpaint provide a release which is stimulating to the imagination and also relaxing. It is inappropriate to ask twos to sit at a table and "perform" as a group. Twos should not be expected to sit and wait until everyone is served, at snack or at lunch, and it is NOT advisable to keep them waiting in line for the toilet. *NOW is their byword!*

Socially the two year old is very much an individual. He is interested in others, but has yet to learn the rules for interaction. Solitary play moves to parallel play, and as he gains the ability to tolerate interference with his wishes he will play in small groups. At first the two-year-old cannot share, and parents are urged NOT to let him bring toys to school (not to be confused with a security blanket—see SEPARATION).

For twos the world is frighteningly big and so they need fences, physical limitations and the security of a solid "home base." A wise teacher builds trust in the two-year-old by giving him freedom and at the same time holding him close with the apron strings of love. (Read: *The Runaway Bunny,* M. Wise Brown, Harper.)

Twos need warm loving adults with quiet voices, comfortable laps—always ready when they need them, welcoming yet not coming on too strong, attending but not smothering with attention. There must be enough adults for each child to identify with one person, "MY teacher." The classroom and teacher of twos provide a warm extension of the home.

THREES—Certain ages seem to represent plateaus in development. Threes and sevens fall into this category. They are not periods of rapid change or violent struggle but of quiet maturing and even growth. Returning to the analogy of the plants, they might be compared with the time of blooming—lovely to look at and pleasant to have around. Twos love to resist. Threes want to conform. They use "yes" as freely as "no." Twos take—threes can give.

Threes have gained quite a bit of self control and will conform to reasonable rules. Cooperative and easy going, they are secure in relationships with others. At this age they are able to enjoy cooperative play with other children, can wait for turns and share toys and can often carry their social techniques into helping others. "Paul will give you the bike after he has a turn" or "John is the father and I am the mother, but you could be the baby." They often go to great lengths to please peers in order to have a friend and become very upset when told "I won't be your friend." Threes are capable of sympathy.

A three year old stands between the physical and social "lumbering" of twos and the gusty exuberance of fours. Not too much, not too little. He has advanced enough in physical coordination to gain new satisfaction in climbing to new heights and is able to sit down for periods of time to develop manipulative skills. He can dress himself, with a little help and he likes to help others. He has a good sense of rhythm. Threes are ready to work. Many threes recognize their names—some will want to copy them.

Initiative emerges during the third year. Their "I can do it myself" is an expression of a new sense of power and should be encouraged but at the same time they are inclined to dawdle, requiring infinite patience. Many a conflict at home is brought on when a parent, in a rush, says, "I can't wait for you to do it yourself." School is the place, sometimes even the haven, where time and patience are afforded this young plant needing room to grow, allowing each new leaf to open by itself.

Threes are eager and responsive—a pleasant interlude before they reach the next stage of disequilibrium which occurs sometime in the latter part of this year... .

The three and one half year old does a complete turnabout. He is in a state of disequilibrium, caused mainly by growth factors. Some of these are poor coordination, stumbling, falling, fear of heights, stuttering, tics, crying, whining, and making demands such as "Don't look!" "Don't talk!" "Don't laugh!"

Because he is socially unsure, he goes about making friends in a backwards manner by excluding others. His group life is stormy and so it is a time when imaginary companions emerge. When the truly delightful three year old disintegrates into an insecure, disagreeable bundle of problems, his bewildered parents often send him off to a pediatrician; or ask themselves where THEY have gone wrong. This is a time to keep in mind that "this too will pass," to give extra doses of love and understanding, equal doses of attention, and as much patience as one human being can muster. Often being forewarned makes acceptance of these changes possible and helps to avoid confrontation over the less desirable traits.

In the child care center, the doors between threes and twos should be opened as soon as both groups have had a chance to settle in; at first for a short period of time, gradually extending the time until doors are open most of the day, allowing threes to go back to be little again, to feel "bigger than." At the same time the twos who mature quickly and are ready for more activities and new experiences are not held back by their less adventurous peers. They can venture into the new world, returning when they have had enough.

FOURS—Fours seem to be bursting at the seams in all four sides of our square. They are restless, whirlwinds of activity, constantly out-of-bounds! There are times when we wish their "I AMs" and I CANs" were not so positive. It is at this age that the physical part of the circle within the square bulges. Fours have great need to use their big muscles and they *do* in running, leaping, and jumping, climbing, hanging and swinging, pushing, pulling, and tugging. Physically rambunctious, they will roll, tumble, hit, punch, wrestle, chase each other, fall down, ending in a heap of arms and legs. The wise teacher accepts this hardworking play as a vital need and makes provision for it or suffers the consequences!

Fours are discovering maleness and femaleness and are greatly interested in trying on many new roles in their dramatic play. While adult tolerance of interchanging sex roles has certainly improved in the past few years, it is well for teachers to remember that in this year fathers, who were able to look the other way when their three-year-old sons played with dolls, may begin to impose different standards at four, with pressure to "be a man" or engage in what have traditionally been considered male sports. Little girls are often envious of maleness and will go to great lengths to be like boys in appearance and behavior. Parents may have to live with a "tomboy" for a time!

The social behavior of the four-year-old is likely to be quite uninhibited. He is bold, brassy, aggressive, noisy and swaggering, likes to swear and is out of bounds with adult relationships. Fours may kick, bite, snatch and grab, and they express their feelings in very explicit terms, both to their peers and adults. "I hate you," "You stink," and name calling are a part of their social patterns; they swagger, boast, and can be defiant and TOUGH. It can almost be guaranteed that at some time during this year they will engage in bathroom talk, and worse. Despite current acceptance in our culture, four letter words still sound inappropriate when they come from the mouth of a child, and even though the meaning may be hazy, there is no question that fours soon learn how to use such language as a manipulative tool. They know and appreciate inappropriateness, and will be as defiant as they dare. Punishment has little chastening effect.

On an emotional level, fours will get along better with other children, are less sensitive, less vulnerable, less demanding. Never stopping for a breath, gusty fours accompany action with verbal outbursts and threats.

Imagination knows no reasonable limits at this age. There is a thin line between fact and fiction and at times they may be very silly. A four-year-old is most creative and shows understanding of real life. Fours are interested in what people do and how adult roles are learned.

Intellectually, a four-year-old tries to sort out real from unreal. He makes real drawings of airplanes. He may be confused about what he sees on television, and what is real, or near, and how quickly it might affect him or his security. At this time, his coordination begins to improve, as do his skills. This is often a catching-up time.

There may seem to be a wider span in the interest of fours than at some other ages. Some have an urgent need to PLAY—hard, active play, and absolutely cannot be persuaded to sit down and work at table activities. Others are so eager to learn to read and write, that they need to be encouraged to expand their interests to the physical and creative. Fours need materials which enable them to try out their own ideas rather than mechanical gadgets.

Parents and teachers of fours need to hold the reins loosely but pull up tight when necessary. They need unlimited patience and the ability to stand NOISE. *Fours are fascinating, frightening, and fun!*

FIVES—*At this age, the child enjoys life.* It is a period of stable equilibrium. Gone is the out-of-bounds exuberance. The five-year-old is secure, calm, friendly and not too demanding, exuding self-assuredness.

Five is a year of awareness. Suddenly it seems that the light breaks through. Kathy, who was blind, had been in nursery school for two years when she asked her mother, "Am I blind?"

"You know, Kathy, I have always told you that you are,"replied her mother, "Why do you ask?"

"Today in school Jackie said, 'You can't play with us because you are blind'. What IS blind?"

Her mother, who thought she had succeeded in helping Kathy to adjust to her difference, started all over again to explain what it means to "see with your hands instead of your eyes."

David looked at Mark and said, "Gee, you're black."

Mark replied, "Gee, you're white.", and that was that!

At four, it seems that children literally do not see differences. At five, they see them and talk about them quite openly.

Television opens doors and fives are more ready to walk through. Fives need to talk about the alarming things they see—riots and violence. The riot in New York is frightening to children who do not know whether New York is just outside their own backyards or far away. News of floods and earthquakes may have a profound effect on young children. Though they realize that their own home is safe, at the same time they wonder, "Will the flood come here?" "Is the earthquake going to knock over my house?" Young children often carry unnecessary burdens of worry or fear as they ponder such questions in silence, not knowing what or whom to ask.

Socially, five-year-olds have a sense of "We-ness" that allows them to work cooperatively on murals and to plan and coordinate projects. They can combine forces, work together, give and take leadership. Their interest in people extends to their professions and the type of work they do. The interest is all encompassing including the economics, exchange of goods and types of service.

When at election time a voting booth is set up, fives vote with great seriousness. They are capable of understanding democratic controls and developing attitudes about them.

Fives are curious, filled with a sense of industry, their wheels humming. They have an insatiable desire to learn and usually carry their interests to greater lengths than fours.

Fives want to read, write, do arithmetic. Many a kindergartner has gone home at the end of his first day of school, devastated because, "I didn't learn to read!"

There is a tendency for adults to think of kindergarten as a preparation for first grade. Too many five-year-olds are hushed, required to walk in a line, sit a whole morning in school by teachers who do not appreciate these lively, active, curious, social, imaginative beings. This is sad and unnecessary. Fives are not PRESCHOOLERS marking time and getting ready for magical age of six. Fives are vibrant, active, learning DOERS. The best preparation any child can have for formal learning is a happy and wonderful busy year of "five-ness."

Post Kindergarten Children

In some child care centers, older children will be present in the mornings until the public schools open and again at the end of the elementary school day. Some will be enrolled during public school vacations, when parents are at work or at school. Sometimes it is possible to have separate staff for these children, but often they will be under the supervision of the regular staff. A few words about age characteristics of older children may be helpful in planning appropriate activities geared to their needs.

SIXES—The six year old child is going through a period of physical body changes which may cause fatigue. Programs should be planned carefully, allowing for alternate activity and rest. As he adjusts to school and new standards which may cause insecurity and fears, he needs reassurance that his teachers DO know where he lives and he WILL go home.

Special friends may be very important but may also be shifted frequently. The six-year-old can have close relationships with only a few at a time. Sixes are quick to observe fairness and will tell teachers, "You're mean!" or "You're bossy !" or "You're wrong!". On the other hand they also lavish affection and praise and will tell teachers how wonderfully artistic, pretty, strong, etc. they are. Models are extremely important, but the six-year-old should be accepted *as he is* and comparison with other cildren should be avoided at all costs.

Intellectually, the six-year-old is building his set of values and needs space, materials and time for imaginative play, free from the imposition of adult standards, but with help close at hand when he asks.

Sixes enjoy all forms of literature and respond enthusiastically to music when it is shared in a spontaneous, voluntary way. They will participate in a joyous manner provided it is not a regimented, directed activity. They should be encouraged to make up patterns and rhythms and compose their own songs, allowing their own creativity to be expressed.

SEVENS—This age group is very similar to the threes. Both seem to be settling in as they quiet down, and are less noisy and violent. They are more cautious and purposeful.

Physically there is an increase in fine-muscle control, for example, they can tie a shoe lace tightly enough to stay tied. Sevens can sit still longer as they enter this period of perfecting skills. Once accomplished in a skill, they will add extra hazards and fancy approaches to the feat. Large constructions will often be well planned and built.

The seven-year-old is more in competition with himself than with his peers and this is not a good time to present competitive sports or new social or mental activites. *Seven should be allowed to set his own pace.*

Socially the seven-year-old is changing. His "I" turns more to "WE" and he truly enjoys working and playing with other children, but he works better in smaller groups where *they* have a chosen leader rather than being under the direction of an adult leader.

Emotionally, seven is very critical of his own work; rather than have it criticized by others he will beat them to the punch by saying, "That's crazy" or "This stinks!" He is very sensitive to riducule, failure or loss of prestige. When the going gets tough, seven will tend

to withdraw, using statements such as, "O.K. stupid, do it your own way. I'm quitting!"

On an intellectual basis, sevens are good listeners and good talkers. They like to make up plays to perform for audiences. Memorizing is possible but they prefer taking roles of characters with their own words and gestures and they are more apt to take time with costumes and properties.

Sevens enjoy stories, poems, riddles and limericks more than at five or six and can understand the moral of fables. Stories with plots and suspense intrigue them. They relish the opportunity to use swears and vulgarities and love rhymes and couplets that are tinged with off-color connotations. This is a good year for creative writing and, if physical effort is standing in the way of setting down their own thoughts, the use of a tape recorder for taking dictation and a willing "secretary" to type these thoughts will help to encourage this creativity.

EIGHTS—Age eight has similarities to age four. Eights are well coordinated, smooth, quick on their feet as the physical side of their square becomes predominant. They have not yet reached the awkwardness of preadolescence; their reactions are sure and secure. This is a good age to teach simple, rhythmic dances and games. Eights have bursts of energy which are like gusts of wind but can also stay with an idea or project. They are most cooperative, especially when they help to initiate the plan.

These youngsters want to be liked socially and are willing to work at it and make some concessions. While a seven-year-old might walk away from problems, an eight-year-old will stand his ground and muddle through. Even though it may involve some fighting and tears, he can accept the consequences and learn from them. During this year, the child begins to acquire social aptitude and insights, learning best from his peer group.

Eights are strong on clubs, expecially the secret type. They become very conscious of "In" and "Out" groups. The eight-year-old forms crushes and chooses adult models. He likes being with adults and enjoys conversation with them.

Emotional development at this age is delightful to behold. The physical exuberance, wide-ranging curiosity and awakening knowledge of self offers rich rewards to adults who accept and understand the eight-year-old's flair of bravado and enthusiasm.

Who Needs Child Care?

The reasons for providing child care are as varied as the persons who use a service. For some parents, the goal is purely to provide a social experience for the young child. they believe that even the most devoted adult cannot fulfill the need of a child for good "shoulder-rubbing" social contacts with his peers.

For others, day care is a vital need; it is indeed the *extended home* for the child of the parent who must work, or is unable to provide proper care. For single, divorced or separated parents, day care provides an invaluable partnership. In these cases, teachers supplement much-needed, missing support.

There is a basic difference between these two groups of parents; one seeking child care by *choice*, the other, through *need*. Both may carry a common burden of guilt for having entrusted their child to someone else's care. Society says:

"Children need their mother's full attention."

"When you became a parent you took on a responsibility."

"There is no substitute for the love of a parent."

All in part true, but society often fails to recognize that life-long parental care need not mean twenty-four hour long "togetherness." The apologetic, guilt ridden parent needs to understand that *it is normal to need to be away from a child.* Furthermore, the child neither wants nor needs to be at home with a parent all day. A mother who questions this should try keeping her child home from nursery school for a few days. By the end of the second day, if not sooner, he will be yearning for the companionship of his peers and to return to the far more exciting and *challenging* life with them. Also, it often happens that after three hours apart, the relationship between parent and child is strengthened, particularly if there can be some carry over from the school activities. One child, who had a lovely home, devoted parents, and many toys expressed her need for nursery school very practically, "but Daddy, my toys don't talk."

We do not suggest that full day care, in a group setting, is right or good for all children. Ideally, each set of circumstances would be evaluated and each child placed in the situation which would best fill his needs. Some would stay home with mother, some might react well to a family day care home, and some would thrive in the environment which provides a social climate and mentally challenging program.

So much for the parents and their respective needs or desire for child care. Let us now turn to the other side of the issue and look at the child care center and its first and foremost need—children! Whether the service is furnished by a tax supported institution or private non-profit or private for profit providers, enrollment is an important consideration.

Enrolling The Child

A child care center, whether private or public, cannot exist without children. Even if it comes into existence because of an established need it may take time for parents to accept it as an answer to their own particular problem. The most effective promotion for a center is through satisfied parents. It takes only one negative response to turn a chain reaction in the wrong direction.

Often, the voice answering the telephone gives the first impression and the director should personally train each person who is allowed to take calls. If the voice is curt, sharp, dull, vague, indifferent or flippant, the caller recieves the impression that this is the attitude of the center. (The training of such personnel should involve some role playing with the more experienced person acting as the caller.) It takes skill and training to put oneself in the place of a parent and show sincere interest, concern and enthusiasm. A director may never know the damage caused by one individual who "knows it all" and who tries to give information outside his realm of understanding. It is best to say, "I'm afraid I can't answer that question. May I take your number and have someone call you back?" or "I think you would find it more satisfactory if you could visit the school. Would you like to make an appointment?" A log book for recording all such inquiries and follow-up procedures would be an invaluable aid in the training of personnel who will be trusted with this important role.

The owner of a private center may find it difficult to say to a prospective client, "We want your child's first experience to be the best possible, and so we urge you to visit many centers, and try to choose the one which is *right* for *your* child." The risk of losing a customer is far outweighed by the sense of confidence that parent will have when he does return to enroll his child. The parent-school relationship is established on a firm footing of TRUST.

First impressions are lasting—and so the warmth of the welcome a parent receives on his first visit will say something to him about the treatment he can expect his child to receive. In a very busy, large day care center a man walked in with a small boy perched on his shoulder. There were several people about—all very much preoccupied with their own business and each one assumed that someone else knew who he was. He stood there, looking slightly embarrassed; he did not have an appointment—he did have a problem—and he needed the attention of someone who could help him with a solution. In this particular case, only the director could really help this man, but until she could be found, someone needed to provide the necessary support and warmth. *Everyone who works in a day care center in any capacity should be tuned in to people!*

It may seem ridiculous to say that the steps to the entry should be swept daily, but it is this attention to detail which speaks for the quality of what goes on inside. The foyer, hallway or office should be attractive, inviting and *clean.* In a particular center, which comes to mind, there was a table (at child level) immediately inside the door which always had some appropriate scene on it. It contained objects which could be touched and admired. The wall behind the receptionist's desk was bright with simple designs and pictures made by children, attractively mounted and changed frequently. News items on a bulletin board conveyed to parents a further impression of the activities of that center and tacked to the board were "What We Did Today" slips (see Evaluation) which invited the visitor to sense some of the activities taking place.

The director did not wait to be summoned by the receptionist, but came out to greet the visitors and the tone of her voice and genuine warmth of her smile and handshake reflected the overall tone of the center. As they walked through her school, she interpreted the program with enthusiasm and obvious pride. She called attention to some of the children's work on display and explained its purpose and motivation. Occasionally, she asked a child or teacher to make the explanation. Her genuine concern for children was evidenced in the way she touched one or slipped her arm about another, admired a new outfit, inquired about a family situation or a new baby at home. To the children she was not "that person who sits in the office," she was their FRIEND!

When a parent indicates positive interest in a school, it is incumbent upon the director to go over each step in the enrollment procedure, to show each required form and explain its purpose. There is a temptation to skim lightly over references to financial obligations, such as payments when a child is absent, vacations, days off due to inclement weather, etc. THIS IS MOST UNWISE. Terms should be clearly stated on the forms and the director should call attention to them and answer any questions thoroughly. Terms for withdrawal should also be discussed. It is common practice to ask for the payment of the first week (or month) at the time of enrollment, and some schools also require payment for the last month. The parent should be given a duplicate of the application he has signed.

For the parent who is still undecided, it is wise to have a packet of materials ready, which might include an application, medical forms, and permission slips and copies of recent parent bulletins. The latter gives a true picture of what goes on in the center; it speaks of ACTION in contrast to an elaborate brochure which often makes unrealistic promises.

Enrolling a child in nursery school often represents a major step to young parents. When this occurs several weeks or months before the actual date of attendance, it is important to maintain contact. This can be done by spacing out the mailing of bulletins with details about health, safety, clothing needs, dates, etc. It is a good promotional gesture to choose a distinctive stationery so that even the child will recognize a letter from "MY SCHOOL."

The director's responsibility does not stop with the formal procedure of enrollment. There is a professional obligation to guide the parent in choosing the best time for admission, particularly when it is a first experience for the child. Again, the director must be careful not to let the need for more children take precedence over good advice.

When the child is enrolled it is important to stress the need for gradual orientation and to describe the procedures to be followed. Some parents will say, "Oh, that won't be necessary, I leave him with strangers all the time and he never makes a fuss." It is not always easy to convince this person that the effort required will be rewarded with the peace of mind which comes when a child makes a good adjustment.

Various procedures for the gradual orientation of a child into a center are described in the following section. There is no tried and true recipe for this process. Each center must develop a workable plan appropriate for its own clientele and services.

Orientation   What is the purpose of orientation? It is an opportunity for the teacher to help the child feel that school is a good place, where there are people who like him, who will take care of him, and where he will find friends. As the child interacts with his new environment, the teacher can observe the behavior, interest in surroundings, and involvement with the parent. These first impressions should not be for the purpose of forming quick conclusions about levels of development but rather, early clues in the solution to the puzzle described in section A and future working relationships among teacher, child and parent.

The following plans have been used in various centers.

A PROMISE—As more and more half-day nursery schools are extending their hours to meet the needs of working parents, the previous concept of a school year beginning in September and ending in June is being replaced with a transient enrollment which takes place fifty-two weeks of the year. *Every day is the first day of school for hundreds of children in child care centers.* Mothers, anxious to get to their jobs, or afraid of asking favors from a new employer, are inclined to argue about the need for gradual orientation. The conscientious director, placing the well-being of the child first, will be prepared to stand firm. This conviction comes from the experience of the author, Grace Mitchell, who recalls: "During World War II, I was involved in setting up a war nursery. Often gradual orientation was impossible. A mother, frantic with worry over her husband, lonely, and desperately in need of employment would call in the evening and ask that her child be picked up the next day. Many a child left home early in the morning, in a strange station wagon, to go to an unknown place, with someone he had never seen before. The emotional reactions were as might be expected, soiling, wetting, vomiting, tantrums, withdrawal, and extreme aggressive behavior. I promised myself then that never again, when the exigency of the war situation was lifted, would I be party to such emotional trauma and that *there would always be a process of gradual orientation.*"

Open House

In a nursery school, where the majority of children are enrolled by the year and begin in September, Open House might be held on the day before school actually opens.

Upon arrival, each parent is given a page of suggestions for simple activities to do with the child. Some teachers provide "busy work" for parents, such as making name tags, labeling clothing, decorating boxes for extra clothing, or assembling the pieces of a homemade game. In this case the intent is to divert the attention of an overanxious or overprotective parent away from the child, giving him a chance to react to the environment in his own way and at his own speed. This allows the director/teacher/assistants to focus attention on the new child.

Student teachers and substitute teachers might be used on this day to cover indoor and outdoor areas and activity centers, allowing lead teachers the freedom to observe the children and talk to the parents about program and goals.

Color coded name cards for the children are a necessity. Colors indicate grouping, "home room," transportation, A.M. or P.M. scheduling, etc. In some cases the parent and child might help to make these tags. Teachers should explain that during the first few days of school it is very important that the child wear a name tag. Attractively decorated, it will become a special possession of the child and he will wear it with pride. Tags taped or pinned to the child's *back* are an aid to staff in learning names and calling the child by name, reinforcing the security of his "I AM!" and "they know who I am." Attaching the name to the back allows greater visibility, as children are often bent over tables, standing at easels or sitting on the floor bending over a work project.

On this special day of orientation, the environment should be carefully arranged, with enough toys available to make it interesting but not enough to cause confusion. Toys with small pieces should be kept out of reach until the children are ready to care for them properly. Covers of games might be on display to suggest their future use. Neatly printed signs and charts in each interest center help to explain the curriculum to the parents. Each interest center should provide some simple activity for the children to do, to handle, explore or create.

Some effort should be made to introduce the children to as many of the daily routines as possible. Cubbies are chosen as the child and mother arrive, marked with names, a picture or a snapshot (previously requested) of the child. The bathroom should be located right away and the teacher will assure the child that, "You may go any time you need to but I will remind you in case you forget."

When juice is served, the children are usually ready to sit together at one table, as long as the parent is visible.

Extra clothing should be marked and stored where the children can see it. Decorated shoe boxes, uniform in size and marked with the same symbol as the child's cubby, can be kept on a high shelf in storage space. Cots and blankets are marked and their use explained to the children who will stay for extended hours.

It will be a bonus to teachers and aides if a staff member can take candid snapshots of parent and child together on this first day. These provide a helpful record to the director and other staff members. During the first few weeks, such snapshots might be used in name games or just displayed on an attractive poster, where the children can find their own picture and some of their friends. Later, these pictures should be attached to the permanent record cards.

Each child should be encouraged to make something to take home to strengthen the bond between home and school. (See Adjustment.)

At the conclusion of the open house, staff, who will be working together, will meet and share their observations and make the first entry on the record cards. (See Observation and Recording.)

The procedure might be identical to the above but spread out over a two or three day period with a smaller number of children coming each day, allowing the staff to become better acquainted with individual children before they all come together as one group.

There will be rare times when emergencies, such as sudden illness or death, make it necessary to accept a child without this introductory process. The director will be particularly sensitive to the needs of this child, providing comfort, reassurance, a soft lap, whatever is needed to let him know that he will be safe and that one person is watching over him.

SUDDEN CHANGE—A father, a busy executive, called a school one night at eight o'clock. "My wife left me, and the housekeeper I employed also walked away today, leaving my son with a neighbor. I have just heard about you and your school. Can you take my boy tomorrow?"

The director explained the usual procedure, expressing sympathy for his problem but stressing the fact that this boy must also be feeling very insecure and deserted. "Yes, I agree," replied the father, "and I will be able to spend some time at the school soon, but tomorrow I have an important meeting, one which I just can't postpone." "Then I suggest," replied the director, "that you bring your son at seven o'clock and stay until you have to leave. Hopefully, by then he will be willing to let you go, but if he isn't ready I think it would be better for you to take him with you and let your secretary take care of him in the next office, than to let him feel deserted again." Because he had no alternative, the father reluctantly agreed. The staff were advised about this child's special needs and made every effort to make the boy feel welcome and to interest him in some activity. He was a bright, alert child. At nine-thirty he smiled at his father and said, "O.K. Dad, you can go now." A grateful and relieved father left, saying, "Please call me at work if you need me. I can see how important this was and I must say I feel very comfortable about leaving my son in your care."

HANDOUT FOR PARENTS—Welcome! Today you are sharing in your child's first day of school—an historical event! Perhaps you are both a little nervous? Relax! Enjoy this first visit. Below is a list of activities for you to join in with your child. We hope they will help you both feel more at ease:

1. Make name tags for both you and your child.
2. Explore the room area. Show him where the bathroom is located.
3. Introduce him to his teacher.
4. Greet and chat with other parents and children.
5. Find the cubby area and point out his very own.
6. Leave extra clothing and a snapshot of your child with one of his teachers, or put them in the cubby.
7. Explore the playground and encourage your child to play on equipment. Please do not urge when he seems reluctant even though his peers might appear to be advanced acrobats and gymnasts. He knows when he is ready.
8. Enjoy some refreshments with him.
9. When he seems comfortable and at home perhaps you can use the opportunity to visit the office to make sure you have completed all the necessary forms:

> Application
> Health Form
> Parent Questionnaire
> Authorization Forms
> Special Needs Form (if applicable)

Also check to make sure you have paid all fees or made arrangement for payments.
10. Is there anything special you think the teacher should know about your child? If you have an opportunity, have a brief chat with your child's teacher alone, or schedule a conference with your child's teacher during these first few days or weeks.
11. During your visit, you will be taken on a tour of the building.

12. PLEASE do not leave your child without telling him. NEVER sneak away! Again, we say, WELCOME to a new adventure!

The First Day

A young child's first experience away from home is as earth shaking to him as the first trip across the ocean to an adult. Feelings of anticipation and excitement are mingled with fear and apprehension. Recognizing this, the staff will consider every tiny detail which might pave the way for a happy experience.

It is important to step into his skin, to try to relate it to a remembered experience such as the first day on a new job.

"I AM NOT GOING"—When this emphatic statement comes from a child who has been looking forward to going to school, who sat on the doorstep waiting for the school bus for the first four days, and who has come home with exciting accounts of events and new friends at school during these first days it is, to say the least, disconcerting. The immediate and obvious reaction is to say, "something must have happened yesterday." But when the anxious parent calls the school and is told that all had apparently been fine, distrust creeps in. "They must be keeping something from me."

Adjustment

"Did you leave your lap at home?"—Fourth-day-itis is a normal, predictable reaction from a young child just starting school. Parents, when forewarned, are better able to cope with it if it happens. Very simply, the child wants to be grown up, to venture out of the nest, but he isn't quite ready to cut the umbilical cord for good. HE needs help in taking this decisive step. This may not necessarily be in conscious thought, but the doubt and hesitation are very real. For the child who is having a hard time making the transition, the teacher might consider the following suggestions:

1. Ask the parent to come in and spend time reassuring and working along with the child.

2. Often, working parents of day care children cannot leave work to stay. Can they come for breakfast? Is there a close relative, neighbor or friend who might come?

3. Objects brought from home may help. David began his first school experience in an all-day program at a time when things were quite mixed up at home. Father had a heart attack and mother had gone to work to support the family. David carried with him his father's necktie, his sister's scarf and an old silk blouse of his mother's. One by one, as he became more comfortable, he relinquished these symbols of home and family.

4. "Homework" assignments bring home and school together, i.e., "Bring something blue from your bedroom." (Pin a note to the child explaining such assignments and inform parents of their significance.)

5. Help children feel important by giving them notes and bulletins to deliver to their homes.

6. Suggest that an insecure child bring a carrot to feed the rabbit. Thinking about the bunny diverts his attention from his anxiety.

7. Invite the parents to drop by the school on the weekend and let the child show "his school" to brother, sister or grandparents.

When all else has been tried, it may be time to suggest a firm stand to the parents, who, in their anxiety, have placed too heavy a burden of choice on the child.

Gene had carried on for three weeks. Mother was ready to make the break. She could see that all was well in school and that Gene needed to be a part of the school, not clinging to her. The teacher suggested that she say to him, "I will take you to school BUT when we get there, I am going to go home. Daddy and I have *decided* that it is good for you to go to school. I know that it is a good place, that you can have fun there. I know the teachers are kind, they all like you. I know the children are your friends. So, I WILL GO HOME!!!"

As expected, he did cry. The teacher put her arms around him and held him firmly while the mother walked away. Then, in a voice so soft he had to stop crying to hear her, the teacher said, "Have you ever seen green noodles?" He looked at her in astonishment. Taking his hand, she went inside with him to where the children were coloring uncooked noodles with paint, later gluing them on paper in different shapes and designs. After watching for a few minutes he joined them. He went home at noon, proudly bearing his paper. He *did not* give in immediately, but each day he fussed with less vigor and soon was one of the group.

For another mother the suggestion backfired. She had made it clear that her son WOULD go to school, and that she would expect him to get into the station wagon when it appeared, even if it meant a scene. As she stood at the door the following morning, he marched bravely down the walk. When he reached the car he turned and came back, smiling. "He forgot to kiss me goodby," his mother thought, whereupon he reached up and pulled her hair, kicked her in the shin, and proceeded to go calmly off to school.

Sarah, the only child of a mother in her late forties, was putting on a real tantrum each morning. "What should I do?" asked the desperate mother. The next morning the teacher said to Sarah, "We will walk down to the car with your mother to say 'good bye'." When the mother drove off, Sarah struggled, screamed and carried on. In a minute she said, "Has she gone yet?" "Yes," said the teacher. "O.K. we can go back to school then!" said Sarah, calmly—and that was that.

For one child who seemed inconsolable, water play was the relaxer. He spent the whole morning playing at the sink full of soapy water, blowing bubbles through a straw and pouring water from one container to another. For another child, the guinea pig was often a source of comfort; it was smaller than she was, soft and cuddly.

There is no single answer to the problem of separation. Teachers must follow their intuition and keep in close communication with the parent. Sometimes it is the parent who needs help. Mothers often find it hard to let go of the apron strings, and may treat the child like a yo-yo, letting go but holding on, saying goodbye but lingering on. "Mommy wants you to be happy, you don't have to stay unless you want to." This puts an impossible burden of choice upon the child, and the teacher or director must be able to explain this to an anxious parent. A teacher will *never* allow the parent to slip away from the child when he has been distracted.

Erik Erikson's "Basic Trust" is never more important than in this initial school experience. The parent must TRUST the teachers—the child must TRUST the teachers AND his mother—and the teachers must TRUST that the parent really wants what is best for the child.

A word of encouragement! Just when parent and teacher are about to give up in despair, the problem disappears. The child settles in as if he had been going for years and all is well. Not infrequently this change comes about when another new child enters, crying, and the once insecure child sees himself as a veteran.

There are different ways of crying, and an experienced sensitive teacher can discriminate between anger, "I'll show my mother she can't do this to me!"; attention seeking, "I forgot to cry for a minute, I must turn it on again"; whiny, fretful crying which says, "This is the only way I have found to get attention"; or real panic which may seem that the parent will have to come and stay until the child is ready to make the break.

When that is the only solution, the teacher should try to put the parent to work. "Would you please get the juice from the kitchen?" or "Could you sit at the table with these children?" Her child can stay nearby but should not feel the full forces of parental attention, anxiety or impatience. The parent can break away gradually: "Miss Jones wants me to go out and get some crackers. I WILL be back in a few minutes" or, "I am going to the store. I will come back to take you home." The time will come when the child will say, "You can go home now." Reassure the parent that this will eventually happen and reassure the *child* that he can grow to make the separation. "It's tough to grow sometimes, it hurts, I know how badly you feel but I know the hurt will go away soon." "You must be a *very* special person to love your parents so very much. They love you, too, and know that coming here is a good thing for you to do."

Often the simplest way to help a child through this period of adjustment is to let him know that you understand his feelings. "I know you feel very sad. You miss your mother." It is best to make a single statement and let it go. Later you might say, "You want your mother. She has her work to do and we have things to do at school. How would you like to make a picture to take to her?"

Keep reassuring the child that the parent WILL come. Above all avoid any suggestion

of criticism such as "You are a big boy now, why don't you stop crying and come and play?"

A mother tells this story:

> When it was necessary to find full day care for my little girl I investigated many centers. With my background in early childhood education I thought I could evaluate and choose the right one but I was wrong. The center I chose was immaculate, well equipped and the director seemed to have a philosophy which agreed with my own. I could not understand it when my child came home in tears every day and woke up at night crying. I asked my husband to drop in during the day to talk to her teacher and observe her there. When he arrived at 11:00 a.m. one day, Joan was not in sight.
>
> "Where is my little girl?" he asked.
>
> "Oh, she is in the crying room." The teacher indicated a room off the classroom with a one-way observation window. Looking through my husband saw Joan scrunched up in a chair weeping. "How long has she been in there?" he asked.
>
> "Oh, nearly all the time since she arrived." (To our horror we later discovered that this meant since Joan had arrived on her first day, and not since she had arrived that particular morning!)
>
> "What have you done to help her? Has anyone given her something to play with? Talked to her? Tried to comfort her or interest her in the program?"
>
> "We don't have time for that. The other children have managed to adjust in a reasonable length of time. Joan knows she can come out when she stops crying."
>
> Our child came home that day and was removed from the center immediately!

A supervisor observing in a nursery one morning noticed a crying child. "Why is that little boy in the corner crying?" she asked. "Oh, he wants to sit in my lap" was the reply. "Did you leave your lap at home today?" she asked. "if I let *him* sit in my lap, every child will want to" was the answer. "Every child doesn't need your lap, but HE does!" advised the supervisor.

Every adult working with children must be ready and willing to extend warm, physical comfort to a disturbed, uneasy, unhappy child. It may be a comforting arm or just a look which says, "I know how you feel; I understand." *No teacher of young children ever leaves her lap at home!*

A Child Goes Forth — Picture yourself as a small child…leaving the nest for the first time, breaking the "umbilical cord" from mother…eager, excited, frightened, anxious. What will make you feel comfortable?

1. An *anchor*…one teacher who is YOURS…one person who knows *you*…calls *you* by name…who lets *you* stay nearby until *you* are ready to venture away.

2. *Sameness*…the *same* things in the *same* places. Cubbies with identification…a color…a picture…or best of all…a snapshot of the child.

3. *Routine*…knowing what is coming next and having someone explain each new experience before it happens.

4. *Limits*…"this is as far as I can go NOW"…literally and in my actions. There is someone who will stop me if I cannot control my behavior…there are physical barriers to stop me if I wander too far.

How can we PLAN to meet the need of this child?

A daily schedule adhered to as closely as possible in the beginning. The *same* people in the *same* places at the *same* time.

CONSISTENT rules. A limited number of activities. Each new experience to be introduced with an explanation of procedures — rules to be observed. (Read: *Curriculum is What Happens,* by Laura Ditmann, pub. NAYEC, Washington, D.C.)

What can the teacher do?

1. Make a color code name tag for every child…and match the color to his teachers.

2. Study the record cards before school opens and KNOW each child's name and something about him. "you have a sister…a little baby sister…do you help Mummy take care of her?"

3. Know whether this child comes to school with his mother, his father, or a driver — and if the latter, know who it is. The teacher will know what time he comes and leaves.

4. The teacher will have talked about and rehearsed and memorized daily procedures so well that these first days will go like clockwork and the atmosphere will be calm and serene. Children are mirrors — they will reflect speech, diction, manners and mannerisms and they will be secure if the teacher is calm and self-confident.

5. The teacher will be aware of the need for coordinating daily plans with those of the total staff.

6. The teacher will stretch—giving some part of herself to each child—never allowing them to be lumped into a 'group!'

The Child with Special Needs "Everyone Is More or Less"

Grace Mitchell tells this story:

In 1949, the mother of a totally blind boy wanted to enroll him in our nursery school at Green Acres. I refused, feeling that my staff and I were not properly trained for this responsibility. A few months later, I attended a meeting of nursery-kindergarten teachers, where the speaker was from the Division of the Blind. She urged us to integrate blind children into our schools. This was during the period when a frightening number of cases of retrolental fibroplasia were emerging, and before the cause had been discovered. She tried to allay our fears, saying, "You need not be afraid of a blind child running in front of the swings. A blind child will not run until he is thoroughly familiar with the environment." Before I left that night I assured the speaker that we would be willing to accept a blind child, and would offer a scholarship, if necessary. A few weeks later, Joy came to us, a beautiful three-year-old with a sparkling personality and no vision. Joy not only brought *joy* to our school, but she opened the way for hundreds of other children who had physical or emotional handicaps.

Now, in 1976, it has been recognized that these early years in a child's life are important years for learning for ALL children, but especially for those with special needs. Their education has been mandated by federal law, and whenever possible they are integrated into private and public school classes. The guidelines we had established before this took place are still applicable. We include them with the hope that they will offer encouragement to teachers and parents and smooth the way for many exceptional children. ALL children are special!

When considering the child with a physical or emotional "difference" think first about what might be termed "normal." Some people have 20/20 vision, some need glasses, others distinguish only light and dark, some are blind. Some people hear the tiniest sound, some have partial hearing loss, others need hearing aids, some receive only vibrations, others are deaf. One person has a physcially well-built, beautifully coordinated body, another is awkward and clumsy and yet another, deformed.

Visual and auditory perception are matters of degree; physical and emotional "perfection" and norms must be determined in the context of each person's life.

Who then can say what is "normal?" Everyone is *more* or *less*, in many ways. Everyone needs to be able to live in a so-called normal world, in as nearly a normal way as possible. The way he is accepted in that world, his way of functioning in it BEFORE he is five years old plays a large part in determining his future.

Children take differences in their stride; often they seem not to notice them. The exceptional child who is able to attend school before he is five has a distinct advantage. Though his family may coddle and protect him, he will have to "earn his way" with his peers. A four-year-old classmate does not give in to the tears and demands of the exceptional child. On the other hand, the young child DOES develop a casual consideration which is not at all like the maudlin sympathy of an adult which is so degrading to a person who is different.

Contrary to the often voiced opinion, young children are NOT deliberately cruel. The life of a so-called "normal" child is enriched by an encounter with one less fortunate. In the following examples, it would be hard to say which child received the most benefit.

Steve was an aggressive, active four-year-old, always pushing to be first and not above using his strength to get what he wanted. One day when the teacher said, "Time to go in for juice now," Steve started off at a run as usual, stopped suddenly, went back to the sand box and walked quietly BESIDE Kathy, who was totally blind. He did not take her hand but talked to her as they walked along, leading her with the sound of his voice.

Lenny was severely disabled, a victim of cerebral palsy. His gait was loose and distorted, his speech almost unintelligible, and facial grimaces which he could not control contributed to an appearance which was, at first sight, shocking. But Lenny had a good mind and an indomitable spirit. He earned the respect of his seven and eight-year-old campmates. Richie was everything Lenny was not; strong, agile, well-coordinated, handsome and popular. As they lined up one day for relay races, the counselor noticed an act which was so carefully disguised he had to see it himself several times to be sure. In each race, Richie carefully aligned himself opposite Lenny, and when their turn came he slowed down just enough to give Lenny a fair chance, but not enough to be noticeable to the other contestants.

Most children accept difference without any great "to do" and that is the greatest gift they can give to the child with special needs. But what about adults? Can they give the same kind of casual acceptance? Not always, and because the attitudes of the children will be influenced by the behavior of the adults, the teacher's willingness to have a special child enter a group should be heartfelt and sincere. It takes a new kind of courage. A blind or crippled child cannot be helped to independence by a teacher who insists on holding his hand. He must be allowed to fall, to find his own limits, develop his own patterns for daily living. Certainly, the adult watches over the safety of the deaf or blind child who may not be aware of danger, but without being overprotective or unduly solicitous.

Before the special child is enrolled at least one, and probably several, visits should be made to the school, allowing everyone who may be concerned with his care to observe him. There is much to learn about his previous experience, habits and special needs before a decision is made. It is cruel to accept a child and decide later that it was a mistake. The exceptional child will be "put down" many times throughout his life span. The destruction of his "I AM" should not start at this early age.

What criteria should be used in determining eligibility?

1. It must be agreed by all concerned that this particular school will be right for this child, and that he will be good for the school.

2. The child must be able to function without demanding more time and attention from an adult than is fair to the other children.

3. If a child must be lifted, carried, or is incontinent and has to be changed frequently, one extra adult should be made available. If it is his mother, she should be willing to take the training offered to volunteers (see training program for parents).

4. A professional referral should be required, with the promise of continued communication and help from the doctor, clinic, guidance counselor or social worker. This is particularly important when the problem is emotional. Often when behavior is becoming intolerable, the professional can give information or advice to the staff which makes it possible for them to continue.

Jay, aged six, refused to take part in any activity. After a reasonable length of time, his mother was called and she disclosed that he was seeing a psychiatrist, information she had not previously shared. The doctor came to school and explained Jay's problem to the staff. "This little boy needs to have a detailed description of each part of your program BEFORE it happens. Take time before each change to explain what will happen next." With the cooperative efforts of a concerned staff, his parents and the doctor, Jay made great strides in that year.

Even when the greatest care is taken before the child is enrolled, there will be cases in which it becomes necessary to "let go." It is very hard for a teacher, who has invested so much time, effort, and 'self' to make this decision. When the director observes that a child is draining the extra reserves of a teacher, it is time to step in and set the wheels in motion for an alternative plan. Sometimes, complete withdrawal is not necessary, but instead the hours can be reduced or additional help provided.

When the Child Is Withdrawn From School

All of the foregoing suggestions are relevant when a director knows before the child is enrolled that a problem exists. But what happens when a teacher says, "I wish you would observe Susan. I can't put my finger on the problem and perhaps there isn't one, but I don't feel comfortable about her."

The director should find time to observe Susan, preferably over a period of several days, and at different times of the day. At the same time, she requests that Susan's teacher or one of the assistants keep a diary, noting in detail Susan's development in all four sides of the square, making special notations of specific incidents to clarify observations. The director is now in the position of a person putting together a jigsaw puzzle, and needs to assemble all of the pieces, carefully studying all the known information on the application and health card. The person who drives Susan is consulted. Perhaps the answers will disclose something about the family:

"Her mother is never there to greet her."
"The baby sitter looks so harsh."
"Her father always brings her to the car in the morning."
"There is a "For Sale" sign on the house."
"I have to keep her on the front seat beside me."

The director stores up these bits and pieces, being careful to give no information and make no assumptions. If, as the picture develops, the director feels that a conference with the parents is advisable, the request is made with great caution, choosing words that will not give the impression that something is terribly wrong. It may not be easy to find the casual tone and words, but this is important! The conference should be held as soon as possible after the request, recognizing that the parents *will* be disturbed. To call on a Friday, burdening the parents with a whole weekend to worry is cruel and unusual punishment and the child may be the target of their anxiety.

At the appointed time, the teacher is freed from the classroom to be present: "I have asked Susan's teacher to join us since she knows Susan much better than I. Notes of observations made of Susan here at school will explain why I asked for this conference." (This is where specific examples are essential; On Tuesday, at eleven a.m., she... .)

The director, while guiding the discussion, gives the parents plenty of time to talk and ask questions. Both director and teacher carefully avoid words which might suggest labels or diagnosis, i.e., "hyperactive," "hostile," "withdrawn," etc. They are prepared to make suggestions for procedures they will now try in school, which the parents can also try at home. They will establish plans for daily communication and for a follow-up conference at an early date.

If the problem is so severe that the child cannot remain in school, the director should be knowledgeable about resources for professional help. A pediatrician or social worker should be the first to be consulted. In all cases, the complete cooperation of the school is promised: "Please tell your doctor to feel free to call us." or "If they would like a written report, we will be glad to send one." or "Perhaps they will send someone to observe — at school."

There are three rules to follow: 1) proceed with caution; 2) make no assumptions; and 3) draw no conclusions. Many times behavior which seems bizarre will straighten out as the child becomes more comfortable in school. Frequently, the mere fact of communication and cooperation between parents and school will solve the problem. *On the other hand, it is unprofessional to ignore serious problems in the hope that they will either go away or with the feeling that "We'll only have to cope with this until June."* Such an attitude is unfair to the child and his parents.

When, for the good of all concerned, the decision is made to request that the parents withdraw the child, the staff will experience some emotional reaction. The personal investment made on behalf of a child makes it very hard to accept failure. Director and staff must reassure each other that every possible effort has been made.

In this case, a detailed, written report should be submitted to the parents, the professional source of referral, and a copy kept in the school's file.

PARENTS

Where the love of the parents, the knowledge of the professionals, and the joy of the child become mingled, there truly is rich soil for growth...

Who Are Our Parents?

How wonderful that the professionals in child care and teaching have, in the past two decades, come to recognize that parents are PEOPLE with the strengths and weaknesses that make the human personality varied and interesting. The care and guidance of a young child in a day care center cannot be truly effective unless each parent is known as someone other than the biological creator or custodial guardian of that child.

Describing a "typical" parent is as impossible as defining a "normal" or "average" child. Each is unique and yet each is a vital contributor to the life of his child. This is evident in the way he views his responsibility toward the education of his child and his attitude toward discipline.

For the purpose of this manual, "parent" defines the person who is immediately responsible for the care of a child, be he biological, adoptive, custodial, foster, neighbor, grandparent or guardian—a parent is that person who, through the daily care of a child, vitally affects his growth and development.

It is easy to type parents and children according to what we know of their social, cultural, or ethnic background. Sometimes teachers over react to a single incident. Seeing a tired mother of a three-year-old slap or yell at her youngster in the supermarket tends to color the attitude of the observer who may forget that during moments of stress all parents are guilty of aggressive behavior and that even the sweetest child has his "bratty" moments.

Creating the Partnership   A working partnership must be just that—working together in every way possible to extend parent into the school and teacher into the home.

We begin by just having the WELCOME MAT out. If a parent does not feel welcome early in the year, he will begin to draw back and leave things to the school. In very subtle ways, the school must keep the mat out:

"Good morning, have you got just five minutes to see our baby gerbils?"

"Come in and see what happened when we put out three colors of paint for the first time."

"You're early today, why don't you hear our story before you take Peter home."

"If you have an extra half hour some morning, come and have juice and watch the children cleaning up; your daughter has the whole crew organized."

These casual comments make a parent want to come a little early or stop in for brief visits. A day care center should never be a parlor for invited guests but rather a country kitchen where the neighbors drop in unexpectedly for a slice of apple pie and to chat. Someone once defined the difference between Eastern and Western hospitality as: In the East when you see a strange car in your neighbor's driveway, you stay away "because they have company." In the West when you see the car you go over and say, "I came over to meet the company." Whether or not Easterners accept the definition as correct, let us see its example and be like *Western neighbors with warm, country kitchens.*

Parent Involvement—It is one thing to talk about parents as partners. What do you do if they don't choose to "dance with you?"

In too many situations, our traditional separation of church and state has unconsciously carried over into separating school from home. There are some who insist that parents should be the alpha and omega of every school situation. On the other side are those teachers who demand autonomous control of the child once he comes through the school door. Both parents and teachers jealously protect their authority, not realizing that they are setting apart the two most important guardians of a child's growth and development. When they work hand in hand, a child recognizes this cooperative relationship and responds to it as positively as a growing plant to the sun.

Parents expect the family doctor, who has spent long years in training, to use his medical knowledge to benefit his patients and the most intelligent parents respect the right of the educator to apply his training to his work; BUT, the good doctor relies on information given him by the parent and doesn't assume that in one short visit to his office he can have all the facts necessary for a complete diagnosis. So, also, the teacher who is realistic knows that if she only has a child for three to eight hours out of twenty four, the other people in his life must have something to contribute. Neither can be of help to the child if they are operating in a vacuum or from two disconnected vantage points.

Professionals must look hard at the growing trend of parents to want in. They are better informed and more demanding than at any time in history, and they are going to insist on a true partnership. Teacher can no longer hide behind the jargon of their profession. Parents who have been reading the latest books, magazine articles, and reports about education want to know what is happening in their child's school and some of them will want to take an active part in the process. They have much to offer, and the teacher has much to share with them.

Emotionally, parents and teachers NEED each other. The growth of basic trust, which is essential to all relationships will be an investment which pays off in mutual understanding, respect and acceptance of human errors. All teachers and parents "goof" occasionally. Mrs. Jackson forgets to tell her husband that she will be working and he is to pick up Susie. By the time the mistake is straightened out, the teacher has been kept waiting an extra hour at the center after a long, hard day and HER patience has worn thin. OR: Miss Harrison has to call Jim's mother and report that he has a large rip in his new trousers, from a nail on the slide, which someone should have seen. It is far easier to explain or admit errors when a groundwork of basic trust has been developed.

Teachers should never underestimate the parent's ability to succeed in raising their children. Avoiding the narrow outlook that only two-parent, middle-income families produce happy, well-adjusted children, they sometimes still tend to look at divided marital status, economic strain or social environment as obstacles which a child must overcome, or from which he must be rescued. Prejudgement of a parent and child should never become slanted by what is known about the family. Though each condition has its influence, it will not necessarily make or break the child's future. A parent with the book knowledge, understanding and potential for raising the perfectly balanced child may still fail miserably at the task.

There are often children who do not seem to belong to their particular family "type"; children who overcome tremendous obstacles of birth and social condition to lead happy, productive lives, or children who just never seem to fit into their particular family configuration.

How Can Parents Serve the School?

Most parents have very narrow vision regarding helping at school. Any activity which gets them involved in a casual but meaningful way, is a good beginning. They need to feel, smell, touch and see a classroom in operation before they can even begin to understand where and how they might be of assistance. Once their interest is captured, individual talents and interests will surface. Many just need to be discovered.

Parents who are busy with other small children at home may be able to set up a calling team for notifying or inviting parents to special events. Perhaps a mother can launder the housekeeping clothes or sew for the dolls. Parents with special talents in music, art, cooking, etc. may want to join the children for a morning of special projects.

Fathers and mothers who come in for a brief talk about their work are a most valuable addition to curriculum and sometimes children are able to visit the place where a parent works. *No work is ordinary to a child* — be it office work, accounting, gardening, truck driving, or plumbing. Watching the simplest kind of job, such as cutting and fitting a linoleum, installing a bathroom, shingling a roof, or changing a tire — is curriculum!

Consuelo's mother came once a week to teach Spanish. The children learned rapidly and looked forward eagerly to her visits. She also helped a non-English speaking child make the difficult adjustment to a new world with a new language.

Debbie's mother made a weekly visit to straighten out the books on the library shelf. If they needed repairing, she set them aside until a group of mothers could be assembled for a work session.

Kathy's mother made frequent trips to the library, so when a teacher needed extra books to supplement curriculum she would depend on Mrs. Jones to get them for her.

A workshop was held one evening for the purpose of making educational games (see Workjobs). Some parents maintained their interest and continued to make games at home for their own children and for the school.

Parents can sometimes be asked to come at noon to eat and rest with the children, while teachers attend meetings and conferences.

Another mother visited industrial plants and stores, asking for materials for the resource center. Devising a system for keeping "elegant junk" in order and still accessible to the children, is a task which could appeal to some parents.

Clothing for the "dress up" corner usually needs to be altered to fit the children. The parent who sews can best help in this area.

Parents are valuable aides needed to accompany children on field trips (see Field Trips).

A boy scout leader brought his troop to repair and build equipment, on a Saturday.

A father, who gave performances as a clown, came to entertain the children. He first applied his makeup before the children so they would not be frightened.

A parent who owned a dress factory donated dresses for a sale to raise money for scholarships; also kept the school well supplied with remnants of material, buttons and trims.

Parents with experience on newspapers or magazines or former English teachers will often welcome the opportunity to put out a school newspaper.

A parent with social work training gave a course in "parenting."

A psychiatrist conducted a discussion on explaining death to children.

A doctor, and on a different occasion, a nurse, put on their operating room garb and explained procedures, with children volunteering as patients. This led to much role playing and opened the door for some very healthy talk sessions.

The resources are there, and parents are willing BUT they seldom respond to a request on a bulletin. It is up to the teacher or director to issue a personal invitation and then to follow through with a cordial welcome; set the stage for the activity and send written notes of thanks, if possible including some of the children's comments.

Hobbies of parents often become the basis for interesting class projects; for example:

Tony's father developed musical instruments out of funnels, hoses, etc. He also played the trumpet. He demonstrated both, taking time to let the children experience with all their senses, ask questions, enjoy.

Dr. Smith, an opthamologist, brought in specialized medical equipment and explained how it was used and what could be learned from it, as she tested the children's eyes.

Jim's mother told a class about computers and gave the children a chance to experiment with statistical research. They made choices between pink ice cream cones and pony rides as they put a needle through punched cards—a real life experiment!

An artist set up her easel and painted in a corner of the room. The children observed, admired, and were allowed to use her brush to add some small bit to the work of art. Painting at their own easels took on new dimensions after that day.

Juan's father was a chef in a large hotel. Wearing his tall, white hat and crisp white suit, he gave a demonstration of breadmaking to the kindergarten which was the forerunner of a variety of baking experiences, and a scientific discussion of "leavening."

Training Program
for Parent Volunteers

For some parents who wish to become more involved in school activities, a training program puts the parent/teacher partnership on a whole new course.

This is usually taught by the director, but individual members of the staff, or parents might also be asked to conduct workshop sessions. Invitations are extended (see Suggested Letter of Invitation to Parents) with a description of the course and requirements. It is usually given in the fall and lasts for eleven weeks. Parents who participate are expected to make some commitment for volunteering once a week throughout the year, but this is necessarily flexible.

The numbers attending should be limited. One week the class meets for instruction and discussion, and the following week are placed in classrooms with a specific assignment. The first part of the next class session is spent reviewing and evaluating their successes and failures. For example, if the assignment is to tell a story, one parent may report, "It was awful. I fell flat on my face. They wouldn't listen and some even walked away!" While another might say, "It was beautiful. I felt as if they were hanging on my every word. When I looked at their shining eyes and saw their attentive expressions, I was thrilled."

The philosophy of this book is based on the development of PEOPLE. Parents and teachers have "I AM'S" and they are also searching for ways to develop their "I CAN'S." Taking and completing a Parent Volunteer Training Course will give a parent a better understanding of the ways children learn and grow, but it also may open new doors which lead to a full or part-time career.

The class leader should remember that most parents have been out of high school or college for a few years and that those years have been filled with the care of home and family. The very idea of 'learning' may be frightening. Some will need encouragement and assurance that they will NOT have written assignments. Outside reading is always voluntary. Some will go to the library and seek additional literature, some will take home the pamphlets provided, but NO ONE will be required to do either. It is beautiful to watch the "I AM" of some of these wary, apprehensive parents develop as the class progresses and TRUST is established. Mrs. I _____ who is very conscious of the fact that she didn't finish high school, shyly contributes from her experience in bringing up a large family, and Mrs. P _____, overburdened and confused by magazine articles on child rearing, grasps with eagerness the solutions Mrs. I _____ offers to everyday problems. Both parents welcome the opportunity to be brought up to date on current knowledge about young children.

When it becomes time to assign parents for classroom experience, they often express concern about being with their own children. Usually, they are given a choice. If they opt to work near their own child, they must be warned to be ready for clinging and/or demanding behavior. It takes a while for a child to be willing to share HIS mother with other children. He must be assured that she IS special to and for him—but once this initial concern has been satisfied, it usually works out very well. Children say with pride, "MY mother is a TEACHER today!"

The parents who are interested enough to stay through the entire course form a nucleus of support and strength for a director. These people are so tuned into the school, the curriculum and the philosophy that they radiate good will and interest throughout the community. In addition, they become a sounding board for evaluation and may often be the ones who can help get a working Parent Council established. They have made a personal investment in the school and begin to feel a sense of ownership—it is THEIR school.

The following is a suggested letter of invitation to parents to participate in the Training Course for Parent Volunteers.

TRAINING COURSE IN EARLY CHILDHOOD EDUCATION FOR PARENT VOLUNTEERS:

You are cordially invited to participate in this course at your child's school, one morning a week for eleven weeks. This course will be given by the director, assisted from time to time by classroom teachers or outside specialists. We believe it is a real service to our parents for the following reasons:

1. It gives them an opportunity to observe other children...a point of comparison. Parents worry—especially with a first child. Is he advanced or slow in development? Is this normal behavior for this age? Through observation and class discussion, they find answers and reassurance.

2. Parents can be better parents if they know more about children. What could be more appropriate than a study of young children? Many parents go on to take courses offered by the state or in colleges. For some, this has been an entry to a new career.

3. Through observation and involvement, parents gain an understanding of the education and experiences their children are receiving.

Enrollment is limited, so please notify the director promptly. There is no charge, but we do hope that those parents who complete the course will continue to give one day a week as volunteer.

In a center where an optional stay-day program was offered, parents who completed the course were given two extra hours for each hour they gave IF the request for such service came from the center, i.e. Mrs. Smith filled in for the new aide so she could attend the workshop.

Outline for Workshop Sessions

Session I   TOPIC: *History and Philosophy of School*
Tour of classrooms and playgrounds, including office, library, resource rooms, kitchen, etc. Explanation of licensing requirements, standards required and those adopted by the school for teacher/pupil ratio, qualifications for teachers. Show and comment on available reading materials.

Session II   ASSIGNMENT: (Classroom Participation)
Observe and record interaction between teacher and child. Come to the next meeting prepared to discuss your reactions and pose questions.

Session III   TOPIC: (Discussion of previous assignment)
Physical Development of the Child: Large and small muscle development and coordination through environment, equipment and curriculum. Discussion of age expectations. Discussion of goals and readiness for formal learning.

Session IV   ASSIGNMENT: (Classroom Participation)
Look for and record examples of large and small muscle coordination. How many different ways? Were they deliberately planned by the teacher? Provided by the equipment? Spontaneous? Imaginative? Prepare a table activity involving small muscle coordination. Observe and record performance of individual children who participate.

Session V   TOPIC: *Social and Creative Development*
Discuss solitary play, parallel play, small group interaction, team effort, sharing, taking turns. Relate to previous discussion of age expectations.

Session VI   ASSIGNMENT: (Classroom Participation)
Choose a particular area, i.e. blockroom, housekeeping corner, to observe. Record conversations, behavior. Look for examples of children helping others. Keep four sides of developmental square in mind as you observe.

Session VII   TOPIC: *Intellectual Development.*
Language development through stories, poetry, verbal expression and sensory games.

Session VII   ASSIGNMENT: (Classroom Participation)
Plan and carry out with children a project which involves more than one activity. Story, poetry, art, music, science. Instructor might use development of *Caps for Sale* by Slobodkina (see Seq. 8, Act. 10). Choose a story or poem and include a related art or unusual activity.

Session IX   TOPIC: *Emotional Development.*
Emotion control. Helping a child cope with daily situations. Expression of emotions in developing personality. Ways of expressing emotions through creative activities. Acceptable activities for releasing strong feelings.

Session X   ASSIGNMENT: Through art, drama, music or creative movement, plan and carry through an experience which is designed to help children express emotions.

Session XI   TOPIC: *Evaluation of Course.* Participants relate own experiences in classroom. Offer criticisms and suggestions for future sessions. A panel discussion by lead teachers who evaluate experiences in working with participants.

Teacher Preparation for Volunteers

Teachers who will share their rooms and their children with trainees must have a clear understanding of the purpose and the content of the program. Some teachers, even though reluctant to admit it, may have 'hang-ups' about parents invading their domain. They need to be helped to see the advantages, and to discuss specific ways to make parents feel comfortable.

PARENT COUNCIL

An organized group of parents who wish to participate actively can be a great source of help and support to the director. It is important that leadership be enthusiastic, energetic, and consistent and it takes time for this to emerge, thus, in a new school it might be wise to wait until the children, staff, and environment have "jelled." In the beginning it is the director and staff who take the initiative in starting a parent council. They know what is needed—the climate they are trying the establish and the needs of the parents they are dealing with.

Once a group is established, some simple by-laws will be necessary to provide for replacement of members and officers and to maintain continuity. Some parents will want to make decisions about the hiring of teachers and the curriculum and discuss purposes and goals. In publicly subsidized programs this is often a requirement. In a private school the director can explain tactfully that such decisions are made by the administration but that suggestions are welcome.

Meetings of the council should take place often enough to develop some spirit—and to enable the members to feel that they are serving a useful function. At the first meeting the director can:

1. State her reasons for wanting such a group and the benefits she feels will accrue to the children, staff and parents.

2. Ask one parent or couple to act as chairmen-pro tem, to get by-laws written and develop a system for electing leaders and a governing board so the organization will continue from year to year.

The following are some of the functions which might be taken over by a parent council:

1. Planning and carrying out a calendar of activities for a full year. (See Special Events.)

2. Establishing committees, for example:

TELEPHONE COMMITTEE—parents who can telephone others with notices of special activities.

EDUCATION COMMITTEE—determine subjects which hold interest for parents and arrange seminars and speaker meetings.

BOOK COMMITTEE—to evaluate new children's books and records and make recommendations for purchase. May also keep books in good condition and act as librarians.

EQUIPMENT AND FACILITIES COMMITTEE—to meet with director and staff to discuss ways of improving and adding to environment. May build or repair equipment (see Fathers' Breakfast,) find and build storage for "elegant junk," or create new and unusual playgrounds.

INTERCULTURAL COMMITTEE—seek out parents of different ethnic or cultural backgrounds and encourage them to share their customs, foods, songs, games and art activities with the children. May also assist a non-English speaking parent to adjust to a new environment.

Special Events at School

SPEAKER MEETINGS: There was a time when parent meetings meant speakers—speakers who dropped their pearls of wisdom on the tired ears of parents who were made to feel unworthy and guilty.

One deadly meeting, with a poor speaker, can turn off all participation in future meetings.

Planning a series of meetings for the year should be a reflection of the needs and interests of the parents in a particular school. If they share in the planning, these meetings will serve a valuable purpose.

SEMINARS: Following the leads from answers to questionnaires sent to parents, plan a series of four to six seminars. These will usually be given by the director but might also be lead by teachers or qualified parents (pediatricians, psychiatrists, dentists, social workers, etc.)

CURRICULUM MEETINGS: These include a very specific description of goals and methods of curriculum with suggestions for ways parents can extend them into the home. Stress value of enrichment experiences — stimulation of language through family discussion and reading to children.

It may be assumed that parents are primarily interested in knowing what is going on at school. At this first meeting, interest centers should be labeled with explanatory signs outlining the goals. Some work may be displayed, with an explanation of the purpose and motivation. Parents should be able to roam about and capture some of the atmosphere of the school. Teachers should be free to visit informally and answer questions about curriculum.

This is a good time to use slides or movies to illustrate curriculum. It must be explained that slides were chosen for demonstration of ideas and that all children may not be seen. If extra staff, substitutes, cook, maintenance person, driver, are invited they should be identified on name tags.

Refreshments can be provided by the children — with emphasis again on the learning experience of cooking.

In one child care center, the educational director had been invited to speak at this first meeting of the year. After a brief question period, parents were served refreshments, which had been prepared by the children and included a large bowl of applesauce and home made cookies, homemade bread and butter made by the children. (The children also decorated paper table cloths, arranged centerpieces and folded napkins.)

BACK TO SCHOOL NIGHT: On this occasion the room is set up as a 'planned environment' and parents "try and test" as the children do. They use the materials available to the children, paint, blocks, collage materials, cardboard and tubes or scrap wood, or they may be led in a creative movement session. A good way to end is to sit on the floor and learn the songs the children sing (with guitar or piano accompaniment, if possible), so they can sing with them at home. Teachers offer the same kind of assistance they would give children. It can end with a discussion of how they felt — and what they enjoyed.

PARENT TEACHER WORKSHOP: Workshops might focus on a wide variety of topics — games, science, holidays (how to plan parties and make simple gifts with children), projects to do at home with the young child, learning simple songs and games, choosing the right books and music for a child, etc.

Every school has staff members gifted in these various areas. A series of workshops led by individual staff members and focusing on a special topic can greatly enhance a parent's "I AM - I CAN" as he relates more effectively with his child at home.

"Come find out about unusual ways to make valentines with your child." This was the invitation extended by a teacher.

FATHERS' BREAKFAST: In a school, where parent involvement was considered a pleasure rather than a chore, a breakfast was held on a Sunday morning for father and child. They planned and cooked breakfast and then the children played or helped while fathers repaired and rebuilt equipment. The interesting part is that teachers, and even the director, were *not allowed* to attend. They were, however, permitted to help plan the work activities. It was enormously successful.

SPECIAL VACATION ACTIVITIES: Might be planned during school vacations. Field trips, entertainment, special classroom activities. In day care centers, older siblings may attend. In others, enrollment will be reduced because parents will stay home during school vacations.

CHILDREN'S ENTERTAINMENT: Fund-raising programs which are planned for ticket sale to the general public require a well-organized parent committee. They are beyond the scope of staff and directors except as advisors. The school office equipment might be used for typing, mimeographing, telephoning, etc. Some suggestions:

Folk Singers — one who specializes in entertaining young children, mingling in the audience and teaching group songs.

Puppet Shows — some puppeteers will show puppets and tell how to make them.

Children's Theatre Group

Zoo-Mobile

HOLIDAY PARTIES: More and more the trend has been to include families in school activities. In one school, a most successful party was held in December; the time was from 6:30 to 7:45. The rooms were decorated by the children, refreshments prepared by the children (with a few extras provided by parents). A few tables were set up with art activites appropriate to the season. Automatic slide projectors were set up in each classroom, showing slides of the children. Entire families came; it was a bit crowded and a bit noisy but no one seemed to mind. With a minimum effort, it was applauded as the most successful party ever!

POTLUCK SUPPER: Sometime in the fall, preferably before Thanksgiving, a Pot-Luck Supper might be planned. This is also an activity for the whole family. The planning and telephoning committee could be one or two parents from each group who would attend to contacting all parents for donations of main course, salad or dessert. The school would furnish milk, coffee, plates and cutlery; parents seem to enjoy sitting at child sized tables for this. The supper should be at the end of the school day, during the week and will be particularly appealing to those parents who work all day and are reluctant to come out again in the evening after feeding and bedding their children. A supper of this kind gives great opportunity for parents to meet others, share their problems and joys while eating together. Experience has shown that this can be the best attended function of the school year.

GRANDPARENTS' DAY: This is a delightful way of introducing the advantages of the nursery school curriculum to members of the family who, through lack of understanding, may have condemned it. It also serves to reassure the grandparents of one-parent children that a vital need is being fulfilled both for the parent and the child. Often, too, grandparents are paying for the schooling. They are entitled to and need special attention and appreciation.

Two invitations are sent to each parent, to be addressed to both sets of grandparents. Parents are urged to send them even if the grandparent lives far away. Grandparents who are unable to attend may write a letter to the child and send it to his school, a 'next best' response.

This event may be planned for a Tuesday after a long weekend when travel is easy and when grandparents often schedule visits with their children. A surprising number will come, even from far away, including great-grandparents. Ask your mothers to serve as guides and hostesses. It is nice if the children cook something special for the refreshment table, supplemented by treats from parents.

The director meets with the guests, briefly, and answers questions. continuous slides also help to explain curriculum. As far as possible the day should be normal so grandparents can see what actually happens in school. Children prepare for the visit by making pictures of their grandparents, writing stories about grandparents and by discussing and dramatizing the role of a host or hostess.

In one school, the children had made pictures of their expected guests, trimming them with buttons, "junk" jewelry, etc. One had white hair (cotton), another bright-red yarn hair. It was amusing to see how accurate their images were when the guest arrived. One child made a lovely picture—and covered it all over with black paint. His story— "This is my Nanny sitting in a dark room."

ANNUAL MEETING OF PARENT COUNCIL: Much of this is planned by the council, assisted by director and staff, as needed. Director and staff give reports of the past year. Committee chairmen are welcomed and special recognition and 'thank you's' to staff and others.

Communications

How often have you found yourself blaming a bad situation on 'lack of communication?' A wise director will constantly check all the lines to be sure they are open and clear.

In addition to the many suggestions offered in the sections on parents and staff, a director may employ some of the following written communications:

1. BULLETINS TO PARENTS

These contain the necessary detail for smooth operation. They should be *dated and numbered* and parents should be warned frequently to check numbers and ask for any they may have missed. It is also suggested that parents have a folder and keep all bulletins for referral. Some parents will NOT read their bulletins—and it is important for the director to be able to say:

"I'm sorry you didn't know there was no school yesterday but it was on bulletins numbered 2, 3, and 4, which were dated Sept. 11, Oct. 15 and Nov. 5. This is our means for letting parents know about these things. Would you check the numbers on yours, now, and let me know if any are missing so I can send you extra copies?"

Including small stories or something to read to the children, will help to insure that the bulletin will be read. It is a good idea to include calendar reminders on every bulletin. It is wise to spread out over the year requests for elegant junk or special items to supplement curriculum. One long sheet, with one hundred items may be tossed aside. A few specifics in each bulletin seem to bring better results.

2. NEWSLETTERS

These are often written by a member of the parent council. They are 'after the fact' reports on special activities related to curriculum, parent meetings, etc. They may include suggestions for home activities.

3. SCHOOL NEWSPAPER

This may be a more sophisticated (printed) piece of material. It is intended to tell more about the 'people who make it happen' and may have interviews with anyone—the director, maintenance man, visiting teachers, student, parent. It is an extension of the educational tools employed by the school. It may include reviews of books for children or for adults, suggestions for places to take children on weekends, recipes and other suggestions for activites parents can share with children in the home. Properly done, this can serve as a valuable promotion piece, but it does require much time and a fair amount of expertise. An editorial by the director would provide an opportunity for sharing thoughts on current issues in education and child care.

THE STAFF

A school may have a beautiful building, the finest equipment and an outstanding playground but it will be totally ineffective without a dedicated staff. Bearing in mind that we look upon the members of a teaching staff as unique individuals, we also know that they must be able to work in close formation and in harmony. In this chapter we have outlined qualifications and job responsibilities as we see them. There will be variations within each school; the fine line between guidelines and requirements is not easy to determine.

The Director

Using the square and circle as a guide, let us now consider the qualifications of a director, reminding ourselves once again of the weavers who caution us not to seek perfection.
Personal Qualifications—*A Director is a special being,* first and foremost a "people" oriented person whose most important task is to establish relationships of mutual trust with parents, children and staff. Integrity and sincerity are two words which might be used in describing a director, and these qualities cannot be worn like a garment during the workng hours; they come from the heart of a person who genuinely likes and enjoys people.

A Director has feelings. "I AM! I CAN!" If this is to be the philosophy of the director who believes that this self-confidence can be instilled in children, then the director must be able to TRUST, believe in and rely on personal competence and judgement. On the other hand a director cannot be so serious that a sense of humor is missing. Keep a light touch. Each day in the life of a director presents new challenges; there is almost never a time when some new unheard of, and unanticipated problem will not demand the best and immediate concern and judgement. This fact of a director's life will either make life interesting or exhausting (sometimes both!) depending on ability to cope, to accept exigencies as they come, and deal with them without losing emotional and physical stability.

A Director has physical limitations. Administering a child care center or nursery school is a demanding, exhausting task which requires constant and boundless stamina. The I CAN! means literally that a director can trust the body to rise to any occasion when it is demanded, while at the same time knowing how to alternate activity with sufficient rest to renew energy. The person who is in command of his/her physical person can muster the "second wind when it is needed, but does not abuse the physical and nervous system. If one "draws on the principal" in the energy bank that the means must be found for renewal and takes care never to "overdraw the account."

Morale is an essential factor in the composition of a staff, and the director holds the key which turns it on or off. If a director moans and groans and complains, the rest of the staff will follow suit. One director put it this way, "When I look in the mirror and I am scared by the tired and bedraggled apparition I see, I go into the staff room and put on fresh lipstick and come out sailing." This director had learned the meaning of "I CAN!"

A Director needs the wisdom of Solomon. Degrees in education are certainly an asset but they should not rank highest on the list of qualifications. What is more important is attitude toward education as a continuing process and a desire for growth in the profession. The highest calling in an intellectual pursuit is the constant seeding and nurturing of knowledge. The director must be the one who reads the articles in professional magazines, scans the book reviews and the education pages of newspapers, belongs to professional organizations, and participates in their activities to assure knowledge of what is going on in the profession. The director goes to conferences, seminars, and workshops and relays all of this enrichment to the staff.

Responsibilities—*A Director is a catalyst.* The director can share ideas and enthusiasm in such simple ways as dropping into a classroom with a bird's nest and showing it to the children, following it up with "there are some books in our library about birds and how they build their nests." Such sharing might well be the spark that fires up a teacher who has become a little stale and yet it does not come as a directive.

The director senses when teachers need revitalization and will try to make arrangements for them to be free to visit another school, browse in a recycling center, or attend workshops.

The school is considered to be a laboratory, and as such a director keeps it amply supplied with materials, as well as ideas and provides for the sharing of both. Staff meetings are held on a regular basis and the times set aside are guarded by a director with the zeal of a mother bird protecting her young.

A director encourages staff to join professional organizations.

The director who keeps staff on their toes need never worry about the education of the children in the school. Attitudes are contagious, and realization of growth is invigorating and exciting. The teacher who is reaching for the stars has stars in her eyes, and the children who see those stars will become attuned to learning as a joyous experience, rather than a chore to be endured.

The Director is a public relations expert. As the first representative of a school, the director will influence the attitudes of the community to the school, while dealing with neighbors, service people, businessmen and other school personnel, public and private. The task of presenting a positive image to the public is one which never ceases. It puts demands on a director to "keep cool" when wanting to "blow my top," to wear a smiling face when feeling anything but agreeable, to try to look at antagonism with the eyes of the antagonist, and to convey pride in the school.

A Director is a salesman. A child care center, whether funded or private, has a service to sell and the director is chief of sales and service. The need to "sell" the school to the customers, the parents who will pay for the service, will continue to exist even though a school may reach the point of maintaining a waiting list. There will always be those who need to be convinced or reassured.

The Director is a housekeeper. Pride in the appearance of a school will delineate the responsibilities which go with this facet of the director's job. It is suggested that a "director's walk" be a regular procedure, a walk in which every nook and corner is inspected with the critical eyes of an outsider.

Maintenance help is essential but in every school there will be many daily chores which cannot wait for attention. The problems of housekeeping are the province of the director but it will be a great mistake to attempt the task alone. This is a clear case of "many hands make light work." However, a director should never feel it beneath the dignity of the position to perform the menial tasks. It is healthy for staff to see their "boss" pick up papers from the floor or playground, wet a paper towel and wash a window, wipe off sticky handprints on the door or wipe out the bathroom bowl.

A director will spend as little time as possible behind a desk, never doing anything which can be allocated to members of the office staff. He or she must be able to say "I can't do this alone, but I have the administrative talent for organizing and leading people and helping them to produce." Although perhaps too modest to say this aloud, a director "knows" it inwardly, and conveys this self-confidence to staff and parents. (See Zoning)

A Director can be a drill sergeant. Sometimes a director finds it hard to strike a balance between democracy and leadership. A staff will be more comfortable if they know where they stand and what is expected of them.

At the beginning of the school year, the director does more telling and assigning, trusting that as soon as the staff knows what is expected of them they will be able to share in the problem solving and decision making. When the director feels a compulsion to preface every sentence with "What do you think?", inviting rap sessions over details which should be routines, a sense of instability pervades the whole school. A parent says to his child, "There are some things which you can decide, some choices you can make, but there are others which I decide and there will be no arguments about them." A director must sense when strength and convictions are required, and be forceful and explicit particularly in matters that relate to health and safety. When it comes to curriculum and teaching techniques, there should always be room for discussion.

Finally, a director will be wise and humble enough to recognize personal shortcomings as well as those of the staff, and know how to capitalize on strengths and weaknesses, while respecting the rights of the individual to be "unique" remembering that the constant goal will be to help others to say, "I AM! I CAN!" A director can be compared to the conductor of an orchestra, eliciting from each instrument its particular tone, charactersitics, and colors at just the right moment; choosing combinations which will be harmonious, but recognizing that occasional dissonance lends vitality and interest to the composition.

The position of a director is an awesome responsibility to be approached with humility. The material rewards will never match the personal satisfaction of a director who can say with conviction, "I AM! I CAN!"

Evaluating a Director's Performance

How can a director be on the receiving end of evaluation, encouraging teachers to speak of his/her weaknesses without losing their respect? If communication is truly a two way process a director will find a way of opening the lines, perhaps saying, "We will have scheduled conferences BUT if you want or need to talk to me about anything please tell me and I will meet with you before that day is over."

This really happened in one center:

M—, a teacher, asked the director for a conference. "I can see you at 12:30 if it will not take too long." "I would rather wait until we have plenty of time," was his reply. The answer aroused her curiosity. "What can he be going to say? Is there anything wrong? Is he giving notice?" With all these thoughts stirring in her mind she soon made arrangements for the meeting.

In a quiet, honest, but not disrespectful manner, M— proceeded to pour out his negative reactions to the staff meeting of the previous week, and to go on to say that he felt very uncomfortable when the director came into his class.

"You breeze through in such a hurry," he said, "and if you do talk to me it is often a quick comment about something entirely irrelevent to what we may be doing. I resent the intrusion in my program. When you can come and sit down, have juice with us, or see what we are doing I will welcome you. Otherwise I prefer that you stay away." Then he startled the director with "The other day after you had been in the room one of the children looked up at me and said, 'Mr. M—, are you afraid of her?'"

When he had gone that director made some self appraisals:

"I am glad that he felt able to speak to me with such honesty. I am chagrined, but not angry. He was not rude. He was trying to help me!

"Have I truly been so carried away with administrative detail that I have forgotten how to be a teacher, so harried that I have lost sight of sensitivity? Have I let JOY turn into jargon?"

In another case, a director arranged for each teacher to spend an entire morning playing the imaginary role of the director, trying to look at environment, program, staff, as if each was responsible. This was followed by lunch in the director's office where they shared an honest evaluation. It was most effective and led to improved performance, greater understanding of the overall functioning of the school, and a new sense of responsibility.

Lead Teacher   In team teaching, which is the prototype advocated in this manual, every member of a team is a teacher and is expected to be contributing to the education of the child. An assistant may very well have the same educational qualifications as the team leader or even an additional degree, but will recognize that leadership is necessary in a team effort. Some one person has to make decisions, and accept responsibility for these decisions. This is so important that when the team leader is absent *one* other person must always be designated to assume this responsibility. Furthermore, this cannot be left to chance, to a casual assignment, "Sue is out today so you take over, Jim," but should be planned in advance of the necessity.

A limited "hierarchy" is essential, even on a team where the emphasis is lateral rather than vertical, but one's position on a team should never be seen as an opportunity for self-elevation, or, on the other hand, as a position of inferiority. In addition to the qualifications for a teacher a team leader has an additional challenge—being responsible for personal performance, but also accepting responsibility for the combined efforts of the members of the team. When morale begins to break down, the lead teacher must bolster it. When one team member goofs off and is not doing her share of the program or routine chores, the team leader has to get her back in line. When parents are complaining about the program, the lead teacher needs to be able to respond by first asking herself and then the team whether the complaints are justified, and, if not, how the team together can educate the parents to their goals.

A problem with the members of a team may be as simple as "Sue looks sloppy," "Tom needs to use a deoderant," "Mimi's hair is a mess" or "How *could* Jane wear that dirty smock?" Does the team leader handle this or take the problem to the director? It takes a different personality, different motivation, to be a leader and there is nothing to be ashamed of when a good teacher says, "This is not for me. My 'thing' is with the children, and I don't want to be responsible for other adults."

An effective team relationship provides each child with a role model—one which might be exemplified in an ideal family. Each member is important, respected, and feels free to contribute ideas and suggestions. The individual members are supportive of one another; if one has a bad day the rest are willing to extend themselves, and know that they can expect the same assistance when it is needed. Each person is proud of the accomplishments of other members of the teams and offers material and emotional support. On a smoothly functioning team problems and differences are a joint responsibility—and routine methods are established for reaching group consensus. Children are extremely sensitive to adult relationships; they KNOW when people like each other and enjoy working together. It gives them a comfortable sense of security to feel this aura of compatibility.

Job Description for a Teacher or Lead Teacher—*Responsibility to the child.*

To see every child in the group as an individual, respecting his right to be himself. A teacher will recognize that the child's experience is limited and that the forces which may have made an impression on his life may have differed greatly from that of every other child.

To be completely fair to every child whatever his physical or personal limitations may be and to make an honest effort to "find something to love" in each one, scrupulously avoiding favoritism.

To be alert to the physical and emotional needs of each child, sympathetic and friendly.

To be constantly aware of the growing needs of each child, offering new and enriched experiences as he reaches each level of development. To constantly seek the perfect "match" for each child. (See Ages and Stages.)

To avoid discussion of the child in his presence.

Responsibility to parents.

To protect the health and safety of each child as a parent would his own child.

To learn as much about the family and home life as will be helpful in working with the child.

To be careful not to jump to any conclusions about parents' methods of training without knowing the facts.

To respect the privacy of parents by overlooking any family secrets the child may divulge.

To respect the parents' right to decide what is best for the child. When this is in direct conflict with school policy, to explain as tactfully as possible, and if there is still disagreement to refer the matter to the director.

To know each child well enough to be able to give the parent a reasonably accurate and concise verbal report when it is requested.

To confine such reports to information about the child, taking care not to make comparisons, or to give any information about other children in the group.

To establish a system for the care of clothing which will keep damage or loss to a minimum.

To call the parents to report any incidents, falls, scratches or emotional experiences. This is in addition to a report by the director or nurse, and reassures the parent.

Responsibility to the members of the team.

To respect each one's right to share in making daily and long range plans.

To provide opportunities for them to ask questions, disagree with policies or procedures and offer suggestions.

To divide chores such as housekeeping, playgrounds, dressing, etc., assuming a fair share.

To look for and draw out every talent and ability of team members, encouraging and aiding them to enjoy satisfying teaching experiences.

To schedule regular conferences for purposes of evaluation.

Some soul searching questions a teacher should ask periodically.

1. Do you maintain at all times a pleasing, neat professional appearance which will be a credit to the school?

2. Do you consistently exhibit warmth toward the children, parents and your fellow workers?

3. Are you cheerful — no sulks or grouches?

4. Have you a sense of humor, even when the joke is on you?

5. Can you keep the tone of irritation out of your voice and your face "loose" when your nerves are strained?

6. Are you free from touchiness so that others do not have to handle you with kid gloves?

7. Do you refrain from listening to and repeating gossip?

8. Can you accept criticism without anger or hurt?

9. Are you cooperative — even when carrying out the plans of others?

10. Are you dependable? Do you do what you say you will, *when* you say you will?

11. Are you prompt at all appointments, in your part of the daily program? Do you respect the time of others?

12. Can you easily adapt to changes in programs, weather, plans?

13. Are you willing to "go the second mile," to do the extra which may not be your job?

14. Can you weigh facts and exercise judgment in making decisions?

15. Are you curious? Do you have an interest in a wide variety of fields?

16. Have you initiative? Ability to get started without prodding?
17. Are you careful not to "judge" children, taking active likes and dislikes?
18. Are you careful not to judge parents?
19. Do you talk *too much?*

Enthusiasm is the secret ingredient! The teacher has to be excited about teaching and the children learning. *Teaching cannot be a duty—it has to be a love.*

A teacher is part of the equipment, blending into the activities and the spirit of the occasion, guiding freedom to changing moods. A teacher is a classroom companion, who, because of age and experience, can extend uses of equipment and activities a little further each day.

A teacher has: twenty eyes all around the head—they see everything; two enormous ears—they hear everything; one smiling mouth; one frown—used sparingly; two India rubber legs; two Indian rubber arms; add a gentle voice, sense of humor, sense of fair play and trust.

A teacher has a sense of beauty, is open to new experiences and has a relish for new tastes.

If a teacher is to foster creativity in children he/she should be an adequate, fully functioning person with a positive view of self—and the ability to identify with others.
And now a few negatives:

A teacher must constantly be on guard against using a child to satisfy personal needs.

A teacher should stop to consider whether methods are colored by personal experience.

Some teachers cannot resist the temptation to be center-stage. They over-use flannel boards, they play the role of actress-magician.

Some teachers see their role as bystanders. They set the stage for action but do not become involved.

A teacher is not a baby-sitter, a jester, an entertainer, or a technician to build little bits of knowledge and skills into parts of a human.

Let the reader now think back as these people did, to teachers who left lasting impressions. There is no definition of a good teacher. Each one will be as different as each set of impressions. A teacher must therefore be true to self—think well enough of his or her self to be free to develop an individual and personal teaching style and character.

The Teacher as a Disciplinarian

Discipline is a harsh word to use in speaking of pre-school children. If all the other factors involved in creating a good environment are in order, discipline should take a back seat. A contented, busy child who has a healthy "I AM," and is able to exert his "I CAN" will not find it necessary to test himself constantly in his social environment. In the same vein, the adult who has a strong "I AM" is able to maintain a calm confidence which the child senses—and can lean against.

One of the first things a neophyte needs to learn is that it doesn't hurt to say "I made a mistake. I was wrong to say NO to you—I just wasn't thinking very well." Too often adults fear that if they retract their threats they will lose face, and thus weaken all future relationships with the child. On the contrary, when they admit error they are teaching the child one of life's most important lessons: that we all make mistakes, that we all have need of a "second chance," that this will continue to be true even when the child becomes an adult. There is no magic that makes a grown-up perfect. What we want our children to learn is that we admit to our errors, and try not to make the same mistake a second time; also that life has its way of doling out penalties for mistakes; we accept them, profit by and learn from them.

The second piece of wisdom for the beginning teacher is that it takes experience to become a wise and confident disciplinarian. The child knows this—and will take advantage of the insecurity of the adult. He has a great need to push against something resistant—it is only by testing each newfound strength that he can recognize his own power, that he can assess his own "I AM." In the fumbling and "feeling out" which must necessarily take place between teacher and pupil the following faces may emerge.

The Queen

Teacher reigns supreme—ensconced behind a desk or façade, daring any ordinary mortal to oppose her slightest command. Every person who reads these words will remember at least one such autocrat—one who aroused such fear that it practically erased all potential for learning. There were always nicknames—used with glee when one was safely outside the classroom or beyond her class—usually prefaced with "OLD LADY".... . Seldom does one see such a person in the preschool, but occasionally an Assistant or Aide who has known school in no other terms will adopt this style.

Joe Friendly

"Kids are great, I love them," says Joe, as he tosses David in the air, "skins the cat" with Harry, and lets Susie throw her arms around his neck and her legs around his waist. Joe doesn't really enjoy the mauling; he has the mistaken idea that the way to "handle kids" is to get down to their level—to win their affection at all costs. What Joe doesn't know is that children really don't want adults to get down to their level. They know that they don't belong there—and they would rather respect them than to meet them on equal terms. It makes them as uncomfortable as if they were allowed to kick or hit adults   and leaves them with a feeling of "something is not right in this situation."

Loudmouth

Mary is related to Joe—she works very hard at this business of discipline—but her voice is her means of attack. Mary can be heard as soon as you approach the school. "Jimmy Jones, get out of that sandbox!" "No, you can't take the bike away from Tommy, he had it first," and "Everyone come in now—time to wash up for lunch." She screams and bellows all day long. However loud her voice may be the children can always top it—and the result is a continual cacophony of children's and adult's voices, accompanied by the rising emotional tone they inspire!

> A kindergarten teacher glared at one of her pupils and in a very cross voice said, "Did I call you? Did you hear me say your name?" So intent was she on what she apparently considered to be an affront to her authority that she couldn't see the bewildered 'Oh, gosh, what have I done now to make her mad' look on the small child's face.

Minnie Milquetoast

Minnie probably grew up in the shadows of an autocratic home. Her "I AM" is practically nil—and she appears to be completely overwhelmed by the boisterous active children she hopes to teach. Minnie is a step ahead of Mary—because when she gains a little confidence she can use her quiet voice to good advantage. Mary will have a harder time remembering to tone hers down.

Nagging Nellie

"How many times do I have to tell you?

"I told you yesterday not to...

"Susie, put on your rubbers. Put on your rubbers, Sue. Have you got your rubbers on yet?"—all in the space of two minutes. Nellie doesn't even hear her own voice, going on... and on... and on.... Neither will Susie who soon learns to "tune out" that continual nagging. Mothers sometimes fall into this trap and with the strain of twenty-four hour duty it may be forgiven, but it is totally unprofessional for a teacher!

Miss Anne—The Teacher (with a capital "T")

Anne is so "tuned in" to program that she doesn't need to worry about whether she will be able to *control* the children. She assumes that behavior will take care of itself if children's minds are challenged. When she does see the need for correction, she moves quietly over to the situation, sizes it up, interfering only if it seems necessary. She knows children need to learn to manage their own squabbles—explore and experiment with human relations as well as cognitive skills. She *will* step in if one child is on the verge of hurting another. Then she gets down to his level literally—*eyeball* to *eyeball* and in a VERY firm voice says "I will not let you hurt Tommy" or "You may NOT take the bike away from Sam—he had it first, but when he is through with it you will be the very next one to have it." Anne will not humiliate a child by berating him in a loud voice before his peers. She will not pour fuel on his already injured feelings by scolding him. She WILL offer him support saying, "I will not LET you do that." He has a right to lean on her, to trust that she will stop him before he goes too far, to know that she will set reasonable limits for him.

Anne knows when to ignore blustering threats, "I hate you. I'm going to chop you up!", to answer with a pleasant "I'm sorry, I do like you." She can answer a defiant "I won't" with a confident and pleasant, "Oh, yes, you will" at the same time holding the child's hand firmly and moving toward the action she had requested.

Anne has the marvelous ability to "get into the skin" of the offending child; to KNOW when he needs the protection of her arms holding him firmly from doing what he knows is wrong, but not so tightly that he feels the constriction of her anger. Anne is saying to a child "I am grown up. I want to help you."

Anne trusts her own ability to say and do the right thing at the right time and to back up gracefully if she goofs. Anne has the light touch which can sense when the healing balm of laughter may be more useful than the abrasive action of anger.

Avoiding the Pitfalls

Kathy is starting off with ten children, moving from classroom to play yard. Her mind has moved ahead, considered the possible hazards. She gathers her children around her and they have a short meeting.... "When we go outside, we need to remember some rules..."

1. Wait for me. You MAY go as far as the big tree, but then you will stop and wait until we all catch up with you.

2. When we get outside, we will use the tree house playground. Another group is using the bikes. When they are through perhaps we can have them.

Kathy doesn't talk about the "or elses" but she knows what they are. Danny does NOT wait for her. She does not yell and scream after him. But when she does catch up with him she says very quietly in his ear—"You did not listen to me. Now you will have to hold my hand for a few minutes while the others play." On the first offense she does not hold his hand very long (a minute is an eternity to a child in these circumstances) but she MUST do something which fixes the idea firmly in his mind that there will ALWAYS be consequences for infractions. The next day, before they start will she say "Remember, Danny, yesterday you ran ahead and I had to punish you?" (Or will she trust him?)

Don't make threats you can't carry out!

Mr. Jim digs his own hole and falls into it. "Jacky, I'm tired of telling you to put on your jacket. If you aren't ready when that taxi comes he will leave without you." So the taxi comes. Now what? Jim is "hoist on his own petard." He can't keep Jacky—he knew he couldn't when he made the threat. He has no alternative but to finish dressing Jacky, and get him into that car. EVERY adult falls into this trap sooner or later—and has to find a way out. Reading these words won't stop him—experience won't prevent it from happening. The best thing that comes of it must be the reminder to the adult that we all make mistakes over and over. *Humility* should be an important word in the adult vocabulary.

"It's a competitive world. They might as well learn to live in it!"

"Come on, Bill, you can put on your boots. See, Sam can do it, and Jill can, and they are four—just like you. Now TRY!" Maybe Bill can put on his boots; maybe Bill should put on his own boots, but the reason is NOT because Sam and Jill can put on their own boots! Being four does not mean that physical and manual dexterity reach a common level. Bill may very well be more advanced in some other area than Sam or Jill. Suggesting that he is lacking by setting him in competition with his peers may have the opposite of the desired effect.

But what can I do? is the plaintive cry of the harried teacher suffering through boot season. "I will end up putting Bill's boots on EVERY day—and with all these children it is impossible!" She might try saying to Bill, "The others are going to hear a story now, Bill, but it takes you so much longer than the rest to get your boots on, I am afraid you will have to get started early" or "As soon as you have your ski pants and boots on, bring your hats and jackets with you to the story carpet. I have a special surprise there!"

Be a Big Boy!

Picture yourself walking along on the main street, loaded with bundles, when you slip on a banana peel and fall, scattering your pocketbook and its contents, tearing your stockings and scraping your knee on the asphalt. You are embarrassed and hurting. How will you feel if some wise adult comes over and says, "come on, get up, that didn't hurt" or "be a big girl, don't cry. Everyone is looking at you!"

When a child falls, it hurts his pride AND his body. The most you can do for him is to recognize this fact. "It hurts. I am sorry. We will go in and put some cold water on it. That will make it feel better." More than anything else he needs the assurance, through your tone of voice, that he is NOT permanently injured, that it WILL feel better in a few minutes, and that you DO understand that it hurts!

"Come on, try it, you'll like it!"

...says the new substitute teacher, as she PUTS little Linda on the slide. Linda, who is NOT ready to tackle this piece of equipment, tenses up, and when she reaches the bottom her leg breaks. Exaggerated? Maybe, but not impossible. Children are better judges than we are of their readiness for new experiences. They may need help. "If you would like to try it, I will hold you all the way down so you will not go too fast" or "This time why don't I just hold your hands?" and gradually Linda gains the confidence which will let her clamber up and down the slide as well as her friends. *Putting a child on a piece of equipment is dangerous!*

"Think before you Speak!"

Easier said than done—but a sign of "teaching maturity." The most important skill an adult can use is the ability to think one step ahead of the present. While the children are still sitting at the table having juice she is thinking of what will happen next, how she will manage the transition from one place to another, anticipate the hazards (which may mean knowing Johnny will take off for the blocks) and thus armed with pre-planning she will be able to keep her voice down and her face serene.

"Why are these boys sitting in your office on such a lovely day?"

The director of a full day care center answered, "They are being punished. They have behaved so badly on the playground that the teachers are at their wits' end. I spoke to the parents and they have talked to their children but nothing seems to do any good."

Inquiry disclosed that these bright, active, four-year-olds were in the center ten hours a day, five days a week. They gave little or no trouble in the morning when program activities kept them occupied.

The following suggestions were offered:

1. Go back to the books and read everything you can find about four-year-olds. What are they like? What are their needs?

2. Have a meeting of all staff who work with these two children at different hours of the day. Talk about the positive things. What do they enjoy most? When do they perform best? What seems to 'trigger' the objectionable behavior?

3. Get them involved in an acitivty which has some continuity. Building or making something which requires them to think, plan, look for materials and bring things from home, such as developing a play which will involve making costumes, props, invitations, etc...and most important, with the objective of a performance.

4. *Greet the parents each night with some* POSITIVE comment. "Tim helped the little ones dress today. Does he help you a lot at home?"

"You would have been proud of Jamey if you had been here at clean-up time. He organized a crew and directed the operation and they all worked very hard for him."

In watching for *positive acts* to relate, staff will hopefully change their negative attitudes toward these two boys.

Asking a parent who has worked all day to scold or lecture to a recalcitrant child is like a mother who greets her husband each night with a demand that he discipline the children for their bad deeds during the day. In the first place, they are going to be anxious about whether the center might exclude the child and jeopardize their jobs, and secondly, they are not in the position to handle punishments for deeds which they have not seen. In either case, the relationship between child and parent is destroyed. The objective of the staff should be to strengthen the family.

Stay Loose   Every true teacher has a philosophy, a set of beliefs about what she is doing, but usually it is in her head and heart. Confronted with a request to 'spell it out' as sometimes hap-

pens in interviews, she may find it difficult to express. It is a healthy exercise in self-discipline to attempt to express one's convictions in words, to assemble them into some recognizable shape.

The philosophy stated in this book is only a beginning. The very nature of the "I AM!" and "I CAN!" theory carries with it the implication that each teacher is also a four-sided individual with strengths and weaknesses. It is expected that some will bulge in one area of interest and shrink in another. It is hoped that each teacher will contribute generously of enthusiasm and talents in special interests and make an effort to grow in those which are less appealing.

As a teacher grows an individual teaching style will develop. Our advice to the neophyte teacher is "Do your own thing!" but "Never let your convictions become encased in cement. Leave the doors of your mind open to new ideas. Let your "I AM" develop to the point where you can experiment with enthusiasm, succeed with satisfaction and fall flat on your face without frustration or a sense of overwhelming failure."

"STAY LOOSE!!"

What is a Teaching Team? The modern medical profession has consistently improved health care by utilizing teams of doctors, nurses, technicians and para-professionals working at different levels of expertise and skills offering better and more efficient care than the old-fashioned general practitioner who tried to be all things to all people.

Members of a staff of teachers using the team teaching approach can also find greater satisfaction, improved efficiency and economy, and at the same time offer higher quality educational programs to children. When there is a balance of talents with each team member providing a special skill the program has variety and strength in each activity area. When these personalities and talents blend into an integrated whole, teaching is more rewarding and harmonious.

In Figure C staff is divided into three teams working under a director whose main contacts are with six people—the three team leaders and three administrative personnel. ABC and abc work as horizontal teams. Teams have easy access at all levels with one another and with team leaders. In each group there is a lead person (shown in dark outlines). These act as backup people for the persons at the next level. A is team leader/assistant director a, a, a would take over in the absence of each team leader.

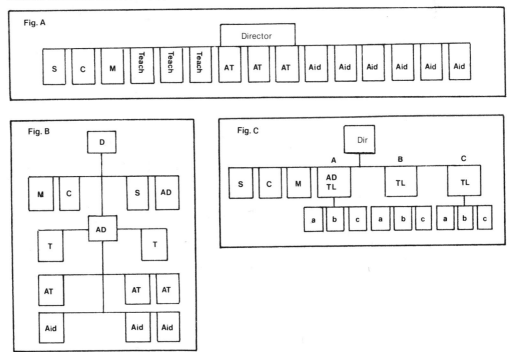

Volunteers   In many centers there will be individuals who, for various reasons, offer their services. This can be enormously helpful, but also calls for a word of caution. More than one director or teacher who eagerly walked into a situation which turned out to be undesirable has found it difficult to back away. It is best to look at the volunteer with the same care one uses when employing a staff member. They will be with your children, and the fact that they are not paid does not enhance or limit the relationship. Motivation is a consideration. Is this to fulfill a need of their own, and is it compatible with your goals and philosophy? Will they make a definite commitment and expect to be conscientious and prompt in adhering to that promise, or will they feel, "I'm not getting paid, so I come when I feel like it."

Would you employ this person if you had a vacancy? If not, would the obstruction be based on personality, appearance, speech, or education? Is it a negative quality, serious enough to be detrimental to your school? Remember, the parent or visitor cannot always distinguish the student teacher or volunteer from employed personnel.

Will this person agree to volunteer and then feel "put upon" when she sees she is not being paid for what she judges to be the same duties?

We do not intend to negate the value of these additional people to your program, only to suggest that such a relationship needs to be given careful thought.

Who are volunteers? Where do they come from?

A retired school teacher was delighted when a day care center opened across the street from her home. She called on the director as a neighbor and when they had established a friendly relationship she explained that she missed daily exposure to little children and offered her services.

"It would be wonderful if you could help us at noon, and through naptime, because that is when we have team meetings." It was a happy situation for both sides. Living alone, she welcomed the opportunity to eat one meal a day with company and she was able to make that her main meal of the day. The children enjoyed her grandmotherly presence and looked forward to her coming during the day. When she could attend meetings, she was able to make contributions based on her long experience. Some of her methods were more traditional than those of the center but she was open to suggestions, and receptive to new ideas.

In another school, a half day nursery in a church, the classroom was used by a senior citizens group twice a month for lunch and a meeting. One elderly gentleman, who happened to arrive early, was thrilled when the children flocked around him and asked, "Are you a grandpa?" His arrival time became earlier and earlier, and finally the director asked him if he would like to volunteer on a regular basis. That, too, turned out to be a happy arrangement.

A caution—With the growing interest in child care, the proliferation of extra adults in a classroom becomes a serious problem. High schools are introducing courses in child care, and request training opportunities for their students. Federal programs, designed to furnish employment which may lead to training for a career, will often seek placements in a center. A director must steer a careful path between the desire to be helpful and responsibility to the children. Basic rules should be determined—and discussed, in advance. Minimum, on-going training should be required, which in itself may serve as a deterrent to the insincere applicant. The format suggested for a Parent Volunteer Program could serve as a base for such training. There will be many fine, sensitive people, who can add to and enrich programs, but their selection and approval is not to be taken lightly.

Student Teachers   A good student teacher program enhances the educational image and scope of a school. The director should find out what teacher training programs exist in nearby colleges and junior colleges and invite the department heads to visit the school and discuss the possibilities for mutual service. The director joins the team who are educating teachers and gives as much as he/she receives from the student.

The teacher also becomes a member of that team and will be a model as some parts of his/her will surely rub off on this fledgling, while sharing philosophy and attitudes towards children and teaching. The way a teacher feels as an individual and about the profession will influence the student. A teacher who is rigid or uncompromising implying that there is only ONE way, may 'turn off' a potentially good teacher.

On the other hand, the teacher who sees this relationshop as a two-way street will reach out for the fresh ideas and additional resources which the student can bring to enrich the program. Helping the professional student to become a teacher is an extension of one's self.

The following suggestions will guide the director in making the most of this experience:

1. Try to have the names of students before they arrive—and when they come, greet them by name.(See Seq. 1—importance of names)

2. Plan to sit down in the *staff room* with students on the first day to explain the background and philosophy of the school.

3. Try to give students some choices in making group assignments. Talk about which age they really want to work with. A student who has just finished a semester with threes may desire some experience with fives.

4. Take a *tour* around the school. Give it as much time and enthusiasm as you do when showing it to a prospective parent.

5. Introduce the student to the lead teacher and other members of the *team*.

6. Explain that the student will be encouraged to work directly with the children, to bring in materials and ideas, but that the student should try to make these fit into the current activities of *curriculum*. Suggest that when observing something he/she does not understand, or approve of, the student should make a note of it and find an opportunity to ask the teacher about it later.

7. Make sure that time is allowed for *conferences* with the supervising teacher and director, and for an occasional break in the staff room.

8. Suggest that the student try to attend weekly *team meetings*, and, if possible, a parent meeting.

9. Explain at the first meeting that the student will be asked to write a letter at the end of the practice session evaluating the experience, and offering constructive criticisms. The supervising teacher will also write an evaluation, and these two documents will be consulted if references are requested at a later date.

Suggestions for Volunteers and Student Teachers

It is recommended that a lead teacher go over these practical "down to earth" ideas with each student on a one-to-one basis, or on occasion ask one of the team to do it. EVERY person who works with children needs to be reminded of the little things, regularly, frequently. Explaining them to others is reinforcement!

1. Treat every child with the same *courtesy, respect* and *sympathy* you would accord to an adult. This means you will NOT talk about them in their presence.

2. *Be natural,* never "talk down to a child." Avoid exaggeration, or overly demonstrative affection.

3. Be *pleasant* and *friendly.*

4. *Be reassuring.* Give legitimate praise without being effusive.

5. Avoid *promises and threats.* If you do find yourself unable to follow through, do it graciously. Children need to know that adults make mistakes.

6. *Avoid competition.* Instead of "Let's see who can jump the highest" say "We'll all have fun jumping."

7. Be *consistent and firm.* Know the "ground rules" and maintain them.

8. Use *simple direct language.* "Come" with hand outstretched. Avoid unnecessary verbiage.

9. Your *tone of voice* sets the tempo for action. EXPECT the child to respond! Walk to him when you have a request or directive. NEVER shout across a room or yard. Let your voice hold a note of mystery and anticipation which will arouse his curiosity and hold his attention.

10. When offering *choices,* make them explicit. If there is NO choice make this clear also.

11. Give directives in *positive terms.* Instead of "Don't shout," say "Loud voices are

for outside. Use your inside voice here." or instead of "Don't touch the food yet" say "Let's put our hands in our laps until we are ready."

12. *Be leisurely*. Instead of hurrying children, plan ahead for time to get from on activity to the next.

13. *Give warnings*. Instead of "Leave the puzzle and wash your hands" say "When you finish the puzzle come wash your hands."

14. *Be understanding*. Give children time to plan and complete activities. Do not direct more than necessary. Do not interfere, make suggestions, or help until asked.

15. Keep your hands *off childrens work*. NO EXCEPTIONS!!

16. *Be patient*. Take time to LISTEN and to care about what the child is telling you, either through his words or actions.

Self Evaluation for Teacher Aides

Adult Attitudes

Do you sit down next to the child so that you are on his level and so that he may see your face and talk to you more easily?

Do you show warmth and affection by patting or putting your arm about a child?

Do you let the child do the talking while you listen attentively to him?

Are you alert to untied shoes, children who need a tissue, children who seem listless or ill?

Do you ask the teacher what to do about a child who is doing something of which you disapprove?

Do you watch for safety hazards and correct them, e.g. spilled water, spilled paint, protruding nails, "wobbly" equipment?

Do you help the child become independent at dressing and undressing time by doing only what is necessary, e.g. buttoning top buttons, starting zippers?

Language

Do you speak clearly and slowly so that the child understands you?

Do you control your desire to talk constantly to the child?

Do you say "please" and "thank you" in talking with the children?

Do you give the child your full attention when he is speaking to you?

Do you use the correct names for things?

Do you repeat important words in English for the child who speaks another language?

When you read to children, do you use expression which heightens the child's enjoyment?

Do you share books with children, discussing pictures and story?

Art

Do you place art materials in an inviting display and encourage the child to experiment with them?

Do you use manuscript writing when you print a child's name on the back of his work?

Do you help children hang up their work when they have finished?

Do you remind the children to wash their hands after painting or clay work?

Do you make certain that the paints are ready for use and of the right consistency at the beginning of each period?

Do you see that the brushes are clean and the paint jars are covered at the end of the day?

Work-Play Period

Do you watch to see that the block building activities are safe?

Do you join in dramatization by participating in planning and acting the role assigned you by the children?

Do you sit with the children who are playing with table toys, listen to them, answer their questions?

The Secretary-Receptionist

Experience has shown that this person is the 'right arm' of the director, often the first voice heard on the phone, and the first impression of a school is transmitted by the receptionist.

In a school there may be many visitors. Some are parents who wish to register their child. Many are professional people who come to visit and observe, for a variety of reasons. Sometimes they come with a skeptical or critical attitude.

In such cases, the secretary-receptionist is a sales person who must learn how to answer an inquiry with enough factual information but never more than qualified to give; to speak and listen with warmth and interest, and to refer to the director for further information.

The secretary is often a business representative and may be the one who accepts payments and keeps delinquent payments at a minimum; may also be the bookkeeper. In every way possible relieving the director of details, enabling him/her to spend more time in the classroom.

Appearance is of prime importance and the receptionist cannot afford to indulge in tastes for casual, exotic or unprofessional attire. Hair, makeup, voice and diction, and smile are important. This is a professional who must take pride in maintaining these assets.

The secretary-receptionist must be able to exercise discretion in using a knowledge of the people (parents and staff), the business (salaries and income), and mistakes which happen in every organization. Finally, the secretary-receptionist must *like people and enjoy children!*

Daily Duties

1. *Greet visitors.* Give them prompt and courteous attention. Screen them before calling director and make them comfortable while they are waiting.
   Keep area in order, adding the extra components of *attractive displays* or a bulletin board and a comfortable chair for waiting visitors. Provide them with educational reading material or a scrapbook with pictures of the children and activites of the school. Add the extra touch of a plant or flowers on the desk and children's art work.

2. *Answer phones.* Give information pertaining to class schedules and tuition but refer all questions on curriculum or philosophy to director. Fill out an *inquiry card* when interviewing callers or visitors seeking information about the school. At all times the receptionist must respond to complaints with sympathy and courtesy. "I'm sure our director will want to know about this. As soon as she can look into the situation she will call you back. RECORD ALL CALLS IN A LOG BOOK. Time consuming, but important. A code can be used for routine calls, i.e., SD = stay day; also record outgoing calls with special notation.

3. *Greet parents* and children as they arrive. Make sure children go into classroom.

4. *Serve as personal secretary to the director.* Discuss any special plans for the day with the director. If trips are to be taken make calls for prearrangements. Check permission slips in files to make sure every child can go. Keep director's calendar up to date. Call attention to daily appointments. Take letters and type for the director. Take care of incoming and outgoing mail, postage and petty cash.

5. *Record extra hours* or services provided, keeping track of stay days or hourly care for children and staff.

6. Keep up to date on memos for *newsletter* placed in the news box. Check with writer if additional details are needed while the incident is fresh. Help prepare and distribute copies of newsletters and bulletins to parents and staff, making sure no one is omitted.

7. Receive *applications* and send *acceptances.* Keep applications of children currently enrolled in a notebook. When a child is withdrawn, be sure to record the reason and then place the application in the permanent file. Prepare record card for each child as enrolled. When child is withdrawn, be sure to get a final statement from teacher on card, have director approve it and place in permanent file. Check return of health card, emergency card and trip permission slips. File for easy access.

8. *Fill in whenever or wherever needed if an emergency arises!*

Assistant Director—Unless the budget can be extended to cover both an assistant director and a secretary, it is strongly suggested that the assistant director follow the previous job description, adding whatever additional responsibilities necessary for training to be a director. A plan should be evolved which would assure that either the director or the assistant director be in the building every moment of the day in which children will be present.

The Cook

When you think about a 'storybook home' what are some of the first visual images which pop into your mind? Which room do you think of? *The kitchen*—a warm inviting place inhabited by a happy, cheerful mother, a full cookie jar and a glass of milk to go with a cookie when you come home from school or in from play. Tantalizing mouth-watering smells that permeate the whole house and come drifting outside from the vent in the kitchen fan.

In a child care center the kitchen should not be hidden but placed in view of the classrooms. A cook whose smiling face tells the children that she likes and enjoys being with them is an important addition to the staff. The cook need not be a professionally trained chef but needs to know or be trained in simple food preparation, economics, and basic dietary rules, perhaps may be a homemaker seeking part time employment, a retired older person, a mother who needs to support family income to help pay her child's tuition, a college student.

The cook is a valuable member of the director's team and should be invited to attend all full staff meetings. His/her knowledge of food and nutrition may suggest contributions to curriculum. Tolerance will be required when an extra bowl, or fancy carrot cutter is borrowed. When the cook realizes the true meaning of curriculum he/she may suggest that the children make the jello for dessert, or fix the carrot sticks. If the cook sees the experiment with stalks of celery in a glass of liquid food coloring the close relationship between the kitchen and the science program will be appreciated.

Pride in personal appearance is vital. It is appropriate and desirable that the cook wear a uniform. This need not necessarily be white—uniforms come in pretty colors—but it must be spotless. The same rules which apply to the nurse and doctor for cleanliness should be considered for all who are preparing food. If hairnets are not required, at least hair should be tied back away from the face.

The cook will keep the kitchen spotless and shining and manage it as efficiently as a business, keeping careful track of purchasing and expenses, making reasonable requests for updating or replacing equipment, going through the proper channels and using accepted forms or procedural outlines.

The Nurse

When a school budget does not allow for this extra service, a director may find a mother who is glad to give part time service in exchange for tuition. It would be very unusual to have a full time nurse, except in a very large day care center.

When a nurse is not available licensing regulations usually require that at least one person trained in First Aid be on the premises at all times. In some cases a nurse who lives or works close by the school can be "on call," a measure of comfort and reassurance to staff and parents.

Maintenance

Maintenance is perhaps the most difficult problem a director has to deal with. Child care is a 'messy' business, and the materials that are important to creative program are most difficult to use and maintain with any semblance of order.

The program is in direct contradiction to an important requisite of child care— absolute cleanliness. The person who does the heavy maintenance, floors, windows, etc., must understand the needs of the program. Communication between the 'users' and the 'cleaners' is important. Often the cleaning staff work at night, but notes can be exchanged, and an effort should be made for occasional face to face conversation.

In a very large center, maintenance may be part of an overall establishment such as an industry or hospital. In the church it may be the custodian, and in the small proprietary school it is usually the owner and members of his family.

Teachers must expect to share this responsibility. They cannot wait for a maintenance crew to clean up a spill, and they should not expect anyone else to keep their tables and counters clean. A teacher who takes pride in the room will not be above wiping finger-marks off the white paint around the door, washing the chairs or cleaning out the cubbies, always enlisting the willing assistance of the pupils.

Where do you look for maintenance personel? Perhaps a high school or college student, a working man who is seeking extra work at night, a woman who wants to earn some extra money and can only leave her home in the evening, a retired person who may also like to fix things and wants to work part time. The last is ideal and the director who finds such a person will agree that *"Next to a good husband, happiness is a good maintenance man!"*

If the maintenance person is to be on the premises while the children are present, several very important factors must be considered:

He/she must like and enjoy being around children. A surly attitude, uncouth habits, bad language, or an untidy appearance will be noticed, and sometimes emulated by the little ones in the center. They have no way of distinguishing between the adults they should or should not copy.

It is important to explain the philosophy and curriculum goals of the center to a maintenance person. They can be of great assistance, and as they participate, they are more aware of the reasoning behind some of the requirements of their work.

Orrin brought in a basket of baby bunnies one day, and took them to each group, allowing the children to look, touch gently and admire them.

When the teacher asked to have the legs of a painting easel shortened, Henry did it right in the classroom and at the same time conducted a class in problem solving with four-year-olds. "How shall we do it?" he asked. Cutting one leg at a time, he stood the easel up and said, "Is it right now? What is wrong? What shall I do next?"

On another occasion, when the teacher had put plastic numerals on the floor to make a clock (See Sequence 5, #90) Henry lay down in the middle to make the hands, to the great glee of the children.

Staff Morale   A school was described as the "Cadillac of all nursery schools" — an interesting simile to pursue! Picture a big, beautiful Cadillac, tooling along the highway, impressive, efficient, comfortable, eliciting favorable comment from all those who *KNOW THE DIFFERENCE*. A school is not a machine, but there are commonalities worthy of consideration. Each has a direct influence on the life of human beings.

The Cadillac is not only useless but positively dangerous without a capable and intelligent driver. In a school, the staff *are* the vehicle — teachers, maintenance, kitchen, office and administrative staff are all functioning parts of a total on-going force. The Cadillac may continue for some time when one cylinder is not functioning but soon other parts will be affected and efficiency impaired.

The staff must be coordinated by a leader who will see the red light flashing a signal to check the oil or water, who will hear and even feel the first warnings of trouble in the engine, who will sense the slightest irregularity in over-all performance and know where to look for the cause.

To continue the analogy, a misguided act or statement which backfires can cause an explosive disturbance. A team member who fails to do his share of the "housework" can be compared to the driver who fails to check the gas tank or water in the battery.

A flat tire, like the negative teacher, holds back the progress of the vehicle. A director who fails to assume leadership is like faulty steering equipment — destination is always uncertain.

If the Cadillac is to give long-lasting, consistent day-to-day performance it must have a certain amount of T.L.C. (tender, loving care), plenty of oil to keep moving parts well lubricated, fuel and water, prompt attention to mechanical difficulties and concern for overall appearance.

In a school, the separate parts are oiled by practices which respect the rights of the individual; a salary schedule which is fair, personnel policies which are clearly defined, division of duties discussed and agreed upon, rather than arbitrarily imposed. Employees need time for brief stops at a station during each daily trip to refuel the tank or cool the engine.

But what happens to the Cadillac when someone fails to put oil in the right place at the right time? When dirt gets in the fuel line or carburetor or when a nail puts a tire out of commission? The same thing that happens in a school when the oil of communication is missing, when the mixture is thinned by lack of opportunity for meetings, or when one individual throws dirt in the working parts, or drops a nail in the driveway.

The beginning of trouble may be hardly noticeable in a car, and so, too, the breakdown of morale in an organization can be so subtle, so insidious that even the perpetrator may not be aware of the seriousness of the act.

"I never gossip. If I have anything to say I will say it to a person's face." he says, self-righteously, and yet, with a shrug of the shoulders or a facial grimace or a sly wink he sets the wheels in motion which can carry the morale of the team to destruction. If you have ever watched Red Skelton's skit, "The Silent Ones," you can appreciate the possibility of conveying thoughts, ideas, emotions, anxieties, and even aggression without ever saying a word.

We talk about concrete and abstract concepts—morale fits into the latter category. *Morale is the business of every employee in the school.*

Positive Grapevine—The director has an excellent opportunity to start a *positive grapevine* at staff meetings which will enhance the image of the 'Cadillac'. It is started simply, by saying:

"There are always so many good things happening in our school which I never see. You may be modest, and hesitate to tell of your successes but you can report about each other in a very positive way. I think it is great when one staff member says, 'Have you noticed what M _____ has been doing with creative movement? I could hardly believe my eyes when I saw J _____ A _____ dancing.' "

"I wish you could have seen the expression on the faces of two children I saw playing a game L _____ had made; they were so absorbed they didn't know there was a soul around. L _____, could you show us the game?

"I think parents are so lucky to have a school like ours. I watched Judy (secretary) consoling little Eddie the other day. He was unhappy because his mother was late. Judy made it obvious that everyone cares for children here."

A positive grapevine is just as contagious as gossip; the ball can roll in either direction but someone has to give it the initial push.

Staff Training & Recruitment

The director is the key to the success of a child care center, but even if he/she has a fair share of ability in all of the areas described previously, plus unlimited physical strength and mental energy, a director still needs the support of a happy, enthusiastic and well trained staff.

How staff is chosen, how personalities and talents are combined on each team is the first major concern of the director. The director must try to help them become one harmonious, supportive unit, calling upon every vestige of experience, and guided by that which is stored in his/her head and heart.

At the time of employment, a director is careful to go over the plans for *pre-opening training* and *in-service training*. If time for training or meeting is on a volunteer basis, the director makes this clear:

"I see our staff meetings as being fully as valuable as a course for which you would pay." She may say, "I do not consider that it is an imposition to ask you to attend, but an added benefit we offer. Your work will be more pleasant and satisfying because you meet and share with your co-workers. I will expect you to carry out assignments. If you cannot give this extra measure of your time and interest, please do not come here to work, because it is expected.

After a person accepts a contract, it is unfair to make unexpected demands on time. If an employee takes a position with a clear understanding of the requirements, he/she can be expected to comply.

What to Look For

In addition to the personal qualifications outlined in the previous descriptions, we suggest the following minimal professional training:

Director—four year degree in Education or closely related field with at least two years experience in early childhood

Associate Director—same, with one year of experience

Lead Teacher—same, with student teaching experience

Assistant Teacher—two year Associates degree, with some courses in Early Childhood Education

Aide—High school plus at least one basic course in Early Childhood Education and a plan for continuing education

Where to Look

The director should keep on file an up-to-date list of teacher training institutions (colleges, universities, community and junior colleges), employment agencies (private and government), and local professional associations, with the name, address, telephone number and name of person to contact. Some notations of past experience with the agency might be helpful to a new director.

In addition to these, the following are potential resources:

Clergymen (they often know of persons who are in need of financial help or looking for a new interest outside the realm of homemaking or regular jobs.)

Other school directors will usually share their list of candidates, especially in an emergency and if you evidence a willingness to reciprocate.

Parents who may welcome this opportunity to earn tuition. (The value of the Parent Volunteer Training program is evident when a vacancy occurs during the year.)

An *ad* in the local paper usually brings a good response, especially if it is designed to appeal to people with varied backgrounds.

Once a center is established the best source is through *personal recommendation.*

If the working conditions are pleasant, and the training opportunities exciting, there will seldom be a need for advertising when a vacancy occurs. Ideally, there will always be someone on the *substitute list* who has been waiting for a full-time position.

Substitutes

As with drivers, the first resource for substitutes will be found within the center. Part time employees are THERE, and accessible for short-term, or hourly replacement.

When an ad is used, every applicant should receive an answer—even when a box number is used. (Just a card saying, "Thank you for your response to our ad. The position has been filled but we will keep your letter on file" relieves the applicant who may be eagerly waiting for a reply.

References

Choosing the best person for each place on the staff is so vital to the success of a center that the director should employ every possible means to help to make this decision. While most of us would admit that we rely heavily on intuition, 'gut feeling', our responsibility to children and parents requires that we go beyond that. Putting together the right combination of personalities and talents is like doing a crossword puzzle, and pertinent clues will be found in references.

When expediency demands that references be checked by phone, we suggest that the written form be used in recording the conversation.

Interviews

The interview should be seen as an opportunity for both director and applicant to share information. Setting the stage for this meeting is important. Seated in comfortable chairs facing each other (NEVER conduct an interview from behind a desk), the interviewer should give the candidate his/her undivided attention, closing off all but emergency phone calls or interruptions. This is not just a matter of courtesy—interruptions often break the line of communication at a crucial point—or keep it from ever really getting established.

Some directors like to provide the applicant with information and materials about the center prior to the meeting—others feel that this will invite "cued responses." We are inclined to feel that future negotiations depend on a platform of TRUST and that a trained interviewer will know when the applicant is giving the responses he "thinks you want to hear."

The successful interviewer trains himself/herself to LISTEN and become a sensitive receiver. Facial expression, body language, and voice quality speak as loudly as appearance, diction and words. To set the applicant at ease, and to put the "conversational ball" in motion, the following questions are appropriate:

What do you know about our center?
Which of the experiences you have listed here did you find most fulfilling?
How do you feel about structure vs. open classroom?
What do you consider to be your strengths in personality and ability to contribute to program?
What would be your weakest areas?
What attempts have you made, or do you plan to make, to broaden the scope of your talents?
Do you have any hobbies or other interests which might be used in program planning?
What is the most fulfilling experience you have had in the past six months?
What kinds of things do you enjoy when you are relaxing?

True communication is more than a series of questions and answers. It is a matter of 'tuning in' on the same wave length—a feeling response. Some interviewers rely heavily on eye contact. Occasionally, one encounters a person whose eyes light up the whole face— literally shining with enthusiasm and sparkling with vitality. The success of such a person in working with young children is almost guaranteed!

You may lose the bright-eyed, eager applicant when you ask, "Have you ever cleaned a child who has had a bowel movement?" or, "Will you be able to mop up when one of the children throws up?", but these are the facts of life in a child care center and might as well be faced honestly, in advance.

THINGS TO LISTEN FOR
(The Four Sides of Development)

INTELLECTUAL	—experiences with children that demonstrate ability and agreement with our philosophy and program —experience in 'team work', understanding of shared responsibility for total program. (Listen, too, for how the applicant talks about his/her former employer.) —experience calling for basic skills of the job (e.g., receptionist in record keeping, meeting public; cook, in cooking in quantity, shopping wisely, keeping records; custodian's past responsibilities for property of others).
EMOTIONAL	—healthy "I AM" with openness to grow and learn from others —realistic "I CAN"—adaptability and flexibility —commitment to seeing things to completion; sense of pride in past accomplishments —vituperative criticism of people or program—is a warning!
SOCIAL	—every member of the staff is a part of the total team and compatibility of personalities must be considered in gathering together the people who will function comfortably and happily with you and other members of your staff
PHYSICAL	—it is important to consider the physical appearance and posture of the applicant. Accepting a casual style of dress does not mean overlooking a sloppy appearance. People often reveal how they feel about themselves by the way they stand or sit— 'body language'. It is necessary also to ask about the applicant's health record, especially if they are taking any medication regularly.

An enthusiastic director, who is excited about the program, must be careful not to oversell the position. It is important to remind the applicant that many hours are involved in routine activities—dressing, struggling with rubbers and boots, helping to clean up messes, and that all of this is PROGRAM and is just as important as the activities described in a curriculum. In schools where there are housekeeping chores these should not be minimized. If the applicant has children be sure to discuss what arrangements will be made if they should become ill. Is there someone at home who can care for them? Would the employee be required to take time off?

At some point during the interview a visit to the classrooms is in order. The reactions (verbal and otherwise) of the applicant to the environment and children will add another dimension to the growing impression.

At the conclusion of the interview a form will "jell" the interviewer's impressions and retain vital information. This is especially important when a number of candidates are being considered.

Contractual Procedures

When verbal agreement has been reached, this should be followed up with a letter of welcome and a written agreement, or as we prefer to call it, an Employment Action Sheet. Space has been allowed here for two salaries. It may happen that a lead teacher in the morning is glad to be an assistant in the afternoon, either for a change of pace or because that is the only job available and he/she needs full time employment. If there is a different salary scale this must be taken into account. This agreement would be accompanied by

    a) Personnel Policies
    b) Staff Handbook
    c) School Calendar
    d) Health Examination Form

Staff manual

    1. Brief history of school including form of organization (private, nonprofit, cooperative)
    2. Enrollment policies (limitations if any)
    3. Written statement of philosophy of education
    4. Personnel policy
    5. Job descriptions
    6. Who's Who on Staff (thumbnail description — place on Organization Chart)

It is suggested that this information be kept in a looseleaf binder, and that all staff and parent bulletins be added, as well as minutes of staff meetings and other pertinent materials. This handbook belongs to the center and on termination should be turned in to the office BEFORE the final paycheck is delivered. It should be kept accessible for easy reference and brought to all staff meetings.

Staff Files

A file folder should be maintained on EVERY employee, and stored for at least seven years. (We have had occasion to refer to them after much longer periods.) This would include:

    original letter of inquiry
    application
    references
    copy of contract
    health examination report (T.B. test report)
    health record (including dates of absence and reason)
    sick leave record (especially important when cumulative time allowed)
    employee's profile
    reports of conferences and self-evaluations
    a picture (this may be just a snapshot or a class picture but proves to be very helpful when a call comes for a reference years later)

Additional Employee Files

In addition, we suggest that some provision be made for keeping the names and applications of applicants NOT hired, separating those who might be eligible at a later date from those who were undesirable. In the latter case, the record should show WHY this person was not accepted.

Termination of Employment

Termination of employment may be at the request of the employee or of the director.

If an employee must resign, ask for two weeks notice whenever possible. If he/she has been unhappy, terminate as soon as you can find a replacement.

Conducting such an interview is never easy, but, again, experience has shown that the maxim 'the coward does it with a kiss—the brave man with a sword' is true. It is far better to start with "I have come to ask for your resignation" and then proceed to elaborate on the reasons, than it is to build up to it, leaving the "victim" squirming with a growing sense of apprehension. This does not necessarily preclude the possibility that at the conclusion of a healthy, two-way discussion, you may decide to try again; it actually opens the way for that discussion at the very outset.

Be prepared for some of the following reactions:

The person who accepts every criticism with seeming sincerity may be the one who explodes when he/she has had time to think it over, or share it with a sympathetic relative. It is quite possible that you will receive an irate, or even abrasive, phone call that night or the next day, from a husband or parent, officials of the Labor Department or employment agency. The terms and reasons for severance will be important if an application is made for unemployment insurance. The sympathy of parents of the children will frequently be solicited, and the director will want to choose words carefully when asked for reasons, trying to be fair to the staff member and still justify the action. Usually, it is best to offer no reasons, other than, "It seemed in the best interest of the children."

Once a person knows they are leaving, they rarely function well and can affect total staff morale, even unintentionally.

Termination Interview

Special effort should be made to conduct a termination interview, inviting the team leader to participate when appropriate. If you decide to ask an employee to leave, be as honest as you can and as you NEED TO BE to explain the reasons. It is never necessary to destroy a person's "I AM" in the process. Give the person job-related reasons, personal reasons, if that is part of the cause, but deal also with the person's strong points and assets, perhaps suggesting other kinds of work or other settings in which you think they might function better.

Discuss your willingness (or UNwillingness) to have your name given as a reference and talk specifically about what you would be comfortable in saying about that person. (You might have to discuss what you will NOT say also.) Discuss what each of you intends to say to other staff and to parents as to the reason this employee is leaving. Try to establish agreement here to avoid conflicting statements later, which would lead to misunderstanding by both teachers and parents. Discuss also what will be said to children and by whom.

A Termination Interview Record should be completed by the director and the employee, one copy to be filed with the original application and other papers (including a Reference Form for future inquiries).

STAFF TRAINING   **Pre-Opening Training**—If gradual orientation is important for the children, it is equally important for staff. The length of pre-training will run from one to three weeks and, to be effective, *no less* than three full days. The square and the circle, representing the educational philosophy and educational programs, are the basis for this orientation program.

An important part of this training session is getting to know others on the staff and blending the personalities and talents into an effective working team.

The content will vary with each school year, but the general themes will remain constant. The overall goal is to give confidence, to strengthen the "I AM" and to reinforce the "I CAN!" so that the staff can move through the first few days of school with serenity.

The indoctrination of staff members in a center with a year-round program presents a different set of problems, but for the traditional program, starting in September, we offer the following detailed suggestions, again hoping that each reader may find something which will be appropriate to the particular situation:

First Day—The director has prepared thumbnail sketches of each staff member and combined them on a "Who's Who" list. This enables newcomers to start with some point of reference. "I see you went to Cragmore—I have a friend who graduated in 19--" or, "You are going to have your own child with you, too. Have you tried it before? Will it be a problem?"

The time span between the first arrival and the last is of CRUCIAL importance. Newcomers feel awkward and inadequate, and their discomfort is increased when oldtimers greet each other with exuberance. Something to do, to eat, to make, eases the situation. Former staff members may be assigned newcomers to greet and later introduce. Team leaders may watch for the members of their team and take them to their own area to look around and get acquainted. Setting the stage for this first impression may determine the success of the first few hours.

When all have arrived, the director can further increase the confidence of newcomers with a short talk about the history and philosophy of the school. Knowing 'how it all came about' puts the present into perspective.

Using the diagram for the philosophy stated in the first chapter of this book, a framework is estbalished for discussions which always relate to the four sides of the square and the goals of encouraging the development of the "I AM" and "I CAN." Continual referral will help the listeners to assimilate their significance.

Getting acquainted is the next step, and a double purpose is served when some of the name games and songs (are learned and practiced) which will be used in the first few days with the children (see Sequence 1). In fact, the entire training program should demonstrate the environment and daily schedule, with a balance of activity and rest, of sitting still and moving around, of listening and discussing, of using and making equipment. *Teachers, like children, learn best when they have a need or desire to know.* These first days stress ideas, thinking, problem solving, combined with defining the structure of necessary rules and limitations, and establishing orderly procedures.

Using every visual aid he/she can contrive (diagrams, floor plans, mockups of building), the director will take the staff through an entire day, from the moment the doors are opened until they are locked up for the night. This is followed by a trip through the building, identifying the various areas previously mentioned. When copies of diagrams are available, they can also be referred to on the tour.

Returning to the central meeting place, the director can speak briefly about the areas observed and review health and safety procedures. To conclude the morning, several role-playing sessions, or open-ended questions posing emergency health or safety situations can be used as a test.

On the first day, lunch will be served and eaten in each team area, following the procedures which will be used with the children. Hopefully there will be at least one "oldtimer" in each area to lead the way, but until the directions in the manual have been read and discussed the practice will not be perfect.

During the lunch period, the director and assistant director will set up cots in the nap area, and immediately after lunch, zoning and nap time will be the topics for discussion.

Next, each team will go to its own area to talk about and start to set up the arrangement of the environment. This is concluded with all visiting each area to hear the plan and compare it with the suggestions offered heretofore. The day ends with music, learning some of the songs, a game and/or finger play, to be used during the first week with children.

Second Day—The first order of business is the distribution of record cards for the children. These have been prepared in advance, and contain the information on the application blanks. Each staff member will be given a share of the children in the team and it will be his/her responsibility to memorize enough of the key factors, to be able to recognize and greet each child with some personal comment. The slightest reference to the familiar gives a child the warm, comfortable feeling that, "She knows me; she was expecting me." For these particular children, this particular teacher will be the anchor mentioned (see The First Day).

The entire section on "The Young Child" will be reviewed with particular reference to procedures to follow at Open House, and the necessity for orientation. Suggestions for Adjustment will be mentioned, but it can be assumed that they will not be fully appreciated until the problems have been faced.

Since it is appropriate at this time to speak of books on the library shelf which will elaborate on ages and stages, this will be a good time to talk about all special equipment, its care and rules for use.

Returning to the central area, children's feelings and emotions will follow the discussion of adjustment problems. The young, or inexperienced, teacher may have some difficulty recognizing the difference between 'acting out' and sheer naughtiness. The section entitled "Behavior—A Second Language" will provide material for discussion.

The basic *Rules for Discipline* may be demonstrated with role-playing techniques or pictures which tell a story.

Ample time should be allocated on this second day for teams to work together in their own areas, setting up and planning.

If a whole week is possible, the entire contents of the manual will be covered—if time is limited, some items such as observation and recording, evaluation, and parent conferences can be postponed until after school has started. It is more essential to practice actual procedures and curriculum activities than to cram everything into too short a time.

Finally, in planning the pre-opening training there should be time allowed for relaxing and laughing together, for meeting in small and large groups to get acquainted, to explore personalities and discover talents, and free times to allow breathing spells, to ingest the heavy dosage of instruction.

Orientation for a Single Staff Member—In every school there will be times when a teacher leaves and is replaced midterm. Too often, the new member is never really trained and plunges into the job as if he/she were pushed off a diving board.

The following procedures suggest that some plan for orientation should be made well in advance. The newest team member should receive the attention and support of all other staff members.

Beginning with the interview which may lead to an offer of a position, the director, who is really anxious to hire this person, may say, "In some ways it is hard to come into a situation after the children and staff have developed a small society, but on the other hand there are advantages. Some of the adjustment problems of the children and interpersonal relationships of adults have been settled and things were really going along very well until this change in staffing occurred. Our first objective will be to make the transition as smooth as possible so the children will not be adversely affected. I would like to explain our philosophy to you.

"I wish I could give you one full day to just observe in the school, but unfortunately we need you now so I ask that for at least one week, you will stay for an extra half hour each day to go over with me the subjects we covered in our pre-opening training at the beginning of the school year. I will choose the order in which I think the information will be most helpful to you. Your team leader will talk to you about the curriculum and how we use the manual. I expect you have already seen some visual evidence of it on the walls.

"Here is the fact sheet that tells about the history and organization of our school It is the same one we distribute to parents and other visitors. This is our 'who's who' sheet which gives names, addresses and telephone numbers of staff. We do not encourage parents to call staff members at home, so I ask you to keep this list in your own folder. It is important for you to have a folder or notebook in which you will keep copies of minutes of staff meetings and staff and parent bulletins. Please note that they are numbered so if you should miss one you can ask for it. I often need to refer back to items in previous bulletins.

"Your job may seem overwhelming at first, and I'm sure you will be tired until you have had a chance to absorb all this, but I can assure you everyone will help and no one will expect more than you are able to give."

The newcomer might also be introduced to the total environment through slides selected to point out the important aspects of the program, to demonstrate the creative approach, to explain what is meant by motivation, to show the simple mechanics for helping a child with painting or getting ready for lunch. The development of this set of slides would be an interesting task for one who enjoys such work. The new teacher could look at them and use them as a basis for questions.

The director should tell as much as he/she can about the arrival of the new teacher, sharing as much of the background given on the application as possible, for example: "After interviewing several candidates, we have hired Ann to take Steve's place. Ann is married and has two children, Susan aged seven and Lawrence who is nine. Ann lives in Brewster and will be riding in with our driver. She has taken three state courses and is presently working towards an associate degree at Community College. Ann plays the guitar and hopes to be able to do some creative movement with the children."

The new staff member is in the same position as the new child: he/she needs to be made welcome and to know that his/her arrival, however sudden, was expected and that he/she is recognized and somewhat known by fellow workers.

Inservice Training—Inservice training can be defined as everything taking place within the school, which is planned and designed to contribute to the professional growth of each individual staff member. A well planned program of inservice training can go far to narrow the gap between lethargy and excitement. Often it makes the difference between mediocrity and excellence in the curriculum. A workable plan, based on the size of the school, the hours children attend, and the daily schedule should be presented in detail to each staff member. The director makes it very clear that full attendance is a condition of employment.

An effective program will serve to STIMULATE, EDUCATE and INSPIRE. Every teacher, no matter how well qualified, needs to expand his/her scope of activities, improve skills, refresh knowledge of proven methods and keep an open mind to new approaches to learning. The classroom teacher who is not afforded this opportunity has a lonely job, always wondering what may be happening in the educational millieu which is new and exciting or even controversial. This teacher gets stuck in ruts, using the same methods and materials in the same way, year after year, and becomes a teacher who starts looking forward to Friday on Monday morning and who counts the years to retirement. This lack of enthusiasm is contagious and the children begin to dread school and they, too, live for the next vacation.

Teachers applying for and anxious to secure a position will agree to comply with the inservice training program schedule with genuine sincerity but as the weeks pass and the responsibilities of a teaching job become more demanding, enthusiasm wears thin for putting in extra hours, especially to attend meetings. The director is cautioned to be firm and at times even hard-hearted on the first occasion when staff members begin to make excuses for absences from meetings.

"I can't come, it's my husband's birthday."

"I need Saturday for my housework and shopping. I can't attend the conference."

When one excuse is accepted, the domino theory goes into effect. To help avoid this, all training schedules and special conference dates should be established well in advance.

A director needs to stress the possibility of sacrifice before the contingency arises. "There are certain responsibilities which are part of our profession. Are you sure your family understands this and will not stand in your way when your attendance calls for some sacrifice on their part?"

Scheduling Staff Meetings—In a hypothetical school with four groups or teams, a meeting schedule might include the following:

One meeting each week with director and team leaders.

One team meeting each week.

One meeting a month (at least) of full staff. This often has to take place in the evening, but is an important link in the chain that strengthens the total structure.

In addition, the following are suggested:

Meetings with neighboring schools in special areas, such as:

Teachers of a particular age group of children

Teachers' interest in discussing environment, curriculum development, staffing patterns, zoning throughout the day, etc.

Once a schedule is established, it is the director's responsibility to see that nothing interferes. Often it seems impossible!

"It's foolish to have a meeting to day, Miss S_____ is sick, we don't want to meet without her."

Sorry, I have some important visitors coming, we will have to postpone our meeting."

"I just couldn't get a substitute for M ____ so I'm afraid you'll have to miss your meeting and cover for her."

All legitimate reasons, but they start a pattern which will snowball. If the rule is, "You MUST find a way," and if the director is consistent, meetings will attain an importance that makes postponement or omission a major catastrophe.

Timing is always a problem. Usually it is best in a day care center to take advantage of naptime, when fewer people are required to sit with sleeping children. Some teams prefer to meet between 7:45 and 8:45, some during lunch hour, and others between four and six o'clock.

When a full staff meeting is held in the evening, there should be some time for socializing. The expense of a supper is justified when it leads to a relaxed atmosphere and open communication.

Full Staff Meeting—How can a director plan for meetings? A clear, concise, effective agenda is most important, drawing on suggestions from the whole staff.

It should be planned with some of the same criteria used in planning programs for young children, with a balance of activity and rest, listening and participation. A change of voice tone helps to keep an audience interested.

Alternating reports with topics presented by the director will help maintain interest and vitality. Remember that messages conveyed enter through all of the senses and employ visual, audial and tactual methods of presentation.

The list of items on the agenda should be numbered in order of importance and an estimate of the time needed for presentation of each one made. The agenda should be copied and distributed to staff, and a copy posted on the bulletin board or it can be written out on a blackboard for reference during the meeting. This serves to avoid overly long discussion or rambling on the part of speakers.

The director sets the stage for the meeting with notes, assembled and ready. He/she might present notices of conferences or workshops, some new books, an idea for curriculum, an item in an equipment catalogue to introduce and discuss, or a sample of an activity observed in another school.

It is essential for one person to act as secretary, and when possible, notes of the meeting should be distributed following the meeting.

Finally, a director must find the right mix of autocracy and democracy. There are times when he/she does issue directives and make statements on policy. There are also times when the director poses questions, presents a problem or offers a topic for discussion.

Too much, "What do you think we ought to do?" can degenerate into fruitless 'rap sessions' while important business is neglected. The members of a staff need a director's leadership, inspiration and encouragement. They need the security of a director's ideas and to know their ideas are respected and welcomed. Staff meetings provide a vital forum for this exchange.

Assignments for Staff Meetings—if one truly believes that staff meetings are in-service training, it will be clear that assignments help to divide the participation and maintain interest. The following suggestions have proved to be successful.

Stretching a Story

The well-loved book *Caps For Sale* by Slobodkina, pub. Scholastic, was used to demonstrate the variety of ways a story can be extended into various aspects of program. One group developed math activities, another, music and movement. The third group looked for opportunities to include language and drama, and the fourth brought in suggestions for art, which included a variety of ways to make the CAPS.

Science Workshop

One group contributed ideas for water play, another for plumbing and the third for electricity. They were first to study the suggestions offered in the curriculum manual, and either demonstrate them by assembling the equipment, or making additional contributions.

Book Reviews

The director distributed several books, which the book committee of the parent group had asked staff to review with a recommendation for purchase. Each team chose two books, read them to children and reported back at a subsequent meeting.

Slide Stories

A parent shared some pointers with the staff on how to take good pictures. Each team was asked to prepare a set of slides on a particular subject. These were shown and discussed, one at a time. Some of the subjects chosen were: MACHINERY, SIGNS, ANIMALS, HORSES, LOBSTER CATCHING. The topics represented hobbies or interests of the persons who took the pictures, which added a special ingredient of enthusiasm.

Writing Reports

On a more serious side, when it was time to make first entries on record cards, each staff member was asked to come prepared to read a sample card about a fictitious child. Fellow staff members were asked to evaluate the contents, from the point of view of a guidance counselor, a supervisor, a new teacher who has just come on the team, and a parent. Teachers reviewed the material in the section on Observation and Recording, prior to this assignment.

Team Meetings—These meetings may include:

DISCUSSION OF INDIVIDUAL CHILDREN

EVALUATING PROGRAM OF PREVIOUS WEEK. How much were teachers able to accomplish as planned? If program went in another direction, how did it get started? Was it profitable?

PLANNING FOR COMING WEEK. Discussion of adminstrative detail should be kept at a minimum. If chores have been evenly divided and assigned (see Workjobs), the team leader should be able to discuss most problem areas with the individual responsible.

The balance of meetings will shift. At times, it will be important to spend most of the hour discussing children, and at other times, the entire discussion will center on program. It is important to have an agenda, and to keep some records of topics discussed and decisions reached. At the beginning of the year, it is usually best for the team leader to take responsibility for the meeting, but when the teams have established secure working relationships, it is good to rotate the leadership.

Conferences with Individual Staff Members—Meetings are essential but cannot take the place of the individual conferences which the director needs to have with each member of the staff. These should be held at least twice a year. Each should be planned ahead by appointment and at a time when there is no pressure. Sometimes it takes a full half hour before any true communication begins.

The door of communication must be open for *all* staff members to receive as well as give. The cook, maintenance man, and drivers will attach new importance to their jobs, feel a part of the team and appreciate the attention of a director who affords them the same courtesy of a conference that is extended to teachers.

January (in a school which began in September) is an excellent time for a conference. It is midway, there is still time to make changes, eliminate minor irritations, make suggestions for professional improvement. Daily communication on the job is NOT the same as sitting down face to face, behind a closed door and having the undivided attention of the director or team leader.

At the end of the year conference, it is sometimes helpful to look together at a reference form and say, "Let's pretend I had to fill this out for you. What would you want me to say?" When there are criticisms they should be dealt with squarely and always followed by positive and constructive suggestions for self-improvement. Honesty and positive mutual evaluation will go far in improving and sharpening the skills of every staff member.

Experience has shown that there are certain times in the year when staff morale takes a dip. February and early March can be precarious, especially in areas of the country where teachers have been struggling with snowsuits and boots. A conference in January forestalls this phenomenon. Anxieties and irritations are surfaced and discussed before they become major aggravations. We have acquired evidence that directors who 'didn't get around to it' have suffered the consequences.

Workjobs for Teachers—A visit to a school was impressive because of the orderly arrangement of supplies and equipment. Shelves were exposed and neat. Materials were accessible, labeled, and those intended for teachers' use on high shelves and those which children could choose at will, down at their levels.

"We have a system of workjobs," the director explained. "Each staff member chose the job he/she found most attractive. Two teachers are responsible for the library center. They put out books which are appropriate to the themes and activities, and change them daily or weekly. If a book is damaged, they put it away until it is mended. (see Book Committee) They keep an inventory, and if a book is lost or destroyed they report it. They enjoy this work, and I think they have helped train children to respect books."

She continued, "Other staff members have chosen areas of the room and take care of everything in that particular area. We discussed what makes a room look messy, such as the accumulation of junk on the tops of cubbies, stacks of papers waiting to go home, articles of unclaimed clothing in the cubbies, etc. We also divided the real housekeeping chores, such as checking the bathrooms twice a day, straightening up the staff room, cleaning paint supplies, etc."

A teacher should not accept a position in a school if he/she feels it is out of his/her realm of responsibility to pick up a mop or a sponge, or even to clean around the toilet, if it is required. Children have accidents and spills and these cannot wait until the janitor comes in after the children are gone. Just as a parent does what needs to be done *when* it needs doing, so a teacher thinks first of the proper environment for children and less of 'what I was hired to do'. A teacher should not be expected to wash floors or windows, but should not be too proud to do it in an emergency. The director of a school will take a fair share, never asking any employee to do anything he/she isn't willing to do herself. The toilet plunger will be a familiar tool to the entire staff!

If it is necessary for one person to forego a given responsibility, and a satisfactory swap or substitute for that chore can not be arranged, it is always a good idea to speak to the director or leave a note. It is better for the director to find a note saying, "I had to leave the room a mess because I had a dental appointment, but I plan to get in early enough in the morning to clean up," than it is to walk in unexpectedly with a visitor and apologize for a messy building.

What can the children do? Far more than most adults allow them to do. What may seem like a tremendous chore to an adult can be great fun for a child, but they must be taught the necessary skills, carefully and patiently.

How often do we say to a child, in our very best unperturbed tone, "Oh, you have spilled your juice. That's all right, get a sponge and clean it up," without stopping to realize that this child has not mastered the simple techniques involved. By following some basic steps with the children, they can become experts in cleaning up their own spills.

The teacher or mother who is not consistent, who teaches the child patiently one day and then performs the task when rushed or impatient, will deprive the child of necessary and valuable learning.

Serenity is a beautiful word. It implies peace, order, respect, a quiet joy in being. We have an obligation to make this a reality for the children who come into our classrooms.

Chapter 2

WHERE DO YOUR CHILDREN GROW?

The gardener chooses the location for his plants with care, seeking the right balance of sun and shade, protection from the elements, traffic and animals. In the same way, we, who nurture the growth of young children, are concerned with safe and convenient access to our buildings, a balance of sun and shaded areas and traffic patterns within the school and on the playground which achieve a smooth flow of movement.

Child care centers can be found in so many different settings that it would be futile to attempt to write for all of them. We assume that every owner, director and teacher dreams about the environment he/she would like to provide, and we offer some ideas, suggestions, questions and guidelines which might be helpful in achieving that ideal.

Once again, we refer the reader to the four sides of the developmental square. Each activity, each area of indoor and outdoor space, and each piece of equipment needs careful examination.

Has the school provided for physcial development of large and small muscles, and for social experiences?

The arrangement of the space will have much to do with the emotional reactions of our children. Is it too controlled? Too open?

Does it encourage exploration and provide opportunities for success?

Will it encourage running and boisterous, noisy activity?

Will it inhibit and restrict normal movement?

Are there places for large group activites such as music and movement sessions, meetings, an open space for when excess energy needs an outlet?

Are there cozy corners where a child can be alone or play with one or two friends?

Are there corridors which invite running? If they exist, can they be used profitably or can the space be broken with some kind of dividers?

The following is an account of an imaginary tour of a school. The conversation between the director and the parents is hypothetical but "real" in that it poses and answers the questions which parents do ask. The reader will hopefully pick up some ideas about the school environment which can extend or be added to their own planning.

As Mr. and Mrs ___ entered the child care center, bright red geraniums in window boxes seemed to offer a cheery "WELCOME!" An attractive foyer extended the message; on one wall mounted (see Seq. 6 #32) silhouettes of children were displayed, children with pigtails and ponytails, snub noses and chubby cheeks.

PARENT: "Are they real?"

RECEPTIONIST: "Oh, yes, they are our own children. They love to look at them and name their friends."

In one corner was a large papier mache ostrich, painted gaily.

PARENT: "Surely, the children couldn't have made that!"

RECEPTIONIST: "The fours had a lot of fun putting that together, the frame is chicken wire. Last month we had an eight foot dinosaur created by the kindergarten."

She invited the parents to sit in a cozy alcove to wait for the director. Several comfortable chairs were grouped around a coffee table, and a coffee urn was on a side table. A rack on one wall held pamphlets of interest to parents, including on *How to Choose A Nursery School,* (N.A.E.Y.C.). Standing at the entrance was a bulletin board with notices to parents, some newspaper stories and a notice of a forthcoming lecture.

RECEPTIONIST: "While you are waiting you may want to look at a recent copy of our school paper. It is written and printed by our parents' group."

At this point, the director appeared and invited them into her office. She did NOT conduct an interview from behind her desk, but sat with them in comfortable chairs.

DIRECTOR: "Let's talk a bit about you and what you are looking for in child care and the needs of your child. Then we will walk around the school; I can explain our philosophy in the classroom where you can see it in action."

The director's office was cheerful and inviting. A small table with two chairs was beside a low shelf on which a few toys and books were arranged. A divider set off one corner shielding a small cot. Seeing the parents looking at it, the director explained, "We do not plan to keep children here if they are sick. Until a parent can come or send someone to take him home, a sick child will stay in here with me. Sometimes they can play with the toys, but if they are really sick they use the cot. I chose that picture to hang on the wall because years ago a child said to me, 'I remember the day I was sick. I liked to look at that picture of two children playing in the sand at the beach. It made me feel better.' "

After a very brief explanation of the basic organization of the school, the director took them into the school—one large room, divided into areas of interest and by age groupings.

DIRECTOR: "We call this the holding area. It is where the children who arrive early stay until their teachers come, and where they wait for their parents at the end of the day. During the day, it is a place for meetings, for use of audio-visual equipment and other special programs. We do have a television set, and the early and late children may watch children's programs, but more often than not they find other things more interesting."

PARENT: "I have heard of day care centers where the children sit in front of television for most of the day."

DIRECTOR: "Oh, yes, so have I, but I can assure you it does not happen here. Our set can also be used for video tapes. We use it for staff training, and occasionally the children like to see themselves. If there is an outstanding program we feel the children should see, we might use the T.V. during the day, but that seldom happens. In any case, it would not be a command performance; it would be one choice among many."

PARENT: "Do you mean the children can just do anything they want?"

DIRECTOR: "If you are thinking of the stereotype image of the progressive school where children are jumping on furniture and climbing the walls, the answer is 'no'. We are trying to teach our children to live comfortably within the limitations of their own society. At certain times of the day they choose their own activities, but when it comes to routines, such as eating, napping, washing and dressing, they are not given much latitude. We TEACH them how to care for their own needs and try to establish routines which will become good habits. We also expect them to respect the rights and property of others."

PARENT: "What do they do besides watch television when they arrive early?"

DIRECTOR: "It is all very low key. We try to think what a child might be doing at home at that time of day and create a similar environment. The reading corner and housekeeping corner are close by, and we usually have one or two table activities available. The children do not wait to be entertained. They quickly form friendships and carry on their own ideas from one day to the next. This whole area is used by the kindergarten. When their teacher arrives they come here and perform little chores, such as watering the plants or feeding the animals. When all are present they hold a meeting."

PARENT: "What kind of meeting?"

DIRECTOR: "Sometimes it includes some singing, some conversation, but it is really a planning session. At first, the teachers will have set up activities and the children are given choices. As the year progresses, the children participate more and more in deciding the program. We have a curriculum, which I will be glad to show you when we go back to the office, but it is intended as a catalyst—not a rigid plan. "Cues" come from individual children or from the nature and direction of the group activity at a given moment."

PARENT: "Suppose a child chooses to do the same thing every day?"

DIRECTOR: "We let it go on for a while. Some children need time to absorb, enjoy, or test ideas and materials. An experienced teacher knows when it is time for diversion. She controls activities by changing the environment. For example, if a child stays too long with trucks and blocks, she simply closes off the block area for a few days."

PARENT: "Won't they all choose to play outdoors most often?"

DIRECTOR: "No, it is like a smorgasbord; at first they may choose all desserts, but eventually our experience shows they will level off and choose a balanced diet."

DIRECTOR: "This area is for fours. They have most of the same activity centers, except for blocks which they share with the kindergarten. We have the large building blocks here and the unit blocks on the other side of the divider."

As they moved to the other end of the building, she called attention to the fact that the plumbing had been installed in the center with a bank of toilets and washbasins facing each side.

DIRECTOR: "The painting area has a floor drain—we do some pretty messy activities and we need to wash up often."

PARENT: "Where did you find these little mops?"

DIRECTOR: "They are adult size with the handles cut down so the children can help. *Cleanup IS program, just as important and just as much fun.*"

A bank of large, cardboard cylinders, each filled with items for creative activities (yarn, ribbons, feathers, string, etc.) had a sign over it "ELEGANT JUNK." The director explained; "We want a variety of materials to be available all of the time to stimulate the child's imagination, but storage of these materials is always a problem. The way in which a teacher displays such items can be compared to merchandising. People are trained in stores to set out merchandise so customers will want to buy. A teacher wants children to be intrigued by materials so they will want to explore and examine them, use them and create with them."

PARENT: "I see many signs. Can they read them?"

DIRECTOR: "Quite a few, by the end of the year. We believe that children learn to read when they want to know, and so we put up signs that have some special message for them. 'Entrance' 'Exit' 'Go around' 'No blocks today' (see curriculum—catalyst or conformist, basic premises).. We change them often. Sometimes the teacher will mix them up, i.e. 'DOOR' on the 'PIANO' to see how quickly someone will notice. Children are quick to ask, 'What does that say?' and will pick out the letters they know. They learn that important information is conveyed through symbols."

As they passed a science area, they saw a table with shelves on both sides on which were seeds, dried beans, rice, measuring cups and scales for weighing.

DIRECTOR: "Sometimes a science area includes plants and animals but we prefer to scatter ours about the building. We try to avoid large groups of children around an animal. We also think this is a nice way for a child to be 'solitary' occasionally. She called attention to a rabbit cage, set up on legs, with a small rocker beside it and several books about rabbits.

DIRECTOR: "At this end of the building we have threes in the back and the littlest ones are in front, nearest the kitchen. We feel that they need to be apart, to have a room of their own, and so you will see that we have six-foot dividers around them. The rest of the dividers are four feet high, which is a wall to the children but enables a teacher to see over them. As time goes on we open a space between the twos and threes for a part of each day. By mid-year, there is quite a bit of going back and forth."

PARENT: "Do the kindergartners ever mix with the twos?"

DIRECTOR: "Yes, as the teachers get to know their children, and the children settle into their environment, the fives are invited to help the little ones dress, to eat with them and sometimes to nap beside them. It is good for some of our children to be chosen for this kind of responsibility. It stretches their 'I AM' and often they can communicate with a little one when the teacher can't. In fact, as the year goes on, the whole building opens up more and more. It is fascinating to see children working in mixed age groups of their own choice."

PARENT: "When you said, one big room, I thought 'how awful.' I expected it to be much noisier."

DIRECTOR: "If we tried to function in that way at first, it would be chaotic. Children need time to adjust to the necessary rules of society, the forerunners of adult laws. This is May, and what you see now is quite different from what you might have seen last November. We have done a lot of stretching, growing, and changing together since then. Did you notice as we walked about that several children were alone? We deliberately plan for small private spaces and talk about respect for privacy, that it is alright to like to be alone and have time to think or daydream, or just relax. Susan was in that big tire with a soft pillow in the middle looking at books. One of our staff made a cloth cover to fit over a rectangular table like a tent. She put a clear plastic window in it to let in light. The other day Carol asked to have the upstairs section of the Wendy House all to herself. "I need my privacy," she said. Jean has been working with those design blocks for almost an hour. In a traditional Montessori school children work on individual mats, it is part of their training. We make provision for it and teach others to respect the individual rights and privacy of their classmates. The majority of young children prefer some companionship most of the time but *everyone* needs to be alone for periods of time."

PARENT: "Mmmmmmm, I smell something good!"

DIRECTOR: "It is almost lunchtime. The children who are going home will be taking their things to the holding area, and those who stay will be getting ready for lunch. If you would like to stay and watch, you are welcome, but you must excuse me, I like to be there to say 'goodbye' and speak to the parents."

The parents left, planning to come back on another day to enroll their child.

A visitor's comment: "I sensed something very special when I came into your school. It was bright and cheery, but more than that, it was the faces of the children and teachers. They looked interested—involved. Everyone seemed busy, and yet it wasn't noisy or chaotic. In thinking about my visit after I left, I couldn't recall hearing a single teacher's voice, giving directions or instructions. The other thing I noticed was that every child did not seem to have to be doing something every minute; some were just watching. I saw two children by themselves, playing a game. One little girl was lolling on a big, soft, furry cushion, looking at books. She was all by herself there for half an hour and no one seemed to feel it necessary to interfere. The children were living while they were learning!"

Planning the Environment

What goes into planning this kind of a learning environment for children? First, it might be well to review and think about the goals described earlier, and the components making up the four sides of the developmental square. No matter where the learning situation presents itself, inside, outside, on the way to school, eating, playing or napping—if the teacher is reaching for goals which extend one or all of the developing areas, the child will benefit.

Within the classroom arrangement of space and equipment is important, i.e., the housekeeping area turned into a beauty parlor, the science area into a Mr. Fix-it shop (see seq. 7 #85) or a woodworking bench in the art area.

Another factor which contributes to the general environment of the classroom is the limit placed on the number of children using any particular activity center. At first, these may be designated by pictures, for example, pictures of four children cut from a catalogue tell that only four can sit here at one time; eight stick figures mark the entrance to the block area; or pictures of six family members are posted at the housekeeping center. Later, these pictures are replaced with numbers. In the beginning, these limits will probably be determined by the teacher but as soon as the children can understand why such limits are needed they can share in the decisions. The child who sees these pictures or numbers is learning that important information is conveyed by using symbols.

> There was a large '5' at the entrance to the science center. Sandy told a newcomer, "Jimmy and Gene came out and Brian and Ben and Jane wanted to go in but that was too many, so Brian is going to come back later." Sandy was learning mathematics—and more!

Traffic patterns are as important in the classroom as in the street. Staff need frequently to analyze the situation, to think about the mechanics of moving a child or a group through the day. Which activities can best be near each other? Surely, music will be removed from quiet areas. Blockbuilding and a family center or store adjacent to one another may encourage cooperative dramatic play. Messy activities should be near the sinks. Science centers situated near the classroom entrance will stimulate the child as he enters each day and looks for something new on display, and perhaps brings something of his own to share with his friends.

About Buildings   Child care centers, unlike public schools, vary greatly in the buildings they occupy. There are centers in churches, old warehouses, storefronts, community halls or recreation rooms, remodeled homes or barns, apartments in housing developments, even Quonsett huts. We have not yet seen one in a tent, but it wouldn't surprise us.

We are presently working with children in twenty-two different kinds of buildings, and have visited many more across the country. For those who may be planning to build or remodel, we can share some of our ideas based on experience.

We believe in the open classroom theory because it allows for greater flexibility in enrolling children. Seldom is it possible to guarantee neat packages of twenty children in each of four rooms, entering in September and remaining until June. When twenty-five three-year-olds and eighteen kindergarten children are enrolled, problems arise. In the open classroom, dividers allow change to accomodate age groups and developmental needs.

In the open classroom teachers do not have to decide between family grouping and chronological age grouping. Groups can move gradually from one to another as needs dictate or as the year progresses. Children start the year with "anchors" and "sameness," staying with the same people, growing accustomed to the same place. When THEY are ready, they can venture forth gradually into a wider world.

In a building with separate classrooms teachers have a tendency to be divisive and possessive, "my room," "my children," "my paste" and "my program."

In the open classroom where dividers are four feet high, they can see what is going on in other parts of the building. Ideas and activities more easily blend among co-workers. As a result, each teacher is challenged with new ideas and they find their work more interesting.

"Eighty to one hundred children in one room! Horrors!" One cannot blame the teacher, accustomed to the traditional confined areas, for such a response. It is true, the challenge to create an environment which is not overstimulating for children is demanding but with proper attention given to acoustics by the planners, and a concerted effort toward the goal of purposeful activity, the noise level does not have to be excessive.

Cooperation and communication are the most important concepts to learn if we are to have an integrated, harmonious society. In the open classroom, these are necessities for children and adults.

Some of the ways space has been divided, (Of all these plans, F seems to be the most satisfactory):

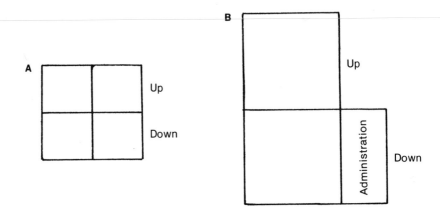

a. Four rooms, either on two floors or in a ranch style building, with the entrance half way between...

b. Two large rooms, on two floors, each set up as an open classroom...

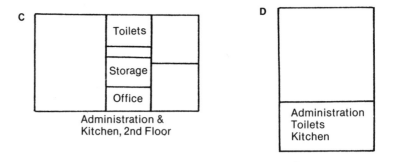

c. One level, with one large and two smaller rooms...

d. One large room with administration, kitchen and toilets in one end...

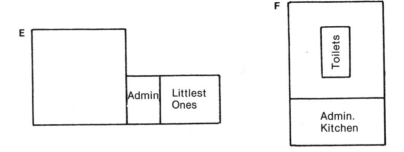

e. One large room, one smaller room with entrance and administration in between...

f. One large room with toilet facilities in the center, facing each side...

G

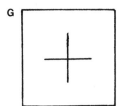

H

Admin. Kitchen	Infant	Toddler	2 s
	Corridor		
	3s	4 s	K

g. One room with walls to the ceiling in the center. The advantage here is that there are eight corners for activity centers and quiet, cozy learning centers...

h. In a center where infants and toddlers are enrolled, the traditional type of school building with a corridor through the middle, was used...

Interest Centers   **Art**—This is the one activity common to all nursery schools, often to the exclusion of other learning which might take place if the environment were more carefully planned. The art area should be accessible to sinks, and on a tiled floor which can easily be cleaned. A floor drain is a great advantage. There will be some provision for painting, either at easels, on large tables or on the floor. Wall easels which permit children to paint side by side, thus enjoying a social experience, are preferable to the standard two sided easels. They also conserve space. Look for the possibility of placing wall easels against a fence, or against the side of a building on the playground. There are many days when painting is enjoyed out of doors.

Usually nearby, but separate from the art area is one devoted to creative activities which take place at tables. Materials should be on low shelves or in containers accessible to children. In the beginning materials will be limited, but as rules are established and learned, the variety can increase. Shelf space or "cubby" style bins should be provided for crayons, paste, white glue, scissors, staplers, paper punches, paper fasteners, and paper of varied sizes and texture including pieces of cardboard and wallpaper. In addition there should be storage provided for a generous supply of "elegant junk" such as yarn, string, ribbon, thread, scraps of dress trims, pieces of cloth, feathers, artificial flowers, beads and sequins, spools, scraps of wood, ice cream sticks.

An ingenious teacher will find many other interesting and unusual items and inviting ways to display them which will motivate children to creativity.

Creativity cannot flourish when children are limited to one or two materials a teacher chooses to "put out" or when cluttered storage and/or difficult access to materials discourages their use.

Block Area—The value of block play cannot be overestimated. Given an adequate supply and a well planned place to use them, blocks are an important tool in providing growth on all four sides of the developmental square. The block area should be located out of the main stream of traffic. There should be room to spread out, to create a whole city or farm or zoo, and ideally, a space where a large building project can be held over for a couple of days.

Unit blocks and large building blocks offer two separate activities and while they may be back to back they should NOT be combined. *Unit blocks* should be on low shelves, divided according to sizes. Replacing them after use becomes a part of the learning experience. Some teachers prefer to start with one or two sizes, and add new shapes gradually as skills increase. Accessories such as people, small cars and trucks and materials for tracks such as cardboard, paper, masking tape, add to the variety of the play. Large trucks and riding toys may be used nearby if they are supervised carefully so that they do not provide distraction and disruption of good block play. Pulleys, ropes, trolleys and dollies are stimulating to block activities.

The large building blocks can be next to the family center. Housekeeping equipment can be shared when a store, hospital, office or some other building is constructed.

Family Center—Nothing can be worse than to see what is called a 'doll corner' stuck out in the middle of a play area, with a stove, sink and table, devoid of accessories for play. Space for a family center should be set apart from other activities. It should offer some semblance of four walls with window cutouts and a door. Inside one would expect to find a table (with table cloth), and at least two small chairs. Dishes in a cabinet or on shelves (never thrown into a box!), cooking equipment, a bed for the dolls (clothed) and clean sheets, blankets and a pillow, possibly a small rocking chair, a broom and dustpan, dress-up clothing and accessories. Each item is kept in a designated place. All items are sized to fit reasonably well and kept clean and in good repair. Extras might include a dressing table and mirror, equipped with razor (minus blades), jars, bottles and fancy containers from men's and women's vanity tables. Hooks and shelves are provided for dressups—a full length mirror is excellent—and telephones are a must!

Science Center—A science center may provide a good buffer zone between the noisy activity of the block area and the quiet of a reading corner or learning center. To may teachers 'science' suggest only animals or plants and both are important in the nursery school as samples of living and growing, but need not be confined to one place. Plants will add a pleasant touch to any part of the building.

In one school, the teacher brought in a large, cut-leaf philodendron from home. This became a palm tree and was the incentive for jungle play, and was moved with pride to various areas of the room. It was treated with care and respect—and after it served its purpose, returned to the teacher's home.

Animals should be in cages—where little ones can not hurt them or risk nipped fingers. Some teachers prefer to use glass aquariums, with wire screening over the top.

The science center should provide space, equipment and work areas for things to look at and act upon. It should have a counter or table space to accomodate two to four children at a time and shelves for equipment and display of materials.

Exhibits shold be changed often. One week it might be stones, another shells or seeds. Various natural grains can be combined with breakfast cereals which have been blown up from the original.

The science center should arouse curiosity, give children a chance to solve problems, experiment and test. Scales will encourage children to weigh the stones or cereals. Rulers and tape measures are necessary equipment, and books which elaborate on the central theme should be accessible.

Woodworking—Carpentry is an activity which calls for careful instruction in the use of tools. It should be limited to a small number of children at one time, with adequate supervision and strict adeherence to rules. It should be located away from any activity which might interfere with safety and concentration. (See Woodworking.)

Reading Corner—Every effort should be made to create an environment which is inviting, quiet and cozy. Dividers might be formed by the bookshelves. A rug on the floor (a piece of real soft shag is delightful), a small rocking chair, table with two small chairs, or a child recliner chair, add to the atmosphere. One teacher lined an old-fashioned bathtub on legs with carpet and put some big, soft pillows in it. Another placed a large, soft pillow in the center of a tire, and still another, threw some pillows into a carge carton. The books should be attractively displayed and changed often. (See Workjobs.)

Soft Area—In one school a platform was covered with a soft, shag rug. Draperies were hung around three sides, and colorful pillows of varied sizes and shapes where stacked on the floor. The soft area was used for small group activites, sensory games and activites, as a reading area, a story carpet, and even on occasion, to allow two angry children to work out their aggression with a pillow fight!

In another school, an ingenious device on pulleys could be lowered over a small stage. It had sheets hanging from three sides. At various times it was a circus tent, a store, a house, a library, an office. The sides rolled up when it was not in use and the frame pulled up to the ceiling. An extra seat from a station wagon provided a low couch. Another sofa was constructed by covering a sheet of plywood with rug samples, setting it up across concrete blocks and adding a few pillows.

Music Center—This should be located where furniture can be pushed back to allow movement. Instruments are displayed on shelves or hanging on a board. Children are taught to use them with respect. Storage for instruments can be constructed, using heavy cardboard cylinders attractively painted and placed against a wall. Pictures or names of instruments might be placed on each section. Extra materials which invite creative experiences, such as scarves, hoops, rug squares, will be close by. (See Creative Movement-Props.)

Water Play—This is one aspect of science which needs its own place. An industrial, hand washing fountain is ideal, if the floor mechanism for turning on the water is replaced with faucets on the center post. Because it is round, it encourages social interaction and stimulates creative use of the materials provided. These should include articles for pouring, measuring, straining, funneling, sailing, whipping or beating, tubes and suction items. Waterproof smocks are a must. (Children cannot be allowed to get their clothing wet and stay wet all day.) A raincoat, worn backwards, may be used.

Sinks, water tables, or large tubs are all acceptable vehicles for waterplay. It is one of the most important (and least expensive) activities offered in a nursery school curriculum).

Playgrounds—The Outdoor Classroom

Often, teachers who are professionally excellent within the classroom suddenly deteriorate into 'child minders' when they go outside on the playground. What are some of the reasons? Perhaps they are tired, or look upon this time as an old-fashioned style recess. To some, it offers a chance to exchange bits of gossip and to chat with other staff members. Some teachers are unprepared for and uncomfortable with outdoor programs, assuming that it must be a nature or science oriented curriculum which must be taught by a specialist. Some are lacking in imagination, a basic ingredient for all good program.

A playground, no matter how small or inadequate, should be an extension of the indoor facility and just as much a laboratory for learning. The same degree of attention to use of space, careful placement of equipment and the job of the teacher in relating to the environment is required. *Children are learning wherever they are;* teachers cannot 'turn off their switches' when they go out of doors.

Every teacher needs interludes of complete relaxation, relief from responsibility, expecially if she teaches full days, but such relaxation should be completely isolated from the children. (*NOTE: the playground is never a place for a coffee or smoking break!!!*)

When teachers are on the playground, they must be observant and sensitive to what is happening with each child. Outdoor learning is as closely related to the developmental square and circle as indoor activity planning. Space and equipment are just as carefully selected and used. A minimum of 75 square feet per child is the usual requirement, but in urban areas this is not always possible. In the city, rooftops or tiny vacant lots can be designed to provide ingenious uses of space and materials, and supplemented with visits to nearby parks. Fenced-in areas, cozy nooks and divisions are needed for control and safety.

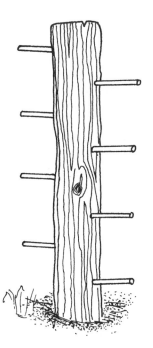

Basically, children need opportunities to climb, crawl, pull, push, wiggle through, run, jump off, walk on narrow boards, swing by the arms—to move! Standard playground equipment usually begins with swings and a slide. There is nothing wrong with these so long as they are not the only selections made. Swings, while relaxing, offer minimal opportunity for imaginative play or a variety of uses. A slide, which is just a slide, is expensive in relation to its value as a means of physical satisfaction, social growth, emotional release and intellectual stimulation. The money might be better spent for building blocks and boards, balance boards, climbing ropes. In one school, the directors had given serious thought to every piece of equipment, making much of it themselves. The slide was incorporated into a total climbing configuration. The child climbed a ladder, walked a plank, with guide ropes for those who needed them, and then chose between going down the steps (a new experience for many children who live in ranch-style homes or apartments with elevators) or sliding down a ramp on the other side. One such structure in another school had a fireman's pole in the middle for sliding down.

Jungle gyms are good for climbing, but again very expensive, and in a very small playground they take up a large proportion of valuable space. Climbing poles with dowels on the sides or plain poles for shinnying serve the same purpose.

The sandbox is, to the child, as necessary as the kitchen is to the homemaker. It is the focal point of the yard, the social center and work area. In a sandbox, engineers and cooks can work side by side. Sensory and social experiences are stimulated. The sandbox should be first on the essentials list and justified, even if it occupies a fairly large proportion of limited space.

Some teachers look upon the sandbox as a 't.v. watching' type of babysitting service. Children are left to content themselves with a continuous program of sifting and pouring. Sand, to be effective, must be combined with water, enough to make it adhere. Sandbox toys need to be carefully selected (eliminate tin shovels and toys with sharp corners) and they should be stored at the end of every day on shelves, in a box or closet, out of the weather. Rusty coffee tins, broken plastic dishes, trucks and cars minus wheels are not good teaching toys for children and they are hazardous. Motivation through new toys and planned projects relating to curriculum activities are as necessary here as in the block corner. HOW LONG HAS IT BEEN SINCE YOU HAVE REALLY LOOKED AT YOUR SANDBOX??

In one school we saw a courtyard with a hard surface in the middle. Bikes and other wheel toys, (Stop and Go signs), traveled on painted, play roads, Enter and Exit signs added to play houses and stores, created an entire community involved in on-going, purposeful, dramatic play. At the same time, other children were busily playing around the perimeter, in the sandbox and climbing in a tree house. The teacher was asked, "Did you decide to have the children build this town?" She replied, "No, the whole thing emerged when I put out some boards and boxes. The children asked, 'What are they for?', I said, 'What do you think we could do with them?' From there they just took off in all directions and the village has continued to grow and be a center for their daily activity."

Traffic patterns on the playground require careful thought. Is there room to move from one space to another without encroaching on the rights of others? Is there space for building with blocks, cartons, planks, etc., without having efforts knocked down by the more active runners? Are there safety zones, or islands where the watchers can be near and yet not into the action until they are ready? Can the total area be adequately supervised by the number of teachers available at any given time? If there are spaces obscured around corners, can they be closed off when supervision is limited? Does the arrangement of space and equipment make possible learning in the areas of music, movement, science, dramatic play, art, building, water play, language development?

The same rules which are important indoors apply on the playground. The basic rules of courtesy and common sense are essential. The common trap for a teacher, when in the open, is to shout across the playground, giving commands and directions. "John, you know you aren't supposed to stand on the swings." or "Come on, Susie, your mother is waiting." or "All the pixies come in and get washed." One loud voice is all that is needed to increase the tone and tempo of an entire group. Putting it bluntly—a loud-mouth syndrome can quickly ruin a relaxed, peaceful atmosphere. When outside, the teacher walks over to a child or group, giving directions or enforcing discipline quietly in a normal speaking tone. Learning happens best in an environment of purposeful activity, not chaotic, noisy confusion.

Children belong outdoors unless the weather is too cold, wet or hot. The decision of when to go out should not be based upon whether the teacher is comfortably dressed for the activity. It is a common sight to see a teacher huddled with arms crossed, shivering miserably while watching children getting their 'outside quota'. Some teachers will stand and scold the child who has no rubber boots, and yet will not be wearing their own on the playground. Professional attire for a nursery school teacher is whatever is practical and comfortable; raingear which is waterproof, boots, warm hats and mittens—these are as much the 'uniform' of the teacher, as the white uniform is appropriate for the nurse, or the hard hat for the construction worker. When, for justifiable medical reasons, it is not sensible for a teacher to go out, the children should not be sacrificed. An exchange with another willing teacher must be arranged. The teacher who sits at the lunch table and refuses to eat the carrots gives the child silent permission not to eat his carrots. A negative attitude will have the same result on the 'going outside' habits of children. The extra effort of planning activities and games may change a teacher's attitude. Many parents have pursued whole new areas of interest led by their children—the same can be true with teachers!

Chapter 3

HOW DO YOU OPERATE A CHILD CARE CENTER?

So many people go through life looking for easy answers, explicit directions, cut and dried solutions, exact recipes. Parents yearn for prescriptions which will cure all of their child rearing problems; and teachers welcome the curriculum guide which gives them a sense of security. These manuals were developed out of a philosophy which emphasizes the uniqueness of the individual's initiative, creativity and self direction; it also stresses the need for continual growth; the satisfaction of earned success.

There is so much to learn—there are so many new doors to open and so many paths to explore, that it would be a foolish waste of time to look only to the future. We study what has gone before, seeking patterns, and hope that they will show us how to avoid the same mistakes.

In this chapter—the "HOW" of running a child care center is discussed. Each practice described is based on actual, down-to-earth, daily experiences. *It worked for someone, somewhere.* It may not work for you in exactly the same way but if you read with an open mind, we trust you will find some useful guidelines.

TEACHING TOOLS

The teacher uses the whole self, voice, body, mind and heart, as a sensitive instrument tuned into ALL of the children. The teacher can never become so intensely involved with one that he/she loses track of what is happening to the others in the group. A teacher is a juggler; while helping Jane clip her painting on the easel or tying Susan's waterplay apron, the teacher is noticing that the blocks are getting dangerously high and might topple over on little Anne. At the same time thinking ahead! "It is 10:30. I think I will give them ten more minutes and then I will allow another ten for clean up. That gives me time to walk around the room and give a quiet warning to each working group.

"Should we have juice at the tables today? Everything seems to be functioning so smoothly, perhaps it will be better to put out the tray and not interrupt them." A teacher needs to be able to separate the thinking apparatus into numerous compartments and have them all functioning simultaneously.

supervision

It is absolutely essential that someone be responsible for every single child at all times, and that the responsibility be handed from one to another as carefully as if the child was literally handed over. We have said that each child, in the beginning, needs to identify with ONE adult, and should be able to break this tie at HIS OWN speed, leaving for a time, but always free to come back for reassurance.

This kind of supervision can be subtle, unobtrusive—certainly we do not want children clinging to adults, or feeling shadowed or overprotected by them; nor do we want to interfere with the flexibility and fluidity of our program, BUT there can never be any relaxation from responsibility.

A true example of "overall but not specific" supervision occured in a day camp some years ago. A counselor at two o'clock FELT a child lying at the bottom of the pool. NO ONE had missed that child. He had been there for TWO hours and everyone thought "someone else" knew where he was.

A visitor to a day care center watched an outdoor program with many interesting activities going on. Staff were placed reasonably well throughout the play area and yet NO ONE saw a little girl go outside the gate. If she had not been spotted by the visitor and had continued on her way towards a busy, city street NO ONE person would have felt responsible. Each one could have said, "But I thought _____ was watching her."

Sometimes it is best to assign certain areas of the playground... "Today or for the next hour, you Susan, will stay inside the building. We will only let children enter through THIS door, and it is up to you to know what is going on in there.

John will cover the sand box area. (This means that if John has a special activity going on, he has to have eyes for other happenings.)

One person—*at all times*—MUST be in charge.

Supervision includes stopping disruptive actions before they go too far. It is NOT necessary for children to scream at the top of their lungs to be happy. When they do, they are actually infringing on the rights (and the nerves) of others. The nearest adult GOES TO THE CHILD and says very quietly and directly TO him, "You are going to give us all a headache if you make so much noise. Find another way to have fun!"

Finally, teachers who teach have little time for conversation with other adults, indoors or out. When they are not involved in program activities, they are observing, making mental notes about behavior, new skills, storing up information—and thinking of the developmental needs of the children.

Supervision is everyone's business—but the responsibility of each individual!

Supervision—in the Director's Absence See also Director's Responsibilities

The immediate health and safety of the children is usually the responsibility of the teaching staff, but the overall supervision of a school rests on the shoulders of the director. Therefore, it is essential that provision be made for every moment of the day, from the time the doors open in the morning until the last child leaves at night. No director can be there all of the time, but some ONE person must accept the responsibility in his/her absence, even if it is only for fifteen minutes while the director is out on an errand. It only takes that long for some emergency to arise which calls for a decision to be made by one reliable person.

It is not enough to say 'When I am gone in the morning, Sue will be responsible, and in the afternoon it will be Bill." The reins need to be literally handed over EVERY time. What are the things this person needs to know?

What to do if a child is hurt?
Which member of the staff is trained in First Aid?
How do you call a parent?
What do you say to avoid alarming them unnecessarily and yet make them know they must come?
Where is the fire alarm? (the fire department may arrive at any moment and ask for a fire drill)
How do you turn off the alarm? (In one case, it went off with a short circuit and no one knew where the alarm was!)
How do you shut off the water if a pipe bursts?

Where is the toilet plunger and how do you use it?

Who understands the total transportation set up, in case problems arise?

What would you do if a teacher reports a child is missing?

Whoever is in charge should know where the director is and whether he/she can be reached.

It is not enough to have a plan for replacement, it should be written and posted in a conspicuous place. Practising emergency procedures through role playing at staff meetings will firm up the need for such precautions.

Signals

What if the tempo of the room is rising? Things are getting noisy. One or two children are acting silly—and the rest are beginning to react. What can a teacher do? One thing he/she will NOT do is to raise the voice and scold, this will be only adding more noise to the rising clamor. Neither will the teacher clap hands and shout, "Children, children !", snap fingers, blow a whistle or say, "Shhhhh!"

> A student was reporting on a visit to a school and said, "I was so impressed with the way the teacher used her whole body to communicate with the children!
>
> "Can you tell us how? What did she do?"
>
> "She didn't seem to have to talk to them. They just seemed to know what to do. I watched her—and she used a raised eyebrow to indicate disapproval—a slight nod of her head to indicate direction, a smile of approval for the child who was settled in—which spurred others along. I saw her take a child by the hand and walk with him to the bathroom door—hand another child his blanket, cover another—she just moved around the room in such a calm, quiet, *pleasant* way."

There are other methods for gaining the attention of a noisy group.

Go to the piano and play one or two notes steadily, rhythmically on the *black* keys. If there is no piano, use two drums or two tone bells.

Have drum signals with different meanings. Call it drum talk i.e., wash your hands, juice time, time to go to nap, let's go outside.

Get out a balloon or paper bag and start to blow it up. Children will stop to see what you are going to do.

Put out the lights. When children stop to see what has happened, talk about noise.

As the weeks progress, the group will *develop an understanding of attention signals,* how many, who gives them, why and when they are used. Developing recognition and response to signals carries into the very important area of safety. Training children to respond to signals is basic education. Talk about street signals and fire alarms.

If play is building up to a high pitch, try to DIVERT it. For example, if blockbuilding is getting too high, suggest extending it sideways with a village and add some accessories.

Start singing a familiar song (Jingle Bells) and when all have joined in tone it down— softer and slower until it is just a whisper.

Stand in front of a few children and *start a motion* (i.e. tapping top of your head). As more children join in, change the motion. When all are participating, slow down and bring to a stop.

When the group is ready to listen to you, it is better to smile and say, "That was fun. Now let's go back and finish what we were doing ", than to berate them or scold.

Group Control: The "Meeting"

> It was the last week in January and the weather had kept the children in for most of the month. It was getting noiser day by day and the teacher found herself using her voice more often than she should. One morning when the children came in the chairs were arranged theatre-style.
>
> "What's this for? What are we going to do?" they asked.
>
> "As soon as the rest of the chidren come, we are going to have a meeting."
>
> All children know that word—parents are always "going to a meeting". One told another as new arrivals came in—and soon all were sitting on chairs, looking very serious. When they were ready, she began.
>
> "Things haven't been going too well around here this week. I went home with a headache last night. Does anyone know why?"
>
> The children responded with giggles and nods.
>
> "Grownup people have to have rules—they call them laws. They say things like 'Don't drive your car too fast.' 'Don't throw papers on the street'. I wonder if we could make some laws for our schoolroom."
>
> The answers came freely—and as they began to make up rules the assistant teacher wrote them down on a large sheet of paper and numbered them. When they were through, she read them all back. They played a

game. "What is number five?" "Which one says 'Don't run?' "

The teacher asked, "How could we use these rules?"

The suggestions were:

"You could say number four—and we would know that it said 'Don't holler.' "

"I know another way," Tommy spoke eagerly, "you could go take a number out of a box and give it to the one who was breaking the rule."

"That's a terrific idea" the teacher praised. "Can anyone think of another?"

By the time they were through discussing the rules, most of the children had the numbers and rules pretty well put together in their minds.

After that, they reminded each other. If Harry ran, Sarah might say, "Number four" and he would look at the paper on the wall and slow down.

(See Seq. 8 # 55)

Transitions

"How can teachers move a group of children from place to place without chaos?"

In an open classroom there will not be many occasions when an entire group will be moving but there are always some. For example, if meeting time is held at the beginning of each session, there will come a time when children disperse to chosen activities. The natural tendency for children, especially if they have been sitting for long, is to make a wild dash. Teachers need to develop a variety of techniques to avoid this. It is far easier to lose a group then it is to get them back into a mood of purposeful activity.

Some teachers use a variety of songs (for Songs to Move Groups, see Action Songs-Music). Many become proficient in creating songs on the spot to fit each special occasion, adding new words to familiar tunes. Other teachers dismiss a few children at a time, suggesting a way for each to go. "Miss B's children will go out like mice. I think it would be fun to have the fours be great big heavy elephants. How will you walk? Be careful, don't step on any of those little mice. I just heard a plane go over. How could you "fly" out of the room?"

NAMES can be used. "All of the children whose name begins with "A" may go." After several movement sessions where names have been tapped out a teacher might say, "I am going to tap a name. It may fit more than one of you. If you think it is your name, stand up." Next tap one syllable names like John, Sam, two syllables, Ma-ry, Ka-thy, three syllable names, Jon-a-than, Cath-er-ine, in between try a few odd ones like Mar-ga-ri-ta.

TAP NAME RHYTHMS with two instruments, sticks and drums, using the drum for the accented syllable.

Send out a group at a time to rhythms which you tap on sticks, a drum or tambourine—fast, slow, heavy, light, running, walking.

Hold up a NAME CARD, each child leaves when he recognizes his own. With fives, a teacher might be able to say, "I will hold up a card. If that person is sitting on your LEFT you may get up. The two of you will leave together. If you see you own name do NOT stand right away. Wait until the person next to you has a chance to try to read it."

Only when you are experienced enough to keep one channel in your mind at least ten minutes ahead of the present will these suggestions become effective. If, in a sudden burst of enthusiasm, you announce, or even suggest, a move without warning, children will react suddenly and spontaneously.

Several observers were watching a four year old nursery class behind the visitors screen. The children were acting out a favorite record "Abeyoyo" (an original story told to his own children by Pete Seeger). It was a beautiful warm May day and the outside beckoned. When the narrator said "And as Abeyoyo came closer the people all ran." The actor *took off*—right out to the playground! The teacher, a sensitive person with a genuine sense of humor, laughingly followed. She had listened to the children's second language. (See Teacher—Are You Listening?)

Temper Tantrums, When Emotions Run High

Adults have varied ways of releasing their own strong emotions. Some vent their feelings on others, leaving behind them a chain of bruised feelings. The boss gets a memo from the president, so he chews out the foreman. The worker gets the backlash, and when he gets home vents his frustration on his wife or child. The dog, recognizing the signs, hides under the bed.

Some find more acceptable means. One lady weeds her garden and as she yanks and pulls weeds out of the dirt she lets her irritation drain out into the soil.

Another puts her anger into practical purpose and washes the kitchen floor. Taking a long walk, alone, will soothe some adults and others can look at the mountains or the ocean and put their problems into perspective.

Children need to be helped to find acceptable ways of releasing their feelings. First they need to know that it is ALLRIGHT to be angry, mad, sad. ALL people have such feelings. We cannot hurt other people but there are things we CAN do.

1. CLAY is a good form of release. Pounding, banging, shaping, twisting, manipulating.

2. WOODWORKING is more than a creative activity. Hammering nails into a block of wood is an emotional outlet.

3. A TACKLING dummy of some kind should be standard equipment in the preschool. A pillow case, or burlap sack filled with leaves, torn paper or old nylons makes a satisfactory punching bag.

4. TEARING old sheets into strips is very satisfying.

5. TEARING up newspapers to fill a paper bag, which then becomes a toy to toss is a means of release.

6. THROWING bean bags or sponges, wet clay or sand at a legitimate target is permissable.

7. FINGER PAINT offers a legitimate form of emotional release.

Bruce was an angry child who had frequent outbursts of language, and physical aggression. One day the teacher said to him "Bruce, you are so angry. Will you draw me an angry picture? Bruce looked at her in surprise. He sat thinking for a few seconds and said, "I can't. I'm not angry any more."

8. WATER PLAY may not be the best method for a child who is having a tantrum, but the alert teacher will see the storm coming and offer it as a release to avoid a crisis.

9. When the children are given a chance to VERBALIZE STRONG FEELINGS it often relieves the tensions within.

"Let's go in here," said the teacher, walking into the staff room with a firm grip on Andy's hand. They sat down at the table and when he stopped crying long enough to listen, she said, "Why don't you tell me about your angry feelings and I will write them down." Faster than she could write he vented his anger and frustration.
When he was through she read it back to him. He listened with great interest.
"What shall I do with this now?" she asked.
"Keep it," was his reply, "I might need it again."

Behavior:
Teacher—Are You
Listening?

Children have a second language! Long before they have acquired verbal skills, they express what they are feeling and thinking through their actions. A sensitive teacher will try to "read" the message a child is trying to convey through his behavior, as suggested in the following cases:

Lisa, generally a cooperative child, was displaying unusual behavior. She destroyed the treasured work of her best friend, knocked down a block building with one fell swoop, and snatched at coveted toys, sometimes accompanying her actions with well-placed kicks. The teacher called her mother to talk it over and suggested, "Do you think it could be because of the baby?" "Impossible," declared the mother, "Lisa adores the baby. When she comes home from school, she rushes over to the crib to talk to her. She loves to help me take care of her. Whatever the problem may be I am SURE it is not that!" The next day, Lisa's mother called back. "I remembered what it said in a book from your library (*New Ways of Discipline*, Baruch) and I suggested that Lisa might like to write a letter to her Granny. This is the letter she dictated, 'Dear Granny, At school there is a green house. Behind the house there is a bush with poison berries. I am going to pick the berries and give them to Susan (baby).' "

Billy, aged three, had always been mischievous but suddenly his behavior was out of bounds. He was destructive and aggressive and constantly testing limits. His teacher called his mother who reported that the same change was taking place at home. "We are at out wit's end. Billy was always such a good boy, and now he is impossible. He is so bold and fresh, and I can't leave him alone with the baby. I am afraid he will hurt her. She is just walking and talking and everyone pays a lot of attention to her. I am afraid he may be jealous." At the teacher's suggestion, the parents left the baby sister with her grandparents and took Billy into the city for a full day. They did a few errands, rode the subway, went to a cafeteria for lunch, and stopped at the museum for a visit to the Planetarium. His mother called the teacher the next day to tell about the excursion. "It was apparent that Billy needed to know he is still important to us. He was an absolute angel! I was so proud when someone stopped by our table to commend us for his impeccable behavior!"

Jeff was displaying atypical behavior. The teacher called his mother, "Is something unusual going on at home? Jeff is not himself. He is alternately staying by himself and teasing or pestering the other children." Mother replied, "My husband is going to have a serious operation on his eyes. We have tried not to talk about it in front of Jeff, but he may sense our anxiety." The next day, she called back, "After you called I asked Jeff if he would like to fingerpaint. I usually sit at the table and paint at the same time. He chose black and brown and smeared and jabbed while he said, 'This is the gucky, mucky hospital where my daddy is going!' We talked about the operation and I gave him as much reassurance as I could but I did not try to pretend I wasn't worried. He seems to feel better now. I hope it will be reflected in his behavior at school."

The reasons for a child's acting out is not always so easily discerned. Mike had not been an easy child from the beginning of the year but by January, his aggressive behavior was endangering the other children. A conference was called with both parents, who were at first very defensive. "It must be the other kids who are teasing him. He never acts that way at home." Mike's teacher kept a diary for one week with specific observations and recording of actual incidents, the time of day, the number of children involved and motivation, or lack of it. At a subsequent interview, she shared this report with the parents. When they heard that Mike with absolutely no provocation and with a smile on his face, ran to a far corner of the building, knocked over a building five boys were working on and scratched one of them on the face, his distraught parents admitted that it was time to seek professional help.

Children have a built-in radar system which tells them how adults are feeling about them. They are not fooled by sweet tones or forced pleasantries. Teachers and parents also have receiving systems, but they are not as clear as the children's. Their receptors have become cluttered with their own life experiences.

Sensitivity to the unspoken language of a child is developed with experience. Adults need to constantly think, "What is going on inside this child that makes him NEED to behave this way?" "How can I help him communicate his needs? Set limits for him which will protect the other children and at the same time let him get rid of bad feelings?"

It is very hard for a parent, in the midst of the pressures and tensions of twenty-four-hour-a-day living, to respond in this way. We cannot condone the quick reaction to an incident such as slapping, yelling, shaming, but we can appreciate it because as teachers, we too want to react with anger when we hear a defiant "I won't" "You stink" or "I hate you, you bitch" BUT we are teachers and our profession has taught us to STOP, LOOK and LISTEN to the messages children try so hard to convey.

Read Hymes, *Teaching the Child Under Six* and *New Ways of Discipline* by Dorothy Baruch.

Sometimes the message is sad, as in the following case:

Jim's mother had to leave him before eight a.m. and did not come back until five thirty. She always seemed to be in a hurry, and looked harassed and tired. Jim was a loveable little fellow, but lacking the joyful exuberance of a typical three-year-old. One day the teacher asked the children, "What is love?" Jim thought for a minute and said, quietly, "Slow." The director invited the mother to come in for a cup of tea when she called for Jim that night. "I have something to tell you, let's just sit and relax for a few minutes. I think Jimmy was telling us something, and I want you to hear it." The mother was visibly upset. "I am so tired," she wailed, "and I never can seem to catch up. I hurry him all the time. In the morning it's rush, rush, rush, and at night I give him his supper and hurry him off to bed so I can get my housework done. I HAVE to work, his father left us and I am our sole supporter." As they talked, the director suggested that this distraught mother might try to have a more leisurely meal with Jim, take time to talk about his day, read him a story or play with him. If choices had to be made, the house should be sacrificed—not Jim. She invited the mother to stop in once a week for a while to compare notes on Jim's progress. Just knowing that someone else was aware of her loneliness and sharing the responsibility for her child helped to lessen the heavy burden which this mother felt she was carrying alone. The difference in Jim was easily observed.

Manners

This story was told by Ruth Taylor Stone, a pioneer in early childhood education. "It was a Saturday afternoon in a crowded bakery. The girl behind the counter smiled at a four year old girl who was waiting with her mother and offered her a cookie. 'Say thank you,' the mother ordered. Shyly the little girl smiled but did not verbalize her gratitude. 'I said, say thank you!' said the mother in a louder voice. As the mother's insistent tone attracted attention, the poor youngster's shyness and inability to comply with her mother's wishes increased. The mother, now sensing that others were watching, grew more and more irate. The girl behind the counter was obviously embarrassed, and the child dissolved in tears."

Was this a bad mother? Probably not, but her 'I AM' was weak. Her mind was set on, "What will they think of me?" The child's smile was enough, she had expressed her gratitude in a manner which came naturally to her. By focusing the attention of strangers on her behavior, the mother was damaging the child's 'I AM'. In front of all those people she was made to feel that she was inadequate in the sight of the one person she most wanted to please—her mother.

Teachers often make the same error. They insist on vocal expressions of the amenities of polite society. "Say thank you," says the teacher as she passes the child another cookie, and even though she does it with a bright smile the tone of her voice puts undue emphasis on mouthing words, rather than on feelings.

Requiring a child to apologize for a misdemeanor fits into the same category. "You hurt Mark, now say you are sorry" or "You must apologize to Mrs. Smith for picking her tulips." Again, the adult who makes this demand is showing more concern for "What will the neighbors think of me?" than for the child. Words said in apology, when the child is either unaware of the actual import of the transgression, or still too angry to mean what he is forced to say, will only teach him that "You do what grownups tell you because they are bigger, or stronger, or because that is the only way you can win their approval."

It may sound trite to say that "manners are caught—not taught", but more is accomplished by setting an example than by making issues over simple situations. If a child fails to respond, the teacher might say "thank you" in a quiet voice. If he does not pick up the clue, it is better to let it go. Given enough time and good examples, children will learn to say these words at the appropriate times and it will happen out of a natural desire to express gratitude.

Can manners be *taught*? Yes, there are ways—fun ways. Children enjoy playing dramatic roles. Just before Thanksgiving, for example, when discussion has disclosed that some children will be entertaining relatives, the teacher may suggest, "Let's pretend that it is Thanksgiving day and Jimmy's aunt is coming for dinner. Mary, will you be Jimmy's mother? Who would like to be Jimmy? Who could be the aunt? What could we use for a doorbell? What should Jimmy do? What could he say? How can he show his aunt he is glad she came?" Some will want to play every role—some will be the audience. After Thanksgiving, there can be further discussion. "Who did have company at Thanksgiving? Did you make them feel welcome? What did you say?"

Five year olds enjoy and are capable of completing open-ended stories. The goal of language development is fulfilled when we give them this exercise. In addition, we respect their opinions and sharpen their thought processes.

Resource Files:
Saving and Sharing

A teacher is an inveterate scrounger who sees possibilities in every thing, and can never walk through the dime store or past a hardware counter without looking for some new item. Visits to rummage sales and walks through second hand stores are filled with the gleeful anticipation of the diver looking for the pearl in the oyster. One teacher confessed, "I have to control myself when walking down the street on rubbish collection day!" Another asks store keepers and gas station managers for their decorations when they take them down. Now that recycling is 'in' scavenging teachers have gained respect for their interest in ecology!

In keeping with this resourcefulness, there is a most important piece of advice one can give to the teacher, newly graduated and beginning a career, or one long in the profession who feels disorganized.

Set up a system, NOW, for recording and storing the ideas you glean from others, the things you read, the results of your "teachable moments!" Make it simple, easy to use and accessible. Otherwise you will find yourself saying on endless occasions, "I remember something that speaker said which would be just right for a lecture, article or parent conference—or did I read it somewhere? If only I could remember where to find it!"

The following suggestions are the result of years of such frustration:

1. Purchase a 5x8 file box and a generous supply of cards. If you are a copious saver, you may want to start out with the two-drawer type which can grow—upward.

2. Set up your system, by topics to begin with. As you use your file you may decide to change the organization of it, but the material will be there.

3. Get into the habit, as you read, or transcribe notes from conferences, courses or workshops, of selecting the 'nuggets' of line, phrase or thought which condense the idea, jogs your own thoughts or stirs your memory. File it away, recording the *source*. You may want to go back and 'put it into context', to read what came before and after, or to find the person who said it and ask for elaboration.

4. Whenever possible make a simple diagram or sketch of an idea. Use both sides of the card when necessary.

5. You should go through your file annually lest a good idea get buried. Weed out the deadwood.

6. In addition to this resource file you should set up a file for your own personal library, using a 3x5 card file. You will save money and great annoyance if you make a card for every book and label with your name. Then make a habit to record the date and borrower's name *every* time you loan a book. Do not expect that your name label inside will insure its return. Check your file cards regularly and request the return of a book after a reasonable time.

7. Pamphlets, magazine articles, papers you have written, speeches, etc. can be kept in a file which holds 8½x11 pages, also available in cabinet form with drawers.

8. If you have sufficient storage space, you will want to save a few samples of paintings or children's constructions which will illustrate points you may want to make at some future time.

9. Complete sets of slides, to be used in innumerable ways, will also need their own special file cabinets. Here, a cross file is essential, because the same slide might well be used to talk about equipment, integration of the exceptional child, or a good day with the 'fours'.

10. Some teachers also make photo albums throughout each school year, an excellent way of illustrating program and its progress, reflected through actual children and events. This is a wonderful tool to use in parent conferences and with the individual child— showing him his own growth and recalling happy times.

11. A large folder for filing pictures, by subject or seasons, from magazines, calendars and posters, will insure that you can always put your hands on the right picture at the right moment.

12. Collect boxes of various sizes and shapes and cover them with fabric or wall paper. These will hold favorite things—collections of all kinds, miniatures, pretty stones or shells, junk jewelry, old watches, buttons—whatever interests a teacher will be of interest to a child when offered as special treats to share, look at and return. One teacher keeps a 'junk box' on a shelf in her kitchen. Here she drops such delights until they can be sorted and arranged for permanence. A similar collecting box in the class room will encourage children to watch for such items. The broken parts of an old toy, a puzzle piece, a lost button, an odd-shaped wood scrap or plastic cap will someday find an interesting new use.

13. One of these boxes might be a 'Tiny Treasure Box'. In it you will have a host of miniatures, small items which a child can look at, touch, play with and carefully put away for someone else to enjoy. It may even enhance the mystery and excitement if each tiny prize is wrapped in colored tissue, or enclosed in a wee bag or envelope. This box is kept out of reach, taken down only on very special occasions for one or two children at a time. It belongs to YOU, but you TRUST the children who share your treasures—an excellent way to teach respect for the property of others. (See "Tiny Treasure Box")

Note: To the reader, who at this point is saying, "that's a great idea, I must do it!" If you don't make a start TODAY, you will wake up years from now saying, "Where did I see, hear, put that?"

Fundamentals of
Taking Slides
(Barbara Delinsky)

A. Technical aspects

1. Camera should be in top working order. Have batteries checked regularly. Have any necessary repairs done as soon as possible.

2. Keep lens clean. Curious children adore exploring with their fingers. Smudges can ruin an otherwise fantastic slide.

3. Hold camera steady

4. Hold camera level. Avoid the discomfort of viewing slanting tables and leaning subjects.

5. Know flash range of camera and keep within that distance. This is THE major factor in proper exposure with an Instamatic, non-adjustable camera. That is, if the flash range is stated to be "4 to 9 feet" objects closer than 4 feet will be overexposed, while objects further than 9 feet will be underexposed. It is critical to keep the center of interest within the flash range.

6. Avoid flash reflections by shooting at a 45° angle (loosely measured) from window, mirror, or other shiny surface

7. Flash may be needed outdoors. An Instamatic always needs a flashcube indoors. In some locations, it may be called for outside, also. If there is an unusual amount of shade, such as in the forest, use a flashcube and keep within the flash range for proper exposure. A flash can never ruin an outdoor picture.

B. Content

1. Determine purpose of slide and choose angle and distance accordingly. For example, to record a particular pencil and paper activity, move in close and aim down to get both the child and his work recorded on the film. To capture a group activity, move back and shoot from a great distance, (within flash range) thereby recording the group IN activity; in such a situation, a tight closeup would lose the general context and purpose for which the slide was taken.

2. Be sure that your slide has an obvious center of interest. This center of interest does not have to be centered physically in the picture, but it should immediately draw the viewer's interest. Beware that the photograph of a group activity often comes out as a mish-mush of action.

3. Choose your background whenever possible. Keep background as simple as possible by choosing the appropriate shooting direction. Avoid bright lights or sun shining directly into camera. Avoid the inclusion of unpleasant or irrelevant objects, such as wastebasket, snowsuit, empty chair, extraneous teachers, visitors or children.

4. Wait for just the right moment. Observing the situation through the camera, wait for the activity's climax, the right facial expression, or the disappearance of an unwanted subject. It is possible to carry on a conversation with the children even with the camera at your eye; they will soon tire of looking at you and turn their full attention to the activity you wish to photograph them doing. Be patient!

5. Always have camera ready. If loaded with flashcube and kept within sight but out of reach, camera will always be available and children will become accustomed to its presence.

6. Keep an open mind for bonus shots. An unexpected happening may vary from the original purpose of the slide but may be well worth recording.

Observation and
Recording

Knowing Your Children—Referring again to the picture puzzle, the fitting together of pieces that make a total configuration, it is essential for each teacher to observe children constantly, always keeping the square and circle diagram in mind.

A casual observer cannot really know what is going on in the mind of a dedicated teacher.

Sally needs the soothing motion of this swing now. She is new and needs time to get adjusted but if she hasn't made friends soon I will have to help her.

There is something interesting going on over in the sandbox. I'm glad to see Jane is taking some notes. I hope she will share them with us this noon at our meeting.

Oh, oh, there goes Henry after John's bike. He will manage to 'con' him into thinking he really wants the truck.

Cappy has been watching something near that tree for over fifteen minutes. I must go over and see what it is.

Today is the first time Jeannie has listened through an entire story. I must remember to tell her mother and make a note for her record card.

Observing is a necessary skill in a good teacher. The second stage of observation is being able to record and later use the results. A pad of paper and pencil should always be at hand, in a pocket or on a nearby shelf. The time to record is *immediately* after the conversation or incident. The 'flavor' will be diluted between seeing and recording if too much time has elapsed.

Some of these notes are dropped into a box of suggestions for a parent bulletin or newsletter. Some are conversational topics for brief meetings with parents as they deliver or pick up a child, but the true value of such notes becomes evident when a teacher writes record cards. Accurate recording about a child is probably the most difficult, and at the same time, the most important function of a teacher. It is not just to have permanent records in the files that these written reports are required—they also improve the quality of teaching. The difference between a good teacher and an excellent one can be equated with the gap between 'observation' and 'perception'. The necessity for accurate recording will constantly send the teacher back for another look.

Does John initiate activities?

If a story is announced, who comes running?

Is Sally the first one chosen?

If I say Jim loses his temper easily, can I say what usually triggers an outburst?

When a teacher writes a report half way through the term, does the report show progress?

Susie was clinging to her best friend in September, has she changed?

Harry was a watcher—Is he participating more now?

Kathy was bossy. Has she learned to use her leadership ability without being obnoxious?

Is it possible that I wrote that Lisa hadn't talked? She never stops talking!

As the teacher writes record cards, he/she will refer often to daily notes. A simple example of an event is worth a paragraph of educational and psychological jargon. For example:

If it is written that Kathy is well adjusted, the reader must ask, "In whose opinion? By what standards?" Whereas a card which says, "Kathy took everything in stride" tells much more.... When Ann and Mary said, "You can't come in to our house," she replied, "Well, I'll have a store over here and you can come buy things from me."

or

Instead of socially mature, the report might read: "Dick is the first to greet a visitor or a new child." He says, "I'm Dick, what's your name?"

or

'Emotionally stable' means little unless one really knows the person who made the judgment. But "When Donna's little brother was hurt in an accident, she was concerned, but she managed very well. She talked about it freely and often", tells a lot about Donna's emotional stability.

Writing, for any reason, requires a certain amount of skill, but this skill can be acquired with practice. A *snapshot* of the child attached to the card is always helpful, but without that, the first entry should make this child come alive for the reader, so each card begins with a physical description, using colorful words which create a visual image of *that child*. Examples taken from actual cards illustrate this point:

Dark-haired, chubby, little Mark has more facial expressions than there are minutes in a day.

Sarah is petite and pixieish.

Jack breezes through the day like a breath of fresh air.

Stuart never runs out of gas.

She is a gorgeous child who moves with grace and a kind of sophistication.

A cheery, chubby, curly-headed, little cherub.

She radiates a *joie de vivre*.

His facial expression is guarded and reserved.

She is a little thing with a bouncing, brown pony tail and freckles on her nose which accent her blue eyes.

As you read these comments, each of these children begins to take shape as a *person*.

Each recording should include some evaluation of PHYSICAL prowess or strength. For example:

He dislikes rough play — is very cautious!

Excellent stamina. Walked to the top of the hill and was not tired.

Has no notion of how to manipulate scissors. Holds a pencil or crayon in fist rather than fingers.

When Bruce finally climbed to the top of the ladder and into the tree house the rest of the children, who had been silently watching, spontaneously clapped. (Bruce was handicapped.)

Observations of SOCIAL behavior might read:

She is usually sitting by herself watching the group.

Sweet, gentle, kind; never pushes or reprimands another child.

Can handle only one friend at a time because she gives full attention.

Not an 'exhibitionist' but loves to 'ham' for an audience.

A designated leader — a good organizer.

Shows concern for others. Asked mother to buy a card for a child who was in hospital.

A leader — full of ideas — others flock around her.

A giving person — offers to help me and other children.

The EMOTIONAL side of our square cannot be ignored. Often it is picked up in other descriptions, and usually the language which tells about this aspect is more subtle, less concrete:

Boastful, but not to the point of being obnoxious.

Could...'Well, what if....' you all day if you would let him.

A moody child who often whines and complains.

Reacts with anger, argument or avoidance, according to his mood of the day.

Lloyd is the kind of child who will stop in the middle of a relay race to smell a daisy.

An angry young man who reacts to slightest provocation.

Has a face which mirrors his feelings.

Has to know in advance what each day holds for him, when and why.

We are all familiar with the parent who evaluates INTELLECTUAL growth in terms of papers and rote recitation of the alphabet and numbers. A teacher has many more ways of determining and recording progress.

Alex wants to *do*. He made a car with wheels and an axle that turns.

When he was making a bughouse the other day he created enough enthusiasm to keep everyone else interested.

He solves his own problems. Does not WANT to be told.

When listening to a story his face provides entertainment.

He is always ready with unique suggestions.

He asks questions until he has properly sorted something out to his satisfaction and then he will end questions by saying 'yeah-uh' to himself.

He adds his own interpretation to something someone else has said.

She is enthralled with learning.

He is constantly trying to figure out how things work, i.e., the lock on the gate, hose connection, etc.

Never initiates conversation.

Precisely finishes what she has begun — even when others try to hustle her.

A teacher who was having trouble writing reports was asked to "pick one child from your group and talk to me about him — right off the top of your head." She described David: "David is the kind of boy who never chatters the way most four year olds do; but when we are having juice, and David talks, the others all stop and listen."

She had given some information about David in three areas — SOCIAL, EMO-

TIONAL and INTELLECTUAL. Such an example will prove to be more valuable for later reference than a whole page of checklist facts.

The tired teacher who sees this recording as an added chore, may ask whether they are really ever used. The answer is positive. For example, the following comment from a guidance counselor: "I see that John Smith was with you when he was four. What was he like then?"

OR: "Jack Jones wants to get into Civil Service and uses your name for reference."

OR: "Kathy Lane is applying to a college. She lists you as a reference."

OR: (and sooner than you think)... Melinda applies for a position as a summer counselor. When you go to the files and pull her card, you will find that the information there is very helpful.

> Patty, aged six, who had attended the same school for three winters and two summers, had a wetting accident on her first day. Her parents were indignant—'something must have been wrong! The counselor didn't show her where the toilet was!' The director was able to show that on the first day of each new experience, Patty had reacted in a similar fashion. Obviously, she was a child who was fearful of new situations.

The writing of record cards involves discipline—self discipline on the part of the teacher. But the director must first determine whether the writers understand the process, so first requires a sample. This is usually followed up with a discussion, and some help.

Secondly, the director is *explicit* about due dates, and will adhere to them, even to the point of withholding paychecks if reports are not forthcoming. He/she will try to make some time available during working hours, although it should be clear that this is not guaranteed.

The director MUST READ THE CARDS! They are read first by the lead teacher, who then hands them to the director with his/her own comments. It is encouraging to the writer to get some feedback and inspires him/her to improve the skills.

Finally, at the end of a term of enrollment, the cards should be checked against a list and then filed. Reports are *confidential* and should never be left lying on a desk or in a classroom.

Some common errors to avoid:

1. Failure to sign (NOT initial) and date each entry. It is important to know WHO made the comment and whether it was in the beginning, middle, or the end of the child's year.

2. Failure to note the date and reason for a late entry or early *withdrawal*

3. Comments which do not cover all four sides of the square.

The following Guide to Development Report is NOT to be used as a checklist, rather it is suggested that those items listed may be used to stimulate thinking.

Guide to Recording Development

(See also Seq. 9, #21—Activities for Testing Skills)

PHYSICAL

> General appearance
> Body type
> Coloring
> Facial expression
> Large muscle coordination
>> Walking
>> Running
>> Climbing, etc.
> Small muscle coordination
>> Dressing
>> Handling scissors, crayons
>> Manipulative materials
> Tempo
>> Fast
>> Slow
>> Jerky

Hesitant
Moderate

SOCIAL

Leader
Watcher
Plays with one child, or in a group
Clings to adults
Ability to share, take turns
Respects rights of others
Resists authority

EMOTIONAL

Aggressive in behavior
  Language
Excessively fearful
  Passive
Dependent on adults or children
Withdrawn
  Shy, but can be drawn in
Stable
Easy-going
  Able to cope with unexpected situations, or easily frustrated
Over-sensitive
Uncontrolled temper
Sulks
Even-tempered or moody
Poised
Exhibits crying, tantrums, high-pitched voice, screaming, uncontrolled laughter, nervous habits (tics, whining, demanding, attention-getting devices)
GIVE EXAMPLES to illustrate your descriptions

INTELLECTUAL

Ability to follow directions
Special interests
Imagination
Awareness of detail
Initiative
Inventiveness
Work habits
  Careless, or with skill
  Excessively neat
  Concentration
  Completes what he starts
  Accepts rules pertaining to use of materials

LANGUAGE DEVELOPMENT

Speaks only when spoken to
Talks only when something to say
Talks all the time, but says little
Can't stop to listen to others
Speaks in clearly defined sentences
Enunciation — special speech defects
Enjoys stories; listening or dictating
Enjoys poetry; listening or dictating
Vocabulary
GIVE EXAMPLES of unusual words used and knowledge of their meaning.

TO BE USED WITH RECORD CARDS

Record Cards—Each child's progress is kept on cards and entries should be made on these cards soon after the child enters in (September, again in February), after the check sheets have been used, and again at the end of the year.

To some parents there is no substitute for daily reports. Nursery school teachers should try in every way possible to make it clear that the scribbles and blobs and collage concoctions which children take home are not to be judged by the appearance but represent stages in development as necessary as creeping before walking, and babbling before speech. Unfortunately, often a teacher's explanation either does not reach the ears of the busy parent or falls on deaf ears. They look at such papers and exclaim, "For that I'm paying all that money?!" Papers also can develop into a false system of communication between the child and parent. When a mother greets him with, "Did you *bring me* a paper today?" the paper becomes a symbol rather than an experience and his efforts take on unfortunate values.

What can we do about this? Children LIKE work. They like the word and its adult connotation, and they really enjoy going through the motions of writing numbers, letters, words in the same way they enjoy playing at being doctor, father, truck driver. IF no pressure is brought to bear, it is not harmful to have a work paper as one of the choices at activity time. When this can be extended to a 'homework' assignment, it serves a dual purpose. In one school where this has been tried successfully, the work paper always has something on the reverse side for the child to do at home.

School papers are important not so much for what they say to the adult in content but what they develop in the child. Putting our thoughts down on paper is just one way of recording our knowledge, demonstrating new skills, using another set of muscles and learning to use new tools (pencils, crayons, paints, staplers, etc.). Teachers must educate parents (and often themselves) to understand good papers. Parents who look at all education as something which must be put down on a paper have a slanted and very limited view of how real learning takes place. They do, however, need constant reassurance of the many other ways with which a child does express his knowledge. If occasionally a child carries home a paper, his parent needs to know how to evaluate and fit such papers into the total picture of development.

RECORD CARDS

GUIDELINES FOR STAFF

WHY?   Permanent record for files
To help director and/or teacher in conferences with parents
To help director know each child
To help director have an overall view of program and its effect on individual children
To help director know staff better
To make it necessary for each teacher to see children as individuals...not as a GROUP
To give teaching team an opportunity to share their feelings about children
To help teachers recognize strengths and weaknesses of individuals so they will know where extra attention is needed
Guidelines for developing program

WHAT?   Three entries a year (October—January—May)
Each entry to give some information on all four areas of development

HOW?   Each staff member to do ten or more cards—changed each time so three entries are by three different people. Write on paper first. Only to be typed on cards after approved by director. Use colorful descriptive language. Paint a "word picture" which makes child come alive.

GIVE EXAMPLES:

One good example may contain all the "meat" necessary. Eliminate all excess and unnecessary verbiage. Make no predictions. Offer no opinions. Record only what you see and can document!

Do not let concern for spelling and punctuation interfere with spontaneity. Let your ideas flow! If your cards are dull, boring...if they all sound alike...if any two cards could fit the same child, they will be returned for rewriting. Treat each one as if it were YOUR child. Be honest...but do not fall into the trap of negativism. There are positive things to be said about the most unloveable child. If there is important information which might be harmful to the child at some later date, record separately...for special file.

This will be your most difficult time-consuming task, but it is also the most important facet of your job. For some of you, it will come hard...but you will be given help and you WILL find that with practice you improve in your ability to observe and record. Best of all, you will KNOW your children!

Request for Child's Records—A child attended school and camp for two years. Three years later a request for information came from a guidance clinic. Using the contents of the child's record cards the director was able to write the following report:

TO:
Director of Social Service
Guidance Center
RE: J _____

Dear _____

J— first came to school in September 1964 at the age of three and one-half attending five mornings per week. He was a very attractive little boy, a bit shy and serious and quite dependent on adults at first. He was very bright, a fluent talker on all subjects but was not particularly interested in creative art activities. At the end of his first school year, he entered into all activities and was a popular member of his peer group.

J— attended the day camp for four weeks in August 1965. He was quite insecure and tense at first and wet his pants several times, but learned quickly to tell his counselor when he needed to use the bathroom. He enjoyed the pool and joined in all group activities. His counselor felt he was a bright, sensitive child and a wonderful camper.

During the next school year, J— continued to progress intellectually and demonstrated a delightful imagination and a great deal of knowledge about the world of space. He knew his colors and used the scissors very well. He was able to tell his teachers when he was unhappy and responded to attention with a big smile. The teachers felt he was a very lovable little boy.

At camp in August 1966 J— was a bubbly youngster whose vocabulary and ability to hold an intelligent conversation made a strong impression on his counselor. His counselor's report read: "J— tackles every activity with no predrawn conclusions as to whether or not he'll like it. He can work very well by himself, but also fits in easily with any child and all members of the group. J— is a very stable person who takes everything as it comes. I've never seen anything get him upset. His apparent intelligence makes him curious and quite imaginative—as evidenced by sessions in creative movement.".

When J— entered his kindergarten year in 1966 he began to show some signs of insecurity. He had frequent wetting incidents and would cry each time. He was quite shy and serious at first. In February 1967 his teachers wrote: "J— has learned to smile, even laugh with his whole being. He enjoys painting, and often dictates stories about his paintings, such as 'What I see from my seat in the bus on my way to school'. One was a happy scene. Another was a robbery, the theft of the family car and two dollars."

The teacher's final report in June 1967 read as follows: "J— is quite delightful. His worries and nervousness are less apparent now although he still comes in to school complaining about a stomach ache every once in awhile. He loves to play outdoors and is very creative in art work. His drawings always have wonderful stories to accompany them. The other day he drew with his eyes closed 'just to see how it would come out', and then invented a story about the picture. He has really come a long way. Listening to a triangle being played J— said, 'It sounds like a giant pin falling down on a piece of paper.' "

We hope that this report will be helpful to you in your work with J—

(signed)
Director

This form should be signed by a parent or guardian before information about a child is released:

I, _____ (parent/guardian) hereby grant permission for the release of information from _____ SCHOOL about my child, _____ _____ to _____ (school, doctor, agency, clinic).

Evaluation

For the children, we have evaluation sheets, folders, and file cards. If all are used faithfully and intelligently the effect a school has had on a particular child will be apparent.

For staff, the self analysis sheet asks questions of student teachers which apply to all of us. The most valuable evidence of individual performance shows in the three methods used to evaluate children. If a teacher has done his/her job well, success in their progress records will be evident.

1. *The parents should be given an opportunity to express their ideas*, feelings and suggestions. This can be at a final parent meeting, through a questionnaire, or through an invitation to express their ideas to members of the parent council who will take them up with the director. We like to think that letters of commendation are representative of *all* parent attitudes, but there is usually some silent criticism which needs an invitation to be expressed openly. Honest appraisal is a necessary facet of every successful organization. It should be sincerely invited, openly received and acted upon.

2. *Children can tell us a lot*. At the end of the school year when we are seeking ways to evaluate the child's ability to express ideas, we encourage them to tell stories or relate incidents, two purposes are served by choosing such topics as:

"Think very hard. What was the best thing you liked at school this year? When you are ready, tell us about it."

or

"Draw a picture of what you liked best and when you are ready to tell me a story, I will write it down. I will put all of the children's stories into a book and later I will read them to the class."

Try the reverse

"Is there anything about school you didn't like? Can you draw a picture of it so I will know what it is you are telling me?"

or

"Let's make a list of the things we liked and then we can put numbers on them to see which we liked most and which we liked least."

When one-to-one conversations are possible, possibly at nap time, true feelings are more likely to emerge.

Accountability—At the time of this writing, accountability is a much used word. Political, social and economic unrest have undermined basic trust. Parents and children are touched by this lack of confidence, and we, who have the temerity to accept the responsibility for the nurture and care of children, carry a heavy burden. We should welcome the opportunity to prove that we are trustworthy. We should not resent pressure for 'proof of purchase' but should constantly seek new tools to assist us in explaining our procedures for evaluating individual growth and collective progress.

Consider the following questions:

What do parents really want?

They want their children to have a good foundation for learning, one which will give the individual child a head start. If it seems as if they are seeing the 'now' in terms of the future, as if their sights are set on entrance to college rather than healthy growth and development, we do not blame or criticize, but accept the challenge for which we were trained. We KNOW the true values of nursery, kindergarten education. We should be convincing when we explain them.

The parent who makes out a sizable check each month wants something more than the scribbles and blobs the child brings home. Another wants to know whether his child will learn to count and recite the alphabet; a third may be focused upon such worries as:

"J— was out of sorts this morning. If he behaves badly will the teacher scold him or give him a little extra love? If he is not feeling well will she recognize the symptoms and call me? He was upset about that new boy who has been hitting him. Will the teacher see it and protect him? If walks in a puddle and gets his feet wet, will someone see that he changes to dry socks?"

What does the director think about?

"So much of my time has been taken up with the administrative detail that I have not been able to observe in the classrooms. How do I KNOW the program is good? Mr. S _____ said he didn't think his son was learning anything. How can I show him what is really happening in our school."

What about the teacher?

The teacher is the one who really feels the pressure of accountability, because he/she is the one who is closest to the child. The teacher may know he/she is doing well, but how can he/she produce evidence of good works which will reassure parents?

What about me? questions the child

The child cannot make his demands for accountability, but if he could state his rights, he might say:

'I want my place in the sun, to be recognized as an individual. I want someone to see ME, to know when I am growing and when I need a little help. You keep a chart which shows I am taller. How do you know I have grown in my ability to solve social problems, to cope with strong feelings, to make my hands do what my brain tells them to do, to know the excitement of discovering and learning?"

The following methods have been tested and proven successful. Each director along with staff, will take from them some one idea or procedure, which may add a new dimension to the methods used in each school.

Many schools keep a folder for each child, starting at the beginning of the year. Large folders can be made simply from two sheets of 18 x 24 manilla paper, taped together, or cardboard. Each month, two or three samples of a child's work are added, crayoned papers, a painting, his way of printing his name, a self-image picture, a dictated story and any other special papers which show progressive development. During a parent conference, these folders aid in demonstrating the child's school work.

At the end of the year, a teacher might say, "This is a self-image picture of John made last September, and he did another this week. He was quite excited when he compared them and he saw how much he had grown. He could also see that he was more accurate in coloring the details of his clothing—see, he even made the stripes on his jersey. It was good for him to see how much he had changed. Look at his name, as he wrote it in September. On this paper, he wrote a whole sentence and signed his name."

The contents of such a folder offer a more accurate and interesting record of a year's development than a written report. Children take them home with pride and parents are pleased to have such a concrete record of achievement.

What We Did Today—These 4 x 6 slips are filled out at the end of each session and posted on parents' bulletin boards. As parents come for their children, they can glance at them to see what had happened during the day.

When the afternoon teacher arrives, he/she is able to see what the children did during the morning and invite conversation about, repeat, or extend the activities.

Directors find these records helpful as a check on program and curriculum.

Teachers are able to look back during their weekly team meetings and evaluate their adherence to plans and overall quality and variety of the program.

Staff Evaluations—The final full staff meeting should be used for evaluation. It is unwise to assume that it will all be effective unless some plan is made in advance. A questionnaire circulated and its results tabulated ahead of time may serve to start a discussion. Role playing may serve as an opener. "Mary, you be Mrs. Jones who is interviewing Jim for a position in another school. Your question is "Tell me about where you worked. What kind of an experience did you have?"

Assign one phase of the school operation to different teams and ask them to give an overall evaluation.

Individual Staff Evaluation—This staff evaluation form is filled out at the end of the year. After it is reviewed by the director it is placed in the individual's file.

It serves the same purpose as the director's annual report in that it makes the teacher THINK about the year, and evaluate her own performance.

This form is also very helpful when a reference is requested. Somewhere it needs to be recorded who worked with whom in a given year. When a teacher retires after many years of service all this information will be needed.

Name of School
STAFF EVALUATION FORM

Name   Date:
School year
Worked with (names of team members):   in   group

Please comment on the following:
1. Organization of people and their responsibilities
    a. Your team
    b. Total school
2. Daily Schedule
3. Teacher Interaction
    a. Flexibility
    b. Communication
    c. Maximum use of special needs
4. Pre-opening training
    a. Was it adequate?
    b. What was most effective?
5. In-service training
    a. What has been most effective?
6. Recommendations for improvement of school. (Please use other side if necessary):

A Director Evaluates His/Her First Year—"When I came on board in July, I felt like a 'piper cub pilot flying a 707'. Terror is a gross understatement for my feelings at that first staff training session, but it was soar or nose dive—I had no choice but to try my wings. I made a lot of mistakes, but I learned a great deal from them *and I am still learning*.

At first I tried to do everything all at once with an equal degree of intensity and perfection—and many times ended up exhausted, accomplishing little. I learned to set daily priorities, plan and pace better, to do what I was doing, one thing, one day at a time.

In trying so hard to build up the "I AM and I CAN" of the children and staff, I didn't seek enough positive feedback and support for myself, so I sometimes felt isolated, and afraid I was doing everything wrong. At these low ego points, I tended to have misgivings about my own intuitions and judgments, and so whenever I went back on my own intuition—especially in dealing with parents or staff—I always regretted it. I learned to take time out to strengthen me and to listen to my inner voice.

In training or more specifically reprimanding staff for unacceptable teaching behavior, I tended to give one too many chances, with the result that more than one teacher hanged herself on the rope I gave her. I learned to balance the soft touch with the hard line approach, to set a uniform standard of competence and uphold it, without feeling guilty if certain people just couldn't make the grade.

As a deep feeling person, I find it fairly easy to understand and share the emotions and experiences of others, a prerequiste in relating to small children and a necessity in dealing honestly and compassionately with adults.

One of my favorite lines goes 'I want to live and help live—hoping never to cease until I die.' To cease before you die is to stop growing, and even in my moments of most extreme weariness and bitter frustration, I know that ceasing to grow is something I simply cannot and will not do. This 200% commitment to life and growth is my best strength and recommendation as a director of a school for malleable children."

A Director's Walk—One benefit gained from visiting another school is that it makes you look at your own school with clearer vision. Periodically a director should walk about the building and grounds, figuratively wearing the glasses of:

A parent choosing a school.

Another school director or staff member.

A neighbor who want to see what goes on in "that place."

A licensing agent on a required inspection.

The fire department looking for hazards and methods for getting children out quickly.

...And finally your very own glasses, which will reflect pride in YOUR school.

HOUSEKEEPING

"Everyone uses the collage materials. They are in my room, but I don't think I should have to straighten up when others leave a mess."

"The ashtray in the staffroom needs emptying but I don't even smoke."

"I left paint jars washed and the brushes clean on Friday, but someone used them and I had to clean them all over again before I could use them with my group."

No maintenance crew, however efficient, can ever take care of the total appearance of a school building and grounds. Every member of the staff, including the director, the receptionist, and the cook will have to do their share if it is to be a place which is attractive and inviting and teaches children something about good housekeeping.

It is essential that this be discussed during pre-opening staff training, stressing the importance of total participation. Duties should be discussed and chosen or assigned (see Workjobs). This cannot be treated lightly. Housekeeping will not "take care of itself if we all do our share" because there will always be people on a staff who do not *see*, who do not know *how* to do the simplest chores, and a few who are prone to "goof off."

When a director sees neglect he/she should be able to go directly to one person, rather than berate the entire staff at the next meeting with generalized complaints. Posted schedules enable a director to say, "Susan, you must have forgotten that this is your day to check the staff room. I was embarrassed when guests came in and the table was covered with junk and the ash trays overloaded."

In some schools staff prefer to choose one chore and stay with it; in others a revolving schedule is set up. In every school duties may differ, but the following check list will serve as a starter for discussion.

Staffroom

Empty and wash ash trays. Make coffee and keep table supplied with cups, sugar, cream. Check shelves, floor and table for personal belongings strewn around. Clean closet during school vacations when attendance is low.

Library

(Usually done by director or secretary). Check weekly. If one person has had a book for a long time ask if they are still using it. If books are missing and there is no card in the box go looking for it.

Bulletin Board

There may be two boards, one with notices, news items, magazine articles, etc. for parents; a second with samples of childrens work. In either case, they should be tastefully arranged and placed where they can easily be seen by children, parents and visitors. These boards should be changed weekly.

Cubbies

Interiors should be kept clear of unnecessary accumulation of clothing, toys, and clutter. Tops of cubbies should have nothing on them which is not useful or decorative, i.e. plants, books in bookends, accessories for an activity.

Toilets

Check three times a day. Be sure they are flushed, and spills around seat wiped up. Check supplies of toilet paper, paper towels, soap, etc. Spray with disinfectant daily and wipe seat and shelf behind toilet with a paper towel.

Cots

Should be stacked when not in use. When properly stored, cots are not an eyesore.

Activity Centers

Each area should be checked at the end of the morning and again at the end of the afternoon session. If used at the end of day, the teacher in charge must see that it is left ready for morning. Check with maintenance personnel to see if the children should stack chairs on table so floors can be more easily cleaned at night.

Floors

Children should learn to pick up papers and other items WHEN they are dropped. It is appalling to visit a school and see a floor littered with elegant junk, scraps of paper, used tissues and parts of puzzles and toys. The teacher sets the example and is insistent that children share in clean-up.

Playgrounds

Bikes and wheel toys must be put away and storage house locked up at the end of p.m. session unless 4-6 teacher requests that they be left out and agrees to be responsible for them. Yard should be cleared daily of papers, and debris of all kinds. Sand and water toys are kept in baskets or boxes and stored in shed.

Livestock

Plants, animals and aquariums require daily attention. Someone must take on this responsibility.

The worst mistake of all would be to exclude the children from these housekeeping chores. As in every other aspect of program, they will have to learn, in easy stages, but the lessons they learn will be more long reaching than the immediate completion of the task. Sharing responsibility for one's "home," remembering to carry out a task without reminders, and recognizing that it takes the combined effots of many people to provide the comforts and cleanliness they otherwise take for granted—these are all part and parcel of living and learning together.

During pre-opening staff training, the staff together decide what needs to be done, what is a fair distribution of chores, when tasks will be performed and where the tools are kept for carrying out the task.

HEALTH

Parents display enormous trust when they leave their child in a child care center. No precaution can be overlooked, no procedure neglected, which justifies that trust. Here we have outlined the basics. In every center there will be extenuating circumstances which indicate the need for extensions of these policies.

Health Forms: Child

Prior to Enrollment (or Employment)

Before a child (or adult) is admitted to the center, it is necessary to have written assurance from a licensed physician that the individual is able to participate in the activities related to the program or position. Regulations and supervision of compliance will vary from state to state, even within a state, but the conscientious director will be motivated by concern rather than external pressure. The following information is needed prior to acceptance:

Report of physical examination
Evidence of required innoculations
Parent information sheet
Statement from the director
Written permission for emergency medical attention
Names and telephone numbers to be used in case of emergency

Health Information for parents (to be included in parent's manual)

Our concern for your child will not be limited to "learning" but will encompass the physical and emotional sides of his/her development as well as the social and intellectual. We ask for your complete cooperation in accepting the rules we have made for the health and safety of each child, and in turn we pledge to you our diligence in maintaining good practices. If at times you are inconvenienced, we ask you to remember that in protecting someone else's child you will also help maintain a safe environment for your own.

Sickness

Please keep your child home under the following conditions: If he/she seems listless, unusually irritable, complains of a stomach ache, headache, or ear ache, or seems to be unusually pale or flushed. It is better to be overcautious than to risk exposing the rest of the children and staff to contagion.

A child should remain at home for forty eight hours after a temperature goes down, and for twenty four hours after a minor upset.

Clothing

It is better to have too much rather than too little. Trust in teachers to use their judgement as temperatures change.

Please send an extra set of indoor clothing (underwear, top, pants and socks) and a pair of slippers or sneakers. It is possible for a child to get wet from without as well as from toilet accidents, and we do not want our children to sit in wet clothing. If clothing is sent home after an accident, please wash and return as soon as possible.

Our children play out year round, and in all kinds of weather. Please send them dressed for active participation. (Rain coats and rubbers on rainy days; ski pants, boots and mittens in the winter.) On very cold winter days we will stay in at first and go out later in the morning when the sun is higher. The station wagons are heated so it is reasonable to let children carry their ski pants as long as they are available when needed.

We teach the children how to dress and undress themselves. Please encourage this at home also. Try to allow enough TIME and express your pride in your child's accomplishments. "I can do it myself" is the natural tendency of the child. When you cheat them out of this satisfaction, you also cheat yourself.

If your child is exposed to a contagious disease in school we will send you a written notice, with instructions for keeping him/her home. If you are aware that your child has been exposed elsewhere PLEASE consult with the director about procedures to follow.

In the event of accident or if your child becomes ill while at school we will follow these procedures:

First aid treatment for minor cuts or bruises will be reported to you by the director or teacher before the child returns home. If we cannot reach you a written report will be sent with the child. We are required to have at least one person on the staff who has an updated First Aid certificate and is available at all times.

If stitches or further treatment seem necessary, we will keep the child quiet while we

1. Call parent at home
2. Call parent at work
3. Call emergency number
4. Call child's doctor
5. Take child to out patient dept. of hospital
6. If time seems to be important we will call police ambulance or the director and one other person will take child to hospital. At the same time someone will be setting calls in motion as above.

It may reassure you to know that because we ARE so conscious of health and safety, these procedures rarely have to be used.

All staff have been trained in procedures to follow and written instructions are posted in the director's office.

Incorporated into our curriculum are basic principles of cleanliness, knowledge of the parts of the body and their care and functions, and the body's needs for food and rest. Our teachers see your children functioning in many ways and under different conditions and in comparison with other children of the same age. If they observe what appears to be a deviation from the norm, however slight, they will report it to the director. If the director observes the child and considers it a matter worthy of concern, he/she will report it to you. On the other hand, we appreciate it when you share with us any information relating to your child's physical or emotional health. It is particularly important for us to know if you are away on a trip, if there is serious illness or death in the family, or if you are contemplating a move or change in family patterns. We respect all such information as confidential, but we know that children are often uncomfortably aware and will express their insecurity in their behavior.

Health Forms: Report of physical examination
Employee Report of TB test
Statement from doctor
Health history
Name and number of person to be called in case of accident or illness
Permission for emergency medical attention
We are not always as careful about obtaining the emergency information for adults as we are for children, but for the rare occasions when it is needed, we should have it available.

Staff Needs: *Relief Periods*

It is the responsibility of the director to make certain that each staff member has some periods of relief during the day. However, a teacher cannot just "drop everything" at a specific regular "break" time. The needs of children do not fall into neat time slots. The timing of a brief respite should be determined by the members of a teaching team and abuse or disagreement of the privilege handled at weekly team meetings. It is "family" business, to be managed within the family.

In a day care center when a staff member has an hour off at noon, the director should urge that person to get away from the building, at least for a short walk. There should be a cot or couch in the staff room or director's office for staff use. It is suggested that medication be given out by the director on request rather than placed in a medicine chest. A teacher who calls for aspirin every day bears watching.

Provision should be made for the teacher who is not well enough to be with children but not sick enough to stay home, especially when sick days with pay are limited. This person might assist with clerical work duties.

Careful records of staff absences, stating the reasons, will have implications for future employment and references.

> One director found this out when a frightened aid came running in to the office. "Mrs. Smith has been acting funny and now she is lying on the ground. I think she may be having a seizure." (It turned out to be a diabetic coma.) In addition to calling for an ambulance the director had to notify a responsible relative and found the teacher's recorded information woefully inadequate.

Health Inspection

Each day immediately upon arrival the child should be carefully checked by the nurse or director or teacher. It is important to have the same person do this, first because it establishes a relationship of trust (the child feels that someone really cares for him and is watching over him), and second because there are chronic conditions which are learned by a person who really knows the child. If a child resists this inspection initially it is best not to attempt to force compliance. If he observes other children cheerfully opening their mouths, and sees that nothing bad comes of it, he will come to it on his own in due time.

Using a flashlight or standing under a direct light the inspector looks at the childs throat for redness, irritation or white patches, at the same time feeling both sides for swollen glands. Signs of rashes, sores, bruises, flushed cheeks or unusual pallor are also indicators. While looking between fingers for a rash or sores, notice "clammy" hands, and listen for a cough or wheeze. Running or red eyes and nasal discharge are warning signs. A teacher who observes any unusual behavior or symptons will confer with the director immediately if a child becomes listless, sleepy, restless and irritable, makes frequent trips to the toilet, stumbles or falls easily or complains of aches in the stomach or ears.

Clothing

Children cannot be expected to take full responsibility for wearing the right clothing, or making certain that it is properly fastened when they first come to a center. These details should be discussed, practiced, and checked daily until habits are formed. Children can learn to help each other with buttons, zippers and boots and thus develop some sense of responsibility for their peers.

Food and Rest

It is the teacher's responsibility to see that the children maintain a balance of activity and rest, i.e. after a vigorous activity they are settled down for a story. Table activities are followed by creative movement or some form of physical exercise.

A mid-session rest may or may not be necessary. Most nursery schools have eliminated the compulsory rest on blankets or mats and use their judgement based on the tempo of the classroom, but in a full day care center there should be a minimum of one hour's rest after lunch. (See Naptime)

The nutritional needs of the child will have been taken into account by the person who plans meals and snacks. Their importance should not be treated lightly.

Personal Habits

Children do not automatically know how to use a tissue, wash their hands and dry them carefully, or care for toilet needs. The teacher should not avoid the responsibility of TEACHING these skills, using every available method. The teacher tells, shows, demonstrates, role plays, uses pictures, provides dolls, and makes health and weight charts.

Curriculum:
Teaching Hygiene

To the many suggestions offered in the curriculum the teacher will be constantly on the alert for opportunities to integrate the principles of health into daily program. It is not necessary to preach. Learning basic facts can be as interesting and as much fun as acquisition of any other aspect of learning, IF the teacher sees program as everything the child has a need and a desire to know.

First-Aid

In most states, licensing requires that at least one person be trained and certified in First Aid, and available at all times. It is the director's responsibility to provide training when necessary. First Aid should be JUST what it says—only minimal treatment until professional help is available.

A daily log MUST be kept of every incident and treatment, however trivial. It is suggested that this be in a hard cover bound book, rather than loose leaf, and that records be stored and kept almost indefinitely. A parent cannot sign away the child's right to bring suit after he is twenty one, and it is possible that a claim will be brought for an injury at a much later date. The report should not be limited to "Johnny fell and got a bump on his head. Applied ice." but should state how, where, and what part of the body was injured (tip of right index finger), and it should be recorded immediately, not at the end of the day.

Procedures for emergency treatment MUST be WRITTEN, DISCUSSED and POSTED in a conspicuous place. Part of the training of each new employee would be to go over this plan.

Attendance

A director who keeps a finger on the daily attendance has it also on the *pulse* of the school. A system of balances and counter balances (recorded by driver, room teacher, and on a chart or graph) will provide useful information. Recording the reason for absence will give evidence of spreading infection. An analysis of WHY a cold spread through an entire class, or car, often helps in developing adequate precautions. A graph will show absentee patterns which have implications for staffing and planning vacation periods.

SAFETY

Safety in the child care center is the responsibility of every member of the staff. There are dangers inherent in every aspect of program, in every moment of the day, and adequate protection calls for constant vigil.

The following suggested plan requires cooperation, concern, and conscientious observation.

At initial staff training give each member a copy of the check list and discuss each item fully, giving examples.

Each week assign a different staff member to do a thorough inspection of all facilities. Check each item and give details of incidents observed or faulty equipment.

The director will assemble reports and discuss pertinent items at monthly staff meeting and report on action taken. Inspection tours should take place at different times of the day. It may be necessary to pay extra time for someone to cover early morning and late afternoon inspections.

Safety Checklist

I. PEOPLE
   1. Did you see children unattended? Children in forbidden areas? Children in dangerous play?
   2. Inadequate adult/child ratio?
   3. Children hurting other children?
   4. Inadequately or improperly clothed children?
II. SURFACES
   1. Are floors slippery from wax, sand or spills, cluttery, dirty or splintery?
   2. Are outdoor surfaces icy, cluttered? Are there hard surfaces under climbing equipment or swings?

    3. Are passageways clogged? Are there obstructions in front of doors?

    4. Is equipment broken or dangerously worn?

    5. Is equipment unsuited to ages of children?

    6. Are there exposed nails, screws, sharp edges or points?

    7. Are there handrails on stairs at the right height for children?

    8. Do doors open out? Do heavy doors have crash bars? Are there inside locks in closets or toilets?

III. HEAT

    1. Are heaters, fireplaces, radiators covered?

    2. Can children reach knobs and turn on burners on stove?

    3. Are pots and pans on stove within reach of children?

    4. What is the temperature of water coming from faucets used by children?

IV. WATER

    1. Are pools fenced and locked when unsupervised?

    2. Are there depressions in the yard which hold rain?

V. TOILETS

    1. Are they clean? Free of odors?

    2. Are seat and lavatory the right height for a child or is a stool provided?

VI. KITCHEN

    1. Clean floor, counters, stove, refrigerator?

    2. Rubbish and garbage disposal clean—adequate?

    3. Cook's appearance—clean uniform? hair restrained?

    4. Evidence of insects or rodents?

    5. Are cleansing agents, insect poison, other dangerous materials in locked storage?

VII. LIGHTING

    1. Are play areas and passageways clearly lighted?

    2. Are electrical outlets either 48" from the floor, covered or equipped with a safety device?

Note: Some new building codes permit only safety glass within 48" of floor.

Procedures for fire drills will be explained and practised at pre-opening training. Thereafter a fire drill should be held at least once a month. There should be one signal used—and used for that purpose only. Children should be alerted to the sound of that signal, prior to the first drill. (See sequence 2, Activity 5)

Timing is of the utmost importance. If the director stands with a watch—and commends those who get out of the building promptly, children will take pride in competing with their own record.

It must be made clear that children do NOT stop to gather belongings, or put on outside garments. That few seconds could be crucial.

Fire drills should be held at different times of day, and in varied weather. Each class, group or team should be assigned a meeting place. Procedures for counting, checking attendance, and reporting to director should be planned and practised. The last adult to leave the building will check all areas; this is crucial in centers where children come for different hours in the day or days of the week.

DISASTER—A log should be kept recording date, time of day and time taken to clear building.

It would be wise to invite the fire chief to send someone to review procedures planned, and where inspection is not automatic to invite him to look over the property.

Other disasters would vary in different parts of the country. Smog alert, tornado or hurricane warning, lost child, dangerous persons loose; anything is possible.

One center director thought she was dreaming when a voice over the phone said a bomb had been hidden in her school. It seemed so ridiculous she hesitated to report it, but of course she did. Within moments the police and fire equipment arrived. The children, who were napping, had sleepily gathered outside. After making a thorough search, the men took a few moments to talk to the children and demonstrate equipment, so the experience proved to be exciting and informative.

Written Arrangements

Precautions:
There must be a list which tells the location of the fire alarm system and all shut-offs (gas, water, heat) in the building.

The fire alarm (which was connected with the fire department) went off at 7:30 a.m. It was embarrassing when the fire department arrived, to hunt for the activator, which could not be located. (See 'Supervision in the Director's Absence!)

The director of a new center will not wait until disaster strikes, to make contact with all of the services he/she might need. One of the first tasks would be to call upon the police department, explain who he/she is and tell a bit about the center and its purpose, hours, ages of children, etc. At the same time, the director could request that a policeman come to the school to talk to the children about safety, and ask that the cruiser check during off hours for vandalism, especially on nights and weekends.

The director should also speak to someone at the medical center, or if a local hospital is to be used, visit to determine the exact location. Most hospitals have an emergency entrance and special requirements.

If a local doctor is the first resource, his/her willingness to be called should be in writing, with information about office hours.

Be sure to have on hand the telephone number of the nearest poison center.

TRANSPORTATION

Between the security of the home and the safety of the child care center lies the public way over which the child is conveyed twice each day. A very small percentage of the children who attend child care centers live near enough to walk, and not too many parents find it convenient to drive them.

In some schools transportation is provided as a service. In others, the concerned director becomes the "arranger" who tries to help find satisfactory solutions to the frustrating, time consuming problems involved in arranging transportation.

We will describe here a number of known systems for transporting children to and from school, and urge all readers to share with their colleagues any new or different methods.

Hired Transportation

How to Find It—
1. A notice in parent bulletins may reach parents who are planning to drive their own child and would be willing to bring other children to help defray tuition costs.
2. An ad in the local paper usually brings a good response. (For example, "Wanted...Responsible drivers to use own station wagons for school transportation. For information call...")
3. In some towns there are taxis or bus companies interested in providing this service.

Things to Consider—
When transportation is hired, through whatever means, the following questions must be considered:
Who will pay for special school bus insurance?
How can the director be assured the car is properly insured?
What assurance does the director have that vehicles are maintained properly and checked regularly for safety?
Will parents pay for service *directly*—or will school handle the billing?
Will charges be by trip? week? month? year?
Will drivers be paid by hour? trip? salaried?
Will parents pay for holidays? vacations? days when driving conditions are hazardous?
When a child is withdrawn will notice be required?
Will drivers agree to accept conditions outlined in "Instructions to Drivers"
Will drivers attend driver training and monthly meetings?

Car Pools

In most schools for small children, there are parents who want to share the responsibility for getting their children to the center. They need help in making such arrangements. In addition to setting up lists and providing addresses and phone numbers, the director may offer the following suggested set of rules; however, one member of the car pool should act as coordinator to call a meeting to establish rules and policies and to deal with problems.

Suggested Rules for Car Pool Parents

1. If your child is not going, call the driver of the day so he/she will not make an unnecessary trip.
2. Have your child ready on time. (If not, wave car on and take him yourself.)
3. When child is brought home, give some evidence that you are there to receive him.
4. Be at home when he returns. (If not, driver will take him to his/her home where you will be expected to pick up.)

Center-Owned Vehicles

Over a period of years, we have found this to be the most satisfactory method, because it gives the director control over the factors which relate to the welfare of the child. Parents also feel more secure when they know the center can set the rules for selection and training of drivers, maintenance of vehicles, planning routes, and setting costs.

It is not unusual for a child care center to own or lease one or an entire fleet of station wagons or "mini-buses." Automobile manufacturers are at last recognizing that this is a needed service and are making mini-buses with built-in safety features (reinforced sides and tops, padded seat backs and seat belt for each child.

In a day care center, it is an advantage to have a vehicle at hand to provide before and after school care.

Hiring Drivers

Where to Look for Drivers—

The director should look first within the structure of the center. The cook, secretary or maintenance person may find that the combination of two jobs makes the salary more attractive.

Parents are also good candidates, especially if, in addition to a salary, some reduction is offered on tuition. Mothers who have children of junior high age are better prospects than those who have little ones. They do not have to be at home at noon or stay home if the child has a minor illness.

People who have worked with youth groups, brownies, cub scouts, Sunday School teachers, are all good prospects and should have desirable personal qualifications.

The following ad usually brings a good response:

"Child care center offers part time employment to men or women who enjoy being with young children. At least five years driving experience required. For further information, call..."

What to Look For—

It is required in some states, and strongly urged here, that all drivers be over twenty one years of age and have at least five years of successful driving experience.

They should be in good physical condition with no restrictions or limitations on their license.

As a representative of the school, the driver should present a neat, clean appearance. (An unkempt, unshaven man in a dirty old sweater or a woman wearing curlers and bedroom slippers will not inspire the confidence of parents!)

A driver should be emotionally stable, able to stay calm under stress and exercise good judgement when quick decisions are necessary. These are nebulous qualities, not easy to ascertain, and the director must use all of the "tools" available to seek the right person.

Job Description—

It is our belief that the INSTRUCTIONS FOR DRIVERS constitutes an excellent job description. Each applicant should be asked to read them carefully before the interview, and the interviewer can choose a few questions at random to ascertain the degree of understanding.

Benefits—Terms of Agreement

If a driver is entitled to sick days, vacations, or fringe benefits, these should be stated in writing, in addition to a statement of tax deductions.

Occasionally drivers think it legitimate to work for ten months and collect unemployment during the summer. To avoid this, the length of the employment period should be made clear in writing.

Termination conditions should be included in the Personnel Policy, Contract, or Terms of Agreement.

Salaries—

Salaries may be hourly, weekly, or contracted for the year. The latter, with regular step raises will keep valued drivers with the center over a period of years, a great source of strength to the director. (It is advisable to pay drivers for time spent learning routes.)

Substitutes—

Whenever possible, a substitute should be introduced to parents and children in advance. It is ideal when each driver finds and trains an alternate, possibly a friend or relative who would not want a full time position. However, in a large center which maintains a fleet of vehicles it may be worthwhile to employ one full time substitute who learns *all* of the routes.

Substitutes should also be paid for time spent learning routes.

Driver Training

At the beginning of a school year, it is as essential to meet with drivers as it is with teaching staff. A child is "in school" from the time he/she leaves the security of home, and it only takes one thoughtless statement or act to counteract the efforts of the teacher.

The INSTRUCTIONS FOR DRIVERS would constitute the main body of the training period. Time should be allowed for full discussion of each item. In addition, the director should go over some basic rules for dealing with children.

During the year, drivers should meet at least once a month with the director. A good time for this meeting is at 9 a.m.

The stage is set with comfortable seating, a large pot of coffee and refreshments. It is a time for listening, for sharing problems. The director will find many opportunities to restate the basic principles of good child care illustrating them with examples.

Drivers who are treated with this kind of respect and who are, after a trial period, salaried with the same fringe benefits given teaching staff, will stay on year after year. "Veteran" drivers often help to find and train new drivers, offer valuable insights into children's behavior, and are usually deeply respected and loved by children and parents.

Many excellent aides and assistants started as drivers who substituted occasionally in the classroom, and went on to further their education and became teachers!

School Traffic

A center director is responsible for planning and practicing procedures for delivering children to teachers in the morning and "collecting" them when it is time to go home.

When a center is located on a busy highway, the location and angle of the entrance are of prime importance. These should be carefully planned and measured. (With a brand-new building, this would probably be required by local authorities. When an existing building is to be used, it may call for some sacrifice to outdoor space for new driveways, or exits to another street.)

It is usually best to have one-way traffic in the driveway. (Expedience for the parent who is on the way to work must be coupled with provisions for the parent who wants to stop and go in to speak to the teacher or director. If the line of cars cannot move smoothly at the busy hours, this might engender ill will and confusion.)

Prodecures for "Drop-Off" Time—A staff member, properly attired for all kinds of weather, should be assigned as a "greeter" who will:

a) Open car door and assist child in getting out, making sure he/she has all belongings. (A pleasant greeting for parent and child is important.)

b) See that children go straight to the building or playground and are received by another adult.

c) Take written messages from drivers and convey them to proper source.

d) Keep a pad and paper to write messages given verbally by parents.

e) Make sure one parent does not hold up traffic while talking to you or entering the building.

"Pick-Up" Procedures

a) Again, it is best to have one staff member available at the close of a nursery or kindergarten session when "pick-up" traffic is heavy. Specific procedures should be planned and practiced.

b) Drivers do NOT go for the children. They stand beside their cars for identification and children are taken to them by staff member.

c) Children enter vehicles on the right hand side *only*.

d) Teachers are equipped with lists of children who ride in each car. They will have written messages about children who might have left early due to special circumstances.

e) Carpool parents display a sign with the names of the children they carry.

For the first few days, children should wear tags which tell the name of the teacher, group, and driver. (These might be color-coded.)

It is most important that all adults are cautioned not to raise their voices, or call to drivers or children.

If all procedures are carefully planned; if all adults are aware of the rules, and if the first two or three days go smoothly, the whole operation will fall into place with miraculous precision in less than a week!

DAILY ROUTINES

"My teachers have time to teach! My staff is not frazzled, harried, exhausted. I am always ready and proud to have people come to visit."

When a director of a child care center made these statements, the glow of pride and confidence were evident. What was the magic formula? It was called *zoning*.

Zoning

What is zoning? A technique so simple and logical, one would suppose such a plan would just happen.

Zoning is—placing each adult in specific places (zones) at specific times throughout the day.

Zoning is—moving children easily from place (zone) to place (zone) while adults stay within a particular zone. When zoning is a smooth, well established procedure, children can move alone and in groups without the guidance of an adult.

ZONING DOES NOT JUST HAPPEN. Each school presents its own set of zoning needs. A director must first spend time analyzing:

1. BUILDING and PLAYGROUND SPACES and how they can best be used (zoned). Each is given a name.

2. DAILY SCHEDULES of staff.

3. NUMBERS OF CHILDREN present in the center throughout each hourly time block during the day. Schedules of staff and children are charted for easy reference.

4. WORK LOADS of teams and individual staff members.

5. TRANSITIONS and ACTIVITY PERIODS when groups of children are being moved.

6. TRAFFIC PATTERNS

Zoning WITHIN EACH TEAM allows one teacher to stay with a last slow child, quietly listening and talking to him. He need not be constantly pressured to hurry because the teacher must stay with the whole group which has moved on. For example: At lunch time, a teacher can stay with one child as he cleans the table and sweeps up crumbs. A second teacher stands by the bathroom to supervise and guide toileting and wash-up. Another is waiting at the napping area, settling and quieting the children on their cots.

Zoning is an on-going process, changing as numbers of children change; extending in scope as children and staff mature and become more responsible. Patterns will need to change as programs and routines fluctuate throughout the year.

In the beginning, the director initiates and establishes zoning procedures, assigning the staff at strategic points. As the school "settles in" the suggestions for changes and improvements will come from the staff. Initially, also, a team leader zones within the team. Adults, like children, need the security of knowing what is expected of them. When routines become a natural sequence, the school day will begin to flow. As the teams become secure, participation in planning will be a group effort.

One teacher described zoning this way, "It is like the coach of a football team who stands at a blackboard and draws a diagram for each play. He assigns each player a number, and a position and gives each play a number. Each player has a special job to do and every play fits into a special place in the game. As players memorize these plays and perfect their individual skills, the games are played with greater precision and success. When a player forgets a strategy or does not use his particular skill successfuly, the game is lost."

Daily Schedule (to be posted in office)	7 am	Assistant arrives (one who can be cheerful in the early hours!) and does whatever is necessary to make the environment say 'welcome'. When the first child arrives there should be two people in the building (see regulations in your state). As more children come in there must be staff for supervision and to meet required teacher/pupil ratio. Children go to a central holding area.
	8 am	A lead teacher (or Assistant Director) stands near door to greet children and speak to parents or drivers who bring them.
	8:30 am	Director arrives and greets and inspects all children who are present and then takes over at door. (See section on health inspections.) As teachers arrive they take children to their own home base.
	9 am	Meeting time. Each team (with possible exception of Babes) has a meeting to discuss plans and choices for the morning. See Meetings, p.
	9:30-11 am	Activity time. See description-sketches page
	10-10:30 am	Snacktime (see section on Snacktime).
	11 am	Stories, music, outdoor play.
	11:30 am	Half the children get ready to go home. The rest get ready for lunch, wash, set tables, etc.
	11:45-12:30	Lunch (see section on Eating with Children).
	12:30	Some teachers find that an interlude between lunch and nap help children settle down. This should be a quiet time—story, records or movement session, ending up on cots. Naptime.
	1:30 pm	Afternoon children arrive. Teachers are ready to greet them, have activities planned outdoors or as far away from sleepers as possible.
	1:30-3:45	Repeat morning instructional program for p.m. children. Day care children function as a separate group with a separate staff.
	3:45 pm	P.M. children ready to go home.
	4-6 pm	Special Programs (see section on End of the Day Activities).

Early Arrivals The teacher who agrees to work from 7 to 9 in the morning and 4 to 6 in the afternoon takes on a different kind of responsibility. His/her *attitude* will either make this time special for children, or an unpleasant alternative to being home. Either they will look upon themselves as 'the poor little things—having to be away from home so long' or as 'very special people'. The teacher who feels "put upon" because he/she is required to work these hours can hardly expect to generate a good feeling in the children.

The atmosphere is all-important. In the morning a sunny room is a real asset and on a dark day lighting should be as bright and cheery as the smile on the teacher's face. The room needs to look ready—which means that the last one there the night before should have left things picked up and neat. A very imaginative teacher will keep a supply of special things which are only used at this time of day. A tiny *treasure* box (see Resource Files—Saving & Sharing Sect. 13; also "Tiny Treasure Box")—a toy or game, a little tea set, a big rag doll or stuffed animal.

Some children will not have had time for *breakfast*. Cereal, milk and juice may be offered to those who really need it.

At first children may need some *table activities*, but as they settle in they will form their own friendships and develop their own plans. A group of children may head for the family center, and take up their play where it left off the day before. Jackie may look forward to this time when he can have the *wood working* bench to himself, and add to his project from one day to the next. *Rules* will have to be established. "We will not take the unit blocks off the shelves, but you may build with the big *blocks*."

There should be a designated holding area for early arrivals, and in some cases, a *television* set will be available for those who want to watch their favorite programs. This is also a restrictive precaution, hopefully keeping two-year-old Tommy from darting into the team areas and scooping all the toys off the shelves! A row of coat hooks in the holding area can be used until the teacher arrives so the children need not go into other rooms to their cubbies. This may be the time when a teacher can supervise the use of the *tape recorder*, and slide projector, while there are only a few children to watch. A *five-year-old* who has been taught how to use it can help to entertain the little ones with special stories on the *film strip machine*. Older children can be encouraged to help the little ones with their clothing and to play with them but should not be required to do so.

The teacher should bear in mind that some people are slow starters in the morning. Children who want to "just sit" or who seem apathetic may be reacting according to their own metabolism and need not be urged to be actively engaged in *group activites*.

The ultimate goal is to create a comfortable, relaxed, homelike atmosphere.

Toileting   The wise teacher will realize that toileting is a time when the greatest teaching skills are needed. However advanced his/her thinking about bathroom techniques and language, the teacher must understand that some education has all ready gone on in the home. The child may have already stumbled up against attitudes toward doing what comes naturally. His mother's face, wrinkled up nose, and the vigor of her hands during the cleaning and changing procedures have told him something about bowel movements and how grownups feel about them. His first impression of "bad," "naughty" and "nasty" may be associated with his bodily functions. The child may have the feeling that this necessary and important function is associated with dirt, shame, rejection, sex, to be taken care of as quickly as possbile and behind, figurative if not literal, closed doors.

He may have found that withholding his movements is his most effective method for gaining approval, or that defecating at the wrong time and in the wrong place is his only way of punishing his parents.

The lead teacher who always sends the child to the bathroom with an assistant or classroom aide is saying something very clearly about his/her feelings toward toileting and teaching.

The bathroom is a place for intimacy, for quiet conversation. A child will often disclose what is closest to his heart, good or bad, while seated on the toilet. It is natural for a teacher to think his/her place is in the arena of the classroom with the group—where the action is, needs to consider what he/she is missing in getting to know and understand children.

Toileting cannot be treated routinely, as something unimportant to get over and done with. It requires careful, considerate thought—going to the toilet is important.

Though started in the home, toilet training continues in nursery school. When a child is ready in all respects for a group experience except for toilet training, the teacher cooperates with the parent in completing the training process. In fact, starting nursery school is often just the extra boost a child needs.

Although schools may not wish to accept a child who is not bowel trained, teachers must expect children to have an occasional accident, especially during the adjustment period. All children are apt to regress in the first weeks or at times of emotional strain and illness.

It is important that children wear training pants. If they come in diapers and plastic pants, they are set apart, 'different'. At first, when a child is wet, the teacher will go with him to the bathroom and change him. As soon as feasible, he takes more and more responsibility for changing, finally reaching the point where the teacher can say, "Oh, you have had an accident. Well, you know what to do. Get your bag from your cubby and go into the bathroom and change. Be sure to put your wet panties into a bag and take them home." Of course, the teacher will keep a watchful eye on the situation, making sure that he is thoroughly clean and has washed his hands.

The child will often quickly master his toilet training at school. The teachers accept 'accidents' casually, without embarrassing or scolding, anger or recriminations. When the child sees others using the toilet he will conform, eager to accept the rules of this new school 'society'.

NOTE: If there is an accident on carpeting, it must be cleaned up immediately. Use paper towels to soak up the urine, and then sponge the spot with warm, soapy water. It is a good thing to let the child help, or at least to show him what was done and explain why. If you do not take care of it at once, your carpet will be disfigured with permanent stains— and will soon acquire an unpleasant odor. (See Seq. 8, # 55 — Bathroom Talk)

Pause here for "Just Something to Think About" by James Hymes..

SUB-TITLE: The Child on the Pot Has His Personality in a Pliable Position

"All I do is toilet kids. I never teach them anything..." "In the early morning we have our creative activities. But with large groups so much of the rest of the day is taken up with routines..." Have you ever heard it?

What do we mean by routines? An activity that occurs many times a day, and day after day after day? Toileting does, so maybe "routine" is a good name for it. Or do we mean something that is done routinely? A job we do to get over with — with no thinking involved, no skill, no planning necessary, no particular results expected, nothing important to the child bound up with it? Toileting is not a routine (Nor is eating, washing, sleeping...).

You have to get some perspective on it. A child is born. He urinates and defecates. He doesn't need any teaching. He makes out alright. But when he is still very young, something new is added. We decided he has to learn. Not how to urinate because he knows that. But how to do it in the way our society thinks is nice...and when we think it is nice...and where...and with what attitude...and what words.

Is it teaching? Is it education? Well...the mother says "No" to the child. It is one of the first times he bumps into discipline. The mother says, "That's right. In the pot." It is one of the first times he bumps into right and wrong, appropriate and inappropriate. (At the college level we call it "Ethics" and give a Ph.D. for it.) The mother says, "Good boy, Johnny." And Johnny, for one of the first times, begins thinking and feeling about the kind of person he is. She says, "Bad. Bad." And little Johnny learns something about the success and failure. Mother makes a face. Baby learns that some things are considered clean and some dirty. Mamma says, "Mustn't touch" and sex rears its ugly head for one of the first times. Johnny doesn't wet his diapers; Mother looks pleased and maybe gives him an extra hug. Johnny gets a lesson in affection. He wets and he wets and he wets. But Mother doesn't like it and Johnny learns that it is a hard world, with tough high standards.

Success, failure, adequacy, inadequacy, clean, dirty, right, wrong, love, rejection, sex, acceptance, shame...My goodness. And it all happens in the bathroom.

And it happens day after day after day, and many times a day. So that all kinds of very important feelings and attitudes get tied up with it and pretty well established even before Johnny comes to our eighteen-months-old group — to say nothing of what has happened by the time he is ready for the fives. Some attitudes are good and we can try to build on them. And some are not so good. We could try, skillfully, to change them slowly and to give them a new start in a right direction. The setting is right. Bathrooms are small, intimate. We can talk with children and laugh with them, starting conversations: we can interpret them, assist them, or let them help themselves or give just the right amount of aid.

But then..."I like to teach. I like to be on the play court. There the kids are doing something. They're learning..." Still...the child on the pot does have his personality in a pliable position.

Snacktime

Little children use up a lot of energy as they 'live and learn.' For Sam, who has barely taken his foot off the gas since the moment of his arrival, snack time is for refueling. For Susie, it is the 'kaffee klatsch' of the neighborhood, and for Mary and Jane it is the adult 'coffee break.' The issue of 'formal' versus 'informal' juice time has long been debated. Some teachers like to gather their flocks around them at a table for a few songs and finger plays — or quiet conversation. Others prefer to set juice out on a tray, where the children can help themselves without interrupting their play. Both have their merits. The former breaks down when the teacher acts as a martinet, exacting unreasonable attention to "waiting until everyone has been served," "saying please and thank you" or sitting until the last child has finished. Such restrictions are unreasonable and inappropriate.

Putting juice out on a tray became so delightful an informal occasion in one school that David, a sophisticated, little youngster, said, "This is a COCKTAIL party!" That was fine until Greg went into his home, staggering, and said, "I'm drunk. We had a cocktail party at school." It was then decided that a more appropriate name would be a 'juicetail' party!

Manners are better 'caught' than 'taught' and so the teacher who relies on "say the magic word" or "you can't have another cracker because you forgot to say 'please' " should serve as a role model, and avoid calling attention to the transgressor.

There can and should be some teaching involved in the routine handwashing that takes place before all snacks and lunchtime. The ritual-like step by step procedures described by Montessori are appropriate. Small children NEED to be taught HOW to wash both front and back—and to dry between the fingers. It is inappropriate for a teacher to tell children to wash their hands and sit down without washing his/her own hands.

Extreme care must also be taken in handling all food and materials. For example, a package of paper cups is opened from the BOTTOM, otherwise fingers will go inside the cups when they are pulled out.

Actually, there is no one right way for snacktime. Whatever suits the mood of the moment, the expedience of the program, makes more sense than following the same rigid pattern day after day.

Snack Can Be a Daily Routine or It Can Be an Exciting Adventure

Preparation for snacks, and cleanup afterward, is an important part of the procedure. Counting the children and the right number of napkins or crackers is a way of learning numbers because you have a need to know. Carrying a pitcher of juice is another way of utilizing Montessori methods. Children should be permitted to pour their own juice from small pitchers which they can handle easily. Two-cup, plastic measures work well. The child must be taught how to hold the pitcher with one hand on the handle and the other on the front, and to pour it very carefully. The teacher says, "Fill your cup half full" and the idea of fractions has been introduced! Certainly it takes longer than if the cups had been filled beforehand, or the teacher had done the pouring, but such routine activities ARE program.

Snacks can be varied, they need not always consist of juice and crackers. Raw vegetables, peeled and sliced, accompanied at times by a simple dip, a small potato or an apple wrapped in foil and baked in the oven, or over a charcoal fire, is an adventure, as well as a snack.

When snack is to be different—especially in child care centers where nutritional values are figured very carefully—a teacher will communicate this intent to the cook, director or nutritionist in advance.

The daily snack sometimes becomes whatever the magic of imagination can produce, i.e. "I am eating a mushroom pizza and drinking root beer" as the child munches his crackers and drinks apple juice.

A picnic, with a special treat, peanut butter, jelly or marshmallow on the crackers, carried to a special corner of the room or playground, makes snacktime special. Snack crackers, taken out of a picnic basket, take on a new identity. Pudding or jello, made by the children, and served in tiny paper pill cups is a snack. In one school, the children took an imaginary six-week tour through different countries, and snacks were appropriate to the country visited. (See "Early Years" October 1974, Pub. Allen Raymond, Darien, Conn.)

> In one school, the teacher had been having real and imaginary picnics with the children. Active, four-year-old twins, who lived in an apartmenthouse found the idea of picnics very exciting. One morning their mother was awakened at seven o'clock by the security guard. He was holding her two little boys firmly by the hand. They had taken food out of the refrigerator and a blanket from the crib. They managed to push the button to the elevator, went down to the lobby, spread out the blanket and were having a picnic—stark naked!

Snacks and the lunch should provide at least fifty percent of a child's daily nutritional requirements in an all day child care center. In most states, licensing requires evidence that these needs are being met. If a qualified nutritionist is not immediately available on staff, this service may be sought at the state or federal level.

Mid-Day: The Zero Hours

The heaviest traffic flow in a combination nursery school and child care center seems to fall between 11:30 and 12:30. Morning children are leaving, but some stay for lunch and then go home. Afternoon children are arriving but some may come in early and be there for lunch. In that case they will NOT rest but those who have been there all morning should. Some children NEED to sleep, some will rest quietly on cots and some just cannot rest. When the afternoon children arrive, they should come into an environment which is as inviting as the morning children found, as clean, as well organized with materials and activities. How can all this happen?

The answer to the problem is found in Zoning.

Eating With Children

Mealtime is as important as any facet of the daily program. it should be a pleasant, leisurely experience. In too many homes, meals are hurried, or the occasion for argument and nagging. There is no excuse for this in the day care center. The day is long enough — there is no hurry to be finished and ready for something else — and there is much learning taking place in a carefully planned mealtime.

It is important for adults to have spent time "thinking out" procedures which will be reasonable, *routines* which are feasible, and once they have been established to maintain them with consistency. (See Zoning)

A suggested plan is offered here. This will not work in every school. The distance from the *kitchen* to the tables, the ages of the children, the number of adults who can sit with the children, are all variables which will have to be taken into account.

PROCEDURES

As the children are washed and ready, they may help:

1. Set tables with place mats, forks, spoons (if needed), napkins, and cups.
2. Put finger foods on the table.
3. When the teacher is ready, put bread on table...pass around.
4. Main course is placed before the teacher, who will serve.

In one center this was a weekly privilege given to a particular child who wore a sign with the words "BIG CHEESE" printed on a picture of a cheese.

Serve *very* small helpings. After a few days, the teacher will be able to judge the capacity of each child. It is better psychologically to have a child come back for seconds and thirds than to leave food on the plate.

Avoid scenes, discussion of dislikes. If a child says, "I don't want any," just say "I am going to put just a tiny bit on your plate. I hope you will taste it," and let it go at that. Eating should be casual — *taken for granted*.

Procedures for clearing tables and serving desserts will vary. Desserts are not withheld until a child eats all of his meal. They are an important part of his nutritional needs. Desserts are NEVER withheld as *punishment*.

Manners are explained — acquired gradually. They are based on consideration of others:

"If you talk with your mouth full, we can't understand you."

"When you take two pieces, there may not be enough for everyone to have some."

"You do not have to snatch. There will be enough for all."

"Please take the first one you touch."

Make no big deal of "Please" and "Thank You". Children will learn by example. Try never to send a child away from the table. If you know he is going to be troublesome, let him sit beside the teacher.

If you treat your children with the same respect you would accord a guest at a dinner party, they will surprise you with their response!

MEALTIME CONVERSATION
by
Margaret Connett
(as printed in Fairbanks Daily News — Miner, Fairbands, Alaska)

1. Keep the lunch groups as small as possible. Groups of five or six children give each child more opportunities to talk.
2. Avoid having two adults at one table. The temptation is almost irresistible to talk together over the children's heads. But also avoid seating children with no adult at the table.
3. Encourage the children to talk with each other rather than only to you.
4. Think up good conversation starters. Ask the children about their brothers and sisters; or what they like to watch on television, or if they have a dog, or what kind of pet they would like to

have. Develop their memories by asking them if they can remember what they had for lunch yesterday, or what they saw on the way to school.

5. Don't accept the children's pointing to food they wish passed to them, or their saying, "I want that!" Ask them to tell you specifically what they want. If a child doesn't know the word you can tell him, "This is jello—now you can tell me!" When he does, give it to him instantly, and tell him "Good for you!"

6. Children can learn concepts and language skills at the lunch table. For example, the teacher can start by talking about the food—what kind of vegetable do we have today? What kind of meat? What do you think we will have for dessert?

This kind of conversation can continue with such questions as, What does it taste like? Is it cold, hot, soft, hard, or crunchy? The group could also discuss colors or amounts.

Nap Time *Attitude of Adult:*

Licensing in some states requires that children in a day care center facility must rest for at least one hour, and, we believe that children really do need this rest. Many of the children who come to the center will have given up naps at home; some may have never known what it is to rest in the daytime. The teacher must recognize this: for some children the idea of nap time may 'turn them off' on the total experience away from home. Sympathy, understanding, 'putting yourself into the child's skin', will be essential factors if your rest time is to succeed.

A good rest begins with the teacher who sees this as a chance to relax briefly and talks about:

"How good it is to *just take it easy for a while*, so we will be able to *have fun* later."

"When we get tired we get crabby and whiney and want to argue."

"Animals know it's important to rest—look at your dog or kitty, they take naps in the daytime."

Set the Stage in Advance:

In a center which offers double sessions, *lunch* should be served early enough so that children are down, and most of the sleepers are sound asleep before the afternoon children arrive.

The arrangement of the cots is important. A space of one foot is required between them. Children sleep 'head to foot', reducing the temptation to talk or play. Some children must be separated, because they excite each other; some will need physical dividers.

Blankets and cots must be marked, and *under no circumstances* is one child ever to use another's. If and when cots are changed, they must be sprayed with a disinfectant.

If a child is accustomed to have a 'security object', i.e. blanket, soft toy or other item at home, it would be foolish not to let him use it at school for as long as he needs it. He will break away from the dependency himself, when he is ready. (See Adjustment)

It is important to remove shoes *unless this is frightening to the child.*

Books, or quiet conversation may be allowed until all are ready; and then, a very definite "now it is time to rest" announcement is made. The room should be darkened, teacher assumes position and attitude of rest, and all are expected to be quiet.

There are various techniques for inducing sleep. Some start by using quiet *music*, but it is best not to lead children to expect this, unless you are prepared to do it every day. Experienced teachers have found that no 'crutches' are necessary. Sitting or lying beside a child, rubbing backs, whispering quietly for a few minutes in serious one-to-one conversation, shaking imaginary sleep dust—whatever methods prove effective are acceptable. The main object is to achieve a quiet rest without 'policing' action. (A child cannot relax when an adult—from a higher position—barks commands such as, "Lie down, John. No, Mary, you can't go to the *bathroom*. I told you to go before rest time." etc. etc.!) When all else fails, try yawning. It is contagious!!

The length of nap should be discussed with parents. Some children would sleep for two or more hours, but if this means they will not go to bed until ten o'clock, parents may want you to awaken them. Suggest that the child be given a few days to adjust to new life patterns before any radical changes are employed.

Nap time is an intimate time—a time for quiet, whispered conversation between child and adult.

A teacher reported, "Today something really nice happened. I was sitting with Chuckie, when he whispered, 'Do you know what makes people grow?' I answered, 'Well, things like food, and rest, and playing in the sun?' 'Nope, want me to tell you?' 'Yes.' 'People grow by loving each other.' "

End of the Day
Visiting a day care center at about four thirty in the afternoon, I saw about twenty five-year-olds sitting in chairs in a formal circle. Some looked very tired, some utterly bored, some blank. A weary-faced adult was reading a story to this disinterested group. On one side of the room, a raspy record player was screeching out nursery songs with no one listening.

On the way home I thought about what I had seen. What could these children have been doing? How could it have been made into a more homelike atmosphere?

At that point my thoughts went like this: I would turn off the overhead lights and have wall lamps (which wouldn't take floor space during the day). I would have someone bring out a bowl of snacks which wouldn't spoil a child's appetite for dinner (cereals or apple slices). I would try to have some fresh faces—or at least teachers who had not already been with these children for five or six hours. Perhaps I coud find some 'grandparents' who would read stories, play table games, or just listen to children who wanted to talk. Perhaps I could find a high school or college student who would come in with a guitar and play, and sing folk songs.

The needs of children at this time of day vary. They do not all need, or want, this as a quiet, relaxed time. One group of 'five-going-on-six' boys proved this point. They began to organize and plan their own activities. One day it was a hospital—complete with operating room. This dramatic play continued for weeks. As soon as the afternoon children had gone, they moved, as a team, into organizing and setting up their hospital.

In addition, there could be table activity with some special materials, such as: 1) baby marshmallows and toothpicks (to make two or three dimensional structures), 2) peanuts in the shell and bits and pieces to make peanut people and animals, 3) acrylic paint—which may be too costly to use freely in the total program, 4) a tray or pan full of cornmeal on a table—to be used as if it were sand in a sandbox.

A clever teacher could make 'doing work' become an anticipated privilege and make a list of specific chores which would vary from day to day. For instance:
1. Get all of the sheets and blankets from the doll corner and wash them.
2. Check all of the puzzles. Come back and tell me if they are all complete.
3. Check the unit blocks. Make sure they are in the proper place.
4. Clean up woodworking bench. Make sure all tools are hanging on the board over their picture. Sweep up sawdust or scraps.
5. Get a dust pan and sweep out bottom part of six cubbies.

It would be most important to follow through—check up when chores were completed, give praise and credit where it is due. It might even be fun to 'hire' workers, and pay them with currency in the form of Cheerios, Fruit Loops and Cornflakes.

Sewing is another activity which might appeal to some children, and could carry over from day to day.

Blowing bubbles with straws—or with a pan full of soapy, COLORED water. Just making a sinkfull of soapy, colored suds is a relaxing experience.

Cooking could happen at this time—sometimes more easily than during the day. Making jello or pudding for the next day's dessert, cutting out cookies with fancy cutters, or puffed rice candy—to be shared as a treat at juice time the next day.

Children could put the sleeping blankets in the washer and the dryer. Measuring the soap and setting the timer is *learning*, and doing what mother does at home is *living*.

In one school, hair combing and styling with a mirror to check results, proved to be relaxing. Each child, of course, MUST have his or her own comb (marked). A mother who calls for a well-combed and washed child should be happily surprised.

If we plan well, children will think "Now that 'they' have gone the best part of the day is to come" rather than, "Those lucky kids—they have gone home and I am stuck here for a couple of hours."

It takes imagination and ingenuity, but the end of the day CAN be special! (See Seq. 6, Activites 61-71.)

Field Trips

It is important to review goals and objectives based on the developmental square in planning field trips. Are all four sides of the square involved? Children need time and "space" to express thoughts, ask questions, digest details. There should be plenty of time for conversation and observation. Avoid taking small children into crowds and rush hour situations. Consider the anxiety and fear of a child lost, even for a brief time, in a crowded strange place. Badly planned trips can unleash unhappy emotions and cause severe emotional set-backs.

What social experiences will be derived? Will the "buddy" system enhance new relationships and build upon friendships? Will parents participate?

Climbing a hill, taking a hike, following a native trail, walking on a beach are good scientific expeditions as well as excellent physical activity. Children are "doers" not "watchers," so trips should take them where they can touch, taste, smell, listen or get in or on or climb over.

A field trip is not just an excuse to "go somewhere" and calling it one will not magically turn it into an "educational experience." Simplicity of content, time to enjoy and plenty of help are good rules to follow. A well-planned trip stimulates the joy and excitement found in the discoveries of a new adventure and it is a good memory for all.

For the Babes

Special thought should be given to the length and value of a trip for the littlest ones. Where the fours and fives may go to the post office, these children will find a trip to the nearest mailbox exciting enough. In most cases, imaginations should be used to make trips exciting which do not go farther than the corner of the school yard, to a neighbor's yard, or within a short walking distance. Just leaving home to go to school is an adjustment, and taking them to other places may only arouse fears and anxieties.

Permission Slips

At the beginning of the year, parents are asked to sign a slip which gives the school permission to take children away from the school property. These are filed in the office and must be checked before EVERY trip. One person should be delegated to make this check before the trip starts. Some parents may not want their children to go.

Identification

List the names of the children in each car, registration and driver of the car and leave in the office. Do NOT change children on return trip.

In one case, a car was involved in a minor accident and the police took the children to the hospital to be checked. When the director of the center received a call, she was grateful to have complete information at hand on the occupants of the car. If the driver had been incapacitated, this would have been even more essential!

Supervision

There should be a minimum of one adult for each five children, and one to four is preferable. Since there can seldom be that many teachers spared, it is a good idea to invite parents to help.

The following procedures are suggested:

1. Invite parents to come beforehand for coffee and a discussion of plans.
2. Have a teacher and/or parent make trip in advance to:
    a. decide on best route
    b. observe points of interest on route
    c. observe possible hazards
    d. talk with manager or host about:
        1. the ages of children
        2. requirements for safety
        3. find out what sensory experiences may be possible, things to touch, manipulate, taste or special sounds to listen for
        4. try to tactfully suggest that a 'lecture' is inappropriate. A few pertinent bits of information, simply and briefly stated, and a willingness to

answer questions will be sufficient

(Many a field trip has been ruined when a well-intentioned guide delivered a 'canned' lecture intended for adults.)

3. Talk about HOW you help children get most from the trip.
   a. do not tell too much—try to think of questions which let children discover
   b. do not expect too much response at once
4. Ask for suggestions for ways to enhance trip
5. Make name tags for adults and children. Each adult should have a different color—matching that of children for whom he/she will be responsible (clothing, scarf of that color, will also help child to recognize his guide).

Teachers Preparation for Trip:

1. Use books, pictures in advance to build interest.
2. Talk about necessary rules for entire trip, door to door. Keep simple but explicit.
3. Have one person delegated to take slide pictures. These will be invaluable in recalling trip with children.
4. Make a list of 'things to look for', such as:
   a. "On the way we will pass a big, red, brick building. Who will see it first? Who will tell us what it is?"
   b. "We will cross some railroad tracks. There will be a yellow sign. See if you can tell us what it says."
   c. "Keep a list of the names of all the animals you see."
   d. "We will go over a bridge. Why does there need to be a bridge there?"
   e. "Look for a place that has a lot of pretty flags. What are they?"
   f. "Watch for a place that sells something we will need when it snows. They are orange. What are they?"

This will greatly reduce the need for nagging supervision of behavior en route.

(See suggested letter to business manager or owner at end of this section.)

After the Trip

1. DO NOT EXPECT immediate reaction or response. Give children time to assimilate—let their impressions jell.

2. DO NOT, as soon as you get back, insist that everyone make a picture of something they saw on the trip. All children do not necessarily react the same way.

On a walk, one boy muttered to another, through gritted teeth, "Don't look! Don't look! You'll have to make a picture of it!"

3. Remember that children are tired, just from the excitement of leaving school. Let them rest before expecting feedback.

4. Later, maybe the next day, divide into small groups and write a group story. Talk about stories having a beginning, a middle, and an end. Read stories to the whole group. See how they are the same—different. Did they remember different things? Some children may want to make picutres to illustrate stories. Put into a book which can be read and re-read.

5. When slides come back and are shown, children will want to go back to stories and compare.

6. Place some object or picture in the block area which relates to the trip, i.e. a pair of oars, a garden trowel, a pair of fireman's boots, a mailbag, or the book on construction equipment which may stimulate block building.

7. Can you think of a way of introducing a science experience related to the trip?

8. Can you think of ways to recall sounds—movements, (i.e. machines can lead to dances), dramatic play?

Walking Trips

If there are more than two children (one holding each hand) there MUST be at least two adults, even if it is only across the street. There should be at least one to four when there are larger groups.

There should be name tags, made in advance, for every child with the school name and telephone number on it. If these are made on thin wood or cardboard, with a coded color scheme, they can be used over and over. In one school I visited, these were on a board near the receptionist's office, and the tag was turned over when the child arrived in the morning and again when he went home. In another school, there was one in each team area and children turned their tags when they went to an activity in another part of the building. The value in this case is not just to keep track of children, it is helping them to:

    a. recognize their names
    b. realize that it is important for someone to know where they are
    c. take responsibility.

Special Walks

    It is just as easy to plan a SPECIAL WALK as it is to just 'take a walk.'

A COLOR WALK: Today we are going to look for things that are red and orange. An adult is always equipped with paper and pencil to write these down as children see them or, when possible, take back samples.

A SOUND WALK: "Let's see how many different sounds we can hear." Record on paper, or better still, take a tape recorder (write them down also as you may not recognize all sounds when you listen later). Build up interest with such statements as, "I know where there is a big rock where we can be very quiet and listen for special sounds."

A SMELL WALK: Plan to walk by a bakery, or restaurant. Know what weeds or natural products have distinctive smells. Smell the water in a puddle!

A TASTE WALK: Not as easy to arrange but can be done with some forethought.

A FEELING WALK: Bark of trees, stones, milk weed, pine needles—"What can you find?" Carry paper bags and let each child collect items to feel. Compare when you get back. Set up a table for the rest of the children to look at and touch. Make a 'feely box' using items children have found.

A MOVING WALK: "Look for something that moves. When we stop to rest, see if you can show us how it moved so we can guess what it was."

COLLECTING FOR COLLAGES: Carry a paper bag and collect bits of wood, feathers, etc. Put together when you return, mounting as pictures.

Suggestions for Field Trips

The following trips were all taken by preschoolers:

Library	Gas station	Park	Pet shop
Post Office	Museums	Farm	Apple orchards
Bakery	Airport	Beach	Horse farm
Supermarket	Zoo	Lumberyard	Pumpkin farm
Firestation	Aquarium	Produce stand	Turkey farm
Arboretum	Factory	Bottling plant	Wildlife sanctuary
Produce Market	Photographer	Florist-greenhouse	Potato chip factory
Fish hatchery	Police station		
Construction—Buildings, roads, sewers, bridges			

The Unusual Field Trip

    1. Computer—mother who worked at insurance office demonstrated keypunch programming.

    2. Motel—father who was manager invited the group for refreshments in the coffee shop after a tour of the facility.

    3. Sugaring-off place (Maple sugar house)

    4. Chinese restaurant—father (owner) opened early before regular patrons, talked to children in Chinese, gave them tiny parasols (from cocktails) and fortune cookies, let them sample fried rice and chop suey, wrote Chinese characters from 1-10. Each child was given his name written in Chinese. At the school the children made Chinese costumes and one was taken in costume to deliver a "thank you" letter.

    5. Train Ride—children were driven to railroad station, rode on a train to city and back on same train. At another school children were put on train at one station and taken off at next.

    6. Apple orchard—children were allowed to gather bags of apples which they made into applesauce, apple jelly, apple pie and apple pan dowdy.

7. Highway department—where the men let children sit on the big trucks and showed them how each works (snowplow, street cleaner, sander, sewer dredger).

8. Parachute Drop—at air base, where chutes are dropped from tower for testing.

9. Hospital—father (doctor) demonstrated many kinds of medical instruments and machinery.

10. Dress Rehearsal—of a high school drama, watching demonstrations of make-up and costuming.

11. Meat Packer—father (butcher) showed processing of animal into various meats.

12. Weather Station—father (meteorologist) showed radars, weather instruments.

13. Airport Fire Station—entire group of 16 fit inside cab of huge foam truck. Tried on helmet of asbestos fire fighting suit.

14. Artist Studio—parents were artists, served a picnic in back yard following.

15. Police Cruiser—*Came* to school yard and officers demonstrated equipment.

Reverse Field Trips

Instead of going to fire station, police department, or construction site, invite their workers and equipment to come to you. Exciting and interesting visits which had many side effects have been:

1. A fire truck: Children were allowed to sit on seat, wear a hat, and firemen explained use of all equipment and gave a talk on fire safety. In another school a child discovered the alarm and set it off (unknowing). The equipment arrived unannounced, to the surprise of the director!

2. An ambulance: Some of the children who associated this vehicle with sirens, accidents, and trouble were afraid. When they were allowed to walk inside, holding tightly to a teacher's hand, they saw that it was not as fearsome as they had imagined. If one of these children should ever have to make a necessary trip in an ambulance, they will be prepared.

3. Police brought an attack dog. He could be patted while policeman held his leash. Then a demonstration of his training was given and it inspired discussion of the need for such trained animals.

4. A father who owned a construction company had his men stop by the school on the way to a job. Children were allowed to sit in drivers seat of a shovel and learned about the use of such equipment.

Suggested Letter to Manager of:

Dear Sir,
The children in our kindergarten would like very much to visit your _____. They are learning about 'what people do at work' and 'why it is important to us'. We recognize that if you allow us to come, it may mean some inconvenience to you, and in order to minimize that and make it most beneficial to the children, we have drawn up the following plan.

1. We would like to send a teacher in advance who would talk with you or a representative about what would be of interest to children, and how much explanation is necessary. Sometimes adults who have long since forgotten what it is to be five years old tend to deliver lengthy lectures, and others talk down to the children. Our children are intelligent and understand a great deal, but their level of experience needs to be taken into consideration.

2. Children learn through actual sensory experiences, so if there is anything they can touch, smell, taste, or hear in addition to the things they see, this all makes the trip more interesting. For example, they were allowed to stamp a letter at a post office, smell and taste bread at a bakery (and then went back and made their own bread), ring up a charge in a cash register, etc. We are also most anxious to find out about the "No-No's" so the teachers who accompany them can keep a watchful eye.

3. We prefer to send them in small groups, but if you said one trip would be all you could extend, we would send a whole class and enough adults to maintain supervision. Part of the training our children receive is respect for property and appreciation of the time and courtesy extended.

I hope you will give our request favorable consideration. If it is more convenient to answer by phone, I can be reached at _____.

Sincerely,

(A thank you from the children after the trip is a must. This may be accompanied by pictures drawn by the children or dictated stories which indicate the impressions received.)

Special Activities During School Vacations

In child care centers where mothers depend on year round service, the doors never can close. Usually attendance drops during public school vacations. Some mothers have older children at home from school who can take care of the little ones and some mothers arrange to have this time off from work. On the other hand, there may be an influx of older school age children for that week.

How will the children who must, of necessity, stay in school feel? Will they envy their peers who have 'time off'? Or will they enjoy special privileges and programs that are not possible when all are in attendance?

What about the staff? Are they tired, disgruntled because they are expected to work? Will they 'put in the time' giving adequate care but with little enthusiasm?

With proper planning, this can be—like rainy days in camp, *the Best!* (See Sequence 11) Time will go faster for staff if they have special activities planned, and have taken the trouble to assemble the materials they will need. (See Staff Meetings) Children will feel as if they have 'visited another school' and arouse the envy of their classmates who 'had to stay home'.

(See Sequence 11—Special Days—Act. 85-100)

Part II

Chapter 4

WHAT: CURRICULUM—
CATALYST OR CONFORMIST

I n Book I, we have set the stage. Children, teachers and environment have come together. What will happen now? It will be living, but how can we be sure that learning will take a positive direction? We believe that if we are going to build healthy attitudes toward learning, the following basics should be firmly established.

Philosophy   In every profession, training and experience are the basic working tools; the first becoming refined and cultivated by the second. There is a third ingredient, however, which is needed to add the polish and a special magic quality to any profession. The philosophy, the sense of value, the belief in what is right, become the mortar which binds training and experience together. The "I AM! I CAN!" philosophy as outlined in Part I, is the yardstick with which we have measured the contents of this curriculum.

Basic Premises   The following basic premises will serve as guidelines for the teacher in planning daily program.

We learn best, and retain knowledge longer, when we have a need and/or a desire to know.

Four-year-old Dick came into the classroom and saw a sheet of white paper taped over the block case. On it was printed "NO BLOCKS TODAY."

"What does that say?" he asked the teacher. She read it to him and they discussed her reasons for elminating the blocks.

Soon Donald arrived. Taking him by the hand, Dickie pointed to the sign: "That says, NO BLOCKS TODAY," he explained. Several times more he was the giver of knowledge about this latest innovation.

Three weeks later, the sign appeared again.

"I know what that says," said Dick, "It says, NO BLOCKS TODAY."

"And that is a K," said Donald.

"That is a B," chimed Betsy, "B is in my name."

This teacher was not attempting to TEACH children to read. She was exposing them

to symbols, letters with a message which had significance for them.

Rote learning creates robots

Learning by rote satisfies the adults—but means little to the child except the pleasure he gains from the adults' reactions to his recitation.

Dr. Peter Wolf of Harvard has said, "There is a possibility that if you train the child intensively in certain routine actions, such as learning letters or counting, you may contaminate the whole excitement of learning."

Excitement is the key word here. Learning IS exciting. The child who can add "I KNOW" to his "I AM" and "I CAN" senses fulfillment—the ultimate satisfaction of need.

Learning comes through INVOLVEMENT.

Learning takes place as a child interacts with his world, and becomes part of the action. He explores the world through his senses, through discovery and curiosity.

The traditional "sit still," "keep still" and "do as you are told" practice takes all the fun out of learning. Children gain satisfaction from solving problems, finding out, testing, and achieving.

Children want to win the approval of the adults who are close to them.

For years we have given children credits and status for good behavior. "Johnny is such a good boy." "Susie is my nice little helper." How much better to give credit for IDEAS. "Did you all hear that?" "What a terrific idea!" "Who can think of another way?" A climate is established where thinking is "in" and when children start competing with each other for good ideas, creativity walks through an open door.

Learning begins where the child IS, starting with the familiar and progressing to new understandings from that which he knows.

Thus it is essential for the teacher to know EACH child, and something about his home, family and experiences prior to attending school.

Children learn through play.

Play is the BUSINESS of childhood.

When he builds with blocks, explores his environment with all his senses, creates with art materials, listens to stories and communicates ideas and feelings, the child is working, as surely as the adult who goes to work.

Play is the process, the means to education. Through play the child (1) experiences, (2) relates the new to the familiar, (3) makes his own inferences, (4) tests his new knowledge, (5) assimilates it—makes it a part of his being. Play and learning are inseparable companions.

Goals and Objectives

By goals, we mean generalized, long range expectations of growth. Objectives are the specific, daily or weekly results we look for as we work with the children.

For example, a teacher may concentrate on RED, ROUND, OVER and UNDER for a few weeks. These are *objectives* leading to the long range *goals* of recognizing colors and shapes and understanding spatial relationships. As teachers plan, they align activities with goals. A well planned activity often will be developing several goals at once.

As we began to make up lists of goals, we tried to categorize them into INTELLECTUAL, EMOTIONAL, PHYSICAL and SOCIAL areas of development but we soon found we were bogged down in cross relationships.

The child develops in just this way. His physical "I CAN!" often becomes tangled up with his social "I AM!;" his emotional "I AM!" relates constantly to his intellectual "I CAN!"

This curriculum is designed to meet the following goals:

I. TO DEVELOP THE PHYSICAL, SOCIAL, EMOTIONAL AND INTELLECTUAL GROWTH OF EACH CHILD.
   A. *Physical*
      1. To increase strength and endurance
      2. To improve muscular coordination and control
      3. To develop physical and mental coordination

        4.   To control bodily functions
        5.   To identify need for proper food, habits of cleanliness and proper amount of sleep
        6.   To recognize and experience relaxation and release of tension
        7.   To use rules necessary for safety

B.   *Social*
        1.   To participate in group activities
        2.   To take turns
        3.   To share personal and school property
        4.   To play role both of follower and leader
        5.   To respect the rights and property of others
        6.   To increase self control
        7.   To accept behavioral limits which are appropriate for group living
        8.   To communicate freely with peers and adults

C.   *Emotional*
        1.   To establish a positive self concept (I AM — I CAN)
        2.   To tolerate frustration
        3.   To delay self gratification
        4.   To channel emotions into socially acceptable outlets
        5.   To increase self control

D.   *Intellectual*
        1.   To listen to and follow directions
        2.   To carry a project through to completion
        3.   To increase attention span
        4.   To seek answers to questions by asking and testing hypothesis
        5.   To recall information
        6.   To solve problems
        7.   To progress through content areas which are compatible with ability and developmental level

II.   SPECIFIC GOALS IN CONTENT AREAS
    A.   *Language Development*
        1.   To recognize the relationship between symbols and ideas
        2.   To recognize symbols as a means for self-expression and obtaining desired information
        3.   To distinguish between fact and fantasy — and recognize appropriate use of both
        4.   To appreciate spoken and written language as
           a.   Practical
           b.   A source of knowledge and pleasure
        5.   To recognize value and need of communication
        6.   To explore a variety of means for communication
        7.   To explore upper and lower case letters and manuscript writing
        8.   To recognize that in our language words are placed on a horizontal base line
        9.   To recognize left to right sequence in reading
      10.   To develop eye/hand coordination
      11.   To increase number of words used meaningfully
      12.   To discriminate between visual stimuli
      13.   To discriminate between auditory stimuli
      14.   To recall sequence of events
      15.   To associate consonant sounds with appropriate letters
      16.   To enjoy and appreciate stories and poetry
      17.   To create original stories and poems
      18.   To enjoy dramatic activity as a means of expression of emotions, ideas, and languages skills

B. *Music*
1. To develop physical and aesthetic responses to
   a. tone
   b. tempo
   c. rhythm
   d. pitch
2. To experience music in a variety of ways until it becomes as natural as breathing
3. To listen with sensitivity
4. To improve auditory discrimination
5. To express ideas and emotions through musical media
6. To match tones

C. *Movement*
1. To know and appreciate the physical self
2. To know the joy of spontaneous movement
3. To utilize body movements in expression of ideas
4. To utilize body movements as a means of communication
5. To express emotions through bodily movement
6. To relate bodily movement to other content areas
7. To relate self to space through bodily movement
8. To experience (as a sixth sense) bodily movement in conjunction with other sensory experiences.

D. *Dramatic Play*
1. To acquire understanding of world and relate self to own society through play which concerns:
   a. family life
   b. life styles of work and play
   c. extension of world through play about other countries, cultures, customs
   d. understanding of differences in people
   e. relationship of animal to human life
   f. means of transportation
   g. means of communication
   h. community helpers

E. *Science*
1. To obtain some understanding of natural forces:
   a. weather
   b. light
   c. heat
   d. gravity
   e. air
   f. motion
   g. machines
   h. space
   i. sound
2. To develop respect for natural environment
3. To develop respect for animals
4. To see balance in nature
5. To appreciate need for conservation of natural resources
6. To develop senses for practical and aesthetic purposes

F. *Mathematics*
1. To identify numerals (seen and unseen)
2. To recognize sequential placement of numerals (counting)
3. To experience and assimilate number concepts
4. To acquire basic understanding of basic math processes through practical daily application

5. To identify and classify geometric shapes (circle, square, triangle, rectangle)
6. To identify and use terms related to time concept
7. To recognize the calendar and the clock as instruments for measuring time
8. To identify and use terms related to direction and distance
9. To develop knowledge and understanding of measurements in weight, height
10. To use mathematical skills in other curricular or environmental situations

G. *Art*
1. To use a variety of materials and art media
2. To recognize and use colors and variations of colors
3. To recognize shapes and see them in environment
4. To express ideas and feeling through use of a variety of materials
5. To increase creativity and self-confidence
6. To work in two and three dimensional levels
7. To appreciate art through exposure to works of contemporary and traditional artists
8. To use plastic media as a means of release and expression

HOW TO USE THIS CURRICULUM

A good curriculum must develop and change with each group of children, each individual child, each individual teacher. It must REACT to experiences, events, accidents, chance visitors, etc. It must have eyes and ears on all sides and sensitive antennae which constantly say to the child and teacher "Hey, look" or "Shhh, listen." It can never remain constant since life is always in motion, changing, growing, shrinking, looking ahead, looking backward. Such a curriculum will change from day to day, month to month, year to year and often, minute by minute. Curriculum takes into account the needs of developing children but cannot be administered as medicine forced upon a sick patient.

The outlines used in this book are intended only as "roadmaps." They help tell where the children are at a given time; they suggest ideas and point out alternate routes; they help show where the children have been and where they are going. It is not intended that any teacher follow them exactly, it is not even desirable. Each person must bring to this curriculum fresh, original, current ideas, following leads within each group, taking cues from each individual.

PROGRAM PLANNING

Visit any three child care centers and you may find at least three different theories about good program. The truth of the matter is that there is no RIGHT way, or totally WRONG way. The important thing is to have a *reason* for the plans.

During the first weeks of school, in one center, we may see children playing with blocks, painting at easels, making collages, and we think, "This is a good school, the children are busy, and seem to be learning." But, if we return to that school several months later and the children are building with blocks, painting at easels and making collages, *at more or less the same level of development*, we are almost certain to witness boredom, aimless ambling about, and probably some negative behavior. The teacher has provided the right environment but has neglected to *extend* it, as the children have developed.

In a second center we ask, "Do you have a curriculum?" "Oh, yes, our program includes science, music, drama, art and language development."

This is an improvement over the example above where not much is stirring, but there is still something missing. The teacher has found enough ideas in the resource books to plan daily projects. The children are learning and probably their faces show evidence of interest, but the teacher does not know WHY her projects were chosen. The *interrelationship* between one act and the next is lacking.

In a third classroom, the teacher *relates* planning to *WHAT* the child should learn, *HOW* he learns, and *WHY* he learns. Experiences are presented in a definite *planned* sequence and both student and teacher are learning. This teacher asks, "What can be added to the environment which will bring about the desired learning?"

In planning a learning experience, these steps may be considered:

1. EXPLORING WITH SENSES
2. RELATING TO THE FAMILIAR
3. SEEING RELATIONSHIPS — LIKENESSES AND DIFFERENCES
4. CLASSIFYING — SEPARATING INTO CATEGORIES

For example: THE APPLE

The teacher shows a round, red, shiny apple. The goal is to help each child assimilate 'appleness'. The children *touch* it, *feel* its roundness, *smell* it. It is cut into pieces and they *taste* it and *hear* the crisp crunchiness.

The teacher says, "Tell me about an apple."
"It's round," says Tommy
"It's red," says Sue
"It's *white* inside," observes Joseph.
"Those little things are *brown*," Jim adds, pointing to the seeds.
"It is sweet, but kind of sour," says Timmy.
"It tastes something like a pear," another child adds.
"How are an apple and a pear alike?" asks the teacher.
"They both grow on trees. They are both fruit," some children respond.
"Can you think of anything else that is round and red?" their teacher asks.
"A balloon," "A ball" … and so on.

On subsequent days the teacher introduces stories, songs, poems; plans cooking experiences with apples; visits an orchard or market to buy apples; displays a granny doll made from a dried apple; deliberately leaves an apple outside during a frost; cuts one up and leaves it to dry; etc… .

Apples have become a part of every area of curriculum; language, science, math, music, and art. The children see apples in a variety of ways. They have begun *a process of learning* which can be carried into each new learning experience.

Such planning rewards the teacher with the excitement of observing growth and development as the child assimilates new knowledge.

A word of caution about planning: *Teachers should be careful not to become so involved with carrying out their plans that they are insensitive to the learning which will come about spontaneously… in the words of one teacher, "The best things just happen!"*

In the well planned approach described, the *teacher* is acting *on* the child, deciding *what, when* and *how* he will learn. But does it allow for curiosity, discovery, self-directed activity? What about the premise that *we learn best and retain longest that which we have a need or a desire to know*? When does the *learner* get a chance to act on *his* environment? Are children simply exposed to a rich environment while teachers wait for something to happen or are the children fed carefully with a well balanced, well planned program? The answer is clear — both approaches working together will offer the child the most successful kind of learning environment.

LISTEN FOR CUES! The chance remark or happening within a classroom of young children is so often the spark which fuses a whole series of creative explosions which can be called learning experiences. Teachers must be watching for such cues, ready to motivate and nurture them. Materials and guiding words or hands should be available at a moment's call. The teacher knows just where the right item has been stored which will stimulate and extend a child's thinking. (See Resources)

Some ideas start small and grow bigger and bigger like a snow ball rolling down a hill, gathering more layers of snow. Some get caught along the way, bumping into immovable boulders (perhaps a teacher who says, "Not now, Peter, it's time for juice"). Some reach the bottom bursting with new layers of snow, where they just melt away in the sun. Teachers must be ready to motivate, to "get more mileage" out of an idea, at the same time knowing when to let go and allow it to "melt away." It is not necessary to "wring learning" out of every classroom experience.

The Train

Some fours had been making trains with their seat blocks for several days. The teacher, seeing their lasting interest, added a suitcase to the block corner and an old fur jacket and bathing suit to the 'dress ups.' She did not call attention to the new additions. She waited. She would not have been concerned if the children had not made any connections, but of course she was delighted when they did. Conversations about, "Where shall we go?" and "What shall I wear?" were stimulated. Children were busy acting. "What shall we take along?" "It's warm enough to swim there." One conversation fused a whole new series of discoveries:

"I'm going to Denmark where my daddy went."

"How?" asked the teacher.

"Oh, on the train," was her response.

The teacher brought in the globe and helped the children find the water parts and the land parts, the United States and Denmark. Soon, one of the children discovered that a trip to Denmark from the United States would not be possible on the train. Their train might take them from Boston to New York (road maps verified this) but to get to Denmark, a boat or plane would be necessary. Ticket sales, train conductors, discussions of air travel; the curriculum for that group flowed, branching off in many directions—and coming back again to the generalized theme of transportation.

Teaching Style

STYLE and INDIVIDUAL TALENTS, the secret ingredients. Each teacher has a specialty, a 'forte,' and developing it will bring creative zest, *STYLE!* Some teachers always have a good story or poem ready to illustrate or motivate; some use pictures to extend an idea; others are collectors of elegant junk and seem to know how to turn such items into magic uses. Children everywhere love and respond to music, rhythm and rhyme, and the teacher who has memorized a repertoire of songs and rhyming patterns offers an extra sparkle of joy to the classroom.

The essence of this curriculum will be found in the TEACHING STYLE of the individual who is the PRIME MOTIVATOR.

LESSON PLANS VS. PLANNING THE LESSON

To many teachers the words "lesson plans" mean a list of "musts" in the curriculum to be accomplished on a given day at a particular time, itemized chores sent down from the "head office" which must be completed by a certain time. Should an exciting or spontaneous event occur and take time away from this daily schedule of events, the teacher must then speed up the process to make up for lost time, if indeed spontaneity has been indulged.

There is a vast difference between lesson plans and planning the lesson.

In a center of about one hundred children the following system achieved excellent, *relaxed,* creative results. There was, to begin with, a curriculum, designed to offer the staff ideas for good program while at the same time setting forth objectives which would insure that the children were guided in a forward motion toward particular goals. This curriculum allowed *ample* room for spontaneity and individual expression from *both* teachers and students, but it established guidelines within which all could grow.

The director met with lead teachers once a week to discuss and plan the following week's objectives. (In a center where several teachers are interacting with the same children at different times of day, such planning is essential if teachers are to pick up where others have left off and to extend each activity.)

Each teacher assumed responsibility for a particular aspect of the program, sometimes focusing on a special area (music, science, cooking, etc.). Plans and objectives were discussed so that each knew the other's plans and could help to extend them. For example: it was good to know when the fives were focusing on transportation so others could then be watchful for items and ideas to enrich their work. If they know a parent is going to take a trip, they can ask for related materials, such as maps, ticket stubs, airline travel packets and brochures. Attention was focused on such particular concepts as colors, shapes, spatial relationships and activities planned, based on a special area of development.

On another day, lead teachers would meet with assistants and volunteers and plan around these general objectives. For example, the fours were working with winter animals. One teacher made plans for a field trip to an aquarium where seals and penguins could be seen, including all arrangements for reservations, transportation, parent volunteers, name tags, snacks at the aquarium, etc. (See Field Trips—Part I)

A second teacher gathered materials for a related art activity (i.e, toothpicks and marshmallows for constructing polar bears, cotton balls, black and white construction paper, bits of furry cloth for making animals, etc.)

A third assumed the responsibility for picking up related film strips and slides at the library and reserved a projector and a projection room for a specific day. The person who would operate the projector was asked to check out the extension cord, extra bulb and screen *before* the appointed showtime.

A fourth teacher went to the library for books, gathered pictures, researched for special events, such as TV programs. Related outdoor activities, such as building with snow blocks, were planned in advance. "Where are the small shovels stored?" "Does everyone have boots and mittens?" As each task was completed it was indicated on a check list in the director's office.

Director and staff could enjoy their weekends knowing that seldom was anyone besieged with last minute requests, such as, "I forgot the toothpicks, can I dash out now?" or "Where's the red construction paper, I planned to use it today and when I looked this morning I found only six sheets!" Nor were there minor irritations, such as, "I was planning to read *that* book and surprise my group with the film strip, Now Ms. _____ is using the projector."

...and, of course, the inevitable "The bulb is out on the projector, my children are all sitting there impatiently and it doesn't work!" or "I used it last week, it was fine then."

PLANNING AHEAD! a wonderful cliche which should be a part of every day. It smooths out the wrinkles in the program and on the face.

DEFINITION OF ACTIVITIES

Just as each teacher will differ in approach to curriculum and teaching style, each will also have individual definitions of the activites described in this curriculum. The following statements express our beliefs.

People In the Curriculum

People! This is a major theme in our curriculum which follows a natural sequence related to the life experiences of the child.

In the beginning, when a child is venturing into a whole new world we try to help him begin to see himself in the context of a larger society. We concentrate on that which he brings with him.

The teacher's task with every new child is to enhance and strengthen a child's own self-image. His name is important to him. It is uniquely his—the label which distinguishes him from another. We capitalize on this symbol of "person" by exploring names in many different ways (see Seq. 1—Name Games, Activities 1-10). Next we deal with his feelings about those close to him, his immediate family. Talking about them, bringing them into school physically and conceptually, strengthens his understanding of "how things are in the people world." At first we limit our discussions to the nuclear family, remembering that the "Dick and Jane" family of primer fame—mother, father, sister, brother and baby are not always typical in our society.

Joe becomes the envy of his peers when he announces that he has FOUR grandfathers and FOUR grandmothers, especially to those who are keen enough to mentally add up presents! (Sequence 2)

Many children are being brought up by single parents and that lone parent is not always the mother, often it is the father. Children can cope with "what is" if they are told the truth.

Our nursery school children have not lived long enough to know what is "different" from the norm. The attitudes of parents and other trusted adults will be the factors which will disturb or effectively guide the child.

As Thanksgiving draws near we begin to hear about members of the extended family. Grandparents are coming or families are taking trips to visit relatives, aunts, uncles, and cousins and new relationships are explored. It is a real surprise to some children to learn that Mummy was once Grandma's little girl. A child will listen eagerly to tales of "when Daddy was just as big as you are now." (Seq. 3)

In the holiday season our "people" thoughts become warm and rosy. We introduce the customs of people in other cultures and countries. Most of these customs will include some form of caring and sharing, giving of gifts and meeting with friends and relatives. We stress commonalities—respect the rights of "differences." (Seq. 4)

These differences gradually flow into a discussion of "Likenesses and Differences." We introduce the idea of differences in people, starting with such obvious things as hair and eyes, height and weight, and going on to differnces in skin color, physical, cultural or language differences.

A discussion of places (Alaska and Florida) may lead to differences in what people wear, and eat, and how they live. (Seq. 5)

This whole subject might lead to discussions of "like" and "dislike," "love" and "hate." We talk about the meaning of friendship. Having a friend is very important to a young child. Some children learn at a very early age to use withdrawal of friendship as a weapon, or a bargaining agent. The teacher rushes in the direction of an anguished howl, and instead of finding a physical injury she hears a wailing child lament "She said she wouldn't be *my friend!*" (Seq. 6)

Within the basic frame of reference outlined above, we can talk about what people do. Starting with fathers and mothers we invite them to school to tell or show what their work is and sometimes we go to visit Johnny's daddy at the gas station, or Susie's father at the motel he manages, or the big building where Jack's mother has an office. (Seq. 6) (See Field Trips)

We visit the people in our own school, the secretary, who lets us try the typewriter or adding machine, the maintenance man and cook. If the school does not have a librarian we visit the big library. The cook's husband is a mailman and he lends us a mail bag and invites us to visit the post office. (Seq. 6)

We extend our knowledge of people to community helpers. Perhaps the telephone man comes to the school to install a new phone, or the electrician or plumber comes to make repairs. We take advantage of every opportunity to ask questions, and play out the role of each one. We talk to the policeman at the corner and the police lady in front of the big school down the street. (Seq. 8)

With the coming of spring we can find out how we get the food we eat. A trip to the vegetable counter, followed by a trip to a market garden helps the child to a new understanding of the people involved in providing our food. If a dairy farm is within trip distance, it is a valuable learning experience to find out how milk gets into the cartons.

Joshua, whose father is a veterinarian, was giving his teacher a lecture about the different animals who give milk:
"Do you know where the milk comes from?" he asked.
"Where?"
'From the cow's gutters!" was the beaming response. (Seq. 9)

Children in our society are continually entertained but we talk very little about the source of the programs we enjoy. Since entertainment and recreation are FUN it is not likely that a child will know that the entertainer is a provider of a service or that this is the way he earns his living. (Seq. 10)

The child, thus, is gradually led through this world of people from his own egocentric concept to a broader realization of where he fits into the total scheme of "peopleness." He acquires a social awareness which will help him to adjust to new situations and which will enrich the quality of his life.

Birthdays

"*Me* having a real BIRTHDAY?" Winnie-the-Pooh

My Birthday Party
Everyone knew when MY birthday came
There was a cake—it had my name
Written in frosting on the top
It was fancy, yummy, and full of glop

And all my friends helped me to eat
This very, very special treat
Then pretty soon it was all gone
We ran and played on our front lawn

It was a happy day you see—
To play and laugh and climb a tree
And blow out candles—one, two, three...
        This was a special day for *me*!

Deborah Mitchell Haney

Next to a child's name, his birthday is very, very important to him. On one day of every year he is the key figure in the family, the center of attention, the special person. In some homes there are privileges—for example, the birthday child chooses his favorite meal or clothing. Most young children consider a birthday a milestone in life and some even seem to feel and act "bigger" and older when the birthday morning arrives. They hop out of bed to experience that first day of a new age. Some will ask, "Mommy, tell me the story of the day I was born."

In school some special recognition is appropriate on birthdays but caution should be taken that it is not overdone. Parents should be informed about the school's policy. It is best not to permit parents to send in cake, favors or other treats for their child's party. This puts in bad positions those who cannot afford it financially or in time commitment. Sometimes such parties have a way of getting out of hand; first one child has a cake; the next has cake and special napkins; the next, cake ice cream, prizes, ballons, popcorn, etc. Such competition is inappropriate for the child and more often expresses the needs of the parent.

In many areas public health laws specifically forbid food being brought into school from home and given to other children since there is no control over sanitary conditions of home kitchens. (Though this does not apply to the child's lunch box it is a good reason to discourage swapping at lunch time.) Persons preparing food for children are required to have certain health certifications such as TB tests. Teachers have no guarantee that every parent has such clearance.

Children are perfectly happy with a simple party with similar treatment for everyone. Should a parent insist on preparing food explain the health rules and invite the parent to come into school and work with the children in baking the cake.

I Don't Want a Party—It should be anticipated that some children will not want a party. Some may even be apprehensive and stay home on that day. Children have been known to burst into tears when their cake was presented. A teacher must be sensitive to each child's wishes.

Some suggestions for birthday celebrations at school:

1. Wherever possible the children make the cake and the birthday child adds the decorations.

2. The birthday child **might receive a balloon or another simple** gift. Most children seem to enjoy wearing a crown **with points or candles marking** their years and trimmed with "jewels," flowers or designs. (See illustration for a simple crown.)

3. The child might be presented with a special birthday badge or a "Miss America" style band or ribbon.

4. The other children might make birthday cards and present them at the party. This is a good way to make use of old birthday greeting cards.

One teacher offered an assortment of boxes and gift wrappings. The children drew or cut pictures from catalogues of presents they would like to give. The "gifts" were wrapped in the boxes. Guessing games and stories were made up as the packages were opened. The children were involved in choosing and wrapping their gifts all morning and at the end of the day from four to six o'clock they enjoyed the "opening up ceremonies."

In another school the children made pictures of the birthday child and stories and poems to go with their pictures. The portrait was dressed in party clothing, trimmed with lace and buttons.

Read: "HAPPY BIRTHDAY TO YOU," by Dr. Seuss, Random House, N.Y. (A silly story about a ridiculous kind of birthday party in the land of Katroo.)
This is read in one home at the party and the birthday child chooses a page each year where the party guests sign their autographs. The book has become a happy reminder of each party as the years pass.
Note: This book may be too long for three's and four's but portions of it are excellent. One teacher suggested breaking the story at the point where the "Hummers and Strummers" lead the birthday march.

"Un-Birthdays" are celebrated for the children whose birthdays fall in months or on days when there is no school. Help these children choose a day on the birthday calendar (see below) when they would like to have a school birthday party.

Post a special classroom calendar with large squares marking dates which can become the BIRTHDAY CALENDAR. Appropriate seasonal figures, seals, symbols, flowers, etc. for each month are pasted on the date of each child's birthday. A special "ceremony" of recognition and pasting on the markers for the month might take place at the beginning of each month.

It is a nice gesture and good public relations to mail a birthday card to each child in the school. In one school an active parent council offered this job to a mother who could not participate in activities at school, attend meetings or take trips with the children. This can be handled by having a card addressed to each child on file in a school calendar date book and kept at the secretary/receptionist's desk. Two or three days before each birthday, these cards are mailed. Summer and holiday birthdays should not be overlooked. This simple gesture can be a major event in the life of a child.
Read: "THE END" from NOW WE ARE SIX YEARS OLD and "Everyone Has a Birthday and Gets Two Presents," from WINNIE—THE—POOH, by A.A. Milne, pub., E.P. Dutton & Co., Inc., N.Y.

SING HAPPY BIRTHDAY!!
and add...

5 5 5 5 5   5 5
Today is Andrew's birthday

5 6   6 6 6 6
It comes but once a year

6   7 7 7 7 7
Let's all sing together

7 6 5 5   6 7   8
Happy Birthday, Andrew dear!

Holidays—Holidays reflect the cultural, religious and ethnic heritage of a country, and help to further mutual respect and understanding among people of varying background. They should not be the foundation of a curriculum but rather one of the themes which add interest and sparkle to daily events. Colorful and interesting activites can be planned around holiday themes.

The sequences suggest ways of relating holidays to growth and development, for example: giving, sharing, joy, relate to Christmas and Hanukah, and love and hearts relate to Valentine's Day. Some of the holidays celebrated in America will be found in the following sequences:

HALLOWEEN	Sequence 2
THANKSGIVING	Sequence 3
CHRISTMAS	Sequence 4
KWANZA	Sequence 4
HANUKAH	Sequence 4
MARTIN LUTHER KING DAY	Sequence 5
VALENTINE'S DAY	Sequence 6
ST. PATRICK'S DAY	Sequence 7
EASTER	Sequence 8
MOTHER'S DAY	Sequence 9
MAY DAY	Sequence 9
FATHER'S DAY	Sequence 10
4TH OF JULY	Sequence 11

Language
Development

All areas of society depend upon communication. Blue collar workers must be able to read and follow directions, listen and react, give directions and explain methods. Executives of large corporations came to their high positions because they were convincing; they had mastered the language and could speak with authority and intelligence. Teachers and parents train children mainly through the use of language.

Teachers in high school and professors in universities are often appalled at the inability of their students to write a meaningful paper, expressing ideas in an organized manner, using language that is clear and concise in conveying the student's ideas.

Those working with very young children have the opportunity and the privilege, of establishing good foundations for language expression. Young children can learn to use full sentences if we do not always accept one word answers from them. They can verbally express their thoughts, and when a teacher writes them down the children are writing, even though they may not actually hold the pencil. When they are ready to guide the pencil they will have already mastered the art of expression.

Talking and writing are much like learning to play a musical instrument. Each requires practice.

Sensitive teachers will seek many ways to make talking and writing a part of the integrated school experience and as much FUN as playing house, block building or easel painting.

1. "READING BOOKS"

In one schoolroom the teacher suggested that each child choose a book and "study" it. Eagerly the children chose their favorite books from the shelves. The room became very quiet and the rustle of pages was the only sign of activity. After ten minutes Chipper said, "Could I read my story? I don't really mean "read" but I can tell from the pictures what it's about."

The children listened intensly.

Next Patty said, "Now it's my turn. This is my best story. She read "I'LL FIX ANTHONY," by Judith Viorst (Pub. Harper & Row).

Language becomes a part of every activity. In our philosophy we stress ideas rather than behavior, we emphasize THINKING, explaining, dictating stories about thoughts, feelings. The child makes language a useful tool for living and learning.

Reading and Telling Stories—Children, to be able to read for information and for pleasure, must be surrounded from an early age with books. As they see grownups and older children reading for pleasure and information they too will want to master the necessary skills.

All nursery teachers read story books to their students but with varying degrees of skill and effectiveness. The following suggestions will improve these skills.

1. Begin by reading the story first to yourself. (One inexperienced nursery teacher, who purchased a copy of Ibsen's "The Doll House" to supplement her school library, was fortunate to have discovered her mistake before she tried to read to the children!) Even the simplest story, intended and illustrated for children, should have the benefit of preview by the teacher.

2. Set the stage. The group should be reasonably settled and comfortable, the wiggles will settle if the story captures their attention. If props for sound effects or visual aids are to be used they are nearby *and organized.*

3. Hold the book open facing the children so all have a view of the pages as they are turned. Even if there are no illustrations the children are learning that "those black marks" are telling the story.

4. The voice is used as a delicate, refined instrument in telling or reading stories. It expresses with an infinite variety of tones the drama, the suspense, the compassion, the humor or excitement of the story.

5. The listeners share the action as often as possible. Being involved gives the child the feeling of "reading" and "telling" the story himself. "Farmer Hezekiah Brown doesn't know what happened to his carrots but WE do, don't we? Shh, don't tell!" ("Smokey's Big Discovery," by Walek.) These listeners know the glee of a shared secret. They reach the end of the story before Farmer Brown and can't wait until he finds out what they already know.

6. Visual aids enhance a story. Porcelain figurines of Peter Rabbit, his mother and Flopsy, Mopsy and Cottontail are treasured possessions in one school. When the story is read the figurines are taken out and the children very carefully handle them, feel the smoothness of the china, admire the colors and then lovingly place them back in their special box. A doll's tea set of delicate blue dishes has survived many years of admiring and handling as "The Little Blue Dishes" from TOLD UNDER THE UMBRELLA, pub. McMillan, is read to the children. In the red box where they are kept there is a small red purse with ten pennies inside to be counted as the story unfolds and also a little pink heart made from salt dough all carefully wrapped in blue tissue paper. (Seq. 4, Act. 8)

7. The teacher who takes the time to learn a story and tell it to the children will know great satisfaction while watching the expressions of wonder, awe, amusement, surprise on the faces of the audience. Their response inspires greater skill in the telling. An additional benefit is that she has a valuable teaching tool available for immediate use. When there is a five minute wait or a group is "high" a well told story may save the day. Telling a story should not imply total recall, or word by word recitation. It is most helpful to memorize the first sentence, to know the sequence of events and to memorize the last sentence. "Oh, I forgot to say that..." makes the thread of the tale go a little limp. If you memorize an entire story and relay it back by rote you will be so busy trying to remember the next line it becomes a recitation and your story will be a bore for both performer and audience.

8. PLEASE! Don't moralize! It really isn't necessary to "heavy up" the ending with "So you SEE children, if Cinderella's sisters had not been so selfish..." or "I'll bet Goldilocks listened the NEXT time her mother told her not to go into the woods." The children will get the moral message if there is one, perhaps not the first time, or even the second, but eventually the story will take on layers of meaning which fit their growing experiences and they should be allowed the excitement of such discoveries. They do not need spoon feeding or adult interpretations. Books should be treasure chests holding beautiful stories and exciting bits of knowledge. They should not represent some strange square vegetable out of which teachers squeeze or wring "learning" which the child is expected to digest. Young children will learn to love books and will approach reading with joy and excitement, if they have good experiences in these early years.

9. Bring your stories to life whenever possible by eliminating 3rd person *grammar*. Instead of "The king told the people he was going to solve their problems," address the audience in the King's very own voice and use other tones or voices for each of the other characters. Tell the rest of the story in a comfortable, pleasant narrating voice. When a conversation takes place between two characters in the story turn your face in either direction giving the impression of two people talking. Telling a story with these embellishments is just as easy and twice as much fun.

10. Use sound effects. In TOLD UNDER THE UMBRELLA, (see Bibliography) Paddy's father comes home every night and jingles his keys in the lock and whistles to let Paddy know he is home. Paddy might come down the stairs by way of the keyboard on the piano or on the xylophone. A cymbal struck slowly becomes the tolling church bell helping to create a visual image of people dressed up and walking in a slow dignified manner to church. Father takes off his overcoat, folds it and places it on the seat beside him, all slowly and solemnly. These sound effects can be produced by preselected members of the audience to add interest and excitement.

11. Most important of all...choose a story *you* really like, one which tickles your funny bone and stimulates you imagination. Your pleasure unlocks the silver chains around the treasure chest of enjoyment.

The Story Carpet

A teacher of very young children had a large fringed couch cover in a tapestry design. She called it her "story carpet." When she took it off the shelf the children began to gather round. Sometimes on a good day the story carpet went outdoors, into the tree house, under a tree, or on a grassy spot. Like the magic carpet of Alladin, the carpet set the stage for an experience which meant pleasure.

The Captive Audience—Too often in the nursery school "story time" means that every child is expected to sit down in front of the teacher and "enjoy." Children should be given a choice in this as well as in other areas of curriculum. Their options must necessarily be limited to activities which will not disturb or distract those who do want to listen, but they should be given alternatives.

"Those who want to hear my story come over here. If you do not care to listen you may look at books in the reading corner, you may play quietly with this game or you may have crayons at this table. You may *not* play in the doll corner, build with blocks or play with trucks because that would disturb us."

A captive audience will often be disruptive and take away from the pleasure of those who wish to listen. "But," the reader says, "when he gets to first grade he will have to sit still and listen."

When children seem incapable of listening the challenge rests with the teacher to seek ways to encourage rather than to force attention. Story Book Development (See Seq. 8, #10)

Props and Visual Aids—Finger Puppets—Finger puppets are a delightful visual aid to supplement stories, finger plays, poems, and songs. They might be elaborate puppets made by adults or very simple creations made by children. Some tiny "special" puppets might be kept in pretty little containers to be used with special stories, songs, and on holidays, birthdays and other special occasions.

Easy to make finger puppets can accompany favorite stories, finger plays, or poems.
1. Five Little Mice: made on a pair of gray gloves with ears, tails and faces sewn on.
2. Five Ghosts: a simple arrangement of kleenex over each finger held on with an elastic band. Draw on faces.
3. Witches: made on black gloves, with separate black hats of paper and tiny brooms sewn to glove fingers.
4. Faces of story characters painted on paper circles and glued to paper rings.
5. Button Puppets: faces painted on buttons and sewed to a 1/4" elastic finger band which fits over fingers.

More Suggestions for Puppets

Sequence	2-25 (Ghosts)
Sequence	3-55 (Tube Caps and Acorns)
Sequence	3-73 (Hobby Horses)
Sequence	4-35 (Rudolph Reindeer)
Sequence	5-23 (Bears)
Sequence	8-10 (Storybook Development)
Sequence	9-85 (Gloves)
Sequence	10-26 (Peanut Shells)
Sequence	10-27 (Spoons)
Sequence	11-121 (Clothespins)

Poetry and the Program—Fortunate are those who were introduced to poetry by someone who loved it and who shared that enjoyment. Too often even the suggestion of poetry stirs memories of rote recitations droning on in a monotonous cadence. Such as, "Oc-to-bers-bright b-lue weather" or "I-shot-an arrow-in-to-the-air" or "This is-the-for-est-prim-e-val."

"I like it but I don't know how to use it."

"When I read poetry to the children they just don't respond."

Total language development includes an appreciation of the beauty of spoken and written words, and so poetry becomes an integral part of any language.

One of the basic theories of how children learn states that we start where the learner is. Reading, singing, dramatizing, drawing pictures of nursery rhymes can become the first step in an appreciation of poetry. The children are soon eager to join in with the rhyming word or complete a sentence "Jack and Jill went up the...."

They enjoy participation in choral assignments.

Variations with instrument, pictures, or puppets, bring the children into the action.

ALL: Ding dong bell, Pussy's in the well.
Q: Who put her in?
A: Little Tommy Green.
Q: Who pulled her out?
A: Little Tommy Stout.
ALL: What a naughty boy was that, to want to drown poor pussy cat!

The teacher might divide the class in half, one side asking the questions and the other providing the answers. Two children might be chosen to ask and answer, especially if the teacher is seeking ways to encourage individual expression. A bell or a gong, dolefully struck, would emphasize the dramatic aspects of this tale. Such expressions as a prolonged groaning "O-h-h-h" after the first line and a "Tch, tch" at the end might be used in one type of choral speech. Another method might be to use these two vocal choruses as an accompaniment by *half* of the class while the other recites the words.

Finger plays are another excellent way to enter into the world of poetry. We play "This little piggy went to market" on the fingers and toes of the infant. Pre-schoolers will giggle all over again when they meet this old friend at school. It can be their introduction to a host of finger plays fitting each season and many new concepts throughout the year.

In the development of language skills we know that children need and enjoy repetition. "This is the House that Jack Built" and "The Old Woman and Her Pig" should be a part of the poetic offerings. The clever teacher who may become bored with such rhymes will devise visual aids to add interest.

Fours in particular are at a stage in their language development when they have a real need to experiment with sounds. This often manifests itself in bathroom talk and even more offensive words. (See Part I, Ages & Stages) One teacher, frustrated by this situation, used the poems of Edward Lear:

"A is for Apple Pie

Pidy

Didy

Widy... ."

Limericks are another style of poetry which children enjoy, but the sensitive teacher will lead children from such literary pabulum into enjoying more sophisticated poems; poems which express emotions ("Pierre," Maurice Sendak); poems which take one into a world of fantasy ("Knitted Things" by Karla Kuskin, "Fish with a Deep Sea Smile" by Margaret Wise Brown), and Rose Fyleman's delightful poems about Fairies. There are poems which express delicate imagery ("First Snow," Mary Louise Allen) and poems to tickle the funny bone ("If We Walked on Our Hands," by Beatrice Schenk de Regniers). Robert Frost wrote the poem, "Last Words of a Bluebird." When this was read in a nursery school one four year old asked for it over and over, and in a very few days was heard reading it accurately to others. We must never underestimate the ability of a child to appreciate the best!

What do we mean when we suggest integrating poetry into the total program? Poetry and music are first cousins. Nursery rhymes are usually put to music. A natural introduction will be to think of ways to combine music and poetry. Using instruments often injects a note of drama into a poem as when a gong or triangle is used for the clock striking in "Hickory Dickory Dock." One child said "Why does the clock always have to strike ONE?" That poem then became a math experience as each child waited and counted to see how many times the clock would strike.

Poetry and art go hand in hand as children illustrate their favorites. Often a poem is prefaced with pictures and discussion.

Science appears in poetry with the "slush" in "Susie's Galoshses" by Rhoda Bacmeister, the *melting* of the "Silly Snowman," and *traction* "Snowflakes Falling." A child entranced by the imagery of Carl Sandburg's "Fog coming in on little cat feet" will be reminded of that bit of poetry when enveloped in a blanket of fog.

Play acting comes so naturally to children that, given the opportunity, they will make many suggestions for dramatic versions of the poems they like. The ultimate pleasure will come to children and teachers when they write their own poems. Methods for developing this art are described in the section on Creative Writing.

But how does the teacher include poetry, and why do some children respond? Appreciation expressed in the face and voice of the person making the presentation will carry over to children and become contagious. There are some basic rules:

1. Never attempt to read a poem until you have read it, *many times*, yourself. If you do not like it, do not attempt to use it. Your feelings will come through to your listeners.

2. Decide in advance whether this is a poem which should have a rhythmic cadence as when "Christopher Robin went hoppity, hoppity, hoppity, hop," or whether the story aspect is most important. Your voice is the instrument playing the tune. If it stops at the end of each line but in the middle of an idea, a sing song version with little meaning emerges.

3. Memorize short poems. You will be rewarded for this investment of your time. Write a poem on a small card and say it while you knead bread, cut wood or drive to school. Keep the card with you for reference in case you get stage struck. Just knowing it is there will give you confidence.

If you do not memorize your poem write it on the blackboard or a paper which you can fasten on the wall and use as TV actors use cue cards. A favorite poem might be hung at child's eye level beside an appropriate picture.

When reading poetry, present each poem alone, as you would a lovely object. Do not confuse the children by reading four, five or six poems about snow on the same day. Present them one at a time, savoring the imagery, humor, or emotional content. We dilute the appreciation of so many experiences for our children by offering too much too soon. Small bites, well digested, will leave a more pleasant and permanent imprint on the developing mind.

Creative Writing—Can young children write poetry? Yes, as surely as they have thoughts and imaginations and express these thoughts in their own words. When we write down these thoughts in poetic form rather than prose the results are often poetry.

A kindergarten teacher had often written poetry for her own pleasure. As she stood at the sink washing dishes suddenly a poem was clamoring to be born. None of her teaching colleagues knew she had this gift until she revealed it one day when she read some of her original poetry to the children. She was encouraged to find a way to share this talent.

She began one morning by just talking about poetry. "Some poems have words that sound the same, they rhyme. Can you think of a word that rhymes with fish?" That first day the children spent a few minutes rhyming words. Next day she offered a number of two line couplets, leaving out the rhyming word to be filled in by the children. On another day the class played a word association game, "I'll say a word and you tell me what it makes you think about. 'HOT!' " The responses were written on a large sheet of paper; "summer, stove, soup, swimming... ." They tried putting some of these words together.

During one discussion time she said, "This morning when I came to school I saw some little flowers just sticking their heads up out of the ground. They are called crocuses. When I saw them I felt happy. I know that spring is coming! Soon it will be warm and we can play outside more and more. Did *you* see any other signs of spring?" The children's responses were listed and her notes for that day read: "While Peter tried to think of more signs of spring to add to our list he rhymed:

"Spring brings swings and things."

He smiled and, after he said it, realized it rhymed. I wrote it down for him. Carol and Laurie came over and began adding to Peter's poem. The results were:

A POEM
by Peter, Carol and Laurie

Spring brings
swings and things
and penguins
and worms and
squirrels and
snakes and
fish in a dish
to make a wish!

On another day the children were introduced to limericks. Many original limericks followed.

On another morning a poem with delicate imagery was offered with the explanation: "All poetry does not rhyme, sometimes it is just a thought, a very special thought, which you want to keep and so you write it down." Then she extended an invitation. "We have all written poems together. Now you may want to write one of your very own. I will keep this pad and pencil in my pocket. If you have a special thought come tell it to me and I will write it down. It might be a happy thought, or sad; about something good, or scary or bad, or maybe an 'I wonder.' " Following that session it was a common occurrence to see a child go over to her and say "Mrs. Smith, I have a poem." She would write it down, always trying to go a bit away from the other children, respecting the author's feelings, which might be revealing or private.

"Would you like to have me read your poem back to you?" she offered; and then, "Do you want me to read it to the others?"

Each day, when the group met for discussion, she read two or three of their own poems. This often inspired others to try.

How did this teacher reach the child who had not responded, who might be too shy or who really didn't seem to have many original ideas?

On a sunny, warm spring day she invited five children to go with her to a place where they could sit on the ground and they talked about:

"What can you see without moving from where you are?"

"What can you hear?"

"What can you smell?"

"What can you feel?"

Then, "Think about all of the things we have just talked about. If you were going to be something else, not a boy or a girl, but something we have discovered here, what would it be? When you are ready, tell me and I will write it down. Please tell me why you chose it."

Mary wanted to be: "A cloud moving fast in the blue sky."

Karen wanted to be: "The sun shining on her back."

Sam wanted to be: "The breeze blowing against his face."

This ended the experience for some. Mrs. Smith concluded by saying, "If you want to put some of our thoughts together into a poem I will write it down." Four of the children went off to play. Donald, who had not offered anything before, stayed and dictated this poem:

Just around the corner

What did I see?

A big brown bear

Looking at me.

Waiting for lunch the next day the teacher recited Donald's poem in a lilting tone: "Just around the corner, what did I see?" "Laurie, what did I see?"

Laurie grinned and replied, "A fuzzy brown caterpillar on a tree." The class made a book of "JUST AROUND THE CORNER" poems, illustrated it and kept it in their library area where it was frequently chosen for reading.

This "Poetry Workshop" took time. It did not happen in one, two or even three days, but almost every day there was a story time when one or two poems were introduced, poems to fit seasons, moods, classroom events, or simple poems that this teacher loved. Her own enjoyment was so genuine that she could have held the children's attention if she had been reading excerpts from the dictionary. Her voice and facial expression were an important aspect of the experience.

Little by little more and more children came to her to dictate poems. One day she placed two chairs at a table in a quiet corner. She announced, "This is poetry day. I am going to sit over here. If you want to tell me a poem wait until you see this other chair empty. When I listen to your poem I just want to hear YOU."

On the table she placed some small, very smooth stones. "What are those for?" asked her first poet.

Some people think it's better if they have something to do with their hands," she replied. Those stones acted almost like prayer beads or a doodling pad; thoughts did seem to come more easily when hands were fondling the smooth stones.

When this teacher was invited to come to read to a class of students in early childhood education, her cheerful, exuberant presentation of the delightful poetry of childhood brought about a new outlook on the part of those students. They were excited and interested in experimenting with poetry. Before the end of the term the students wrote and compiled a complete book of original poems. Following are some of those poems:

ELECTRIC JEWELS

At night when I look out at the city
I see a jewelry display set against
Black velvet before me.
In the distance the street lights
look like diamond earrings.
The airport runway looks like a queen's tiara.
The red lights on the radio tower
could be a ruby necklace.
"See," I said to myself, "you really
don't have to be a millionaire to have jewels.
You don't even have to be Elizabeth Taylor!"
(Carol Glavin)

and: SCOTT'S QUESTIONS (as he took his first walk on a forest trail)

"Where, oh where are the baby deer?"
"Not here — not near — not here."
"If I went deep into the woods,
wouldn't I find them there?"
"Do you think they'd come if I called to them?
If I promised not to scare?"
(Connie Greenman)

(See also Seq. 8, #16)

Language Games—There are many games, activities and tools to help children learn words, concepts, enlarge vocabulary and master the art of conversation. Following are some suggestions and guidance in using them according to ability and ages. Some games are as simple as finding the rhyming word to a jingle; others as difficult as arranging pictures to form a sequential story. The transitions and experiences of each day run more smoothly for the teacher with a game or simple activity for every occasion; to make waiting less tiresome when program hits a slowdown or snag; to play at the luncheon table; to while away the last half hour in late afternoon; or to play outside on the playground.

The keen observations of the teacher will serve as guides to know each child so that he can be helped with his individual language needs through the skillfull use of a variety of language games.

Dramatic Play—Are you trying to help a child who does not engage in conversation? Stay near him for a day and listen. Somewhere—in the housekeeping area, the block corner, on the playground, or while he is fingerpainting—something will happen which will give a clue to his reticence.

Ruth Taylor Stone, a pioneer in nursery education in America, told a story of an incident which happened in her school. It was at the beginning of World War II. One morning, Rosie, normally cheerful, but uncommunicative, came in, hung her coat, and went straight to the easel to paint. Her face was cloudy, her expression determined, her back stiff and tense as she scrubbed and rubbed and jabbed with black, brown and purple paint. An observant teacher stood nearby and heard Rosie muttering, "I hope to hell they don't take him in the draft!"

The following day Rosie came in to the classroom with her usual smile. Again she wanted to paint. This time, however, she chose bright colors and her strokes were free-sweeping arcs. Her body motions were relaxed and graceful. As she painted, she almost sang, "They didn't take him. They didn't take him!"

The teacher took a valuable cue from Rosie and guided her class through a series of art experiences asking, "How would you paint angry?" "How would you paint happy?"

"What colors make you feel sad?" She combined painting with movement and music. She played sad music ("Largo"), mysterious music ("Hall of the Mountain King" from the Peer Gynt Suite, Grieg), strong rhythmic music. Some children moved with the music, others painted, all talked about feelings. The teacher then led them into creating improvisations and dramatizations of favorite stories. Rosie became a part of these sessions. She was now ready to express her ideas and act out her interpretations.

Each child has some key which unlocks his abilities to express, communicate, create. The sensitive teacher never ceases searching for those keys.

Puppets are often successful teaching tools in helping the non-verbal child. Somehow it is easier to speak if it is not YOU, but an image held on your hand or perched on your fingers. The puppet is doing the talking and can say ever so much more than you would dare! (Adults find this to be true when they use puppets for a role playing discussion of parent-child-family relationships.)

Choral speech is a catalyst for some children. It is easier to be one of a group when no attention is focused on any one speaker. Reading familiar stories to which choral sound effects and responses have been added is an excellent introduction to verbal expression.

Dramatic play is not only a means of developing communication. It is a source of great fun for most children. It may be as simple as "you be the mommy, and I'll be the daddy," in the housekeeping area, or the doctor making the baby well during hospital play. Often dramatic play grows naturally out of a movement and thinking session or a spontaneous act.

Instant costumes (see Seq. 3, #9), simple accessories, puppets and a few props all help to create a play acting center where children can enter into a wonderful world of make-believe! (Read "Nurturing Challenging Activities," by Wagner, Allen Raymond, Darien, Conn.)

Tiny Treasure Box—Imagine the delight of a small child at peering into a tiny box filled with miniature treasures—dolls, cars, a shiny jewel, a china kitten. Such tiny treasures act as stimulants to spur language development; as relaxing peacemakers to an unsettled child during homesick moments. (See Part I—Separation-Adjustment.) Miniature treasures in a box help to tell a story or serve as storytelling puppets.

We all see pretty boxes or containers and tuck them away for future use. Most of us are attracted to miniatures; china people and animals, charms, dime store and joke shop items, cocktail favors, advertising gimmicks, doll house furnishings. Put these treasures into a pretty box and create a tiny treasure box.

It is not used as a toy or for daily activity but is only taken out for special occasions. When the contents are always the same children take great delight and pride in naming the items and finding a remembered object.

Sometimes the treasures are changed and new surprises are added from time to time. On returning from a vacation trip the teacher gathers children around and after telling of travel adventures takes down the treasure box and from her pocket a tiny package. Inside the children find a pink seashell and it too is added to the box.

Specialized boxes enhance language or other skills. A collection of rhyming objects; several round items; a box filled with soft touchables; seriated items from small to teensy or light blue to dark blue. Kindergarten children might make up spelling boxes containing items with names they can spell—cat, hat, cup, pin.

A treasure box might even have a joke to trick an unsuspecting teacher or child. A box in a box in a box in a box....

Music Throughout the Day

"Music is fun and music is as much a part of everyday living as breathing and talking, as block building and sand cooking, as dressing and eating, as running and resting, as looking at clouds and feeling grass, as crying and laughing."

(Emma Sheehy, Living Music with Children)

In planning a curriculum for young children music is woven into the fabric of the entire day. Every interest center provides some opportunity for musical expression. Judy in the housekeeping area sings softly to her baby doll. Experimenting with tuning water glasses and auditory discrimination game introduces music into the science center.

Children who have had ample opportunity to explore and experiment with painting are introduced to a new dimension of artistic expression while painting to music with varied moods and tempo.

The teacher watches and listens for cues for the *teachable moment*. As a group of children chant or sing spontaneously, the teacher picks up the beat of a movement with a drum or sticks and makes it a shared experience. Four children playing with clay begin to pound it in unison and as their teacher uses a drum to accentuate their rhythmic patterns their faces reflect pleasure in her participation.

Children who are happy and content will sing. Mimi and Joan, swinging side by side, combine the joy of movement through space with the satisfaction of having a friend as they sing "up, up, up" and "down, down, down." Their voices climb up and down with the musical chanting. Robbie discovers a bounciness to the balance board and jumps chanting "bounce, bounce, bounce." The teacher joins his chanting and may add a new idea with "Bounce, bounce, bounce, and JUMP!" Mark joins in the fun. Soon a line forms with each child taking his turn saying, "bounce, bounce, bounce, and JUMP." The game becomes much more dramatic when the teacher gets the cymbals and accents the "Jump" with a crash.

"It all sounds so easy," sighs the self-described "non-musical" teacher. It IS easy for the teacher who is prepared to believe she is capable of SOME simple musical experience. She starts where SHE is and grows along with the children, working in a climate of freedom and FUN.

When a musical experience gives pleasure, sooths fears, allays tension, or brings joy to a single individual it is good. It does not have to please everyone at the same time or in the same way.

Singing with Young Children—Singing and childhood go hand in hand. Singing is not reserved for special time slots—it is woven throughout the entire day. We sing as we go through necessary routines such as dressing, napping, washing; we sing as we move from one activity to another, from one place to another; we sing on our school buses and in our station wagons as we travel to and from school; and we sing as we walk out on a field trip or hike. We sing to convey and reinforce ideas, we sing for sheer exuberance, we sing to express our moods; and as we sing together the seeds of harmony and unity are sown.

What are appropriate songs for young children? We choose songs for:

(1) A general feeling of content—"Hey Betty Martin" gives you a happy, contented feeling.

(2) Some aesthetic value—Children will love a song for sheer beauty. Even if they can't reach the standard they will go toward it. The lullaby "Fa-la-na" (Seq. 7, #39) is tender and sweet, but real—on a child's level.

(3) Brevity and simplicity of form—The younger the children, the shorter the phrases should be ("Mary Had a Red Dress," *Songs to Grow On*, Landeck, pub. Sloane).

(4) Repetition of words, tune and rhythmic pattern ("Frere Jacques," "Old Mac-Donald")

(5) Rhythm—vital and definite ("A Hunting We Will Go," "All Night-All Day")

(6) A melody that is easy to sing—with not too many large intervals ("Star Spangled Banner" and "Thanksgiving Day is Coming" are *negative* examples.)

Start with the Familiar—When choosing songs to sing with young children we turn first to the familiar folk tunes which have been passed on from one generation to another. They belong to everyone; they are easy to learn, within easy voice ranges and have a simple basic rhythm. They have lasted because they came from the heart; they grew out of real life experiences.

Sea chanties were sung by sailors who led a very monotonous life. Confined to ships for months at a time, far away from home and loved ones, they were overworked, often badly treated and underfed. As they swabbed the decks, climbed the ropes, and polished the brass they sang to keep up their spirits. They rhythms of the chanties were a vital force in many of the shipboard tasks.

The cowboy riding the expanses of the great western ranges sang to himself, to his dog and to his herds to dispel the loneliness and to calm the resless animals. As we sing his songs we FEEL the rhythm of his horse, loping along. (Play "On the Trail" from the Grand Canyon Suite of Ferde Grofe.)

The men who built railroads across this vast continent, and the blacks who picked cotton under southern skies, spoke to us of the physical hardships they endured through the songs they have handed on to us. These folk tunes depict the very fibre of a developing nation and are a priceless contribution to our national heritage. As they are introduced to our children with brief explanations of their origin and uses, the child begins to have an awareness of his country's history. (EXPANDING THE WORLD)

How to Introduce a New Song—Though some schools still advocate teaching a song by rote we are most emphatic in our objections to this method. It is unnecessary. It squeezes the joy out of singing, and it takes music out of the natural flow of events and sets it apart as a lesson to be learned. When the leader says, "Now I will SAY the words, and you SAY them after me, one line at a time," children and adults tune music out.

A new song should be offered as if it were a surprise package, wrapped in bright paper. "I know a song about a clown, all funny and fat, with a feather in his hat." Listen, I will sing it to you." The teacher sings it through once—and "Now this time when I sing it if you remember some of the words, help me," or just indicate with a gesture that her listeners may join her. If there is a recurrent phrase (i.e. A-HUM, A-HUM in "Froggie Would a Courtin' Go") they will sing that part and soon will know the whole song.

Some teachers, out of nervousness, preface their songs with much clapping of hands, calling to attention and explanation.

"O.K. now everyone. I have a new song. Now everyone listen. John, you aren't listening. O.K., now here it is." Instead of all the preamble if she simply starts singing, looking into the faces of those nearest her, some of them will join her and the rest will follow.

What of the teacher who says, "But I'm not musical. I can't carry a tune. I can't sing or read a note." FIDDLESTICKS! Everyone can sing or chant the songs we all sang on the playground as children. Everyone has sung, "We won't get home until Morning" or "Farmer in the Dell" and those familiar tunes are a starting place for the most unmusical teacher. If she really can't recognize or carry a tune she can find someone to help her tape a few songs and use this until the children learn. Then they will carry the tunes. There are many fine recordings by well known folk singers and children can sing along with them until they learn the songs. We believe that it is better for children to sing with the most inept leader and risk learning a few tunes inaccurately, than to be denied the fun of singing.

One teacher who could play the piano introduced each new song by playing it for several days while the children were resting. The children absorbed the melody and when the words were added the song was quickly learned because of the previous exposure.

Tempo and tone are as important as the tune. There is a tendency to adopt the dragged out half chant of the playground, "Li-ttle-Sal-ly-WA-A-Ters" and if a song is intended to be light and gay like "Hey Betty Martin" it destroys the quality. Children sing most comfortably in the keys of C and F and most adults can sing at that level, but again, through nervousness, have a tendency to start all songs an octave lower. It is a good idea to have a tone bar, or even a bell tuned to middle C to help in starting a song, until the range comes naturally.

Finally, a teacher needs to carry some songs in her head, songs to suit many different moods and events, so she can respond to special moments with a spontaneous outburst of song. Such moments are lost while she frantically hunts for the right book and page. Learning two or three songs in each of the following categories will greatly enhance a teacher's use of classroom musical experiences:

Familiar Tunes for Making Up Your Own Words
Songs for Daily Routines
Songs to Move Groups
Silly Songs for Experimenting with Words and Sounds
Songs for Appreciation of Beauty
Songs for Making Motions and Dancing
Songs to Stress Spatial and Temporal Concepts

Action Songs

One Finger Keep Moving
Put Your Finger in the Air, Aiken Drum
Teddy Bear
Hokey Pokey
Looby Lou
Heads, Shoulders, Knees and Toes
Bear Went over the Mountain
B-I-N-G-O
Eensy Weensy Spider
Little Mice are Creeping
Let Everyone Clap Hands Like Me
Whole World In His Hands

Under the Spreading Chestnut Tree
Rock-a-my-Soul
Rock a bye Baby
Wheels of the Bus
Michael Finnegan
I am a Fine Musician
Thorn, Rosa
Thumbkin
Coming Round the Mountain
John Browns Body
My Hat She Has Three Corners

For Repetition and Sounds

This Old Man
Old MacDonald Had a Farm
B-I-N-G-O
Hole in the Bucket
Bought me a Rooster
Allouette
Polly Wolly Doodle
Supercalafragilisticexpialidotious

Pretty Songs

Kum Ba Yah
Whole World In His Hands
Down in the Valley
You Are My Sunshine
Hush Little Baby
All Night, All Day
Michael, Row Your Boat Ashore
Jacobs Ladder

Music for Rhythms and Movement

Skaters Waltz
Greensleeves
Lara's theme
Love Makes the World Go Round
Sunrise, Sunset
Time to Remember
Eidelweiss

When the Saints Go Marching In
King of the Road
Raindrops Keep Falling on My Head
Zorba the Greek
In the Forest (Herb Albert)
Pop Goes the Weasel
Mexican Hat Dance

Rounds

Row, Row, Row Your Boat
Three Blind Mice
Chairs to Mend
Make New Friends
Why Couldn't My Goose?
Rose, Rose
Little Tommy Tinker
Kookaburra (Cook-a-burra)
Frere Jacques
White Coral Bells

Humourous Songs

Cat Came Back
Did You Feed My Cow
Fox Went Out on a Chilly Night
Lollipop Tree
Animal Fair
There was an Old Lady
John Jacob Jingle Hymen Smith

Familiar Tunes to Use for Original Songs

Frere Jacques
Farmer in the Dell
Twinkle, Twinkle Little Star
Go In and Out the Window
Bear Went Over the Mountain
Mary had a Little Lamb
What Shall We Do When We All Go Out
Let Everyone Clap Hands With Me
Clap, Clap, Clap Your Hands
Oats, Peas, Beans and Barley Grow
Goodnight Ladies
Looby Lou

Pop Goes the Weasel
Row Row Row Your Boat
Three Blind Mice
Jack and Jill
The Muffin Man
Jingle Bells
Ring-a-Round the Rosy
Did You Ever See a Lassie
Little Brown Jug
Old MacDonald
Skip to My Lou

Make a Motion Songs

Punchinello
Theres a Little Girl in the Ring
Ha Ha This-A Way

Instruments—Rhythm bands went out with "circle time" in the nursery school. It is inappropriate for young children to sit or march banging and clanging away on musical instruments. What emerges is a cacophony of distorted sounds. There are music books and records that suggest that we arrange children according to the instruments and conduct them as if they were in an orchestra, each section playing at an appointed time or all together at others. While this *may* have value for children seven or eight years old it is not good musical training for young children. It is fatiguing, overstimulating, and in general, uncreative. Children have a lot of experimenting to do before they are ready for such directed music.

What DO we do with musical instruments?

Begin by presenting them one at a time, each with the dignity and importance of a precious Stradivarius violin. Pass it around for the children to touch and listen and experiment. For example, when sand blocks are rubbed together very lightly they call to mind lightly falling rain. If you start rubbing them slowly and increase the speed they have the sounds of a train. Coconut halves clapped together are a galloping horse and are a fun surprise to add to a song about cowboys or ponies.

Bells might be introduced two or three at a time, each with a different tone. Collect a set of various bells such as elephant, cow, sleigh, bells of Sarna, a dinner bell and an old fashioned teacher's desk bell.

As each instrument has been presented the growing assortment might be displayed on a table and likenesses and differences and individual characteristics discussed: "Which ones do you shake?" "What is metal?" "What makes more than one sound?"

When using instruments expect children (and adults) to test them, try them out. To say "Hold your bell very still until we are ready," asks the impossible when children are given instruments for the first time. They must be allowed to experiment and find out what they can do. Anticipate this with, "When I give you these sticks I know you will want to try them. See how many different sounds you can make with them. When I hold my sticks way up high like this please STOP and LISTEN to see what I am going to tell you." If this STOP signal is played as a game for a few times the children will take pride in not being caught when the signal is given. It is better to anticipate the need than to try to get the attention of the group by shouting over the din.

Instruments can be used for sound effects with stories and poems, to add drama to creative movement, in math for counting patterns, and in combinations of sound and beat that will create harmony.

A music center takes as much thought and planning as any other interest center.

If we want children to treat instruments with respect we must set the stage with proper care and storage. How many times have you seen a basket or carton filled with a jumbled assortment of bells, sticks, cymbals, drums, etc. Have you ever searched frantically through such a collection seeking the hanger for the triangle or shuffled to the bottom for the striker?

Sticks should be arranged by sizes in attractive containers. Triangles can be hung on hooks; finger cymbals placed in dainty little boxes which suit their delicate sounds; anklets or wrist bells kept in a separate bag or box and drums in a special place on a shelf. Until rules are established and learned most of these instruments will be out of reach with just two or three at a time laid out on a low shelf.

Teachers and children can construct their own shakers, drums, anklets. In one school each child owned his own complete set of stickes, claves, sand blocks, bells and maracca. Each set was kept in a shoe box which he had decorated and marked with his own name. These instruments could be used whenever the child wished and they were frequently played. They took an extra pride in caring for them because they had made them.

Also reference: (Seq. 3, #21-23—Drums), (Seq. 4, #53—Bells), (Seq. 5, #57—Rattles and Shakers), (Seq. 10, #35—Hummer-Drummer), (Seq. 11, #31-43—African Inst.), (Seq. 7, 53, 57.)

Creative Movement—Movement, *the sixth sense*, is best developed in the *context and rhythm* of daily living. Humans cannot explore and develop the other senses—sight, smell, taste, touch or sound, in isolation. They must be learned in the day to day events of work, play, and rest. Movement is also an integral part in the discoveries and creations of the other five senses. All of life *IS* movement.

The development of movement, the body's language, into an active, vital, creative sixth sense should become a part of every classroom activity. Stories, games, songs, clean-up, playground antics, painting, dramatic play—each involves body language. Watchful, sensitive adults can translate such language into creative movement.

> Thus a child learns; by wiggling skills through his fingers and toes into himself, by soaking up habits and attitudes of those around him, by pushing and pulling his own world.

Frederick Moffitt
New York Department of Education

Creative movement is used to *follow-up, expand,* and *reinforce* concepts throughout the daily program. Spatial concepts (on, through, around, over, behind...) are involved in almost every movement experience. On a day when the children had been talking about animals, their likenesses and differences, their eating habits, their homes, the "cues" for movement were obvious—this was a day to "dance" animals into their body language.

This is the *integrated approach* to creative movement.

Music and movement are like happily married partners, each able to function alone but with added joy when they are together. Children enjoy dancing to the music from their favorite classroom records or exploring space and motion with music from classical symphonies and ballets or modern jazz and rock records.

If one of the onlookers gazes out the window and shouts, "It's snowing!" the teacher can pull the class out of its traditional rut by saying, "We'll have to plow the streets and push out all the stuck-in-autos."

"Plows" and "tractors," "shovelers" and "sliders" may be accompanied by "Swan Lake" but they are *moving*—creatively.

In the phrase creative movement it is the "creative" which scares away many excellent teachers. The word creative suggests artistic talent and the "I can never draw a straight line" attitude sets in as they slip away to sit and watch from the sidelines. This in unfortunate, for movement is as simple as bread and butter, as accessible as crayons and paint. Art and motion become graceful partners as children translate body motions on paper with brushes and paint or explore colors and "the way they make you feel."

Movement is for EVERYONE who can nod his head, clap hands, wink an eye, shrug a shoulder. The growing popularity of modern dance has confused many into thinking that creative movement and dance are one and the same thing. Though modern dance IS creative movement, creative movement does not exclusively mean "dance." The "creative" simply means awakening the consciousness to the wonders of body motion. How does it move? Why? How fast or slow? How does the body come to rest? Awaken? What shapes can the body become? How does it stand when happy, terrified, sad? Can it be a carrot? A machine? A cat? A flower in the wind?

Can motion ever be separated from sight, sound, smell, touch, taste? NO, NEVER! Students and teachers of nearly every philosophy acknowledge that children learn through sensory experiences. Montessori made sandpaper letters and by tracing around them with a finger children gained another impression. Through movement we can seek ways to feel letter shapes and number with our bodies. For example, "Think of a number of ways to express the letter "s." Can you make it with your fingers? With your whole body? How could two people make it? Use two different parts of your body to make "s." Think of some action words that begin with "s." Which could you do standing? Sitting? Use ropes to make "s." How could we walk on them? Around them? Make an "s" pattern into a dance. What kind of music shall we use? Put large sheets of paper on the floor and paint "s" with musical accompaniment.

Creative movement begins where teacher and child are..."just doing what comes naturally" as Annie (Get-your-Gun) sang. It may be as simple as, "What could we do with our fingers? How many different ways can we move them?" While seated around the table at juice time or at the beginning of rest when each part of the body is relaxed one at a time ending with a soothing y-a-a-a-a-w-n.

Whenever bodies, attached to imaginations, are involved in exploring and discovering, creative movement is happening!

Read "Body Movement???," by Rita Abrams, pub. B.A.Y.E.C. (35¢), Boston Mass.

Creative Movement Activities Using Props:

Hoops-Seq. 1-32	Pictures (Emotions)-Seq. 6-55
Pumpkins-Seq. 2-32	Scarves-Seq. 6-72
Balls-Seq. 2-35	Boxes-Seq. 7-41
Hoops-Seq. 2-37	Eggs (Plastic)-Seq. 7-48
Scarves-Seq. 2-39	Pictures (Machines)-Seq. 7-49
Elastic-Seq. 3-54	Paper Streamers-Seq. 7-51
Ballons-Seq. 3-56	Film-Seq. 7-68
Boxes-Seq. 4-55	Cords & Ropes-Seq. 8-29
Drums-Seq. 5-46	Netting-Seq. 9-28
Bean Bags-Seq. 5-57	Colors & Scarves-Seq. 9-32
Elastic-Seq. 5-61	Cartons-Seq. 9-35
Tissue Paper-Seq. 5-63	Hoops-Seq. 10-31

Art In the Classroom   Many teachers of young children withdraw when music and science are mentioned but they beam and relax when the art program is the topic for discussion. It would be nice to think that daily activities were equally divided among the major areas of interest and skills but in practice, art related activities take up about fifty percent or more of the program, limiting the child's introduction to a wide variety of experiences.

Why this heavy concentration on art activities? Perhaps it is because we are more comfortable using our hands than our voices or bodies, and even at times, our minds. Part of the problem also relates to the fact that teachers feel they do not have to "explain" their art projects. They call everything "creative" seldom taking the time to evaluate the value of their projects. Art then becomes so much busy work—keeping the children happy. It is easier to put out paints, crayons and paper then to plan an integrated day in which art fits into the total program.

We know that children will benefit by experimentation with a wide variety of materials, textures, colors, shapes, tools. When we surround them with media to which each can respond, in his own way, we help them work their way through the developmental stages which follow in a natural sequence. Just as the child creeps before he walks and experiments with sounds before he talks, so also he goes through many stages of experiencing with all of his senses the materials which he can later use to represent his thoughts and emotions.

Adults find it difficult to appreciate the scribbling or blobs of paint on paper, applied with brushes, fingers, and sponges which children proudly carry home. Admiring relatives exclaim over these creations ascribing unwarranted values to them, thus giving the child false notions about his work. At the other extreme, is the adult who remarks on the waste of time and materials it took to make them and disdainfully tosses the creation into the wastebasket.

"But if we don't send papers home the parents think their child isn't learning anything." It is the teacher's job to help parents understand that knowledge isn't expressed on paper. (See Record Cards) A teacher who has goals and values firmly established will be able to explain the purpose behind all of the experimentation. Conversations with the parents will satisfy them that she knows what she is doing. Often this means reminding them that the emphasis is on the process and not the product. This is not to suggest that papers are never allowed to leave school but they should not be required as "proof of learning."

Whether a child is painting at the easel, fingerpainting, modeling, making a collage, or building a structure his right to "just be doing" should not be challenged. When we ask "What is it?" we often put the burden on him of making it "be" something, because he wants to please us, or thinks we expect it. A teacher can show interest by commenting on some aspect of the work.

A kindergarten teacher had been watching Tommy play with blocks and trucks through all of September and October. He refused any suggestions that he might want to paint. One day she said to him cheerfully as she tied a smock around his waist, "Today it is your turn to paint." Tom went dutifully to work, applying one color after another until the paper was nearly covered. His teacher came back to stand and watch him for a short time and commented, "That is a very pretty shade of blue." Tom looked up at her with an engaging grin and replied, "I don't know what it is either!"

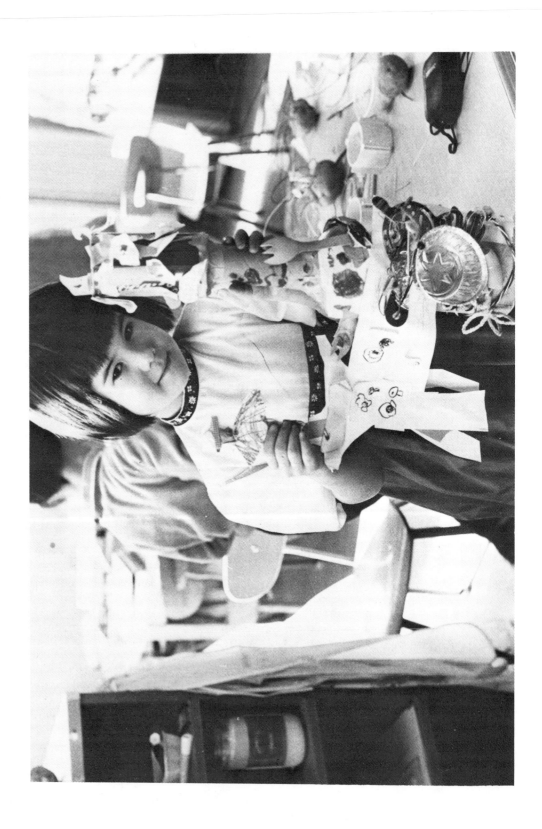

An adult NEVER lays a hand on a child's work! She does not "show how" or "touch up" his work so his parents will think it credible.

"Teacher, can you help me make a rabbit?"

How would you respond to such a request without refusing to help? Here are some suggestions. Discuss what rabbits look like, how they feel, what colors they are, what shape. If you have a real classroom bunny go look at him. Talk about "round" body, "round" head and long pointed ears. Make suggestions to lead the child in the right direction. "Here are some cloth scraps and some cotton balls." Lay out scissors, glue, stapler. Ask questions which will stimulate his ideas but leave room for discovery.

Suppose the child has come to you with a picture of a rabbit saying, "I want to make one just like this." Explain to him that "Everyone doesn't make a rabbit in the same way. You have your own way and it is the very best way for you. Your bunny may not look exactly like the one in this picture but it will be very special, just as this one is, because YOU made it."

And don't forget to look for poems which will add another dimension to his discoveries about bunnies:

"Every little bunny rabbit
Has this funny little habit
If he stays or if he goes
He wrinkles, wrinkles up his nose"

When the picture is completed, don't be surprised if your budding artist suddenly announces, "It isn't a rabbit—it's a milk truck!

See Seq. 11, #102-Arts and Crafts.

Note: See "How to organize and use Found Materials in School Art Activites" by Chandler Montgomery from *Art for Teachers of Children*, pub. 1967 by Chas. E. Merrill Books, Inc., Columbus, Ohio.

THE PAINTING
by
Helen E. Buckley

Once a little boy was going to paint a picture
He put the paper on the easel,
And he looked at all the jars of color
In front of him.
"What are you going to paint?" asked the teacher
"The sky," said the little boy,
"I'm going to paint the sky."
"Good," said the teacher,
"Do you have enough blue paint?"
And he took up the blue brush
And made a wide band across the top of the paper.
"There," he said, "There is the blue sky,"
And he looked around for the teacher,
But she had gone.

Then the little boy looked out the window
To see if his sky looked like the real one.
And it did.
But was the sky ALWAYS blue?
The little boy put down the blue brush
And thought about the sky.
"Sometimes," he thought, "Just before night,
The sky is pink—and a little purple."
So he took up the pink brush
And then the purple,
And pretty soon there was a sunset on his paper.

Then the little boy remembered winter.
And how the sky looks when the snow comes down.
So he took up the white brush
And made soft snowflakes over all

The blue and the pink and the purple sky.
And some of the snowflakes melted
To make more colors, and the little boy felt happy
Like he always did when the snow came down
In the wintertime.

And just as he was about to put down his brush
And be finished, he remembered a day in summer
When the sky grew dark.
And he remembered that he had been a little scared
And he had run to tell his mother about it.
So now he took up the black brush
And painted great storm clouds
With flashes of red and orange lightning
Streaking through them.
"It's thundering, too," said the little boy softly to himself
"Boom! Boom! Boom! And the wind is blowing!"
And he made the rain come down—hard rain—
In long green lines across the sky,
And all the colors ran together in rainbows
At the botton of his page.

"Now I will make the sun shine,"
Said the little boy to himself,
And he made a big, round sun in the middle of the paper.
But the painting was so wet,
And there were so many colors in it,
That the yellow sun turned brown in the sky.
But the little boy didn't care—
His picture was finished
And it was just the way he wanted it.

He looked around for the teacher,
And pretty soon she was there—
Standing by the easel and looking at all the colors:
All the blue and pink and the purple;
All the white and the black;
All the red and orange and green;
And the yellow that had turned brown.
The teacher looked at all the wet and dripping colors
Which had run together
In the snow and the wind and the rain
Of the little boy's painting.

And she said: "My goodness!"
"I thought you were going to make the sky"
"I did," said the little boy,
"I made all the skies I know about"
And he took his picture off the easel
And put it carefully away to dry.

Helen E. Buckley is Associate Professor of English at the State University of New York College at Oswego, N.Y. and is author of two recently published children's books.

Painting Techniques—There will be some who will question the methods we are about to describe for TEACHING children how to use the tools we provide. It is our opinion that the artist cannot create a masterpiece until he learns how to hold a brush and mix his paints; the musician cannot compose a symphony without some knowledge of the "tools of his trade." We are not afraid to use the word "teach"; some adults are still bumbling along because no one ever taught them to do the simplest, most basic things, such as sweeping a floor without stirring up the dust, washing the middle of the back, or cleaning a bunch of celery! It is the WAY we teach children that detracts from, or enhances, their pleasure in creative experiences.

Materials, paints, brushes, easels are kept in 'ready' condition at all times. As with every other teaching tool or toy, these painting tools are a valuable asset to the classroom. If they are in disrepair, difficult to set up, crusted with paint, etc., they will not receive proper use and the child will acquire some false notions of the care of materials.

It should be the task of a teacher, assistant or volunteer parent to keep paint mixed and ready for use. Paint can be mixed to the proper consistency in quart containers and liquid soap added as a thinner instead of water. The paint will then wash out of clothing easily. Small containers are filled daily and emptied into storage containers at the end of each day. Brushes are *never* left standing in paint and, after washing, should be stored with handles down.

Most easels come equipped with trays to hold paint pots but some teachers find them inconvenient. The brush handles stick up over the lower portion of the painting and are easily hit and tipped over. The child inadvertently mixes colors by dipping the brush into the wrong color.

A better method is to put the paints on a table beside the easel with a mixing pan, wet sponges and a rinsing pan to clean brushes between colors. The child is encouraged to mix his own colors and can easily see the shades as they are blended in a low, flat dish.

Once a child has been taught a few simple techniques of cleaning brushes, wiping the brush on the side of the pan to prevent dripping and mixing to create his own colors, he is free to paint often and creatively.

A drying rack or line should be nearby so children can hang their own work to dry.

A low shelf or table or floor space is easier for younger children to use as a drying area. Newspapers should be laid under easels and drying areas before beginning painting activities. Smocks and aprons are a must. These can be made from shirts worn backwards with the sleeves cut off, or simple apron smocks of poly with cloth edge bindings and ties.

One enterprising teacher made a drying rack which came down from the ceiling with a rope and pulley arrangement. Lest it strike someone on the head, it could only be lowered to a height which required the child to climb on a platform to clip on his painting. An example of ingenuity in combining science, art, and physical activity.

To stimulate interest and conversation at the easels, arrange them side by side rather than back to back. Construct a long easel from a 4 x 6′ plywood panel along the outside of a building. Slant the trough away from the building. This is good for mural painting or for four or five to paint together. A child who has not shown interest in painting may try it outdoors with a friend beside him.

Natural materials such as flower petals, leaves, grass, pine spills, weeds and sticks can be used as brushes and for rubbing colors. A variety of colors and shades can be created from moist soils; charcoal from a camp fire or rotted wood and rocks substitute for crayons. Indians and pioneers obtained their colors for dying and painting from berries, roots, vegetables, fruits, and clay. It is an exciting experience when children can also make their own colors. To lend variety various forms of painting (such as string painting on finger painted or sponge painted papers) can be combined.

Printing Objects—
    sponges
    meat grinder parts
    sea shells—keys
    jewelry—mesh bags
    cotton balls
    cloth scraps
    cans and bottles (caps and bottoms)
    wood textures
    vegetables and fruits (carved)
    rolling pins

String Painting—Fold a piece of paper (9 x 12″). Some children will need guidance in folding and smoothing the fold. Open paper and arrange a string (approx. 12″) in any shape or pattern on one side of the fold. Remove string and dip it into a saucer of paint and rearrange on the paper, leaving about one inch extended from bottom. Explain the directions using a dry string first. Fold the paper over the string, hold it firmly with one hand, and with the other, pull out the string. Open the paper, remove string and set the open painting to dry. This process develops listening, following directions and manual dexterity. Spatial relationships and concepts are emphasized—this side, that side, the other side, inside, on top of, over. After a child has mastered the technique he can experiment with various weights of string and yarn and more than one piece or color at a time. ("Can anyone think of a different way to do this? How could you make it look different?")

Blot Painting—Fold a paper through the middle and smooth carefully. Open and place several "globs" of paint on crease. Fold top over and smooth carefully. Open and dry. Observe how each child will use this medium in a different way. Some have tiny dots, looking almost like measles, others choose vivid colors and use them in combinations. The activity can be extended into creating blot pictures. When the paintings have dried children study them from various angles to see if a realistic object is suggested by the blots. Magic markers or crayons are used to outline these areas creating scenes, animals, shapes. Another variation of this is to wet a sheet of paper and drop water colors or dry paints onto the surface. Paints spread out and mingle to create designs which can be outlined into pictures.

Finger Painting—Finger painting is introduced after children have had an opportunity to paint with brushes. It requires more adult help and supervision than other art media and should be presented to a few children at a time when assistance is available. A low metal topped or formica table or one covered with a plastic sheet serve well as a painting surface. The table is divided into sections with tape and the children paint directly on the surface. When designs are completed, if the child wishes to make a "lift off," lay a sheet of paper over the design (newsprint is best), *rub* gently into paint and peel away.

It is not unusual for children to refuse to engage in this messy activity. Some have repugnance for "getting dirty," others have been taught so well to stay clean that they cannot enjoy finger painting. A teacher can sometimes choose the right moment to help a child by putting her hands over the child's and painting along with him. With this gentle persuasion, one little girl went at the paint enthusiastically. Soon she was back to show the teacher, her forearms covered up to the elbows with paint. "See," she cried gleefully, "I am wearing green gloves!"

Painting with Cars

Robbie and Billy, aged five, refused all attempts to interest them in "that messy stuff." One day they were invited to come and see what was happening at a table where children were using red finger paint to draw hearts with their fingers and make lift-off valentines. The teacher thought perhaps the additional process might intrigue them but to no avail. Remembering that they loved cars, she gave then each two small cars and said, "How would you like to drive these cars through the red paint?" They looked at her in amazement, "You mean we really can? You're kidding," Billy grinned in surprise.
Soon both were tracking roads and curves and spin-offs into a lovely design in the red paint.
"Hey, Billy," shouted Robbie, "we're doing this all the time now. It feels good! It really feels good!" (See Seq. 6, #45)

Vary the finger painting experience by placing papers on the floor to change the kinds of strokes. Try painting with toes, elbows. Paint with objects such as combs, forks, spatulas, brushes, etc. Paint to the moods of music. Ask a child to make a motion while the others paint it.

Use dried fingerpaintings as backgrounds for collage or string paintings. Add texture to finger paints by stirring in rice, sand or salt.

Recipes for Fingerpaint

I.	II.
6 cups water	Liquid starch
1½ cups wheat paste	soapflakes
½ cup soapflakes	powdered paint
powdered paint	(mix directly on paper or table
cologne or oil of wintergreen	top with hands)
(few drops as preservative)	

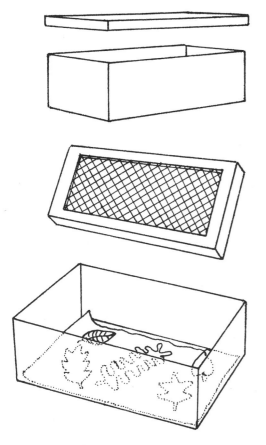

Screen Painting—Construct a frame about 9″ x 12″ and about 2″ deep. Tack wire mesh screen to the top of the frame with small brads. Screen frames can be made from picture frames and sturdy boxes. (See sketch.)

Set up designs by arranging objects on a piece of paper under the screen. Use a toothbrush dipped in paint to brush over the screen causing the paint to spatter in a fine spray. Carefully remove the screen and when the paint has dried, lift away the objects. Use natural objects such as leaves, pine cones, shells, ferns. Supplement cognitive activities by using screening medium to teach shapes, letters, numbers, names. Create snow flakes by laying lace doilies or hand cut paper designs under the screen.

A variation of screen painting is SPRAY PAINTING. Put a fairly thin mixture of tempera paint into a spray bottle and use to spray pictures. Arrange designs as in the screening techniques.

Plaid Paintings—Introduce this activity by looking at pieces of plaid fabric. Is anyone wearing plaid? Examine threads going each way. What happens where the colors cross? Pull threads from a small swatch and form plaid by laying the loose threads into the plaid design. How can you paint a plaid picture?

Use different sized brushes to paint stripes down and across a paper in different colors to create a plaid design. Stretch white sheeting over a frame or embroidery hoop and draw on plaid designs with crayons, iron with warm iron. Place wet strips of crepe paper crossing each other on white sheeting. Colors will "bleed" off and leave plaid designs on cloth.

Straw (Blow) Painting—Drop thin paint on paper and blow into designs using a straw.

Comb Painting—Use several varieties of combs. Dip into paint and draw designs. Vary by finger painting on a tabletop and drawing designs with combs. Lift off designs by laying paper over wet paint and lifting off prints. (See RAIN PAINTING—Seq. 8, #44.)

Roller Painting—Make a wire handle to fit through hair rollers and use as paint rollers to create designs. Roll on deodorant bottles can also be used for roller painting.

Marbling—Fill a square shallow (2″-4″) sided cake or lasagne pan with water and drop oil-based paints onto the surface. "Swirl" the paint into a design if desired or leave as it falls in spots. Lay a sheet of hard surfaced paper (glossy, finger paint stock) on the surface of the pan. Lift off and lay flat to dry. Prints can be hung but this will cause running and change the design. (Look in old books for cover liners done by marbling.)

Rubbings, Relief Painting, Lift-offs
Rubbings—Children can explore the many textures of the environment and at the same time create beautiful and interesting works of art by using the techniques of relief, lift-off, and rubbing. Rubbings and reliefs are done simply by laying paper or finely woven cloth over any object which has texture and rubbing over the surface with crayons, chalk or charcoal. Below are some suggestions.

FLOOR AND WALL TILES
ROUGH FORMICA
COINS
STYROFOAM TRAYS
TREADS-STAIRS, SHOES, TIRES
CRACKED DRY MUD

LEAVES, STONES, BARK AND OTHER NATURAL OBJECTS
STREET CRACKS-PAVEMENT
SCREENS-ONION BAGS
BASKETS-STRAW AND PLASTIC
METAL SIGNS-RAISED LETTERS
CRUMPLED FOIL
WOOD SURFACES
GRILLS
BRICK WALL
FABRICS-ALL KINDS
BOOK COVERS
EMBOSSED SURFACES
CORRUGATED PAPERS
LEATHER
SANDPAPER SHAPES

Rubbings can be used just as they come off or combined with other things in art objects. The texture of the environment awakens new interest when it has been rubbed and observed. (See Seq. 11, #18—Tombstone Rubbings)

Note: An art teacher once said, "Crayons with paper on them limit creative possibilities at least 75%." It is not recommended that teachers tear paper off all the crayons but insisting that papers be kept intact and the crayons used only on the ends limits them as creative tools. Children should be encouraged to rub them along the sides.

Relief Paintings—By combining two different media children can create lovely designs and pictures called relief or resist paintings. This is similar to the way engravings are made. Wax crayon is first used to color the entire surface of heavy paper or cardboard. The surface can be all one color or a combination of many colors in a picture or design. The best results come from heavy application of the wax crayon. Next the surface is painted with tempera, generally black but other dark colors will work as long as the crayon is obscured by the paint. When the paint has dried the surface is scratched away with a fine point. Old ball point pens are excellent. Also experiment with metal forks, combs, blunt scissors. As the paint scratches away the colors come through. Designs and pictures against the dark background have the look of fine etchings. Fancy cardboard boxes with brightly colored surfaces can also be used as "Scratchboard" creations. The color is scratched away to reveal the white base beneath.

A simpler method, possible for very young children, is to make a picture with crayons and paint over it with black paint. The picture will show through and creates an unusual and attractive effect.

Lift-offs—This is an elementary form of painting. When a surface has been painted either with brush or finger paints and is still wet, a sheet of paper is gently pressed onto the surface. Pat gently or roll a rolling pin or cardboard tube lightly across the surface. Lift the paper away and the excess paint will leave a reverse print. This is an economic way to stretch paper and paint supplies.

Textured surfaces can also be explored by using clay as the medium for lift-offs. The clay is pressed onto the surface and pulled away to reveal the imbedded designs. Dentists make impressions in just this way. Plaster of Paris can be poured onto textured objects such as pine needles, tracks, sand patterns, rough cloth swatches to create castings.

Sculpture—Children need time to experience materials with all of their senses. The accessibility of play dough has, in too many cases, given it too prominent a place in the teacher's planning. It is an excellent sculpture medium and has the advantage of the additional fun of making it, but there are many other modeling materials, each offering a particular advantage.

Real *clay* should be available in all schools. It can be controlled in texture and when properly cared for will last a long time. It can often be purchased locally (look in yellow pages under "pottery") but can also be ordered from educational supply catalogues in quantities from five to fifty pounds, often in powder form. Once mixed it should be kept in a clay crock, or metal pail covered by a wet cloth. The daily chore of keeping the cloth wet could be given to the children.

Pieces of masonite, $12 \times 12''$, make good clay boards, one for each child. Linoleum sample squares will also work well. Children should use painting aprons or smocks when modeling. The clay should be wet, just enough thicker than mud to be able to form shapes. Each child is given about a cupful to work with.

Just manipulating the clay is enough for quite some time. Children enjoy the sheer satisfaction of squishing and squeezing the clay. A teacher who is sitting at the table may start making snakes and balls. Some children will observe and try. A nest, or bowl, made by pressing down the center of a ball is usually the next step. This can be followed by "I know another way to make a nest," and the teacher makes snakes and coils them round and round, smoothing the sides into a bowl. Making several balls and stacking them (snowman) will lead into the making of animals. If the teacher has been careful not to make samples or to stress the right or wrong way or the good or bad results of each child's efforts, representation will come gradually, as each child is ready. *Stress the process, not the product!*

While clay appears to be very messy it is actually quite easy to clean up. The secret is to treat it as you do mud, let it dry and then it will brush off clothing and from the floor.

1. *PLAY DOUGH RECIPE:* This can be colored with vegetable coloring and used in the same way as clay.

2 cups flour
1 cup salt
food coloring in water
Add until pliable (about 1 cup water)

2. *SALT DOUGH RECIPE:* Sometimes there is a need or desire to make something to last. Salt dough will harden without baking. It will crack or break if dropped, but it can withstand quite a lot of treatment.

1 cup flour
2 cups salt
Roll out — let dry in sun or oven — can be painted

3. *SAWDUST SCULPTURE RECIPE:* If this is prefaced by a trip to a sawmill, carpenter's shop of furniture factory the experience is enhanced. Shavings, or curls, collected at the same time can be used for collage, curls or simply for "What can we do with this?" Like salt dough sawdust clay gets very hard and can be painted or shellacked.

a.
2 cups sawdust
1 cup wheat paste
Water to hold mixture together. Will get very hard.
b.
1 part flour or wheat paste
2 parts water

Mix flour and water and heat until clear and thick. When cool, add fine sawdust until a thick modeling material is formed.

c.
Add sawdust to liquid glue to form a thick paste.
1. modeled

2. Spread flat on wax paper and cut into forms like cookies.

Material can be sawed, filed, whittled, or sanded.

4. *PAPIER MÂCHÉ:* Papier mache are French words meaning mashed paper. When

dried it is a very light and durable material. (A good activity for young children if extended over a long period.) Tearing the paper, just for the sake of tearing on one day, then mixing it with water and paste on another are very satisfying experiences. (See recipe below.)

a. *MÂCHÈ SCULPTURE:* Mush and squeeze the mache "batter," shape into forms, dry, and paint. (See Seq. 1, #23.)

b. *MÂCHÈ "LAYERING":* Construct forms by bending chicken wire into shapes and cover with layers of mâchè. Tear newsprint or paper towels into strips, dip into a thin solution of wallpaper paste or wheat paste and lay over the frame, adding several layers until the desired thickness and shape are achieved.

c. *MÂCHÈ RECIPE:* Tear newspaper or paper towels into small pieces. Soak for several days. Add wheat or wallpaper paste to a mushy consistency. Add 1 tsp. boric acid per pint of water to prevent mildew. Add a few drops of oil of wintergreen for a preservative.

5. *GRANDMA'S SALT BEADS*

1 cup salt
½ cup cornstarch
½ cup boiling water
1 drop food coloring
1 drop perfume or toilet water

Mix salt and cornstarch. Add boiling water and coloring. Cook over moderate heat until thick, stirring constantly. Add perfume and mix well. When cool enough to handle, form mixture into balls. Run a thick pin through the center of each ball and place upright on a corrugated piece of cardboard to dry, string on heavy thread.

6. *SILLY PUTTY*

2 parts white glue
1 part liquid starch
add color if desired

7. *WOOD SCULPTURE:* Given an assortment of small pieces of wood of all shapes and sizes, including spools, dowels, throat sticks, popsicle sticks and toothpicks and some strong adhesive (preferably glue), children will create with the same imagination and absorption that they give to painting or other plastic media. Until they have had ample time to explore the properties and discover the potential of wood no motivation is required or advisable. In time they may wish to work on a group project.

In one kindergarten this took the form of a small town called Woodsville. It started with the January curriculum and a suggestion that homes be explored. The village occupied a space 4′ × 4′ and grew much larger before it was completed. Each day something new was added to the village and more sentences added to the story book which was posted on the wall behind the sculpture. There were roads, streets, houses, garages, a firehouse and swimming pools. Later a zoo was added. One day the children went for a walk to look at doors and roofs, to see how they were alike and different. "I don't think we could turn off Woodsville," said the teacher, "they come in each morning so excited and motivated with new ideas of additional buildings they want to make!"

In another day care center wood sculpture became a very relaxing end-of-the-day activity. (See How: End of the Day.) It started on a large piece of heavy cardboard (tri-wall). The children just glued and glued, adding pieces at random, outwards and upwards. When it became too heavy to lift up on the shelf and take down again the project came to an end. But soon another was started. The children did not ask for it every day, it was like knitting, something they chose to do when they were in the mood. (Seq. 9, #52—POUNDING BLOCK and Seq. 5, Act. 41.)

Woodworking—Woodworking enables a child to work off strong emotions by pounding and sawing. It is an excellent way to strengthen math concepts and develop manual dexterity and eye/hand coordination. Some children will become creative at the woodworking bench even though they have resisted all other art media. Many feel great personal satisfaction as they become skilled in using tools and learn new techniques.

Woodwoking can be dangerous. It is not recommended for the threes and always with close supervision with fours and fives, at least a one-to-four ratio. Threes can begin such activity as driving nails into blocks of styrofoam. Provide them with pieces of styrofoam, large flat headed nails, hammers which are not too heavy and unwieldy and plenty of close supervision! Just pounding the nail into the styrofoam is a beginning experience. For variation draw designs with magic marker and nail on the lines.

Children will be frustrated by saws which are not sharp enough to cut, hammers too light to drive a nail and screw drivers too worn to turn a screw.

NOTE: Left-handed children will have difficulty tightening *screws which are threaded against the natural wrist motion.* Removing *the screw will be easier for left-handed children.*

Woodworking activity is probably best held off until after the winter holidays. By this time the children have gained in maturity and are capable of accepting rules of safety and use of tools and materials.

By mid-year children begin to show enthusiasm for "real learning" and are ready for new experiences and skills. In colder climates children will be inside more and this vigorous inside activity brings many of the same rewards as active outdoor play.

Establishing a Woodworking Center—Where? This is a noisy activity. Where will it cause the least interference? It should be away from traffic and closed off securely when not in use. When children are at work can they be supervised by a teacher near enough to be doing something else?

The workbench must be of the right height and solidly built. Tools should be hung on a board, each one over a silhouette or outline marking its proper space. Rules for the care and use of each tool must be explained and rigidly enforced. The tools are not toys in use or in fact.

Nails are sorted into containers by size and weight. A heavy magnet attached to the bench by a rope serves to keep the floor clear of nails. Box nails small and medium finish, 6 and 8' lbs. common, and roofing nails work well. (Roofing nails are aluminum and will not adhere to the magnet.) Supply wood screws of assorted lengths and thicknesses.

Bench Accessories

1. two vises—fastened to bench
2. two coping saws
3. one box coping saw blades
4. one brace—assorted bits
5. four claw hammers
6. two rip saws—16" or 18" blades
7. one smooth plane
8. 2 screw drivers
9. one small tri-square
10. two compasses
11. two rulers
12. four pencils (large, soft, black)
13. two pkg. medium grain sand paper
14. Screws—different sizes
15. one pkg. carpet tacks
16. blue nails
17. $1^1/_4$—two " nails
18. water based paint (less messy than oil)
19. white glue
20. dowels—different sizes and lengths
21. soft pine wood (different widths and lengths.) (Masonite, plywood and any other hard wood will frustrate child to extent that he may not try again, and will thus miss a good experience.)

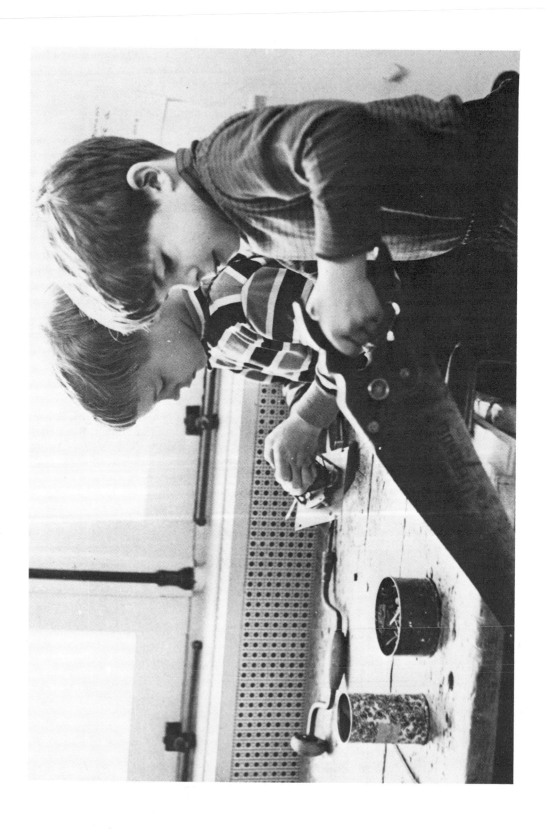

Sources of Wood

Visit local lumber company, woodworking shop or furniture factory or the woodworking department in trade or public schools which may have short ends and scraps. Ask at construction site where workers often pile scraps in one spot on location to carry away but do not take without asking. Usually they are interested in helping children and will save special pieces of trim and scraps. Go back if you can show them something the children have made. *NOTE: You might even find a young student who will volunteer to come in and work with children.*

Ask parents for spools, scraps and ideas for more resources and assistance in teaching.

Wood Curls

Five children stood around the teacher as she was showing them how to use the plane in the carpentry center.

"Looks like curls" said Dana, "too bad they aren't blonde like Cindy's." The teacher got a shallow pan of yellow paint and put it on the table. Cindy dropped some chips in and all watched as they took on the color. More colors and more wood curls were added. Paper towels were laid out to dry them on. The wet chips created wonderful shapes. What fascinated the children even more were the pretty designs they left on the paper. They began to place the curls in special order to make more designs. When they were dry, some were mounted on construction paper of a contrasting color.

Weaving and Sewing, Dyeing—It is not usually wise to introduce paper weaving until children are four. Start with plain colored construction paper, weaving in contrasting colors and fairly wide strips. As children gain in skill they can have larger papers, narrower strips and weave in several colors. For ecology and variety use strips cut from magazine covers and catalogues.

Sewing cards are fun, even better if you make your own using a paper punch.

Children can sew around the edges of pillows and stuffed animals using large needles and yarn or coarse thread.

The idea of weaving might begin with unraveling a piece of coarse cloth. Making mats with strips of paper, bamboo slats and paper or oil cloth mats will serve to teach a process, but offers little change for creativity. Plastic webbing, vegetable bags, can be woven with yarn using large needles, bobby pins, or toothbrush handles. Large needles can be made from old tooth brushes. Cut off bristles and file away "stubble" then form the end to a blunt point and thread through the hanging hole at the other end. (See Seq. 9, #72)

Hoop Sewing—Sewing can also be an activity which appeals to young children as seen in the following description which happened in a group of young fours.

"I placed some squares of bright colored burlap, needles threaded with yarn and some embroidery hoops on a table. I sat down, picked up a hoop and placed it over the material and started to sew. Mark sat down beside me, silently watching.
Finally he said, "Can I do that too?"
"Sure," I replied, "pick out a piece of cloth and a needle and I will help you get started."
My only instructions were, "When the needle pokes his head up on this side, he must poke it back down on the same side." Soon there were six children busily sewing. (I only had six hoops.) Michael was the only one who asked for and completely used up three different colors.
Karen and Cindy took another square and another color of yarn when they had finished with the first one.
Elaine preferred not to have the needle go back down on the same side.
When she found she couldn't get the hoop off I watched as she carefully cut the yarn, leaving a sort of fringed look. She was pleased with the results, calling attention to the fact that hers was different.
The squares of burlap were mounted on contrasting colors of construction paper and made a colorful decoration on our wall. (See Seq. 11, #3)

Tie Dyeing—Tie dyeing is a technique of dyeing designs in cloth by tieing off or knotting sections of the cloth before dipping the fabric into the dye. With practice, experimentation and experience unusual designs can be created turning ordinary white sheets and old dress shirts into attractive garmets or fabric.

Very young children might begin with the:

a. SCRUNCH AND BUNCH method—simply bunch sections of fabric together and wrap rubber bands or string tightly around the fabric at random. Squeeze several colors of undiluted dye into the bunching before dipping to add unusual shapes.

b. TIE KNOTS in sections of the fabric. Squeeze additional colors under the knots before dipping.

c. ROSETTE KNOT—Pinch a section of fabric and wrap the base tightly with an elastic. For concentric circles ("sunburst effect) add more rubber bands.

d. DONUT KNOT—Made a rosette knot then push the center of puff through to the other side and tie with elastic. Suggestion: Squeeze undiluted dye into the center of the knot before dipping.

Collage—Many a parent has been puzzled by a "work of art" proudly carried home which appears to be an assortment of junk stuck with a great deal of thick paste to a sheet of construction paper. Not wishing to discourage artistic expression, there is an uneasy reaction. "What is it?" "It looks like a waste of paste." "How can I hang it up," and father sputters 'Is this what we are paying to have him do all day?"

Collage stems from the French word coller meaning "to paste." French and German artists invented it early in this century and the notion spread around the world. What is the function of collage in the preschool? Unfortunately it has become a crutch for nursery school teachers. It is easy to dump an assortment of junk on a table, suggest to the children that they paste it on a paper or cardboard, and label the result as "collage." Used as a legitimate art media it should be presented with thought given to children's needs and developmental levels. For threes, tearing or cutting paper and pasting the pieces onto a larger paper is the beginning of collage. This process may be repeated over and over, with each child finding his own way. Some will build the papers up, one on top of another; some will carefully place each one keeping them separate, and some will choose large pieces and let them hang over the edges. This is a good time to emphasize process and minimize results.

Gradually more and more materials are introduced and with each one there is exploration, conversation, problem solving. Cloth and paper of different textures, buttons, feathers, dress trims... . As the children experience, experiment and place the materials in a way which they find pleasing, they are assimilating the notions of balance and symmetry. They are discovering techniques and media for attaching their materials—paste, glue, staples—and because there is no "right way," no established or imposed standard to follow, they are allowed to be truly creative. The teacher guides their development by putting out particlular materials or combinations of materials. In this curriculuum manual new concepts are chosen, for exploration as the year progresses. Shiny and dull, smooth and rough, scratchy and tickly, hard and soft. Many of these concepts can be explored through the medium of collage.

As in every carefully planned program the method of presentation is important. Scissors may have blunt points but should be sharp enough to cut easily. Sticks or brushes are offered for pasting so that collage materials do not adhere to sticky fingers. Materials are arranged in a box cover in the center of the table or smaller individual boxes provided for each child to use in gathering his own assortment. A place for drying the completed pictures is necessary. The storage area for the assortment of materials is organized, *labeled and accessible.* Materials are changed often and special surprises added on occasion. Setting the stage for success can make this experience valuable for the young child.

Displaying Childrens Art Work—Display in a school should be as carefully planned as interior decorating in the home. Pictures are hung straight, with an eye to grouping. Sculptures and other constructions are set off to advantage by placing them on cloth, or colored paper. A cardboard box or carton painted inside and upended makes a satisfactory shadow box for exhibiting works of art. Mobiles should hang where they are free to turn and catch the light. Transparencies are hung in windows. Sometimes it is possible to hang a picure where it will be reflected in a mirror.

Finger paintings, string, spatter or blot paintings are enhanced when mounted on construction paper which draws out their colors. To conserve paper cut out the center portion of the backing. The outer square is placed over the painting as a frame. Frames can be made from corrugated cardboard, box covers or cardboard painted or covered with cloth. Clear plastic or contact paper stretched over a painting preserves it and adds a finished look.

Where there are attics, garages, cellars and second hand furniture shops, there are usually old picture frames which can be cleaned up, painted and hung in a special place to display a child's painting. These can be changed frequently so every child can have his picture in this place of honor at some time. Children are encouraged to reach new levels in their painting when they see them attractively displayed.

Hang it all!—While we encourage display of a child's work it should be seen as a means to self-development, not an end, and never as visual evidence of the teacher's proficiency in her profession. Her classroom walls tell that story. A visitor who sees Halloween drawings on the wall after Thanksgiving or dusty paintings with torn or curled corners tacked to the walls in a haphazard fashion must wonder about the teacher's attitude and ability.

"How can you get the pictures away from the children to display them? My children insist on taking everything home," teachers will ask.

The teacher establishes a rule during the first weeks of school that papers do not *always* go home. Samples of each child's work will be kept in a folder to show progress, interests, creativity and manual dexterity during parent conferneces. Though every paper may have some significance in the developmental process it is not necessarily a work of art deserving praise or display by parents. The child acquires a false sense of the worth of his work when it is treated as if it were another Picasso. HE knows it was just paint on paper and he was content with the process. When adults whom he respects give it the "rave treatment" his self-respect may turn into self-adulation.

Even more detrimental to a child's feelings about himself is the tendency for some teachers to feel that they must "touch up" a child's work before it can leave the school. This says very clearly to a child "It is not good enough." He may translate this into "*You* are not good enough" and be discouraged from further effort. Laying hands on a child's work to fix it up, complete it, or make it more realistic is an absolute "*no, no*" for all teachers, students, volunteers *and* parents!

Creative Mess—Ecological Distress
Norma Cushman

Is your paint polluted?
Are scissors scattered?
Materials all jumbled
Like it hasn't mattered?

Look at your picutres
Outdated? Askew?
The way things look
Sure tells on you!

The classroom can say
"Come play and work"
Or it can shout
"This teacher's a jerk!"

The state of the puzzles
The books and the paste—
Do yours reveal care
Or careless waste?

The piles of collage stuff
The hammers and saws
The house and the block things—
Do they stick out like claws?

While children are working
There'll be a nice mess
But have you arranged things
For clean-up finesse?

No need to be prissy
Too fussy or prim
But a sense of order
Is more than a whim

For freedom of choice
In a room that's chaotic
Can bring teacher and children
To a point that's neurotic

So, if you've had the impression
That tidying up is a bore
That is just doesn't matter
About materials or floor

Think again of pollution—
We've given nature a mess
Is your array really creative
Or ecological distress?

The classroom setup should include a well organized plan for storing the papers to be sent home. This might be an attractively decorated box in which rolled up paintings can be placed or a shelf near the door reserved for the purpose. A basket hung from the ceiling with a rope and pulley is useful where floor space is limited.

In a school were the classroom joined a long inside hallway each child was given his own space with his name over it and chose the pictures he wished to display.

Every teacher should walk into her room from time to time as if she were a visitor. What kind of impression will she receive of the art programs, of creative output? Fresh ideas? Sensible organization? Conservation of art materials?

Coloring Books—A coloring book destroys the I AM! I CAN! instead of building and strengthening it. Outlines to be filled in say to the child, "*This* is the way it should look." They teach the child to be passive and take orders, to lose confidence in himself and *his* ideas. As he fills in the figures he need not *think*, be original, or creative.

Coloring books stress the point of view of one person, emphasizse a *right* and *wrong* way and inhibit creative activity. When they are given to children in a nursery school or child care center it suggests a clear example of "Goofing Off" on the part of the care giver.

Science   Words of Teacher: "Oh, I can't teach science!'
Words of Wisdom: "Nonsense!"

    Can you brush your hair and create static electricity? (physics)
    Can you dig around a tree and find its roots, bugs, worms? (biology)
    Can you bring snow balls inside to melt? (physics)
    Can you measure the ingredients and bake a cake? (chemistry)
    Can you mix blue and yellow paint to make _____? (chemistry)
    Can you blow up a balloon and let it jetpropel itself around the room? (physics—engineering)
    Can you plant seeds and watch them sprout? (biology)
    Can you go to a chicken farm and watch chicks hatch? (sex education)
    Can you find three different kinds of rocks on the playground? (geology)
    Can you give a demonstration on hand scrubbing? (hygiene)
    Can you pick up nails with a magnet? (physics)

Then…YOU can teach science!

Furthermore…You can and will become an expert on *exploring* and *explaining* the world around you. There is one rule of self-training in science to follow:

    Always ask WHY.

…and if you are lucky your "why" will come before the child's "why" and you will have a chance to go to a library in search of the answers. There are hundreds of basic books on science written for YOU who say, "I can't teach science."

Science surrounds you as does the air, speaking of which, if you sneeze, yawn, or burp YOU are a scientific experiment. Did you ask "Why did I sneeze?" If not, you missed a whole unit of curriculum.

Science Goes Through the Year—Of course no decent scientist would sneeze his way into developing a biology curriculum, so a little planning is in order, at…Science through the year.

At first your tiny self-centered cells (the children!) need training in a few basic rules of personal hygiene, housekeeping, playground safety and ecology. If you spend all of the first month in handwashing procedures before meals, after toileting and painting you will have had a successful science program. Montessori delineated several different steps to proper hand scrubbing beginning with putting the water in the basin and ending with drying every finger. A demonstration of how to use a paper towel to its fullest capacity is an excellent introduction to classroom *ecology* and introduces the idea of absorption.

The capillary action of a sponge in soaking up a spill is science. Sorting the blocks according to size and shape into their proper places on the shelves is Math.

Next you give your first demonstration of paint mixing magic by combining ? + ? = orange. As you cut and scoop out pumpkins you demonstrate chemistry by mixing a batch of pumpkin cookies and roast some seeds, saving some for planting. When skeletons appear grinning and dangling be ready to seize the opportunity to further explore "ME" with a mini unit in anatomy. Squeezing arms and legs, rubbing ribs and spines, and tapping craniums is ANATOMY. (Seq. 2) It is exciting to find your very own structural timbers. The human anatomy theme carries over to houses as you look at a house under construction, see its "skeleton" of rafters and joists and watch its "skin" of siding go on over an inner coat of insulation.

Dramatic changes in weather, plants and animals are taking place as seasons change, so take advantage of crisp autumn days to explore outside. Talk about hibernation, collect seeds and pods, press leaves, cook apples! Bring in a sleeping bag and take turns curling up inside to show how cozy hibernation underground can be. What blanket helps keep houses warm in winter? Where have the birds gone? WHY???

Holiday excitement brings many edible treats, so why not concentrate on a biology/chemistry unit of stirring and baking, tasting and smelling. Stars will stimulate an astronomy course. Create a "moon walk." (Sequence 3, #44)

In some areas of the country science curriculum falls from the winter sky. Science helps us discover likeness and differences in color, weight, shape, temperature, people, taste, smell, touch, etc.!

FEBRUARY is the heart month, and you listen for the thumping inside you. Can you operate a pump? Perhaps you can borrow a portable sump pump. Go to a construction site and look for pipes and wires. Where do they go, what do they carry? Compare with human nerves, veins and arteries. (Sequences 6 & 8)

Set a pan of iced water or juice on the table. Any condensation?

Hold a pan cover over boiling water. What forms inside? Set on table on sheet of paper, lift and look. (Sequence 6)

BLAST OFF! with a balloon (Sequence 7, #78)

Bring forsythia and other branches of flowering shrubs indoors and force them to bloom. Watch for the first signs of spring.

No playground is complete without a section of gutter to prop up and course water through (Seq. 8, #45—Gutter Projects). Tiny mud dams built around drains collapse when a flood of water from a hose pushes against them. Tiny sailboats wisk over a puddle and galoshes and rubbers dry out by the radiator.

Baby animals enter the school family and ducks demonstrate a whole new way to wiggle our anatomy.

Mud is first-class science. Hunt for and identify tracks, make plaster castings of them. Make hand and feet casts for anatomy classes.

Farming provides an abundance of scientific themes. Sprouting seeds, burrowing insects, the good smell of soil, planting, cows being milked—there is so much to explore. Have a picnic and see how many insects come to lunch!

You may be sneezing your way into science class when pollen counts are high. (Seq. 10, #57, 58, 59, 60).

Math and Shapes—With new knowledge of the capacity for early learning, teachers know that mathematical concepts are interesting and important to children. Math includes *recognition of numbers,* enabling the child to know his address and phone number. *Counting* is math, not for the sake of reciting numbers by rote, but when there is a reason for wanting to know "how many" as when counting out napkins or cookies. Math includes understanding the *concepts of quantity.* A child needs to assimilate fourness, in addition to being able to recognize it and make it.

Seriation is an important part of a math program. The child needs to know and comprehend *"more than"* and *"less than,"* larger and *smaller,* as he arranges objects and people in order of *height* or *weight.* We observe and sort colors from *dark* to *light*; listen to sounds from *loud* to *soft,* and gradually come to understand the total concept of differences in *gradation.*

Shapes in the math program help prepare the way for reading, starting with the simple shapes; the circle, square and triangle. We lay the groundwork for recognizing the difference in letters (b, d) through this early recognition of shapes. Shapes help a child to order his environment, recognizing similarly defined areas. "That round box," rather than "that thing on the table." (Communication through description.)

Much of this curriculum is not new; many have taught such ideas in the early years. The difference is that we are consciously looking to specific goals and objectives, to give children a solid foundation which will later alter their attitudes toward education and learning. Not "You have to know this for first grade." BUT—"You have discovered a new idea!"

Color—Imagine "colorless." Create a wall sized image in your mind of NO COLOR. Try to draw a picture of something lovely in nature using NO COLOR. Take ten minutes and write down all the things you did today that involved the use of color:

got dressed, matching ensemble—shoes
put on makeup
set table—matched cup & saucer
admired fall foliage from kitchen window
identified 5 birds in trees
sorted laundry
made beds—chose linens for each room
made dress—matched designs, threads, trim
bought salad greens, white bread, yellow vegetables
cut and arranged flowers for dinner table
played Monopoly with children
polished shoes
cleaned & reorganized jewelry box—matched earrings
brushed teeth—identified brush by color
played checkers with husband
watched a beautiful sunset!

Our concern with color runs through the entire year. Nearly every activity can be enriched by a color concept. Guiding children in learning and ENJOYING the world of color can be a vital tool in a teacher's hands.

Colors must be used in comparison with other colors, but there will be times when emphasis can be placed on particular colors. Learning to name colors by rote is ridiculous. "Color is experience."

Eating a red apple, or orange
Wearing a green dress & matching ribbons
Having blue eyes and blonde hair
Seeing Robin Red breast
Watching white clouds in blue sky
Picking yelow daisies & purple violets
Carving orange pumpkins
Wearing yellow slickers & red boots
Being black
Seeing silver Christmas stars sparkle
Riding an orange bus
Waving the "red, white & blue"
Running to the window to watch fire engines
STOPPING at red lights
Going with green
Running to red swings
Twirling pink streamers
Playing color lotto
Finding your blue & yellow coat
Sitting on the green rug
Mixing yellow jello
Seeing a rainbow!
Painting red!

Colors are everywhere! In this curriculum particular emphasis is placed on certain colors in each sequence and these color themes are planned to correspond with other activities:

Sequence one: red, yellow, green—tied in with traffic signals

Sequence two:	orange, black, yellow—Hallowe'en, fall foliage
Sequence three:	gray, brown—turkeys, fading foliage, Puritans
Sequence four:	red, green, white, gold, silver, blue—Christmas, Hanukah, Kwanza
Sequence five:	white—all variations of white—sun and shadows
Sequence six:	red, white, blue, pink, gold, silver—Valentines, patriotic themes
Sequence seven:	pastels, shades of green—Easter, spring, St. Patrick's Day
Sequence eight:	gray, silver, blue—rain, water
Sequence nine:	shades of purple, violet—pansies, lilacs, violets
Sequence ten:	blue, white—boats, all bright colors in circus themes

Goals at the end of the year might be:

1. recognition of colors
2. recognition of shades and tints
3. knowledge of mixing colors (What two colors make orange?)
4. names of variations in a color (purple, violet, lilac, orchid)

Animals—Pets in the classroom are a valuable source of learning for young children. Caring for animals, cleaning cages, checking food and water supplies, thinking about who will care for them on weekends—all help to develop responsibility, sensitivity, and compassion for the creatures of the animal kingdom. Many children begin to assimilate the emotional thrust of death through their association with animals.

Some schools offer sign-up sheets where children, with parental consent, can request to take the guinea pig, gerbils, or bunny home for a weekend or during school vacations. Parents are able to determine from such home visits whether they are able to take pets into their homes on a permanent basis. Some soon find that they do not want house pets. Their refusal is easier to explain to a child when they have had the actual experience.

Some teachers cannot have animals, either because they do not enjoy them or school rules forbid it, but they may be able to allow a child to bring in a pet, or set up a reverse loan from home to school, for a day or perhaps longer. (RULES must be established BEFORE the guest animal arrives.)

Visits to a pet shop are exciting. (See Field Trips, Part I) the owner is consulted in advance so the class can go at a time when the shop will not be busy, and he can give his attention to their questions. The children should know in advance whether they will be allowed to pet any of the animals.

OCEAN MURAL

In one school a visit to an aquarium led to a series of experiences for children who lived far away from the ocean. The threes who went loved the dolphin show. When they returned to school they made a beautiful mural. Using wide brushes they painted blue, green and white on the background. Then fish constructed from foil of different colors were set swimming in the water. A teacher brought in a collection of shells, sea moss, sea weed and small pieces of drift wood and a star fish. They talked about each item and looked at pictures in a book to discover where the sea things might fit into their mural. A large sheet of clear contact paper was crumpled then and pasted on over the mural creating the effects of a sparkling sea. The entire picture was framed in a border of construction paper. The effect was striking.

Each month of curriculum suggests some wild animals to be introduced. Children often have some very distorted images of animals from stories, films, television. They observe fanciful creatures who carry on conversations, solve complicated problems, think and act as humans. While such stories may be legitimate entertainment children need "straight" information. There are many excellent wildlife films which show animals in natural settings.

Creative movement, dramatic play, puppets, sensory experiences all help the child to understand animals. When a child "roars," "crawls," "snarls," "climbs," builds a nest with mud and straw, he begins to see the world as an animal might.

The most important attitudes to foster in a child toward all animal life are respect, sensitivity and compassion.

Some animals which are "cute" and cuddly in appearance are really dangerous and unpredictable. Which animals help us? Why do animals kill for food?

Tiny classroom pets are often a child's first exposure to animals. Helping children relate to animals, to understand that they have feelings, likes and dislikes and peculiarities, becomes a foundation for the child's future feelings toward all living things.

Cooking with Children—Eating something you have invented yourself somehow adds to its flavor, and while adult cooks do tire of their own cooking and enjoy a change, children never seem to tire of their own concoctions.

It's fun to measure (math), mix (chemistry), cook (magic), and taste (sensory) your own food. Just the conversation of a cooking session is well worth the effort and mess. Somehow preparing and eating food always becomes a social occasion. Preparing materials, scrubbing up (hygiene) before and after, following a recipe (pictoral or written) develops reading skills, and the ability to follow directions and sequences. "What happens if you leave out an ingredient or add too much of another?"

The simple process of mixing a prepared pudding is enough for threes. Fours make cakes, helping to beat the eggs, measuring the liquid, counting out the ingredients, licking the batter bowl, setting the timer, dividing the finished recipe into portions—all of these activities add to their skills.

Older children can become very proficient in following simple recipes and attending to all the related tasks of preparing a meal. And what satisfaction they glean from the finished product! Nothing makes as great an impression at a parent meeting as a tray of classroom cookies. "Did you eat my cookies?" will be the first question a youngster asks when parents return from their visit to school.

There are times when the whole group can be involved in a cooking activity or preparing cookies for a parent meeting. At other times 4-6 children need help with a complicated recipe. They must have careful supervision when using knives, beaters, parers and ovens.

Recipes printed on large cards, with words and pictoral representations of ingredients are very useful. Cover the cards with plastic wrap or clear contact and devise a way to hang them near the mixing center when preparing a recipe. Children can help to find or draw pictures to illustrate the cards. Store the cards in a box or binder.

Cooking materials (bowls, beaters, measures, spoons, etc.) should not double as toys at water play or in the housekeeping corner. Like the collection of rhythm instruments, they deserve careful use and respect. Each hangs or sits in a special place, clean and ready for use. It is most frustrating to find a tool missing when a group of eager children is waiting to cook.

NOTE: If your school provides meals and has its own kitchen the cook should always be consulted before borrowing from kitchen supplies. In general, it is best to have the classroom cooking center fully supplied with basic equipment. Larger items (stove, beaters) are easily shared as long as pre-planning with the cook is arranged.

Cooking, when properly planned and executed, is good program. It can, however, become a crutch or an easy way out for a teacher who has limited resourcefulness. Food, costly or not, should be used with as much respect as paints, clay or paper products. It must have a purpose when it becomes a part of curriculum. Activities involving cooking should be approved by the director, especially when the products used are "far out" or expensive. In a child care center the dietician should be included in planning since cooking in a daily curriculum may sometimes become a part of nutritional requirements. Even when cost is separate from her budget the cook can often help with purchasing. She needs to be included when meals and program supplement each other.

One kindergarten teacher took her classes on imaginary tours of many foreign countries. Each week the children planned and prepared a meal appropriate to the country they were visiting. Meals were approved for cost as they came from the cook's budget and were carefully checked for nutritional balance and value. (See *Early Years,* Oct. 1974).

Food in art projects: In the past, children enjoyed "playing" with and creating art projects with various food stuffs. "Cheerios" (and other cereal), pictures and marshmallow men, gumdrop puppets, mosaics from seeds and beans, fingerpainting with pudding, chocolate sauce and jello...all such projects may occasionally still add sparkle and fun to curriculum, but teachers should always consider the appropriateness of using such material in a frivolous and wasteful manner, lest we find ourselves teaching children the wrong lessons. As long as children anywhere suffer from hunger and starvation, we must teach our children to treat all food materials with respect and resourcefulness.

Expanding the World   Just a few years ago it might have seemed incongruous to include information about foreign countries and cultures in a pre-school curriculum. Television, the ease of travel and increasing respect for the young child's ability to comprehend that which he cannot see has extended his world to its farthest corners.

It is important to remember that we are not trying to teach children about the actual location of Africa, or "how far away is Japan?" We explore and extend each child's contacts with other cultures and customs through his own family, through trips to restaurants, through movies and television specials and often from daily news broadcasts.

Recognizing and understanding that cultural differences are acceptable and exciting is a vital part of expanding the child's world.

See Field Trips.

Chapter 5

WHAT: SEQUENTIAL DEVELOPMENT

FROM APPLES TO KOALA BEARS

When this curriculum was first written, it was planned around the twelve months of the year. The authors and the *many* teachers who helped to test and develop the activities are all located in New England, where schools open in September and close in June.

It was, then, natural and useful to develop the activities according to this particular school calendar. Children come in September, "Beginnings," when apples are ripe and fall leaves are brilliant red and orange; they celebrate Christmas, Kwanza, and Hanukah in December; tumble in snow during January and February; watch the awakening miracles of spring during April and May; and swim and camp during July and August.

The activities suggested, therefore, follow a logical order of progression and reflect the distinct four-season climate and traditional American holidays which occur through the twelve months.

But as we began to consider extending our ideas beyond our own geographical area, we realized that many would not fit into this field of reference. As our thoughts and ideas stem from our surroundings, so your planning will be a reflection of your life style and locale. If we write extensively about apples in autumn (September in New England) and if apples only appear in supermarkets in your area, we are sure you can transfer the suggested activities to the familiar—pineapples? pomegranates? sugar cane? koala bears?!

If this progression implies a "tight, *planned curriculum*," with no room for creativity—spontaneity, *this is not our intention.*

The success of this SEQUENTIAL DEVELOPMENT of activities will depend on each person's ability to let it reflect geographical areas, classrooms, cultures, personal talents, and *the familiar world of each child.*

The sequences build one upon the other, while at the same time having value separate and alone.

5A. SEQUENCE ONE

Can you remember your first day of school? Always there was a sense of excitement over new clothes, a new pencil box, new expectations and some apprehension. "Will I have a friend?" "Will I like my new teacher?" "Will they like ME?" "Will it be hard?"

As adults we experience some of these feelings on the first day of a new job. Even though we are happily stimulated and challenged, we are sure to suffer some feelings of uncertainty.

One thing that reassures is *recognition*.

In a school for young children it is imperative that *every* staff member, bus driver, teachers, aides and the director of the school let each and every child know he/she was expected and welcome. "She knows my name!" "My driver knows where I live and where my daddy works!" "My teacher said my dress was very pretty!"

It only takes a very little assurance to break the tension and though it may take a long time in some cases for total ease and acceptance, each little moment of comforting friendliness and care builds this person's "I AM."

To help the children gain a sense of identity we focus on stories, rhymes, songs, games and rhythmic patterns based on each *child's name*. *Self image* pictures are made with paint, crayons and collage materials and saved for comparison later in the year. All *children are weighed and measured* and six months later they will be surprised to see how much taller they have grown, how much bigger they are!

The first *shape* introduced in this sequence, is *round;* the first *color, red*. These *familiar* concepts offer a variety of ways to explore the classroom, the home and the neighborhood in between. It will be easy for each child to have successful learning experiences with round and red.

An *apple* is a delicious and popular *food* which is both round and red. This first sequence offers suggestions for many activities based on apples. An old adage tells us that "an apple a day keeps the doctor away," (or gives us good health) but we want children to realize that *cleanliness* is important to good health, so the guidelines will suggest ways to TEACH children *when* and *how* to wash their hands carefully.

Throughout the year the curriculum sequences will suggest many ways to teach *safety*, but in the beginning the focus will be on traffic and *traffic signals*.

Name Games   For an explanation of why we use NAMES in games and songs read "PEOPLE IN THE CURRICULUM." (See index listing for ideas through the curriculum sequences.)

1. *ROLLING A NAME:* Children sit on the floor in a *circle*. The teacher rolls the ball to someone saying the *name* ("I am rolling this ball to Robert. I am rolling the ball to Kathy.") When the children become familiar with the game, they each take a turn. Short periods of this game are better than one long session. A good change of pace at frequent short intervals. (See Seq. 9, Act. #27)

2. *GUESS WHO:* "I am thinking of a girl in a *red* dress. Who can say her *name?*" (Response from one of the children.) Child who responds continues, choosing another child and selecting a particular characteristic. In the beginning, another adult might need to offer first two or three answers.

3. *MIRROR, MIRROR ON THE WALL:* Child stands before a *mirror*. The others find as many ways as possible to describe him "John has brown shoes." He has blue eyes." "He looks sad," etc.

4. *LOST CHILD:* One child is a police officer; another a mother or father. "Officer I have lost my little girl," (goes on to describe her.) Officer finds the child by relating the description to a child in the group. OR: Child approaches policeman and says, "I am lost. I live at (address), in a white house. My telephone number is... ." (See Seq. 6, #12, 13)

5. *RHYMING NAMES:* Make rhyming ditties with *names.* "I am Matt. I wear a hat." "I am Paul, I'm very tall." Or: "Jack, Jack, touch your back." "Harry, Harry, go find Mary." After each child has exhausted all the possibilities with his own name, he can work with classmates' names.

6. *COMPLETE SENTENCE:* Encourage the children to answer questions with complete sentences, (My name is _____) instead of a one word answer. Habits are more easily formulated when started early in the year.

7. *MY CLASSMATES:* First child (Harry) goes to another, touching on shoulder and says, "I came to school and I played with Jean." They form a line. Jean says, "I came to school and played with Betty." Betty joins the line, touching and naming Harry and Jean and adding a fourth child. The game continues with each new child touching and naming those who came before and adding a new one.

8. *NAME TREE:* Plant a many twigged, leafless branch in a pail of dirt or plaster of Paris. Write each child's name on cardboard apples (they can color one side), and hang on the tree. The teacher (or a child) removes the apples at the end of each day. Each morning the child finds his name on a tray and hangs it on the tree when he arrives. Make new name tags using seasonal motifs (i.e. pumpkins, turkeys, stars, mittens). As the year progresses one child can be assigned to hang all of the names as children arrive. Look at names left on tray to see who is absent. Count names on tree and names on tray. Record on a chart and report to teacher.

9. *WHO IS IT:* Take slides of children, or ask children to bring one from home collection. Show on screen and talk about "who it is," "what he is wearing," "what she is doing," "where he is," "who is with him."

10. *MATCH-A-NAME:* Arrange snapshots of children on a large sheet or card. Hold up a name card and choose someone to find the matching picture, or mount pictures on cards and play matching game with name cards, individually or in small groups.

11. *COMPARING NAMES:* Who has the longest? shortest? same as anothers? What names rhyme? Sing *The Froggie Went A-Courting,* for names that rhyme with _____. Think of a name that begins with (letter). (Put three names together in rhythmic patterns. Clap the rhythms.) Example:

Ahummmm   A humm
The first to the wedding was Kathy Brown
She was all dressed up in her very best gown
A hummmmm   A hummmmm

12. *DRAMATICS:* Dramatize some of the nursery rhymes, leaving the concept word for the children to fill in, as "Jack and Jill went _____ the hill." Later when the children are completely familiar with the words, emphasize the rhyming word as, "Jack and Jill went up the _____."

13. *NURSERY RHYMES:* Some practice and understanding of spatial relationships can be developed by using the various nursery rhymes. Emphasize the position words when teaching the rhymes.

Concept	Nursery Rhyme
ON BESIDE	Little Miss Muffet
UP DOWN	Jack and Jill

14. *MAKING BOOKS:* Give each child a blank book in which he can draw, paste pictures or copy words. Put his *name* on the cover in the way you want him to write it eventually. (K'GARTEN)

15. *THEME BOOKS:* make a *round* book. Cut round sheets of paper and staple them together. Put child's *name* on cover. Help the child find pictures to paste inside that show *round, red,* myself, small—big, worms and other.

16. *STOP, LOOK AND LISTEN:* (SAFETY)

> Stop, Look and Listen
> Before you cross the street
> First use your eyes and ears
> Then use your feet

17. *TRAFFIC LIGHTS:* (TRAFFIC)

> I love to skip, skip, skip
> I love to hop, hop, hop
> But when I see a red light
> I stop, stop, stop.
>
> I look to the left
> I look to the right
> And then I push the button
> on the traffic light
>
> If it's red and yellow
> Then I know
> That it's surely safe to go.

18. *TRAFFIC SIGNS:* Use cardboard circles of red, yellow and green as traffic lights to indicate whether an activity center is open or closed. Make a large cardboard rectangle (illustration), trace three circles on each side. Color the top circle on one side red, the bottom circle on the reverse side green, suspend from a hook in each area—expose green side when the area is open, flip it to red when the area is closed—also yellow (slow) 'lights' can be placed in areas where children are apt to run (i.e. hallways).

19. *THE LITTLE RED HOUSE:* (Traditional)

One bright fall morning, a little boy asked his mother, as I know you have asked *your* mother many times, "What can I do, Mommy?"

His mother, who knew lots of happy things for boys to do, smiled and said, "You know, I think this is just the sort of morning to spend looking for the little red house."

"What little red house?" asked the little boy.

"Oh," replied his mother, "the little red house with no doors and no windows and a star inside."

"No doors and no windows and a star inside?" asked the little boy. "What kind of house is that?"

"A very special house," answered his mother.

"How can I find that little red house?" asked the little boy.

"Well, you might walk over to Grandma's house and see if she could help you," suggested his mother.

So the little boy put on the warm, blue sweater his mother had knit for him and he started out to visit his grandmother, who lived down the street and around the corner.

As he walked along, he looked very carefully at the houses he passed, in case one of them might be the little red house with no doors and no windows and a star inside. He saw lots of houses, but not one of them was red, and everyone of them had windows and doors. "What a funny house that little red one must be," he thought.

Soon he came to his grandmother's house. It was white with green shutters, so he knew *it* wasn't the house he was looking for. He stood on tiptoe and rang his grandmother's doorbell.

"What a lovely surprise!" his grandmother said when she opened the door. "Come right in. What brings you out so early in the morning?"

"Grandma," said the little boy, "Mother says this is just the right sort of morning to spend looking for the little red house with no doors and no windows and a star inside."

His grandmother laughed. "Your mother should know," she said, "for it was on a morning just like this long ago that I sent *her* out to look for that little house."

"How did mother find the little red house?" asked the boy.

"As I recall," said his grandmother, "Mr. Wind helped her. Why don't you go out in my backyard and ask him to help you."

So the little boy went out into his grandmother's yard. He stood under her big old apple tree and called, "Mr. Wind, Mr. Wind, please help me find the little red house with no doors and no windows and a star inside." At that, Mr. Wind, high in the top of the apple tree, chuckled. When he chuckled the leaves whispered together and the branches swayed, and down fell a beautiful big red apple, right at the little boy's feet.

He picked the apple up and looked at it carefully and then he began to chuckle, too. "Thank you, Mr. Wind," he called as he ran to knock on his grandmother's back door.

"Grandmother, grandmother," he called, "I think I have it!" He put the big apple on his grandmother's kitchen table. "It's red and has no doors and no windows," he said, "but is it a house and does it have a star inside?"

"Yes," said his grandmother, "it is a house, and a very special house it is, too. It is the home for tiny apple seeds—seeds that can someday grow into strong new apple trees with lots and lots of beautiful little red houses on them."

Then Grandma took the apple and washed it. She rubbed it with a soft cloth until it shone. She took a sharp knife and cut across the apple. There, to the little boy's surprise and delight, were the tiny seeds, nestled safely in a beautiful star.

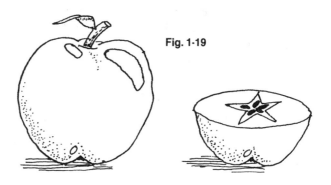

Fig. 1-19

20. *RED—DEVELOPING A COLOR THEME:*Develop a red area in the classroom. Hang red curtains, streamers or tissue paper in a window and cover the sill with red paper. Add a red geranium. Ask the children to gather red objects and pictures from magazines. Play guessing games with the collection of "reds" and make a red book from the pictures. Perhaps a red mat and some cushions can help to create a red cozy corner for reading "Whose Little Red Jacket?" by Mary McBurney Green, pub. Franklin Watts. A monkey puppet wearing a red jacket will help to brighten and surprise the audience at the end of the story.

Put some red objects along a trail of red chalk and have a treasure hunt for red. A long red thread might be used to make a trail or some red foot prints might alternate with green prints to reinforce "left-right" concepts.

At snack time serve a red surprise on a red dish while sitting on a red blanket.

Give each child a portion of red jello powder to mix in individual red paper cups (or make red popsicles from fruit juice).

21. *RED:*

> Red marbles
> smooth and round
> Red flowers
> on the ground

Red shoes and
stockings too
I guess I just
don't like them *blue*!
Is RED your favorite color, too?

Deborah Mitchell Haney

22. *ROUND AND RED:*

What is red?
What is round?
Look at all the things
We have found!

Harriet Chmela

23. *PAPIER MÂCHÈ APPLES:* Tear toilet paper or newsprint into small pieces. Add flour and water mixture until soft and gooey. May be used instantly. Mold like clay—the more it is worked the softer and smoother it gets. It is fun to make a mess and the tearing and ripping of paper is only part of this very satisfying group experience. Form into apples, dry and paint.

24. *PLAY DOUGH APPLES:* Using recipe for Play Dough (See Sculpture), form apples dry and paint or tint the dough before forming. These can also be baked.

25. *FIVE RED APPLES:* (Traditional)

Five red apples, hanging on a tree
The juiciest apples you ever did see
The wind came past and gave an angry frown
(Hold up hand, palm outward, fingers extended)

And one little apple came tumbling down.
(Tuck in one finger)

(Four red apples, etc.)

(Tuck in finger each time an apple falls.)

26. *WHERE OH WHERE:* (to tune of Paw Paw Patch)

Where oh where is little (name) etc. As children are found they are added to the group.

27. *WHERE IS SUSIE?* (to the tune of Thumbkin or Frere Jacques)

Where is Susie? Where is Susie?
Here I am. Here I am.
How are you today, dear?
Very well, I thank you.
Now sit down. Now sit down.

(Teacher sings question and child stands up and answers. If group is very large, call two at once: "Where are George and Harry?" "Here we are," etc.)

Variation: Who Is Missing? (to tune of Frere Jacques)—Children have heads bowed and eyes closed. The teacher taps one or more children on the head while she sings "Someone's Missing." When the child is tapped, he leaves the group, quietly, and hides. At the end of the song, the class must look around and decide who is missing.

Who is missing?
Who is missing?
You don't know.
You don't know.
I'm not going to tell you.
I'm not going to tell you.
Can you guess? Can you guess?

28. *THE MORE WE ARE TOGETHER* (NAMES): This is a good exercise for the teacher who is trying to learn names of children. She goes around the circle, *touching* and *naming* each child.

The more we are together, together, together
Oh, the more we are together, the happier we'll be
For it's Johnny and Kathy and Harry and Debbie
Oh the more we are together the happier we'll be.

29. *GOOD MORNING LITTLE YELLOW BIRD:* (Traditional)
Teacher sings to each child using some color they wear. "Good morning, little (yellow) bird..." Susan answers, "My name is Susan Applebee. I'll tell you true."

30. *RIG-A-JIG-JIG:* Children form a circle and choose a leader who walks around inside the circle, singing:

> "As I was walking down the street,
> Down the street, down the street,
> A little friend I chanced to meet
> Heigh-o, Heigh-o-o, Heigh-ho."

Standing before a child, the leader says in a loud, clear voice, "What is your name?" Child's answer will complete sentence, "My name is Kathy." They take hands and skip or run around outside of circle while all sing:

Rig a jig jig and away we go, away we go, away we go
Rig a jig jig and away we go, Heigh-ho, heigh-ho-ho, heigh-ho!

The leader returns to the circle and the first child becomes the leader and chooses another partner. Children should be clapping or swaying while the couple go around the circle so that they are all involved.

31. *JACK IN THE BOX:* Children scrunch down. Teacher recites in a mysterious voice:

> Down in a box there lives a little man
> He waits and he waits as quiet as he can
> Un-til the lid goes POP!

At the final word everyone pops up.

32. *EXPLORING WITH HOOPS* (SHAPE): Explore *'round'* with hoops. Put on floor in middle of circle. What shape is it? Is it like the ball? How is it different? How many ways can you think of to walk around it? One foot in—one foot out. How can you go through it? Over top of head? Up over feet. Lay flat on floor and walk through. If able to have one for each child, dance with hoops, holding in front of, over head, swinging on arm. Do a dance with three poeple holding onto a hoop. Use lively music. Use balloons and balls with music. (See Seq. 2, #37—Hoop-La)

33. *BEING ROUND:* How many ways can you make round with your body? Fingers? Arms? Whole body? Two people? Many people? A wheel rolls. Can you roll? Another way?

34. *APPLE TREE DANCE:* Ask the children to act out the following:
Tree with outstretched branches. Branches are heavy with apples.
Apples fall from tree....plunk!
Apples bounce on ground....roll.
Reach up and pick apples and bend over to put in basket.
Pick up apples on ground.
Carry apples in a bag.
Carry apples in a basket with two hands.
Walk with an apple on head.

35. *INNER TUBE SEAT:* Fill the center of an inflated inner tube with a colorful pillow to make a comfortable seat in your library corner. (SCIENCE)

36. *MIRRORS:* Use mirrors to enhance self-image. Many children have not seen themselves from top to toe and are fascinated when they look into a full length mirror. Use a large sheet of shiny aluminum foil in which child can see reflection. Compare reflection in a puddle or tub of water with mirror reflection. Use double mirrors which let the child see back of himself. Prop mirrors up on tables so children can draw pictures of themselves.

37. *MY HEIGHT AND WEIGHT:* Make height and weight charts with a space for each child. Allow enough time between weighing and measuring (approximately 3 months) so the children can see the dramatic growth spurts which occur during these early years. The heights for each child should be indicated *separately.* (See chart example below.) (MATH)

HEIGHT & WEIGHT CHART

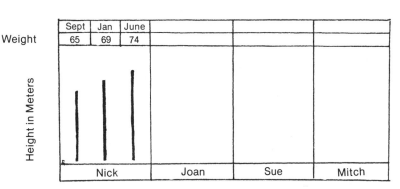

Fig. 1-37 .

38. *TREES:* Make a tree exhibit. Collect and display different kinds of leaves, seeds, bark. Collect seeds and use for art projects. Collect leaves, use for seriation games, trace, press, rub. Paste many to a paper tree trunk to make a mural. Find leaves of same shapes and different shapes. Make bark rubbings (Read *Johnny Maple Leaf,* Alvin Tresselt, pub. Lothrop). (See Seq. 8, #102; Seq. 9, #89) (NATURE)

39. *ONE, TWO, BUCKLE MY SHOE:* Use this traditional counting poem but extend it by encouraging original ideas from children—"One, two, who are you?" (K)

40. *PETS:* Pets are an excellent way to introduce discussions (HEARING) of animals. Do you have a pet? a puppy? What is his name? Pretend you are a puppy taking a nap, under a tree. Where is the tree? Think…what is it near? The house? the street? Close your eyes and imagine that you are a puppy. What do you hear?

41. *PAINTING ROUND AND RED:* The children cut large and small circles and paint with large and small brushes. Use the terms *large* and *small* interchangeably with *big* and *little*. (SCIENCE)

42. *WEATHER:* Make it a habit to discuss the weather each day. Ask the children to tell you what kind of day it is. Construct large weather chart on which the children place the proper symbol or picture to illustrate the weather (i.e. an umbrella, a smiling sun, Jack Frost).

43. *CALENDAR:* Making classroom calendars and talking about them is an activity too often belabored by teachers. It is sufficient to introduce the concept of the calendar and the fact that we change the name of the month and the numbers change each day. The class might make its own calendar and change the dates daily. The children will pick up the concept.

44. *DAILY SCHEDULE:* What is the very first thing you do when you get up in the morning? the next? the next? Another day: "John, what do you do *before* breakfast?" "Susan, tell me about your breakfast. Who was there? What did you eat?" "Mark, tell me what you did *after* breakfast and *before* you came to school." (TIME)

45. *GOOD MORNING!* Say "Good morning" in different tones. Happy—sad—angry—sleepy—excited—hurried. Children try it themselves. (CONCEPTS)

46. *PASTING ROUND AND RED:* Cut large and small circles and cover with red, scrunched up pieces of red tissue. (For toddlers)—Find and cut out red parts of magazine ads or pictures. Paste on a large, red cardboard circle.

47. *VEGETABLE PRINTING:* Slice *beets* in half and use to print on white cotton fabric. Cut a *potato* in half. Dig out a round center portion; dip in paint and print.

48. *PRINTING WITH ROUND:* Print with round shapes of different sizes using bottle caps, bottle covers, cardboard rolls, buttons. Homework:

> To foster observation skills, ask the children to look for round objects at home. What can they find in the kitchen that is round? What is round in their bedroom? Can they bring a list of round items that they cannot bring to school?

(SHAPE—SIZE)

49. *RED REFLECTIONS:* Tape a large circle of red cellophane in a sunny window and watch the red reflection on the floor. Lay various colors of paper over the spot to observe color blends.

50. *ROUND:* Serve round cookies or crackers for snacks. Different sizes, too.

51. *ART:* Make a traffic signal light from an empty milk carton by pasting on circles of red, yellow and green. Or: Cut three circular holes in the carton and paste red, yellow and green tissues over the holes. Cut out the entire side of the carton opposite the tissue-covered holes. Play STOP, GO and WALK games using the traffic light backlighted at the appropriate color by a tiny flashlight.

52. *SETS:* Introduce the concept of sets by putting out crayons, apples, pebbles, cardboard shapes, blocks, etc. Use a large variety of objects, then, when the children build up some skill in identifying sets, use objects of the same kind, but in various sizes, colors, shapes; for example, use round, square and rectangular blocks. (MATH)

53. *LOLLIPOP:* Construct lollipops by pasting circles of colored paper on a throat stick. Give to five children. "It" is chosen to leave the room. One child and lollipop is removed. "It" returns and guesses what color is missing and who held it. (COLORS)

54. *LOLLIPOP TREAT:* Some special day after playing the lollipop game, read this poem and have real treats:

> Little Jack a Dandy
> Had a stick of candy
> Every time he took a bite
> A piece went quickly out of sight
> Little Jack a Dandy.

55. *APPLES:* If possible, obtain by taking a trip to an orchard, sometimes can pick up drops, or buy at fruit stand or grocery a variety (Mackintosh, Baldwins, Delicious, etc.). Sort by size, weight and color. Have a tasting session of the various kinds of apples. Blindfold, and see if children can tell differences by taste. (MATH)

56. *APPLESAUCE—CIDER:* Cook applesauce, apple jelly, apple pan dowdy, apple wrapped in foil on charcoal fire.

> Visit a cider mill.

> Cut apple open—talk about seeds. Flowers in spring. Worm in apple. Ask "Which is worse—to find a worm in the apple you are eating or to find half a worm?" Some fours will get the joke. (Test of intelligence) (COOKING)

57. *APPLESAUCE:* A group of threes were invited to a neighbor's yard to pick up apple 'drops.' They filled a basket and carried them back to school.

> "What could we do with the apples?" asked their teacher.
> "Eat them!"
> "Find the star inside." (See Seq. I, Art. 19)
> "Cook them."
> "If we cook them, what will happen?" asked the teacher.
> "They'll get mushy," responded Gregory.
> "What do you call mushy, cooked apples?"
> "Applesauce."
> "We could make applesauce. It's hard work but we'll have lots of help," said the teacher. "What should we do first?"
> "Wash them, so the dirt gets off," replied Bob.
> The group counted, washed, cut, cooked, mixed, seasoned, and strained the apples. While cutting up the apples, 'half,' 'thirds,' 'quarters,' were discussed. As the apples cooked there was a tantalizing aroma as the children waited for the timer to ring.

Using a tri-pod strainer set over a bowl, they were able to take turns with the pestle "mushing" and "gushing" the sauce.

"What could we do with the seeds?"

"Plant them or throw them away," replied Lisa. The children tasted the cooked apple but most did not like the flavor. "It's not sweet."

"How could we make it sweet?"

"Honey tastes sweet," said one. "What else?"

"Sugar." The sauce was sweetened but none of the children suggested cinnamon. Lisa offered to bring some from home when the teacher mentioned that it could be added to the sauce. The sauce was spooned into small jars and each child shared some of his cooking at home with his family.

"Best sauce we ever had!"

58. *MYSTERY TABLE:* Set aside one table or shelf on which you can put objects, a magnifying glass and picture reference books to encourage the children to discuss and explore independently. This Mystery Table can be a springboard for field trips and special projects if you keep its contents changing constantly.

EXPANDING THE WORLD

59. *TRAFFIC DETAIL:* Talk about traffic safety rules and dramatize on the playground. Use parked staff cars to illustrate the problem of small children running from between two parked cars. Reinforce with small cars in block corner. Go see a traffic light in operation. (SAFETY)

60. *BUS RIDE:* Take the children on a short bus trip. Have them watch for traffic signals, traffic policemen, meter maids and count signal lights. Watch for STOP signs at this time.

61. *POLICE:* Discuss the job of policemen and policewomen — what they wear, what they do, the various kinds of police work, as patrol, clerical, detective work. Most children are familiar with the many aspects of police work because of their television watching. Three's, four's and five's are at an age when the neighborhood policeman is really a friend.

Tell stories of rescue and safety work.

Invite a policeman in for a visit and to show some of the items used in their work, such as badges, radio/rescue equipment and guns.

A guided tour of the police car will include demonstration of flashing light, siren, radio and radar.

Stress the importance of asking a policeman for help when lost.

Visit a police station and/or busy street corner to watch policemen at work.

Discuss school crossing guards and policewomen.

5B. SEQUENCE TWO

Now that our children have good feelings about themselves and their capabilities, we can extend our interest to *family units.* We will discover that all families do not have a father, mother, sister and brother and dog, Spot, and that there are differences in family living; that families work and play together, love one another, disagree, help each other and miss each other when they are separated.

We have surely assimilated 'roundness' and if we have a new shape, the *triangle*, we will have the parts for making *Hallowe'en jack-o-lanterns,* and that leads us to our special color—*orange.* We will find many ways to explore *'over,' 'under,'* and *beside;' 'long,' 'short,' 'loud,' 'soft,'* and the abstract concept of *fear.* Many of the traditional activities of Hallowe'en are frightening for young children, and talking about the difference between *day time* and *night time,* how it looks and sounds, and how it makes us feel, will open the way to healthy discussion. Clouds can be a part of that talking and observing—white clouds in a blue sky, threatening black and gray clouds—and we might EVEN go outside with our family some night to see clouds in front of the moon.

And, of course, CATS! With songs, stories, poems, movement and dramatic play, we will experience 'cat-ness.' It is time for us to think about good health habits and cats furnish us with a good model; they wash themselves, drink milk and take naps.

Fire prevention day will be coming soon, so that will be our focus on safety.

Pumpkin seeds, milkweed seeds, apple seeds—this may be the time when our science corner will be filled with things to look at, read about, make, weigh, count, and cook—and all starting with seeds!

We have a busy time ahead; of course, all children will not absorb everything outlined here, but the exposure will be there, and we will try to make the most of every "teachable moment!"

1. *MY FAMILY ALBUM:* Make a photo album by constructing family member portraits from wallpaper or construction paper. Use sewing scraps, lace, buttons and yarn to dress and adorn. (FAMILY)

2. *MY FAMILY:* Cut out family members for younger children or supply magazines (for

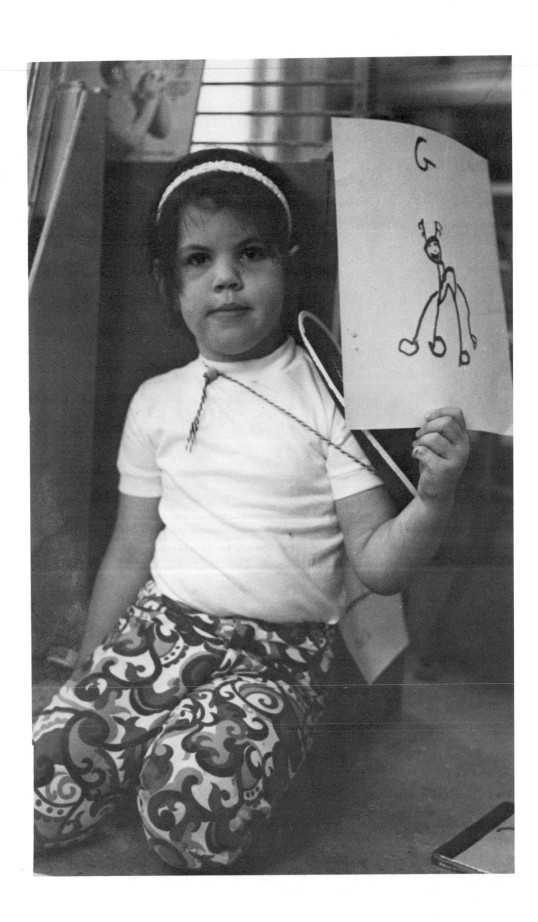

5's). Each child finds a picture for the members of his own particular family group. Paste on a large sheet or into books. Add stories and comments which children dictate about their families. (FAMILY)

3. *CLAY FAMILY:* The children make families with clay. While they are fashioning the figures, have a discussion about family relationships, e.g. Grandmother is daddy's mother, daddy was once a little boy. (FAMILY, LANGUAGE)

4. *FAMILIES:* Children learn that classmates lives are different from their own. Discuss family sizes and activities. Ask each child to describe the people who live in his house. Discuss one parent families. Lead the children in a discussion of the daily activities of each member of the family. Stress the ways in which family members help each other every day.

5. *FIRE DRILLS:* Instructions for evacuation should be posted in several areas.

Read the fire drill procedures to the children and show them where these are posted. Let them hear the sound of the school fire alarm. Talk about PANIC. Stress the importance of walking and taking immediate action when fire is suspected. Walk through an imaginary fire drill and then warn the children that some day soon there will be a real drill. *Plan this drill within the next few days.* Reinforce the procedure again in about a week. (Following these drills, the director should have unannounced drills.) Show how many minutes evacuation took on the clock or a stop watch. A kindergarten class might keep a log and try to improve their efficiency record. (See Safety)

6. *FIRE AND FIREMEN:* Stress the DANGER, but also help children to recognize the need for fire. What causes fires to start in houses? Learn the work EXIT. Look for EXIT signs in school and ask children to watch for them in public places. Talk about the need for a plan to EVACUATE a burning building. Many families neglect this important safety lesson. If children talk about their school activities, parents may be stimulated to carry through at home. Make EXIT signs by pasting letters on oak tag, printing or painting them in red to make signs which the children can take home and post in the appropriate places. Local fire departments often supply safety materials, such as TOT FINDER signs, and are usually willing to come to school and give safety talks and demonstrations.

7. *CLASSROOM FIRE STATION:* REAL fireman's boots, helmet and jacket may be available from the local station. (Perhaps a relative of a child will arrange for a loan of such items.) Hoses, a bell, cartons painted red for fire engines and stations will help stimulate discussion and dramatic play. In the block area, build neighborhood houses from small cartons or blocks, and use toy cars and fire engines to answer fire call. Add hydrants and talk about the danger of blocking them with illegally parked cars.

Outside, lengths of discarded garden hose, ladders, a bicycle siren, and a climbing structure or carton which can become a fire station will stimulate fire play.

8. *FIRE STATION:* Going to the fire station is inappropriate for very young children (2s and 3s). They are sometimes overwhelmed by the size of the trucks, and if an alarm sounds while they are there, they may be very frightened. Some fives will enjoy the trip, but it should be optional and with a high adult/child ratio so a child who is uneasy can be taken out or have a tight grip on someone's hand. Sometimes the fire department will allow an engine to stop at the school.

9. *S-O-S or FALSE ALARM:* Tell the story of *The Boy Who Cried Wolf* and then retell it as *The Boy Who Rang False Alarms.* Stress the danger in such activity. Walk to an alarm box. Play 'false alarm' games (make them up using alarm clock). This helps children become accustomed to sudden ringing of loud bell.

10. *OPERATOR-DIAL 0 FOR FIRE:* Use real disconnected phone (or accurate toy phone) and pre-recorded tape for operator, to practice dialing to report a fire. If fire is in your house—leave building IMMEDIATELY and call from some other phone. Practice telephone calls for "I am lost," "I am hurt," "Mommy's fallen down and can't get up," etc. Many a young child has used "0" to get such help. If your school has an inter-com telephone set up, such calls can be real practice sessions.

11. *YES AND NO BOOK:* Bind several sheets of construction paper into a book; green in one section, red in another. Make a large "YES" on the green cover, and "NO" on the red. NEXT: Discuss all the "NO's" with children and make a list of them. Do the same with the "Yes's." These discussions will take several sessions. Put pictures and words (NO RUN-

NING) into the book. Refer to the book when rules are broken, use to make up stories, keep available on the library table for easy reference. Children love to find the "No's" and "Yes's" to dramatize classroom events. Talk about relation of RED, GREEN to YES, NO.

12. *SPARKY, THE FIRE DOG* by Deborah Mitchell Haney

> He was just a squirmy puppy
> When he came home with me,
> With SPOTS on *every* part of him—
> His head, his tail, his knees!
> He loved to wag his tail and jump
> He'd scramble like a mouse
> And when he grew to be a dog
> He lived at the firehouse.
> He loved to sit beside my dad
> Upon the big, red truck,
> But when the sirens screamed "We-e-eeee"
> He'd hide his tail and duck!
> He'd help the firemen wash the trucks
> He *always* would get wet,
> He'd watch them shine their boots and hats
> When lying on his mat
> And when the station house was quiet
> He would chase the neighbor's CAT!

13. *THOUGHTS ABOUT HALLOWEEN AND THE VERY YOUNG:* It is that time of year when the frost is on the pumpkin and unfortunately, a frosty chill has settled on the sensitivity of many adults. Older children are hooting, howling and screaming as they prepare for the scare orgy of the year. Fathers recall how they once "jumped twenty feet into the air" when some horrible ghost chased them through the cemetery on Halloween.

Mothers stich monster costumes. Teenagers plan horror shows and decorate the playroom with webs, black lights and echo chambers. Older brothers stand before mirrors and paint their faces with bloody scars and slashes.

In the midst of all this fear glory sit the quivering twos, threes, fours and fives. Some are curious, some anxious, and *many are really scared.* Some have never heard of skeletons and ghosts that can really walk through walls. Many have never been outside on Halloween or put on a mask. But now their turn has come to pull a rubber mask down over their faces, urged on by older siblings who tease. "You can't go out trick-or-treating without a mask!" (How long has it been since you donned a mask? You might be surprised at the discomfort just from a physical standpoint.)

Some may think the point is overstated. Others might observe that children watch television horror shows daily without experiencing nightmares. True, but watching such events from the comfort of the living room sofa is not at all the same as experiencing them first hand in the darkness.

Look carefully at your observance of Halloween. Are parents or older children guilty of teasing? "Oh, for heaven's sake, put the mask on; it's supposed to be scary!" or "Don't be a baby still scared of the dark." Are older children teasing and scaring beyond reasonable limits? Does your young child really understand the make-believe part of Halloween?

To the very young Halloween goblins may be just as real as Santa Claus and they may just as readily accept the idea that ghosts can walk through the walls as that of the Santa who slips down the chimney. One image brings them joy and presents, the other may be causing fears. Think about that and help your young children enjoy a Happy Halloween.

14. *SETTING THE SCENE FOR HALLOWEEN!:* Start with yourself by wearing something ORANGE, whether a silk scarf tied around your neck or a whole pumpkin suit. 'Dress' the room and relate it to, and with, pumpkins in as many ways as you can. Use pictures, orange objects, jack-o-lanterns, pieces of orange carpet, round orange circles for sitting on or placemats, games. Perhaps you have an orange cloth for the table. You may

want to get a plastic jack-o-lantern for games. Gather balls, hoops, coins, beads, buttons, masks, and other holiday items. Perhaps you'll serve pumpkin cookies, orange gum drops, oranges, orange juice.

Do the children know what a pumpkin is? Have they seen a real one? Sitting in a circle on the floor, see how many ways you can explore. Where did it come from? How does it grow? What color is it? What shape is it? Is it heavy—light? Does anybody have one at home? Is there another one in the room? A picture of one? Can you tell a pumpkin story— poem—song?

15. *PERKY PUMPKIN:* Using a sheet of orange construction paper, make a paper jack-o-lantern in the following way: Tell the children about a little man and his cat who wanted to build a house for themselves on Halloween. They first found a large piece of orange paper, and since they wanted the front of their house to be extra strong and in the shape of a semi-circle, they folded the paper in half and rounded off the corners to form a semi-circle.

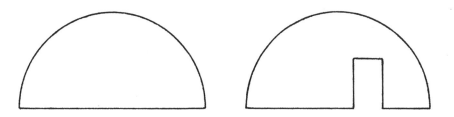

Fold paper at bottom. Then they cut a rectangular door through the double thickness and a small square window to the left of the door.

The cat needed a smaller door that he could open and close by himself, so the little man cut a small, square door to the left of the larger one.

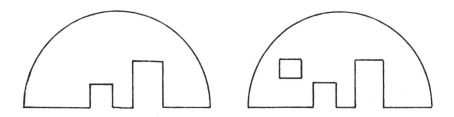

They opened up the semi-circle, by mistake and imagine what they saw! A jack-o-lantern!

16. *PETER, PETER, PUMPKIN EATER:* Teach the children this traditional nursery rhyme.

17. *HALLOWEEN MURAL:* On a large piece of brown paper, help the children construct a Halloween scene, perhaps involving a dark sky, a bright moon and stars and a black cat on a fence. Suggest that each child draw the character he will be portraying on Halloween and paste the picture on the prepared mural, or tie in with a story or poem. (GROUP ART PROJECT)

18. *FREE FORM ART:* Give each child a paper which has a free form line drawn on it. Ask the children to use the line as a start to draw a Halloween picture. If he chooses to dictate a story about it, print in on the reverse side for him. Read these stories to the group during meetings. For variation, ask the children to draw their own free form lines and

trade papers with a friend who will complete the picture. Suggest that they turn the paper in all directions and look at it upside down, sideways, diagonally, etc., before they try to complete it. When all have finished, ask them to notice how many different ways the lines were used.

19. *MASKS:* Many young children are afraid to wear a commercial Halloween mask or find them uncomfortable. (See Act. 13) If you can help your children create masks of their own, you can help relieve much of this concern. They may not wear them as young children often do not like to put things over heads or faces, but they will be proud of their creations. (See Seq. 11, #28 — African Masks)

20. *MAKING FACES:* Put out an assortment of orange and black circles, triangles and crescents. Look into a mirror. Look happy — sad — mad. What happens to your mouth? Can you make a face on your pumpkin to match your mirror face? (ART)

21. *PAPER PLATE MASKS:* Use paper plates to make masks, using collage materials for features and hair. Long strips of colored cloth (fun to tear) make excellent hair. Attach to a small tree branch or dowel (for handle). (ART)

22. *PAPER BAG MASKS:* Use bags which fit easily over heads. Cut out eyes, nose and mouth. Lay out a collection of materials for decorating (yarn, cloth, buttons, construction scraps). (ART)

23. *HAND GHOSTS:* Draw around child's hand on white paper. Mount on black paper.

24. *BAG-O-BONES, Harriet Chmela*
   What's that dangling from that tree?
   A grinning back at you and me?
    Is it real? IT SURE LOOKS SCARY!
    That's a skeleton, "Oh, don't be wary.
     He's not real like you and me,
     He's just a bunch of bones, you see."

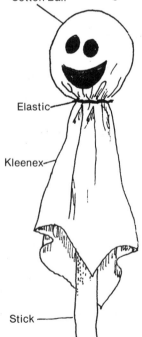

Fig. 2-25

Cotton Ball

Elastic

Kleenex

Stick

FINGER PUPPET GHOSTS

25. *FINGER PUPPET GHOSTS:* Wrap kleenex over a cotton ball on a stick or over finger, with elastics around 'neck.' Draw on face. (FINGERPLAY)

26. *HAUNTED HOUSE:* Ask children to draw a house with their eyes closed. Talk about chimneys, doors, windows, etc. Open eyes and see a queer, wiggly, *haunted house!* (ART)

27. *WINDOWS A-GLOW:* Make two identical pumpkins from orange construction paper and cut out features. Put tissue paper between the two; when placed on the window they glow in the light. (ART)

28. *HALLOWEEN DISGUISE KIT:* For use as parts to a costume, cut out paper moustaches, beards, eyebrows, etc. and decorate an old hat with feathers, lace, fringe, paper flowers, etc.

29. *TAPING STORIES:* (ADULTS) Make tapes of stories and poems you feel you will be able to use to develp curriculum. The tapes will be more interesting if different voices are used — ask older children and adults. Let kindergarten children listen to them alone or in small groups.

30. *SPEECH CLARITY:* To aid in achieving speech clarity for your children ask an assistant to take notes on speech problems and clarity of each child while you are eliciting responses from the class.

31. *PUMPKINS:*
   a. Children sit in a circle on the floor.
   b. Ask, "What can we do with our hands? Creep them on the floor, crawl slowly with fingers, stretch each finger. Walk on floor with fingers. High steps, hopping steps, jumping. Reach up with fingers. Wiggle them. Bring them down slowly like raindrops. Put fingers together to make a tent with them. Bring them together, clap them. Put fingers together, intertwined. Pretend you are writing, painting. Oh, oh, there is something stickly on your fingers. Oooh, Gooey! Pull it off! Try to shake it off! Wash your hands and dry them carefully, wiping between each finger.

c. What do you think about when we say Halloween? (Pumpkins, jack-o-lanterns, ghosts, witches, black cats, owls, skeletons).

d. "Who knows where we will go to get a pumpkin. Maybe to a farm or market?" (At some point the teacher will make sure that all children know that pumpkins originally come from a farm, but for this session the movement is more important.)

e. Walk to the farm. Go through the woods. An owl says, "Whoo! Whoo!" Stop and look up and try to see him. Say, "Who, who are you?"

f. Walk on. See the black cat. Walk like cats, slowly, softly, arching our backs and hissing.

g. At the farm. Find the pumpkins growing on the vine. Make a vine on floor with children. Some can be pumpkins growing on the vine.

h. Feel each pumpkin. "Is it rough, smooth, hard, soft, bumpy? Pick up a small one and shake it. Does it rattle? What shape is it? What color is it? Is it like anything else you have seen? Show me how big it is with your arms. With your fingers. Two people use your arms to show me a great big pumpkin."

i. "Choose a big pumpkin. Lift it up. Oh, it's very, very heavy. How do we walk when we carry it home? How could two people carry it together? Could you roll it? What might happen if you did? What if we put it on a wheelbarrow and pushed it home? What else could we use to carry it?"

j. "When we get home we are very, very tired. We will make the pumpkin into a jack-o-lantern another day. Now just lie on our backs and close our eyes. Let one hand dance like a skeleton. Make both hand fly like witches."

Session might end with the game *Old Gray Cat* (Making Music Your Own).

32. *JACK-O-LANTERN:*

a. Form a circle. Warm up with shaking like a skeleton and stretching like a cat.

b. Stand up and join hands and run to center of circle, saying O-O-O-O-O-O-O-O! Back up saying WHISH-SH-SH!

c. Sway back and forth, moaning and groaning. Ask, "How do Hallowe'en witches fly through the sky?" Ask children to show different ways, one at a time. "Let's all try flying, but be very careful, don't bump into each other." (Play spooky music.) Come back to the circle.

d. "Now let's lift our pumpkin out of the cart. Put it on the table and cut off the top. Save it for a hat! Scoop out insides. Gooey! Icky! Spread the seeds on paper to dry. Cut out the eyes and nose and mouth carefully. Put in a candle and light it. Carry the pumpkin over and put it on the shelf.

33. *MOUSE AND PUMPKIN:* Read *Mousekin's Golden House* by Edna Miller, pub. Scholastic.

Use the story to explore different kinds of movement. Seeds and cranberries popped on the ground. Cat walking softly, Owl swooping down, Mousekin jumping into the mouth of jack-o-lantern, wind whistling and snow blowing. Pumpkin doors settling lower and lower. Mousekin sleeping.

Dramatize the story in mime, no words. Choose music to accompany different movements.

34. *BALLS:* (See also Seq. 5, #16)

a. Stand in circle and warm up ending on floor.

b. Pass a large ball to the right when music ascends. When music descends, start passing the ball to the left.

c. Make a chalk circle in center and place ball in it. Take turns trying to knock it out with another ball.

d. Stand up and bounce like a ball. Bounce an imaginary ball. Throw it to a friend. Catch a ball. Catch a *big* ball, a baseball, a tennis ball, a ping-pong ball. Throw a basketball.

e. Get down on the floor and curl up like a ball. Roll like a ball.

f. Stop and rest on backs.

35. *FINGER EXERCISES:* Stretch fingers. Bend them, make fists, circles, tap nails on floor, make fingers walk, one finger on each hand, two fingers, three fingers, four. Tap

louder, getting closer and closer. Now going away, work back to one finger. (See Seq. 6, #48)

36. *HOOP LA!* A hoop was introduced to the nursery group for the first time. The teacher held it up. "What is it?"

"An O"—"It's round"—"It's a circle."

She laid it down on the floor and asked, "Who can go around it?" Robby walked around the outside. "Can anyone go around it a *different* way?" she asked, stressing the word *different*. Sally walked around the inside. Jim walked with one foot inside and one foot outside. Mary hopped around it. David walked inside and out crossing feet. Kim walked ON it. Beverly slid her feet along over it sideways with her feet on the hoop. "Can you go through it?" the teacher asked. Jim picked it up and dropped it over his head. Robbie stepped in the middle and pulled it up over his head. "I can think of another way to go THROUGH it," the teacher said. After a few seconds of serious thought, Karen walked over one side and out over the other, without moving it from the floor. "What else can you think of to do with this hoop?" their teacher asked. "I can jump over it," said David, and he leaped over the whole hoop. Christine rolled it around her neck—and then her waist. "You said it was a circle. What does it make you think of?" asked the teacher. "A wheel"— "A hubcap?" said Robbie as he picked it up and rolled it. Christine picked it up and jumped along on two feet, bouncing the hoop in front of her.

David used the hoop as a steering wheel and, adding sound effects, went roaring into another room and fell on the floor in an "accident," lying perfectly still.

37. *FIREMAN AT WORK:* Develop a movement session around fireman's duty. He's sleeping. Alarm! Jumps out of bed into clothes, pulls on boots, slides down pole, runs to truck (each person has a special pre-determined job), drives to fire, pulls hose, sprays water, climbs ladder, rescues people, puts on mask to go inside, returns to station, polishes truck, etc.

No more fires, the engines are back in their barns and all the equipment is polished and put away. The firemen climb out of their heavy boots, hang up their slickers and hats and go to their fire stations to rest.

38. *FIRE! FIRE!* Two creative movement specialists conducted the following session, based on fire: (See Seq. 6, #72; Seq. 9, #32)

Following the warm-up session, the children were gathered into a large circle. Some were invited into the center of the circle. Some of the inner group were given red, yellow and orange scarves to represent fire; others were given gray, white and black scarves representing smoke. The outer circle children were the firemen.

The inner group was told to pretend they were fire. "the fire, with red, orange and yellow scarves will kindle and begin to rise and become a big flame. When the fire is put out and dies down, the smoke will rise. The children who are smoke will stay down until the fire goes out."

Children on the outside were told that they represented firemen and fire engines. "How does an engine sound? Make those noises. What do firemen use to put out the fire? Pretend you have hoses. What are some of the noises water makes on fire? Make those noises, too."

The outside ring came to life circling round and round the fire as it rose. The hoses squirted and wooshed at the fire. Sirens and bells sounded. The fire rose higher and higher, brilliant scarves crackling and waving in the air.

"The fire is just beginning to die down, slowly, slowly. There's just a little flicker of light now. The smoke is rising in little puffs, now it's all smoky. There's lots of smoke. We need more water until the smoke is all gone and there are no more flames or glowing embers left." The smoke and fire disappeared under the crouching children, and the fire department gradually slowed and quieted until all was quiet.

39. *ANATOMY CLASS:* At Hallowe'en, introduce a skeleton (from the dime store) and hold an Anatomy Class. Give 'Mr. Skeleton' a class name. Since he cannot sit on a chair with the children, string him up so he can be operated by strings. What is he made of? Can he stand? Sit? Walk? Ask, "Do *you* have bones? Where?" Ask the children to feel, touch, bend, squeeze, rub—to discover what's inside.

40. *SKELETON BUILDING:* On a large piece of paper trace a child's shape. With chicken, turkey, pork chop, beef bones, or with sticks, construct a skeleton inside the body shape.

NOTE: If using real bones boil and scrape thoroughly, *then bake about ½ hour at 300° to kill bacteria. Real bones make a very interesting structure and children who have done this were fascinated with them.*

Show pictures of real skeletons of animals, fish and people. An imaginary animal could also be designed from the bones.

41. *HOUSE SKELETONS:* Talk about the house; how is it like a skeleton? Show pictures of or visit a construction site to see the framework of an unfinished house or skyscraper.

42. *MY SKELETON:* Talk about the various bones inside. Using white paper strips and a circle for the head, ask the children to construct a skeleton on a black sheet of paper using the strips to represent the various bones.

43. *TOOTHPICK SKELETON:* Ask the children to draw self-portraits and paste on toothpicks to indicate their bone structure.

44. *X-RAYS:* Show an x-ray picture. Hang in a window or back to a light. Note likenesses and differences to jack-o-lantern/skull head.

45. *WINDOW X-RAYS:* Paint some windows black. When the paint is dry ask the children to dip their fingers into water and trace skeletons onto the paint. This can also be done on a tabletop, using fingerpaint.

46. *DRY BONES:* Teach the children the old, favorite song, *Dry Bones,* and ask them to touch the various bones in their bodies to correspond with the lyrics of the song.

47. *DARKNESS:* Talk about night and dark. Are they scary? Why? Turn out lights and have children pass various objects around in a circle. See who can guess what is being passed. Teacher walks around circle, touching one child who speaks a word chosen beforehand ("scary," "ghost," "Hallowe'en"); others try to guess who spoke.

48. *PUNCHING GHOST:* Make a ghost by stuffing a sheet with leaves or torn newspaper. Be sure to tie it securely so the stuffing will not fall out when it is used as a punching bag.

49. *CLOUDS:* Take the children outside on a bright day to observe the sky and clouds. Discuss color and shape as well as cloud movement. Can the children discover what makes the clouds move? Can they see differences in the color of clouds? Can they suggest ways to make clouds?

50. *CATTAIL CLOUDS:* Use cattail down or milkweed silk to make transparencies. Glue on blue for clouds. (ART, CLOUDS)

51. *CLOUD PRINTS:* Using bits of sponge, cotton balls, cloth scraps (of various textures) glued to wood blocks or can bottoms, dip into white paint and print cloud designs on sheets of blue paper.

52. *ORANGE DAY:* Relate familiar objects to the color of the pumpkin. Ask children to wear orange. Have real oranges and orange juice. Finger paint on a table top with orange. (COLOR, PUMPKINS)

GAMES: Place several orange and green objects around the pumpkin. Ask the children to put an orange-colored object on top; a green one beside it. Who can find the orange crayon in the box? Sort out green and orange. Take an orange walk.

53. *PINE NEEDLE ART:* Put pine needle spills out on a table. Compare them to leaves. What could you make with them? Brooms? Skirts? Trees? Make a collage by arranging the needles with other kinds of evergreens and leaves. (ART)

54. *LEAF RUBBING:* Collect many varieties of autumn leaves and evergreen spills. Place between folded manila paper and rub with flat side of crayons. (TOUCH, LEAVES)

55. *TREE ARMS:* Trace around arm and hand of child on brown paper to make a tree. Sponge paint to make bright, fall leaves on branches. (LEAVES, ART)

56. *TREE MURAL:* Cut out a wall size tree. Children dip hands into paint to print on leaves. Pieces from an incomplete jigsaw puzzle or torn scraps of gray and brown construction paper can be pasted on to simulate bark. Glue real leaves to the tree and observe the changes over a period of time. (TREES, LEAVES, ART)

57. *LEAF COLLECTION:* Collect many different kinds of leaves and have a sorting session. Classify, according to color and shape. Kindergartners may learn names. (LEAVES)

58. *LEAF TRANSPARENCIES:* Place leaves between waxed paper (keeping waxed sides together) and iron gently. These transparencies can be hung in a window. (LEAVES, ART)

Variation: Cut around the shape of the leaf, leaving about 1″ of the paper as a border and hang the leaves as mobiles. (If plastic sandwich wrap is used, no ironing is necessary.)

59. *LEAF POEM:*

I like to rake leaves
Into a great big hump
Then I go back a little way
Bend both knees and....JUMP!

60. *ORANGE SURPRISE:* Help the children discover orange in the following ways:

Finger paint: place two separate globs of red and yellow finger paint on a table top. As the children mix the colors watch orange appear. (See Fingerpaint) (COLOR, ART)

61. *COLOR MIXING:* Mix red and yellow play dough or salt dough. (See Sculpture)

62. *WATER MIXING:* Using vegetable coloring, prepare jars of red water and yellow water. Provide children with eye droppers or straws and small clear plastic jars. Mix until they make a third color—orange. (Show the children how to use a straw as a dropper by cutting the straw into short sections, dipping the straw into the liquid, blocking the top of the straw with a finger and releasing the liquid by removing the finger.) Print or paint with red paint on bright yellow crepe paper to reinforce the color make-up of orange in the children's minds.

63. *BLACK ON YELLOW:* Print with black paint on bright yellow crepe paper. (COLOR, ART)

64. *FEELY BOXES:* To help discover sensory perception cover the outside of boxes or cans with various textures of paper or cloth. Prepare some with the same texture on all surfaces and others with different textures on each surface. Use a variety of shapes and boxes. A soft, feely box, for instance, may be covered with a soft material and contain soft objects, such as a velvet covering and a few cotton balls inside. A rough box could contain rough objects, etc.

Put assorted items of various textures and shapes into a large box or carton in which has been cut a hand hole large enough for a child to reach inside. The children reach in and identify the textures or shapes of the objects they grasp. Some texture suggestions:

Cloth:		Paper:	Other textures:	
Burlap	Linen	Brown wrapping	Mud	Sand
Canvas	Muslin	Cardboard	Clay	Sawdust
Corduroy	Net	Corrugated	Papier mâchè	
Denim	Nylon	Crepe	Finger paint	
Felt	Percale	Construction	String	
Fur	Plastic	Egg carton	Styrofoam	
Flannel	Rayon	Newsprint	Glue	
Leather	Satin	Tissue	Yarn	
Wool	Velvet	Wallpaper		

65. *PUMPKIN SEARCH:* Take children to a farm to select a class pumpkin. It would be ideal if the pumpkin could actually be picked from the vine, but even a visit to the vines would be helpful. If a farm visit is not possible, take a trip to the supermarket or to a produce stand. The important thing is to have the children participate in the purchase wherever it is made.

66. *PUMPKINS:* Talk about round, starting with the pumpkin, adding ball, apple, orange, beads, marble. A circle is round—sit in a circle—sit on circles drawn on the floor with chalk or tape. Bring in a feely box or round 'treasure box' filled with familiar, round and circular objects (pennies, rings, bracelets, buttons, marbles, beads). Can they find

some of each? Sort out round and circular. Is anybody wearing circles? (Shoes have eyelets.) Are any parts of your body round? Which? Walk around the room. Around the pumpkin. Can you make a circle with your hands? Your body? (ROUND, PUMPKINS)

67. *CLASSIFYING ROUNDS:* Using the same objects, as above. Put all the round things in the box. Find all the things you can eat. Put the circles in the box. Put the round things on some circles. Put the buttons in a bowl. Bring two *different* colored objects—three the same. Call attention to the fact that the class often sits in a circle and a cirlce is round. The feely box (see Activity #66) can be filled with only round objects to reinforce tactically the round shape.

Ask the children if anyone is wearing circles. Some might have on polka dots, while all shoes which tie have eyelets. Suggest that the children make circles of their bodies. (ROUND, PUMPKINS, LIKENESSES/DIFFERENCES)

68. *CARVING PUMPKINS:* The teacher cuts the pumpkin into sections and the children scoop out the seeds. Place the sections upside down in a shallow pan in about one inch of water. (Refill as needed.) Bake in a 325° oven for 45 minutes or until soft. Cool and scrape pumpkin from the shells.

69. *TWO PUMPKINS:* Put two small pumpkins (approximately same size) side by side. Measure and weigh. Compare. Carve out one and set outside. Place the other in refrigerator. Check both each day. What changes are taking place? Talk about decay, withering, rotting. (PUMPKINS, TEMPORAL)

70. *PUMPKIN GAMES:* Using the pumpkin, and perhaps a hoop, develop games with 'IN' and 'ON.' Add other concepts (over, under, behind, in front of, etc.) slowly, as they grasp each. Hide your collection of now familiar rounds and cirlces in and on each other. "Take the candy drop which is 'on' your plate and put it 'in' your mouth." "Sit 'on' the orange circles and put your hands 'in' your lap." (CONCEPTS)

71. *SCARECROW:* Rake leaves and stuff an old shirt or a decorated pillow case to form a scarecrow. Encourage games, plays, stories using "Mr. Scarecrow" as a prop. Do children know what a scarecrow is used for?

72. *MILKWEED:* Ask the children to collect milkweed and be sure each child has one. Let them open the pod, find the seeds, and either blow them away or watch the wind blow them away. This activity is best done out of doors! Talk about how the milkweed seeds are carried and why. Discuss the fact that seeds are always protected by something, some kind of covering. (Try to get the children to volunteer that apples and pumpkins have seeds protected by meat and skin.)

Collect some milkweed pods to take back to the classroom, place them in plastic bags and hang them up where the children can watch them and see what happens when they dry out. (Don't put them into a vase as they will burst open and seeds will fly all over the room.)

73. *BABY SEEDS:* Use this poem to conduct a movement session:

In a milkweed cradle
Snug and warm
Baby seeds hiding
Safe from harm
Open wide the cradle
Hold it high
Come Mr. Wind
Help them fly.   (Author unknown)

74. *MORNING, AFTERNOON, NIGHT:* Discuss when you have breakfast, eat lunch, go to bed, brush teeth, wake up, etc. Introduce clock. Look for pictures which show activities or items which might be used at a particular time of day. Ask the children to arrange pictures in the sequence they would be used. Add clock pictures indicating various times of day. Ask children to match clocks with picture groupings. (TEMPORAL) (See Seq. 5, Act. #58, 59, 60, and 88-95)

75. *PUMPKIN COOKIES:*

2¼ cups sifted flour	½ cup shortening
¼ tsp. nutmeg	1½ cups sugar
½ tsp. cinnamon	1 egg
2¼ tsps. baking powder	1⅓ cups mashed
¼ tsp. ground cloves	cooked pumpkin

Mix the dry ingredients together. Blend in the shortening, then the egg. Add the pumpkin and mix well. Drop by tablespoonfuls onto a baking sheet and flatten the dough slightly with a spoon. Bake in a pre-heated 375° oven for about 15 minutes or until done. Decorate with orange-colored icing and raisin eyes and nose.

76. *COOKING WITH PREPARED MIXES:* Using prepared mixes (79) simplifies a cooking experience for the very young or perhaps with a larger group. For older children and a more extensive "cooking from scratch" experience, see Activity #80.

77. *PUMPKIN RAISIN MUFFINS:*

1 (30 oz.) can Pumpkin Pie Mix

2 pkgs. (17 oz.) Nut Bread Mix

1 egg, beaten

1 cup golden or dark raisins

2 tsp. sugar

1 tsp. cinnamon

Combine the first four ingredients and blend until just moist. Spoon into greased muffin cups and sprinkle with sugar and cinnamon mixed. Bake at 400° for 15 to 20 minutes.

78. *PUMPKIN MUFFINS "WINSKY:"*

1 egg	½ cup sugar
½ cup milk	2 tsps. baking powder
½ cup mashed, cooked	½ tsp. salt
pumpkin	½ tsp. cinnamon
½ cup butter, melted	½ tsp. nutmeg
1½ cups sifted flour	½ cup seedless raisins

Beat the egg slightly with a fork. Stir in milk, pumpkin and butter. Blend dry ingredients and stir in just until flour is moistened. (Batter should be lumpy.) Fold in raisins. Fill greased or pumpkin muffin cups 2/3 full. Sprinkle 1/4 tsp. sugar over each muffin. Bake 18-20 minutes at 400°. Makes 12 muffins.

79. *PUMPKIN BREAD:*

3 cups sugar	1 tsp. cinnamon
1 cup oil	1 tsp. nutmeg
4 eggs	⅔ cup water
3½ cups flour	2 cups pumpkin
2 tsp. soda	¾ cup walnuts
1½ tsp. salt	

Combine sugar and oil. Add eggs and beat. Add dry ingredients with water. Add pumpkin last. Fill 2 loaf pans 2/3 full. Bake at 350° for 95 minutes.

80. *SEEDS:* Brown pumpkin seeds in butter or oil. Sprinkle with salt. Eat! String pumpkin seeds to make necklaces; alternate with macaroni, beans or popcorn.

81. *JACK-O-LANTERN ORANGES:* To make tiny jack-o-lanterns cut off stem end of an orange and hollow out the pulp. Draw a face on the shell and cut it out using sharp, pointed scissors.

5C. SEQUENCE THREE

Many children in a mobile society have little opportunity to establish close relationships with *relatives* outside the immediate family. *Thanksgiving* is often a time for *large family gatherings* when grandparents, aunts, uncles and cousins come for visits. Children learn about *visiting and being guests* as well as *hosting company.* Anticipate some of the situations which may occur through dramatic play based upon the many ways the visitors will *travel* to get to their destinations.

Children will experience *cooking* for large family gatherings and special holiday menus and much about *pumpkins.*

The first *settlers* in America and the *Indians or Native Americans* who were there to greet these *Pilgrims* and their first Thanksgiving together will be themes for many classroom activities. Teachers should be careful to separate *cultural myths* from accurate information in discussions about Pilgrims and Indians.

Introduce the children to Indian culture by helping them to enjoy:

1. *POW-WOWS AND POTLATCHES:* Pow-wows are meetings or councils of Indian tribes, usually held before some tribal undertaking. Potlatches are lengthy feasts given to the tribe by a member aspiring to be chief.

Story time and discussion time can take place on an Indian blanket (or your version of one) with the tribe sitting cross-legged, Indian style, and a campfire of sticks illuminated by red foil or tissue paper to lend atmosphere. The teacher, as the chief, might wear some type of Indian dress (a headband around the forehead with a feather stuck in the back). (Suggestions for simple costumes—Activities 4-12)

One topic of discussion might be the important role the Indians played in the first Thanksgiving. Clarify the words "Indian" and "Native American."

2. *INDIAN SYMBOLS AND TRIBAL NAMES:* Design tribal symbols and make up badges for each little Indian. Help the children choose a tribal name and a tribal color. (Relate the idea of tribes to families, and more particularly, to their school family.) Illustrated below are some Indian symbols and their meanings, which may be used.

3. *INDIAN NAMES:* After the chiildren have decided on a tribal name and colors, hold a pow-wow to choose Indian names for the children. Some suggestions to give the children so they can work out their own names are as follows:

> Robert found an Indian arrowhead, his name might be Good Hunter.
> Betsy has such long braids, we could call her Betsy Long Braids.
> Steven is the tallest so he might be Cloud Toucher.
> Lisa has a tiny voice. Her name could be Whisper Speaker.
> Other possibilities include Golden Curls, Deep Blue Eyes, Freckle Cheeks, Good Thinker and High Jumper.

4. *DRESSES AND VESTS:* Can be easily cut from brown paper or grocery bags. Cut the bottom for a fringed effect and decorate the body with circles and rectangles, cut from foil or tissue.

5. *TUNICS* can be made from old sheets, folded lengthwise, with the shoulders of the tunic cut on the fold. If sheets are not available, old shirts can be used. Remove the collar and cut the sleeves short. Fringe the sleeve edges and the bottom. Decorations can be put on the tunics in several ways:

a) Designs can be crayoned on cloth, then ironed in.

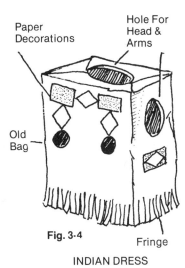

Paper Decorations

Hole For Head & Arms

Old Bag

Fig. 3-4

Fringe

INDIAN DRESS

Hole for Head

Fig. 3-5

INDIAN TUNIC

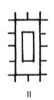

= MAN—HUMAN LIFE

= BROKEN ARROW—PEACE

= CROSSED ARROWS—FRIENDSHIP

= SUN SYMBOLS—HAPPINESS

= BIRD—CAREFREE, LIGHTHEARTED

= BUTTERFLY—EVERLASTING LIFE

= RATTLESNAKE JAW—STRENGTH

= SUN'S RAYS—TRUTH

= BIG MOUNTAIN—ABUNDANCE

= 4 AGES—INFANCY, YOUTH, MIDDLE AGE, OLD AGE

= SNAKE—DEFIANCE

= CACTUS FLOWER—LOVE

= TEEPEE—TEMPORARY HOME

= HEADDRESS—CEREMONIAL DANCE

= ENCLOSURE FOR CEREMONIAL DANCE

= DEER TRACK—PLENTY GAME

= RAIN CLOUD—GOOD PROSPECTS

= RAINDROP/RAIN—PLENTIFUL CROPS

= MORNING STARS—GUIDANCE

b) The cloth can be painted by attaching it to an easel or stretching it over a table. (If possible, use natural dyes from berries, beets, coffee, tea, fruit juices or even the juice from pumpkin pulp.)

c) Hammer color spots into the cloth, using peas, vegetable skins, leaves, grasses, crayon chips, etc. (Let the children try using the style of hammer used by the Indians—a flat-surfaced rock.)

6. *BIRD COSTUMES* which resemble the Indian bird costumes can be made by using a slip or plain dress as foundation. To the foundation, sew on rows of feathers made from crepe paper which has been fringed. Take one sheet of crepe paper, fold it lengthwise and cut a fringe of feathers as shown in the illustration. Add tiers of feathers until the costume is as long as desired.

INDIAN BIRD COSTUME

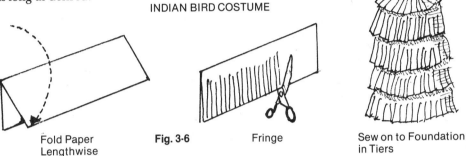

Fold Paper Lengthwise   **Fig. 3-6**   Fringe   Sew on to Foundation in Tiers

7. *HEADBANDS* can be made by the children by decorating strips of cloth with beads, jewelry, colored scraps or feather. For younger children the strips should be long enough to tie in back. Older children can sew a piece of elastic on each of the ends to make a snug-fitting headband. Discarded leather belts and corrugated paper strips also make good headbands.

8. *MOCCASINS* for little Indians are made by cutting off the bottom of a foot-sized paper bag, according to illustration (at right), fringing the front flap and tying the moccasin on with a string. The flap and sides can be decorated with Indian designs.

9. *AMULETS:* Drop blobs of plaster of paris on waxed paper into rounds about one and a half inches in diameter. When hard, paint with acrylic paint. Put a paper fastener in before dried and hang around neck with length of gimp.

10. *MASKS* can be made from medium sized paper bags or small cartons which fit over the face and head. Decorate the head masks with papier mâche, tissue or foil designs.

11. *HEAD MASKS* can also be made from plaster of paris strips, wrapped around a blown-up balloon and dried. When the plaster dries, the balloon can be deflated and removed. The back half of the shape can be cut away, holes pierced on either side, and elastic inserted through the holes, across the back, to hold the mask on securely. Eyes, nose and mouth holes should be cut and the mask decorated. (See Seq. 4, #50)

Decorations of Cloth, Beads, Paper, etc.

Fig. 3-7

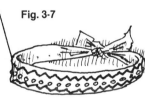

INDIAN HEADBAND

SPECIAL REMINDER
Be sure to provide a safe place for each child's costume, mask, etc. If separate boxes can be secured, encourage them to decorate the box with their tribal name, their Indian name and symbols.

12. *WAR PAINT* can be made from red clay, berries, charcoal, shaving cream, eye shadow.

13. *TEEPEES* can be made from throat sticks, inverted cone cups, with pipe cleaners or toothpicks or sticks gathered outside covered with construction paper.

14. *BRACELETS:* Cut a band of cardboard one inch wide and fasten ends with masking tape. Cut a colored paper napkin into strips. Dip each strip in liquid starch and wind around ring. Build up several layers, letting dry between layers. When complete, paint with Indian designs.

Fig. 3-8

Tie on Shoe with String

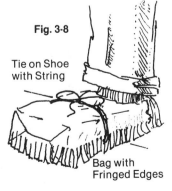

Bag with Fringed Edges

MOCCASIN

15. *INSTANT COSTUMES:* Make with large sheets of cardboard or poster board. They should be large enough to cover the whole child, but not so cumbersome that he cannot hold it up. Cut a hole for the face and decorate the panel to represent the person (fireman, queen, storybook character, etc.) or animal desired. Use cloth scraps, trims, buttons, furry fabrics; add tails and fringes of yarn or paper.

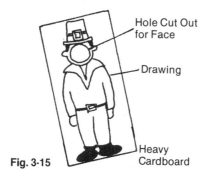
Hole Cut Out for Face — Drawing — Heavy Cardboard
Fig. 3-15

Child Holds Costume in Front of Him

16. *BEADS FOR NECKLACES* can be made from salt dough (see Sculpture) balls. Each must have a hole for stringing put in before it dries. When dry, the beads can be painted. Dried lima beans or other bean varieties also make interesting necklaces. The beans should be soaked overnight in dye and strung while wet on bead floss or fishing line. Colored macaroni and cranberries are two more variations.

17. *INDIAN VILLAGE:* Divide class into groups (tribes) and construct an Indian village, each group making its own 'temporary home,' using the various types of shelters suggested.

a) *Sticks tied together* and covered with sheets, old canvas or tarpaulin, burlap bags, cardboard panels. Paint on designs.

NOTE: A see-through teepee of clear poly with bright leaves and grasses to decorate it would be an especially pretty sight.

b) *Lean to's* from sticks and boughs or cloth and cardboard.

NOTE: Protect cardboard structure from weather with poly.

c) *Tents* to make of any shape from ropes and blankets or from natural materials. (See illustrations.)

BARK LEAN-TO

Bark from Sticks

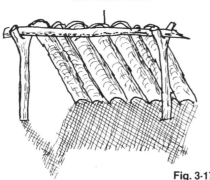

Fig. 3-17

LEAN-TO-FRAME
(Thatched Lean-To)

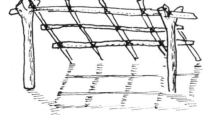

TEEPEE

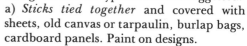

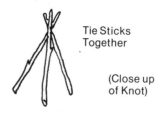
Tie Sticks Together

(Close up of Knot)

General Pattern for Canvas

Cover with Canvas and Decorate

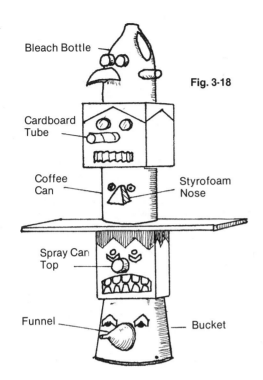

Bleach Bottle

Fig. 3-18

Cardboard Tube

Coffee Can

Styrofoam Nose

Spray Can Top

Funnel

Bucket

18. *TOTEM POLES:* Anchor a pole about 2 inches to 3 inches in diameter. Set into cement, over which totem sections can be 'threaded.' This makes the totem secure and perhaps even permanent depending upon construction materials. It can be a colorful sculpture on your playground. Build sections from cartons, large spools (what else?). Perhaps this will be an inter-tribal activity, each making one unit with a grand assembly to put it all together.

Decorated cartons can be separated by brightly colored plastic bottles and reels. Flat boards can be painted and bored to slip over pole and give 'arm' effects between boxes. This totem pole was made by kindergarten children. They used such materials as: tops of spray cans (nose), cardboard tube (nose), nut cups (eyes), egg cups (teeth), metal roll ends from a copying machine (eyes), styrofoam packing material (nose), corrugated cardboard strips (mouth and teeth), plus old cardboard boxes and plenty of bright paint to create a six-foot totem pole!

19. *BEAN MOSAICS:* Make a design or picture on a piece of cardboard, Apply one kind of dried bean, peas, rice, lentils, barley, etc., at a time. Shake off residue and let dry before applying another kind.

20. *SAND PAINTING:* Dye sand in different containers. Apply as described above. Be sure to work on a paper which can be lifted up and excess poured from one corner back into container.

Indian Instruments

21. *HOOP DRUMS* may be constructed, as follows:
Bend stiff, sturdy cardboard into rings and stretch heavy cloth or plastic coverings over both sides.

Saw heavy cardboard tubes into three or four inch sections and stretch inner tubing, canvas or leather over them.

22. *TOM—TOM:* Make tom-toms from hollow logs, sticks or steel drums. Also, tip plastic wastebaskets, bowls, pails and dishpans upside down for different sounds.

23. *HAND DRUM:* Make hand drums from coffee cans (and other cans) with both ends removed and replaced with plastic lids. Paint with enamel and decorate. Attach string or gimpe handles. Give each child his own drum; they may be introduced on special occasions and kept in safe place.

24. *PIPES AND CALUMETS:* These are the traditional symbols of Indian peace talks, conferences, pow-wows, friendship. Hold ceremonial pow-wows as get acquainted sessions. Each is given a ceremonial fancy straw and as a bowl of bubbles is passed around the circle and the great chief (teacher) calls out his name, each takes a turn blowing a "friendship" bubble. Another assistant might tap the rhythm of each name as the rest chant it.

25. *PEACEPIPES:* Can be simulated by attaching a plastic straw to a stick, then decorating by winding paper, cloth, or string down the length, being careful not to crush the straw. Add feathers, streamers, a tie to hang the pipe around the neck!

26. *WAMPUM NECKLACES:* String from colored macaronis, seeds, spools. Make Indian badges and designs from seeds, feathers, macaroni, stones.

27. *THANKFULNESS:* Record children's thoughts about thankfulness. Make them into booklets, poems, stories. Ask children to illustrate their feelings.

28. *VEGETABLE AND FRUIT QUIZ:* Pin a picture of a fruit or vegetable on a child's back. He stands with back to class and tries to guess what it is by asking questions of his classmates. (See #74)

29. *BOUNTIFUL BASKET:* Use real fruits and vegetables for many, many games of counting, seriation, sorting, etc. Introduce less familiar foods, such as unusual squash varieties.

30. *RESTAURANT MENUS:* Make menus by pasting pictures of food items on cards. There should be about six foods on each card. Have corresponding pictures of individual

foods in a play kitchen. Children seat themselves at a table; the appointed waiter takes orders chosen from the menu cards. He goes to the kitchen to fill orders by selecting appropriate matching pictures. These he serves his customers on paper plates. Encourage complete sentences in conversations, i.e. "I would like peas and apples." "Here is your hamburger and a dish of peaches." (See Seq. 8, #17)

31. *TRAVEL POSTERS:* Discuss faraway places where relatives live. What are these places like? Climate? Houses? Scenery? Choose three or four places and divide the class into small groups to put together travel posters from magazine pictures or drawings of each place. Cut large letters from magazines to make the name of the place. Older children may wish to make their own individual posters. Use the posters as props in railroad stations, and for story telling about, "My uncle is coming to visit from Chicago.

32. *TRAINS AND BUSES:* Provide props and stories to encourage imaginary trips by train and bus. Arrange seat blocks in rows to make an aisle, make tickets, schedules, fare boxes and stations. Use rhythm instruments to create sounds of trains and buses. Discuss where the children are going—how long will it take? where will they eat? where are the bathrooms? beds?

33. *GRANDPARENTS:* Ask each child to tell about his grandparents, giving a physical description, telling where they work, what are their hobbies, where they live and the stories they tell about the child's parents, when the parents were young. Write down the dictated comments and make into books which the children may illustrate. Cut magazine pictures of people or use drawings by the children as cover art. (See Grandparents' Day.)

34. *ELECTIONS:* Children can begin to understand the idea of making group choices by voting through simple elections at school.

> One group voted (behind a sheet) for a snack of "ORANGES" or "APPLES." An excited youngster announced that evening at supper—"We voted oranges!" His parents had been absorbed in political election campaigns for weeks and suddenly he was proud to be included in the election process.

In another classroom, the threes dropped a round or a square paper into a slot to choose "round" or "square" crackers for a snack. The "ballots" were sorted and counted to find out the "election results." An added "referenda" item consisted of making a mark on the "ballot" with a brown crayon indicating "peanut butter" on crackers.

One teacher made a voting booth out of a large carton which became a very popular way to decide issues throughout the year.

It is fun to have a "popularity" contest between two major candidates for the presidency. Posting news items and magazine articles helps to reinforce and stimulate interest in current events. But children will gain more from elections which offers a chance to vote about something which affects their daily lives in a tangible manner. (See Seq. 11, #91—Storybook Day)

35. *CHOICE BOARD:* A system used to train children to make activity and interest center choices at the beginning of the day. The "voting machine" or choice board is a board (see illustration) on which each child has a square labeled with his name. The interest areas (BLOCKS, HOUSEKEEPING, WATERPLAY, etc.) are labeled with signs, each a different color, and the numbers of children allowed there at a particular time.

BLOCKS-4   HOUSEKEEPING-3

Fig. 3-35

Tickets or "ballots" are color coded to correspond with each area and the number of tickets for each area will correspond to the number of people allowed to use it at a given time.

Each child chooses the area where he wishes to work and puts a ticket in his name square. When he is finished in an area, he returns to the choice board, removes the ticket from his space and makes another choice.

A teacher might also make the choices before the children arrive in order to start an individual or a group in a particular activity.

The number of children using an area can be controlled daily by the number of tickets offered by the teacher. For example, extra tickets are offered for special projects, such as carving a pumpkin, which might be limited to three children. This is explained to the children during the meeting at the beginning of each day.

Chris	Ann	Beth	Extras
Amy	Mike	Nancy	
Laurie	Ray	Andy	
Bill	Dan	David	

Fig. 3-35

Velcro Patch →

36. *AUTUMN WHISPERS:* Ask children what words make them think of Autumn (fall). List the words, such as leaves, pumpkins, chilly, color, raking, etc. Each child may want to draw a picture of his particular word and others may try to guess what the word is. (See also Autumn: Theme and Variations—Act. 42, 43)

37. *BARE TREES:* Show pictures of trees without leaves. Ask children how they think trees must feel when they lose all their leaves. Record their answers and read them back.

38. *SIMPLE INVITATIONS:* Children decorate colored folders with pictures they have drawn or cut out and paste a mimeographed message inside. Older children may print 'PLEASE' or 'COME,' etc.

39. *FAMILY TREE:* Hold lunch table and 'meeting' discussions and talk about grand-parents, aunts and brothers and sisters. You might construct a family tree in the following way: (PROJECT FOR PARENTS)

Tree Chart—cut trees (▲) from large size construction paper. Make leaves by tracing hands, rubbing real leaves and cutting out impression, or tracing patterned leaves. Each leaf represents a person in the family. Each person has a place on the tree. The grand-parents (or great-grandparents) are at the roots, and each family group occupies a special place on a branch. The child is at the very top. (SHAPES, COLORS)

40. *HOUSE CHART:* Give each child a large square of paper to serve as a house. Also give him a triangle for the roof and squares or rectangles for the windows. He now can paste his house onto a large sheet of paper. Ask the children to either cut pictures from magazines or draw faces representing family members and paste these pictures in each window of the house. The whole family may also be fitted into one large picture window.

41. *HOLIDAY TABLE:*

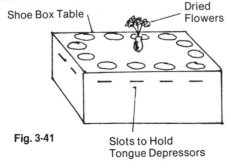

Shoe Box Table

Dried Flowers

Fig. 3-41

Slots to Hold Tongue Depressors

Provide a shoe box for each child. To make holiday tables, ask the children to cut horizontal slits one half inch down onto the sides from the edge of the box bottom. (See illustration.) These slits should be just wide enough to hold tongue depressors or small, wooden ice cream spoons. Paste simple table decorations on the box. The family members, represented by the tongue depressors, can be decorated with cloth, faces and yarn hair. When decorated, the family takes its

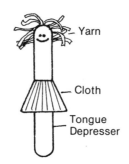

Fig. 3-41

Yarn

Cloth

Tongue
Depresser

assigned places around the table. A piece of tape on the underside of the box, across the wood of the spoon or the tongue depressor, will keep each family member upright and seated properly. Reinforce spatial concepts by discussing who sat beside whom, who sat across from whom, who sat down first, etc. Each child might bring his shoe box family to visit another's and thus see the different interpretation of customs. Add toy cars, buses, trains, planes and boats to surrounding area so children can select type of transportation used by family members coming to visit.

42. *AUTUMN: THEME AND VARIATIONS:* A single theme word "autumn" was suggested to a class of five-year-olds and their teachers. The following ideas were the results of a "brainstorming" session. Many were used to develop activities in several areas of the curriculum.

GENERAL IDEAS

Golden leaves	Indians	Storing nuts
Thanksgiving	Feathers	Sleeping
Turkey	Flying South	Squirrels
Pilgrims	Migration	Pine needles
Mayflower	Harvest	Chilly
Frost	Hibernation	Fog
Rake	Anti-freeze	

HIBERNATION

Animals gathering food	Insulation (fur, what keeps a house warm?)
People gathering food	Gathering seeds
Tunnels (chippies sleep in them)	Classifying things (floaters, stickers, animals)
Bears in Caves	Cocoons and butterflies
Deep freezers	

MIGRATION

Birds	Maps	Gathering Seeds
Climates and Seasons	Suet and Peanut butter feeder	Classifying seeds
Winter birds	Flocking	Travelling
Feeding winter birds	Bird feeders	Flying and planes

FROST

Lacy pictures	Ice	Gray skies
Anti-freeze	First snow flurries	Mittens and hats
Lace doilies (frost pictures)	Bringing plants inside	Temperature, cooler, chilly
Cloudy sun	Dews and Fogs	weather
Dripping windows	Sneezing	Coughs
Storm windows	Breathing on glass	Frost bite
Fuel and furnaces	Condensations	

43. *AUTUMN HAIKU:* A simple poem like the one below might also stimulate program ideas. (The poem was also the result of the "brainstorming session" described above.)

In fall the frost comes
leaving lace on window panes
putting things to sleep.

Carl Chmela   Age 11

44. *SPACE WALK:* Toss feather, blown up ballons or sheets of paper into the air to observe 'weightlessness.' If possible show a movie in slow motion. Ask the children to walk as if weightless, relating to astronauts walking in space. Tie tethers to belts and confine space walk to length of tether. (SPACE)

45. *MOON WALK:* Place the bottom half of a large appliance (SPACE) carton (sides about 18″ high) in a small, confined area of the classroom. Fill half full with styrofoam packing bits. The sensations of walking through, lying in, rolling in, tossing this 'moon scape' are a marvelous stimulant to understanding what moon walking in a weightless state might be like for moon explorers. There is also the added fascination of the *static electricity* generated in the styrofoam bits and causing them to cling to the astronauts.

46. *ROCKET FLIGHT:* Ask the children to imagine they are rockets with pointed cones (hands together over their heads) and blast through space. In discussion, have them compare the difference between a rocket moving through space and an astronaut moving through space. (See also Seq. 7, #78 — Balloon Jets.) (SPACE)

47. *INDIAN WALK:* Explain that Indians going through the woods on a hunt walk very quietly. Their soft-soled moccasins made this possible. Have the children take off their shoes and walk as quietly as possible over a newspaper trail. Try the same activity outside on various surfaces, (grass, pine needles, leaves and pavement). (INDIANS)

48. *DRUM TALK:* Explore various rhythms by sending and answering the same patterns between two (or more) groups. (*Indian Red Feather*, recorded by Young People's Records, good source material). Use a variety of drums and strikers. (See Drums, items 21, 22, 23 of this sequence.) (INDIANS)

49. *STAMP:* Conduct a session with such statements as: "Stamp big, big holes in the ground. Fill the space with your body. How many ways can you put your WHOLE self on the floor? Push your arms through the walls, ceiling," etc. (See #57)

50. *WHAT'S INSIDE MY BOX?* Ask the children: "Imagine a box, a big box, a teeny box. How big is the box? Show with your hands. Put something inside; is it something heavy or light? Lift the imaginary box and see if we can guess how heavy it is by the way it is lifted. Think: Big boxes can hold feathers. Tiny boxes can hold rocks. Pass the boxes around. Carry a big one with a friend. Move them in wheelbarrows, in carts."

51. *BOXES:*

> One teacher used boxes, as follows: The teacher emptied a bag of many boxes of different kinds, sizes and shapes on the table. "What are we going to do?" Anne asked, picking up a stocking box. "How could we make it *longer*?" asked the teacher. Bobby picked up a necklace box and placed it *next* to the *first*. They used masking tape and fastened them *together*. Judy added another *smaller* box to that. "How can we make it *wider*?" Nina and Bobby placed a box on each side and taped them. "Could we make it *higher*?" she asked. Anne and Bobby discussed how to make it *higher*. They taped one of the *longer* boxes upright on the original structure and another *smaller* one *on top of* that. "How many boxes are left?" They counted "*four*." "Which one is the *smallest*? biggest?" "Which one would hold the most?" There were two separate covers. Lisa said, "This one's *square*." Ellen said, 'This one's a *rectangle*." By this time, eight children were standing around the table. "Let's tape the rest on," the children said. "It looks like a building!" two children exclaimed. "Let's make an apartment house," said Bobby. They added the rest of the boxes and put their creation on the table to be admired. (See Seq. 7, #109.)

52. *WHO'S WALKING?* Cut, and paste in folders, pictures of people of various ages and occupations, such as: babies, older people, astronauts, divers, dancers, soldiers, etc. Give each child a folder and ask each to walk in the same way as the person pictured in his folder. The other children guess the age or occupation of the person being mimed.

53. *TRAIN SOUNDS:* Use sandpaper blocks, sticks, bells and oral sounds to simulate sounds of trains. Start slowly, pick up speed, climb a steep hill, belch steam, whistle at crossings. Play a recording of real, train sounds, if possible.

54. *ELASTIC HOOPS:* Use half inch, dressmakers elastic sewn in a looop (about 5 yards). Variation — Cut sections of rubber from large inner tubing. Explore motions with the elastic such as:

    a) Standing or sitting in a circle with everyone holding the elastic. Change the shape of the elastic by moving about while still holding on.

    b) Make sounds by 'plucking' the hoop. Change these sounds by stretching and relaxing the hoop.

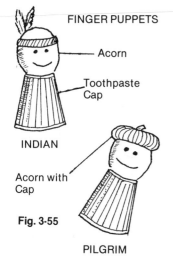

FINGER PUPPETS

— Acorn

— Toothpaste Cap

INDIAN

Acorn with Cap

Fig. 3-55

PILGRIM

c) Create shapes by stretching the hoop around two, three, four and five people. (See Seq. 5, #61)

55. *TEN LITTLE INDIANS:* (TEN LITTLE PILGRAMS)
Sing this traditional song, changing words to sing about Pilgrims. Make Indian finger puppets by gluing acorns, with caps, into the top depression of tooth paste caps. (Little fingers will fit into the bottom of the caps.) Attach paper strip headbands and feathers. Use acorns with caps, painted black, to create Pilgrims or settlers. (MUSIC)

56. *BALLOONS:* Begin with a circle, standing.
Blow up a balloon. Let it go. "Watch, listen, what happened?" (REPEAT)
"Let's pretend you are balloons. I will blow all of you up into make-believe balloons. I'll start with your feet. (She blows a big puff into a balloon.) "Your feet are getting very tight, very, very stiff and tight." (Another puff.) "Now your knees are getting tight, now your hips and your tummy are tight-tight-tight. Your hands, arms and shoulders." (Puff.) "Now your neck, your head, tight, tight, very tight, right up to the tip top of your head."
"Now I'm going to let go of the balloon. All the air will go out and it will fizzle down to the floor. Ready? Let go!" (Children exhale air with a noise and spin around, landing on floor.) (MOVEMENT)

57. *PATTERNS IN RHYTHM:* Make hand and foot patterns by tracing around hands and feet (or shoes), on heavy paper or cardboard. Cut around the patterns, punch hanging holes in the top and use them to "write" rhythm patterns—hand patterns are clapped, foot patterns are stamped. The children take turns setting up rhythm patterns by hanging combinations of clapping and stamping rhythms on a row of hooks (or standing them in a blackboard tray). Group copies the rhythms "composed."
Vary the activity for older children by using letters F and H to represent the rhythms, add "S" for snap, "N" for nod, "B" for bell, etc. This is an excellent activity for developing reading readiness.

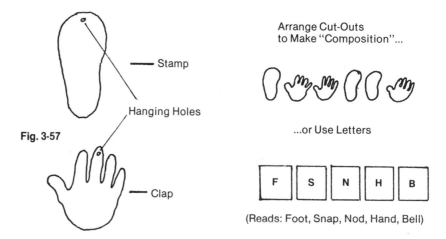

— Stamp

Hanging Holes

Fig. 3-57

— Clap

Arrange Cut-Outs to Make "Composition"...

...or Use Letters

| F | S | N | H | B |

(Reads: Foot, Snap, Nod, Hand, Bell)

SENSORY EXPERIENCES

58. *WHAT HAVE I HERE?* Put 4-6 objects into a bag or box. Put identical objects into another bag or box. Have one child put his hand in and describe the object he feels. He does not take the object out. Another child tries to find the matching object in the second bag from the description given by the first child. (TOUCH)

59. *SMELLING SENSATIONS:* Place portions of various items with different scents in small containers, such as pill bottles. Use spices, herbs, perfumes, extracts, coffee beans, pine spills, sawdust, onion, vinyl leather, etc. (SMELL)

60. *SMELLING HUNT:* Hide an onion, which has been cut in half; spray a corner of the room with perfume, spread some coffee grains in a corner; put some orange slices under a sheer cloth, conceal a cake of scented soap, and have a smelling hunt. (SMELL)

61. *EARS CAN TELL:* Place a collection of objects on a table behind a screen. Use metal,

glass, plastic, paper, liquids. Child goes behind screen and uses various combinations of objects to create sounds. 'Metal hitting wood,' 'metal rubbing paper,' 'water dropping on paper,' 'wood scraping metal,' etc. Other children try to guess how sound has been made.

62. *SOUND CHAMBER:* Drape a cloth over a table or use a large carton as a sound chamber. Children sit under table or carton while others create sounds as described in previous activity. The enclosed space acts as an echo chamber, magnifying the sounds. Use plastic glasses held up to ear and against the surface of the table top, carton or wall, as ear-phones magnify the sound.

63. *VOCAL SOUNDS:* Analyze indoor and outdoor sounds. Talk outside, inside; speak softly. Discuss the differences. Inside sound hits wall and ceiling and bounces back. Out-side sound moves off into space. Experiment with megaphones, cones, shouting into boxes, cans, etc. Use drums in demonstrations.

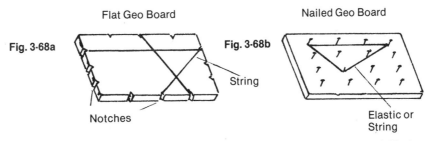

Fig. 3-65

Refrigerator Rack

64. *TASTING PARTY:* Place small portions of a variety of foods in styrofoam, egg carton sections, using such foods as, raw vegetables, candy, fruit, cheese, cooked and cold meat chunks, sugar salt, spice. Each child has his own tray and as he tastes each variety of food, he comments. Likes and dislikes are noted on a tasting chart, wall chart. (TASTE) .

65. *VIBRATIONS AMPLIFIED:* Tie two pieces of string, each about 1 foot long, to the corners of a refrigerator, stove or cooling rack. The child holds a string in each hand and puts his fingers in his ears, leaning forward a bit so the rack does not touch the body. Another child strikes the rack with a variety of objects (spoons, pencils, wood blocks or drags a fork across it). The sound will travel through the string. (See Seq. 9, Act. #50)

66. *BALANCE SCALES:* Construct various types of balance scales to weigh and sort objects by weight.

Use a balance beam or plank across a block, to weigh and sort children of equal weights.

Use blocks as weights on a balance beam. (MATH)

67. *BALANCE SWING:* Children weigh each other and large objects, using sandbags as counterwieghts.

68. *GEO-BOARDS:* Construct, as follows, and use to construct intricate, geometric patterns by stretching elastics or string over pegs, nails or grooves:

a. *FLAT GEO-BOARD:* Make equidistant grooves or cuts around the sides of a square of sturdy cardboard or masonite. Use string, wound through grooves to make various geometric shapes. (See Fig. 1.) This flat-style geo-board can also be used to make rubbings. After string is in place, lay a piece of paper over board and rub with crayon to make shape impressions. Then use a magic marker to outline shapes left by crayons.

Flat Geo Board   Nailed Geo Board

Fig. 3-68a   **Fig. 3-68b**

String

Notches   Elastic or String

b. *NAILED GEO-BOARD:* Hammer rows of finish nails partially into square of wood, being sure that they are evenly spaced. (See Fig. 2.) Elastic or string may be used to create geometric shapes.

69. *POINT TO POINT:* Create large squares, triangles, and rectangles by stretching lengthy elastic loops of 1/2" elastic from point to point, within the classroom. Have children identify shapes. A star shape may be created by stretching two elastic triangles around the legs of children standing in a circle. (See Activity #54, ELASTIC HOOPS.)

70. *HORSE MURAL:* Draw an outline of a large horse on brown paper. Cut it out and hang it on the wall. Children cut out small, paper swatches of brown and gray from magazines or clothes swatches from old clothing and paste them on the horse. Features and

TURKEY HANDS

Fig. 3-72

details of the horse may be drawn in with a magic marker. Before entire form is filled, with color swatches, leave two or three spots to be filled with white or black swatches to make a spotted pony. Spots may be outlined in heavy yarn. Add reins of an old leather belt, yarn mane and tail.

71. *TURKEY MURAL:* The same procedure as above may be followed in making a turkey mural. Feathers, tissue paper, cloth or paper scraps, leaves, paper feathers, or grasses may also be used. Turkey feather effect can also be made by gluing on the *separate* sections of a large pine cone.

72. *TURKEY HANDS.:* Trace around childs open hand to make the body of a turkey. Color fingers "feathers" bright colors, add a turkey head.

73. *HOBBY HORSES:* Make heads from suggestions below and attach to sturdy stick or broom dowel. (Use discarded tool and broom handles.)

    a) *Man's sock* stuffed — add fringed cloth or yarn mane and button eyes and nostrils.

    b) *Paper bag* stuffed — add paper fringe and features.

    c) *Folded cardboard* — add cloth, yarn or paper fringes, draw features.

Fig. 3-73a   **Fig. 3-73b**   **Fig. 3-73c**

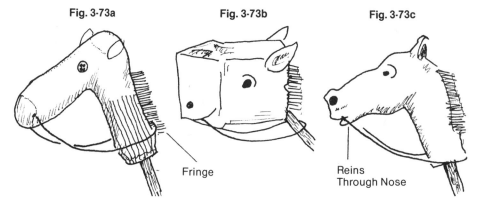

Fringe

Reins
Through Nose

74. *VEGETABLES:* Shop for many varieties of vegetables. Discuss which vegetables grow above the ground, and which below. Which have leaves that we eat? Match each vegetable to a color swatch. (Ask at a hardware store for paint chips). Read *Up Above and Down Below,* by Irma E. Webber, Young Scott Books, in connection with this activity. (See #28.) (FOOD, COLOR)

75. *HARVEST MURAL:* "Shop" in magazines and seed catalogs for colored photographs of vegetables. Plant a vegetable garden by taping two cardboard strips across poster board to make pockets to hold vegetable pictures. Label top strip 'Above ground' and bottom strip 'Below ground.' Put pictures of beets, potatos, carrots, etc. in underground pockets, and beans, lettuce, celery, etc. in above ground pockets. (FOOD, COLOR, GARDENS)

HARVEST MURAL

Garden

Fig. 3-75

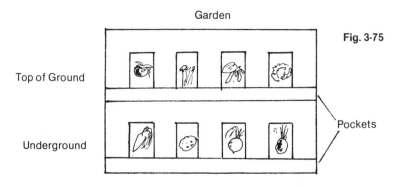

Top of Ground

Underground

Pockets

76. *BAKED BEANS:* Follow package directions and bake beans slowly, the old-fashioned way. This will be a two-day project. Can be left overnight in a crock pot at low heat. (See Seq. 11, #100.) (FOOD)

77. *CORN BREAD:* Explain the importance of corn to the Indians. Grind some kernels between flat stones. Supplement with enough commercial corn meal to bake into cornmeal recipes, such as corn bread and Indian pudding. Taste home-ground meal and commercial meal before mixing together. (See Seq. 11, #100.) (INDIANS, FOOD)

78. *YEAST BREADS:* Make bread, and while the dough is rising, read *The Duchess Bakes a Cake,* by Virginia Kahl, (Scribner). Yeast breads are good projects for all day children. It involves mixing, rising, punching, rising, baking and EATING. (See Seq. 11, #100.)

79. *CRANBERRIES:* Cranberries may be used in nut breads, cookies, sauces and jellies. Show pictures of cranberry bogs and describe the raking process. Serve cranberry sauce on toast or ice cream. Plan a field trip to see a cranberry bog or processing plant (Write Ocean Spray Co., Bryantville, Mass. for brochures and information.)

80. *NUT HUNT:* Hide different kinds of nuts around the classroom. To eliminate failures, section off a special area for each child. Children search for the nuts, count and sort into categories (use egg trays). (Sing 10 little walnuts, to tune of 10 little Indians). (MATH, SERIATION, FOOD, ART)

    Crack them open for a snack.

    Save walnut shells to make Walnut Whimseys. (See Seq. 4, #19).

    Put some in a jar and guess how many.

81. *MAYFLOWER:* Fill Walnut shells with cookie or cornbread dough, bake. When cooled, stick in sails made of paper triangles on toothpicks. Gumdrops, marshmallows or dried prunes might also be used as cargo. (PILGRIMS, FOOD)

82. *RAISINS:* One group held the following discussion:

Some children were eating a raisin snack. Their teacher asked, "Where do you suppose these raisins came from?" "Did they always look like this?"

Someone thought the raisins grew on trees and several others agreed.

"Did you buy them in a store?"

"Yes, these came from the supermarket, but they did not grow there," she responded, and the subject was dropped for the moment.

The following day, the teacher put a basket of grapes on the table.

"We are going to make raisins!" Jeffrey said, "I asked my grandfather last night and he said, 'You dry up grapes.' "

They hung the grapes from the sash of a very sunny window. During the next two weeks the children watched as the grapes began to wilt and wrinkle, noting changes in color, size and texture.

One day, David asked, "Can I touch these fuzzy things?"

The grapes were taken down and placed on a tray. "There are so many," Sally said and they all counted the grapes. One by one the grapes were picked from the stems and placed in piles of ten. David wrote down numbers for each pile. There was much conversation—"They feel crinkly." "They are all wrinkled." "They are smaller."

"What has gone out of them to make them smaller?" the teacher asked.

Arnold guessed, "It must be water if they are dried."

"Now can we eat them?" asked Mark, "but first tell me, are they Jewish?"

As they ate the grapes, descriptive vocabulary included, "sweet," "sour," "good," "delicious," "sticky to touch and taste."

"Do all grapes come out the same way?"

"No," said Bobby, "The green ones come out a different color."

83. *HARVEST TABLE:* Set a table with paper plates with various foods pasted on them. Practice table setting with real dishes and silver, checking to be sure each place has a complete setting. Do the settings correspond with the seats? Practice counting out each piece set. (ART, MATH)

84. *PLACEMATS:* Arrange seeds, grasses, leaves, feathers and pine spills on 12″ × 18″ construction paper. Spray or spatter paint over arrangements. When paint is dry remove arrangements.

85. *NUMBER LINES:* Hang a clothesline and use snap pins to attach 4″ × 4″ squares of cloth, oil cloth or cardboard with several sets of numerals, 0-9, printed on, For children

who may have difficulty operating pins, put numbers on folded squares of cardboard. Use the numberline to arrange numbers in order or make child's own telephone number. (MATH)

86. *CLASSROOM UNIVERSE:* The following story describes an activity which was not pre-planned. The events happened spontaneously and the after effects, the 'fall out' into other areas of program were extensive:

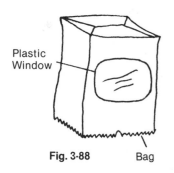

Plastic Window

Fig. 3-88   Bag

The kindergarten climbed an *imaginary,* grassy hill during a creative movement session. There was much movement of hands and feet. When the tired climbers reached the top, they lay down in the soft grass to rest and look up at the sky.

"What can you see?" the teacher asked.

"Sky." "Clouds."

The group discussed the colors of sky and the differences between night skies and daytime skies.

The word "universe" was used by the teacher. She asked, "What do you think universe means?"

One child resonded, "It's forever and ever."

"How would you like to make your own universe?" the teacher invited.

The children were so eager to begin, they almost forgot to descend from their make-believe hill. This group was accustomed to gathering their own materials from the shelves and bins. Each one chose his own materials to contribute to the classroom universe. Stars, sun, moon, planets and rocket ships were constructed from a great variety of materials and suspended from the ceiling. The globe, representing earth, was placed beneath the other heavenly bodies. The planets even rotated realistically as the heat from the radiator rose and caused them to turn.

ROCKET SHIP

Cardboard Nosecone and Fins Attached with Tape

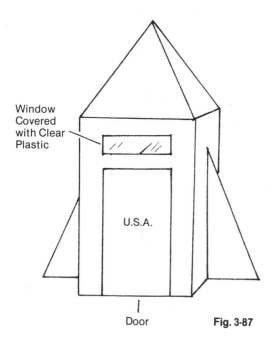

Window Covered with Clear Plastic

U.S.A.

Door   **Fig. 3-87**

87. *ROCKET SHIP:* Construct from an appliance carton large enough for children to stand up in. See illustration for suggestions:

Attach cardboard nose cone and fins with tape.

Paint with bright colors and add insignias (NASA, USA, etc.) name (APOLLO) and national flag. Fins and cone might be covered with foil.

Add an instrument panel inside, constructed by gluing or nailing spools, wood bits, plastic caps and knobs to cardboard or wood. Discuss what each knob is used for and label (i.e. LIFT OFF, OPEN HATCH, FIRE ROCKET #1, etc.) Decide what rules are necessary for the use of the rocket ship (only 4 children, location, etc.)

88. *SPACE HELMETS:* Make from large size grocery bags. Or use hard hats, motor cycle helmets; also see Seq. 4, Activity #50 for papier mâchè masks which fit over head.

89. *SPACE SUIT:* Make from child size overalls, add insignia patches, gloves and heavy shoes or boots. Make oxygen tanks by attaching oatmeal boxes or large cardboard tubes to straps which fit over shoulders (similar to back packs), or a back pack can also be used, as is, with "survival" items inside.

90. *SPACE FOOD:* Prepare a balanced meal in a blender (raw vegetables or cooked rice, beans or vegetables). Put in small plastic bags and eat as an astronaut would by squeezing the bag. (Consult blender cookbooks for ideas.)

91. *PLANETS:* Make balls with crumbled newspaper and cover with foil. Suspend from ceiling or on a bulletin board (in the rocket ship area). Name them and talk about size, where they are, how far from earth, what they are made up of.

92. *SATELLITES:* Construct by poking small dowels or straws through styrofoam balls. Attach pipe cleaners (antennas) to a one pound coffee can. These two satellites are very close to the actual sizes of some of the real satellites used for communications. Suspend the satellites with the planets (see Activity #91 above). Talk about the use of satellites, how they get in the sky.

93. *DAY AND NIGHT:* Illustrate by shining a flashlight on a turning ball. Talk about the light and dark sides of the earth and moon.

94. *BINOCULARS AND TELESCOPES:* Make binoculars by taping two cardboard tubes together and one long tube for telescopes. Punch holes in sides and insert yarn or string for neck straps. Cover each end with clear sandwich wrap or plastic held in place with tape. Use foil to cover the rolls.

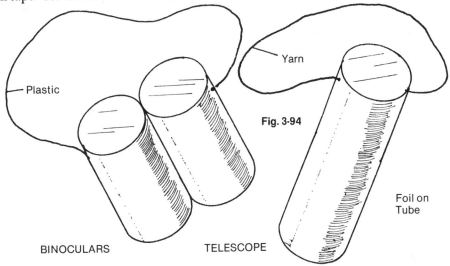

Plastic

Yarn

Fig. 3-94

Foil on Tube

BINOCULARS   TELESCOPE

For more ideas for space activities, see *Introducing Children to Space*—The Lincoln Plan, a handbook compiled by National Aeronautics and Space Administration, published by U.S. Government Printing Office, Washington, D.C. 20402.

95. *COLOR TEAMS:* Talk about fall colors. Make a list. Divide class into color teams. Look for pictures and objects they can bring in of their color. Use also as homework. Perhaps color tickets or badges could be distributed to each team. Provide a special collecting box for each color collection. (COLOR)

96. *CANS FOR COLOR:* Collect vegetable and fruit cans with colored labels. Use as sorters for like colored objects, such as small vegetable pictures mounted on oak tag, for crayons, for leaves, for playing store games. (VEGETABLES)

97. *CREPE PAPER DYE:* Children make dye by soaking crepe paper in water. Lay wet streamers on cloth so the colors 'bleed' into a design. When dry, the teacher can iron and finish edge. Use the cloth for special parties, a theater curtain, doll's bedspread or curtains.

98. *MITTEN LINE:* As cooler weather approaches, give each child two snap clothespins to paint with acrylic or decorate by gluing on sequins or small beads. When dry, string the pins onto a line and stretch in front of cubbies or over a radiator. Each child has his own mitten hangers.

99. *MITTENS:* Make paper mittens by drawing around child's hands, cutting out shape, punching holes in wrist end and tying pair together. Good activity for threes. Sing *The Mitten Song.*

100. *SCHOOL TOUR:* Tour your school building, visit offices, maintenance shop, cellar, storage rooms, roof, staff rooms, director's office. Look for signs which identify special areas or give directions. Make signs for your own room, such as: EXIT, ENTER, STOP, ONE WAY, QUIET.

101. *TURKEY FARM:* Visit a turkey farm and collect feathers for art projects.

102. *AIRPORT:* Visit an airport. Before the trip, make a list of things the children will expect to see. Take the list along and check off as many things as are found. On your return, ask the children what they saw which surprised them, what they did not expect to see and did. Use magazines and travel folders to write and illustrate an airport book. (See Seq. 7, #145)

103. *RAILROAD STATION:* Ride a commuter train between two stops. Plan to have cars waiting to pick children up at the end of the ride. Make booklets and stories as suggested above.

104. *BUS RIDE:* Ride on a city bus.

105. *STABLES:* Tour a riding stable, horse farm or race track stable area.

106. *POLLS:* Visit a polling station. Along the route look for campaign signs. Get permission beforehand from election officials as children are generally not allowed in voting booths during voting. Hold a school election. Make a voting booth with a large carton or building blocks. (See Activities #34-35)

5D. SEQUENCE FOUR

During the *December holidays* families are often together *sharing* visits and *gifts*. Such holidays are also internationally celebrated and the curriculum offers suggestions for ways of looking at the *global family*. Many schools have children of various *ethnic and cultural origins* and parents who will share their cultures through active participation or by lending materials can enrich the program and expand the cultural horizons of the children. *Holiday customs* may be different, but *joy, gaiety, giving, sharing and lights* are some of the themes common to many cultures.

1. *HOLIDAY STORIES:* Tell or read to children traditional stories of Christmas, Kwanza and Hanukah. Discuss with them the many ways people of other countries observe these great festivals. Tell them about the customs of Mexico, Scandinavia, France, etc. Several traditional stories and poems follow:

2. I. *CHRISTMAS STORY,* by Grace Mitchell:

There was once a king whose name was Herod. He ruled in a land called Judea, near where Israel and Palestine are today. Herod was a very severe and strict king. He made a law that all of the people of his country had to go to the villages where their parents and grandparents had been born and write their names in a big, black book, called a census book. This was because Herod wanted to charge every person a tax to live in Judea. He would punish anyone who did not go to be counted and pay the tax.

Many of the people lived far away from the places where they had been born. In those days there were no cars, planes or trains to travel from place to place. The roadways were rough and it took many days of hard walking to reach the towns where the people were counted and paid their taxes.

There were two travelers, whose names were Mary and Joseph. They had a long way to travel. They had a donkey; he was little but his back was strong and he carried Mary all the way. Mary was soon going to have a baby and Joseph walked beside her, guiding the little donkey over the rough and narrow pathways. After many days they came to Bethlehem, the town where Joseph's grandfather had lived. They were very tired. It was cold and they were hungry. Mary needed food and rest. It was near the time when her baby would be born.

Joseph comforted her and said, "I will find you some warm food and a comfortable bed in an inn." But Joseph did not realize how many others had come to Bethlehem to be counted. The inns were crowded; there were no more rooms. Joseph and Mary went from one to another asking for a place to rest but each time Joseph knocked at the door, the busy innkeepers would snap at him rudely saying, "No room! No room!" Some even slammed their doors. (It was a busy time and they had forgotten their manners.)

Finally, Joseph and Mary came to the very last inn at Bethlehem. It, too, was filled. Poor Joseph begged, "Please, I must find a place for my wife, Mary, to rest, for her baby will soon be born."

The innkeeper's wife stood nearby and heard his pleading. She looked at Mary and felt sorry for her. "You could go into our stable," she said, "it will be warm and there is fresh hay to make into a bed. I will bring you some food."

Joseph and Mary were grateful for this kind woman's offer. They went into the stable and found it warmed by the heat from the animals' bodies. There was a cow, an ox, some sheep and goats and Joseph's own little donkey. They fixed a bed in the manger with sweet, fresh hay. Late that night, just when the animals had fallen asleep, they were roused by the tiny cry of a newborn baby. A baby boy was born to Mary and Joseph. Mary wrapped him snugly in clean cloth and laid him in the crib. She named him Jesus.

Later, some wise men and shepherds from far away came to bring gifts to the new baby. They had been told that Jesus would be born and that he would grow to become a great king. They wanted to share in the celebration of his birth.

Jesus did grow up to become a very great man. He went as a teacher throughout the country and taught people how kindness and love toward all mankind would bring happiness and peace to the world. This happened a long time ago, nearly two thousand years ago. Still, people remember the lessons of Jesus and each year on December 25th, Jesus' birthday, some gather to celebrate the event.

Christmas is a happy time when people share gifts, songs and special foods. It is a time to remember those we love and to practice sharing and kindness.

There are special signs and symbols of Christmas which you will see as people begin to decorate and prepare for their celebrations. The star is the sign of Christmas because on the night when Jesus was born, a very bright star shone in the skies over Bethlehem. It was called the Star of Bethlehem. The shepherds who came to see the new baby carried long sticks, called crooks. They used them to guide their flocks of sheep over the rocky hills. Candy canes look very much like tiny shepherds' crooks. When you see bright canes hanging on the tree, think of the shepherds who brought Jesus his very first gifts and of the sheep which kept him warm in his little straw-sweet crib. Perhaps the soft 'baas' of the wooly sheep lulled him to sleep under the bright star.

3. *HANUKAH STORY,* by Grace Mitchell:

There once was a wicked king named Antiochus. He was a very proud king. "I am the greatest king of all," he said. "When my people walk near me they will bow down before me." The people did bow to Antiochus for they were afraid of him and his cruel punishments. He had many soldiers. The soldiers marched from town to town watching to see that the people obeyed the harsh laws of Antiochus and bowed before him and his statues.

In a village called Modin, there lived a man named Mattathias. He had five sons, Judah, Jonathan, Jochanon, Simon and Eleazar. (Suggest counting with fingers.) Mattathias and his sons were Jews and they believed only in God. They prayed to Him in their temples. They refused to bow to Antiochus. They were not afraid of him.

Antiochus was very angry when he heard of this. He ordered his soldiers to go to the village and fight Mattathias and his sons. Many of the villagers heard that Antiochus' soldiers were coming and they fled into the hills with Mattathias and his sons to form an army. This little army hid in the caves on the hills. They chose Judah, the eldest son, as their leader. He was called Judah Maccabee, Judah the Strong.

The army of Antiochus reached the village of Modin, and when they found none of Mattathias' men there, they broke into the temples and destroyed many of the beautiful things inside. They tore down the temples of Jerusalem, smashing the altar which was sacred to the Jews. When the army in the hills heard of this, they were outraged and they went into Modin to drive away Antiochus and his men. They fought bravely and defeated the army and drove them away from their lands.

The women of Modin cheered their brave men and welcomed them home from their successful battle. Together the villagers cleaned and restored the temple and refilled the oil lamps which were always left burning in honor of their God. But they discovered that the oil for the lamps had been spilled by the soldiers and that there was so little that it would only burn for one day. They sent a messenger to run through the hills and into another village for more of the precious oil. It was a long, hard journey and would take at least eight days. The Jews in Modin waited patiently, watching the flickering lamps, knowing that they could not burn until the messenger came with more oil. While they waited they made food for the tired army, a special food called latkes, pancakes made from potatoes.

To the amazement of the villagers, the little lamps continued to burn. One day passed, two days, three—still the lamps burned. By now the messenger was through the mountains and crossing the wide valley below. On the fourth day he reached the village where he bought the new oil. It would take four days to return to Modin.

When he returned he was surprised to find the lamps of the temple still burning. God must have made the lamps burn on. The villagers celebrated, saying this was a miracle of God. They danced, sang and offered feasts in honor of their God for the miracle of lights, Hanukah.

Ever since that day so many years ago the Jews have celebrated the miracle of the lights. On each day of Hanukah they light one of the eight candles of a candle holder they call a Menorah. In the center stands a tall candle called the shammes. On the very first day of Hanukah, the shammes is lighted and with it the first of the eight candles. Each day another candle is lighted from the shammes flame until all eight are lighted on the last day of Hanukah.

During this festival of lights, the Jews have many special celebrations. They bake latkes and eat them with applesauce or sour cream. The children are given special Hanukah gifts and money which they call gelt. They play games with a dreidel, a spinning top made for Hanukah.

Hanukah days are happy days, days for joining with family and friends in gift giving and feasting, days for remembering the happy miracle of the lights—Hanukah.

4. *MISS GOODWINKLE'S TREE,* by Harriet Chmela:

There was once a little, old lady who lived in a very little house with a white, picket fence around it. It was at the end of a dead end street in a very quiet neighborhood. In the front yard grew a little, green fir tree. There were several families along the street with young children. The children often came to play under the little fir tree and run sticks along the fence to make a rat-a-tat-a-tat. The little old lady, whose name was Miss Goodwinkle, enjoyed the children, for she lived alone and they were pleasant company. She often gave them cookie snacks and lemonade, which she always made with a little extra sugar just for them. In the winter her cocoa was always the very best on the street after skating parties, because she would add—not one, not two, but three marshmallows to melt into the rich, hot chocolate.

Miss Goodwinkle knew all the children by name and often told them stories about their older brothers and sisters and their fathers and mothers, for she had known them since they were children, too. She even knew some of their grandparents. She would often say, "I used to go sleding with your Grampa," and "Your Gramma and I walked to school together."

Every year, at Christmas time, each house along the street held a friendly contest to see who could make the prettiest display outside. One day, in front of a yellow house with a porch all around, a beautiful tree was decorated with colored, glass, Christmas balls. (This was Joseph's house. He and his father had gotten up very early that morning and trimmed their tree. Joseph was seven, and this was the first year his father had let him climb high on the ladder to hang some of the ornaments at the very top of the tree.)

The next evening, just as the children were going out to look at the evening stars and make Christmas wishes, they were thrilled to see another beautiful tree. It stood in front of Peterson's house. David and Donna, four year old twins, lived there. They were waving and grinning from their steps as neighbors cheered their tree. It was all hung with garlands of golden rings with a beautiful star on the very top. The twins had made the rings and hooked them together. They were very, very proud of this tall Christmas tree because they had helped to decorate it.

Two days later, when the neighbors were hurrying home, they were treated to still another surprise. Kathy and her older brother had stayed home all day to decorate their holiday tree. It was a blue spruce, the tallest in the neighborhood. It was covered from the very top to the lowest branches with bright lights of many colors. Some of the lights even blinked at the onlookers as they stared at the branches. Kathy was in the first grade and, with the help of her mother, she had climbed high on the step ladder to hang some of the lights. She shouted with delight as her father turned on the lights and the tree sparkled with lovely colors.

Miss Goodwinkle smiled as she stood on her front porch and watched her happy neighbors admiring the beautiful Christmas trees. She looked at her own little fir tree.

"You know, little tree, I think you need a little trimming. Tomorrow I'll be out early and you will need strong branches to help me with my surprise, so sleep well tonight."

The next morning Miss Goodwinkle tied a patchwork apron around her tiny waist and began to bake. She made Christmas cookies in just about every shape you could think of — stars, circles, diamonds, birds, Santas. Each one was sprinkled with sparkly candies. She made lots of popcorn, and late that afternoon she strung it into long garlands, and then she took the cookies and garlands outside and used them to trim the little fir tree. It was the most delicious looking tree, almost like a gingerbread house. Just right for nibbling! Then she remembered something else and scurried into the house and returned with a red and white box. Inside were twelve striped candy canes with a delicious smell of peppermint. When they were also hung on the little tree, she stepped back to admire her work. "You do look good enough to eat!" she said.

Miss Goodwinkle went inside to rest in her rocking chair and wait for the children to discover her surprise. She fell asleep, for she was very tired after her long busy day. Just as the sun was beginning to set, she awoke to hear cheerful voices outside.

While she had been sleeping the children had discovered her surprise. Sure enough, the little fir tree was good enough to eat and that is *just what they did!* By the next day, all of the delicious cookies and canes were nibbled away.

But there was something extra special about the little fir tree. It had one decoration that none of the other trees had. The children had left the strings of popcorn and each day the little tree was filled with beautiful birds, singing and pecking at this winter treat.

On Christmas Eve each year the first prize was given for the most beautiful tree. "Miss Goodwinkle, you have the only singing, chirping, peeping tree on the street. You have won the prize." The prize was always the same, the neighborhood carol sing was held before the winning tree. Miss Goodwinkle's birds were treated to a special concert.

5. *THE LITTLE SPRUCE TREE*, adapted by Grace Mitchell:

On the night in Bethlehem when the shepherds and all creatures came to adore the child in the manger, trees from many lands wanted to do the same. Some came from nearby, like the cedar, the olive tree and the palm tree. Others traveled from distant lands. The birch and the elm came, the willow and the strong oak.

But none had come as far as the little spruce tree. It had traveled all the way to the Holy Land from the North Country. When it reached Bethlehem, it was so tired it could hardly stand.

All the trees were bigger and made fun of the little spruce.

"How bare it looks," the olive tree laughed, proud of her own white blossoms.

"How dark it is," said the white birch.

"You haven't any leaves," said the maple, shaking her own scarlet and yellow leaves.

"You are so ugly," said the graceful palm tree. "We cannot let the Christ child look upon such an ugly tree. Your needles are sharp. You might get too near and harm him." So all of the trees made a circle around the little tree, doing their best to hide it from the Babe in the manger.

Only from above in the sky could the little tree be seen. The stars looked down; the bright Christmas star which had led the shepherds to the manger and many others. They felt sorry for the poor little tree which had traveled so far, and was now hidden in the dark.

But there was something about that little spruce tree that the others couldn't hide. It had a wonderful fragrance — a smell that was like no other ever known. The fragrance reached the little baby and He smiled. Then, at that very moment, a rain of stars fell down from the sky upon the little spruce tree. They landed on all of its branches where they sparkled and twinkled. The other trees stepped back in amazement.

"It is the most beautiful tree of all," they cried.

The little baby gazed at it in wonder and then blessed it with a smile.

Do you know what he wished when he looked at that tree? I think he wished that such a beautiful tree might always shine on his birthday.

6. *THE JOKE*, adapted by Grace Mitchell:

Santa came down the chimney with a bounce and a whoosh! There were three stockings hanging by the fireplace, a green one for a boy, a red one for a girl and a little blue one for baby sister. Santa went right to work. He put shiny pennies way down in the toe, then a golden orange, some nuts and candies and lots of toys. At the very last he stuck a silver trumpet at the top of the green stocking, a pretty little doll peeped out of the red stocking and a soft cuddly teddy bear for baby. When he was all through Santa stepped back to look at them. They were all lumpy and humpy. They were SO FULL of goodies!

"Now that's what I call full," said Santa, "no one could put another thing in any of those stockings!"

"I could," said a tiny voice.

"Who said that?" cried Santa.

"I can," said the little voice again. When Santa looked all around he saw a wee little gray mouse on the hearth.

"You?" laughed Santa, "a little bitty pipkin like you! I'd like to see you do it. In fact, if you can get even one more thing in one of those stockings, I will give you the biggest, fattest, Christmas cheese you ever saw."

"O.K.," said the mouse in his squeaky little voice, and he nibbled a hole with his sharp white teeth in the toe of the long green stocking. "I did it. I did it," squealed the little mouse, dancing around Santa's feet. "I put a hole in the stocking!"

"Ho, ho, ho, you certainly did! You played a big joke on me. And I will keep my promise, so here is your cheese."

Well, that little mouse invited his mother and father and sisters and brothers and grandmothers and grandfathers and aunts and uncles and cousins and friends and neighbors to a cheese party and they ate and ate and ate until they almost burst! And when they were full, they still had some cheese left! Now, wasn't that a clever little mouse?

7. *HOLIDAY STORIES AND POEMS:* There are many traditional stories for Christmas and Hanukah. Some may be too long or too old for the very young but should not be omitted. Telling a short, simple version and *using visual aids* is an excellent way to bring such stories to them.

8. *THE LITTLE BLUE DISHES:* from *Told Under Blue Umbrella,* pub. McMillan. Use as visual aids toy tea set (blue), a small red purse, holding ten pennies (count out slowly—children help) and a pink heart made of salt dough. (See Sculpture)

9. *WHAT IS KWANZA?* Kwanza is an African holiday which has been adopted by members of the Afro-American population in America. The celebration lasts seven days, from December 25 through December 31 and in many homes takes the place of the traditional Christmas holiday. Kwanza means "First Fruits" and in Africa takes place at the end of the harvest season. After the crops have been harvested, the people come together to pay tribute to the fruits of their labors. In America, because we are basically not an agricultural society, some changes have been made. We use this time to celebrate our fortunes which we have come by through hard work at school and on our jobs. We remember our ancestors and give presents, which are all hand made much in the same way as they did in centuries past. This also serves to help us combat commercialism and the thought that money means everything.

At this time we also reflect upon certain principles, which are basically essential for any group of people to lead healthy, happy and productive lives. The heart of Kwanza is the "Nguzo Saba" or the seven principles of life, which are:

1. Unoja—Unity
2. Kujichagulia—Self determination
3. Ujima—Collective work and responsibility
4. Ujamaa—Cooperative economics
5. Nia—Purpose
6. Kuumba—Creativity
7. Imani—Faith

10. *HOW IS KWANZA CELEBRATED?* The first thing necessary is a Kwanza table. The table may be placed in the living room or family room. Mats placed on the floor serve just as well, in addition to being an attractive center in the room. What goes on this table is as follows:

A straw mat which symbolizes the base of the family or household.

A straw bowl or basket in which tropical fruits are placed, symbolizing the fruits of our hard work all year long.

Dried ears of corn—You need an ear of corn for each member of your family, or for members hoped for, i.e. unborn children.

Seven candles—Red, black and green candles, one to be lit each day of Kwanza when the family comes together to discuss the principle of the day.

A communal cup—A wooden cup which is filled with wine and is shared at meals or is given to your guests after they have entered your house during this time. (A cup should always have something in it, apple cider will do.)

Each day the family plans a meal which is eaten without utensils, or with your right hand. One member of the family may be responsible for the menu each day. Use foods that can be eaten with fingers. Before the family eats, everyone gathers around to light the candles and discuss the principle of the day. For instance, if the principle is collective work and responsibility—Ujima—we talk about what it means to us; how we have participated in this principle in our lives through the year as well as how we can make this principle more of a reality in the year to come. Each member drinks from the communal cup and the meal is then served. (The discussion may take place at, before or after dinner.)

After the discussion, one member of the family is presented with the handmade gifts from the other members of the family.

Kwanza is a time to reflect upon our lives and be thankful for our fortunes and existence. It is also a time to reemphasize the principles and values that we work to incorporate into our lives the year round.

If it is a party, each person invited is requested to make a contribution in the African communal tradition.

11. *KWANZA: CELEBRATION OF THE FIRST FRUITS:* Ask the children if they have ever heard the word *Kwanza*. What does it mean? Does anyone have a similar celebration in their home? Do the children think such a celebration is important? Talk about Nguzo Saba, the Seven Principles of Life (see What is Kwanza? above). Choose one, such as Unoja—Unity, and relate it to such classroom events as coming together for meeting time and story time.

Gather a collection of Kwanza materials (above activity). What do they mean and how could they be used in the classroom? Ask the children about the kinds of music they like and use when they celebrate holidays. Talk about the way Africans and Afro-Americans use music when they celebrate. Use African music (Olatunji records) and rhythm sticks to celebrate Kwanza. (See Seq. 11 for more ideas on Africa.)

12. *FEAST FOR KWANZA:* Sit on a straw mat or pillows and serve finger foods consisting of fruits, vegetables and nuts. (See Gift Giving, Seq. 9, #11.)

13. *HANDS:* Make prints by dipping hands in black paint and print on colored paper or cast in plaster of Paris or salt dough. Mount with poem:

Sometimes you get discouraged
Because I am so small
I always leave my fingerprints
On furniture and the wall

But every day I'm growing up
And soon I'll be so tall
That all those little handprints
Will be hard for you to recall

So here is a final handprint
Just so you can remember
Exactly how my fingers looked
In '76—December

Though this is a simple activity for the very young, the prints make nice gifts.

14. *NEW CARDS FROM OLD:* Cut old cards and paste holiday motifs onto construction paper folders. Children may dictate messages to go inside. Make folders to fit commerical envelopes or staple and use one side of folder for address. Take children to post office or mail box to mail their cards.

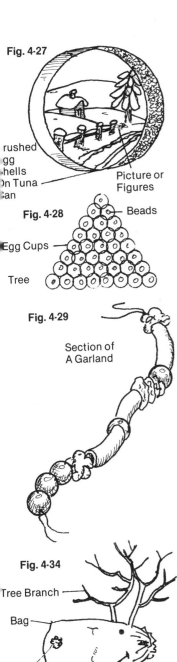

Fig. 4-27

rushed
gg
hells
n Tuna
an

Picture or
Figures

Fig. 4-28

Beads

Egg Cups

Tree

Fig. 4-29

Section of
A Garland

Fig. 4-34

Tree Branch

Bag

Red Tissue

Cardboard
Tube

Fig. 4-35

15. *WHAT IS JOY?* Ask each child his definition of joy. Write definitions as message inside a child-made card.

16. *GREETING CARD GAME:* Use holiday cards to make a matching lotto game. Cut card in half, give child one set of four to six halves and ask him to find matching halves.

17. *GRANDMA'S SALT BEADS* (See Sculpture #5): Use the beads as ornaments, jewelry; put several together to make puppets, make seriation games. (ORNAMENTS)

18. *TREE TRIMMERS:* Make cardboard, or construction paper (also parts of used greeting cards) ornaments in various shapes and put letters, numbers or names on one side. Each child chooses one, and if he can read the letter, number or name, he may hang the ornament. These can also be used as a matching lotto game; child looks for matching item in a duplicate set.

19. *WALNUT WHIMSEYS:* Put tiny surprises inside empty walnut shells. Glue the two halves together, leaving short length of string from one end for hanging, if desired. Spray-paint or leave plain. Whimseys are distributed and opened for surprises at holiday parties.

20. *SALT DOUGH DECORATIONS* (See Salt Dough recipe in Sculpture, #2): Roll and cut into various shapes using cookie cutters. Bake at 325° for 30 minutes. Make hole for hanging before the shapes harden. When they are dry and hard, they may be painted and trimmed with sequins, glitter.

21. *TRIANGLE STARS:* Print stars using triangle shapes. Note difference in number of points in Star of David and regular star shape.

22. *STAR PRINTS:* Use cookie cutters and various printing materials cut in the shape of stars. Dip and print stars on paper, cloth, card folders and other art projects.

23. *ORNAMENTAL SMORGASBORD:* Cut out seasonal shapes. Paint with water colors and when they are dry, serve up a smorgasbord of materials to decorate them, such as: glitter, beads, buttons, cloth scraps, foil scraps, etc.

24. *POD SCENES:* Spray paint milkweed pods and allow to dry. Paste tiny scenes from greeting cards inside or use as cradles for tiny dolls.

25. *CONES:* Paint pine cones with thinned glue and sprinkle with glitter.

26. *EGG SHELL TRIM:* Spray crushed egg shells with gold and silver. Glue onto cardboard shapes.

27. *CAN ORNAMENTS:* With a can opener, remove both ends of small, shallow cans (tuna). Paint glue on the outside and roll in crushed egg shells. Put small clay figures, dried grasses, or pictures from greeting cards inside.

28. *EGG CUP TREE OR WREATH:* Cut egg carton into cups. Spray paint and glue them onto large triangles (trees) or cut out circles (wreaths). Glue or pin beads into the centers of cups. Stick small pine cones in between cups.

29. *GARLANDS:* String macaroni, cereals, popcorn, cranberries or paper chains to create garlands.

30. *WRAPPING PAPER:* Print shapes on sheets of newspaper or brown bags to use for gift wrapping.

31. *CURLY CIRCLES:* Use a paper punch to make several holes in 3" circles of assorted colors of construction paper. Then paint glue on both sides of paper. As the circles dry, they curl into odd shapes. Hang as ornaments or string in garlands using straw sections to keep them separate.

32. *SHAPE MURAL:* Draw stars, triangles and cubes on large sheet of paper. Children fill in shapes with pasted foil scraps of different colors from green. Outline each shape with yarn in contrasting shade. (A good activity for twos and threes and at the end of the day.)

33. *STARRY SKY MURAL:* On lower third of a large piece of dark blue paper, paste black rectangles and squares of various sizes to represent building silhouettes. Silver or gold stars may be stuck on the sky, or stars may be printed on by using star or triangle shapes dipped in yellow and white paint.

34. *REINDEER (Rudolph):* Stuff paper bag with newpaper. Insert antler made of bare tree branches and tape with masking tape. Stuff bag into top of tube and secure with masking tape. Put on red tissue nose— paint eyes and mouth.

35. *SANTA MADE FROM STARS:* Materials—Red construction paper for star, cotton for beard and hat; color boots and features black.

36. *HOLIDAY TREES:*

   a) Ice cream cone inverted, cover with green frosting, decorate with fruit loops or candies.

   b) Make cone-shaped tree of popcorn stuck together with frosting.

   c) Ask children to dress each other (or an individual child) as the tree. 'Tree' is wrapped from neck down with green crepe paper streamers, then decorated with paper decorations. Use tree as "prop" or character in telling holiday stories.

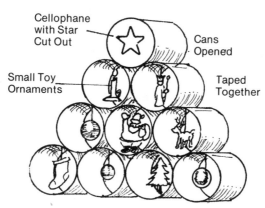

Cellophane with Star Cut Out

Cans Opened

Small Toy Ornaments

Taped Together

Fig. 4-36

d) Glue popcorn on green triangles.

e) Fold and staple a sheet of heavy paper into a cone, decorate.

f) *WIRE TREES:* Bend chicken wire into cone shape and stick or weave evergreens or green tissue into holes. Decorate tree.

g) *CAN TREE:* Cut out both ends of several juice cans of the same size. Stick cans together in a pyramid with tape. Spray paint resulting tree and hang or place tiny figures and ornaments inside each can. Some cans may be filled with crumpled cellophane, others may be covered on one end with colored tissue or painted plastic covers. Suspend tree or place it where light shines through.

   h) *TRIANGLE TREES:* Cut triangle shapes from green paper, magazine pictures (green parts) or cloth and paste onto a large mural to create an evergreen forest effect or use triangles to fill a large triangular shaped tree. Add trimmings to tree.

37. *COAT HANGER SANTA:* Bend coat hanger into oval shape. Pull nylon stocking over it. Paint on features and make cotton beard.

38. *EGG CUP SLEIGH:* Use egg cup sections from egg cartons. Runners are made from pipe cleaners bent into shape and glued to egg cups.

39. *WEAVING:* Fold construction paper and cut into strips, as shown. Open out and weave dried grasses through slits.

40. *EGG CUP BELL:* Hang tiny bell on pipe cleaner. Push through decorated or painted egg cup. Bend top of pipe cleaner to hang bell.

41. *CRADLE:* make cradles by cutting oatmeal or salt boxes, as shown. Fill with straw or flannel and put a sock doll inside.

42. *SOCK DOLL:* Stuff foot or toe of an old sock with cloth, forming the head of the doll. Tie a ribbon or pipe cleaner at the neck. Either use buttons or material scraps as features, or draw them on. Use yarn for hair. Wrap doll in piece of flannel.

43. *PAPER LANTERNS:* Fold a sheet of paper in half lengthwise. Cut slits (see Fig. 1). Unfold and shape into cylinder (2), staple seam. Add handle.

44. *BELL:* Fold several sheets of paper in half and draw bell shape using fold as center (see Fig. 1). Cut out and attach (sew) several bells together at fold.

45. *SILVER TASSELS:* Use foil scraps about 12″ long and 4″ wide. Cut slits, roll tightly around pencil, staple top (include a yarn hanger).

46. *PAPER CUP BELLS AND BASKETS:* Attach hanger and small ornament or bell to inverted cone-shaped cup or attach handle to form candy basket.

47. *MENORAH:* (See opposite page)

48. *TISSUE PAPER ORNAMENTS:* Fold tissue papers and colorful wraps in half and make cut-out designs, as in making paper snowflakes. (Make several folds before cutting, if desired, for more cut-outs.) Unfold to the half fold and hang over string lines strung across and around the room. Mexicans use these simple decorations along with Spanish moss to deck their holiday halls. Newsprint can be painted or left plain (comics) to achieve attractive hangings.

SLEIGH

Egg Cup

Pipe Cleaners

Fig. 4-38

Cut Slits

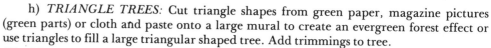

Fig. 4-39

EGG CUP BELL

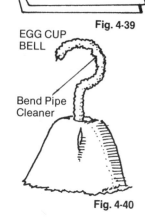

Bend Pipe Cleaner

Fig. 4-40

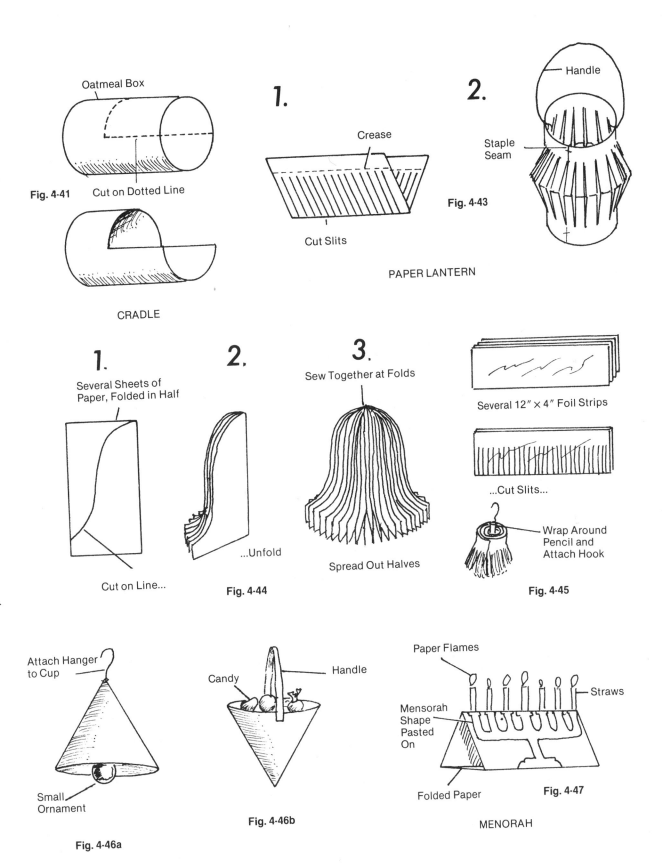

Oatmeal Box

Fig. 4-41   Cut on Dotted Line

CRADLE

1.

Crease

Cut Slits

Fig. 4-43

2.

Handle

Staple Seam

PAPER LANTERN

1.

Several Sheets of Paper, Folded in Half

Cut on Line...

2.

...Unfold

Fig. 4-44

3.

Sew Together at Folds

Spread Out Halves

Several 12" × 4" Foil Strips

...Cut Slits...

Wrap Around Pencil and Attach Hook

Fig. 4-45

Attach Hanger to Cup

Small Ornament

Fig. 4-46a

Candy   Handle

Fig. 4-46b

Paper Flames

Mensorah Shape Pasted On

Folded Paper

Straws

Fig. 4-47

MENORAH

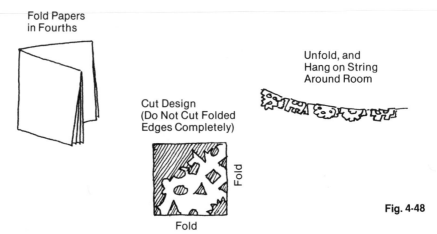

Fold Papers
in Fourths

Unfold, and
Hang on String
Around Room

Cut Design
(Do Not Cut Folded
Edges Completely)

Fold

Fold

Fig. 4-48

49. *TISSUE FLOWERS:* Cut three five-inch circles of colorful tissue. Poke a hole through centers. Insert pipe cleaner into holes and twist end into a loop to hold. Crinkle and twist paper to make flower. Use fringed yellow paper or yarn for flower center.

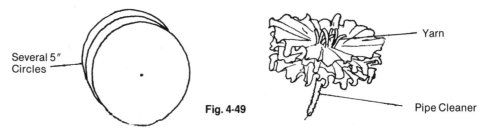

Several 5″
Circles

Yarn

Fig. 4-49

Pipe Cleaner

50. *PAPIER MACHE MASKS:* To make a Mexican holiday mask, cut several layers of newspaper into an oval shape to fit a child's face. Cut one-inch slits around outer edge, overlap edges at slits and staple so oval forms a bowl shape. Apply layers of mâchè (see Sculpture, #4) or use plaster surgical tape strips, drying between each layer, until the mask is built up to a sturdy thickness. Mâchè can be layered over a *large* balloon. When hardened, cut hole in bottom so mask fits over child's head. If newsprint is used, make final layers from paper towels to provide a plain surface. Cut out eyes, nostrils and mouth to fit feature of child. When mâchè is hardened, paint and decorate the mask.

Fig. 4-50

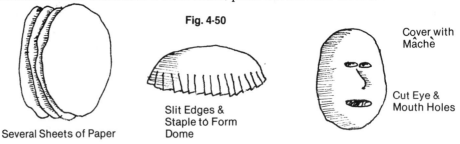

Cover with
Mâchè

Cut Eye &
Mouth Holes

Slit Edges &
Staple to Form
Dome

Several Sheets of Paper

51. *SAWDUST DESIGNS:* A traditional way of decorating streets and plazas for holiday, religious posadas (parades). Floral and geometric designs are outlined in chalk along the parade route and then filled in with sawdust.

52. *BELLS:* Show several kinds of bells. Use pictures and take trips to see bells in churches, public buildings, music stores. Play a recording of bells. Invite a group of bell ringers to give a demonstration.

Children dance to the accompaniment of *Jingle Bells* or other appropriate music, in the following ways:

a) Three commercial, metallic bells sewn on to 1/4″ elastic, or strong bells onto nar-

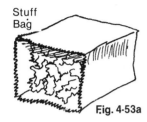

Stuff Bag

Fig. 4-53a

Cover with Mâchè

Fig. 4-53b

Remove Stuffing and Paint

Fig. 4-53c

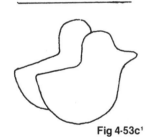

Fig 4-53c¹

Fig 4-53c²

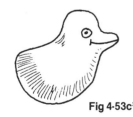

Fig 4-53c³

row ribbon to make wrist or ankle bells.

b) Small bells hung on pipe cleaners, or wire inserted through center of sections of egg cartons, small juice cans, paper cones, etc.

53. *PIÑATAS:* This favorite Mexican holiday treat may be constructed in the following ways:

a) Puff out paper bags. Stuff with tissue to hold shape desired. Cover with strips of starched tissue. Remove stuffing when dry. Decorate.

b) Blow up balloons and cover with mâchè (see Activity #50)

c) Make duplicate shapes, such as stars, birds, animals, etc. from large pieces of tissue (three or four thicknesses), painted newsprint or wrapping paper. Staple the two shapes together at edges and stuff with shreds of paper to hold out shape. Cover this with starched wet paper and allow to dry. When dry, remove stuffing.

Stuff piñatas with wrapped candies or other small treats. Decorate cardboard tube to use as striker for breaking open pinata. (Read *Nine Days to Christmas,* by Marie Hall Ets, Viking Press.)

54. *TOP SPIN:* Children spin around like a top without touching anyone. If you touch, move to side.

55. *DANCING GIFTS:* Children decorate cartons with collage, gift cards, paint, ribbons, or wrapping papers. The cartons are open at top and bottom so they can be "worn" around a child; holes cut in the sides serve as "handles." Children fit inside the "packages" and become dancing gifts. Smaller boxes might be worn on feet for a different dancing effect. Add a dancing tree and create holiday stories. How does it feel to be a present? How would a box move or dance?

56. *GIFT CHARADE:* Using large carton, child decides what type of toy or Christmas present he would like to be and gets inside box. Other children pretend to wrap present, tie ribbon, etc. On "Christmas morning" the children 'open' the present. Toy comes out and the children guess from his actions what type of toy he is. (See also Activity #61.)

57. *TEN LITTLE CANDLES:* Sing tune of Ten Little Indians substituting various themes: candles, stars, reindeer, boxes, etc. Use as counting game. (MATH)

58. *THE TWELVE DAYS OF CHRISTMAS:* Use visual aids to hold up for each verse. Substitute December themes for gifts listed in song. Use children's names—use motions, i.e., "On the first day of Christmas, Robert danced like this (jiggle). He jiggled, jiggled. etc. (NAMES)

59. *TWINKLE, TWINKLE LITTLE STAR:* Use with star shapes in assorted sizes (big, bigger, biggest), (small, smaller, smallest) and fit words to tune so children can take turns rearranging stars by size.

60. *DID YOU EVER SEE A TOY?:* (Tune: Did You Ever See A Lassie) Put a collection of toys in a large box or behind a screen. As group sings the song, children take turns choosing a toy and holding it up. (Good for threes.) Older children choose toy from box and match it to picture cards of same toys spread out on the floor. When all the toys are matched with pictures, game ends. (May have a few extra pictures which do not have a matching toy.)

61. *SOUND AND MOTION MATCHING TOYS:*

a) The children stand in circle and warm up.

b) The teacher plays a music box (if possible, one that has a moving doll). Ask children to talk about different toys and move like each one! Be wooden soldiers, dancing dolls, rag dolls, drums, trumpets, balls, puppets on string, wind up cars. The "toymaker" winds up each toy and rest guess what toy it is. (See also #56.)

c) The teacher gives out scarves to one half of group and instruments to the other. The children with scarves experiment with motions (no music). Children with instruments watch. When they see something they can identify with, they join that person and combine sound with movement. Try in reverse, motion from music.

d) Each child makes a motion "Who can think of a sound that fits that motion? Make a sound with your body, not an instrument."

62. *HERE WE GO ROUND THE CHRISTMAS TREE:* (Tune: Mulberry Bush) Vary words to suit, "This is the way we cut the tree." "…we carry the tree…trim the tree," etc.

(MOTION, MUSIC)

63. *HOLIDAY SONGS:* Suggested as a good resource: *The Fireside Book of Children's Songs,* collected and edited by Marie Winn, pub. Simon and Schuster, N.Y.

64. *HANUKAH O HANUKAH:*

3 3 3 3 6 3 3   3   3 2   1 2 1
Hanukah O Hanukah Come Light the Menorah

3 3 3 3 6 3 3   3   3 2   1 2 1
Hanukah O Hanukah Come Light the Menorah

1   2   3   2   1 1 1 2 1 7   6
Come and Light the Candles so Shining and Bright

1   2   3   2   1 1 1 2 1 7   6
Come and Light the Candles so Shining and Bright

(last line grows softer)

Note: − 7 indicates below middle C.

65. *DREIDLE GAMES:* Use dreidles to develop many kinds of concept activities. Put colors, numbers, letters, names, shapes on four sides and spin. (CONCEPTS)

66. *MENORAH LOTTO:* Give each child a Menorah drawn on a card and nine separate, yellow candle flames. Teacher holds up numbers, names, colors, etc. to be identified. Child who guesses correctly lights one candle by placing cut-out flame over candle on card. Vary by having several sets of cards of yellow flames with numbers 1-9 on them. Children take turns drawing from pile and as numbers are drawn 'light' (place yellow flame on) the Menorah. *(NOTE: Number 20 might be represented by star on base of Menorah.)*

67. *TREE LOTTO:* Construct a large tree from cardboard and paste on 24 motifs from cards. Make up a matching set of playing cards. One for each of the 24 motifs. Put numbers 1-24 also on the cards. Cards are divided among children. Teacher points to a number on the December calendar and children try to find matching number and match to tree pictures. Continue until tree is all decorated. Children may help each other in finding matches.

68. *EVERGREENS:* Collect many kinds of boughs and sprigs. Use for art collage. Stuff into tiny pillows for sniffing. Dip into paint and press between folded paper for designs. Use for crayon rubbing. (SENSORY)

69. *MAGNETS:* Place nuts, screws, nails, bolts and washers into egg cups. Sort and use with magnets. Mix with non-attracting items and sort. Use "yes" and "no" signs on sorting trays. Extend activity for 5's by making books about magnetism using pictures of objects which are (are not) attracted by magnets. (SCIENCE)

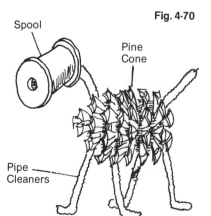

Fig. 4-70

Spool

Pine Cone

Pipe Cleaners

70. *PINE CONE ANIMALS:* Construct a variety of animals, by wrapping pine cones with pipe cleaners, forming legs, tails, antlers, etc.

71. *CINNAMON TOAST:* (This activity is especially good for the very young.) Make toast. Brush with melted butter and sprinkle on a cinnamon and sugar mixture. May be put on in two ways: Put sugar in shaker and sprinkle on cinnamon, or put a mixture of cinnamon and sugar in same container. To make this activity special, color milk with food coloring and have a 'pink' tea party.

72. *CALENDARS:* Toward the end of the year (December) ask parents, business and other associates for old calendars. Use the numbers and pictures in a variety of activities. (See Seq. 5, #96, 97)

Expanding the World   73. *CHRISTMAS DISPLAYS:* Plan a trip to see a special holiday display, many are animated. Such a field trip will require *much supervision* in crowded stores. Call ahead and the department store manager may offer special help, suggestions and even treats from the store.

74. *CHURCHES AND PARKS:* In many areas, towns have special outdoor displays featuring animals and Santas. Check to see which are nearest to your school.

75. *PLAYS AND FILMS:* Watch for special childrens' plays, musicals and films which you might attend on a field trip. Most libraries offer free films and sometimes projectors and screen.

76. *PIPE ORGANS:* Arrange two or three trips to local churches and synagogues. It may be possible to go when the organist can present a brief demonstration and show the various parts of the pipe organ.

5E. SEQUENCE FIVE

Likenesses and differences are important concepts in many areas of development. When children are learning to read they need to be able to distinguish between b and d, m and w, 3 and 8. The activities in this sequence begin to examine likenesses and differences through looking at *people who are different* in the way they look, speak, work and live.

Weather and climate, homes and the clothing and lifestyles of people differ greatly between such *hot* places as *Florida,* and *cold* places like *Alaska.* The *snow and ice* of *winter* in the north and the sunshine and *oranges* of a *Florida vacation* will be explored through the activities of this sequence.

LIKENESSES AND DIFFERENCES

1. *TWINS:* Discuss identical twins with the children. Show pictures and tell stories about them. Have some real twins come to visit if possible.

> A two year old looked with amazement at identical twins who had just joined his group and said, "One poople can't be two pooples!"

2. *WHO'S WHO:* Arrange children according to height, weight, hair color, clothing, etc. Use seriation and matching to demonstrate likenesses and differences.

3. *CLIMATE DIFFERENCES:* Discuss differences in climate and how climate affects people. What people live in cold places? Hot places? What do they wear? What kinds of houses do they live in?

Use a Vue-Master to make a display of various kinds of homes or use magazine pictures or to illustrate variety of homes.

Read *The Eskimos Knew* (see Bibliography).

4. *EVERYONE IS DIFFERENT:* Point out to the children the fact that everyone is different in some way. Discuss the advantages. (Read: *Black is Beautiful,* by McGovern, pub. Scholastic, and *Black Is Brown Is Tan,* by Arnold Adoff, pub. by Harper & Row.

5. *THE ALL-THE-SAME-PEOPLE* by Grace Mitchell:

Long, long ago in the land of make-believe, there lived a wise and a kind king. He tried very hard to make everyone in the kingdom happy and content. He provided every household with plenty to eat, warm clothing and good friends. He gave parties on holidays and special days. The castle tables were filled with delicious food and sweet treats and the grand castle halls rang with joyous entertainment.

Still, the people complained. Each one wanted to be like someone else. Not one was satisfied or happy to be just as he was. They would gather and grumble, whining and pining.

"I'm too fat" said Silly Sam, "Why couldn't I have been thin like Skinny Sue?"

"I hate my curly red hair" cried Debby, "I wish it were yellow and straight like Betsy's."

"Too tall, too tall," groaned Timothy, "If only I were small like Andy, I could get into so many nice, cozy places."

"Everyone can see the parade but me," whined Willie. "Now if I were only tall like Tim... ."

And so it went. *No* one was satisfied, *No* one was happy. No matter what the good king did for his people, they continued to moan and groan, whine and wheeze, cry and complain.

One day the desperate and unhappy king called the people all together in the large hall of the castle. "My good people," he said, "I have listened to all of your sad stories and the constant complaining. I have tried every way possible to bring each of you happiness. When you are unhappy I, too, am unhappy. I have searched for ways to make you happy. I think, at last, I have found the answer. Tommorrow, when you awaken, you will find a surprise."

The people went to their homes very excited. "What a good king we have. He is always trying to bring us happiness."

Each one went to his bed and dreamed about the wonderful surprise that was to bring them happiness on the very next morning.

As the sun rose, the people jumped from their beds and rushed to the village square. The stared at one another, for to their surprise, everyone looked like everyone else! The only way to tell mothers from fathers, brothers from sisters, neighbors from neighbors was by the sounds of their voices. It was *very* confusing. Little children went from look-alike mother to look-alike mother, tugging at skirts and crying, "Mama?" The look-alike mothers tried to sort out their look-alike children. A group of boys tried to play ball but the teams were all mixed up as every player looked like every other. The village teacher got her pupils all mixed up.

At sundown of that very first day, the King looked out the castle window. There on the lawn below sat hundreds of his people. He stepped out onto the balcony. Only sad, very unhappy faces looked up at him. At last, one man stepped out and came before the King with a deep bow.

"Oh, king," he said in a very sad voice, "we were so wrong to complain. We have come to beg you to restore us, each to his own appearance. Please, make us each different. We know now that it is good to be different, and to be satisfied with ourselves just as we are."

The wise king nodded but he did not smile. "Go home and sleep. Tomorrow is another day."

Slowly, the people plodded home and crept into their beds, feeling quite ashamed of themselves. When the sun rose the next day, everyone was exactly as before. Each person of the kingdom *was different!* Some were tall, some were short, some had curly hair, some had straight hair and some had no hair at all! Each one, plump or skinny, quick or slow, was happy to be just as he was. Never again did anyone complain about the way he looked.

That night the castle halls rang with laughter. The king gave the biggest party ever to celebrate. The people were happy to be the different kinds of people they were!

6. *MARTIN LUTHER KING DAY:* Discuss how Dr. King expressed his love for all men and relate this to the concepts love and hate, friends and enemies.

Find pictures of Dr. King and make a collage, bulletin board or book. (See book list for suggested reading.)

7. *ESKIMOS, BEARS AND MICE:* (See Instant Costumes, Seq. 3, Activity #9.) Make an instant costume of bear, mouse, Eskimo child, twins. Children use these in front of mirror to make up stories and plays.

8. *ESKIMO DIORAMA*: A young boy used a shoe box, turned on its side, to create an Eskimo diorama. (The class had discussed the length of day in the far north, midnight sun and long nights.) He painted the inside back of his box blue and pasted on a yellow sun. He made two igloos by wrapping surgical tape over balloons, one for dogs and one for Eskimo people. He made dogs, seals, a boat and sled from clay. While the clay was still wet, he attached a piece of yellow yarn to the sled, "so they would have something to pull it with." (Example of intelligent thinking which should be noted and filed to use when writing reports, see Observation and Recording-How, #11.) The box cover was placed in front of the diorama to represent the ocean and he made clear that the boat and seal went in that part. He made an Eskimo man from a plastic spoon with trousers and a poncho cut from heavy cloth, tied around the middle with yellow yarn. Some gray, shaggy, fur-like material from an old coat was glued all around his face, and boots were cut from grass-cloth wallpaper and attached to the pants.

9. *IGLOOS:* Igloos are no longer used and have become a part of the cultural myth surrounding Eskimos. They were used in olden days on seal or whale hunts. Use the ideas in

the curriculum in the same way that teepees and wigwams (Seq. 2) are included pointing out relationships and comparisons, and explaining that such homes were a part of the 'olden days' of Indians and Eskimos. Suggestions for constructing igloos.

a) Miniature igloos: Experiment with using sugar cubes put together with frosting, or styrofoam cubes and glue.

Construct cubes from snow blocks made by packing snow in milk cartons and freezing. Cover a balloon with papier mâchè or surgical tape. When dry, cut out entrance — paint white. (Seq. 4, #50)

b) Child-size igloos:

For large, indoor igloo bend chicken wire into round, roofed shelter and cover with papier mâchè. (This project is better for older children.)

If you have a geodesic dome on your playground, put a wet sheet over it and let it freeze. With next snowstorm you may pack snow over it.

10. *READING READINESS:* It is not unusual for fives, and even some fours, to be reading and writing. While we do not attempt to 'teach' them, we do tell them how to spell a word when they want to write it, give the meaning of a word if they ask, and create situations which make them want to know what a sign, or statement on the blackboard, says. The teacher's job is to provide environment, exposure and encouragement without pushing, prodding or propelling toward mastery of the three 'R's. Many of the language arts activities in this sequence involve beginning reading.

11. *WORD BAG:* Hang a shoe bag, or a set of pockets made in a similar fashion, on the wall, giving each child a pocket. Cut cards to fit pockets on which children, with the teacher's help, can record their own special words. Cards may be used for story-telling, spelling, copying, sorting, matching to pictures, etc. Children might want to draw or paste a picture on one side of the card identifying the word.

12. *STORY SEQUENCES:* Cut out pictures from old story books or a set of drawings to illustrate popular children's stories and mount them on cardboard. Distribute pictures from one particular story to the children. Ask each child to show his picture when his part of the story is read or told. When the story and pictures have become familiar, ask the children to arrange the pictures in the order in which they come in the story.

13. *SILLY STORIES:* Mix up the story pictures used in the above activity so that pictures from two or three different stories are together and ask the children to make up silly stories to go with them. For example, "Goldilocks found the three little pigs in Grandma's bed and the wolf blew the house down."

14. *SILLY PICTURES:* Mount a magazine picture on cardboard and add an object that is out of context. For example, show a picture of a girl playing in snow scene wearing a bathing suit. Use to stimulate conversation and stories. Include one or two in a set of pictures and ask children to find the silly ones.

15. *RHYMING:* Use familiar nursery rhymes to play rhyming games. Read the rhyme. Repeat the rhyming words. Ask the children to add other words with the same rhyming sounds.

Make up new verses to expand old poems.

List the class names and list rhyming words for each name. Compose a class name poem from the results. Try to think of action words when rhyming, to add motions to the activity. For example, "Jack, Jack, bent his back." "Fred, Fred, touched his head." "Susan Costello, find something yellow." (See Seq. 6, #48 and Seq. 7, #16.)

16. *ROLL AND RHYME:* Children sit in a circle. One rolls a ball to another and says a word such as 'cake'. The child receiving the ball says a rhyming word 'take'. He then says another word and rolls the ball to another child who must think of a rhyming word. Continue in the same manner.

Older children might be seated in two rows facing each other. They try to make the rhymes quickly to keep the ball rolling back and forth down the rows. When it reaches the end the rhyme is changed.

17. *ANOTHER WORD:* Stimulate language growth by asking, "What's another word for car?" "Cat?" "Kitty?", etc.

18. *TAKE A MESSAGE:* Develop concentration skills for oral language development by

sending one child out of the room and then asking a second child to deliver a message to him. The first child returns to repeat the message. Stress accuracy and complete sentences.

19. *BRAILLE:* Introduce and demonstrate the use of braille. Make bean pictures. Draw pictures in clay and describe by touching. Make sand castings of letters, numbers and shapes.

20. *NEWCOMER:*

> In one school there was a sudden change of teachers. They happened to be opposites in physical characteristics. The new teacher called attention to their differences: "I am tall. She was short. We look different," she said. "Miss Jones liked the block corner here, but I am moving it over near the window. We like things to be different. Miss Jones had juice at 10:30, but I get hungry before then, so we will try it a little earlier," to point out how people think and act differently.

21. *THE THREE BEARS:* Vary this popular childrens' story by dividing the children into three or more groups, each one with a special choral response to add drama and sound effects to the story as you read or tell it. For example:

> Group 1 says: "Humph!" (in a very gruff voice) whenever Father Bear is mentioned.
>
> Group 2 says: "Yes, indeed." (in medium voice) whenever Mother Bear is mentioned.
>
> Group 3 says: "Me, too. Me, too" (in high squeaky voice) when Baby Bear speaks.

The activity may be introduced in the following way:

Once upon a time there were three bears. There was a big, gruff father bear. He was very large and always wanted things *just so.* He always found something to grumble about. His favorite was "HUMPH" (Say it with me "HUMPH," make it sound very cross. Use your biggest Father Bear voices, without shouting.) Then there was a mother bear who was always worrying. She fussed about whether things would be *just so* for Father Bear. She worried about Baby Bear. If you listened you would hear her say very often, "Yes, indeed," in a middle-sized voice and shaking her head. (Can you nod your heads and say, "Yes, indeed" in middle-sized voices?)

Baby Bear was just like lots of children. He always wanted to do just exactly as his parents did. No matter what Father Bear did and no matter what Mother Bear suggested, Baby Bear would say in a big, squeaky voice, "Me, too! Me, too!" etc.

Variations suggested by the children, such as puppets and other sound effects, may be used to suit this and other favorite stories. As the children get the idea, the teacher should encourage their own original responses.

22. *TAPING STORIES (CHILDREN):* This is a good time of year to use the microphone and tape recorder. Children who are familiar with a story (*The Three Bears*) can take turns doing the various parts, in their own way. Play this tape back later in the year and observe if children can recognize each other's voices. Tape the story again to observe the difference.

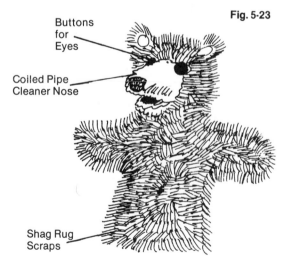

Fig. 5-23

Buttons for Eyes

Coiled Pipe Cleaner Nose

Shag Rug Scraps

23. *BEAR PUPPETS:* Make puppets from samples or odd pieces of shag carpeting cut into bear shapes. Dress and trim with beads for eyes, real clothes. Use in telling story.

24. *SHOE TALK:* Gather a collection of all kinds of shoes, high heels, sneakers, ballet slippers, bedroom slippers, fireman's boots, golf shoes, baby shoes. Place in the center of a circle. The children take turns miming various ways shoes might be used, or how you would walk in a particular shoe. Others guess which shoes a child is wearing by the way he mimes. Entire group move around room, demonstrating each shoe's character as leader holds them up in turn.

Use the collection as a discussion point about why shoes are worn, why each kind is made in a particular way. Discuss what materials the shoes are made of and how they are made. Compare shoes of various materials. (In one school, a parent who was a shoe manufacturer, brought materials and used them to explain shoe making.) Read *Choosing Shoes,* by Frieda Wolf, *Poems to Grown On.*

25. *CINDERELLA:* Tell the Cinderella story and dramatize by the following activity: Children sit in a circle, everyone removes one shoe. Shoes are placed in a carton. Each child in turn takes a shoe out of the box and goes in search of the "Cinderella" or "Prince Charming" to whom it belongs. This activity might be extended to reinforce left/right concepts and shoe tieing skills.

26. *MATCH-A-SHOE:* Divide class into two groups. All shoes are removed and placed in four large cartons, two cartons for each group. Left shoes are put in one carton, right shoes in the other. A child from each group runs to one of his team's cartons, takes out a shoe and tries to find its mate in the second carton. Team to match shoes first, wins. (RELAY RACE, 4's + 5's)

27. *SHOE TOSS:* Line up all the shoes in rows and let children take turns tossing a ball of paper into them. Numbers may be marked on toes with chalk to keep score.

28. *HOMES IN NESTS, SKYSCRAPERS, TRAILERS, AQUARIUMS:* Whether snail or fish, elephant or human, all living creatures have a home of some sort. Even nomadic tribes carry tents or erect temporary shelters. The variety and number of homes corresponds to the many creatures who inhabit them. A learning center developed around the home theme can provide many days and weeks of curriculum, stretching from 'myself' to igloos, from winter hibernation in a bear's den to the life support systems of outer space. Discussion, picture collections, books about the homes of animals and people are the basic materials needed to establish such a learning center. What kinds of homes do people live in? Houses, cottages, huts, cabins, castles, palaces, apartments, condominiums, mansions, duplex, motel, hotel, trailer, dormitory, prison, houseboat, tent, teepee, wigwam, hogan, igloo? How many different kinds of houses do the people in the classroom inhabit? What different things are houses made of? What kinds of houses do animals live in? Nest, den, coop, cage, lair, cave, hole, burrow, hutch, barn, stable, shed, web, rookery, hive, lodge (beaver's)? Does a fish have a house? What kinds of materials are used for animal homes? (HOMES)

29. *MY HOME:* The home is a very important part of every child's environment. His house is unique as he creates it through his memory of it. He thinks about home while he is away from it at school. At first, he may just think of his own room and toys, but he soon begins to understand the other rooms of his house. He separates his own from others. He learns what belongs to him and what belongs to others and to the whole family. In school, children can be encouraged to describe their houses and families and thus to develop pride in their own homes. (HOMES)

Pictures

Pockets

Fig. 5-29

30. *WHERE DO YOU LIVE?* Put pictures of farm, ocean, jungle, house across the top of large sheet of cardboard. Under each one make a pocket (see sketch). Children cut out pictures from magazines of people, animals, fish, etc. Mount them on construction paper and label and back with "fish," "cat," "dog" to be placed in pocket under correct heading.

31. *MY ROOM:* Children make large posters with pictures of things in their rooms. Supply them with catalogues and magazines from which they can cut pictures of as many objects as they can think of that are in their own rooms at home.

Variation: Ask child to close eyes and describe a room in his house. Others guess which room.

32. *MY HOUSE:* Make individual scrap books out of construction paper. With littlest ones, cardboard covers and pages may be pre-cut by teacher in the shape of a house. Kindergartners will want to do it themselves. Bind with string for easy page turning and so that the book will lie open flat. Each page represents one room of the house and the children paste in pictures cut from magazines or catalogues of appropriate furnishings.

Paper doll people may be included. Rooms can be decorated with wallpaper, lighting fixtures, windows, doors, rugs, etc. Color of covers (house exteriors) may be chosen by children depending on the color of their own houses.

The outside of the house (covers) may be decorated with shrubs, doors, windows, mailbox, doorbell, street address, etc.

Cardboard covers can be painted and sprayed with clear lacquer to keep paint from rubbing off.

(A good activity for older children in a center which has after school care.)

33. *FURNITURE LOTTO:* Make large, lotto cards picturing various rooms of a house. Divide cards into five to ten sections depending on age group. Cut out pictures of items of furniture, appliances, accessories, tools, etc. from a catalogue and mount on oak tag or construction paper in sizes to fit lotto squares. Each child is given a lotto card and takes a turn drawing from the stack of pictures to fill his card with items pictured for appropriate room. A group discussion of what item goes where will teach concepts necessary for playing the game.

34. *MOVING DAY:*

On the first day back after their winter vacation, the children arrived at school to find the walls were bare and the furniture have been left piled up to facilitate cleaning. Teachers might have gone in, arranged the rooms, put up pictures, set up activity centers, but they deliberately left it empty. As soon as the children had arrived, they had a meeting. The teacher said, "This is your school. How would you like to have it? Should we put things back as they were? What changes could you suggest?"

Ideas began to pop! Following discussion and a plan chosen by the group, all became involved in rearranging and moving furniture.

David said, "Gee, this is really heavy. It didn't look it."

"I don't think this can go through the door. Maybe if we tip it it won't be so square," suggested Mary.

"It's going to seem funny not to see the doll corner in the same place," another mover said.

As the days passed, other changes were made and with each move the staff observed learning:

"That chair is too big to fit through the door."

"It's too heavy to go up the stairs."

"There used to be room enough for four people, now only two at a time should be in here."...

(Read in Part I, Curriculum—Catalyst or Conformist, Section 2. Basic Premises.)

35. *FURNITURE DISPLAY:* Children make books of "Things to Sit On," "Things to Eat With," etc.

36. *CHAIRS* by Clea Chmela

A chair is bare
unless you sit in it.
Your mother
will knit in it.

Some chairs will rock,
But most are straight.
Some chairs talk;
They "squeak" with weight.

A chair at the table
Is never just right,
Too high or too low
Too big or too tight.

Some chairs are squeezy,
weezy and light;
But some are called "easy"
and those are just right!

37. *TODAY IS KITCHEN DAY:* Over a period of several weeks special days may be set aside, such as Kitchen Day, Bedroom Day, Bathroom Day; for example:

a) *Kitchen Day* you might plan to cook and introduce special appliances, i.e. blenders, toasters, waffle iron, can openers, Dutch oven, etc. If possible, plan to tour the school kitchen.

b) *Bedroom Day* can be dedicated to discussion of bedroom furnishings, including sheets, blankets and pillows. Develop loud and soft concepts by have a quiet, cuddly day with quiet, sleepy stories on a blanket. Talk about feathers. Demonstrate bed making.

c) *Bathroom Day* can start with the dolls getting bathed. Have a discussion of plungers and plumbing, sewers and traps. Older children might discuss the hygienic history of bathrooms, open sewers, etc. (See Seq. 8, Activity #53-56)

38. *APARTMENT HOUSE MURAL:* Make a tall mural of an apartment building on a large sheet of paper, divided into apartments, one per child. Ask each to furnish his own apartment with pictures or drawings of the things he would like in his apartment.

39. *HOUSE MURAL:* Make a class mural of a house, perhaps including a garage and yard. After class discussion, divide the house into several rooms. Have groups of children furnish each room with wallpaper, furniture, accessories, etc. drawn or cut out from magazines or catalogues.

40. *FLOOR MAP:* On a large piece of paper, make a floor map of the classroom. First draw the general layout of the room indicating placement of windows and doors to orient children. In discussion, reinforce the one-to-one concept of a picture for each area or item in the room. Then using pictures drawn or cut from toy, or other catalogues, paste on items of furniture in proper locations, indicating the special areas of the room, such as block shelves, book corner, doll corner, sink, etc. (See #42 — Blue Print)

41. *WOODSVILLE:*

Woodsville was a village which occupied a space 4′ × 4′ and grew much larger before it was completed. Each day something new was added to the village and more sentences added to the story book which was posted on the wall behind the sculpture. There were roads, streets, houses, garages, a fire house and swimming pools. Later a zoo was added. One day the children went for a walk to look at doors and roofs to see how they were alike and different. The 'spin-off' from this project carried into every aspect of program.

Children nailed and glued jar covers, bottle caps, corks, screws, wires, small blocks of wood to a small board. Some of the sculpture was painted. It became a miniature city, a machine, and whatever else imagination dictated.

The projects lasted for many weeks and when finished, the panel was hung on a wall, a very attractive 3-D wood sculpture. (END OF DAY)

42. *BLUEPRINTS:* Make a blueprint of the classroom. On a large sheet of blue paper place unit blocks in proper locations to represent various classroom furnishings, such as piano, tables, workbench, etc. Label each block with masking tape. When children are satisfied that they have placed the blocks accurately, ask them to draw around each with white chalk. Remove the blocks and transfer masking tape labels to outlined areas. The results should be a fairly accurate "blueprint" of your classroom.

Show the children some real blueprints or room layouts from decorating magazines.

43. *WINTER SPORTS:* Cut magazine pictures of winter sports and make into books.

44. *WHERE, OH WHERE:* To the tune of "Where, Oh Where, Has My Little Dog Gone," sing:

"Oh where, oh where has my snow man gone
Oh where, oh where can it be…"

45. *I'M A LITTLE SNOW MAN:* To the tune of "I'm a Little Teapot," sing:

I'm a little snowman
ROUND and fat
This is my broom and
This is my hat
Sun comes along and shines so hot
That now I'm just a very damp spot!

46. *DRUM TALK:* Child is appointed a leader and beats a pattern on a drum. Other children repeat pattern on the floor with sticks. Children beat on different sizes and shapes

of plastic wastebaskets, pails and dishpans. Talk about differences in tone. (See Seq. 3, #21, 22, 23.)

47. *BIG WORDS:* Put new, big words on a large wall chart. Encourage older children to make the letters. This is a good time to recall how names were tapped out. Beat drum, shake bells, clap hands or tap sticks to accompany words, i.e. Co-op-er-a-tion: ____ ____ ____ __ _____.

48. *WHAT CAN WE DO IN THE WINTERTIME:* Ask this question of the children. One child might demonstrate skating, another sliding, another skiing, etc. Each child becomes completely absorbed in his own movement.

5   5   5 5 5 6   5 5   3
What can we do in the wintertime

4   4   2   5   5   3
wintertime, wintertime.

5   5   5 5 5 6   5 5   3
What can we do in the wintertime

4   2   1 7   1
when we all go out.

We can skate in the wintertime

etc. etc.

We can ski....

etc. etc.

49. *SKATING TIME:* Develop a movement session or dramatize from the following poem by Deborah Mitchell Haney:

SKATING TIME

We waited patiently each day
As winter came around
To take our skates down to the tree
Beside the skating pond.

I asked my mother, "Is it time?"
I really couldn't wait.
And then one day she said to me,
"*Today* we'll learn to skate."

The air was very, very cold.
The ice was very slick.
We sat beneath our little tree
And put our skates on—quick!

We slipped and slid across the ice
And sometimes I would fall,
But skating was so *very* nice
It didn't hurt at all!

50. *PAPER SNOW BALL:* Make a paper snowball by crumpling tissue or newspaper and covering it with tissue and scotch tape. Throw it, push it with nose, push it with stick, play baseball, hockey, basketball (toss into wastebasket), roll, pick up and drop, etc. (See Seq. 6, #63.)

51. *ING WORDS:* Make a list of words ending with 'ing'. Put on wall: push-ing, rest-ing, run-ning, crawl-ing, sing-ing, cry-ing, skip-ping, talk-ing, jump-ing, eat-ing, etc. Let children choose one to do. Make pictures to illustrate words. (See Seq. 7, #67.)

The kindergarten children had been experimenting with "ing" words. They made a list of motions—running, swinging, sliding, rolling, falling, which the teacher wrote down on cards. They defined the motion words with body movements. Later, the teacher gave them crayons and a large sheet of paper. "How could your crayon show swinging?" "I do not mean to make a picture of someone swinging. Do not lift the crayon from the paper but move it to make a pattern or design of the motion." They colored in parts of the resulting designs with crayons and then painted over the entire paper with dark paint to create resist paintings. (See Relief Paintings.)

Another day they made the "ing" motions with finger paint—one day they listened to records to find music which would 'fit' a motion—in one class, a pianist played and the children guessed what motion she had in mind-another time the teacher varied the music and they changed the pattern as they colored on a piece of mural paper.

52. *SHADOW GAME:* Play shadow game to music. One child pretends he is another child's shadow and copies his every movement. Accompany with march or dance music.

53. *SHADOW TAG:* One child tries to stand in another child's shadow as he moves around.

54. *ANGELS IN THE SNOW:* Play angels in snow. Twirl child (gently) around by one hand. He falls in snow and makes an impression. Do same thing indoors—freeze in position.

55. *SNOW DANCE:* Children move with sliding, skating, skiing motions; walk on snowshoes; walk in deep snow. Talk about machines used in snowstorms—plows, snow blowers, snow loaders, dump trucks. Ask children to think of ways to move like machines. Several children may work together, i.e. snow loader and dump truck. Use the following variation of "Polly Wolly Doodle."

> I can jump, jump, jump
> I can jump, jump, jump
> I can jump, jump, jump all day...etc.

Substitute appropriate verbs—slide, skate, ski, etc.

56. *LIKENESSES AND DIFFERENCES:* Begin with a circle. Move all parts of the body, one at a time. Then move the whole body at one time using the following suggestions:

stiff/loose	heavy/light	slow/fast
big/small	sweet/sour	
bumpy/smooth	hot/cold	

How would you express the following with your body? Use parts and then whole body.

loud/soft	high/low	one foot/two feet
tall/short	hopping/jumping	one hand/two hands
wide/narrow	moving/stopping	

57. *BEAN BAGS:* (See Seq. 11, #155, 156, 157) Begin with circle, warm up. Introduce bean bags. "What can you do with it?" Toss and catch. Toss to a friend. Toss and clap before catching. Put on head, walk and run. Pass to left, to right, under legs.

One person plays different rhythms on a drum while the rest walk around the room with a bean bag on their heads. "When it falls, you sit down."

Animals: Ask who can move like a snake? Like a bunny? What other animal can you think of? How would it move? "One person move and let us guess what animal you are." "Find a place in the room for your animal house. When music plays, come out of your house. Listen for the right kind of music. If you are a mouse, will you move to the same music as an elephant? As a bunny?"

58. *THE CLOCK SONG:* Use the following chant with activities below (modulate voice to indicate size and sound of clocks):

> Great big steeple clocks go "Tock, tock, tock, tock"
> And the little mantel clocks go "Tick tock, Tick tock, Tick, tock"
> And the little tiny watches ticking through the night and day go
> Tick a tick a tick a tick a tick a tick a tick.

59. *CLOCKS FROM BLOCKS:* Hold up a block and say, "If this were the steeple clock what size block would you choose for the mantel clock? For the wristwatches?" Use three sizes of dowels or sticks to tap clock rhythms on blocks.

60. *CLOCK MOVEMENTS:* Experiment as follows:

Steeple clocks are stamping feet.
Mantel clocks are clapping hands.
Wrist watches are finger snapping, or tongue clicking.
Steeple clocks are big body movements, with arms extended sideways or over head.
Mantel clocks are shoulders or hands.
Wrist watches are eyes blinking, or fingers moving.

61. *ELASTIC:* (see Seq. 3, #54.) Children sit, or stand, in circle holding elastic and move, stretch, push or pull or pluck elastic. Make sounds with mouth, such as ou-ou-ou and i-i-i-i when pushing and pulling; ah-ah-ah and e-e-e-e when pushing up and down. P-p-p-plucking when plucking. All get inside elastic and go round and round, saying choo-choo-choo. Lean back on elastic; sit down and put around feet. What else can you do?

62. *CHRISTOPHER ROBIN,* by A.A. Milne: Use poem in a rhythmic sing-song voice—clap it, use sticks and other instruments.

63. *SNOWFLAKES,* a poem by Elizabeth L. Cleveland. This is an excellent poem to use to develop a movement and dramatic play session. Read the first four lines and use with tissue paper snowflakes. Develop the drama by choosing children to be snowplows, drivers, shovelers. A group might make the sound effects. Cars start hard, wheels spin. Develop ideas from discussion of children's experiences.

64. *STORY TELLING:* If a car happens to get stuck on the way to school and the wheels are spinning, talk about traction.

Make up a story about "The Day Our Car (Bus) Got Stuck"—make illustrations.
Tell the story on tape with the help of the children as narrators and sound effects.

65. *WHEN SNOW FALLS,* by Deborah Mitchell Haney:

When snow falls—sometimes I think of fairy queens waving their wands
Or, maybe, fluffy feathers from snow-white swans.
Or balls of cotton falling gently to the ground
Or even apple blossoms shaken gently from a tree
Or softly falling stars that glide by me
When snow falls down,

so

silently.

66. *HOKEY, POKEY:* Good movement song to learn left and right.
LOOBY LOO also good for left and right concepts.

67. *RIGHT/LEFT:* To help children learn RIGHT from LEFT, use some of the following methods:

a. When helping him put on shoes, say "Lift up your right foot." Squeeze the foot. "Now lift up your left foot." *Do not* squeeze the left. Do the same with mittens, coat, sweater, etc. *Always* squeeze the right, never the left. *Point* to the left hand (foot).

b. Ask the child to: raise his left hand; put his left hand out to the side; look at left hand; keep looking at it; turn toward left hand; go after it; spin around after his hand; touch the wall with extended hand; mark a spot on the wall and face it. Say, "That's *correct*, you are turning toward your left (right) hand. That means you are turning left (right)."

Give encouragement with "Good," "Try again" and follow this procedure in various activities until the child can follow simple right/left orders, remembering that his knowledge will be quite fragile. He may respond correctly two or three times, and then be confused. NOTE: *Never* use the word "right" to indicate "correct." Use "good," "fine," to prevent confusion. (See also Seq. 10, #30.)

Snow, Ice, Temperature

68. *EXPLORING SNOW:* When snowy weather comes, watch for every chance to explore its various qualities. It can be heavy and wet, dry and fluffy, hard and crusty, etc. Discuss why the quality varies. Look at snow through a magnifying glass or microscope. Melt snow.

69. *SNOWFLAKES:* Catch snow flakes on black velvet or felt, and study under magnifying glass. Look at snowflake photographs in scientific journals or books. Cut folded paper hexagons or circles into snowflake designs. Use spyrograph designs and compare.

70. *SNOW SCRUBBING:* Winter clean your floor with snow. Scoop snow up in buckets. Heat on the stove and use the water to scrub, just as the pioneers used to do.

71. *FREEZER SNOWBALLS:* Freeze a snowball in your freezer. Color snow and freeze it. Melt and observe time and results.

72. *SNOWMEN:* Make a small, three or four foot snowman outside. Collect additional snow in plastic buckets and bring inside to make another snowman of the same size. Set the "Silly Snowman" in the sink, or container large enough to hold the melted snow. Use the following poem.

73. *THE SILLY SNOWMAN,* author unknown:

> Once there was a snowman
> Who stood outside the door
> He thought he'd like to come inside
>   And play upon the floor.
>
> He thought he'd like to warm himself
> By the firelight red,
> Thought he'd like to climb upon
>   A big white bed.
>
> So he called the North Wind
> "Help me, Wind, I pray,
> I'm completely frozen,
>   Standing out all day."
>
> So the North Wind came along
> And blew him in the door
> Now there's nothing left of him
>   But a puddle on the floor....

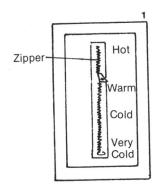

Fig. 5-79

74. *SNOWPLOW:*

A teacher was having difficulty in getting a child to do his share in putting the blocks away. She tried many of the usual techniques: "Who can bring me this shape?" "I need someone to find all of the long ones to fill this part of the shelf," etc. The child would not cooperate until she said, "I wonder what would happen if a snowplow (bulldozer) came along?" With great delight he "plowed" all of the scattered blocks into a pile by the block shelves and then helped to stack them.

75. *SUNGLASSES:* Make sun glasses by cutting narrow slits in strips of cardboard. Tie string or elastic on ends. Wear outside in bright sunlight. Discuss glare of the sun on snow. (ESKIMOS)

76. *FRICTION TEST:* Put sandpaper on one side of a block of wood. Rub on table. Turn block over and rub smooth wood on same surface. Wax the smooth side of the wood and try again. Pull a heavy load over the ice on a sled. Discuss friction.

77. *FRESH WATER FROM SALT:* Explain the fact that Eskimos look for blocks of ice that are bluish in color. These are blocks of sea water that have frozen, melted a little and frozen again many times. Each time melting takes place the salt slowly works its way out. Melted blue ice makes fresh drinking water. Follow up discussion with this experiment: (ESKIMOS)

Fill saucepan half way with fresh water. Add three tablespoons of salt—stir—taste. Put lid on pan and boil water. Remove lid and replace it with a plate turned upside down. Allow water to cool. Taste fresh water formed on plate.

78. *MELTING, FREEZING, EVAPORATING:* Fill a one quart jar with snow. Allow to melt. Mark jar to show water level when melted. Place jar in freezer. Mark the ice line when water is frozen. Melt water and check the new level with the original water mark. Place jar on radiator and allow to evaporate. Observe residue left when entirely evaporated. Discuss processes involved and results. Compare these water cycle activities with natural phenomena, such as clouds, rain, puddles, floods, droughts.

79. *THERMOMETER:* Simulate indoor thermometer with red zipper sewn between two strips of cloth (see Fig. 1) or a loop of bias tape fed through oak tag (see Fig. 2). Hang it on

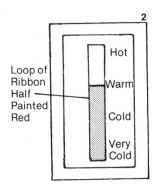

the wall and label beside it very cold, cold, cool, warm, hot, very hot. Move zipper each day according to outside thermometer.

TALK ABOUT THE DANGERS
OF *THIN* ICE

80. *ICICLES:* Observe icicles on the roof. Discuss what caused them. Point out their beauty as well as their dangers. Melt and evaporate icicles in shallow pan. Observe residue. Discuss how icicles can be made.

81. *FISHING THROUGH ICE:* Cut fish from leather or plastic scraps and attach a paper clip to each. Put in tub of water and freeze. Break through ice and fish with magnets on string.

82. *LINEAR MEASURE:* Measure classroom floor, table top or rug, etc., using objects found in the classroom, such as blocks, shoes, string or sticks. Make charts showing the length of each item measured. For instance, "The table was one and a half lengths of string, 16 of Robbie's shoes, 24 of the long block." At the next session, put out an assortment of accurate measuring tools, such as tape measure, yard stick, meter stick, 12-inch ruler. Re-measure items and record results on another chart. Discuss inches, feet, yards, meters. With older children, you might explain early measuring methods and the use of feet, strides, knuckles, hands.

83. *LIQUID MEASURE:* Dramatize the necessity of measuring by deliberately shortening the juice supply in the pitcher one day. Pour full cups all around until the juice is gone and there are still empty cups. Ask, "What can we do? How can we all have some?" Pour all the juice back into the pitcher and re-pour, putting less in each one so that all have some. Discuss the possibilities of how to measure, using the cups and pitcher.

One day later, use a glass bottle as a measuring tool. Using colored water, fill juice cups with the water until it is all distributed. Then cup by cup pour the water back into the bottle. As each cup is poured, mark the side of the bottle to show how much the quantity has increased. Count the number of cups poured into the bottle. Place corresponding numbers on the bottle. Another day use this bottle to serve the juice and once again shorten the supply. Ask, "How can we be sure there will be enough to go around?" Perhaps then you will divide the full cup measure marks into half cup markings. Explore all the possibilities of the measuring bottle. Give the children small bottles, cups, tape and colored water to experiment in making their own measuring bottles.

Another time provide children with measuring cups and milk cartons in half pint, pint, quart, half gallon and gallon sizes. Ask them to find out how many times one volume of liquid will fit into various containers.

84. *DRY MEASURE:* Use a standard measuring cup to weigh objects of various kinds (flour, beans, rice, nails, sawdust, sand). Make a chart showing the differences.

85. *INSULATION:* Discuss how people and animals keep warm in cold weather. Demonstrate insulation by having children put on winter coats in warm room. Ask them how it feels, and why. Talk about the heavy coats that animals grow to protect them during the winter months, and how they shed them (molting) in the spring. Discuss building insulation. If possible, visit a building under constrcution to show how and where insulation is used.

86. *CLOTHING THERMOMETER:* Talk about the clothing of people living in various climates. Collect a set of pictures from clothing catalogues, magazines, travel folders showing many kinds of clothing worn in various climates and according to weather conditions. Make charts showing temperatures, climates, weather and put the clothing pictures in appropriate columns. Use as a 'thermometer' telling what clothing is needed today. Use as a game. Design lotto cards around the same idea. Make a simple map showing your area and others much hotter or colder. Paste the appropriate clothing pictures in the various areas of the map.

87. *FASHION SHOW:* Place an assortment of clothing behind a screen—warm weather, cold weather; costumes from foreign lands; hats, etc. Two or three children at a time, dress up and come out to tell where they live, are travelling, weather conditions, etc.

VARIATION: Use paper dolls and clothing pictures in the same manner. Child tells where his doll lives and/or why he is dressed in a certain way. Or teacher provides paper dolls and clothing pictures and asks, "Your doll lives in Mexico and is travelling to Alaska. What will he need to take along?"

Clocks 88. *NUMBER SEQUENCE:* In preparation for clock study, make a set of sturdy cards with numbers one through twelve. Use in sequence and counting activities. Children may arrange scattered numbers in numerical order; or, arrange cards in numerical order, have one child leave the room, and while he is gone remove one number. When he returns, have him try to guess which number was removed.

89. *CLOCKS OF ALL KINDS:* Collect pictures and draw many kinds of clocks—wrist watches, alarm clocks, steeple clocks, etc. Arrange a set of pictures slowing modern clocks at various times from 1:00 to 10:00. Ask if anyone can find the clock which shows the time on the classroom clock. (See Seq. 7, #89c.)

90. *CLOCK NUMBERS:* Make a large circle in chalk on floor. Place plastic or cardboard numbers indicating hours on a clock face and large cardboard pointers to use as clock hands. One child 'sets hands' by moving pointers to two numbers. Children march around the circle to music. When the music stops the children who are at the designated numbers make a motion, such as hopping or clapping. The other children then join in. Ask if children can identify the numbers. As numbers are learned, ask if they can identify the time.

Have two children lie flat on the floor representing the hands of a clock. Have them indicate the time shown on the classroom clock, what time we go home, what time we have lunch, etc. (See Staff, #15—Maintenance, last paragraph.)

91. *CRAZY LAND,* by Deborah Mitchell Haney:

> Ticks 'n' talks,
> Knocks on blocks.
> Flocks of ox?
> Locks on rocks.
> ....Fox near docks?
> A BOX that TALKS?
> Socks on hawks
> Ticks 'n' tocks
> A funny world
>   with *FEET* on CLOCKS!

92. *PICTURE CLOCKS:* Instead of numbers on the clock, place pictures of various activities throughout the day—juice time, naptime, lunch, etc. Explain that the long hand is the pointer to watch.

93. *SHADOW CLOCKS:* Mark a time line on a sunny window sill and time activities according to the shadows cast across it at various times. Time activities according to window casement shadow marks along the floor. Mark the spots with tape and picture of activity.

Record seasonal changes in sunlight by marking a time line showing the shadow line as it appears on the same day of each *month*.

94. *SAND CLOCK:* Use an hour glass and an egg timer in various activities. Play games using the three minute timer. "Can you do this puzzle before the sand runs through?" "How many times can you run around the sandbox before the sand stops?" Cook three minute eggs. How many turns of the timer will it take to cook hard boiled eggs?

95. *PAPER PLATE CLOCK:* After demonstrating half, quarter, whole with apple, blocks, cuisennaire rods, cup, etc., make a paper plate clock and cut into quarters to teach quarter past, quarter of, half past...

Calendars 96. *CALENDAR PICTURES:* Collect a set of calendar pictures which show the various seasons, holidays, natural events. Talk about why each picture might have been chosen to represent a particular month. Look in magazines for pictures which might go with January. Can you find some pictures to go with December, last summer, early spring?

97. *CALENDAR LOTTO:* Mount six calendar sheets on cardboard to create lotto cards (use months with the same number of days). Make two sets of cards with numbers 1-31. One set is used as a drawing pile, one is dealt to six players. Teacher reads cards from the drawing pile and the children match theirs to their calendar card. The first to use up all his cards wins the round.

98. *COUNTING DAYS:* Explain that clocks count the hours and calendars count the days. Use the classroom calendar to show the days and how the numbers are used as counters. Mark the day of each month off as they pass.

Cut old calendars and use the numbers to construct new calendars.

Place two milk cartons beside a calendar. Place a set of beans or pebbles, etc., in one carton, one for each day of the month. Remove one pebble each day and put it in the second carton. Explain that when the pebbles are all gone from the first carton, the month will be over.

Children may decide how many pebbles are needed for each month by laying one pebble on each numbered square on the calendar.

99. *SUNDIAL:* In some quiet area of the playground, which gets day round sunshine, make your own sundial. Use a stake with string or rope to mark out a large ring (4 ' to 6 ' in diameter.). Put a 6 ' stake in the center as the shadow pointer. As the days come and go, 'calibrate' your clock by placing markers (rocks) as the points where shadows fall on the hours. Markers can be painted with numbers. Markers might be holes dug out and filled with cement and numbers etched in. (See Seq. 8, #67.)

Sensory Activities

100. *HEARING:* Demonstrate differences in sound using the following activities:

Play low and high on piano. Have children move up and down accordingly.

Blindfold children and ask them to identify sounds such as tearing paper, pouring water, using egg beater, striking metal, wood, etc. Differences in voices could be pointed out in the same manner.

Make a set of pictures of objects that make a sound, such as typewriter, bus, dog, bell, etc. Hold up pictures and ask children to make the appropriate sound. Or reverse the activity by having one child make a particular sound and others find picture to match the sound.

101. *SIGHT:* Sharpen the children's powers of observation with the following activities:

a) Have children line up in two teams. While the players in one team have their backs turned, the others each change something in their wearing apparel. The first team then tries to guess what change was made.

b) Hang a sheet and place a bright lamp behind it. Place various objects in front of lamp to project shadows on the sheet. Have children guess what the object is. Children's silhouettes could be projected in the same way. (See Seq. 6, #32.)

c) Use paint sample chips from a hardward store, wallpaper samples or cloth swatches for color seriation, pattern matching, sorting, etc. (Do not use lead based paint chips.)

102. *BLIND TRAIL:* Make a blind trail with string or rope, either around the classroom or outside on the playground. Let children walk along it blindfolded and identify specific things along the way, such as bathroom door, block corner, sink, easel, or swing set, sandbox, climbing pole, etc.

103. *A WALK IN THE SNOW:*

It was the first day back at school after a major snowstorm. The children were excited because everything looked different. As they entered the classroom the teacher read this poem:

The First Snow, by Mary Louise Allen
(Poems to Grow On)

Snow makes whiteness where it falls.
The bushes look like popcorn balls.

The places where we always play
Look like somewhere else today.

She suggested that they take a walk outside. The school was on a farm with a wooded area. They listened, and observed the stillness, the closed-in quietness all around them. They listened for sounds of wild life. They heard trucks on the highway and a snowplow that was still working to clear a side street. The sounds of cars were muffled by the snow. They looked for tracks in the snow. The children found trudging along in the deep snow very hard and tiring. (This was relived later in a movement session.) The children noticed how the snow was piled in drifts and that some of the ground was almost bare in spots. They talked about wind. They observed the contrast of white snow in the crotches of trees and lying along the branches of the dark trees and found some bushes which looked as though they were covered with popcorn balls. As they looked at pieces of play equipment completely covered by snow, the children conjured up imaginary creatures out of the shapes.

Winter Gardens 104. *SWEET POTATO VINE:* Set the narrow end of sweet potato in glass of water and place in a closet or some other dimly lit place until it begins to sprout (approximately ten days). Then move it to a sunny spot. Keep replacing water to prevent stagnation.

105. *CITRUS TREES:* Soak seeds from citrus fruits overnight and plant in potting soil. Keep them well watered, in a sunny place.

106. *ONION PLANT:* Put three toothpicks into large onion and suspend over a small glass of water, so that only the bottom of the onion is in the water. Place in a sunny window and watch it sprout leaves. Replace water frequently. When roots form, transfer to a flower pot of rich soil. (An avocado pit can be sprouted in the same way.)

107. *PINEAPPLE PLANT:* Slice off top two inches of a pineapple, leaving green top attached; allow to dry for ten days. Plant it in damp, sandy soil. Keep it moist. After it begins sprouting roots (about one month), transplant it to a larger pot of sandy potting soil.

108. *POPCORN:*

Pop it! Eat it! Explore it!

Put some in a paper bag on the table. Feel outside of bag. What does it feel like? Have children take some out and feel. Make list of words to describe its smell, feel and look.

Popcorn pictures—Make pictures on dark paper pasting on popcorn. Point out hard kernels which didn't pop. Can we plant them?

Plant a kernel of plain corn, a kernel of uncooked popcorn and a kernel of cooked popcorn in three paper cups. Observe which one grows.

109. *SNOW PUDDING:* (Serve with custard sauce)

1 envelope plain gelatine	*Custard Sauce*
½ cup cold water	1 cup milk
1 cup hot water	1 egg yolk
juice of one lemon	⅓ cup sugar
¾ cup sugar	pinch salt
1 egg	½ tsp. vanilla

Soak gelatin in cold water 5 minutes. Add boiling water and stir until dissolved. Add strained lemon juice. Chill until mixture begins to harden. Meanwhile, beat white of egg until stiff and add to slightly hardened mixture. Beat until spongy. Chill and serve when hardened.

110. *SNOWFLAKE PUDDING:*

1 cup sugar
1 envelope unflavored gelatin
½ tsp. salt
1½ cup milk
2 cups whipping cream, whipped
1 tsp. vanilla
1-3½ oz. can (about 1⅓ c.) flaked coconut

Thoroughly mix sugar, gelatin and salt in saucepan. Add milk. Stir over medium heat until gelatin and sugar are dissolved. Chill until partially set. Add vanilla, fold into coconut. Fold in whipped cream. Pile into mold. Chill until firm (at least 4 hours). Unmold. Makes 8 adult servings.

111. *POPSICLE JUICE:* Fill a paper cup with juice and fit with a popsicle stick held in place by slitting a circle of cardboard to fit over the cup top. Write each child's name on a stick. Freeze.

112. *FUN WITH POPCORN:* The teacher spread a white sheet on the floor. "What is that for?" the children asked, gathering around. "We are going to make popcorn a different way," he replied. Placing an electric popper in the middle of the sheet, he explained, "I am going to leave the cover off. When the popcorn starts to pop out, it will be hot, so we will have to have some rules." He gave each child a sheet of newspaper on which they wrote their names with black crayon. These were placed around the sheet. A sign was placed at the entrance to the area which said STOP—DO NOT ENTER and a low barrier was placed under it. "When the popcorn starts to fly around you will want to reach for it, but you may only have that which comes near you."

Then the teacher put some oil in the popper and poured in some kernels which he referred to as seeds. The children talked about what was going to happen. They curled up on their papers like seeds and imagined that it was getting warmer, then hotter and hotter. When the corn started to pop, so did they. They ate only the popcorn that came near them. The teacher brushed some towards those who were not getting their fair share. They talked about the seeds that did not pop and tried some of them a second time and then took the remaining kernels and scattered them outside for the birds. A discussion related the experience to the energy crisis, talking first about the kind of energy going into the popper, and also about the energy that made the seeds burst open. When the popcorn was flying all over, one child said, "It is snowing." Later they made snow pictures using popcorn. (See #108.)

113. *POPCORN PEOPLE—EXPECT THE UNEXPECTED:*

In one center a director heard a terrible thumping and loud squealing coming through the ceiling. In dismay she went charging upstairs to quiet the explosion of classroom noise. The class had just had fun with popcorn (see activity #112). Following the spontaneous reaction of one exuberant four-year-old, all the children and teachers were "being" popcorn. The director, too, was soon bouncing and jumping around on the "hot" floor as she became a kernel of corn being popped into a fluffy white piece of popped corn.

5F. SEQUENCE SIX

People need people, a child needs a *friend,* a friend is someone to *love.* The *emotions* of *love and hate* are opposites and there are many feelings in between which affect our daily lives. We send *Valentines* to friends through the *mail. Letters* need an *address,* a letter carrier and the *post office* to reach their destination.

Doctors, nurses and other people who help to make us well work in *hospitals. Presidents* and other *national leaders* help to govern us. People need people in many ways.

1. *DOCTORS, NURSES, HOSPITAL WORKERS:* Discuss and list all the medical people and describe their jobs. What do they do? Where? What experiences have your children had? Dramatize and write a story of a sick child, the mother's care, the call to the doctor, an emergency trip to the hospital.

2. *EMERGENCY SQUAD:* Who are they? Ambulance drivers, policemen, firemen. What equipment do they use? Vehicles, stretchers, sirens, oxygen. What is an emergency? List, and add pictures of each—Fire, drowning, trapped, wild animal loose, lost child. (DRAMA)

3. *HOSPITALS:* A visit to a real hospital is the VERY best introduction. Sometimes parents who are doctors and nurses can host such a trip. If the basic areas are visited and explained, the apprehension and sometimes fear connected with hospitals can be eased. Play hospital games, have discussions, try to discover what fears, what misconceptions, etc., your children may have.

4. *NURSE:* Invite a nurse to come in and talk and give a check up. Give the children time to ask and answer questions.

5. *MY TRIP TO THE HOSPITAL:* Have any of your children been to the hospital? Can they relate their experience? Find out as much as you can, write it into a story to be read and illustrated by children. Ask questions to extend, such as, "Where do you sleep? Alone? Did your mother stay all might? Visitors? Food? Bathrooms? Bedpans? Needles? Medicine?" Climax by pointing out such things as, "You did have pain but it went away," "You were homesick but people came to visit," "What were the happy things?," "You were brave," "You were sick and the people in the hospital helped you to get better," and so on. A child's very own version of his stay can be invaluable in gaining a child's eye view of a hospital.

6. *HOSPITAL MURAL:* Children find, or draw pictures relating to hospitals and sickness to paste on a large sheet of paper. 'Speech bubbles', such as those used in cartoons, may be added to include children's comments as spoken by figures in the mural.

7. *OUR OWN HOSPITAL:* Encourage dramatic play be suggesting that the children set up their own hospital in the classroom. The children may want to use the following equipment:

> Beds or operating table—seat blocks or cots with sheets, etc.
>
> Uniforms—men's white shirts with sleeves cut short for doctors, nurses, etc. Headbands, caps, johnnies for patients. (Provide hooks for uniforms.)
>
> Medical equipment—stethoscope, ace bandages, bed pan, basin, even bed table.

8. *THE TEACHER'S ROLE IN DRAMATIC PLAY:* In activities such as that described above, the teacher's role should be minimal. With appropriate questions ("What could we use for...?") she can help the children develop their own ideas, observing and guiding as necessary.

9. *MEDICINE CHEST:* Discuss the dangers and the positive uses of medicine. Perhaps each child could make a DANGER poster to put on his own medicine chest at home. This might serve as a reminder to parents to then check the contents of cabinet and secure toxic items with a lock. The following might be sent home with children:

Dear Mom,

    Please post this sign on our medicine chest to remind me of its
DANGER

                              Love,
                              Tommy

10. *A VISIT TO THE HOSPITAL:*

Walking into the interest center, usually reserved for housekeeping by the fours, I discovered that something new had been added. Along one wall was a low bed made from a stretcher covered with a clean white sheet. Hanging on hooks were spotless, white men's shirts, with the sleeves cut off. The teacher introduced me to Dr. Dangle, one of the children, who wore a uniform (shirt worn backwards) and a headband. "Are you leaving, Dr. Murphy? Hang your uniform up on the hook, please," she said to another child.
Two little girls wore similar uniforms. One had a doctor's headband, the other a nurse's cap.
Two seatblocks had been put together to make a bed, and one nurse was attending to the doll patient in it. "She has a temperature," she said to us with a very serious expression.
"We have a pretty pink jacket here if anyone wants to be a patient," said the teacher, holding it up. Dr. Dangle seemed tempted, but finally decided to keep to his profession. Karen came in and headed for the bed.
"Remember the rules, said Dr. Murphy, "we do not put our feet on the bed."
On the vanity table there was a collection of empty bottles, sprays, pill bottles. They were in constant use.
A real stethoscope, donated by a doctor parent, was used frequently. A popular item was the box of ace bandages. "My sons were all athletes so I have plenty of those," the teacher explained. Nurse Alice was wrapping one around a doll patient.
"Yesterday Miss Smith was the patient, and was well bandaged," the teacher told me.
"What are those things on the wall?" I asked.
"Pictures," replied the children.
"Collage," said the teacher. They were made of throat sticks, cotton balls, Q-tips, bandaids and gauze pads. One child had made his into a face, with a bandage necktie.

11. *IS IT JUST PLAY?:*

In another school a group of fives waited each day for the early bus children to leave, then quickly assembled a hospital with large building blocks, reproducing it just as they had left it the day before. It had an office, an operating table, an elevator, etc.
"This has been going on for over a week now," explained the teacher. "I have nothing to do with it. I stay nearby in case they need me. They don't want any more adults hovering over and directing them. *By midafternoon they have had enough teaching for one day.*"

12. *ADDRESSES:* Talk about addresses. Ask each child where he lives. Some children can remember their entire address, others only the name of the street; older children can write some part of theirs. List each child's name and address on a chart and read them off, filling in the missing part, after each child tells his own. Play LOST CHILD—Seq. 1, #4 to reinforce addresses. Use a labeling machine with individual children to make address labels for cubbies. (LANGUAGE ARTS)

13. *MY ADDRESS:* As a simple "homework" assignment, ask each child to bring an envelope from home. Ask parents to put a stamp inside the envelope and not to stick it on the envelope. Ask each child to write or dictate a message, draw a picture or make a Valentine to enclose and send to someone at home. In a few days ask about these letters.

14. *WRITING A LETTER:* Write a letter to your class and mail it, and when it arrives talk about where you wrote it, where it has been, who brought it to the school. Ask the children if they could write a letter together to someone, such as the mayor, prominent community person, another class or a parent. (The teacher should enclose a personal note explaining the project and requesting a response.) Address, stamp and mail the letter; if possible, walk to a nearby post office or box.

15. *LETTER CARRIERS:* Ask the children to tell what they know about letter carriers. What do they do? Where? How does your mail come? Invite a letter carrier to come into the classroom and tell about such work and show mail bag and some of its contents.

16. *POST OFFICE:* Talk about the post office and associated vocabulary: letters, stamps, postmark, sort, route, addresses, parcels, delivery. Take a trip to the post office; call in first and make an appointment and arrange for a tour, telling ages and number of children you will be bringing.

17. *PRESIDENTS AND OTHER NATIONAL LEADERS:* Ask: "Who is the president? What do presidents do and where do they live?" Look for the names of past presidents on signs, money, stamps and on maps. Point out street names and public buildings named for presidents. Ask older children about the differences among presidents, kings, emperors and dictators.

18. *FRIENDS:* Discuss friendship. What does it mean to be a friend? Am I a friend? Why do we like our friends? Talk about being *your own* friend, taking care of one's self, self-respect, self-love. Read the poem *I'm Glad I'm Me* by Ruth Peterson.

19. *FRIENDS—ENEMIES, A DISCUSSION:*

> When talking about friends, allow plenty of time for talk about enemies.
> What makes you get angry?
> What makes you get mad at your best friend?
> Why do you like your friend?
> How would you feel if everyone got Valentines and you didn't get any?
> How do you feel when you aren't chosen?

20. *RELATIONSHIPS AMONG CHILDREN:* Teachers should observe significant relationships within the group. Does the child play with a lot of others or gravitate toward one special friend? Is he leading his friend or dependent on him? Which children are disliked by all? Why? Which are ignored? Why? Which are liked by all? Why? (See Observations)

21. *EMOTIONS:* List words for emotions and define through language, drama, art and movement. Besides facial expressions, how else can we see how people feel about situations? Look at pictures of people and notice their body posture and the position of hands and feet. Look for pictures about happy things. Ask: "How does that picture make YOU feel happy?" Look for pictures that cause sadness. Make books, using such pictures and ask children to dictate stories for each one.

22. *FACES:* No part of the human body tells as much about our thoughts, feelings, moods, emotions, as the face. The face can say, "Hello. Come talk to me," or it can say, "Leave me alone, I feel sad." It is a remarkable network of nerves and muscles which can be stretched into smiles, frowns, grimaces. Eyelids can alter communication just by being lowered. Mouths indicate moods by the turn of their corners, which can be thin or tight or expand into a smile. Faces have wrinkles—nature's way of etching time and experience. We can help children know others and themselves by exploring faces.

23. *FACES MURAL:* Find pictures of all kinds of faces, young, old, happy, sad, black, white, etc. Discuss each one. Make a large mural of the collected pictures.

24. *SELF PORTRAITS:* Use mirrors to experiment with making faces. When children have discovered how they look when they are happy, sad, angry, etc., ask them to draw pictures of themselves in various moods.

25. *FACES OF SOAP:* Mix a variety of paint or food coloring into several bowls of whipped soap flakes. Supply each child with an oval-shaped piece of paper on which they can make faces with colored soap flakes. The first layer might be pinkish for skin color. When the first layer has dried, brown eyes may be added, red mouth, yellow hair, etc. Allow each layer to dry before adding another. Features will hold their shapes.

26. *THOUGHTS—BRAINS:* Talk about thoughts. Where do they come from? Have each child tell a happy thought, a sad thought and an angry thought, a frightening thought. While illustrating a facial expression or body pose to go with each thought, the teacher asks the children to complete such sentences as:

> "I'm very happy when I am _____." or
> "It makes me sad when _____."
> These can be made into a book.

27. *MY THOUGHT:* After numerous activities and discussions about faces and feelings, a child might want to share a personal thought or feeling with his teacher on a one-to-one

basis. In such a case the teacher might say, "Your thoughts and feelings are very special. I am glad you want to share them with me. I will write them in my special, private book and I will not tell them to anyone else unless you want me to." When a child trusts his teacher with his confidence in such a way, the teacher must be sure to respect the child's privacy. These thoughts are not shared with other staff members.

28. *POEMS WHICH TELL EMOTIONS:*

Emotions, author unknown

a.   Angry, angry, angry!
     So angry that I kick the air
And stamp my feet and pull my hair.
Now isn't it curious,
     That after feeling so furious,
I feel very good once more?

        b.   Here am I
           Little Jumpin' Joan
           When nobody's with me
           I'm all alone!

                c.   My mirror is a tattletale
                   And tells just what I do;
                   For when I frown and scowl
                       a bit
                   It says, "Oh my, see you!"

Daren, by Helen Campbell

Teacher, I am mad
And I'm glad.
Lisa won't play
It's MY turn with the clay
Jack hit me first
MY picture is the worst!
Why can't we go out?
What is the story about?
Put on my snowsuit
Zip up my boot
I hate Jack
I'm *not* coming back
Teacher, I'm mad
And it's making *you* sad.

29. *PILLOW FIGHTS:* In one day care center, the director set up a 'soft' area with shag carpeting and surrounded with draperies. In it she put sofa pillows of varied sizes and shapes. On occasion, when two children were having a disagreement she would suggest that they go into the soft area and have a pillow fight. Anger and frustration turned into hilarity and giggles.

30. *VALENTINES:* Discuss heart, love, heart throb, heart beat with the children. Ask why, and to whom, we send messages of love on Valentine's day. Research as many ways as possible to make Valentines and center your observance of Valentine's Day around these activities. For young children, much of the fun is in the making.

31. *WHAT IS LOVE?* Write answers and make into books or use as valentines with illustrations. (See Activity 13-My Address.)

32. *SILHOUETTE:* Attach a spotlight or strong flashlight to a table or some other piece of furniture, so that the beam is focused on wall at a proper height. Seat child so that his shadow is cast on a piece of white paper taped to the wall. Draw around shadow cast by child's head. Have paper large enough to include entire head so that pigtails, etc. are part

of silhouette. Paint silhouette black. Child may paint silhouettes, but for younger children it is best if the teacher cuts them out. Children may also paste silhouette on card to be used as Valentine.

33. FINGERPRINTS: Children dip fingers in red, pink, or purple paint and make hand prints as Valentines. Print left hand and right hand on separate hearts and join together for front and back covers of Valentine, with verse inside.

34. *WAX VALENTINES:* Cut out two heart shapes from clear wax paper. Chop, grind, pare or grate old crayons. Mix crayon chips with confetti and foil scraps. Sprinkle mixture on one heart, cover with the second heart, making sure waxed sides of the hearts are together. Press with warm iron. Attach paper-clip hanger for stained glass window effect or include several hearts in a mobile as Valentine gift or room decoration.

35. *OLD FASHIONED VALENTINES:* Offer children a selection of bits of cloth, lace, trims, buttons, jewels, etc. to paste on paper hearts.

Red/pink—Mix red paint with white to create many shades of red and pink. Use to paint hearts, stencil hearts, print hearts, etc.

36. *VALENTINE BOX:* Decorate a large box, using red and pink scraps of cloth or paper. Add variety of bits of foil, lace, felt, trim, hearts, etc. Use the box for class Valentines or to play post office games. If box is used for class Valentines, however, make sure that each child gets the same number of cards to avert tragedies. (Read poem: *When You Send A Valentine,* by Mildred J. Hill.)

37. *VALENTINE PIÑATA PARTY:* Make a pinata (see Seq. 4, #51), appropriately decorated, to serve as the climax of a class Valentine party. Teacher may use it for gifts to the children, such as tiny candy hearts stuck on small lace doilies, individually addressed.

38. *VALENTINE PUPPET OR MOBILE:* Cut a red heart for head, add features; a larger heart for body, tiny hearts for hands and feet. Use pipe cleaners or paper fasteners to attach arms, legs and neck; hang with yarn.

39. *NEIGHBORHOODS AND VILLAGES:* Go for a walk and look at nearby yards. Discuss what each child has in his yard. Divide a sheet of mural paper into four sections. Four children work on a section with each having one section for his own house and yard. "Do you have a garage? Car port? How will you get into it from the street? Where will the streets be? Between the houses? Around the houses? Is it a dead end street? A circular street? Will you have fences between the houses? If you build a fence does it mean you don't like your neighbors? (Neighbors walk across my lawn.) Neighbor's children, pets, get into my garden." Read Robert Frost's Poem "Fences Make Good Neighbors." Think about leaving all four yards open and having one swimming pool, one outside fireplace, one set of playground equipment. What might be a problem? What kinds of rules do you think would be needed? When they are ready children draw their houses, streets, etc. Play with small cars, paper dolls, pets. Make a book about their discussions, results. Put it on the library table.

40. *ROAD BUILDING PROJECT:*

In one kindergarten, Russell and Joel asked for the small matchbox cars. "We need roads for them to go on," they said.
"How could you make them?" asked the teacher.
They talked about roads and Russell suggested using brown paper. Four boys went with the teacher to where the large roll of brown paper was kept and tore off a six foot length.
"Is it wide enough?" the teacher asked.
"Much too wide," they answered and asked her to help them cut it. They got a ruler and measured, folding the paper into quarters and taking turns cutting on the folded lines. It was time to stop so they rolled up their papers and put them on a shelf with a sign that said, "Do not touch."
The next day they came in bursting with enthusiasm and eager to continue. The teacher had put out a book, *Building and Wrecking Machines* (Zaffo). They looked at the book, naming the machines, but soon they were anxious to return to their road project. Joel arranged two sheets of paper in a 'T' shape. "Do you know what an intersection is?" asked the teacher. Jim did, he placed one length across another. "How could we make a dead end street?" was the next question. The fourth length was cut in two and placed to form two dead end streets.
Joel said, "We should have a white line and one yellow line that doesn't connect." "Why?" asked the teacher. Jim tried to explain, but she said, "Show me."
The discussion had ended that day with much talk about accidents, so the next day she put out some red

cross arm bands, a first aid kit, and a sign that said, 'Ambulance', but they were ignored. These boys were too anxious to get on with their building. They put the roads back as they were and went on. "Hey, we need a stop light at that intersection," said Joel. "We could make one," said Danny. "I haven't got time, I have to build a bridge" said Joel. Sarah and Karen were watching. "We could make it," Sarah said. They went off to make their stop sign, using a milk carton. They remembered to put a button on the side for pedestrians to push.

Chris said he wanted to make buildings. One boy made a hospital, another an apartment building. They used all of the available blocks and all of the space. The teacher decided that it was important to leave the project standing for a few days, even though this left a limited area for other activities.

In this school a different group came in the afternoon, so a discussion followed as to whether they should be allowed to use the block village. Some said, "No," some said "Yes," and some said, "Well, o.k., but they have to be careful." They decided on some rules which the teacher write on a large piece of paper and hung on the wall. The next day they rushed to their 'city' and found it undisturbed. The afternoon children had admired it, but did not play with it. They seemed to recognize that it belonged to someone else, and did not offer to add to it.

When the morning group came in the next day the teacher told them this and suggested that they should not take up the space for too long. That was Thursday and they decided to take it down on Friday.

This was a total learning experience which went beyond learning how to make roads and buildings.

41. *TABLE TOP VILLAGE:* Use assorted small boxes as houses, churches, garages and buildings of all kinds to make a miniature village on a low table-top or sand table. The buildings may be painted and pictures of windows, doors, landscaping shrubs, etc. painted or pasted on or cut out. Streets may be made of black paper, roofing, felt or strips of shingles. Details may be added as suggested by the children, such as trees, street signs, house numbers (addresses), etc. If the village is built on a table top, it has the advantage of underground space for tubes hung underneath representing gas, water and sewer lines.

Fig. 6-41

42. *OUTSIDE VILLAGE:* A child-size village may be constructed outside with the use of large cartons. One carton could serve as an apartment building where everyone lives and others as fire station, store, school, garage, etc., where they go to work.

43. *AUTO SHOP:* Put out a box of pre-cut paper circles and rectangles of various sizes which children can use to construct pasted picutres of cars and trucks. Or provide a table full of small boxes, round pieces and paper fasteners with which they can make three dimensional vehicles.

44. *PAINTING WITH CARS:* Use a large sheet of brown paper about 36" square or more, or give each child one small sheet, 18" × 24". Dip wheels of small cars into paint and roll across paper. (Show finished product to someone outside the classroom to see if they can tell how it was done.) Some of these might be framed and hung (See Art & Painting with Cars #5)

45. *MOBILE BEANO:*

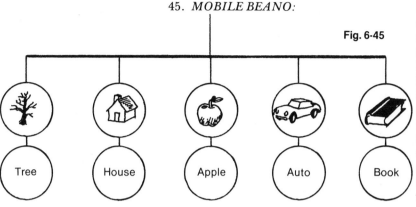

Fig. 6-45

Tree House Apple Auto Book

Make a set of beano cards with nine spaces, each with a picture of a familiar object, i.e., dog, house, tree, flower, sun, shoe. Make a set of cards with the corresponding words. Using the cards, construct a mobile, matching the picture with the word. Corresponding word cards are placed in a stack. One at a time the children draw from the stack and try to match the word with the picture on their beano card as they refer to the mobile chart. This activity helps to develop the ability to adjust to reading from blackboard to writing and back to board, a common method of instruction in later school years.

46. *PUZZLES FROM CALENDARS:* Children paste calendar pictures or posters on cardboard. On underside of cardboard draw intersecting lines. Children cut out cardboard along lines to make puzzles. The numeral portion of a calendar can also be made into a puzzle for use by children who are more adept at recognizing numbers. Put each puzzle in a separate box. (See Seq. 5, #96, 97)

47. *FIVE FINGERS:* While working with a small group of children, have each child hold up the fingers of one hand. Ask questions such as, "Who can say a word that rhymes with ball?" "Who knows a word that sounds like down?" "What word goes with mouse?" Each time a child answers correctly, he puts one finger down. The first to have all five fingers down wins.

48. *PEOPLE STARTS WITH P:* To introduce the children to letter sounds, initiate the following activity: Start by saying, "When I was driving in my car, I saw a policeman," then, "When I was driving in my car, I saw a policeman and a paper bag," "When I was driving in my car, I saw a policeman, a paper bag and a papoose," etc. Children repeat one by one, each adding a word beginning with 'P'.

49. *I WANT TO BE A FRIEND OF YOURS:*

5 5 5 5 8 3 3 3
I want to be a friend of yours

2 2 3 2 2 1 6
Mmmm and a little bit more

7 7 7 1 2 2 2 2
I want to be a pal of yours

7 2 1 6 6 5
Mmmm and a little bit more

5 5 5 5 1 3 3 3 1
I want to be a little flower

2 3 2 1 6
Growing round your door

7 7 7 7 7 7 7 7 7 7 7 7
I want to be your mother, father, sister, brother

5 5 5 6 6 7 1
Mmmm and a little bit more.

50. *PUNCH, PUNCH, PUNCH:* (Tune: Tramp, Tramp, Tramp Along the Highway) (ANGER)

Punch, punch, punch, I punch the big bag
Punch, punch, punch, I hit it hard
I may have to punch all day
But when all my punching's done
I will find that all my anger's gone away!

51. *DO KNOW THIS FRIEND OF MINE?* (Tune: Oh, Do You Know the Muffin Man?)

Oh, do you know this friend of mine?
This friend of mine, this friend of mine?
Oh, do you know this friend of mine?
His name is Geor-gie Lincoln.

Oh, yes we know this friend of yours,
This friend of yours, this friend of yours,
Oh, yes we know this friend of yours,
His name is Geor-gie Lin-coln.

52. *INSTRUMENT SOUNDS:* Display and demonstrate five familiar musical instruments—big and small bells, drum, shaker, tambourine. Choose five children to go out of sight and ask each one to play an instrument. Children in the group try to guess which instrument was played.

53. *HIGH AND LOW:* Put out five or six instruments of the same family but of different pitches and ask children to arrange from high to low (drums, bells, tone bars, shakers).

54. *ACTING OUT EMOTIONS:* Show picutres depicting various emotions. Ask children what sound they would make to show a particular feeling. How would you move? Ask the children to move the way the picture makes them feel. Tell children to walk around very fast and when music or drum stops, to freeze into a state portraying sad, angry, etc.

Ask children, "Show me how you would move if: you lost a puppy; if you had broken you mother's best dish; if you had just found a whole dollar bill; if it was your birthday and you were going to have a party; if you saw your brother playing with your train after you told him not to; if your mother had been away for a whole week and you saw her coming in the door."

55. *WALKING ON ICE:* During very cold weather when it is slippery, develop a movement session around walking on ice. Use with music, such as: *the Skaters' Waltz by Strauss. Practice gliding, skating, falling, slipping, etc.*

56. *LADDERS:* With four foot ladders placed flat on the floor, ask children how many ways they can think of to walk on it. Through rungs, hopping or jumping? On rungs? On edges? On one edge? Use drum to accompany children's movements. Ask the children to try dancing in a row or playing follow the leader on the ladder, accompanied by record with fast rhythm and strong beat.

57. *LITTLE CHARLIE BROWN:*

1 1   3 4   5
Little Charlie Brown

5   5   4 3   1
Lay your cover down

1 1   3   4   5   4
Little Charlie Brow-own

5   5   4 3   1
Lay your cover down

6   5   4 5   1 1   1
Fold one corner—Charlie Brown

6   6 5 5   4 5   1 1   1
Fold another corner—Charlie Brown

1 1   3 4   5
Little Charlie Brown

5   5   4 3   1
Lay your cover down

58. *JACK AND JILL:* Dramatize familiar rhyme. Dance it. Tap it with sticks. Walk with partner in first part. Jack spins round and round then falls (cymbal). Jill falls. Jack gets up, helps Jill up, walk away.

59. *ENERGY CRISIS:* Children are often bursting with extra energy at the end of the day. Try to find a place where the pushing, pulling and running, and, in general, noisy, muscular activities can take place. Decide where you might create a 'gym', an area large enough for wrestling and tumbling. The area should be as far as possible away from the quiet area. It should be easy for the children to move equipment and furniture to set it up each day. Teachers should hold a meeting with the children to introduce the area and discuss simple rules for its use. These rules should be numbered and written on a large poster which is hung in the area. Children and teacher refer to rules whenever the need arises. They will soon learn to do this on their own. Adults should not have to control or give constant supervision but must be nearby and watchful. Following is a list of some games and activities which might be offered:

60. *BASKETBALL:* Give the children a trash can or large basket and some beach balls. or dishpans and tennis balls. The group can establish the rules, teams and scoring system. (Check at local junior high school within walking distance for schedule of sports events. Games at the junior high level usually take place from three to five o'clock. They are often very exciting and youngsters can cheer and shout for their favorite team.)

61. *HOCKEY:* Set up hockey cages using cardboard boxes, waste baskets or block chairs. Use small brooms as hockey sticks.

62. *OBSTACLE COURSES:* Set up "over," "under," "around," "between" type courses, using whatever appropriate furniture or equipment is available. When the children have become creative with their own ideas, introduce a timer or stop watch to add to their fun.

63. *HOP SCOTCH:*

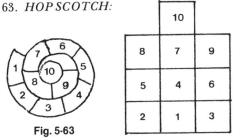

Fig. 5-63

Use the standard street versions or create your own patterns for hopscotch. See illustrations. Make patterns with rug squares, tape markers, drawings on large sheets of cardboard or paper, chalk marks on linoleum, etc.

Animal or flower shaped patterns may also be used. (See Seq. 9, Act #65 for Daisy Hopscotch)

64. *RELAY RACES:* Form teams and hold relay races as suggested:

a. Bean on a straw—carry a large bean by sucking it up with a straw.

b. Paper stamp—each player has two sheets of paper, numbered 1 and 2. When his turn comes he steps on 1 and puts 2 down. Then he steps on 2 and puts 1 in front, etc.

c. Potato on spoon—Carry potato on spoon in relay.

d. Egg carton—Place 12 small objects at one end of course and an egg carton at the other. Children carry objects, one at a time, until carton is full.

65. *STREET GAMES:* Play—Giant Steps, Red Light, Red Rover.

66. *TOWEL SNATCH:* Each player has a towel or bright scarf tucked into his belt or trousers at back. At signal, players try to snatch each other's towels away. Last one to keep towel, wins.

67. *BALLOON STAMP:* This is played the same as towel snatch except that a balloon is tied to the ankle of each child, and players try to stamp on and pop each other's balloons.

68. *BOWLING GAME:* Milk cartons, long blocks, plastic soap dispensers, cardboard tubes, etc. may be used as pins in bowling games. Marks for pins and starting lines can be taped to floor.

Construction Paper
Wrapped around Container
or Paint

BOWLING ALLEY

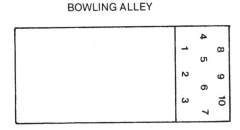

Fig. 5-68

69. *BLOW BALL:* Blow ping pong ball or small balloons from one end of course to another, or put two rectangular tables together. Set one team at each end; children try to blow ping pong balls over the center crack. Sides of the table might need to be lined with blocks to prevent ball from going offside.

70. *SCARVES:* (See Seq. 2, #39 and Seq. 9, #32).

a. Begin with a circle, warm up.

b. To the tune of *I've Got Rhythm* sing, "I've got a head, you've got a head, I can shake my head, that's what we can do."

c. Introduce scarves. Chiffon scarves or pieces of nylon net are best; they are light and inspire dancing.

d. First, explore color. Then shape. With the song, Little Charlie Brown, (#59 this section), you can discover that folding two corners turns a square into a rectangle, and folding two corners again makes another square. If you start by folding one corner across you make a triangle, and you can keep on making smaller and smaller triangles.)

e. Ask "What else can you do with them?" Let each child think of a motion. All try, then choose someone to pick out an instrument to accompany the motion.

f. Put on a record and dance using many different motions.

g. Move with scarves sitting in chairs or lying flat on backs on the floor.

h. After waving them back and forth, around and around, up and down, around heads, on the side, and in big circles, think of ways to wear them. (Brides, kerchiefs, girdles, sashes, bandit masks or shawls.) A pianist can accompany each one with appropriate music. Sometimes the music comes first and suggests the action.

i. Toss them into the air and catch them as they come floating down or toss them back and forth with a friend. And always, when the session is over, the children fold the scarves up and carefully put them away.

j. Large pieces of light, silk cloth or parachute cloth are ideal for a different kind of scarf session. Children stand in a circle holding the edges. Raise and lower the silk. Stand under it. Twist and run with it.

Fog, Steam, Hearts

71. *FOG:* Talk about fog. How does it feel and smell? What makes the fog? Clouds can be described as banks of floating fog. Have you ever flown through a cloud or driven through fog? Was it hot or cold? Can we make fog? What happens when you open the freezer door on a warm day? Read Carl Sandburg's *City Fog.*

72. *STEAM:* Discuss steam. What makes it different from fog? Can we make steam? Demonstrate with a whistling teakettle. Blow up a balloon and release the air. Relate it to the way the water in the kettle boils and pushes air through the kettle's whistle. Point out that steam works for us. Talk about and show pictures of steam trains, steam iron, pressure cookers.

73. *STEAM AND FOG:* To demonstrate steam and fog, fill a pyrex jar half full of boiling water. Cover jar and put an ice cube on the lid. Observe results.

74. *CIRCULATORY SYSTEM:* Activities involving skeletons (see Seq. 2, #40-48) might suggest similar projects involving the circulatory system.

75. *STETHOSCOPE:* Use a real stethoscope to listen to heartbeats. Feel pulses. Listen to heart beats of any small animal you might have. Discuss the heart, comparing it to a pump.

Compare rate of heartbeat when quiet and after running and jumping.

Older children might compare living and non-living things.

Read *The Dead Bird,* by Margaret Wise Brown, pub. Young-Scott.

76. *CORAL GARDEN:* Warning: This activity is only for children who are mature enough to handle the *poisonous* substances, (ammonia, bluing).

Common red brick	4 tbsp. water
4 tbsp. salt	1 tbsp. ammonia
4 tbsp. liquid bluing	Food coloring

Break brick into egg size pieces and arrange in shallow dish. Mix the ingredients in the order given, in a glass bowl: salt, bluing water ammonia. Pour solution over bricks, be sure all undissolved salt is used. Put dish in *permanent* place where it will *not be moved* after the coloring has been added. Drop food coloring on brick. The coral garden should start to grow in at least one hour. It changes color as evaporation takes place. Adding another teaspoon of ammonia every few days will keep the garden growing.

77. *CHARCOAL GARDEN:* Warning: This activity is only for children who are mature enough to handle *poisonous* substances (ammonia, bluing).

A garden similar to the coral garden above may be made by placing several pieces of charcoal in a low bowl. Pour over the following solution.

¼ cup water
½ cup bluing

¼ cup salt
1 tbsp. ammonia

Place it where it will not be disturbed. Add food coloring to the different parts.

78. *PEEK-A-VIEW:* Cut and mount pictures of familiar objects. Cover pictures completely with another sheet of paper in which you have cut a hole two inches in diameter. Can the children identify what the whole picture is from seeing just what's inside the hole?

79. *ONE TO TEN (LOTTO):* Make up sets of lotto cards using only numbers 1-10 and a corresponding set of chips or markers to cover the card squares. Six or eight squares on each card will be sufficient to hold the attention of young children. Younger children will need to see the chip to recognize the written number. Older fours and fives will begin to play without seeing the chip. As these older children master 1-10, add cards and chips with higher numbers. (See Seq. 5, #97).

80. *MATCHING NUMBERS:* Put matching sets of numbers in two bags. First child reaches in, finds number and identifies. Second child finds matching number in his bag. Letters may also be used.

81. *PAPER CONSERVATION:*

One class talked about conserving their supply of paper by using only one sheet a day, or using what they had wisely. Cindy (5) showed her paper which she had folded to make eight sections and said, "Now I can make eight different pictures." These same children agreed to bring in paper bags and try using them for painting and other art projects. ("HOMEWORK" was remembering to bring in bags.) The bottoms were cut off and the sides opened. Then the bags were smoothed with a warm iron and piled neatly on the paper shelf.

Flowers
82. *FORCING SPRING:* Cut some forsythia and pussy willow branches. Put them in water and force the blooms. Compare with the number of days it takes the *outside* forsythia buds to open.

83. *POOL GARDEN:* Plant an indoor garden in a small, plastic swimming pool. Later, transplant the seedlings outside. Marigolds and petunias are hardy seedlings.

Cooking
84. *COCONUT MEAT:* Where do coconuts grow? How do they feel? Drill a hole in a coconut to empty milk. Shred and dry some meat. Serve some chunks. Compare with packaged coconut. Use shell bowl. Save shell halves to make 'clopping' sound rhythm instruments.

85. *COCONUT OAT COOKIES:*

1 cup butter
1¼ cup brown sugar
1¼ cup rolled oats
1½ cup flour
½ tsp. baking soda

¼ cup corn syrup
1 unbeaten egg
1 cup coconut
¼ tsp. salt

Cream butter and sugar, add egg and syrup, beat. Mix in dry ingredients and drop by spoonfuls on greased cookie sheet, two inches apart. Bake in pre-heated oven at 350 degrees from 8 to 10 minutes.

86. *CHOCOLATE COCONUT BALLS:*

2 cups sugar	3 cups quick oats
½ cup butter	6 tbsp. cocoa
½ cup milk	1 cup fine coconut
1 tsp. vanilla	½ tsp. salt

Bring sugar, butter and milk to a boil. Add oats, cocoa, coconut, salt and vanilla. Mix well. Drop by spoonful on waxed paper to cool. (Make about 50 cookies)

87. *UNCOOKED COCONUT BALLS:*

1 pkg. cream cheese	food coloring
1 tbsp. butter	½ cup coconut
2½ cups powdered sugar	

Cream butter and cheese. Add sugar, coconut and coloring. Form into small balls, and coat with coconut.

88. *ORANGE JUICE:* Squeeze juice from oranges. Many children have not actually seen this done or tasted the natural sweetness of fresh squeezed orange juice. Save the seeds to count and to plant.

89. *FROZEN JUICE AND DRY CONCENTRATES:* Mix frozen and dry concentrates and compare with fresh.

Taste a little concentrate. Talk about concentrates. How are they made? Where? Why? Measuring is an important part of this activity. Make a mistake on purpose and taste the result of too much water added. Save out some of the concentrate to correct the error. Leave one fresh orange out and let it dry up to show one reason for the convenience of frozen and canned juices.

90. *ORANGES/A COMPARISON:* Bring a variety of oranges and compare flavors, sizes, skin thickness, seeds, colors. Include tangerines, tangelos, navel, juice oranges, temple, etc. Compare with canned juice, canned orange sections.

91. *GRAPEFRUIT, LIME, LEMON:* Study as you did oranges. A pitcher of lemonade is a surprise when extracted from one tiny lemon. Try with plastic lemons. (Save plastic lemons to make maracas.)

92. *CITRUS TASTE-IN:* Make many kinds of citrus fruit juices. Have a tasting party. Plant a variety of seeds to compare plants. List words used: sweet, sour, bitter.

93. *GINGERBREAD ORANGES:* Scrape all the pulp out of one half orange. Fill shell half full of gingerbread mix and bake.

94. *CITRUS PRINTS:* Half sections of citrus fruits dipped in paint and used to print on paper or cloth make attractive designs.

95. *FLORIDA AND OTHER WARM PLACES:* If this is the time of year when some people go to Florida or some other warm place, extend the idea with such activities as:

Find Florida and other places on a map.

Talk about the climate.

What would you wear in Florida?

What kinds of things can they grow there?

Discuss citrus fruits, coconuts, etc.

Relate to language arts and science activities.

96. *AN IMAGINARY TRIP:*

A group of children were taken on a trip to a zoo. The teacher wrote a short story about the trip, taking care to keep the narrative simple and familiar to the children, and using the children's names frequently.

The next day, before reading the story, each child was given a piece of paper and a magic marker, in case the story inspired pictures. As the story was read to them, they nodded as they recognized their names. When the teacher came to the part of the story abut riding on the little train and feeling a bit cold, Billy said, "I didn't feel cold. Did you, Laura? Did you, Paul? Did you, Robert?" The children, so addressed, looked up rather startled. When the part about feeding the pony came, Robert held up his hand, showing how one has to keep one's palm flat when feeding a pony. When Gerry heard his name as the person who had peanuts to feed the monkeys, he said, "Yes, I had 'em! A man gave 'em to me."

Besides these audible responses to the story, a series of pictures by the children also expressed other memorable moments. An assistant put names and titles dictated by the artists on each one.

The story ended with goodbyes to each child getting off the bus at his home stop.

With the story and pictures together, the children made a book which they looked at and read again and again.

(NOTE: It was an arbitrary decision on the part of the teacher not to wait to draw the story out of the children. They had often gathered following such trips to share in telling about their adventures and show various souvenirs. On this occasion the teacher decided to tell the story.)

97. *GEOGRAPHY LESSON:*

Some threes went for a walk to a nearby farm. "Some people would call it a hike," said their teacher. "It's quite a long way. How else might we have come?" she asked, taking pad of paper and a pencil out of her pocket (*indispensable* for *all* teachers) and writing down the ideas, from bicycles to snowmobiles, until finally fourteen different means of transportation had been listed.

(In that particular class, there were seven children who had come from other countries.)

Daily, the talk went on about transportation. Susie's mother brought in a very large world map which was hung on the wall. Each child who had come from a distance had a card with his name on it placed at his own country and a piece of colored yarn was stretched from there to the location of the school on the map. In some cases, the children had visited other countries on the way, and the yarn was anchored in each place along their route. The map became very colorful. When the maintenance man took a winter vacation in Bermuda, he sent the children a card. When he returned his yarn route was placed to show where he had been. When one of the teachers went to Florida, another yarn was added.

What was the point of all this? Is it necessary to teach geography to the three year olds? What will be left when they get into the upper school grades?

Had there been any pressure, any intent to teach, or if every child had been required to participate, it might have been wrong. But this experience was very real to the children who were interested.

It would be very hard to say how much they understood of distances or abstract locations on a map. However, whatever learning took place will serve as a foundation for whatever learning is to come. Perhaps they will remember this experience when they study geography, perhaps they won't, but they were interested and involved and enjoying the discussion and activities which followed. As a result of this, some of the parents came in and shared aspects of their culture with the children.

98. *POSTCARDS:* Ask parents to send postcards when they go on trips. Make into scrapbooks with a sentence for each card—"John's father sent it from Florida." "Kathy's grandmother sent it from London."

99. *TRAVEL BOX:* Cover a shoe box with a map and set up a file by country or state, and use as postcard file. Use for discussion and referral. Put a map on wall and pin each card to its place on the map. Or make a postcard tree or fill one bulletin board with postcards.

5G. SEQUENCE SEVEN

Many *babies* are born in hospitals as explored in Sequence Six. *Animal babies* are born in the *spring*, along with *new growth* in all of the natural world. What is it like to be a baby? How do older siblings in nursery school feel about the baby at home?

Up to the recent past, traditionally fathers have gone to work and mothers have raised children and taken care of the home. Today these *work roles* are reversed or interchanged.

Fathers' and mothers' work encompass a great variety of *occupations*. Factories and offices use *machines* from such *simple tools* as pencil sharpeners and screw drivers to such *complex machines* as computers, drill presses and looms.

Wind and *magnetism* are natural "tools" which can be harnessed by man to make work easier.

**BABIES—
OCCUPATIONS**

1. *BABIES:* Discuss and show pictures of babies of all kinds, human and animal. Talk about eggs and chicks, nesting and nursing. How are animal babies alike or different from human babies? In size, weight and development? Discuss differences in parental care and family size.

2. *BABY FACES:* Ask children to bring in baby pictures of themselves. Display on a bulletin board, perhaps with a recent picture of each child. Include teacher baby pictures.

3. *BABY MURAL:* Construct a mural of baby faces cut from magazines. Talk about which baby has the sad face. Which is the fattest? the thinnest? the happiest looking?

4. *BABY PARTY:* Have a special party and invite mothers and babies, or ask one at a time. Serve pudding or jello to the older children and possibly to some of the babies. Tape sounds the babies make. After visiting babies leave, discuss all the special attention they required, the time it took, the regular class activities that were left out in order to care for the babies. This might help some children to understand the extra time and attention their younger siblings require of the mother and father.

5. *"I DON'T LIKE BABY":* Often a new baby at home causes unhappiness for his older sibling at school. (See How: Behavior.) Small signs of discontent, and perhaps even open rebellion, manifest themselves in a variety of ways. Sometimes children will express disappointment and resentment at school, and never at home. Watchful teachers can help the child and parents through group discussion dealing with the feelings of jealousy, guilt and loneliness. Discussions should deal directly with problems. Dramatic play is also helpful. Parents should be told if the child discloses these feelings at school.

6. *BABY CARDS:* When a baby arrives at the home of a classmate, the children might make stories or poems and send cards. Cut pictures from magazines and use baby cards as materials.

7. *BABY CARE:* Some children have no babies at home. If it can be arranged, invite them to a special demonstration of bathing, dressing, powdering and feeding a visiting baby. Have them help in as many ways as they can. Before and after the demonstration, 'talk' through the steps, using a doll.

8. *I'M THE BABY:* Have a movement session imitating all the ways babies sound and move. Use the tape made at the baby party to refer to sounds. The children may lie on their backs and wave their hands in the air, kick their feet, gurgle, burp, whimper, creep, crawl, roll over, cry, waddle, fall down.

9. *I CAN! BABY CAN'T!:* Hold discussions about what your children can do that babies cannot. List on charts and add pictures. (Baby creeping—child walking, etc.) This is a

great ego booster for 'left out' feelings of older brothers and sisters.

10. *ANIMAL BABY LOTTO:* Make lotto cards of pictures of baby animals. Make individual cards of animal parents to be matched with the baby. (See Seq. 8, #91.)

11. *BABY CHICKS BORN IN CLASS:*

In one school a large incubator was installed, and eggs were watched carefully and anxiously for several days. It was important to plan the timing so the eggs would hatch while the children were present and not on a weekend.

The long anticipated day came. The process went on all that day. Children took turns coming from all over the school to watch in awe as baby chicks pecked their way out of the shells. They emerged all wet and scrawny. They gradually changed in appearance as they dried. The children heard the cracking shells and the tiny cheeps. It was a thrilling experience for teachers as well as children.

NOTE: Before planning such an adventure, arrange for a home for the babies and for the hens which will follow. Some hatcheries will loan hatchlings and take them back, as well as provide the necessary equipment and advice. (See Activity #48 in this Sequence.)

12. *PARENT OCCUPATIONS:* Discuss the various occupations of class parents. If possible, invite parents to come in and talk to the class about their work, showing tools and other special equipment used and pictures of their office or factory and of people at work there. Arrange, where possible, to visit a parent's place of employment.

13. *SPIN AND MATCH HATS:* Make a game board or lotto cards using magazine pictures or drawings. Make a spinner for center of game board (or matching cards for lotto). Give each child a set of cards (about 3 or 4) with pictures of hats, uniforms, symbols, tools, etc., which relate to the occupation pictures, i.e., stethoscope—doctor, a shovel—contractor, tractor—farmer, apron—cook. Children spin to match their set of cards.

14. *ALPHABET OF OCCUPATIONS:* Ask children to try to name occupations beginning with each letter of the alphabet. Draw or cut pictures to match and put together a book. Captions might include children's own names:

Henry's mom is an accountant.
Robbie's aunt is a baker.
Helen's dad is a contractor.
Beverly's dad is a director.

15. *OFFICE JOBS:* Many parents are employed in offices which include the same operations as the school office, secretaries, janitors, cooks, presidents, vice-presidents, accountants, etc. Take a tour of the building and make word cards for each job. Following the tour, invite each worker (on separate days) to come (or take class to visit them) and describe all his duties, showing special tools, books, machines, etc. which he uses in his work. (This is a good way to explore occupations with younger threes.)

16. *RHYMING:* Make up one or two line verses to develop rhymes, or read familiar poems, leaving off rhyming words for the children to finish. Examples:

"Let's make a wish" said the...
"I love bologna" said the...
"What good luck" said the...
"I want to hear" said the...
"I got loose" said the...
"I have my hat" said the...
"Let's go in the lake" said the...
"I'm too big" said the...
"Come in my house" said the...
"There were an awful lot of us" said the...
"I want it right now" said the...
"Goodbye, goodbye" said the...
"I've lost my hair" said the...
"That's very funny" said the...

More examples:

> When I get into my bed
> I pull the covers over my _____
>
> It is raining hard today
> So we cannot go out to _____
>
> I like to play, I like to sing
> I like to do most _____
>
> I got up very early today
> Dressed myself neatly and went out to _____
>
> The birds are singing, twee, twee
> I see their nest up in the _____
>
> The rain is raining all around
> It falls on the roof and it falls on the _____

(See also Seq. 5, Article #15.)

17. *MY FAVORITE THINGS:* Play a song from the *Sound of Music* and make up a class version. List all favorite things, cut or draw pictures and make into books. (BOOKS)

18. *WORK SEQUENCE:* Use a series of pictures showing a particular job being carried to completion. For example, a shovel digging and filling a truck, the truck dumping, the forms for concrete, the stages of construction, the finished building. Lay them out on a table and ask children to arrange according to sequence. Some companies and factories may have such photos available in their advertising literature. (SERIATION)

19. *PAY FOR WORK:* Make up activities using blocks, crayons, play money, crackers, etc. to serve as rewards for work, illustrating how parents receive payment for their work. Discuss how such things as food, clothing, gasoline, schooling, etc. are paid for with money earned. Perhaps you can set up work teams to clean the room, sort crayons, hang up mittens, stack the blocks, etc. and have a "pay day" following. You might give "raises" (an extra cracker) for special work. (END OF DAY)

20. *CHILDREN'S STORY TIME:* When the children in the group are familiar with the classroom library books, set aside a special time each day when one or two children may choose a favorite book and 'read' it to the class. Some may bring books from home. Keep a record of who has had a turn but assure the children that this is strictly voluntary. (Read *Show and Tell*, Early years, February 1973, p. 35, pub. Early Years.) (ORAL SKILLS)

21. *PROBLEM SOLVING:* Give each child 9″ × 12″ paper, scissors, staples, paste, and ask how they can make the paper LONGER?

22. *SURPRISE PICTURES:* Using paper scraps or torn scraps, ask a child to close his eyes and choose one. Mount on contrasting color. Look at it. What does it make you think of? Finish into a picture, using crayons or magic markers. Perhaps add a few choice pieces of beautiful junk.

23. *BIG MACHINES:* Using boxes, cardboard, corrugated scraps, telephone wires, buttons, etc., have children work in crews of two or three to create machines. Each crew has to decide what their machine does and report back to class. Allow plenty of time for construction and reporting. With resulting machines, set up an inventor's display. Encourage oral descriptions of machines. Also encourage audience to ask questions. (MACHINES)

24. *THE YELLOW BULLDOZER,* by Deborah Mitchell Haney:

> The yellow bulldozer down the street
> Can't seem to get enough to eat!
> He grumbles when he wants some more
> And pushes dirt across the floor
> Of where a brand new house will be
> Right next to that big apple tree
> —I hope he doesn't growl at me!

25. *BRIDGE CONSTRUCTION:*

The purpose of this project was to determine how well the children (5's) could follow instructions to complete a pre-planned project. Each child was to build a bridge by pouring two concrete piers which would hold a road bed and two ramps.

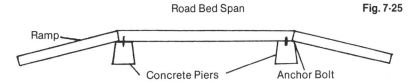

Road Bed Span   **Fig. 7-25**

Ramp

Concrete Piers   Anchor Bolt

On the first day the group held a meeting and the teacher described the plan which would be carried out over several days by a series of specific steps.

First, each child built a *model* using unit blocks. They were asked to get specific sizes and numbers of blocks. They named the various parts of their models (piers, ramps, roadbeds).

On the second day they mixed and poured concrete for the piers, using plastic bottles cut off as forms and setting in the anchor bolts. They held the bolts against the thickness of the boards to determine how high they should be set. The concrete was like "gush," "mud," "cakes." They were surprised the next day to find how hard and heavy the forms had become.

On the third day, they built the ramps and span by measuring and cutting lengths of 3″ wide boards. Holes were drilled in the ends of the span and ramps, to fit over the anchor bolts. The ramps and span were painted black "tarred."

On the fourth day, the teacher cut away the plastic bottle forms and the children assembled the bridges. White lines were painted on the roadbeds and the bridges were added to the block corner. (BRIDGE)

26. *CONFETTI PICTURES:* Draw a picture or design using Q-tips dipped in thinned glue/water solution. Shake on confetti. Place picture in tray before shaking confetti and work on newspapers to save work and waste.

27. *LULLABY FOR REST,* by Glenn Abramson:

Now it's time to rest
Like robins in a nest.
Tuck our heads beneath our wing
Close our eyes to everything
Now we rest. Now we rest.

28. *FIVE LITTLE TURTLES:* Make felt or bean bag turtles, or make from mittens or socks. Stuff with cotton and sew on button eyes. Tie toes and top of sock to make head and tail and add cloth (felt) feet. (See Seq. 11, #155.)

29. *WIND POEMS:*

My Friend the Wind
by Deborah Mitchell Haney

My friend the wind
Didn't come today
I waited with
My kite to play
I know he'll come another day.

The Wind
by Deborah Mitchell Haney

He tapped me
on the shoulder
I turned around to see
That no one was around that day
Except—the wind—
And ME!

Wind Song
by Harriet Chmela

A wind came through the pines
  Making the needles rub together
    into a spring wind song.

The downy feathers on a baby duck's back
  ruffled and tickled him
    He turned to say, "Who's there?"

Across the smooth surface of the pond
  the breeze riffled a ripple
    sending a message to the other bank.

Resting on the quiet surface
  The little duck began a-bobbing
    As the wind rippled past.

He jumped in surprise when
  A pine cone shook loose
    and PLOPPED into the water.

Yellow cat a-prowling in the reeds
  perked her head and listened
    to the tune played on the cattails.

30. *VOICE PRINTS:* Tape children's voices. Play back at juice time. Guess who is talking. (See Seq. 5, #22.) (SOUNDS)

31. *SPRING—THE OUTDOOR CLASSROOM:* When spring comes and the sun is getting warm, teachers and children who have been cooped up indoors welcome the chance to spend more hours on the playground, but does this mean program activities come to an end?

It is all too easy for staff to think of this as the old fashioned 'recess', a time to stand around watching children play. A professor in an early childhood program called it "putting them out to grass." We do not deny that children need time to PLAY, but we have said throughout these books that play is the child's *work*. He *learns* through play, and learning will not stop because of a change in environment. What special activities challenge a child's interests and offer opportunities for making choices, for solving problems, for improving physical dexterity and social skills? Suggestions follow which may serve as sparks to trigger imaginations:

Take a green walk and bring back as many shades of green as you can find.

Mix paints to match.

Use the materials you find (pieces of wood, stone, leaves, flowers and earth) to make pictures, collages or mosaics.

Mix and color plaster of Paris and fill small paper or plastic containers. While still wet implant natural materials.

Use materials from woods or seashore to press impressions into wet sand. Fill imprints with plaster of Paris or wax.

Use 'messy' materials such as finger paint or clay, or dip hands or feet in paint for prints to make a mural.

Woodworking is great outside but requires the same careful supervision outlined in the section on woodworking.

Sewing, weaving or working with string or gimp are good warm weather, quiet activities for the end of the day.

Hang a large loom on an outside wall and a supply of weaving materials. Some chain fences can be used as looms.

Take advantage of every opportunity to test concepts. Set up obstacle courses. Take creative movement sessions outside. Hold relay races.

Take juice and crackers for a 'picnic' to a far corner of the playground with the "story carpet." (See Reading and Telling Stories, #12.)

32. *IMAGINARY PICNIC:*

As the teacher handed out two crackers to each child she said, "Here is a tuna fish sandwich, and this one is ham and cheese. I have some delicious peanut butter and jelly, also." The children sat with sparkling eyes waiting to see which kind they would get. The next day they were invited to ask for their favorite sandwich. They were having an imaginary picnic under the trees on their playground. (See Seq. 9, #19, 106.)

33. *SANDBOX:* Clean out all of the rusted and timeworn sand toys and put in some fresh sand. Set up a system for wetting it down each day. (There is not much you can do with dry sand except sift and pour.) Just as you motivate block play by planting a suitcase or some other object in the block area, so you promote new and imaginative sand play with the addition of a piece of hose, blocks of wood, screen, shells, etc.

34. *PIPE PROJECT:*

In one school, some pieces of pipe were catalysts for sandbox activities:

We took a walk to where they were building the new high school. There was a pile of short lengths of pipe on the ground which the workmen said we could have. The pipes were added to the sandbox equipment which totally changed the content of the play there for weeks. There were sewer, plumbing, street and building projects developing day after day.

35. *PUSSY WILLOW* (Tradtional):

  1 1   1 1 1 1   2   2 2 2 2   2
I know a little pussy, her coat is silver gray

  3 3   3 3 3 4 4   4 4 4 4 4
She lives down in the meadow not so very far away

  5   5 5 5 5 5   6   6 6 6 6 6
She'll always be a pussy, she'll never be a cat

    7   7 7 7 7 7 7   8   8 8 8 8 8 8
Cause she's a pussy willow, now what do you think of that?

    8   7   6   5   4   3   2   1
Mew, mew, mew, mew, mew, mew, mew, mew, *SCAT*.

(See Activity #119.)

36. *IN THE SPRING:* (Tune: Sur le Pont d'Avignon)

  1 1   1   2 2   2
In the spring, in the spring,

   3 4   5 1   7 1   2 5
Children playing, children playing

  1 1   1   2 2   2
In the spring, in the spring

   3 4   5 1   2   7 1
Children playing laugh and sing

    1   1   1 1 2   1   1 1 1 2   1
And they all do this way, Yes they all do that way.

37. *THE ROBIN:*

Robin in the apple tree sings
Wake up! Wake up! It's time to grow,
Crocus stirred down under the earth
And poked their heads up through the snow.

38. *WIND INSTRUMENTS:* Talk about wind instruments. Play the record *Tubby, the Tuba.* Can some parents bring in and demonstrate wind instruments? You can make a

sound like a wind instrument if you blow into a piece of graden hose. Press lips tightly together. Blow through kazoo and across bottle tops. Fold wax paper over combs and "buzz."

39. *FA LA NA NA* (Italian lullaby):

    3 4 5 3 7   5
Fa La Na Na Bambine

    3 4 5 3   1 7 5
Fa La Na Na, Belle Bambine

    3   4   2 2 2 3   1   1
Close your eyes and do not peep now

    3   4   2   2 2 3   1   1
Close your eyes and go to sleep now.

    2 3 1 1   2 3 1 1   2 3 7   1
Fa La Na Na, Fa La Na Na, Fa La Na Na (last line dwindles away very slowly and softly)

40. *THIS IS WHAT MY DADDY (MOTHER) DOES:* (Tune—*Mulberry Bush*)

Compose a class song around the theme of parent's work. Include work inside and outside the home.

41. *TURTLE TROT:* Children pretend to be turtles by crawling along the floor balancing 'shells' on their backs. Shells can be made from flat cartons, sheets of cardboard, paper plates, etc.

THREES: Crawl around room trying to keep objects on back.

FOURS: Two children race with objects on back.

FIVES: Relay race. Child hands object from his back to next contestant. (MOVEMENT)

(Read: *Tommy Turtle*, Poems Children Will Sit Still For, pub. Citation.)

42. *WHO IS THE TURTLE?:* The children hide their eyes and are asked not to peek. One or two children are sent out of the room. They come creeping back under a carton. Others guess "Who is the turtle?" The carton can be decorated with green paint and spots with turtle feet added. (CREEP/CRAWL)

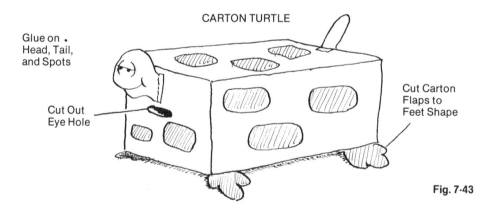

CARTON TURTLE

Glue on .
Head, Tail,
and Spots

Cut Out
Eye Hole

Cut Carton
Flaps to
Feet Shape

Fig. 7-43

43. *TURTLE RACES:* Make several carton turtles (as above) and use for races.

44. *THE BUNNY WIGGLE:* Make gigantic pom-pom bunny tails by cutting magazine pages into strips up to the binding. Bend and staple the binding back to form a pom-pom. Attach a string so tail can be tied around waist. Add rabbit ears by taping ears to a cardboard headband. Do the bunny tail wiggle. Shake and hop to bunny-hop music. (See Seq. 9, #36 and Seq. 10, #3 for Pom-Poms.)

45. *TORTOISE AND HARE RACES:* One child in a large cloth bag, and another under the carton 'turtle shell' have a race. Tell the folk story of the tortoise and the hare.

Bunny Ear
Headband

Fig. 7-44

46. *JACKIE JOHNSON HAS A MOTION:* Substitute children's names to the tune of Old MacDonald.

> Jackie Johnson has a motion
> We can do it, too
> Jackie Johnson claps his hands
> And we can do it, too
> With a clap, clap here and a clap, clap there
> With a stamp, stamp here, and a stamp, stamp there
> With a twist, twist (shake, hop, spin, etc.)

47. *ROLLING:*

> *Rolling*
> by Deborah Mitchell Haney
> I rolled and rolled
>   down the hill
> And landed in
>   some daffodils
> It wasn't really hard, you see
> My friend the wind
>   was pushing me!

48. *INSIDE AN EGG:* Collect empty plastic egg containers such as those Easter candy or hosiery come in. Give one to each child. Ask them to feel, open, look inside the egg and think about how they might get out if they were tiny chicks growing inside. They might:

> Tap inside with fingernails
> Make pecking noises with their mouths
> Roll up in a ball and pretend they are inside an egg
> Peck on the shell — break out all wet and bedraggled — shake dry
> Walk like tiny chicks — walk like a chick one week old, saying "peep"
> Walk like a mother hen, clucking and calling her baby chicks who come running

On another day become hatching baby ducks. Swim in a row behind the mother, bobbing heads down in the water with tails up. (See Activity #11. Read: *What's Inside,* by Barbara Hazen, pub. Lion.)

49. *MACHINES MOVE:* Make a set of picture cards that involve action. A child chooses one, looks at it and dramatizes its action, making sounds at the same time. Other children guess what it is. All make motion. Ask what instrument could be used that makes that sound and motion. Snowplow? Use fire engine, typewriter, tractor, steamshovel, etc. One day all pictures could be of electrical appliances, etc.

50. *BUILDING A MACHINE WITH MOTIONS:* Use the following suggestions to build a machine with the group:

> Form a circle and warm up

Talk about machines, all kinds. Invite each child to think up a machine and demonstrate its motion, add sounds.

Make machine sounds, one at a time around the circle. Put all the sounds together. Use voice or body sounds. Add sounds made by various instruments.

Create one giant machine using the whole group, one at a time. Each child becomes a machine part and makes a motion attaching himself to the whole (physically touching another child).

Take the machine apart (using 'screwdrivers', 'wrenches', and other tools) until it is all separated and its parts are sitting in the circle once again.

51. *PAPER STREAMERS:* Introduce colored streamers. How many different ways to move with them? What instruments would you choose for your motion? Hang crepe paper streamers outside on trees, swings or fences and watch as the wind blows them. Start wind movement session with a circle:

Shake hands hard. Shake them right off! Shake feet—shake heads, up and down, back and forth—shake hips—shake knees.

Button up your coat and put on your hat—let's take a walk—walk as if the wind were pushing at your back. Walk into wind—oops! wind stole your hat—chase it—put your foot on it. Missed. Try again, put your hat on tight this time.

Take a big breath—a lot of air—reach up and pull down an armful of air. Put some in your pocket—put some under your feet—what will it make you do? Blow yourself into a big balloon—burst and break on floor.

Trees have a trunk and you have a trunk...Move from the middle and sway with the wind. If you were a birch tree you might bend way over. If your trunk is thick and strong like an oak, perhaps only your branches move. What part of you could be the leaves?

Pretend it's a nice sunny day. There is a light breeze and only the leaves are stirring. Now the sun goes behind a black cloud. The wind is blowing so fast it is bending me way over. Some of my branches are breaking off. This tree is pulled up by the roots and falls over on the ground. What a terrible storm. I think it was a hurricane! (See Seq. 9, Act. #40.)

52. *FLYING TO THE MOON:* "How do you think it would be to fly to the moon?" Use this question with a small group (4-6), write answers, add illustrations and make into a book.

53. *RHYTHM PATTERNS WITH ART:* Play records with varying rhythm patterns. Children use wax crayons and large paper on the floor and draw designs reflecting the musical rhythms: fast, slow, lilting, short beats, long beats, high notes, low notes. Suggest that they may use dots, dashes, lines (wavy, vertical, horizontal) and that they change crayon colors to suit the music. Later, children may paint over crayon designs with black or dark shades of tempera. This is RESIST PAINTING.

54. *WIND DANCE:* Children create wind by running with crepe streamers or scarves. What makes the streamers float?

55. *FLYING KITES:* Make the motions of flying a kite:

Plastic Squeeze Lemon...

Fig. 7-57a

running to launch
tugging on the line
unwinding the string
being the kite
fluttering to a dive
soaring

56. *KITES:*

Kites
by Deborah Mitchell Haney

We took a day
My friend and me
To make a kite
for all to see
But when we finally let it free...
It landed in our neighbor's tree!

...or Bandage Box

Fig. 7-57b

57a. *RATTLES AND SHAKERS:* make shakers for the story with squeeze lemons, band-aid or typewriter ribbon boxes. Fill halfway with sand, rice, marbles, pebbles, beans, and analyze the sounds. Arrange from loud to soft. Develop a vocabulary for the different sounds of the shakers: "scratch," "swishy," "rattley," "jingly," etc. Have children use shakers to accompany the story which follows.

57b. *PAPER SHAKERS:* Cut about 6 inches of fringe in an 18" (approx.) strip of paper and wrap it around a cardboard tube at the end. Use a variety of papers for different sounds (crepe paper, newsprint, foil, brown bag). "What happens when you blow through the other end of the tube?"

58. *RATTLE THE TIGER,* by Harriet Chmela:

Once upon a time there was a tiger whose name was Rattle. He had a "swishy" tail and a deep "rattley" voice. One day Rattle was walking through the dark jungle "swishing" his long tail and growling in his deep "rattley" voice. Suddenly he heard a "scratchy" noise in the tangle of bushes behind him. He stopped still and "swished" his long tail. The tiger listened ("shhhh"). (Two sand blocks rubbed together make "shhhh".)

He crept toward the "scratchy" noise, trying very hard not to "swish" his long tail, or "rattle" his deep voice, but he did "swish" ever so softly and "rattle" just a bit. He stretched his long striped neck as far as he could and peered into the bushes. Then he saw a little motion and heard a little "scratching" sound and a tiny little "swish." The tiniest, stripiest, sweetest little tiger Rattle had ever seen peered back into Rattle's deep green eyes. The tiny tiger wagged his teensy tail with the teensiest "swish" and said "Hello" with a teeny "rattle." Rattle tried very hard to "rattle" "Hello" back without frightening the tiny tiger. He sat down on his tail so it would not "swish" and frighten the tiny tiger.

"I'm lost," the tiny tiger "rattled" softly. "Please take me to my mother."

"Where does she live?" "rattled" the big tiger.

"Near the pond with the "swishing" grasses," he replied.

"I can take you to her. I drink there every morning," softly "rattled" the big tiger. He picked the little tiger up ever so gently by the loose soft skin at the back of his neck. (Have you seen mother cats carrying their kittens like that?) Rattle walked quietly back through the jungle carrying the tiny tiger and "swishing" his long tail to keep away the buzzing insects. (Can YOU buzz?) He could not "rattle" because his mouth was full of the little tiger's fur.

When they reached the deep blue pond with the "swishing" reeds he put the tiny tiger down onto the soft mossy ground. The little tiger wobbled over to his mother who was so happy to see her baby. In fact, they both "swished" their tails so fast with joy that they fell down and rolled over and over on the ground.

Rattle "swished" his tail and "rattled" his voice until he, too, rolled over.

Everyone rattled and swished and jingled.

NOTE: You may want to use this to introduce some new puppets or stuffed toys as a mid-winter surprise. Make up more adventures to fit your collection of sound makers.

59. *BODY-MIND STRETCHERS:* Mark two lines on the floor about six feet apart. Pretend to crawl through a pipe from here to there. The pipe is big enough to walk in now, if you bend over. Now it is small so you must crawl on hands and knees—now on your stomach.

60. *THE GUMBALL MACHINE:*

"I can make a gum ball machine," said Randy (age 5). "You sit on the floor with your legs out in front of you. That's the machine (pointing to his torso), your legs are the spout where the gumballs roll out." He made a circle above his head with his arms. "This is the glass dish holding the gumballs."

61. *HAT SNATCH GAME:* One child sits in the middle of circle with eyes closed and a hat on his head. Rest of group sit with hands behind their backs. "It" sneaks up and snatches hat and hides it behind his back. He returns to the circle. The rest recite:

"Such a cold and windy day
Northwind blew your hat away
Tell us snowman if you know
Where did Mr. Northwind go?"

Child in center tries to guess who is holding hat.

62. *PEOPLE IN ACTION:* Show pictures of people in action, calling attention to the positions of feet and arms. Ask children to assume the same position.

63. *ACTION WORDS:* make name cards for children, and action cards (jump, run, skip, etc.). Hold up one of each and ask child whose name is shown to perform the action.

64. *BODY LANGUAGE:*

>Move across the floor on your knees
>What part of your body can you use to pick up something?
>What part of your body can you use to wave?
>What part of your body can you use to push?
>Your hands are stuck together. Pull them apart.
>Your hands are stuck to your knees. Pull them away.
>Run without getting anywhere.
>Reach up on a shelf and get something.
>See if we can guess what, by asking questions about it.

65. *SOUNDS WITH STRAWS:* Pinch the end of a straw and make a diagonal cut to bring the end to a point. Blow through the straw to make sounds. Straws cut at different lengths will make different sounds (pitches).

66. *THE BOSS AT CENTRAL CONTROL:*

>a) Begin with circle and warm up.

>b) "Everyone bosses children. Father says, 'Don't eat with your mouth full.' Mother says, 'Wear your raincoat and rubbers.' Big brother says, 'Get out of my way.' Sister says, 'Go away, you can't stay in my room.' " "It isn't easy being the youngest member of the family, always being bossed by someone bigger. But there is a way you can be the boss. Up here, inside your head, is a brain and it's like a control center of a rocket ship. It sends messages out to all parts of your body. A message says, 'Feet walk' and they walk. It says, 'Hands fly like birds' and the hands fly. Your brain sends the messages, so you are really the boss. Let's see what kinds of messages you can send out from your control center. Can you send a message to your elbows? We call that a motion. Send a message to your knees."

>Each child takes his turn as boss and others copy his motions.

67. *ING MOTIONS:* Begin with circle and warm up.

>"Today let's think about words that end in 'ing.' Running is one. How do we do it? Now who has another?" Go around group with each child adding another 'ing' word.

>"Do your 'ing' word very fast, now s-l-o-w-l-y.

>"Sit on the floor. Change weight from one side to the other, reach, reach, stretch, cover as much of the floor as you can. Take a big space. Cover as tiny a space as you can. Lie flat. Move arms, legs—fast, slowly, ride bicycles. Sit in circle linking arms, swaying left and right and making sounds in unison.

>"Think about the 'ing' words you hear in the morning. A neighbor walking, bacon frying, shower dripping, windshield wipers swishing." (See Seq. 5, #51.)

68. *MOTIONS IN SPACE:* Show a movie, speed it up and slow it down to slow motion. Run it backwards.

>Stand in a circle, warm up.

>"Walk, use ALL space in this room, walk in every direction. Walk very fast, as fast as you can without running. Now v-e-e-r-r-y slowly, use slow motion, every part of your body moves in slow motion. Walk like space men on moon, lift feet high. They are very light, almost floating, now light as a feather. Light as a cloud sailing along in the sky. While you are up there in the clouds become a glider. It looks like an airplane but it has no motor. It sails around like a bird—like a big seagull and comes slowly down to earth.

69. *WIND:* Wind affects people emotionally, makes some flustered, irritated, stimulates and excites others. Teachers should expect children to be "high" on a windy day and be alert to those who will enjoy going out and reveling in it—and those who need waterplay or some very relaxing activity.

70. *WIND INDICATORS:* Discuss wind and how we know the wind is blowing. Ask children to suggest indicators using the five sense. Trees bend, dust flies, pressure on back, whistling trees, air swishes out of balloon, smells from distant smoke stacks, salt spray and flower aromas, clothes blowing on line. Does wind sound different in different trees? Can you hear the tree branches rubbing in the wind?

>Look for some flags flying.

>Find a weathervane and see in which direction it is pointing.

>Wet finger and feel direction of the wind.

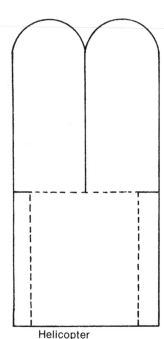

Helicopter
Cut on Solid Line
Fold on Dotted Line

Fig. 7-77

Paper Clip

(Read *Hi Mister Robin* by Alvin Tresselt, Lothrop Pub., for "whistling wind" and *Gilberto and the Wind* by Marie Hall Ets, Viking.)

71. *WIND WORK:* How does the wind work? Look for pictures of windmills, kites, power generators, pin wheels, sail boats, hair dryers, musical instruments, aircraft, fans, clotheslines, weather vanes... .

72. *WIND STORMS:* What are tornadoes? Hurricanes? Typhoons? Perhaps you can name local windy days after class members as the weather bureau names hurricanes. Describe the days as well—Breezy Betsy, Whistling Will, Puffy Paul, Sighing Sue. Make a poem from the results.

73. *BLOWING BUBBLES:* Cut off the tops and bottoms of metal cans. Dip one end in soap bubbles and blow through the other end.

74. *DOLLS' CLOTHES WASH UP:* Wait for a windy day and (accompanied by the appropriate working songs) wash, rinse, and hang to dry all the dolls' clothes. Hang outside and inside and compare the drying times and results (soft, stiff). Sing *This Is The Way We Wash Our Clothes,* tune of *Mulberry Bush.*

75. *PARACHUTES:* A parent may be able to provide a parachute or sometimes they can be purchased at an army surplus store. Use to expand scientific experiments with wind. You can make parachute with four nylon (sheer) curtains sewn together or construct small parachutes from silk or tissue paper.

76. *HELICOPTERS:* Read poems and stories and show pictures of helicopters. Compare with other aircraft. Move as a helicopter—airplane. Take imaginary trip. "What will you see? How do you think it looks when you look down from a helicopter?" Construct one from a carton.

77. *HELICOPTER TWIRLS:* Make by cutting the shape shown in illustration. Cut along dotted line, bend, fold down one side in one direction, other in reverse direction. Attach a paper clip to bottom as a weight. They spin as they are dropped.

78. *BALLOON JETS:* Stretch a fishing line or nylon string between two points, one low enough for children to reach. String a 3″ or 4″ section of plastic drinking straw onto the line. Inflate a balloon and stick it to the straw section with a piece of masking tape folded sticky side out. Let go of the balloon so the escaping air will push straw and balloon along the line. This is one way to explain guided missiles traveling along a radio beam. (See Seq. 3, #86-94—Space Activities.)

Balloon Jets

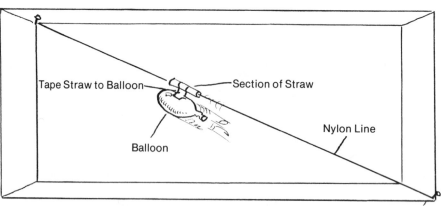

Tape Straw to Balloon — Section of Straw

Balloon

Nylon Line

Tack String to Opposite Corners of Room
(Note: Inflate Balloon Attaching to Straw)

Fig. 7-78

79. *WHAT IS A MACHINE?:* What is a machine? The word conjures up the picture of a black shiny, noisy, smoke-belching, snorting contraption bolted to the concrete floor of a large ugly building beside the river. We all realize the importance of these contraptions and that life would be impossible without them.

"Machine" is a very big word and a more thorough look at its definition reveals a "Mr. Machine" of many personalities. The active day and avid curiosity of children bring them into frequent contact with machines of many kinds. Helping them to recognize, understand and use these machines is another way of nurturing the growing edge. It is often said that the young child will sit "banging a wooden spoon on a kitchen pot" in joyful abandon, oblivious of the fancy, expensive, colorful, motorized, talking toys provided by doting parents. The colorful design and built-in jingle of a toy workbench cannot begin to upstage a *real* hammer or screwdriver. How can we better serve and share in this natural fascination with the ordinary?

80. *WEATHER VANE:* Construct a simple weather vane outside to show wind direction.

81. *WIND SOCK:* Construct a wind sock with nylon stockings to indicate wind direction.

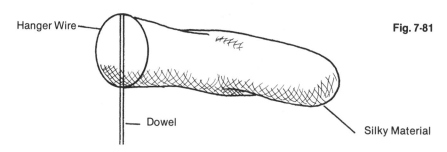

Hanger Wire — Dowel — Silky Material

Fig. 7-81

Cut Circle into Spiral— Hang from Dowel

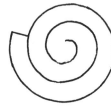

82. *HEATMOBILE:* Cut round piece of smooth, shiny paper into a spiral as in illustration. Thread a 6″ thread into one end and tack other end onto a stick. Remove shade from a lamp and hold this spinner over the bulb. Air heated by bulb will rise and spin mobile. Try over a radiator or hot air heater. Don't *tell* why—*ask*.

83. *SIMPLE MACHINES:* Simple machines fall into six categories—we would probably call them tools—but every tool is a kind of machine. The machine makes the tool work. It is these six simple machines that we will explore: the LEVER, the INCLINED PLANE, the PULLEY, the SCREW, the WHEEL AND AXLE and the WEDGE.

84. *TOOLS:* Display a collection of simple tools. Show each one and how it works. Learn the names. Show how people need each tool. Do something within the understanding of the children. Let each one try the tools. On another day, put the tools out on the table to see if they can name them.

Play a movement game, each one trying to move as one of the tools and the other guess which tool.

Draw around tool, using it for a pattern.

Draw pictures of tools and make charts showing their use.

(See tool list in Woodworking section.)

85. *MR. FIX-IT SHOP:*

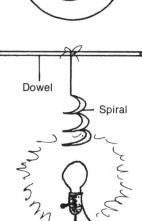

Dowel — Spiral — Lamp

Fig. 7-82

A teacher set up a second bench near the woodworking area. Over it a sign read "WE FIX ANYTHING" and nearby a chart which read "THINGS I CAN FIX." This chart listed the ideas dictated by the children of things they had fixed in the shop and sometimes at home. The shop was equipped with a few simple tools such as screw drivers, wrenches, pliers (you might add sections of wire with prongs and clips at the ends for "checking out electrical problems").

The bench was kept supplied with old appliances and small objects such as clocks, radios, old razors (electric), hair dryers, etc. Two or three children could work there puttering and tinkering and repairing. The conversation and enthusiasm made the shop a favorite activity center for the children.

86. *LEVERS:* The lever is probably the oldest machine in the world. The prehistoric grandfather of every *lever* was the *tree branch*. Neanderthal man used to pry open the front door of his cave. Here are some of the latter-day levers: hammers, crow bars, can openers, screw drivers opening paint cans, teeters, weighing balances, pliers, scissors, hinges, shovels, and oars.

"Put some blocks in a box and try to lift it." Imagine a four's delight at the discovery that he really can.

a. Using the *broom handle* for a *lever* and a pile of blocks as the *fulcrum* let the children test their strength.

Fig. 7-86a

Fulcrum

b. His classmates out on the playground have just discovered they can move mountains, at least the bottom boulders in the foothills, using a *crow bar*. Use one scaled to a mini-giant's size, like a *wrecking bar*.

c. Now try that box of blocks on one end of the *teeter*.

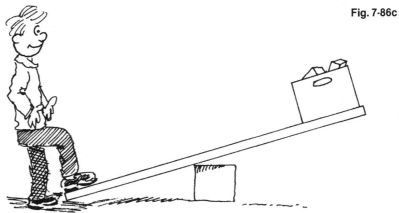

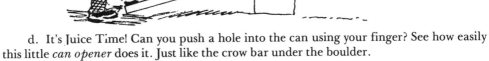

Fig. 7-86c

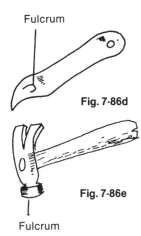

Fulcrum

Fig. 7-86d

Fig. 7-86e

Fulcrum

d. It's Juice Time! Can you push a hole into the can using your finger? See how easily this little *can opener* does it. Just like the crow bar under the boulder.

e. "Tommy drove a nail into this board, can you pull it out with your fingers? Can you find a lever on the workbench that could?"

f. "When you dig into the sand with your *fingers* are they becoming levers? The *shovels* are also levers."

87. *TONGS TO TWEEZERS:* The small muscles of hands, fingers and wrist can be strengthened and trained through a series of activities using tongs of many sizes. This activity can be planned as a progressive series for each age group starting with the threes on item h. and working up to more difficult tasks such as item f. with the fives.

a. Salad tongs (one hand) — serving foods, picking up large items.
b. Fire tongs (two hands) — picking up large items such as blocks or empty boxes.
c. Clothes pins — snap (one hand, fingers) — hanging items on a line.
d. Clothes pins — push — one hand-fist) — hanging items on a line.
e. Pliers — (one hand, wrist) — pulling nails, cutting wire, turning bolts.
f. Tweezers-blunt end — (fingers) — picking up small items such as rice or *Cheerios*.

g. Nutcracker (fist)—opening nuts, turning small screw caps (teachers will find this a handy tool for opening sticky bottle caps.)

h. Sugar or Ice Tongs (fingers)—picking up small items such as cotton balls and sorting them into egg cups.

i. Strawberry huller (two fingers)—hulling strawberries!

j. Toast tweezers (see next item)

88. *TOAST TWEEZER:* Glue two tongue depressers together at one end with a ½ " segment of dowel (½ ") in between. Decorate the sides with tiny designs using acrylic paint. Use to lift hot toast from the toaster. Toast tweezers are a simple-to-make gift.

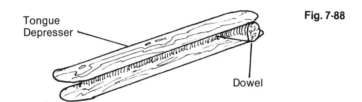

Tongue
Depresser

Dowel

Fig. 7-88

89. *WHEELS AND AXLES:* Put some blocks in a box and ask the children to try and push it across the floor.

a. Next put some *rollers,* dowels, round blocks, large juice cans, small logs, even pencils, under the box and push! Keeping the rollers under the box and going straight takes teamwork. (*You* have also discovered a much easier way to shift heavy furniture around!)

Fig. 7-89a

If you can locate an old hand *wringer* it will be very useful in squeezing out soggy mittens after spring puddle play.

b. A rolling pin from the kitchen is another "tool" the children can use in making cookies.

c. The Lego gear set is an excellent introduction to *wheels as gears.* The wheels and gears of a clock work in much the same way.

"What keeps the clock ticking?"

Roll some narrow strips of paper tightly around a pencil. Now let it go.

"What happens to the coils?"

"Can you find the coil in the clock?"

"How does it get wound?"

If you are going to let a younster take apart a clock be sure the main spring cannot fly out and cause injury.

d. Did you use an *egg beater* to make those cookies? Did anybody notice the gears?

e. The inside of the *pencil sharpener* has a set of *internal gears.*

f. Dump the sand into the *wheelbarrow.* Give it a ride. Add more sand until there is a heavy load. "Can you still push it?" Both *levers* and *wheels* will help.

g. *Waterwheel:* Show pictures and describe uses. Read: *Mechanical Man* by Beril Backer, pub. G.P. Putnam.

90. *PULLEYS:* Attach a rope line between two pulleys.

a. Send messages back and forth from doll corner to construction site in the block corner. Develop language skills as the children send and receive message words which they have hung on the lines with clothespins (lever).

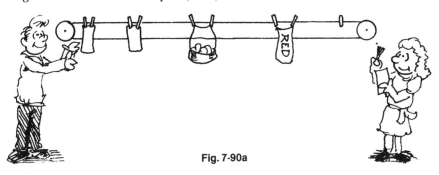

Fig. 7-90a

Fig. 7-90b

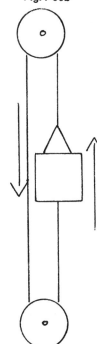

Use the pulley line for a puppet show.

b. *Elevators:* The children in the treehouse can use a pulley line as a freight *elevator* for hauling supplies up and down. Take a field trip to see a skyscraper under construction. Some department stores have cage elevators and you can go to the top floor and watch the large cables and pulleys in operation.

c. *Pulley Book:* Flagpoles, clotheslines, ski tows, fan belts, dentists drills, cranes and radio dials all use pulleys. children might make a Pulley Book by collecting pictures of pulley machines.

91. *INCLINED PLANE AND WEDGE:* "Ramps, sloping roads, chisels, hatchets, plows, air hammers, carpenter's planes—all of these are examples of the fourth basic machine: the inclined plane and its active twin brother, the wedge. In the broadest sense, the wedge includes all devices for cutting and piercing. When a wedge is sliced in half you get the inclined plane. The sharper the knife, the easier the cutting, the gentler the slope the easier the climb.

a. Construct a series of *ramps* at several pitches, a wide plank and the schoolhouse steps is an easy substitute. Take turns rolling a barrel up the various pitches or put some blocks in a box (or the wagon) and pull it up the slopes.

"Which slope was easier?"

"How far does the barrel roll when you let it go down again?"

b. Chip designs into boards with a *chisel* and carve in soap with a *knife*—both are examples of wedges.

c. Take a trip to a farm to watch *plows* and *harrows—trowels* and *shovels* are wedges with levers as handles.

d. *A jackhammer* is a very noisy wedge, a *needle* a very quiet one.

e. *Teeth* are used as wedges when they bite into food!

Fig. 7-91

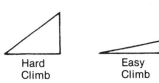

Dull   Sharp

Hard   Easy
Climb   Climb

92. *Screws:* The fascination of wheels and axles might soon be overcome by the versatile personality of the screw. A screw is not a "simple" machine since it depends upon another machine, a lever, for its operation. The screw works in two ways, raising weights and fastening objects.

a. Put some blocks in a box and borrow a *jackscrew* from a neighborhood construction company and see how easily fours and fives can turn it up and down on the jackscrew. If your *piano stool* is the wind-up kind you have been riding up and down on a perfect jackscrew all this time, so get up and give the "box of blocks" a turn on it.

b. A nut rides up and down the *bolt* in much the same manner.

c. Children will discover the holding power of *screws* when they screw them into a board beside their wedge "cousins," nails and try pulling each out with the hammer.

d. A carpenter's clamp and a bench vise are screws.

93. *CAR LIFT:* Using a *jackscrew*.

Use ½" boards. Make a box with three sides and bottom. The size depends on the scale of the toy cars in your own block corner, probably about 8″ × 6″ × 6″ high.

You will need 2 top pieces, one for the top of the box, one for the platform.

One of the sides is left open to operate the lift.

Drill center holes in box top and platform to fit the bolt, about ½″ shank.

Slip the bolt up through the box top, head down. Attach the top to the sides of the box.

With a nut on either side of the platform secure the platform to the lift.

The lift is now ready for business, reach in and turn the bolt and the lift rides up and down. You will need a detachable board to use as an entrance-exit ramp.

94. *THE MOTORCYCLE:* Janie's mother came to school on her motorcycle to show it to Janie's classmates. They did not take rides but each child sat on the seat and tried on the helmet. "Let them try on your jacket, mother" Janie requested and her mother took off her jacket and let each child try it on. They explored the motorcycle closely, chattering and pointing out every detail. Later they created a motorcycle without any suggestion or help.

95. *MACHINE SHOP MIX-UP:* Place many simple machines on a large table, egg beaters, clock, pencil sharpener, door knob, can openers, casters, water faucet, scissors, knife, needles, hammer, wrench, etc. and sort them into boxes marked for each type of machine—LEVERS, WHEELS, SCREWS, etc.

96. *MACHINE TREASURE HUNT:* Place the same assortment of machines around the room and see how many the children can recognize as machines.

97. *VILLAGE SQUARE:* Following a series of field trips turn the block corner into the village square and deliver the tools of the trades to the proper (cardboard) shops. BAKERY (beaters, spoons, cutters), maybe the baker will reward with cookies!; CARPENTER SHOP (hammers, saws, nails, clamps); SCHOOL (pencils, sharpeners, scissors) TAILOR (scissors, needles, tailor's wheel).

98. *WHOSE MACHINE?:* At circle time hold up an assortment of machines like those above and see how many workers the children can identify with the machine.

99. *PICTURE MACHINE HUNT:* Using the endless variety of pictures from magazines and books, see how many simple machines a child can find.

100. *PULLEY GAMES:* Devise a variety of ways to use the cross-room pulley:

"How many green objects can you pull over to the doll corner?"

"I'm sending over a word (hammer, pencil, cracker, hat, scissors). Can you send back the object?"

"Would all the children here today send over their names in the basket?"

101. *CARBURETOR:* Obtain a small carburetor and let the children take it apart and put it back together.

102. *CAR #6:* Make garages using small boxes which will hold small cars. Put corresponding numbers on the garages and cars. Ask the child to park the cars in the right garage. (MATH)

103. *THE SNOW PLOW:*

The teacher put out a carton and the book of *Giant Things That Go* (Zaffo). "Let's look at these pictures and see what we might make with this box," she said. Four children turned the pages, talking about the pictures and decided to make a snow plow. They had to decide how to attach the plow to the main body; to decide what was needed on the dashboard of the vehicle. The only time they needed help was in fastening a steering wheel on the tube they had inserted for a steering post. The teacher helped them wire it on but there were wires coming out of the center of the tube. "That's all right," said Jack "that can be the horn," as he covered them with a circle of black paper.

Magnetism 104. *MAGNET EXPERIMENTS:* Set an aluminum tray up on blocks on table so magnet can be drawn underneath. Do the same with a sheet of cardboard, plastic or glass tray (with or without water in it at different times). Experiment with magnet, drawing various objects along the trays. Cut a large square into the center of sturdy cardboard box and tape paper over it. Shave iron filings onto the paper. (Grate your own, using steel nails and coarse file.) Reach into the box and draw magnets under the paper to make the filings 'dance' into patterns.

105. *MAGNET HUNT:*

Wally knocked on the side of the stove.
"What's this made of?" His teacher asked, "What does it feel like? Is it hard or soft? What kind of noises does it make when you hit it?"
"Is it metal?" Wally asked.
"There is something in this room which helps you find out if things are metal," the teacher answered.
Wally glanced around the room and his eyes fell on the giant magnet on the science table. He ran and got it.
"I can use this magnet."
"If you like I can help you make a list of things which are metal," the teacher offered.
Carol came over and joined them. In the next twenty minutes they tested every area of the classroom with the magnet. Wally and Carol made a long list of metal objects which the teacher wrote on a chart. Later, as Wally told the class about the experiment, the teacher read the list.

106. *MAGNETIC BALLOONS:* Inflate balloons and rub all over with wool cloth or against a wool sweater. They will stick to things. Try this without rubbing the balloons. Put several magnetized balloons into a large carton. They will jump away from each other (repel). This is static friction electricity. Magnets with like poles will do the same thing.

107. *DEMAGNETIZATION:* A new teacher complained that a new set of magnets did not work. "They were O.K. yesterday," she said. An experienced teacher discovered that the magnets had been placed in their storage box all facing in the same direction. They had *demagnetized.* "If you store magnets with the like poles together they will demagnetize each other."

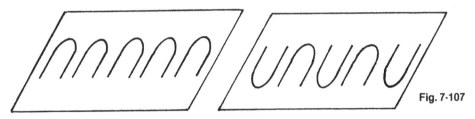

Fig. 7-107

108. *FISHING WITH MAGNETS:* Cut fish shapes from paper, plastic covers or foil. Attach two together with paper clip between. Attach a magnet to the fishing line. Waterproof fish can be put into tubs and pans. Extend to language arts by adding numbers and letters and children's names to the fish.

109. *TUBES AND BOXES:* Every household acquires a wide variety of boxes, tubes and other pieces of cardboard of various shapes. Ask parents to save them for you. When collection is large enough, place it in the middle of the floor and say, "What can you make?" Children who have had experience in an environment where creativity and imagination are encouraged will set to with vigor and their results are often astounding. (see Seq. 11, #92)

110. *THE DISHWASHER:*

"It's a dishwasher," John explained to his teacher.
"See, this is where the pipes are for the water to come in and this is where the wires for the electricity come. The water goes out here." Pointing to a tiny red circle, he said, "This is the light that goes off when the dishes are dry." (MACHINES)

Colors and Shapes

111. *GEOMETRIC PATTERNS:* Fold an absorbent paper towel several times to form a square. Dip each corner into food coloring. Unfold towel, hang to dry. Experiment with folding in other shapes, dipping other parts in color.

112. *DOT-TO-DOT:* To develop eye-hand coordination and numerical order, connect dots to make designs.

113. *TORN PAPER SHAPES:* To develop small muscle skills, show and talk about different shapes and demonstrate how they can be torn from paper. Ask child to tear a shape and mount on a contrasting color.

114. *SHAMROCK DESIGNS:* Make shamrock potato prints. Compare shamrock to clover.

115. *COLOR LINES:* Ask two children to stretch red (or other color) yarn between two red (or other color) objects in the room. Tape color footprints in zig-zags and swirls around the room. Ask children to walk the "red path" (yellow, green, etc.)

116. *COLOR MATCH UP:* Put color patches (chalk, paper, rug squares, cloth) on the floor to correspond with colors of children's clothing (include everyone). Ask the children to stand on the color which matches what they are wearing.

117. *PAINTING GREEN:* Add white, black and/or yellow to green paint to make shades and tints of green. (SCIENCE)

Animals
118. *NICE MICE:* Read stories and poems about mice. Follow up by making mice with pussy willows. Glue pussy willows on paper, add tails and ears. (See #35)

119. *PUSSY WILLOW:*

PUSSY WILLOW
by Deborah Mitchell Haney

> Always a pussy—
> Never a cat
> Soft and grey
> And not *too* fat!
> Warm and cozy
> Smooth to pat
> And she won't scratch you
> Imagine that!

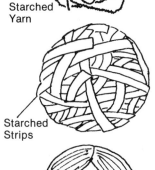

Starched
Yarn

Starched
Strips

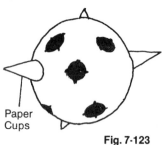

Yarn

Paper
Cups

Fig. 7-123

120. *IMAGINARY ANIMALS:* Draw a make believe animal. Give it a name and tell a story about it. Create animals another day with a selection of elegant junk. (LANG. DEV.)

121. *TURTLES:* The little, red-eared variety of turtle often found in pet stores are carriers of a highly contagious virus 'salmonella.' Symptoms in children are fever, stomach upset, headache. The sale of turtles is regulated. A reputable pet shop will observe the observation period required to assure that your turtles are free from infection. (SAFETY)

122. *PAPER PLATE WEAVING:* Cut four slits in a paper plate toward center and weave yarn over and under each section of the plate. (ART)

123. *BALLOON SCULPTURES:* Dip short (10"-24") lengths of string or yarn in starch and wrap around inflated balloons, Criss-cross lengths for added strength. When dry, balloon is deflated. The result is a lovely, open-work, lacy shape. (Fig. 1) Use as hanging decoration.

VARIATION: Cover a balloon with strips of cloth dipped in starch, for closed sculpture which can be painted when dry. (Fig. 2) Use colorful cloth instead and glue on trims.

VARIATION: Large size balloons can be covered in same manner with several layers of plaster tape, used for molding casts. Strips are dipped in water and laid over balloon. When dry, balloon is popped and hard shape remains. The balloon sculpture may be used as head mask, painted in bright colors and decorated with yarn hair, foil details, etc. They can also be used as piñatas. (Fig. 3 and 4) (see Seq. 4, #50, 51)

124. *POTATO SCULPTURES:* Combine potatoes with toothpicks, small nails or pins to make sculptures using straws, screw eyes, buttons, beads, cloth and trims, wire bits, dixie cups.

125. *POTATO PRINTING:* Cut or scratch designs into flat surface of potato—*brush* on paint and use as printer. (Dipping potato directly in paint tends to cause blotting.)

Growing Things
126. *GROWING GRASS:* Sprinkle grass seed over the top of a sponge. Place sponge in a shallow can or dish and keep moist. Put in light place. Within a few days the sponge will be covered with growing grass.

127. *SPROUTS:* Edible sprouts from seeds, such as alfalfa, almonds, barley beans, buckwheat, corn, lentils, mung, etc. are easy to grow. Wash seeds well and place in a bowl

of warm water, four cups of water to one cup of seed. Soak overnight, drain, retaining liquid to be used as soup stock.

Put seeds in sprouting container and rinse thoroughly. (A sprouting container may be a commercial variety or a one quart glass jar with a clean layer of cheesecloth, nylon net, or stocking or plastic screen over the top. Container must be large enough for growth and air circulation.) Drain off all excess water and keep in a warm, dark area where temperature will remain even.

Sprouts should be rinsed and drained two or three times daily and most will sprout within two to three days. Sprouts are ready when seeds have opened and *shoots* are well developed. They can be eaten in salads, soups, omelets, casseroles, breads and cake.

Place bean, pea, flax, grass or other seeds in a variety of growing containers to demonstrate the ideal conditions necessary to cause germination.

    a. Place between wet blotters. Keep well watered for seven to ten days.

    b. Place around the sides of a glass jar which has wet cotton in the center. (Cotton keeps the seeds against the sides for better viewing.)

    c. Place seed in a jar of water. Some submerged, some above water. (GROWING)

EXPERIMENT: Put one of each of these growing suggestions in different conditions:

    a. full sun

    b. dark closet

    c. refrigerator

    d. outside

Observe and chart (children draw illustrations, find picture of mature plant):

    a. which germinates first (use several kinds)

    b. which need water

    c. which need sun (will germinate in dark-underground)

    d. which need air (those under water 'suffocate')

128. *POTATOES AND BEANS:* Both grow easily and rapidly with little care. Beans, expecially, sprout within two or three days and children can watch the growth process as leaflets unfold and develop.

129. *CUTTINGS:* Take cuttings of geraniums, begonias, coleus. Talk about how some plants can be divided over and over (shared), extending their beauty to an ever widening circle.

130. *MARIGOLDS:* These are hardy and usually successful plants to grow from seed.

131. *CARROT SPROUTS:* Read *Smokey's Big Discovery* by Walck, pub. Preston. Discuss color and shape of carrots. Put carrot tops in dish of water to sprout. Cut carrots in half, dig out center and fill with water. Hang in window. Green sprouts will grow from bottom. Watch and record daily growth.

132. *ROOTS AND SPROUTS:* Root sweet potatoes, potatoes, carrots, avocado and garlic cloves over water, by filling container with water to touch the bottom of vegetable. Hold vegetable in water by spearing with toothpicks from four sides to rest on container.

133. *GREENHOUSES AND FARMS:* Visit a commercial greenhouse and a farm to observe plants in various stages of growth, soil preparation, plowing, fertilizing, planting. Plan to bring home a large plant from which to make cuttings. (see Activity #129)

Food   134. *GREEN FOOD:* In honor of St. Patrick's Day, serve a completely green meal. Choose from lettuce, celery or pea soup, olives, artichokes, limes, green gelatin, green beans, broccoli (raw or cooked), mint jelly, green frosted cakes, green candies, pistachio nuts, cole slaw, pistachio ice cream... (see Seq. 8, Act. #84, for Green Eggs.)

135. *SIMPLE SPROUT SOUP:* Make chicken or beef flavored bouillon and add sprouts, rice or noodles, sautéed onions and/or other finely chopped vegetables.

136. *RAISIN COUNT:* Put 3 raisins on a cracker. Child eats one. How many are left? Vary and use to develop math skills at various levels and stages. (MATH)

137. *WHAT'S IT MADE FROM?:* Put out bowls of uncooked rolled oats, raw rice and a lemon. Children touch and smell. Give each child a small portion of a lemon cookie. Ask which of the items was used to make the cookie. Repeat with an oatmeal cookie and a rice

cracker. Vary the experiment with other cereals and food.

138. *CARROTS:* Cut into new shapes for snacks—dice, triangles, crinkles, rounds.
139. *NO COOK PASTEL CANDY:*

> ⅓ cup evaporated milk
> ½ cup margarine
> 2½ cups confectioners sugar (sifted)
> Add drops of food colors to create pastels

Scrub hands well. Knead ingredients into smooth mixture. Shape into funny faces—bunnies, turtles, ovals. Decorate with chocolate bits, small candies, coconut, etc. Refrigerate until cold and firm.

140. *PISTACHIO:* Read "Pistachio" by Blair Lent, pub. Little Brown. Serve pistachio nuts or ice cream. Serve lime jello, mint jello, lime sherbet and green candies to discover some of the ways green might taste. (See #134)

141. *Ireland:* The Irish are noted for their gift of story-telling. Celebrate the 'Wearing of the Green' with story telling by gathering on the 'green' (carpet or blanket) and creating your very own folk tales. Spin yarns of such places as Tipperary, Ulster, Shannon, Barrow, Kerry, Killarney, Donegal, Down, Dublin, Cork, Galway. Just the sounds of such Gaelic places will bring out a rich brogue in everyone. Practice *rrrr*rolling 'r's to make up rhymes. Take imaginary trips to the famous places of the Emerald Isle.

142. *BLARNEY:* Try a little. Coax and flatter, using all the nice words you can list... "If you don't use a little blarney, it won't work." Can the children use "blarney?" What is the Blarney Stone? Have a blarney day when every one showers flattery on everyone else.

143. *LEPRECHAUN:* Leprechauns are famous in Irish literature for their magic powers in finding treasure. Plan a real treasure hunt with many little leprechauns hunting for treasure. Serve LUCKY CHARMS (or other treats) at the end as a special treat.

144. *THE EMERALD ISLE:* Why is Ireland green? Rain, rain, rain which makes the rolling hillsides and fields blossom with shamrock. Try seeding some clover. Press leaves between sheets of waxed paper to make your own lucky charms.

145. *AIRPORT:* Encourage dramatic play by offering and suggesting ways to turn part of the room into an airport. Suggestions: A step ladder might become the control tower, a long, board a runway for rolling planes. (Tongue depressers taped to cards turn them into planes.) Help the children write to airlines for posters of giant jets. Free postcards are usually available at ticket offices.

Make a "this is your captain speaking" and airline stewardess tape on a cassette and use as part of a transoceanic flight. Serve refreshments, show a movie while in flight. Land for a stopover and outside play during the long flight. A well planned trip might take all day, from ticket sales to welcome home party and greetings, as parents come to pick up the passengers at the end of the day.

Suggested materials: luggage (one for each passenger, use cartons with string handles), tickets and baggage checks, food trays from box covers, box lunches, slides of foreign countries, blankets and pillows (stuff cases) for inflight rest, costumes (pilot hat), pilot's control panel drawn on a box.

146. *MACHINES:* Suggested Field Trips

There are many field trips you can take to see how simple machines and complex machines made up of many simple machines do their daily work and make hundreds of products used in classrooms and homes. The larger factories usually provide excellent tours but frequently restrict them to larger groups and older children. There are so many ways you can introduce young children to a fascinating variety of busy machines simply by knocking on the doors of the local shops where work and products of all kinds from shoe repair and hair cutting to candy making and printing are on view. Some smaller shopkeepers will even turn off noisy machines for closer inspection. (Try the YELLOW PAGES as your tour guide.)

Construction Sights put many *levers* to work digging, lifting, pushing and pulling.

Skyscrapers going up: *Cranes* needed! (Also for unloading and loading at docks.)

Sawmills and Carpenter's Shops: Any local mill or shop puts *cutting* and *planing* tools to work on many jobs and *belt pulleys* help turn these cutters and planers.

Loading platforms at busy stores and factories move supplies up and down *ramps.* You will see many kinds of moving devices at work there.

Chutes are frequently used to funnel feed to cattle and poultry at a farm.

Dams and *irrigation sluices* funnel water.

Sand and Gravel pits use a combination of *shoots, belts, ramps* and *conveyor belts* to move sand and stones.

Houses on the move are lifted up on *jackscrews.*

Cider Mills squeeze out cider with *screw presses.*

Dams at small streams use giant *screws* and *gears* to raise the gates.

5H. SEQUENCE EIGHT

Spring comes with the bursting of *buds* and the *plowing and seeding* of *farms. Baby birds* and some animals are incubated in *eggs.* Sun and *rain* are vital to all growth.

Water and its sources, from tiny *streams* to the expanse of the *oceans,* is important to all forms of life. When children are properly dressed, *a rainy day* offers many possibilities for extending classroom activities outside.

Stories and pictures about *storms* and *floods,* which occur when winter snow and ice melt during the spring, are carried in *newspapers.* Bulletin boards and books made from news items can be used to stimulate discussion about *current events* in the world beyond the school.

Newspapers are *printed* on presses. How is this different from potato printing?

Many people work as *weather men* and *climatologists,* predicting storms, warning about floods and aiding farmers with agricultural advice.

Street *workers* clean out *catch basins* and repair damaged *roads, dams and bridges. Plumbers* install and repair *pipes* and *sewer lines* through which water courses and is controlled.

1. *PLUMBERS:* Ask a plumber for a box of pipes, joints, traps, etc. Perhaps a plumber will be willing to come show how these items are used. Lay out blueprints or plumbing plans. Do not try to explain—just put on table near box of fixtures. Children may relate to what they find in box. Some may ask for and learn the proper names for the pieces. Go through building looking for similar pieces.

If possible, open and clean out a trap under a sink so children can see what goes in and observe how strainer stops it from clogging.

Put some plaster of Paris and some clay into a piece of pipe to show how it adheres to sides and clogs the hole.

Show different compositions of pipe—plastic, copper, lead, rubber hose.

(You are not trying to teach science of plumbing, but exposing children to functional world. Some will absorb more than others. Such learning is foundation for future learning—some part of it will be retained.)

2. *SELF IMAGE—A NEW LOOK:* Self image pictures do not have to be a once-a-year project. In the beginning of the school year (Seq. 11) we draw around each child and invite him to color in his features, clothing and hair. The way in which he completes his picture will tell us about his manual dexterity, eye for color, powers of observation for details. (One child carefully drew in the stripes of his socks.) If we write his comments about his picture we often learn something about the way he feels about himself.

In Seq. 6, we talked about emotions and again, drew around the children. This time the figures are nude and the children proceed to dress them with paper, cloth, yarn and other materials. (Fringed newspaper and ravelled yarn from old sweaters make excellent hair.) Questions give added incentive: "How would you dress for a fancy party?" "What would you wear to work in a factory?" "A garden?" "A construction site?"

At another time the children might take turns drawing around friends and dress another person's figure. This will require looking at each carefully, noting eye color, articles of clothing, hair style, etc. This stimulates good training in making observations and translating them onto the figure.

If these past self-images are available later in the year a comparison will often reveal growth. "Look, I didn't even put in my nose when I was little!" "I can't even wear that dress now, it's too small." "I remember those buckle shoes, they were new when I came on the first day of school."

Hang the figures up and see if they have gained in height.

3. *ELECTRICIANS:* Ask, "If you were an electrician how many things in this room could you find to repair?" List and separate those requiring a special kind of repair service (i.e. telephone).

4. *PEOPLE WHO FIX THINGS:* A collection of trade magazines will supply many pictures of people repairing things. Cut, mount and label these. Can the children determine whether the pictures show something under repair or being built? Ask at hardware, plumbing and electrical supply houses, trade unions, lumber yards, for literature containing such pictures. Watch for possible field trips.

5. *APRIL FOOL'S DAY—SENSE OF HUMOR:* See *Early Years,* pub. Early Years, Darien, Conn. (April 1974) for "Welcome April," Activity #1, p. 67. Developing a sense of humor, tricking, teasing for fun.

6. *TINY KINGDOM IN THE GRASS:* Read *In The Grass* from TOLD UNDER THE BLUE UMBRELLA, by Dorothy Baruch, pub. MacMillan. Stimulate imaginations about bugs, creepers, and crawlers. Construct tiny creatures from egg cartons, tempera, pipe cleaners and clay. Suspend or pull on strings. Create insect sounds with instruments. (See Seq. 10, #'s 46, 47, 49, and 50, for art ideas with insects, Seq. 9, #'s 84, 85, Ant Farm, also Seq. 11, Activity #62, 63, 64, and 69.) (BUGS)

7. *TOE TICKLING:* Read *The Feel Of Things* by Mary G. Phillips from TOLD UNDER THE BLUE UMBRELLA, pub. MacMillan. The boy in the story goes outside in bare feet to discoveries of the way things feel on bare feet. City children? No grass? PRETEND! Make it a dramatic play game. (SENSORY)

8. *LANGUAGE STRETCHING:* Post some pictures of flowers, foods, children, scenery, animals on the bulletin board and invite discussion of their contents. Note on a large sheet the over-worked words used, such as nice, big, pretty, good, cute. Next, try to think of other words to describe these same pictures. Make it a game during discussion to ring a bell or sound a gong when an over-worked word is used. (LANGUAGE DEVELOPMENT)

9. *EASTER EGG TREE:* Use real branches cemented into bucket and hang on blown eggs, (see #82) or painted and decorated paper ones. Hang also with paper birds. After the holiday, use branches outside as nesting material for birds (bits of string and grasses). (See #92, Birds in a tree.) (BIRDS)

10. *STORY BOOK DEVELOPMENT:* Use the following suggestions based on *Caps for Sale,* by E. Slobodkina, pub. Scholastic, to extend other story books with a variety of activities.

a. Read the story to lay the groundwork for follow-up activities. *Do not try it all at one time.*

b. Talk about peddlers. What do they do?

c. Make hats with colored construction paper. Take an imaginary walk and find things to make imaginary caps. Return and list all the things you found.

d. Place all the paper hats you have made in a cloth bag and let children take turns carrying it over the shoulder to peddle the caps to the others.

e. At another time everyone becomes a monkey. They climb and cavort saying, "chee, chee." They wiggle under and climb on top of furniture, swing from the jungle gym. Sometimes a monkey falls out of a tree.

f. Experiment with the story in many such ways until all have 'tried on' the characters of the peddler and the monkeys. Then re-enact the story, choosing one peddler and one monkey to fall out of the tree. Conduct a problem solving discussion: "The monkeys thought they had played a trick on the peddler. The peddler thought he had tricked the monkeys. What do you think?"

g. Construct a mural of the story drawing in the basic scenery and 'dressing' it with the characters of the story using bits of paper, cloth and other materials for monkeys, peddler, hats.

h. Extend the story into as many activities as possible, counting, recognition of coins and colors, expressing emotions, taking turns, drama, movement.

Concepts: On top of, back to (tree), threw *down*, looked *up*, looked to *left* and *right* and *behind* for hats.

Sensory: Talk about what peddler saw, smelled, heard—when he walked into the country. Make cardboard monkeys and cover with fuzzy cloth or cut from carpet squares for touching experience.

Math: How many caps? How do you know? Count the monkeys and match to hats, demonstrating a one-to-one correspondence. How many caps of each color? How much will you charge for your hats? more? less than? Make play money and sell hats.

Science: Balance hats on heads. Talk about scissors grinder, peddler, grindstone. Bring in electric knife sharpener.

Music: Teach song, *Chairs to Mend.* Use sticks or drum for walking, maracas or tiny sticks for monkey talk. Use blocks for "sh-sh-sh" when peddler is sleeping. Play notes on piano or xylophone as peddler shakes fists.

Movement: Mime entire story—NO words.

Problem Solving: Who played a trick? Peddler? Monkeys?

11. *MONKEY TREE:*

A teacher made fuzzy monkeys from cardboard, covered with fabric and pipe cleaner tails as hangers. She made jackets and caps of various colors, each with string hangers. The figures had numerals and letters for matching games. She made a tree of real branches cemented into a can. (A cardboard tree with pockets along the branches could also be used.) The children played a variety of games, matching coats and hats to monkeys, finding numbers or letters which matched. The monkeys, arranged by numbers 1-12 (one was at the top and twelve at the bottom of the tree) were used in many games for concepts and skills.

12. *SIMPLE POEMS:* Use the verse below to stimulate simple Haiku or Cinquain verses from the experiences of the children: (WRITING POEMS)

Shower came
  In I came
    Blue sky came   (Unknown)

13. *ALPHABETS AROUND THEMES:* Develop alphabets around themes, such as seasons, occupations, foods, rooms, (kitchen). Example:

Spring Alphabet
by Clea Chmela

A is for Ants	N is for Nests
B is for Butterflies and Bees	O is for Outdoors
C is for Caterpillars	P is for Puddles and Pansies
D is for Dandelions	Q is for Quacking
E is for Eggs	R is for Rain
F is for Flowers and Frogs	S is for Sprinkles and Spiders
G is for Gardens	T is for Tadpoles
H is for Hives and Honey	U is for Umbrellas
I is for Insects and Itch	V is for Violets
J is for Jumping Frogs	W is for Wind
K is for Kites	X is for eXercise
L is for Lions and Lambs	Y is for Yellow-Forsythia, Sun
M is for Meadows and Mice	Z is for BuzzzzzzZzZZZZZ

14. *GROUP POEMS:* The two poems which follow were inspired by a walk in the rain. Develop class poems, using ideas of the children. Rhyming and meter are not essential to every poem.

15. *SPRING HAS COME CALLING,* Harriet Chmela

How does rain smell?
How does it taste?
Trim delicate webbings...
With rain-pearls all laced?

Hear how rain clatters
On rippled tin roofs.
Puts shine on the pavement
And polishes red boots.

Watch the rain rushing
Through grates in the gutter
"WATCH OUT" for the muddy
Or your mother will sputter!

See earthworms a-wiggle
From holes filled to the top.
Crocus buds in the garden
Are ready to POP.

Buckle your raingear
Go puddle-sail boats
Keep dry in slickers
And bright yellow coats.

Out come umbrellas
Ponchos, so'westers
Rubbers and hip boots
Protect puddle testers...

...Look in the pathway
The driveway or yard
For tracks you can mold
With plaster all hard.

Look at the rain fall
Straight down or slanted?
Look for the bud tops
Of tulips you've planted.

Watch when the sunshine
Through clouds comes a-peeping
Then look for the rainbow
And baby birds peeping.

Don't hide in the house
When April rain comes a-falling
For it's time to announce
That spring has come calling!

16. *RAIN POEM:*

HAVE YOU EVER WALKED IN THE RAIN?
by Helen Campbell

Have you ever walked in the rain?
I have...
The raindrops beating on my hat,
My boots sloshing through a puddle
And the wet, wet feeling on my face.
Have you ever walked in the rain?
I have...

Have you ever walked in the fog?
I have...
It closes in softly about you
And makes you open your eyes wide
To peer into nothing
Have you ever walked in the fog?
I have...

Have you ever run in the wind?
I have...
The rush of noise about your ears,
Hair whipping your head
The feel of fresh air warming your skin
Have you ever run in the wind?
I have...

17. *RESTAURANT:* Make *menus* by pasting three or four pictures of food items to cardboard or construction paper folders. (Hot dog, milk, fruit, cake, etc.) (See Seq. 3, #30.)

Make *order pads* from papers stapled together or use commercial ones.

Make up matching sets of food pictures shown on menus and paste to construction paper or cardboard squares (old playing cards) for use in the 'kitchen'.

NOTE: Menus (make 8-10) do not all have to be the same but each item shown should have a corresponding picture in the 'kitchen.'

Some children are *customers*, some are *waiters*, some are *cooks*. (The ratio of four waiters, four customers and two cooks seems to work well.) A *cashier* with play money can also be added.

Waiters take orders, depending on skills and age levels by:

a. writing simple words on pads

b. drawing pictures of food ordered

c. making a symbol   etc., which corresponds to the same symbol shown by each food pictured on the menu.

Cooks fill the orders by finding the matching food picture and serving them on paper plates.

Waiters serve the plates to customers. (Carrying plates on trays is a good balance and large muscle activity.)

Customers pay for food with play money. Paying concept may also be extended by adding prices (in dollars) or simple numerals (1-10) to the items pictured on menus. Child then matches his payment in play money to the amount shown.

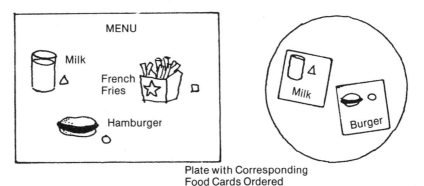

Fig. 8-17

Plate with Corresponding
Food Cards Ordered

18. *STRING DANCE:* Give each child a piece of string (about 6') to lay out into shapes on the rug or grass. Each in turn chooses one of the string sculptures and imitates its shape with his body.

19. *KITS-IN-BOOTS:* Read *Puss In Boots.* Modify for younger children. Bring in real big boots. Walk in them. Walk in imaginary boots. Dramatize the story. What workmen wear big boots? What for?

HOMEWORK: Find a picture or think of a way some workers wear boots.

20. *A TRUE BOOT STORY:*

Near one school there was a pond where the ducks lived. Where the water had receded there was a very mucky, muddy place around the edge. One day the children wore their biggest boots and did something special. They went down to the pond and walked in the mud. SQUOOSHED, PLOPPED, SMOOSHED in the mud! (Their teacher had tested it in advance to be sure they wouldn't sink in too far.) The children experienced the pull of the mud. They discovered they had to work hard to walk when they sunk in with every step. The mud made a squish and a pop, a sucking sound.

They cleaned out some of the debris and other objects that had been thrown into the pond. (ECOLOGY) They looked through a magnifying glass at the tracks the ducks had made. Plaster of Paris foot casts were taken of the duck prints. On another day, the children put a pan of damp sand on the playground near the pond and called the ducks, luring them with bread scraps. The bread was placed just beyond the pans of sand and some of the ducks took a route right through the pans. Plaster prints were cast of their footprints. (ART)

When the children returned they washed some of their boots in a pan of water. Others were set outside to dry in the sun. They discovered that the mud brushed off easily when it was dry.

Inside, the group talked about their experience and made a list of new words, mushy, muddy, mucky, squishy, icky, etc. (LANGUAGE) They took an imaginary walk using instruments to reproduce the sounds of walking over the wooden bridge to get to the edge of the pond. (MUSIC-DRAMA) They had to bend way over to walk under the bridge; this was extra hard in the mud. (MOVEMENT-CONCEPTS) They imitated the sounds of the boots pulling out of the mud.

Many other activities followed the walk in the mud. One day the children made bird's nests. (See Nest Building, #28 and 89.)

On another day they used cords shaped in circles on the floor to make imaginary stepping stones in a brook and jumped from one to another. Then the cords became puddles and the children jumped over them, splashing through them. They even pretended someone had fallen into the pond and used a cord to pull him out. (DRAMA)

21. *RHINOCEROS RIPPLE:* Read *Rhinoceros Skin* from Kipling's *Just So Stories,* pub. Airmont. Make yourself very, very tight. "Tight, tight, tight, squeeze! Now let go! Loose, loose, loose, flappy and flabby!"

22. *LEG WORK:* How many ways can you use your legs? What occupations rely on legs? How many different ways can you walk? In what different ways do animals use their legs?

23. *FEET:* Put corks on floors. Remove shoes and stockings and try to pick up with toes. (SMALL MUSCLE)

24. *BABY BIRD:* A baby bird has fallen out of its nest. Can you walk very softly to pick it up so you don't frighten it?

25. *WALKING:* Walk under a low bridge. Walk through mud, puddles, jump across a brook, climb a slippery hill, fall down, get mud all over your hands and arms, wash it off.

26. *PUDDLES:* Make puddles on the floor with hoops or cords or use rug squares. Walk through them with big boots on. Jump from rock to rock in a brook.

27. *RAIN DANCE:* Ask children to close their eyes. What would it feel like to be a rain-drop? Lots of little soft pattering drops? Show this with your fingers. Now it is raining hard. It is thundering (beat on drums or rattle a large sheet of aluminum or sheet metal.) The rain is coming harder and harder. the wind is blowing, and now the storm is over.

28. *NEST BUILDING WITH MOTIONS:* "Let's be birds and build a nest. Birds do not have hands. How can you pick up things without hands? With your mouth? Between your toes?"

29. *CORDS AND ROPES:* Using 6 feet (approx.) sections of cord or rope, make into circles on the floor. Walk around inside, outside. Sit in your own little circle. Put cords on the floor in a line and walk as if on a tightrope. Step one foot after another, heel and toe. Sideways. On toes. Or heels. Hop back and forth over the line. Accompany all of these with drumbeats.

Develop into a dance using three of the motions and different beats. (A dance always has a beginning, a middle and an end.) Perhaps you emphasize the end with a crash on the cymbal. Feel the beat as a group. Make cords into numbers, letters, shapes and patterns. Ask everyone to look at a shape then pick it up and ask who can walk using the same shape. Draw a pattern on paper or blackboard and ask children to copy on the floor using cords.

30. *UNDER THE UMBRELLA:* Read *My Red Umbrella* by Bright, pub. Morrow, and use the theme to develop a game of catching things and people, underneath. Make an umbrella from a hoop, cloth and string. It can be made to go up and down from a hook or small pulley in the ceiling. Use this same idea as a movement game. Dance under the umbrella. How many children can fit under?

31. *HUMPTY DUMPTY:* Read the nursery rhyme and choose children to act out the parts. Make costumes for various characters. (See Instant Costumes, Seq. 3, #9.)

32. *BODY NOISES:*

a. Warm up in a circle.

b. "Today we are going to try using our bodies instead of instruments. We could have a whole band, or an orchestra, and if we are very smart we can compose some patterns which we can call an orchestration. Let's start with one we all know." (CLAP) Go on taking turns or using some suggestions:

Snap fingers—tap
Pound chests with clenched fists
Stamp feet
Fingernails on floor or desk
Knuckles on floor or desk
Flat of one hand and two hands on floor

Flat of hand making circular movement

Feet shuffling, stamping, tapping

Mouth sounds: whistle, hum, kiss, click tongue, siren, swish, inhale and exhale. Say oooo or ahhh as if you were excited, happy, angry, sad or scared.

What else? Can you think of another way?

Build a sound up to loud and take it back down to soft.

c. After experimenting with sounds, divide the group in two and 'play' two different sounds at once, teacher acting as the conductor. As group learns to follow the conductor continue dividing into 3, 4, 5, 6...sections.

d. Combine sound sections with a story, each one contributing its own effect, sometimes two or three at once, sometimes entire 'orchestra.'

e. Experiment with dynamics, staccato, legato, fast (vivaci), slow (largo), to introduce real music terms.

33. *WHAT CAN YOU DO WHEN IT RAINS*? Some of the happiest times of childhood are spent in the rain. Rain intensifies all the senses and brings out the shine of everything. Smells and sounds seem magnified, objects look and feel different. A pebble which looks dull and gray in sunlight becomes a colorful faceted 'jewel' under the water of a puddle.

Visions of mud, tracks, soggy shoes and clothes have convinced some mothers that a child shouldn't go out and play in the rain, even though he may be well equipped with sophisticated rain gear and a closet full of drip-dry garments.

Take advantage of rainy days. Talk about how they affect people — what they can do. When it is fun, when it is a bother. Read some descriptive poems and books about rain and draw pictures to illustrate them. (See Seq. 11, #122.)

34. *RAINY DAY, A PARODY* by Harriet Chmela:

Sun, sun go away
We must have some rain today
Noses pressed against the pane
Waiting for some dripping rain
We need the sun
It makes things grow
But without rain
They'd wilt you know
So, sun, sun, go away
We all want some rain today!

35. *RAIN GEAR:* Children should be properly dressed for rain activities, especially their feet. (Shoes are expensive, protect them.) Rubbers, boots, even plastic bags in an emergency are good protection. On a warm day, the best foot gear for rain is nothing; take children outside barefoot — if conditions are suitable. A barefoot paddle through puddles, on wet grass and pavement and into MUD is great fun. Cut sheets of plastic into ponchos for those without raincoats. (See #7 Toe Tickling.)

36. *RAIN HATS: Do not improvise on head gear,* especially with plastic; though your version may be safe, a child's may not. *Only* hats *go on heads.* Hats should not be traded or borrowed.

37. *WATERPROOFING:* Read about waterproofing in the book *The Chinese Knew* by J. Levine and T. Pine, McGraw-Hill. Why do we wear raincoats? Stretch a handkerchief over a glass. Pour water over it slowly. Do this with an old sweater, piece of plastic, rubber, loose cloth. Does the water go through some things faster than others?

38. *EXPLORE NATURAL SURROUNDINGS IN THE RAIN:* Is there a spider web all jeweled with water droplets? Has something similar happened to the chain link fence? Has the rain created drip patterns around buildings? Reflections are everywhere. Look for 'upside down' in puddles. Drop pebbles in to 'shatter' reflected buildings and faces. Watch rings spread out. Can you count the rings? Which makes the best reflection — a dark pavement or a light one? Can children relate this to how mirrors are made? Window reflections day and night? Why do birds fly into windows?

(WHERE DOES RAIN COME FROM? Read *You and The World Around You* by Selsam, pub. Doubleday.)

39. *SENSORY EXPEDITIONS:* Divide your group into four groups. Take them out separately with four different assignments. Smelling group—Listening group—Touching group—Looking group. Take each to the same areas to explore with their special sense. Have a meeting to discuss what each group discovered.

40. *RAIN SOUNDS:* Listen to rain falling on different surfaces: stretch over shoe boxes (or other small boxes) aluminum foil, tissue, the box cover, plastic, what else? Set the box in the rain. Listen. Tape each experiment. Play back and guess which box was being recorded. Write down words used to describe various sounds.

41. *PITTER, PATTER,* Harriet Chmela:

> Pitter, patter, drop and scatter
> Making puddles as it drops
> Pitter, patter, clitter, clatter
> On tin roofs and metal tops
> Pitter, patter, plitter, platter
> Yellow slickers, bright red rubbers
> We can wade, it doesn't matter
> Hello, RAIN, here come the mudders!

42. *TARPAULIN TREAT:* Stretch a large sheet of plastic over an area of playground. Many activities will take on brand new character while sitting under it with the rain pattering down. Read poems or stories about rain with real sound effects overhead. Watch the puddles develop and spill off the edge.

43. *RAIN DROP COUNTING:* Take a sheet of manila or similar soft paper and hold it under the rain for a short time (count to 3, 4, 5, etc.). Pull it in and count the drop marks to determine density of rain falling at a particular moment. Have rain drop races to see who caught the most drops in 10 seconds. Notice slant of rain and correlate with wind direction. Measure depth of rainfall by collecting it in a container.

44. *RAIN PAINTING:* Put some globs of finger paint on a sheet of paper and let the rain create a design, or, sprinkle dry poster paint on paper and hold it under the rain. Try easel painting in a light sprinkle.

45. *GUTTER PROJECTS:* Set up some gutters and study 'rain hydraulics.' To make gutters, nail three boards to form a channel and staple on a plastic lining. Hold rain gutter regattas with small boats. Place gutter under a downspout to catch its deluge of water.

Watch gutter activity around the playground and neighborhood. What kinds of things are carried and caught by storm sewers and culverts? Build a simple tunnel by burying a large 3'5" section of pipe under the sandbox. Ask a plumber for a section of broken sewer or drainpipe, or build a section of tunnel by using one of the gutter sections with a top nailed on. Discuss where the water goes.

46. *MAKING A CLOUD:* Place a dish of hot water in a cool room or outdoors. The steam you see is actually a cloud. This is the way clouds are formed. Cold air meets moist air and the warm air loses some of its water to form clouds. Use sponge to show how clouds spill over into raindrops when full.

47. *CONDENSING RAINDROPS:* Fill a saucepan with ice cubes and hold over boiling teakettle. As hot steam hits cold pan it condenses into raindrops; when the bottom of the pan becomes *saturated* with drops, they drip off. In a similar fashion clouds become saturated and make rain. Not all clouds cause rain.

48. *FLOODS:* Talk about floods. Demonstrate by building earth dams in sand table or box, and flood away. Watch the newspaper for stories about flooding. Collect pictures and discuss.

49. *DAMS:* Make a dam. Talk about beavers and how they make dams. Show pictures of man-made dams. What are they for? How are they put to use? If there is one near enough to walk or ride to, take a trip and see it. Make one in the sand table—or the play yard.

50. *LAKES, STREAMS, PONDS, RIVERS, OCEANS:* Talk about the difference be-

tween a lake, pond, brook, stream, river. Use words like smaller, wider, etc. What makes the oceans different?

51. *PUMPS:* Take a walk to see gas pumps. Ask the station attendant to explain how it works. Show where the gas tank covers are which are removed to fill the underground tanks. How does the gas get to the station? Introduce a meat baster and siphon at the water play table. Demonstrate pumps with a real pump (mechanical), mounted on a barrel. Many people use sump pumps and some are portable. Borrow one and set it in the yard for a demonstration of electric pumps. If the school has a washing machine or dishwasher it may be possible to use their pumps to show how they work. What other things are pumped? Use a tire pump to pump air into a tube. Use a vacuum in reverse to pump air into a large plastic bag. How do straws work? Your heart and lungs? Oil furnaces? Do cars use pumps? How? Campers use foot pumps for air mattresses.

52. *TOILETS:* Go to a house under construction when the plumbing is being installed. Follow the pipes from bathroom and kitchen to the basement area. Take the tank cover off a toilet and observe the inside mechanisms. Flush and watch it refill. If plumbing in the school is exposed in the basement, take a group down to listen to water rushing through the soil pipes as the upstairs toilet is flushed.

53. *SEWER PIPES:* A new school building addition was being constructed while the children were there to watch the whole procedure. At one point in construction the children saw a hole in the floor with a pipe going down from it. They poured water from paper cups into the hole. Then they went to the basement to see the same pipe. Some poured water above and those who were below heard it and saw where it went. Later, when the toilet bowl was in place, they discussed the previous experience. When the entire system was installed, they went to the basement again and when someone upstairs flushed the toilet, they were able to hear and feel water coursing along the pipes.

54. *EXPOSED PLUMBING PIPES:* In most new buildings, pipes are carefully hidden away within the partitions with but a few exposed to view in the basement. If you are fortunate to have an older building where pipes are exposed to view, take advantage of many opportunities to talk and learn about their functions. One school had many such "ugly, old pipes" and a clever teacher painted the network running across the ceiling, up, over and down walls in black paint, creating a design against the white ceiling. One large pipe in a hallway was painted white and the teachers added bright red candy stripes, barber-pole style, to accent it. Pipes might be effectively painted in a color-coded manner, i.e., red for hot water, blue for cold, black for drain and soil pipes, yellow for gas, etc.

55. *BATHROOM TALK:*

"The toilet bowl is running over!"

The teacher ran for the plunger and discovered that a large wad of toilet paper was the cause of the flood. Several children came to watch the plumbing procedure. "I guess we need to have a meeting," commented the teacher. "Meetings" to discuss problems were a common event and the children arranged the seat blocks theater-style and gathered for the discussion.

When they were all settled, the teacher said in a very serious tone, "This meeting is to talk about what goes into the toilet."

With these four-year-olds, bathroom talk was prevalent, but always in a secretive manner. Now they were being *asked* to talk about such things. Their faces revealed their surprise. At first they were reluctant but once started they were *very* explicit. Their answers were accepted by the teacher and when they observed her serious expression their silliness subsided.

Then she gathered the group around her at a low table. "This is a plumbing experiment." "Experiment" was also a familiar word for they had often tested ideas by experimentation. On the table was a large glass bowl with a funnel set into a small glass so that it would stand upright inside the bowl, but the flow of water could be observed. First, the teacher ran water through the funnel. Then she took a wad of toilet paper and put it in the funnel. One of the children was asked to pour water into it. Only a trickle came through and as the water continued to pour in, the funnel filled and ran over the top.

Following this experiment, another discussion was held about the proper use of toilet paper. They decided how many sheets were necessary and counted off four. As the roll of tissue was passed around, each child tore off four sheets.

That evening at home Karen said, "We had a meeting because something serious happened at school."

Leigh observed, one day at school, "Something terrible happened at home last night. My brother put too much toilet paper in the bowl and it went over."

Debra observed, "The water won't come up because there is too much paper inside."
Jon said, "If you take paper out the toilet will flush." Laura added, "You don't put paper towels in the toilet."

56. *SEWER LINES:*

In a nursery school, the city had to run a new sewer line right through the property. The project started in September and was not completed until June. There was cause for anxiety for the safety of the children and in some ways the project might have been considered a disaster. But as the work began the staff discussed ways of taking advantage of the project for program experiences, with the following results:

As the machines were digging the children imitated them in movement and sound.

There were days when the machines did not work and the children were able to go near the area. They looked at the various layers of dirt being turned over. Walking on the heaped-up dirt was a new experience in moving on a very rough terrain, which they called "mountain climbing."

As the project continued, there was much discussion of what the big pipes were for and where the sewage would go. In this case it went to a sewer treatment plant some miles away.

The interest in the project was reflected in the choice of books, in sand and water play, in art objects.

57. *FLOAT OR SINK:* Place objects of various kinds (crayons, cork, nail, plastics, string, rock) beside the water table. Provide two sorting trays marked "FLOATS" and "SINKS." Children sort objects.

Make simple boats by attaching paper sails to a variety of flat objects of paper, wood, plastic, metal. Children float the boats. Which worked? Why? How long? Why not? Draw and paste picture charts, divided into floaters and sinkers, using magazines for source pictures.

58. *DISPLACEMENT:* Float a large plastic container or bowl in water. Fill to limit with variety of objects (stones, nails, sand, shells, foam). Mark the sides to show amount of water displaced by loading. Ask the children to watch the tub sides as they climb in for bath. What happens? Put water in the sink and add the dishes. What happens? Look for pictures of large vessels or write to steamship lines. Some may show displacement marks, or go to a dry dock and see boats with marking on sides.

59. *LIQUID MEASURE:* Provide: measuring cups, dial-platform scale, assorted classroom containers, milk cartons and mayonnaise jars in half-pint, pint, quart, half-gallon and gallons. make charts showing how many times one volume of liquid will fit (or not fit) into others. Find the weight of contents by weighing container alone before weighing it with contents. Use the cartons and jars with marking tape to design a classroom set of measures from experiments using standard measuring sets.

60. *STANDARD MEASURE:* Place several large pails all the same size, or gallon cans, in water play areas. Place an assortment of smaller containers (plastic tubs, kitchen cups, jars of odd sizes) nearby. Ask children to choose one of the smaller containers and using it as a measure, fill one of the pails with water or sand. Keep a count of the number it takes to fill. Show many different kinds of measuring cups and test to see if all hold the same amount even though they look different.

61. *CHALK PAINTING:* Chalk or paint on pavement and watch the rain's effect. Drop dry paint into styrofoam egg cups. Have one color, two color, three color combinations. Set under the rain and study the results. (COLORS)

62. *RAIN PRINTS:* Collect leaves, plastic shapes (cut plastic covers into triangles, squares and stars), socks, gloves, etc. Lay these objects on a sheet of colored construction paper and place under rain for a *short* time to make dry patterns.

63. *RAIN WRITING:* Attach strips of masking tape to construction paper to make letters, numbers, children's names. Place in rain until wet. Remove the tape to reveal the magic writing. Repeat the same experiment on a sunny day. These 'fading' prints will take several days.

64. *TISSUE PAPER TRANSPARENCIES:* Make tissue paper flowers and put between two raindrop-shaped pieces of waxed paper. Add just a touch of paste to hold in place. Press with warm iron (with waxed sides of paper inside) and hang in window.

65. *UMBRELLAS:* Make with cupcake papers and pipe cleaners.

66. *TINSEL RAIN:* Use foil and plastic holiday tinsel to make rain pictures, Hang them in shadow box panoramas to make rain effects.

67. *STEPPING STONE NUMBERS:*

A new school building was under construction and the teachers were taking full advantage of the opportunities presented for curriculum. After the machines came for excavation they examined the various layers of soil, talking about the different textures and the creatures who lived there. When the forms were set into place, many similar or related activities began to take place in the sandbox. Then the really exciting event occurred...the cement mixer came to pour the foundations! As the children watched, they commented on the "squishiness" of the cement. The following activities took place in the program:

THE CHILDREN MIXED CEMENT:
    a) Equal amounts of sand and cement were mixed in a wheelbarrow.
    b) Water was added, a little at a time and mixed into a thick consistency.
    c) Each child took a turn at the mixing.
    d) Each child filled a paper cup with cement.
    e) As it began to harden they made designs or printed their initials in the cement with a stick.
    f) The cups were set in the sun to dry.
    g) The next day the cups (forms) were torn away and each child had his own cement block.

The children wanted to make something for their playground. They decided to make a stepping stone walk. The teachers helped them make a wooden form, which was filled with cement to make each slab of the walk. They pressed small squares of tile (pebbles could also be used) into the slabs to form numbers. Then the maintenance man helped them dig out enough soil to place the slabs in the ground, making a *stepping stone number walk.*

After ten years, this walk is still in use, a permanent contribution of that class. When they return for visits, they recall the experience with pride.

68. *BIRD BATH:*

A class of children had been watching the birds feeding, nesting, raising young. Their teacher asked, "Did you know that birds like to take baths?"

"Where?" "How?" "Can we watch?" asked the curious children. "We could plan and build a bird bath on the playground," the teacher invited. Plans were discussed and the work began.

First the children went into some nearby woods belonging to the school. With the maintenance man, they chopped down a cedar tree and they helped saw off the limbs to make a log. They helped carry the log back to the play area.

Next they dug a hole, which took many days with each child taking a turn. Each digger (excavator) stood in the hole to measure the depth until it was the required three feet deep. The pole was cut to the proper length. Then the children searched for small rocks to be added to a cement base, and gathered a supply near the hole. The pole was centered and steadied in the hole using the stones, the area around filled in with the remaining stones. They mixed a batch of cement and poured it in, over and around the rocks until the hole was full. When the cement had set, a bird bath basin was attached to the pole. Finally, flowers were planted around the base.

This bird bath project took most of the springtime. No one was ever coerced into helping but there were always a few children who asked, "What can we do today to build the bird bath?" Many youngsters enjoyed watching the activity. When children can feel that they have made such a contribution to their school, they receive double benefits. But if children are pushed too hard for participation beyond their span of attention or the product becomes more important than the experience, these benefits are diminished.

69. *THE BOAT "HEAVE TO! WE SET SAIL ON THE TIDE!"*

Kathy, age three and a half, came into school with a boat magazine. Her teacher sat beside her and together they looked at the pictures and talked about them. Several other children joined them and they each contributed some comments about boats from their own experiences.

The teacher asked, "Would you like to make a boat?"

"Yes," replied the eager gathering of threes.

"What kind of boat shall we make?"

"Let's make a sailboat. My daddy has a boat just like this one in the picture," replied Kathy.

Four sheets of brown construction paper were taped together and children defined the shape of the boat with crayons and cut it out. Then they asked for white paper and made a sail. When the director of the school came into the room and saw it on display, she asked, "Who made this sailboat?" The children were pleased and very proud.

"We need a name for our boat," said one of the children. Many were suggested but it was agreed that since Kathy brought in the magazine, she should name the boat.

Kathy chose the name Victoria. "That's my mommy's name." The teacher printed VICTORIA on the boat. On another day, as the children looked at the boat pictures, the teacher asked, "What makes the boats stay on top of the water?" The children searched the room, testing different articles to see which would float and which would sink. The teacher did not attempt to go into the scientific explanations. It was sufficient to discover that some things float and some do not. The teacher made a list of 'sinkers' and 'floaters' and hung it on the wall over the sink. These threes were not readers but they understood that the black marks on the chart were symbols which said something about their experiment.

One day the children came to school and found a refrigerator carton on the floor. Their teacher had drawn an oval in black crayon on the side. "It's a boat!" exclaimed the first child to arrive. Soon several were cutting out the center with large shears. This was hard work for threes but the teacher was amazed that she had to give very little help. Their enthusiasm carried them along during this difficult manipulative task.

"Can we paint our boat?" they came to ask.

The following day the boat was set on newspapers and large brushes and cans of paint laid out. "What color do you want?" As might be expected, several colors were requested. Everyone had a turn and the completed boat was decorated in designs of many colors.

For several days the boat was the center of dramatic play as the children climbed in and out, chattering, sailing, taking trips, fixing, fishing.

Then one morning the children found a full-sized set of oars standing in a corner. "Oars. I know what they're for. We have them in our boat," exclaimed George.

"Can we use the boat?"

The oars were very long and heavy and it took a lot of *cooperative* effort and *problem solving* to get them to the boat in the center of the floor. Then they had to figure out how to put them to use. Seat blocks were placed on either side of the 'cockpit' and two inside. With two children holding on inside, the oars resting on the sides of the boat and others holding on, it became almost real. Now everyone wanted to get into the boat crew. Another set of seat blocks were placed in the *stern*, not the *bow*. These words stimulated a discussion about the 'bough' of a tree, and a 'bow' from the waist and the 'bow' of a boat. (See #98.)

The children sang *Row, Row, Row Your Boat* and *Michael Row the Boat Ashore*. With this came the highlight of the whole adventure. Michael, a shy three, had been slow to adjust to school and had never really become involved in any of the groups' activities. He was always an onlooker. But when he heard them singing *his* name, he grinned from ear to ear. They were singing about him — to him. He was IN!

The Victoria remained a center of activity for many weeks. Some days it was a sailboat as they sang *We'll Sail the Ocean Blue*. On other days the sailors contrived a steering wheel and engine sounds roard forth from the holds below.

(All this happened spontaneously. How tragic it would have been if some overly conscientious teacher had said, "We can't 'do' boats now. It is October and we will 'do' Hallowe'en.") (See Seq. 10, #43, 44 and 45.)

70. *NUMBER LINE:* Make a number line with masking tape on the floor and space numbers along the line. Play games such as: Stand on 5, stand on the one BEFORE 5, AFTER 6, then move to a smaller number. Walk on every other number and say them out loud as you go. Walk on the numbers missed and say them out loud.

71. *SUNKEN SHIPS:* Put an empty bottle into the water table. It floats. Next, tip it slightly so water begins to go in. What happens? To demonstrate how sunken ships can be raised, put a tube or hose down into the bottle and blow air into it. As water is displaced with air, the bottle will come to the surface.

72. *MAKING A BROOK:* Remember a sparkling cold brook and the feel of it as it rushed against and parted around your fingers? Did you lick the finger off, tasting the sweetness of fresh woodland spring water? Did you wipe the chilled hand against your jeans? Wouldn't it be wonderful to trickle a brook through a corner of your playground? Is there a way? Do you have a hose? Some drain tiles, pebbles, plastic sheeting, a section of gutter? If you do, there is a way.

The best way to set the stage is to take a field trip to explore a real brook. See, hear, feel, touch the brook and its surroundings. If you cannot go to a brook, use pictures, slides, stories, poems, films to create the idea of a brook for the children. Ask the children for suggestions about how a small brook might be built on the playground. Find the place best suited. It need not be large, should slope and have a water supply reasonably close. Consider where the water will run off. Use a dry well filled with sand or pebbles, a street drain or any spot with good drainage. You should be able to turn off the brook when necessary.

You will need some sand and pebbles for the brook bed. Large sheets of plastic can be used to line the bed so water will run and not soak into soil, or a movable brook can be made using sections of gutter or wooden troughs lined with plastic. Plastic is stuck to wooden pieces with epoxy. Hang a gutter from a tree or fence and run water into it from a hose or create sloping waterways with wooden blocks. Supply shovels and trowels for digging. Use carpenter's levels to check slope. Older children can map playground before building the brook to decide the best location. Use the map as a site plan when digging the brook. Part of the planning will include organizing into various crews of workmen. If you need parents, handymen, driver, students — people who can come and give extra help for such an occasion — send out invitations. When the day arrives to begin work, use the map and carefully describe the construction. Divide into small work units and, depending on how you are proceeding (the kind of brook) and the sequence of events, give each crew an adult assistant and begin work. Remember, brooks aren't built in one day. On construction days, pack sandwiches in lunch boxes (fruit trays, shoe boxes, bags, real black lunch boxes) so the crew can eat at the site. Appoint a water crew to bring water to the thirsty workers. Sing work songs. Wear plastic name tags and hard hats. Travel to the site in 'trucks,' 'bulldozers.' Children can be cranes, dump trucks, shovels during creative movement. Make special work rules. Have a pay day. Measure sand by pailfuls. Count nails. Measure wood and gutter lengths. Check with a long tape to see if boards will fit and hoses will reach. Bring ceremonial bucket of real brook water for the ribbon-cutting ceremony and first run off. Try rest time outside on blankets at the site. When the brook is complete, return to the real brook and find some mossy stones, waterlogged branches, some real moss and ferns, a few real brook pebbles for landscaping. Celebrate with a ceremony—naming the brook. (See Seq. 11, Act. #70-76.)

73. *FOLLOWING PATTERN:* Cut a variety of shapes from assorted colors of the construction scraps. One child chooses ten and arranges them on a bulletin board or lays them out in a pattern on floor or table. Other children then choose from the collection and assemble a matching sequence of colors and shapes.

74. *COLOR LIFTS:* Collect magazine (and seed catalog) color photographs of good quality (i.e., animals, spring flowers, landscapes, insects, etc.). Cut circles from clear contact paper (before removing backing) which will then fit inside a plastic lid (coffee can or smaller). The shape should fit inside the rim. Follow these steps:

    a. Cut clear contact to fit inside rim of coffee can.
    b. Lay over picture to adjust area to be "lifted."
    c. Peel backing from contact paper carefully.
    d. Hold one edge up and gradually press contact onto photo. Be careful to avoid air bubbles.
    e. Should a bubble occur DO NOT try to lift and correct. Sometimes a pin prick will let out air and bubble will go with a little wrinkle.
    f. Rub flat with throat stick.
    g. Pull lift away SLOWLY.
    h. Press and rub lift smoothly onto plastic lid.
    i. String and hang lifts in window.

75. *TRANSPARENCIES FROM PLASTIC:* In empty, plastic pill bottles or clear, disposable drink glasses, put some shaved crayon, small pieces of crayon, beads, shells, a marble, sequins, plastic (Bake-it) crystals, glitter—or any combination of these. Place on an aluminum pan protected with foil in about a 275 degree oven. Bake until they melt into flattened shapes. Cool and puncture a hanging hole using a thick, heated needle or cake tester. Hang in windows, as necklaces or attach pin backs. Use in color games or for mixing colors (as with color paddles).

76. *EGG SHELL PICTURES:* Save and dry cracked egg shells. Fill small bowls about half full of water and add food colors. Stir in crushed shells until color adheres, strain and dry on paper towels. Paint thinned glue onto construction paper in free form designs, or paint glue over pre-drawn pictures (a house with a green shell roof and yellow shell walls); flowers, faces, geometric designs, etc. Shake shell bits onto glue to create attractive mosaic pictures.

77. *CHICKEN HUNT:* Buy or make tiny fuzzy yellow chick to fit under or in a plastic egg. One child hides chick in one of several eggs in a basket. Other children try to guess where it is. Finder gets the next turn to hide the chick.

78. *EGG ROLLING:* Have egg rolling races with plastic eggs. (GAME)

79. *CHANGING SHAPES:* Give each child a *sheet* of paper and ask, "How can you use ALL of this paper and make it into a different shape?" Put a pile of paper strips (different colors) on table and ask, "What can you make?" Suggest pasting onto 9 × 12 manila.

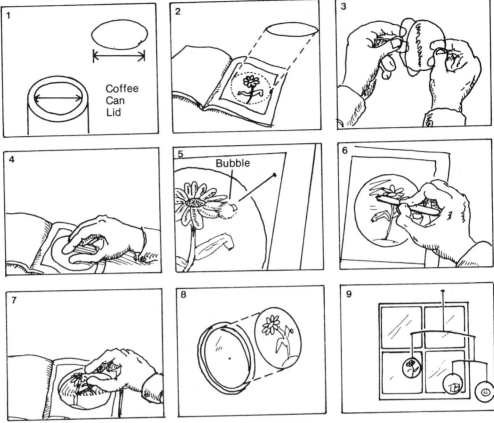

Fig. 8-74

Coffee Can Lid

Bubble

Fig 8-82

With Needle
String Thru
Buttons & Tie

Some may make flat designs, others 3-D pictures.

Put out paper strips, tape, straws, glue, staples, paper punch. "How can you make this paper stand up?" (CONCEPTS)

80. *EASTER EGGS:* Children mix pastel shades, using white with the tempera paints. Cut big egg shapes from cardboard (about 8"-10") long). Paint the shapes with the pastels. When dry, decorate with scraps of lace or trim, or use construction scraps and pinking shears to cut paper trims, or use dry markers and make zig-zags, swirls, ripples, etc. Each child can make two eggs, one to take home, one to put into the EGG-SCOTCH basket. (see Activity #81 below). Make a basket by decorating a carton or weaving paper strips, or crepe streamers or cloth strips through the holes in a plastic laundry basket. This basket can also be used for egg hunting games, i.e., "find the blue egg with the yellow flowers on it."

81. *EGG-SCOTCH:* Make matching sets of two eggs each, as described above. (Wall paper samples and cloth scraps glued to cardboard offer a variety of patterns.) Lay out one set in a meandering pattern around the room. Child draws one egg from the basket and finds the match on the path.

82. *EGG BLOWING:*

(a) Puncturing and Blowing: Using a heavy but sharp needle or hat pin, puncture several holes to break a larger one in both ends of an egg. Then insert a cake tester or nut pick and 'swirl around' to break up yolk. Hold egg over dish and blow hard in other end. Rinse out shell several times by submerging in pan of water (make bubbles), and shake egg to swish water around. Blow out water and rinse again. Remaining egg will rot and smell if not completely washed out.

(b) Painting and Decorating: Set egg into a small juice glass, can or styrofoam cup from egg carton while decorating to balance and prevent smudges from being handled.

(c) Make hangers: Thread a double string with bead or button at loop end, through two holes, using long darning needle. Knot a bead or button on top end.

83. *EGG TREATS:* Serve scrambled eggs from your egg blowing. Add cubes of cheese, ham or hotdog slices.

Break and separate eggs into separate bowls. Cook the yolks (add a few whole eggs), into scrambles or bake into a custard. Whip and sweeten the whites, perhaps color with food color and serve alone as a meringue treat in a cone, or serve on top of custard or jello.

84. *DR. SEUSS SPECIAL:* Color scrambled eggs with food tint and serve them with ham and a giant helping of fun as you relive the pages of *Green Eggs and Ham,* by Dr. Seuss, pub. Beginner Books (see Seq. 7, #134) (EGGS & HAM)

85. *ROCK CANDY:*

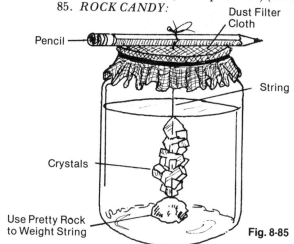

Pencil — Dust Filter Cloth
String
Crystals
Use Pretty Rock to Weight String
Fig. 8-85

Stir sugar into water over low flame until no more will dissolve. Pour into jar. Cover top with gauze or tissue paper to keep out dust. Hang string in solution as shown in illustration.. Place in quiet window and watch but DO NOT DISTURB. In time sugar crystals will begin to form on the string. New words: evaporation, crystals. Mark solution level on the jar to show evaporation. Don't move jar while marking it. This can be done daily with small strips of tape. When a good supply of crystals (rock candy) have formed, break into bits and serve. Try adding food colors in water to create colored crystals.

86. *MARSHMALLOW ANIMALS:* Put toothpicks and marshmallows on table. Talk about color, shape, feel, tast. Encourage conversation about things child might make from the materials. All will not make the same animal. Expect dragons, snowmen, bunnies, and people. You could limit the activity by saying "make an animal" but if a child said "I have a different idea—do I have to make an animal?" encourage his individuality. If he asks for some material you haven't provided but which he knows is in the elegant junk supplies, compliment his GOOD THINKING. (See Activities 87 and 88.)

87. *CREATIVE THINKING:* Encourage, respect and value the products of magination (creative thinking). Watch for the child who always has to look and see what someone else is doing and help him. Think about why he does it. Observe to gain insight. You can say, "Yes, that is nice. It's pretty much like John's. I know you have GREAT ideas. See if you can make a different kind now." Don't pursue it or demand it, but think about ways of freeing that child to become himself and not to have to copy.

88. *ART PROJECTS WITH FOOD:* When using foods such as marshmallows, raisins, chocolate bits, cereals, etc. in art projects (Activity #85) avoid unnecessary waste. Also, expect children to eat or taste some of the materials. Set the limits *before* the activity so *all* of the art project doesn't get eaten! Say, "I have put three marshmallows on a small dish at each place. These are for eating if you wish. Use the others to make your (animal)."

89. *NEST BUILDING:* Mix grasses, pine needles, small twigs, feather bits with 'loose' mud into a stiff 'batter' and shape into a bowl or nest shape. Set in a sunny place to dry. Line with feathers, grass, cotton. Set in a secluded place on a tree limb. Watch to see if any birds come to nest. Look for real nests and watch for parent birds gathering nesting material.

90. *NESTING SUPPLIES:* Children hang bits of string and yarn on bushes and low limbs for birds to gather. String can be lightly woven into mesh bags and plastic vegetable baskets or wire mesh, which are hung outside.

91. *ANIMAL FAMILIES:* Compile a set of animal pictures of parent and baby in separate pictures. Children match baby animal to its parent. Arrange various animal families into sets (cats, sea mammal, bird, reptile) or animals with wings, with fur, etc. (See Seq. 7, #10)

92. *BIRDS IN A TREE:* Crumple tissue papers into balls and wrap around with pipe cleaners to create a bird's body. The wire serves as hanger and also as feet. Make wings, beak and tail from construction paper (or feathers found outside). Hang the birds on bare branches which are secured in a cement base.

93. *PICTURE PUPPETS:* Collect small pictures of animals from magazines, mount on cardboard and attach holding sticks (tongue depressors). Children choose a picture 'puppet' and imitate the sound of the animal or choose an instrument which best imitates the sound. Make stories to go with the puppets and fit them together. When telling or reading stories about animals, ask if there is a puppet to go along with the story and appoint children to hold them up at the appropriate times in the story. (DRAMATIC PLAY)

94. *HANDS AND PAWS:* Discuss the many uses of hands and paws. Compare the various ways different animals and birds make use of theirs. Ask about tails, fins, beaks, claws, etc.

95. *TRACKING:* Many animals leave clues behind that tell how they move around. Animal footprints or tracks in snow or dirt are clues that you can search for. Spring mud and the moist pond-side soil are excellent places to cast footprints with plaster. Can children guess what animals made these tracks? Notice that many animals place their hind feet side by side when they are hopping or jumping. Ground-living animals usually put their front feet down one after another. The hind feet of both tree climbing and ground living animals are usually paired. Nature library books will have pictures and descriptions of tracks and the kinds of animals who make them. Set out shallow pans of tempera paint or put a puddle of paint on pavement and spreads sheets of paper nearby. Lure ducks, geese, chicks with bread so they will walk through paint and leave tracks on paper. (Act. #20, A TRUE BOOT STORY)

96. *PLANTING:* Plant seeds in paper cups or flat, large sea shells, and keep a daily log of their progress. Children can use pictures rather than words to show progress. Use notes in the log to develop a story about how plants grew. When did first leaves develop? If some did not, ask why? Were they watered every day? Did some tip over and need replanting? How tall were the seedlings after 5 days?

97. *TRANSPLANTING:* Set houseplants and seedlings outside to start flower gardens. Visit a greenhouse to see and smell the young plants in many stages of growth. Ask "How do plants grow so well in cold weather in a green house?"

98. *BARK:* Some children were cleaning up their schoolyard during a spring ecology walk. They found many pieces of bark which had fallen from dead branches. They discussed with their teacher why it is not good to pull or strip bark from live trees. It was compared to the skin of people or animals. Dogs were mentioned because they 'bark!' Some of the bark was taken inside and used for art projects.

99. *BEES:* Read *Bees and Beelines* by Judy Hawes, pub. Thomas Crowell and Co. Discuss: budding flowers, nectar, pollen (see Seq. 10, #57-60), hive, swarm, the importance of bees in ecology, orchards, stinging, etc. Eat honey in a variety of ways: honey comb, on toast, in milk, on ice cream.

Visit a field, flower garden, apiary or science center with bees to watch bees at work.

During a movement session: Pretend to fly *straight* to hive. "How would you zig zag home?" "You are heavily loaded with nectar and fly all *wobbly.* Circle the hive carefully in case there are dangerous wasps attacking.

100. *TREES:* Celebrate Arbor Day by planting a tree.

101. *GROWTH OF TREES:*

In order to show the various stages of growth in trees and to indicate the amount of growth each year, a teacher dug up seedlings of pine (white) trees, each from a different year. The pines were easy to dig and transplant and grow in pots and garden. The students also set up a display which showed a pine cone and its individual "leaves" and seeds. They grew a pine from seed. (See Seq. 9, #89).

102. *SOIL TESTING:* Discuss the idea that plants get nourishment (food) from the soil as people do from food. Fill one container with good loam, the other with sand or gravel. Plant seeds or small plants in each. Do the same experiment in sunny and shady spots. Plant a small garden outside following the same procedure. Compare the growth of plants in both soils. Experiment by enriching soils with fertilizer.

5I. SEQUENCE NINE

Concepts about *growing things*, first in the classroom and then in the yard outside the school or at home can be extended through visits to *farms, nurseries, dairies, fish hatcheries, bakeries* or *canneries*.

Children are beginning to discover the *food chain* from *farms*, to *supermarket* to their own dinner table or lunch box. In some locations, the emphasis will be on the fishing industry, in others, citrus or fruit orchards.

As children discover the many forms of *food production*, they are enriching their concepts of how people help people. They will also witness that people *care for, feed and protect plants and animals* in many of the same ways that parents feed and protect children.

1. *PEOPLE WHO PROVIDE FOOD:* In exploring the occupations of people who provide food, the curriculum is once again based on the idea that learning begins with the famliar. Take a closer look at the environment near your school. If it is located near the ocean, the fishing industry could be a starting point.

Some schools are near large truck gardens, orchards, farm stands, grain fields, dairy farms. Many children are familiar with the harvest season but often have not seen the beginning of the growing season, newly ploughed fields, irrigation ditches in operation, seeding machines, fertilizing procedures, baskets full of seeds, cultivating machines.

City children can gain much from visits to wholesale produce markets, meat packing houses, large distribution warehouses of supermarket chains. Dairies, canning factories, bottling plants, packing houses and other food processors often provide tours and literature and sometimes films and colorful charts.

Cooperative food buying groups; perhaps the parent of a child in your school belongs to one and can explain how the cooperative works.

Tracing any food form from its source to table is an excellent way to stimulate curiosity. (See #17)

2. *FARMERS:* Display books and pictures related to farming. Use them as a basis for discussion and stories about farming. When the children have had time to absorb their ideas, develop language activities around the theme. For example, think of words which describe farms: make stories and poems using the list. Create *This Is A Farm* book by putting each word on a page and illustrating its meaning. Sort words into categories, such as WORK WORDS, ANIMAL WORDS, SOUNDS, PRODUCTS. What kinds of farms are there? (see below)

WORK WORDS	SOUNDS	PRODUCTS	FARMS
plow	tractor	milk	dairy
sow	animal	carrots	potato
hoe	bird	grain	orchard
water		butter	grain
weed			

3. *IMAGINARY PLAYMATE:* Children bring an imaginary playmate along on a walk or picnic. Each in turn describes and introduces his friend, what he likes to do, eat and play. He may dance with his friend. On another day, the group composes poems and stories about their adventures with imaginary friends (see also *TALKING A* PICNIC. #19).

The Orient

4. *TRAVEL TOURS:* Set up displays of books, records, toys, dolls, food products (cans with colorful labels), art objects (fans, calendar pictures), travel brochures of the Orient. During discussion find the countries on a map and globe. How would you travel there? What language is spoken?

5. *IMAGINARY TRIPS:* Using the objects on display for ideas take imaginary trips. Discuss what we take along, what we will wear, eat and what language we will speak. Offer a selection of pictures from folders and magazines about travel to children. fold a large sheet of paper as a travel folder and help them paste up their own brochures. Post brochures in an area of their own which can serve as a travel bureau. Make travel posters in the same way and post. Children take turns selecting a brochure and telling the class about the trip they can take. Ask someone from a travel bureau to come in or take children there on a field trip.

6. *STORIES OTHER CHILDREN ENJOY:* Ask the parent of a foreign child to come in and read a story from his own country in the native language, then tell the story in English. Compare it with similar favorites of your own country. How is it different? the same? Show the pictures. Are the children dressed as we are? Do they look the same?

7. *CHINESE HAT:*

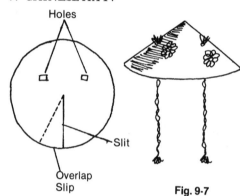

Fig. 9-7

Use wallpaper or heavy wrapping paper. Cut a large circle. Make a cardboard pattern for children to trace around or attach a string to pencil and use as a compass. (Children will also enjoy making circle designs on paper or in sand with a string compass.) Paint or past designs on outside of hat. Overlap slit edges to form hat and staple. Six inches from the edge, make two holes for the ties. Reinforce hole with cardboard squares or tape. Attach bright, braided strings or ribbons or heavy cord.

8. *KIMÓNOS:* Create oriental costumes from sheets and curtains. Decorate with textile paint or tie dying. Tie with bright sashes. Make paper sandals from brown bags or heavy wrapping paper. Have a tea ceremony sitting on a mat on the floor. Try eating with chopsticks ("hashi" in Japan)

9. *BOY-GIRL DAY:*

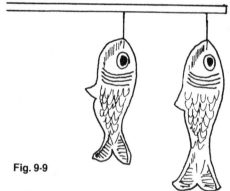

Fig. 9-9

These are national holidays in Japan. Children fly kites in the shape of fish. Choose a day to celebrate. Talk about what boys do and what girls do. Make bright fish kites by cutting two sheets of crepe or tissue paper into fish shapes, taping or stapling edges together and stuffing the inside with crushed paper. Fly from a stick with a short string. In front of each home, fish kites are flown from a pole (Koinbori-paper fish). Big fish means Father—small one means child.

10. *TOSS CUPS:* Construct by attaching a string with a button on the end, to the bottom of a small juice can. Child tries to catch the button in the cup. (CHINA, TOY)

Mothers' Day— May Day

11. *GIFT GIVING:* In many schools children are encouraged to make gifts for parents or relatives on special occasions such as Christmas, Valentine's Day, Mother's and Father's Days. Fostering the principles of giving and sharing is good curriculum for young children, but adult planned projects with the expectation or demand that every child participate is

not appropriate. Some children simply will not wish to make presents and it is fairly certain that every child will not want to make the present selected by someone else.

What goals should be involved in making gifts? Thinking about others, giving pleasure, using our own talents to create a gift rather than buying one, expressing appreciation, expressing love. Such ideas might become a part of daily discussions leading up to the idea that some children might like to make gifts. A variety of suggestions coming both from teachers and children are offered with the necessary materials. When children *choose* to make gifts as an expression of their care and love and no pressure is brought to bear on quality or perfection, it is an indication that the curriculum has real "heart."

12. *SIMPLE GIFTS:* (See Seq. 7, #88)
    a. Decorating containers for small plants
    b. Making containers for artificial flowers (see May Baskets)
    c. Making place mats, using paint, crayon, tie dyeing or weaving paper strips
    d. Writing poems and stories and mounting on papers decorated by the children. Writing a poem inside a hand print of a child. (See Seq. 4, Act. #13)
    e. Artificial flowers (see May Flowers in this sequence)

13. *JOHNNY JUMP-UPS:*

In one school Johnny Jump-Ups, which look like tiny pansies, grow wild and spread rapidly. Each spring the children help their teachers dig up one plant for each child, being careful to leave enough so more will grow another year.

14. *BEGONIA CUTTINGS:* One class took cuttings from a large begonia, the "mother plant" and rooted them. The small plants were put in small pots which the children had trimmed. Half of a plastic, egg-shaped container might also be used as a hanging planter.

15. *MAY BASKETS:* Offer a collection of small boxes, bits of junk jewelry, beads and buttons, ribbons, lace and trims. Trim boxes into May baskets. Teacher has a collection of small surprises wrapped in tissue (trinket, tiny toys, candies wrapped in shiny paper). Each child chooses one surprise for his own basket and the teacher adds some sweets. The children may visit other classes to share the may basket treats, or present them to mothers who have come for a tea party to celebrate Mothers' Day or May Day. (See illustration below for suggestions for making May baskets.) These baskets may also be used as containers for artificial flowers or for picnic baskets.

Fig. 9-15

Margarine Tub

Onion Bag

Paper Bag

Paper Plate

Cardboard Folder

Paper Lantern

Woven Construction Paper

16. *MAY BOX PICNICS:* The boxes decorated above may be filled with picnic lunches. One group invites another (or visiting parent) to come to a picnic. Each child chooses a partner to join him at lunch. (This might be a way to entertain some children who are visiting your school during their spring orientation days in preparation for fall entrance.) (See Seq. 10, Activity #69.)

17. *SEQUENCE PICTURE STORY:* Make up picture stories of production, processing, sale, preparation and final product of an item of food. For example: a cow, field of grass, milking machine, barn, bottling plant, market, money, food product of milk, such as ice cream, cheese or milk in a glass or on cereal. Mount pictures on heavy paper and use to make up stories and poems.

This activity may be followed up with a cooking session which involves using the product in more than one way.

18. *GOOD MORNING, SAYONARA, GUT MORGEN, BONJOUR:* Ask a parent who speaks another language to teach a simple phrase, such as "good morning." Use it throughout the day in various games, discussions. Write it on a chart beside a corresponding picture, i.e., a Japanese lady in kimono—"Sayonara." Another day, ask for another phrase and add it to the chart. Make up charts for each language and/or charts which show the same phrase in many different languages. (FOREIGN LANGUAGE)

19. *"TALKING" A PICNIC:* Spread a picnic blanket on the floor and talk about a picnic. What will you bring? Each child brings something. (Encourage complete sentences in response.) Make a list of items suggested. Later find or draw pictures of them and see if children can remember which items they suggested. Put the pictures on the blanket in the order in which they might be served. (See Seq. 7, Activity #32 and Seq. 9, Activity #106.) (DRAMA)

20. *FOOT FLOWERS:* Children take off their shoes and stockings and trace around their own or each others feet. Paint and cut out. Add stems and leaves. Take one 'foot flower' home and leave the other to decorate the classroom. (CONCEPTS)

21. *TESTING SKILLS:* (Activities)

a. *REPEATING A SERIES:* Start with two numbers or words (colors, objects, animals, etc.) and add one at a time. "I went to the store and I bought... ." Child takes turn with teacher in adding item.

b. *STRETCHING IMAGINATION:* "Would you find an elephant in the bathtub?" "Why not?" "The airplane stopped at a red light." Or make up a story, one child starts and each child adds a part.

c. *MEMORY CONCENTRATION:* Place articles on table. Rearrange or take one away while child has back turned.

d. *PROBLEM SOLVING:* Pose a problem, such as "If you were lost what would you do?" "If your mother left you alone in the living room and you jumped on the sofa and fell and broke her favorite dish, what would you do?"

e. *OBSERVATION-DISCRIMINATION:* Have a series of objects to explore likenesses and differences. How many does he see? Color? Shape? Use? Size?

f. *CATEGORIZING:* Give series of words or pictures and ask which do not belong. For example: orange, cake, baby, bread and lollipop. Chair, tree, table, bed, bookcase. Try first with pictures. Next try with words.

g. *FOLLOWING DIRECTIONS:* (Kindergarten) Make a poster with step by step directions using pictures and/or words for making a soldier hat or other simple project. See if child can follow directions to complete project.

h. *RECOGNIZING PROPERTIES:* Show child a familiar object and ask him to tell you about it. Write down his answers. How many of its properties did he see? Color? Use? etc.

22. *LETTER BOXES:* For older children, mark a set of boxes with consonant letters. Use for sorting objects or pictures of objects beginning with consonants. Ask the children to find something in the room for the T box, for instance, or to bring something from home for the R box. Remind them that the object must fit into the box. Some kindergarten children may be able to arrange objects in alphabetical order before putting them into boxes.

23. *PEN AND PICTURE PALS:* Compose a class letter and mail to children of the same age group in another school. Exchange recipes, poems, pictures, etc. Try to develop a regular correspondence and, if the school is near enough, plan for an exchange visit when the children have become well acquainted by mail.

24. *ANIMAL SOUNDS IN SONG:* Children can mimic real animal sounds. Create your own "MacDonald's Farm" record by recording their noises. Make visual aids to go along with tape. As you sing the song, each child in turn holds up a picture or puppet and the tape makes the sound. The procedure will take coordination as the tape is synchronized to the singing or turned on and off at the appropriate times. After a few straight runs, mix up the pictures and enjoy a nonsense version as a horse goes, "quack, quack" or the pig goes, "moo." (MUSIC)

25. *ORIENTAL MUSIC:* Children compose songs at the piano by simply playing only on the black keys while others create dances or play other instruments (bells, gong, drum). Give each song a name relative to themes, i.e., The Dance of Fu Lee's Cricket, The Kimono Waltz, Rice Harvest Dance, Fan Flutter, etc. (ORIENT)

26. *SPRING SONG:*

When the children were waking up from their naps, the teacher often sang to them, "Lazy Mary Will You Get Up?" Sometimes she added her own lyrics, she sang, "Oh, what a beautiful day." Sara responded, "To go outside and play." As the children were putting on their shoes and socks, the teacher sang the song which she and Sara were making up. She wrote the words on the blackboard. Andrea sang them over and over and then added: "To have fun and run." Jimmy added, "All day in the sun."
As the days went by they sang their song often. Later they added more lines:
  "What a beautiful day
  We can tell it is May
  The birds in the trees
  Sing in the breeze.

27. *NAME SONGS:*

The 'music lady' came into the kindergarten. In previous sessions the children had clapped their names, moved to their names, made little dance steps to the rhythm of their names.
"Today," she began, "we can do something different with our names. We can make little tunes with them. Christina, you have such a long, pretty name, how could you sing it?" "Can I sing my whole name?" Christina grinned, and sang, "Christina Anderson."
"What a lovely tune," said the teacher, "I am going to write it down in a special way and show you how it looks in music the next time I come."
Each child sang his very own name song and each was written in the teacher's notebook as they had sung them. On her next visit to the class, she was greeted with enthusiastic questions about the songs. "Did you bring our songs?"
The music teacher showed the children the papers on which she had printed their names and over each name were written numbers of the corresponding notes which they had sung to her. She went to the piano and marked each key with its note, with #1 representing middle C. She took each child to the piano in turn and showed them how to read the numbers and play their names. During the following days the children took their name songs to the piano and found the notes. Some made pictures to decorate the songs.
One day the teacher said, "Please bring all the songs to the piano and then sit with your backs to me while I play them. If you hear your song, stand up. This time she added some simple chords with her left hand making more complete compositions but taking care to keep the basic tunes clear. Most of the children knew their own names and some recognized songs of classmates.
The expressions on the children's faces when they heard their own songs showed the delight and the very special feelings they had on hearing their names set to music.

28. *NETTING IMAGINARY CREATURES:* Begin with a circle and talk about fairies, gnomes, leprechauns, imps, etc. Ask "How do they move and sound?"

Introduce pieces of colored net. This material, used to make dancing costumes, comes in many beautiful colors. Ballets can be improvised by using these as costumes. Children will choose the color they think is appropriate and decide how they want to wear or use it. The quality of the material seems to inspire creativity.

Experiment first while sitting. Then standing. "How does it feel? Move? What colors? Put two colors together to make a third."

"Now move with your net, use all the room space."

"Move slowly—move fast. Return to circle."

Play a record. "When you feel a dance in the music, you may choose a spot in the room to make your dance. How many different dances will we make? Return to circle."

"Find a partner (guide them) and make a dance using two. (Three, four, five, six.) Return to circle."

"Find a spot and lie on your back, making the scarves dance in the sky." Play a quiet record with slow tempo. "When the music stops lie quietly with the net over you. When I whisper, 'Now all the fairies are sleeping,' sit up very quietly and fold your net into a square. I will come and collect them." (Or "go to the closet and hang each net by a corner on its clothespin.")

29. *TRACKING THE FAIRY GNOME'S HOME* by Deborah Mitchell Haney

> Through the grassy fields we'll roam
> Searching for a fairy-gnome
> We'll c-r-a-w-l along to find his tracks
> When—suddenly—behind our backs
> We'll hear a funny little giggle
> And he'll jump up and down and wiggle
> Knowing that we're coming there
> He'll have a picnic lunch to share
> Like Kings and Queens we'll be dressed up
> —Drinking *tea* from a *buttercup*!
> We'll dance and sing and play for hours
> Making crowns of springtime flowers
> In his secret springtime home
> We'll whisper to our fairy-gnome
>
> And if *you're* tracking fairies too—
> *Look out!* One *might* be tracking *YOU!*

30. *HERE IS HOW THE FLOWERS GROW:* Children never tire of 'sprouting' from seeds and 'growing' into flowers. Develop a creative movement ballet from this theme. Suggestion: Cover 'seeds' with a blanket, attach 'green leaves' to arms, or 'blossom hats' to heads, or tuck bright scarves up sleeves, down necks or into pockets to be pulled out into 'blossoms' as flowers reach full bloom.

31. *HOW DOES COLOR FEEL?* Use pieces of nylon net (see Activity #28.) Talk about colors. What does yellow make you think of? Feel like? How would you dance purple? Black? White? What kind of music would you want? Read a favorite story and improvise costumes using only the dancing nets. Toss them into the air, back and forth, hold them on a string and dance. Blow up balloon and let air go out. How can you dance that? (See Activity #32.)

32. *COLORS AND SCARVES:* A teacher put out a box of scarves. Each child (8 children) was invited to choose one.

"Look this is light green, lighter than yours," Michael said to Steve, who held a dark green scarf.

Robin wrapped hers around her wrist, "This is a bandage because I have a cut."

"Red is my favorite color," Alice said as she chose a red scarf.

Kristen tied hers around her head as a kerchief and announced, "I'm going to church."

"I can crumple mine up," Ricky said, pushing the scarf into his fist.

"Mine can fly," Danny squealed, tossing his bright, blue 'bird' into the air and watching as it fluttered down.

Joanne directed the class with, "Let's play a game, You have to mix them all up and choose another color."

More experimentation and conversation followed and then the teacher played a record which had three very different rhythms on it. The children danced and moved with their scarves in a variety of styles. (See Seq. 2, Activity #39 and Seq. 6, Activity #72.)

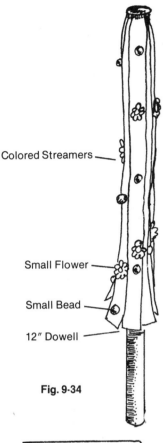

Colored Streamers

Small Flower

Small Bead

12" Dowell

Fig. 9-34

33. *ANIMALS IN MOTION:* Following a discussion of farm animals, move as they do. Take turns guessing, "Which animal moves this way? Which instrument goes best with each one?" List all the words—waddle, trot, flutter, lope, etc.

34. *MINIATURE MAY POLE:* Tie or glue ribbons and streamers to a 12" dowel or pencil. Attach buttons, tiny flowers, bells, beads, to streamers. Use them as rhythm twirlers by rolling them between the palms to make the ribbons 'dance' or use in miniature May Pole scenes by mounting them in a base of clay or salt dough and trimming them with paper flowers, elves and animals. (See Dragon Dance)

35. *DRAGON DANCE:* In the orient, children guard the crops from birds and evil spirits by shaking bells and rattlers on the ends of poles, while walking through the fields. Spirits are also driven away during the 'dragon dances' by noise makers.

Paint and decorate cartons big enough to fit over children. Hook five or six together with a rope and add a long green tail made of cloth or crepe streamers. Make a FEROCIOUS head. Tie bells and other rattlers to the sections and add 'scales' from metal plates. Trim with streamers, bells, paper fringe. (See illustration)

Dance about the school and yard welcoming in the spring. Other children shake pom-poms and rattlers at the dragon to help drive away evil spirits. (See Activities #82 and 83.)

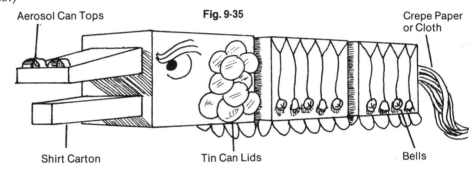

Fig. 9-35

Aerosol Can Tops

Crepe Paper or Cloth

Shirt Carton

Tin Can Lids

Bells

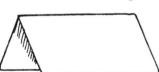

Fold Crepe Paper

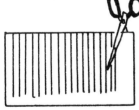

Cut Slits

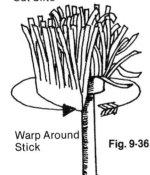

Warp Around Stick

Fig. 9-36

36. *POM POMS (see Seq. 10, Act. #3):* Fold sheet of crepe paper, painted newsprint or magazine covers. Make slits in paper. Wind tightly around a stick and tape securely.

37. *MAY POLE:* Make a May Pole with an aluminum pie plate. Punch holes around the edge of pie plate and tie in pieces of yarn with small bells attached. Put a nail through center of pie plate into top of broomstick. Pole can be held by one child while the rest dance around. Decorate an umbrella and use in the same way.

38. *FENCES AND WALLS:* Bring in a collection of pictures of fences and walls. Talk about each one. How would you get from one side to the other? Create a dance from the motions. Ask children to make books of their own drawings. Take a walk or trip to see how many different kinds of fences and walls you can find.

39. *MAKING A DANCE:* Use the music to *A Tisket A Tasket* (or other familiar rhythmic song.)

Form groups of four facing each other. Make up a dance. It must have a beginning step one), a middle (step two), and an end (step three). Example:

A tisket a tasket a little yellow basket
(walk in circle holding hands)
I had a message for my firend
(turn to right and hand a message to partner).
And to her I did take it
(Use as many motions as fit your tune.)

40. *STREAMERS AND HOOPS:* Tie streamers to hoops to create dances. (See Seq. 7, Activity #51.)

41. *PRINCESS BRITHDAY PARTY:* "Some fairies have been invited to your party. They

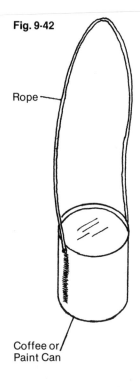

Fig. 9-42

Rope

Coffee or Paint Can

are so pretty. Each one has on a different colored dress, soft, pretty, light, floaty. All of you go to the other end of the room and come back. BE fairies on your way to a party. Come to the party again, only this time carry a birthday present in your hands. Is it a big present? Is it heavy? Is it light? Is it something you will carry under your arm? In one hand? Or in two hands? Stop where you are. Let's all look at Meg walking with her present and see if we can guess what it is? Let's try to guess what Kathy is giving to the princess for her birthday. Who has something different that you want us to guess?"

42. *STILTS:* Make stilts by tying loops of rope through large size cans. Rope loops should be long enough to be held taut when child stands on can.

43. *I AM GROWING:* Make some colorful charts to show growth in various areas, using such topics as: (SELF-IMAGE)

> I CAN tie my shoes
> I CAN button my coat
> I CAN write my name
> I CAN finish what I start, etc.

44. *GRASS WEAVING:* Weave grasses, long day lily leaves, ribbons or strings into plastic vegetable baskets. Add ribbon handle. Make wall hanging by weaving grasses through strips cut in squares of cloth or paper.

45. *EASEL LIFTS:* After a whole year of painting projects, easels are a collage of colored drops and splotches. Use as color lift panels, wet paper towels or white tissue, pressing them against paint on easel so that colors blot or tape white tissue onto the easel so that colors blot when you paint tissue carefully with water. Remove and hang up to dry. Use to make paper flowers and in other art projects.

46. *IRRIGATION EXPERIMENT:* Plant a small garden on the playground, preferably some distance away from a water source. Lay out a supply of materials to use for an irrigation project, such as shovels, trowels, hoses, sheets of plastic (to line ditches), troughs, buckets. PROBLEM: "Can you bring the water to the garden?" Follow up by discussing problems, successes, discoveries, etc. Ask how farmers get water for their gardens. (See Seq. 8, Act. #72.)

47. *EROSION:* Experiment: Use a sand table, sand box or fill a large box lined with plastic with several different kinds of soil, each in its own section (loam, sand, grades of sand, sawdust, clay). Children drop water on the soils from different heights and with different forces to create erosion effects. Go for a walk and look for signs of erosion, the edges of paved country roads, runoffs from highway embankments which have not become fully seeded. What do highway crews use to prevent erosion? Look into plant pots, has watering caused erosion? What can we do to prevent it?

48. *PERSPECTIVE:* Use a set of slides to show how near objects look larger than those far away. Ask: "If you are drawing or painting trees, how can you make one look farther away than another?" Try it with mountains.

49. *VIBRATION PRODUCED SOUND:* Observe the following demonstrations:

> Pluck a rubber band
> Pluck a guitar
> Tap a drum
> Place hand on larynx and hum
> Tap a tuning fork
> Hold a ruler on edge of table with 5″ hanging over edge. Bend to cause vibration.
> Make an instrument by putting rubber bands of different widths around a shoe box.

50. *SOUND TRAVELS THROUGH THINGS:* Demonstrations (see Seq. 3, Act. #65):

One child jumps on ground or floor, others place ears to ground to listen. Try sending jumper to another area where he cannot be seen. Count jumps. Can listeners tell how many?

Hold yardstick to ear and hold clock at other end. Try with metal curtain rod.

Hold pencil in front of face and scratch on end. Hold one end between teeth and scratch.

Make telephone with two tin cans and a string.

51. *PEANUTS TO PAPER:*

> Some four year olds made peanut butter, starting with the whole peanuts in the shell. They removed the skins, put the peanuts through the meat chopper and added salt. They had made a very special treat for their midmorning snack.
> The next day, the teacher brought in her blender and they put the shells in and chopped them very fine. Then they went into the playyard and gathered old leaves, a few scraps of paper, and some of the fine mulch from the cedar chips which covered a section of the playground. This also went into the blender. They filled the water table half full and added their dry, chopped pulp, stirring it until it was thoroughly soaked. (This was a good social experience, the water table provided space for several children at once rather than having them work with smaller pans.)
> Next, they took pieces of wire screen, about 6″ × 9″, (taped around the edges for safety) and dragged them through the 'mush' until the screen was covered with pulp. They placed the screen pieces on a piece of cloth and put another piece over them. Using a rolling pin (or a large bottle) they rolled the pulp to remove the water and flatten it. The next step was to iron over the top piece of cloth until the pulp was dry. The children removed the cloth and carefully lifted off a coarse sheet of paper. Read the book, *The Chinese Knew,* Pine and Levine, McGraw Hill.
> On another occasion, the parents came to the school and went through the same process one evening. They tried it with different mixtures. One used small pieces of linen cloth, shredded, another a combination of sawdust and paper. They mixed their individual pulp experiments in plastic dishpans instead of the water table. (See Seq. 11, Act. #94.)

52. *POUNDING BLOCK:* A large tree stump made an excellent pounding block for threes to hammer in nails. The nails were easily removed and re-nailed many times. The children could stand (two or three) around the trunk and talk as they pounded.

53. *CARD PLAY:* A deck of playing cards suggests many obvious uses for learning numbers, sequence, sorting, counting. One teacher played a simple game with threes. They sat around a bucket and tried to toss cards into it. They counted how many went in, how many on the floor, how many left to toss.

54. *BUBBLES:* Cut out both ends of large, medium and small coffee tins. Dip into a basin with sudsy water from liquid detergent. Sweep the can through the air rapidly to push the bubbles out.

55. *SALT EXPERIMENTS:* Children need no formal introduction to salt since it is a part of their daily lives. Stress the fact that salt is one of the important minerals left behind by seas of long ago. Our bodies need salt. Salt is used in making soap. Chlorine, which comes from salt, is needed to make water pure. Help children discover the properties of salt, listing each as the children investigate. Salt is odorless, white and in crystalline form; it dissolves in water. Pour some salt in a glass of water, it disappears, but you know that it is still there because you can taste it in the water.

56. *ROCK SALT CRYSTALS:* Half fill a metal jar cover with soil from the garden. Add several teaspoons of salt to a glass of water and stir, stopping when the salt still remains at the bottom, even after long stirring. Pour some of the clear salt water on the soil. Put this mud-like mixture in the sun to dry, or set aside in a warm place. A loop of copper wire placed on the mud will cause a necklace of crystals to form on it. After mud dries, large crystals, or rock salt can be seen on the mud.

57. *DE-SALTING WATER:* Freeze salt water to make it salt free. Mix 2 teasp. salt with a pint of water. Put the mixture in the freezer section of your refrigerator. Leave it there until about ¼″ of ice has formed. Remove the ice, rinse it off, and then taste it. Does the ice taste salty? To check your results, do the same experiment again. When the ice has formed, separate it from the water and rinse it off. Then boil the ice and the water separately. In which pan is the salt left behind? This experiment should suggest a way in which to get fresh water from salt water.

58. *ACID TEST:* Certain minerals, called carbonates, fizz when acid touches them. The fizz is caused by a gas, carbon dioxide, which is given off by the minerals. Minerals that give off carbon dioxide are called carbonates. Baking soda is a man-made carbonate. Vinegar contains a weak acid. Try a few drops of vinegar on baking soda, it will fizz. Now

try a few drops of vinegar on a crushed egg shell. Does it fizz? Now try table salt and vinegar.

59. *EVAPORATION:* Add a tablespoon of salt to a quart of hot water in an open saucepan. After children taste the solution, boil it ten to twenty minutes, then cool and have them taste it again. The fact that it is saltier can give them concrete evidence of how salt is removed from the sea by evaporation. The boiling and evaporation, then tasting process, can be continued until only the salt crystals remain in the pan.

60. *DEFROSTING:* Salt and its effect on ice can be demonstrated in a simple investigation. Using candy or kitchen thermometer, compare the temperature of plain ice water and a salt-ice mixture. This is the reason salt is applied to highways in freezing weather. Did any child suggest this?

61. *DENSITY TEST:* A stone weighs more than a piece of wood of the same size. A quart of water weighs more than a quart of oil. Scientists say that a stone is more dense than wood and that water is more dense than oil. An object can float in a liquid only if it is less dense than the liquid. To prove this, place an egg in a glass of water. If it is perfectly fresh, so that there is no gas in it, the egg will sink to the bottom. But if you dissolve 2 tbsp. of salt in the water, the egg will float. Adding salt makes the liquid more dense than the egg. Now stick a thumb tack into the end of a pencil. This weights the pencil so that it will float with the point upward. Make a mark on the side of the pencil where the water line comes. Float the same pencil in a glass of strong salt water and notice that it now rides higher. This is because salt water is more dense than plain water.

62. *BUYING VEGETABLES:*

The housekeeping area had been converted to a store and store play went on for several weeks, with the children bringing in empty cans and packages to sell. During a cooking session they were talking about making a salad. "What shall we put in our salad?" The children listed vegetables that grow on top of and under the ground. Each child was to bring in something to go in the salad. In addition, the teacher took several children to a produce market. "We have only one dollar to spend," she said. Cindy pointed to the sign over the cucumbers, "That says the cucumbers are two for 49 cents. 49 is next to 50 and half of 50 is 25 so we can buy one cucumber for a quarter. Two quarters make fifty cents!" "These are radishes," said Jack, "We need a bunch of radishes. They are two for 39 cents. One bunch would be 20 cents."

"The tomatoes are 39 cents for a basket of small ones and 49 cents for a pound of big ones. We will get more if we take the basket," said Jane.

"Let's ask the man to weigh as many of the big ones as we could get for 39 cents and decide," the teacher suggested. They did, and bought the basket.

"The lettuce is wrapped in cellophane," said Kathy, "It is not very much and it is 39 cents. Will we have enough money?" The children counted out the cost of their purchases and found they were short. The clerk was so fascinated by what he was seeing and hearing that he wanted to donate the difference, but the teacher saw an opportunity to learn about credit and charging. They went back the next day with the money.

But could the children have read cucumbers and radishes if the signs had not been over the real thing? Yes, because they had been making lists of vegetables to hang over their store and since they had a reason to want to know, most of the children could read the words.

Measure the value of this experience against reciting the alphabet and counting up to one hundred!

63. *PETAL DESIGNS:* Cut petal shapes and make into designs. Carve shapes into potatoes and use to make prints.

64. *GIANT PETALS:* Cut five or six large petals from cardboard. Decorate with tissue scraps, construction scraps, cloth scraps. Trim edges with lace or strips of fringed paper. Assemble into single flower.

65. *DAISY SCOTCH:* Draw hop scotch on ground in shape of a daisy. Pick dandelions to use as hop scotch 'tossers' and play "Daisy Scotch."

66. *FLOWERS ON THE GROUND:* Draw petal shapes on the ground and decorate with dandelion blossoms, red maple flowers, green leaves.

67. *FLOWER DESIGNS:* Draw around real petals and leaves to make designs on paper.

68. *BLOCK PRINTS:* To make printing blocks: Cut shapes from inner tubes, paste to wood blocks. Carve designs in soap or linoleum.

69. *FLOWER SERIATION:* Pick dandelions or other flower in various stages of bloom. Ask child to arrange in order of growth.

Fig. 9-65

70. *PURPLE TO LAVENDER:* Have a mixing session to create as many shades of purple

as possible. Sing *Lavender's Blue,* and as your own color appears create your own version of the song, *Lavender's pink, silly, silly* or Lavender's fuschia willy, willy...Lavender's orchid, frilly, frilly...Relate darker shades to deeper tones. (SENSORY)

71. *TEXTURE AND TECHNIQUES—ONION BAGS:* You can do many different things with plastic onion bags.

    a. Weave with pipe cleaners

    b. Weave with yarn, using blunt needle, bobby pin, toothbrush needles (see Act. #72).

    c. Make crayon rubbings through paper laid on top

    d. Cut open and stretch over four nails in corners of a frame and use as weaving base.

72. *TOOTBRUSH NEEDLES:*

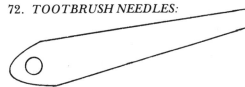

File the brush end off and shape to blunted point. Use hole in handle as 'eye' for threading.

73. *PURPLE SANDS:* Use beach sand and divide into several batches, coloring each a different shade of purple, with vegetable dyes. Dry in oven. Use to make sand pictures by shaking onto designs drawn on paper and painted with a thin mixture of white glue. Shake sand from salt or pepper shakers or use egg carton cups and dolls' spoons. Work on newsprint or large tray and remind children to shake excess back into containers.

74. *PURPLE MURAL:* Cut magazine pictures printed in shades of purple into scraps. Class constructs a giant mosaic flower by pasting purple bits onto a flower shaped mural.

75. *FLOWER COLOR MIXING:* Lay out a variety of real flowers in purple shades and experiment with mixing paints to match them.

76. *FLOWER RELAY:* On a lawn full of dandelions, divide into two or three teams. Line up—first child runs and picks a dandelion, runs back, hands to next child, he runs and picks a second flower, runs back and hands these two flowers to the next child. He runs and picks another flower and hands the three flowers to the next child, etc. First team to pick full bouquet of ten dandelions wins.

77. *FARM ANIMALS:* List on a chart as many animals as the children can name. Children find magazine pictures or draw pictures of each animal to paste on chart. Discuss each animal separately and list its uses, i.e., work, pleasure, food, etc. Compare the animal to machines which may have replaced it, i.e., tractor, plow—replaced horse drawn plow. Serve some of the foods the various animals produce. (ANIMALS)

78. *LIVE ANIMALS:* Borrow a baby pig, lamb or goat for a few days. (If you consider buying an animal, think about who will care for it on weekends and vacations and arrange for a permanent home when the animal is too big to be kept at school.) Ask at a nearby farm for the loan of a baby animal during growing season and then return it when summer vacations begin.

79. *STAND UP FARM:* Cut or draw animals and paste on construction paper. Add bits of cottom or fuzzy cloth, string tails. Construct barns from cartons. Arrange animals and barns to set up a stand up farm.

Fig. 9-79

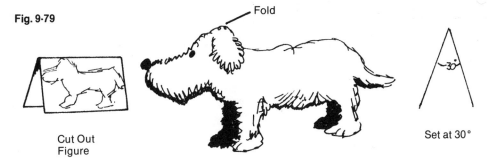

Cut Out Figure

Fold

Set at 30°

80. *CORK ANIMALS:* Assemble a collection of corks, matches, nails, pipe cleaners, buttons, paper, yarn, into animals.

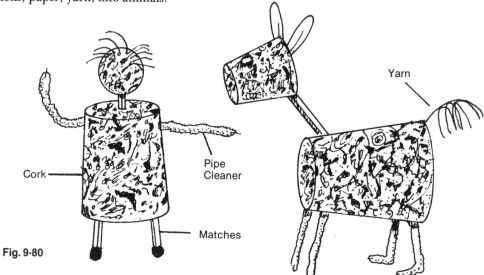

Yarn

Cork

Pipe Cleaner

Matches

Fig. 9-80

81. *COWS:* A teacher drew a cow on the side of a dividing screen and hung a rubber glove as the udder bag and filled it with milk. The children 'milked' the cow.

82. *MINI-DRAGONS:* String together blocks of styrofoam or spools of varying sizes. Use straw sections as spacers. Add pipe cleaner legs and antennae and construction paper 'fins'. Paint green and add features. (See Dragon Dance, Activity #35.)

83. *DRAGON:* (LIFE SIZE)

A large, six foot papier mâchè covered dragon-shaped form was covered with scales by gluing egg cups over the entire body section. This was then painted with 'dragon green' and the result was a marvelous reproduction of *Puff, The Magic Dragon.* (Can also be made by sewing or stapling cartons together.) (See Activity #35.)

84. *ANT FARM:* Fill a one gallon jar, or similar large, glass container, with soil. Find an ant hill. Shovel the surrounding dirt and debris into jar. Cover the jar with dark paper to encourage the ants to make tunnels. Place some cotton on top of the dirt and pour a little water on it every few days. Feed the ants crumbs of bread and cookies, honey or sugar water.

85. *CATERPILLAR-COCOON-BUTTERFLY:* Use an old pair of cloth gloves. On the back of the right glove, glue a caterpillar made of soft, furry fabric. The left glove is covered with glue. Sprinkle on glitter, include fingers of glove. Add a pair of wings on the back, stiff enough to stand out. (PUPPETS)

Fig. 9-85

Stand with both hands behind back. Bring right hand around slowly creeping. "I'm so-o-o-o tired." Open thumb and forefinger for yawn. "I thing I will go to sleep." Caterpillar crawls up around on arm, neck and face and then back down and as he disappears behind the back says, "But when I wake up I want to be a butterfly." After a pause, a butterfly comes fluttering out from behind. Follow up with information about cocoons and butterflies.

"Let's go to sleep"
The little caterpillar said
They tucked themselves into their beds
 (fold fingers into palm)
They will awaken bye and bye
 (slowly unfold and hold up fingers)
Each one will be a lovely butterfly.

86. *ESCAPED PETS:* (CAPTURING) Hamsters and other classroom pets spend much time trying to get out of their cages. Sooner or later they succeed. Here is a way to recapture them.

1. Make sure all cats are removed.
2. Close all bathroom doors as the pet will search for water.
3. Don't waste much time in trying to find them as they can hide under or in anyplace where they can fit their heads, do not be deceived by how fat their bodies seem.
4. The Trap: Place several plastic buckets or waste baskets (smooth sided) in various areas around the building. Place them near kitchens or pantries. Construct a stairway up the sides of the tubs, using blocks. Or make ramps up to the rim, using screening. Place some food and nesting material in the buckets. Do not put out deep containers of water which may cause small animals to drown. Rub carrots or crumbs on the ramp or stairway to leave food scents. Leave a trail of food scraps leading to the traps. Check the traps each morning. Hamsters, gerbils and mice are nocturnal and will probably go hunting for food during the night. Let the children help you!

87. *FLOWER SEEDLINGS:* Visit a nearby store and purchase a packet of flower seeds, pansies, portulaca, sweet peas, marigolds, etc. Prepare planting soil by sifting and sterilize it by baking at 350 degrees for half hour to kill weed seeds. Put soil in planting trays and plant seeds. Make a wall chart of procedures and keep records of seedlings' growth. Include and chart the planting instructions. As the plants grow, encourage children to record the process in pictures. Perhaps each child can make his own notebook. When seedlings have reached the suggested size for safe transplanting, transfer to outside gardens.

88. *SEE SEEDS GROW:* Take two pieces of glass (approx. 4″ × 6″). Cut paper towel to same size. Make a wire holder as shown in sketch. Lay towel on one glass. Sprinkle on seeds. (Bird and grass seeds grow quickly). Lay on second piece of glass. Tape or hold together by elastics. Place in wire rack. Set in shallow pan of water. Water will seep through towel (capillary action) and seeds will sprout. Keep moist.

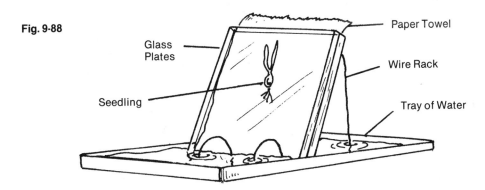

Fig. 9-88

Glass Plates

Paper Towel

Wire Rack

Seedling

Tray of Water

89. *MAPLE WING SEEDS:* Collect the wing seeds from a budding maple. Take off the dry husks to expose the seed. Why does it have wings? Plant and watch for germination. Find saplings under a large maple at various stages of growth. Transplant in pots. Measure. Find a larger, three or four foot sapling. Measure around a large maple. Look at maple furniture. *Enjoy* the seed wings. Spin between fingers, drop from a high place and watch them flutter down. Place on paper and add lines to create creatures or designs. (See Seq. 8, #102—Growth of Trees.)

90. *PICK A FLOWER:* Make slits in cover of suit box. Children make flowers with stems to fit into slits. Write letters or numbers on backs of flowers. Take turns picking a flower. If

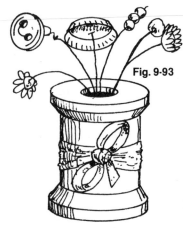

Fig. 9-93

a child recognizes a number, he can hold the flower until a bouquet is gathered. If not, he must put the flower back into the 'ground.' Flower is not yet ready to be 'picked.'

VARIATION #1: Each child picks a flower (numbered 1-10). Group then must put itself in numerical order (or alphabetical order if using A-Z).

VARIATION #2: Letters on flowers are used to spell words. For example, one group holds flowers and children take turns 'picking' and arranging their own names.

91. *DRAWING FLOWERS:* Provide a selection of real flowers. Children choose and arrange flowers and draw them with crayons, chalk or paint. Mount or frame with construction paper.

92. *FLOWER RUBBINGS:* Make pictures by rubbing the colors from real petals and leaves of flowers.

93. *TEENY TINY FLOWERS:* Collect spools, telephone wire, buttons, trims, bottle tops, beads, junk jewelry bits. Fill one end of spool with clay and decorate outside with cloth, paint or paper stamps. Make flowers from buttons and beads using wire stems. On May Day these little bouquets make dainty gifts.

Food

94. *MILK PRODUCTS:* Make a chart display of milk products, using pictures and drawings. Visit a supermarket and set up teams with lists to find and purchase dairy products. Return and serve as smorgasbord or tasting experiment.

95. *MILK:* How many ways can the children think of to serve milk. Set up "chefs" for the day, committees to meet with teacher and make and serve a milk treat for the snacktime for a week's time. They could arrange:

> Chocolate Pudding Day
> Whipped Cream Day
> Strawberry Milk Shake Day
> Cream Sauce on Toast Day

96. *MAKING BUTTER:* Use three different methods for churning butter to demonstrate how machines have changed the process and made it simpler and easier. Use three half pints of cream, a covered jar, a hand beater, and an electric beater. Divide the class into three groups, each churning butter by a different method. Time the processing of each method. One group takes turns shaking the jar churn. The second uses the hand beater, and the third the electric beater. Serve some of the resulting butter salted and some unsalted. Serve on hot rolls, bread or toast. Perhaps a parent has an old fashioned churn which you can borrow, or for display only. Most old wooden churns still have the buttermilk aroma lingering inside. Show pictures of old churns and ask at a dairy if there are pictures of their churns available.

97. *MAKING ICE CREAM:* Borrow a hand cranked ice cream maker, divide the class into teams. Though the process takes time it is well worth it. Save this for a special event. Most cookbooks have recipes for refrigerator or freezer ice cream, but try to hand crank yours, if possible.

ICE CREAM RECIPE
(Not so *old fashioned* but much more reliable)
You can buy a powdered ice cream mix for hand mixers. To it is added milk. Chill the mix for one hour and pour into mixer. Ice cubes with salt sprinkled over them will serve as a substitute for rock salt to chill the mixer. When the cranking becomes very difficult, the ice cream is ready. This will take about one half hour.

98. *WHO INVENTED ICE CREAM?* Ice cream is believed to be a Chinese invention. Originating as water ices some 3,000 years ago, it was brought to the West by Marco Polo. In America, George Washington made it....Mrs. Alexander Hamilton served it; Dolly Madison made it popular. The first ice cream cones probably appeared at the St. Louis Fair in 1904.

Oriental Recipes 99. *HSING-JEN-PING:* (Almond Cookies)

INGREDIENTS:

½ lb. lard	2½ cups flour
¾ cup sugar	½ tsp. baking soda
2 eggs	½ cup almonds, sliced
1 egg, lightly beaten	

PREPARE AHEAD: In a large mixing bowl, cream lard and sugar. Add eggs, one at a time, then almond extract and yellow food coloring. Combine flour, soda, salt and sift in bowl. Mix by hand until fairly firm dough forms. Divide dough in half and shape into two fat cylinders. Roll them on lightly floured board with palms until each is about 12″ long and 1½″ thick. Wrap in waxed paper and chill at least three hours.

TO COOK: Preheat oven to 375 degrees. Cut chilled dough crosswise into slices ¼″ thick. Lay 1″ apart (ungreased cookie sheet). Press almonds gently but firmly into the centers. Brush with a thin film of beaten egg, and bake 10 minutes until golden brown. Makes about 8 dozen cookies.

100. *HSI-MI-CHU-KENG:* (Hot Orange Pudding)

INGREDIENTS:

½ cup pearl tapioca	2½ cups cold water
1 large orange	¼ cup sugar

PREPARE AHEAD: In a small bowl cover tapioca with ½ c. cold water, soak 4 hours. Peel orange, remove membranes, break into small pieces.

TO COOK: In 2 quart pan, combine 2½ cups water with sugar. Bring to boil, stir until sugar dissolves. Pour tapioca (drained) in pan slowly, stirring constantly. Cook two minutes, until thick. Add orange, reboil. Serve hot.

101. *SUKIAKI:* Serve a variety of foods in chunks, such as meat cubes, fruit cubes, raw vegetables cut up, bread cubes. Arrange around a selection of dips (ketchup, relish, dressing, powdered sugar) in bowls. Children use toothpicks to serve themselves (miniature chop sticks?). This meal might be served on a low table and children sit around it on mats.

102. *HSING-JEN-TOU-FU:* (Almond float)

INGREDIENTS:

2 pkg. unflavored gelatin	SYRUP: 2 cups water
1¾ cup cold water	½ cup sugar
1½ cups cold milk	GARNISH: 6½ oz. can Mandarin oranges
1 tbsp. almond extract	1 lb. can litchi nuts

This is a modern version of a classic Chinese dish. The original recipe did not use almond extract or gelatin. The jelling agent in the original was agar-agar, a type of seaweed, boiled until it dissolved, producing a clear, flavorless aspic. Because agar-agar produces jellies of varying consistencies, it is difficult to use with any precision. Instead of almond extract the ancient Chinese crushed whole almonds, soaked them in water and squeezed out the liquid.

DIRECTIONS:

1. In pyrex bowl sprinkle gelatin over ½ c. cold water, soften 5 minutes.
2. Bring 1¼ c. water to boil and add to gelatin. Stir until dissolved and clear, add milk and extract. Pour mixture into flat 7½ × 12 dish. (Custard should be about 1½ inches thick, 3 to 4 hours in refrigerator until set)
3. Make syrup with sugar and water. Boil and chill—it will be thin.
4. Assemble: Cut custard into diagonal slices, then diamond servings. Serve on plate. Garnish with oranges and nuts—pour over syrup.

103. *RICE FARMING* by Harriet Chmela

Pepe is a young boy of the Philippines. He lives in a small barrio (village), in a nipa house. The house is raised on bamboo stilts and is thatched (covered) with dried nipa leaves.

Each Filipino family keeps animals for food and work. Pigs and chickens live under the house and a large, brown carabao (water buffalo) is tied to the nearby coconut trees, when he is not hard at work in the field with the family.

Rice is the chief food of the Philippines. The villagers must work hard the year-round to prepare the fields, irrigate the paddies, plant and cultivate the plants and harvest the rice. Every member of a Filipino family shares in some part of the rice farming.

Pepe lives near the Banaue Rice Terraces in the Mountain Province of the Philippine Islands. The rice is grown on terraces which cling to the steep sides of the mountains, forming stairways into the clouds. These terraces have been farmed for over 4,000 years by the descendants of the Ifugao tribes who first began to carve the stepped terraces out of the mountains.

Children are very young when they first begin to go with their fathers into the rice fields to help in the work. Pepe was just five when he first rode along on the back of the sway-backed carabao, which he calls Putik (the muddy one). Putic loves to roll and bathe in the cool mud. Pepe guided Putik through the paddies as his father carried the heavy wooden tilling plow and rope for the long day of work.

During the day, under the hot sun, Pepe went often to a well to bring cool water to his father and the carabao. As he bent to dip the cool water he splashed some over his back. He took a long drink from the half coconut shell which he used as a dipper.

Pepe and hs father wore wide brimmed coolie hats to protect their heads from the hot sun. At lunchtime, Pilar, his older sister, came with food and drink. It was very hard to return to work after the short lunch break. The thick mud of the paddies was hard to plod through and their backs ached with bending and straining at the ropes behind the heavy plow.

At last the brilliant orange and red sunset behind the far mountain tops signals to Pepe and his father that it is time to go home for supper and rest. They gather with the many other rice farmers and talk quietly about the long day and the hard work as they wind slowly down the steep mountain pathways among the rice paddies.

Pepe's mother Maria and his sisters, Angelista, Carmen, Estrella and Pilar, can see the farmers coming down the slopes and they go to the outside fireplaces and begin to prepare a supper of rice and fish. For dessert they have fresh bananas and pineapples which grow in the rich tropical forests which surround the village.

Nearly 200 people live in this village. Many are Pepe's cousins. He has six brothers and sisters who are away at school or working in larger cities on the islands. Only five children live in the nipa hut.

When the harvest season comes, many of the villagers who have gone away to school and to work, will return to the village to help in the harvest. Though the harvest work is very hard, this is a happy time. Friends and relatives come together to work side by side during the day and to celebrate with feasts, dancing, story telling and songs during the evenings. It is the time of many traditional festivals.

Some of the workers carry guitars into the fields to sing, cheering the workers. The bright cotton scarves tied around the coolie hats of the women, the bobbing up and down and the swaying rhythms of the bending workers and the slow motions of the crews as they move along the terraces make a colorful sight down across the mountainsides. Here and there a guitar carries a song out across the valley. As always, the carabao, Putik, plods along pulling the heavy wooden cart filled with rice stalks.

When the rice has been cut it is dumped in a large open space in the center of the village. There the small white kernels must be threshed (pounded) from the stalks with flat boards and the brown hulls must be winnowed away from the kernels. To do this, the rice is heaped in large, round, tray-like baskets and tossed into the air. Pepe's sisters Angelista and Estrella have learned to weave these baskets from his grandmother. The wind blows away the hulls leaving the heavy kernels to settle into the basket. Chickens and birds flutter about the workers' feet picking up the dropping hulls and kernels.

Many days are needed to harvest all of the fields and the villagers, young and old, work side by side until the harvest is complete.

Here is a Filipino song which tells of the hardships of the rice farmer:

Planting rice is never fun
Bent from morn to setting sun
Cannot stand and cannot sit
Cannot rest for a little bit.

Read *The World of Rice* by Mark Boesch, pub. E.P. Dutton and Co.
(The authors express their appreciation to Charito Lapus, a native of the Philippines for supplying information for this story.)

104. *RICE:* A student teacher made a measuring game which involved pouring rice from one container to another. "It was a flop" she reported to her supervisor. "They just wanted to mess around with the rice and it got all over the floor." The supervisor responded, "Perhaps the children needed more experience with rice before they could use it for other purposes. Think of what you might have done first." The following ideas developed:

Put a large tray of raw rice in the middle of a table. Touch it, taste it, smell it. What sounds could you make with it? Have several covered containers available (cardboard, metal, plastic) and shake rice in each one. Sift through hands into tray and table. What instruments sound most like that? (Sand Blocks)

Can you make a mountain with it? Can you make a hole in it? What happens when you try? Look at it through a magnifying glass. Another day, cook several cups of rice. Repeat all of previous experiences. NOW can you make a mountain, a hole?

There are many ways to cook rice, try some: Rice pudding, boiled rice with butter, brown sugar and cinnamon, boiled rice with tomato sauce, boiled rice with soy sauce, boiled rice mixed with chopped, cooked vegetables and meat chunks, rice with sprouts. (See Seq. 7, #127)

When the children have had a chance to explore the basic properties of rice as described here, they will enjoy it as a medium for measuring and weighing. The same rules apply as when working with sand. Work on trays or newspapers for easier clean up. Pour from pitchers, cups, through funnels. Weigh cooked and raw rice and record observations on charts. What happens to the cooking water?

Dye portions of dry rice by shaking with tinted water, dry thoroughly, then glue in mosaic pictures.

Use in small muscle manipulation games. With fingers and tweezers count grains 1-12 into egg cups or place on colored spots as math sets. (See Seq. 7, Act. #87f.)

1 2 3 4 etc.

Outline designs with rice kernels.

Make a set of graduated sound shakers using plastic, metal, and cardboard containers (of various sizes).

105. *THE RITTLER:*

In one school a music shaker "leaked" away all but one kernel of rice and unknowingly, during a music session a child picked up this shaker to make a great rhythmic entry at just the right point. The ridiculous little "rittle" of the one kernel, sent the class into hilarious laughter. It became a special treat to play the rittler! (See Seq. 7, Act. #58.)

106. *PICNIC, PICNIC, WHO LIKES ANTS?* Preparation and planning are the best part. Where can we go? To babes, a corner of the yard or a very short walk to a grassy spot is an adventure. The fun is packing a basket with crackers, peanut butter, juice. Plan to look for a special color, or smell, or listen for sounds and record them on paper or with a tape recorder. Build up anticipation: "I know a place where there is a huge rock. I think it is big enough for all of us to sit on while we have our picnic." or "I know a place where there is a magic carpet (moss)," or "Today we will have our picnic in an enchanted forest." Use your imagination—make an exciting adventure of a very simple experience. Watch the ants. Did they come to your picnic?

NEXT DAY: Follow up, recall, verbalize, vocabulary, remember details, put into proper sequence. (See Seq. 7, #32, and Seq. 9, #19 and 106.)

Read: *Picnic on the Hill* by Miriam Clark Porter from Read Me Another Story.

107. *GARDEN SUPPLIES:* Visit a garden supply house where they sell flats of small plants, following a talk about gardens, making a garden, planting seeds, etc. Discuss the various items for sale and how they are used. Pick out a trowel or rake for your own gardening. Buy flat and plant in yard tubs or large boxes lined with plastic.

108. *NEAR NEIGHBORS:* Take trips to local foreign establishments, such as oriental restaurants, gift shops. Set up displays of Japanese fans, Kimonos, Indian Sari, Bells of Sarna, Dolls, Books, records and toys of these countries. Take trips to a travel agency to obtain color brochures.

109. *CHINESE RESTAURANT:*

A kindergarten teacher visitied the owner of the local Chinese restaurant and explained that her children were talking about China. He invited them to come during the morning when the restaurant was closed. He talked to them in Chinese, wrote each child's name in Chinese on a piece of paper which they proudly carried back to school, gave each child a small paper fan and a fortune cookie and demonstrated eating with chop sticks. He also gave them two quarts of chop suey, which they had with their lunch that day.

110. *MAPLE SYRUP:*

In a New England town the owner of a farm invited groups of school children each spring to see the entire process of extracting maple syrup from trees, demonstrating each step. Inside the sugar house they saw syrup and observed the various stages of sugaring off. Everyone was served vanilla ice cream with real maple syrup on top.

5J. SEQUENCE TEN

Our world is filled with *entertainment*. Do children realize that people get paid for entertaining them by playing baseball, singing on television, making movies or acting as *clowns* in the *circus*? These are occupations, *"work" that seems to be play. People who entertain us* have children who need their care and live in homes just as those people who work in offices or factories.

There are also people needed to help entertainers who are never seen, such as *cameramen, costumers, make-up* and *hairdressing specialists.*

As summer comes, many families go on *vacations* to swim and ride in *boats.*

Many children will leave our care and go on to other schools. They have grown in size, abilities, and achievements. As they look at slides, pictures, samples of art work, writing and books they have made throughout the year, they can see dramatic changes in growth. Even more dramatic are the results they can witness as they stand by height charts which show growth of several inches and "weigh in" several pounds heavier than previous measurements — visible evidence of a growing I AM! and I CAN!

1. *FATHERS:* "My father wears a _____ hat!" Using many kinds of hats, plan an activity around fathers' occupations. Each child might choose a hat and demonstrate his father's work. (DRAMA, LANG. DEV.)

2. *CIRCUS PEOPLE:* Describe and discuss the many jobs of circus entertainers, clowns, acrobats, animal trainers, etc. Dramatize and wear costumes of each.

3. *POMPOMS:* (Yarn)

Fig. 10-3

Construct by winding yarn around small pieces of cardboard. Cut the loops at one end and remove cardboard, fastening the uncut edge by winding with thead. Use left over mittens or old sweaters and unravel them to get crinkly yarn for pom poms. Use poms to decorate clown hats and costumes. Make clown pictures and decorate with miniature poms made from ball fringe or cotton balls. (See Seq. 9, #36, POM POMS, PAPER.)

4. *FABRIC CLOWNS:*

Cut clown shapes from colorful cloth scraps. Add circles for heads and for arms and legs, cut collar — cuffs. Add triangle shape hats. Paste onto colored paper or hang from trapeze stick.

5. *CLOWNS,* Clea Chmela:

At a circus	One wore rags
I saw the clowns	Some wore lady's gowns
Some were happy	The sad,
Some wore frowns	The happy,
Some had floppy hats	The silly
Some wore crowns	CLOWNS!

Fathers' Day Gifts   6. *TWINE HOLDER:*

Use a medium size, clean ice cream carton (round). Paint and decorate with sequins, glitter, buttons, feathers, etc. Paint a face on the carton and cut out the mouth for the string hole. Ears can be made from light cardboard pieces, glued into place. Make a hat from the lid and decorate with feathers.

Fig. 10-6

7. *WOODEN SPOON BOOK MARKER:* Use flat wooden spoon, ink, colored yarn. Draw a face on the spoon with ink. Glue on the yarn for hair Use small buttons on the face for features, red button for nose, etc.

8. *ROCK PAPERWEIGHT:* Rocks of different sizes and shapes are used. along with ink, enamel, paints or magic markers. Study the rocks and select one that has noticeable characteristics or shape that resembles a figure or face. Wash and clean the rock and then color or decorate as desired. Varnish to protect design.

9. *TALENT SHOW:* Ask each child to think of an 'act' to entertain the class. All who perform will describe their plan to the teacher beforehand. Each act is given a name and listed on a program. Children gather props and rehearse for the performance.

Stress the simplest kind of entertainment. "Betsy, you make such beautiful clay animals, can you show us how?" or "John can jump through two hoops." or "Pauline can sing the dolls a Spanish lullaby."

Use puppets, stuffed animals, rhythm instruments. Some may form groups, others compose simple plays or skits. Some may dance to records.

All are invited to be involved in some way—making and selling tickets, serving as stage crews and managers, making costumes and posters, helping with makeup and costumes. Theatre manners such as arriving on time, no talking or rattling papers, no shifting seats, etc. should be discussed before the performance.

Fig. 10-7

10. *LIVE THEATRE:* Attend a performance of a musical, play, or concert at a nearby junior or senior high school. Ask about attending an open rehearsal. Perhaps the group can watch the costuming and makeup procedures backstage before a performance or the performer or make-up person can come to school to demonstrate.

11. *VIP-S:*

a. Mount news photos on cardboard (famous people such as the President or entertainers). Project pictures on a television screen (see illustration). Children take turns being projectionists and viewers, guessing who is in the picture.

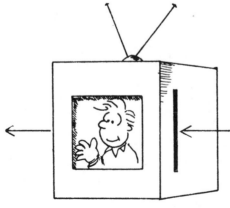

b. Use box also to show circus animals, numbers, letters, childrens' pictures in various games and for "shows."

c. Project a series of pictures which follow a sequence and ask a commentator to tell the story as pictures are shown.

d. Show an entertainer in a distinctive costume (clown, ballerina, etc.). Children describe the action.

Fig. 10-11

12. *NEWSCASTERS:* Listen to a news cast and discuss what makes news, i.e., events, people, happenings, some local, some far away. Choose two or three reporters, equipped with home-made hand mikes to go around room (local) and school (regional) to collect news. They return, and at newstime report the days events to listeners. "John built a road which completely filled the block corner." "Susan fell from the slide and had to have first aid treatment on a scraped knee." "Joan's picture of sea life was chosen to hang in the special art area of the lobby." Some news teams might work with others in preparing their reports, such as in drawing illustrations, maps, etc. Inlcude a weather man, entertainment critic. A teacher might follow a reporter with a camera and gather photos. (This is a good way to collect snaps for a photo display in preparation for a parent meeting or special event.) (LANGUAGE, ARTS)

13. *BRIDES:* Add lace curtains, bridal veils, long white slips and nightgowns to dress up clothes. Show pictures of brides and weddings. Talk about marriage.

14. *TEMPORAL CONCEPTS:* During these final days of school, relax and reminisce, talk about the "good old days" way back last September, January, March. How have we changed—grown—developed? What have we learned?

Look ahead to summer, to next fall, new school experiences. What will first grade be like? Kindergarten? Are you coming to camp? Returning in September?

Develop these temporal concepts of yesterday, today, tomorrow, around your very own school experiences.

15. *LOOKING BACK:* Ask children to tell what they liked best during the school year. Write and read stories based on this theme. Make a poster of pictures and ideas about Best Likes or Favorite Things. Draw pictures of Favorite School Activity, Best Day, Best Friend At School, etc.

16. *LOOKING AHEAD:* Ask children what they would like to know or, what they want to learn or do next year. Develop discussions and stories around this theme. These will be especially helpful as program developers for next year's returning students.

17. *DEAR TEACHER:* Help children who are going on to new teachers to compose a letter containing information, such as "What I learned this year," "What I like most," "Things I can do," "My favorite books, songs, games," "What I need to know." Wherever possible, send these to the teacher (parents can help to supply names and addresses). Perhaps the child will enclose a self-portrait and description of himself. Such letters will be an aid to teachers when the child is registered in fall.

18. *I GREW!* Using the developmental growth charts for concepts as guides, devise activities to teach each child in various areas. Without making these testing sessions, but tying each into classroom activities, observe and take notes on each child's progress. Follow up with a one to one conference with each child and discuss his accomplishments, victories, growth indicators. "You can climb the ladder," "You learned seventeen letters," "You can write your name," "You don't cry when mommy leaves," "You know red, blue, brown, yellow...".

Follow up with parent conference (See #30 and Seq. 9, #21 and GOALS)

19. *SUMMER UN-BIRTHDAYS:* Have a super celebration of summertime birthdays complete with crowns, cake, songs for all those who have them during the vacation. (See Birthdays)

20. *SPRING CLEANING:* Children will gain by sharing the responsibility for end of the year clean up as they help with the packing and labelling of equipment to be stored, mending toys and books and games. Threes can wash and dry dolls' clothes or take a trip to the laundromat to clean drapes and rugs. Fives can mend books and sort puzzle pieces. All can scrub and wash equipment and store toys and games in cartons with labels. Raking and cleaning sandbox, washing slide and tree house.

21. *TREASURE GRAB BAG:* Display all unclaimed toys, games, books, art work. Children and parents are asked to claim. If there are still lots of leftovers (enough for each child), have a grab bag. Put each item in a grab bag or wrap them and take turns drawing for treasures.

22. *MINI CIRCUS:* Set up tents, stages, rings (use hoola hoops) and hold a mini circus. Suggestions follow: (See Seq. 11, Act. #98)

a) Paint CLOWN faces on children and let them take turns doing silly acts.

b) Dress in COSTUMES and march in circus parade.

c) Set up an OBSTACLE COURSE for balancing acts by putting down planks to walk on (flat and on edge), ladders, ropes (on ground), or even a chalk line. Wrap a long pole with bright cloth or tape to use as a balance pole. Tie streamers on the end.
NOTE: Use this activity to test spatial concepts and motor coordination.

d) ANIMAL TRAINING—Divide the class into two groups, animals and trainers. Each trainer chooses an animal and develops an act. Animals can have tails, trunks, ears, etc. Each trainer in turn does his act in the center ring with cape. A big carton might be used for a cage.

e) SCHOOL PETS—Some children might choose a classroom pet and talk about it. "This is a guinea pig. His name is Jolly, and he lives in a small cage. We feed him carrots." Note child's ability to narrate a story, sequences, sentences, poise, etc.

f) FAVORITE ANIMALS—Set up a display of stuffed animals brought from home. Each child makes a cage, writes a label and chooses a space in the Animal Tent to display his animal. Make a tent from blankets (see African Safari #52 this sequence).

23. *FISH GO TO SCHOOL:* Talk about a school of fish. Make a large fish and put the letters of the alphabet on it. Make a small fish, each one with a letter. Attach a paper clip to each small fish. Put all the little fish in the bottom of a box and fish them out with a magnet on a string tied to the end of the pole. The children then place the fish they catch on the large fish, matching the letters. When completed they have a "school." VARIATION: Paint numerals on jar lids and vary activity using numerals. (LANGUAGE GAME)

24. *UPPER AND LOWER CASE LETTERS:* Make two columns on large posterboard with lower case letters in one column, upper case letters in the other. Do not put pairs opposite each other. Glue a length of colored yarn with a loop tied on free end, to one column. Put a cup hook beside each letter in the other column. Child finds matching upper and lower case letters and attaches the yarn to the proper hook. (READING, READINESS)

25. *CONSONANTS:* Make two sets of cards, one with consonants and the other with pictures of objects beginning with consonants. One player holds up letter card and the child who holds up corresponding picture card, gets a point.

26. *PEANUT FINGER PUPPETS:* Break peanut shells in half to form thimbles, making one for each finger. Put a face on each shell with ink. Place a shell face on each finger tip and make conversation with puppets.

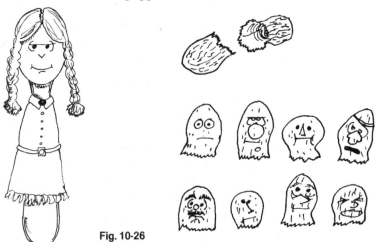

Fig. 10-26

Fig. 10-27

27. *PLASTIC SPOON DOLLS:* Use plastic spoons, colored ink, yarn, cloth if you wish to dress the doll. Paint features of doll on rounded side of spoon. Glue on yarn for hair. Paint on clothes or use cloth to make them. Fasten to fingers with elastic bands and use as finger puppets.

28. *BALLOON MESSAGE:* Tie a postcard wrapped in a plastic bag to the end of a helium balloon, with the address of your school written on it, along with a request for the finder to return the card, telling where it landed. Use a map to locate the place if card comes back.

29. *GROWTH REPORTS:* (See #17 this Sequence and Seq. 9, #21 and GOALS.) At this time of year you are writing the final entries on your student reports. It is important to record as many specifics as you honestly can. Play games on the playground, while you are on a walk, as well as in the classroom, which will test for such knowledge as:

> Can the child tell time?
> Can he dress himself completely?
> Can the child tie?
> Is the child reading?
> Can he recognize colors?
> Can he recognize shapes?
> Can he recognize temporal relationships?
> Does he really know what yesterday, tomorrow, next week, a year mean?
> Does he know the seasons?
> Can he distinguish appropriate signs, clothing, etc.
> Can he demonstrate spatial relationships?
> Can he recognize numbers and letters, visually, audially, tactilely?
> How many concepts has he mastered?

The following story demonstrates some imaginative ways to check on individual children.

30. *CHALLENGE:*

In one school the fives were having a meeting. When it was time to move to another activity, the teacher said, "I have a new game. It is called Challenge. I will give each one of you a special way to go to the tables." Another teacher recorded the results. Her directions were: John, put your LEFT hand on your knee and your RIGHT hand on your ear and walk to the table."

"Susan, put your RIGHT hand on top of your head and walk around the table and sit down beside John."

"Dick, put your LEFT hand on your spine and your RIGHT hand on your hip and go through the door and come back and stand under the clock."

It was fascinating to watch their faces as they thought about the challenge and carried out the directions. No comment was made about mistakes—it was kept on a "game" basis. In addition to testing the concepts, the ability to listen and to follow directions is important. Some children can do two things, and some many more. Some can't listen, think or act in sequence.

Another day this same teacher said, "Mary, tap your finger on your nose and spell your name." To the teacher's surprise, Mary, a very bright child, could NOT spell her name. Mary looked confused for a moment and then drew it in the air. She could write it, and recognize it, but she had not learned to relate visual and audial perception. The teacher had not suspected this and was then able to work with Mary individually.

31. *HOOPS:* (The Circus) (See #22 and Seq. 2, Act. #36.)

Warm up in a BIG circle using the whole room.

Talk about circus animals and entertainers.

Experiment with suggested ideas.

Divide the group into the animals of their choice. Each of the animals may have a trainer and work as a team. Have a rehearsal session in private corners. Play some circus music. Return to circle.

Say, "I am going to give a hoop to each person. When you have yours, find a spot to perform your circus act in the hoop. When I blow the whistle, return to the big circle and sit in your hoop."

Three ring circus acts may be performed by older children (K's) in the center of the circle, three at a time.

Vary the circus by having part of the group use instruments as the band.

32. *GOING TO THE ZOO (CIRCUS, FAIR):* Play "I am going to the zoo." (LARGE MUSCLE)

HOW WILL YOU GO?
   a) "I will hop"
   b) "I will hop and jump"
   c) "I will hop and jump and spin"
   d) "I will hop and jump and spin and run"

33. *WIGGLE AND SQUIRM:* Snakes and worms offer ideas for motions, for comparisons, likenesses and differences.

34. *BOAT MOTIONS:* Move as tug boats, sail boats, tankers, row boats, motor boats, canoes, kayacks.

35. *HUMMER-DRUMMER:* Materials: one cardboard tube from a paper towel roll, two rubber bands, some waxed paper, scissors and adhesive tape.
Directions: Cut a hole three inches long and one inch wide in the tube, 3" to 4" from one end. Place a 6" piece of waxed paper around the tube so that the hole is covered. Make sure the waxed paper is rolled firmly around the tube and then taped or held down with rubber bands. Cut a round piece of waxed paper and fold it over the end of the tube that is nearest to the side hole. Place a rubber band around the paper that is folded over the tube end or secure it with tape. Wrap some tape around the open end of the tube. Place mouth to open end of tube and hum into tube. The vibration is magnified by the waxed paper over the holes. To make a drumming noise, tap lightly with fingers against the side while humming. (Do not "share" mouth blown instruments.) (INSTRUMENT)

36. *SNAILS:* Use the snail-limericks below to stimulate movement and dramatic play. Hold snail races under "snail shell cartons."(See Seq. 7, Act. #41, 42 and 43.)
   VARIATION: Turtle races under cartons. Encourage children to compose limericks.

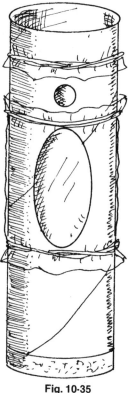

Fig. 10-35

SNAI-LIM-RICKS by Deborah Mitchell Haney

> There once was a snail named Fred
> And all he could see was his head
> He'd carry his home
> Wherever he'd roam
> —Including his pillow and bed!

> There once was a snail from Vienna
> With two very curly antenna
> He was happy to see—
> He could watch his t.v.
> While crawling across a banana!

> There once was a snail named Mel
> Who lived in a deep, damp, dark well
> —Except for his head
> He was *always* in bed
> He never came out of his shell!

SNAILS by Deborah Mitchell Haney

> Snaaa-a-a-ils...
> are all taaa-a-a-ils...
> They're BIGGER than nails
> (and smaller than whales!)
> BUT
> no-thing—is—sl-o-o-wer than
> sna-a-a-ils.

37. *RUG SAMPLES:* Ask a carpet store for discontinued samples. Use for a variety of games and activities. Some suggestions:
   a. *LARGE MUSCLE DEVELOPMENT:* Make a hopscotch with squares. Walk with them balanced on heads. Jump over a row of them, adding one more to row each time.

b. *CONCEPTUAL DEVELOPMENT:* Arrange on floor, walk on them, around, between, over, sideways, backwards, on tiptoe.

c. *VISUAL AIDS*: (See Seq. 8, Activity #10 story Book Development.) Make into caps and other visual aids for stories and poems.

d. *MATH, SCIENCE, GAMES* Cut into strips of varying lengths and widths for seriation. Cut into different sized circles, squares, etc. for seriation.

Arrange according to color shades

Cut circles into pie sections (fractions).

Make into textures game or use for FEELY BOX.

Use to play bean bag toss, mark each square

with a numeral and keep score. (See Seq. 1, Activity #155.)

38. *SHAPES ON SHAPES GAME:* Cut large shapes from construction paper. Children form teams (triangle team, circle team, square team, etc.) and hunt around room for objects of that shape to paste or draw on their construction paper. Might also use rug squares (above) and collect objects to place on each.

39. *SHELL SHAPES:* Use real shells to press shapes into wet sand or mud or fill with plaster to make castings or roll sandbox into a smooth surface and choose a small group of children to create a sand and shell design using shells as molds.

40. *CLOWNS:* Put out an assortment of circles, triangles and rectangles for children to make into clowns. If child says, "I need a smaller one" (or larger one), ask him to look for an object to use as a pattern. See illustration. (SHAPES)

Fig. 10-40

41. *RAINBOW:* Read "A Rainbow of My Own" by Don Freeman, pub. Viking and introduce a prism. Experiment with "catching" a rainbow reflection by placing a glass of water where the sun can shine through it and create a prism of colors.

42. *COLOR SORTING:* Divide a table top or cardboard into color sections using paper or paint. (A round surface can be divided into "wedges.") Offer a collection of objects (bottle caps, crayons, spools of thread, buttons, small toys, rug and cloth samples) for children to sort into the color swatches.

43. *BOAT WORK:* Display pictures (or mount on flash cards) many kinds of boats. (Liners, battleships, tankers, canoes, tugs, barges, sailing boats). What are they used for? Pleasure—work—travel? Use in seriation games, "which is larger?" "goes faster?" Read *The Story About Ping,* by Marjory Flack, pub. Viking (about houseboats). (See Seq. 8, Activity #69)

44. *BOATS FROM CORKS:* Make boats by driving nails through corks, add sails. Use also, walnut shells, plastic dishes. (See Seq. 8, Act. #71.)

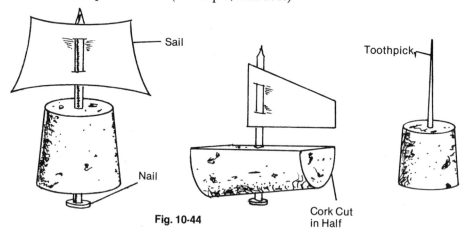

Sail

Toothpick

Nail

Cork Cut in Half

Fig. 10-44

45. *BOATS WITH MAGNETS:* Make a small paper boat with paper clips around edges. Use a magnet to steer it. Put paper clip or other small metal object on sheet of paper and make it move with magnet under paper.

46. *BUTTERFLIES:* Finerpaint on table tops or plastic sheets. Teacher precuts large papers in shape of butterfly and children make color lift-offs from table. Older fours and fives can cut butterflies using folded paper (as when cutting hearts). Tie strings on butterflies to make kites or tie on to sticks.

47. *EGG CARTON CATERPILLAR:*

Directions: cut six leg holes (about $1/2$ inch) in each side of outer edges of egg carton lid. Roll up a section of newspaper about 7" long and thick enough to fit into the leg holes. Bend this in the center and insert through two leg holes, side by side. Bend at each end to resemble feet. Complete six of these until all leg holes have been filled on each side. Cut out head from folded cardboard. Glue it to front of carton. Leave a flap on back for gluing egg carton to caterpillar's body. Pain or color caterpillar. Add pipe cleaner antennae, button eyes, pull string .

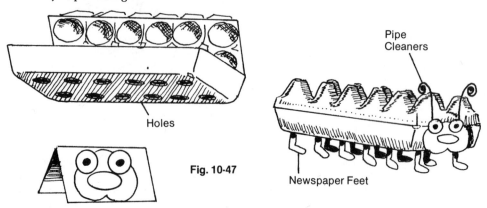

Holes

Pipe Cleaners

Fig. 10-47

Newspaper Feet

48. *FISH:* Draw a large fish on colored paper and cut out. Draw a small outline inside and cut slits. Weave contrasting paper strips into slits. Hang fish from string.

Glue two paper fish together and stuff with newspapers or nylons.

Fig. 10-48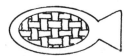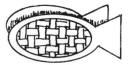

49. *GIANT INSECTS:* Create a collection of imaginary insects from elegant junk (wire, pipe cleaners, buttons, cotton balls, beads). See sketches for folded paper insects.

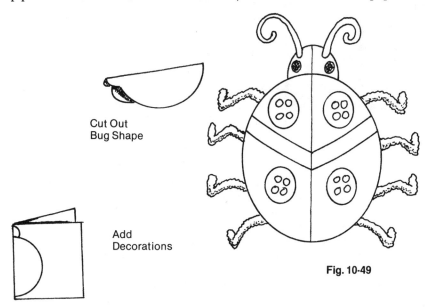

Cut Out
Bug Shape

Add
Decorations

Fig. 10-49

50. *IMAGINARY INSECTS:* Drop paint blobs onto colored paper, fold and rub. When dry turn into imaginary insects by sketching in wings, legs. (ART)

51. *BUMBLEBEE MOBILE:* Cut a foam egg carton into 2 cup sections. Color stripes on one section, draw a face on the other section. Cut wings from construction paper and glue to the section between the cups. Add pipe cleaner antennae and legs. Suspend several from a thread in a mobile arrangement or hang from a potted dead branch.

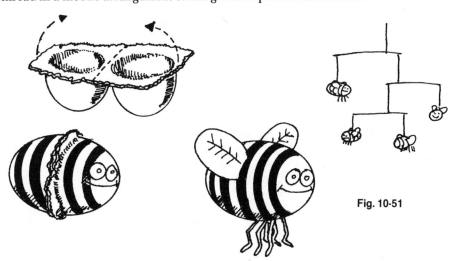

Fig. 10-51

52. *AFRICAN SAFARI:* Talk about safari and Africa. Use toy animals. Each child hides one in room or yard. Using white paper bowls as safari hats and a wagon or carton with rope pull as 'capturing cage,' go in search of the wild animals to use in circus. (See Act. #22.) (AFRICA)

Fig. 10-54

53. *PEANUT ELEPHANT:* Elephants love peanuts. Draw a large elephant for a mural and fill in with peanut shells pasted on. Shelling peanuts, separating shells from nuts and pasting them on the mural are good activities for twos and threes. Count peanuts, bake into cookies, chop and serve on ice cream, or make peanut butter. (See Seq. 11, #94.)

54. *CIRCUS ANIMALS:* Children draw their favorite animal on large sheet of paper. Strips of black paper are pasted over the animal to make a cage. Wheels can be added to create the effect of a circus wagon. Wagons can be displayed around the room and hooked together into a train. Wagons might also be decorated with fancy borders and scrolls, rickrack or lace.

55. *SAWDUST ANIMAL SILHOUETTES:* Color sawdust in jars with thinned tempera paint. Dry on newspapers. Draw animal silhouettes on cardboard, paint with glue and sprinkle on sawdust.

56. *SAWDUST CLAY ANIMALS:* Follow recipe for sawdust-clay (see Sculpture) and create animals. Afterwards make cages from boxes which have been painted and decorated as circus wagons. Add wheels.

57. *POLLENATION:* Ask: What is pollen? Do bees eat it? Do the bees "eat flowers?" What is nectar? Pollen is a fine dust which flowers form in order to fertilize. Nectar is a sugar-like liquid or sap which the flower produces to feed itself. There is always an extra supply of nectar. Bees take the nectar for food. They store the extra in their hives (as honey) to feed their young and the adult bee colony, during the winter months. The pollen dust of flowers must be carried from one flower to another in order for fertilization (seeding) to take place. If the blossoms are not fertilized the fruits and vegetables which the plant forms will not develop.

When bees land on the flowers to drink nectar, the tiny hairs on their legs and body pick up pollen dust. As they go from flower to flower gathering nectar they shake the pollen off which fertilizes the plants.

Introduce the idea into creative movement session. Bees buzz from flower to flower and shake pollen off bodies and legs. (BEES)

58. *SPRINGTIME SNOW,* Harriet Chmela

> The flowers are spitting pollen
>   It's floating from the trees.
> The grass is bursting pollen,
>   and pollen...
>   makes...
>   me...
>   ...SNEEZE!

59. *POLLEN EXPERIMENT:* Make some busy bees by twisting pipe cleaners for legs, around a ball of paper. Dip the legs into cups of flour to illustrate how the dust (pollen) clings to the fuzzy legs.

Make chalk flowers on floor or pavement. Sprinkle some flour in the centers. Children walk through the flowers. Does the pollen get carried from blossom to blossom in tracks?

60. *POLLEN LOTTO:* Make a set of lotto cards with four to six simple flower designs on each, which have circular centers of different colors. Make matching sets of colored circles. Children draw from the deck and match to flower centers on lotto cards. Flowers which have matching centers are "pollinated." Flower centers might have bits of yellow cloth or

yarn stuck on representing bees. Game might be varied by making centers of varying shapes as well as colors.

61. *ANIMAL CRACKERS CAKE:* Bake a circus merry-go-round cake, frost, and stand up animal crackers around the top. Use as a special treat after the mini-circus festivities. (See #23 and Seq. 11, #98.)

62. *BERRY PICKING:* Pick seasonal berries and use in a variety of recipes. Have a berry festival. Some local farms invite pickers in after major crop is harvested.

63. *LEMONADE:* Squeeze fresh lemons (taste); add water (taste); add sugar (taste); separate into five or six portions in glass containers and add variety of food colors to make a RAINBOW OF LEMONADES.

64. *RAINBOW SANDWICHES:* Make open-face sandwiches of various shapes, using creamed cheese blended with a variety of seasonings and food colors. Children might add faces with olives, pickles, chips, diced vegetables, etc. Serve with rainbow lemonade. Cut loaf endwise. Fill each layer with a different color spread. Chill and slice.

65. *AFRICA:* Read and display pictures of African wild life. National Geographic magazines are an excellent source of pictures. Talk about the familiar animals, such as elephants, giraffes, lions, monkeys, and introduce the unfamiliar animals. (See Seq. 11, #27, 28 and 45.) (ANIMALS)

66. *VACATIONS:* "Where are you going this summer?" Talk about beaches, camping, travelling, motels, tents and trailers. Play "packing the suitcase and packing the car" games for various kinds of trips. What will we need to take to the beach? The mountains? Tenting? Decorate shoe boxes to represent a tent, car, trailer, suitcase. Use magazine pictures of various sizes of travel items and sort into appropriate boxes.

67. *TRAVEL LOTTO:* Help the child develop travel games to take home and use on trips. Make lotto cards using pictures of things to watch for and check off. Cut familiar roadside items from magazines or draw them. Use pictures of houses in various colors, dog, service station, mountain, lake, boy on bicycle, flag on pole, man walking, etc. Glue on card. Each rider has a set of cards and the first one to find all items, wins.

68. *TRAVEL LAP ROADWAY:* Construct a mini car roadway inside a shallow box (about 12" × 16"). Line with cloth or paper, paste on roads with black paper strips, tunnels with tubes, houses (small boxes), and gas pumps (toothpaste caps). A small matchbox vehicle travels the mini roads.

69. *GUIDED TOURS:* Help the fives plan a guided tour of kindergarten for the fours. Fives answer questions fours may have about the next year and serve a special treat. This activity should be as 'child-planned' as possible. (See also Seq. 9, Act. #16)

5K. SEQUENCE ELEVEN

During the *summer vacation* at a child care center, the program may need to be extended to include *older children*. The *age span* of staff members may also widen as volunteers and assistants, counselors and junior counselors are added to include *teenagers* and *young adults*. These people of widely varied ages come together to assist and guide each other, engage in healthy competition, enjoy happy times and learn to cope with some of the frustrations of *living together as a family*. Taking this age profile as a model, the suggested activities are designed to give children a sense of family unity. (These curriculum ideas are suitable for children up to age ten.)

As the people change, so too must the environment and focus of the program. Manipulative materials and tools for intellectual development are set aside, and the *emphasis changes* from learning to *fun* and *adventure* with a touch of *suspense, mystery* and *surprise*. We know that children will be gaining intellectually but we are more concerned with their physical, emotional and social growth.

Changing the physical environment in a center will be a major step in helping the children to feel that it has become a totally different place to come to during a summer vacation. If they have been in attendance from eight to ten hours a day during the past several months, it is possible to give them a totally new experience by setting up *outdoor activity centers* which focus on nature and science and by establishing *arts and crafts areas* in the classroom to replace the interest centers which were used during the regular school program.

A summer program can best be built around *themes* which allow children to escape from their own world into a land of make believe, as they become *pioneers and explorers* or travel to *different countries* to join the natives in their customs. It is healthy for children to "get out of themselves" and walk in another's shoes for a time. Staff, also, will benefit from the change, for example:

One day care center in the city was housed in a three story brick building which surrounded a paved courtyard. On a Friday before the summer vacation began the children were told that when they returned on Monday there would be many surprises in store for them and *everything* would be different. Over the weekend the entire staff and some volunteers helped to change the environment. School equipment and materials were packed, labeled and stored. (See Seq. 10, Act. #20.)

The staff had decided to begin their summer program planning by developing activities around an Indian theme. Banners with colorful motifs were hung about the courtyard and a teepee constructed in one corner. The rooms were decorated in a similar fashion using posters, artifacts and costumes which related to the theme. Children of the different age groups were assigned to areas which would be new to them, adding to the feeling of complete change.

Though some of the staff remained the same, on Monday the children returned, their "teachers" had become "counselors." To add to the surprise, these familiar people were now costumed as Indians in head bands, war bonnets, moccasins and tunics. The children were delighted and awed by their new surroundings and their enthusiasm was immediate and contagious. (For Indian ideas, see Seq. 3.)

PIONEERS 1. *PATCHWORK:* Collect items of outgrown cotton clothing, perhaps one from each child. Cut in patchwork squares and sew into a class picnic blanket, story cloth, banner, flag, doll's blanket. Each one will have a part of his own cloth in the blanket. Talk about quilting bees, pioneers, etc. Older children can help with simple stitching.

2. *BRAIDED RUGS:* Using heavier materials from old clothing, cut or tear into strips and make braided items, such as a small welcome mat or a wall hanging.

3. *WEAVING:* Use strips of old cloth for weaving. Staple warp strips across a frame of wood, or a sturdy cardboard box, and weave in weft. Weave on the diagonal as well as right angle, to vary designs.

4. *HISTORICAL THEMES:* The following themes are based on early American history. The idea is not to teach history but to help children relate to other lifestyles and events from earlier times.

1620	1.	The First Settlers-Pilgrims — Pioneers
1755	2.	Pennsylvania Roads — River Highways
1767	3.	Daniel Boone-Kentucky-Cumberland
1775	4.	Revolutionary War Times and Heros
1803	5.	Louisiana Purchase-Lewis & Clark-Explorers
1830	6.	The Mountain Men-Trappers-Hunters-Kit Carson & Jim Bridges
1840	7.	The Oregon Trail-Wagon Trains-Indian Wars-Emigrants-Westward Ho!
1849	8.	The Gold Rush
1850-60	9.	The Railroads-Communications-Pony Express-Stagecoach-Telegraph
1870-80	10.	The Cattle Country-Buffalo-Cowboys-Chisholm Trail-Cattle Drives-Outlaws-Sheriffs-Wyatt Earp-Jesse James, Billy the Kid, Bat Masterson, Wild Bill Hickock, Calamity Jane
1860-80	11.	The Sod Busters-Homesteading-Indian Wars-Custer-Wounded Knee-Little Big Horn-Sitting Bull-Cavalry-The Cherokee Strip

Dramatize these early days with a different sequence of activities based on each of the themes. Each activity might be set up in a DIFFERENT area of the school building, playground, adjacent woods, fields, etc. Each one is given a name, such as Pioneer Hollow, Cumberland Gap, Minuteman Woods, Wagon Trail, Telegraph Hill, Sod Busters Glen.

5. *PIONEER-PILGRIM PICNIC:* Construct a small shelter. Read a story about Pilgrim days, make a patchwork picture, each child adding his own square of cloth to make a large, colorful mural. Plant corn in a hill and fertilize with fish.

6. *DANIEL BOONE HATS AND VESTS* from old cloth, fringed, or brown bags with paper fringe. Explore for "wild" animal signs in the woods. When you reach Cumberland Gap or Old "Kaintuck," sing folk songs, eat cornbread snacks, sleep on a bed of pine needles.

7. *MAKE A TRAIL:* Move obstacles and clear paths for trikes or wagons around the playground using ramps and bridges over make-believe rivers. Carry lunch over the "River Road" or "wagon trail" and serve on the banks of a newly discovered and named river or lake. Send scouts on a return trip and bring a new group of settlers over the trail for lunch.

8. *TRAIL MARKING:* Encourage children to think of many ways pioneers can mark a trail. Keep in mind protecting the environment, avoid unsightly paints, damaging trees and shrubs. How could child mark the trail to a secret place so only he can find it?

9. *REVOLUTIONARY WAR:* Most towns have historic museums, homes, battlegrounds. Plan a field trip to such places to reinforce with simple stories of historical persons. For example: Games relating to Paul Revere—use play lanterns and establish signals of other kinds to see if opponents can guess which way the 'British' are coming. Discuss freedom, independence, flags and Minutemen.

10. *ROADS AND RIVERWAYS:* Using sandbox or large gravel or soil area, build a contour map of pioneer territory, Pennsylvania, Homestead Gap, Louisiana Purchase, Oregon Trail. Make mountains, valleys, rivers, lakes, etc. Add trees, trails, bridge, small wagons (See #11). Use the map for games of "What's the shortest route to Cumberland Gap?" or "How many bridges to cross before we get to Kentucky?" Make up stories of pioneer travel, using the map as visual aid.

11. *WAGON TRAIN:* Construct covered wagons by attaching wheels and covers from paper cups, cut in half. Attach cardboard or plastic horses to pull. Use for sandbox and block play.

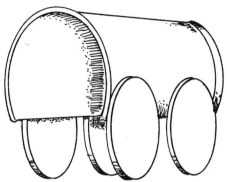

Fig. 11-11

12. *MOUNTAIN MEN:* Play on hill, explore, climb, set up camps, have cookouts in the mountains. Walk softly so as not to disturb animals.

13. *GOLD RUSH:* Create some gold nuggets by spray painting sand and small stones and burying them in sandbox. Children dig and pan gold, putting small shovel fulls in shallow tins to rinse and sift out gold. Follow up with a weighing activity to determine how much each panner discovered. Use a balance scale to divide the gold.

14. *PONY EXPRESS:* Organize relay teams of express riders, each team with identifying colored arm bands. Send them running with messages over a route set up so it winds around the entire school yard, between two points (Kentucky Ridge to California Gap). Time each team to see who gets message through first. Groups of express riders wait at various stations (name them) and grab the message from the tired riders and carry it on. Refresh runners at a water stop with sips of water.

15. *OLD TRAINS:* Tell about how the railroads crossed the west and how two rail lines met and were connected by a golden spike. Use long ropes or poles and build a track from two far points on playground. Children go off in teams to find sticks to lay rails. When teams meet have a "hootin-hollerin" celebration with refreshments. Old trains had water and fuel stops along the route. Passengers got out and bought refreshments at wayside inns. Children might construct an inn along the route using a large blanket or square of seatblocks and give it a fancy name. Display pictures of old trains and sing railroad songs. Make old trains from decorated cartons which fit around child.

16. *CATTLE ROPING AND BRANDING:* Use hoola hoops on ropes as lariats and bags or pillow cases filled with leaves as cattle and have a steer roping contest. Child tosses hoop to catch the steer, pulls the cow in and brands it. Make brands from carved potatoes on sticks, dip in paint to brand. Other printing devices can also be used.

17. *CATTLE DRIVE:* Some children are cows (add horns and tails) and some are cowboys. Cattle are driven over the Chisholm Trail, cowboys have to outride and surround to control stragglers. They have to be corraled and fed at lunch time. Develop a long dramatic session around an "all day" (about one hour) cattle drive. Use a marked trail as the route.

18. *TOMBSTONE GAP:* Make gravestone rubbings at a nearby graveyard. Cover stones completely with shelf paper attached with masking tape. Rub with large crayons, chalk or pieces of charcoal from your own cook fires. *Call town office to obtain permission.* Use the opportunity to talk about ancestors, Pilgrims.

19. *SOD BUSTERS:* The name sod busters came from the busting up of hard sod land of midwestern plains. This activity will demonstrate the difficulty and hardship these early farmers underwent.

Cut sod from a small section of grass using an area which can be replanted as a flower garden, or replace with tree or shrub. Build a small sod house, using boards as door and window lintels and roof. Thatch over roof with reeds and straw. Make windows by rubbing brown paper with vegetable oil. The effect is very similar to the windows of pioneer days.

20. *DUSTBOWL:* Each child draws a garden on a sheet of paper and plants it on the floor. When all gardens are in, turn on a fan. What happened to the gardens? This will dramatize what happened to topsoil of western plains. Turn activity into game by asking children to find their gardens again. Could work in two or three teams, each racing to get their gardens back in place once again. Use different colors of paper to separate team gardens and mark off each team area with tape on floor.

Firebuilding

21. *FIREBUILDING FOR A COOKOUT:* Children have a natural interest in fire and particularly in its creation. Though children are at times impatient regarding fire, it is necessary to include fire prevention and the care of fire into program. Children need to learn what people do around a fire and the rules. Successful and consistent firebuilding takes much patience and practice. Children five and older should have the opportunity to help build and light a fire at some point during the summer.

Fire should be built *only* on sand, rock or dirt which has no roots or other combustible material nearby. Cookout grills can also be used. Building a fire requires three types of materials:

TINDER (finger wood) is used first because it catches fire very quickly and burns rapidly. Tinder includes small, dry twigs no larger in diameter than a small child's finger. It does NOT include newspaper, leaves, grass, or other materials like lighter fluid.

KINDLING includes wood which is dry and ranges in diameter from finger to thumb. It is usually 6-12 inches long. Kindling should snap when broken.

FUEL includes pieces of wood and charcoal. The lower dead branches of trees are a good source. Green and rotten wood are poor additions to fire. Soft woods burn very quickly, hard woods burn slowly.

IT IS NECESSARY TO HAVE BUCKETS OF WATER AND SAND KEPT NEARBY TO EXTINGUISH A FIRE!

22. *BUILDING A FIRE:*
   a. Have a fireplace ready.
   b. Collect tinder, kindling and fuel.
   c. Have safety pails ready with water and sand.
   d. Keep the wind at your back.
   e. Take two sticks of kindling to form an angle in the fireplace.
   f. Pile tinder in the angle created by the sticks *lightly* so that there is air.
   g. Light the wood at the *base* of the pile because fire burns upwards.
   h. As fire catches add tinder until the fire is brisk.
   i. Add kindling one by one where the flames are strongest.
   j. Gradually increase the size of the wood.
   k. Gradually build fire in shape of teepee.
   l. Slowly add fuel.
   m. When fuel is burning well, cooking can begin.

Always make sure your fire is OUT completely before leaving the campsite or fireplace.

23. *MILK CARTON COOKING:* You can cook in a milk carton by cutting off the top, fill with water and set right in coals to boil foods. (The water becomes heated first and carries heat away from carton.)

24. *BOX OVEN:* use a heavy carton which has a central divider. Line *all* surfaces with heavy foil. Line flaps to serve as oven doors. Stand on end so divider forms a shelf. Place a pan of coals below and cook above.

25. *FIRECRAFT SUGGESTIONS:*

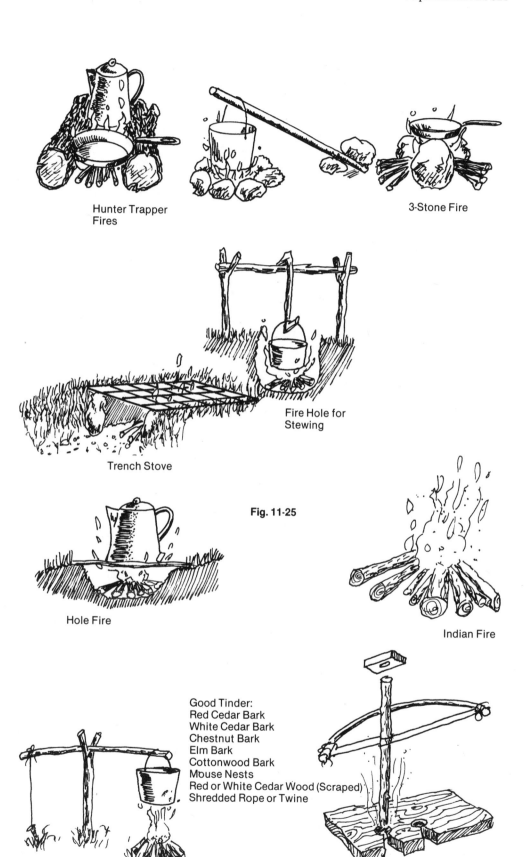

Hunter Trapper
Fires

3-Stone Fire

Fire Hole for
Stewing

Trench Stove

Fig. 11-25

Hole Fire

Indian Fire

Good Tinder:
Red Cedar Bark
White Cedar Bark
Chestnut Bark
Elm Bark
Cottonwood Bark
Mouse Nests
Red or White Cedar Wood (Scraped)
Shredded Rope or Twine

26. *KITCHEN CRAFTS FROM NATURAL MATERIALS:*

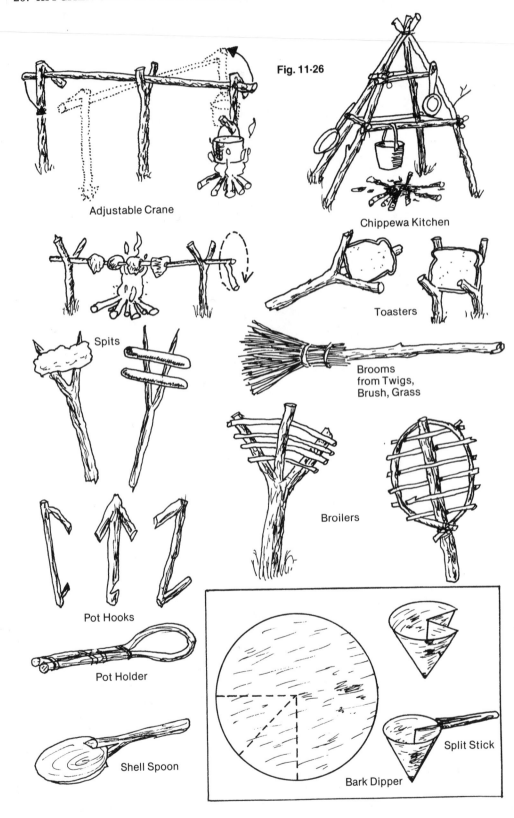

Fig. 11-26

Adjustable Crane

Chippewa Kitchen

Spits

Toasters

Brooms
from Twigs,
Brush, Grass

Broilers

Pot Hooks

Pot Holder

Shell Spoon

Bark Dipper

Split Stick

27. *AFRICAN NAMES AND LOCATIONS:*

1. Hausa	10. Kikuyu
2. Yoruba	11. Tuareg
3. Watusi	12. Pygmy
4. Shilluk	13. Egyptian
5. Ethiopian	14. Ndebele
6. Herero	15. Masai
7. Zulu	16. Ashanti
8. Berber	17. Bushman
9. Moroccan	

28. *AFRICAN MASKS:* A common form of African art is the ceremonial mask based on religion and the daily life of the tribesmen. Sometimes these masks combine features of man and animal. They are worn by witch doctors and chiefs and ceremonial dancers. Headdresses, painted, carved and decorated with feathers and flowers, are used with masks in dances. Headdresses and masks can be made from decorated:

Mâchè	War Paint	Bunches of leaves, tied
Bags	Shallow box lids	Paper and metal plates
Cloth	Small cartons	Pillow cases

(See Seq. 4, Act. #50 — Papier Mâchè Masks, and Seq. 2, Act. #19, 22 — Masks.)

29. *SWAHILI:* Read *Moja Means One* and *Jamba Means Hello,* by Muriel Feelings, Dial Press. Both books are written to illustrate simple Swahili words.

30. *ANASI:* Traditional African folk character. Many stories written about the adventures of Anasi the spider.

(See KWANZA: Afro-American holiday; Celebration of the First Fruits in Seq. 4, Act. #9-12.)

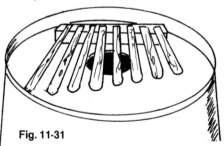

Fig. 11-31

31. *THUMB PIANO:*

Use heavy paper bucket and four tongue depressors. Cut a hole in bottom of bucket. Beside it, glue on a small scrap of wood and then glue on the tongue depressors in a variety of lengths—glue on a top scrap of wood. Vibrate tongue depressors with fingers.

32. *PEBBLE MARACAS:* Sort out several sizes of pebbles. Place each different size in containers to create a variety of sounds.

33. *TAMBOURINE:* Materials: Tops from six or eight bottles (pop), a pie tin, and as many nails as you have bottle tops. Remove cork centers from tops. Nail tops loosely to pie tin by bending ends of nails. Brass paper fasteners may be used in place of nails. (You can also fasten with wire.) With hammer and nail, puch hole through top and corresponding one through pie tin. Draw wire through holes and twist the ends of the wire together. Allow for slack to make the tops rattle.

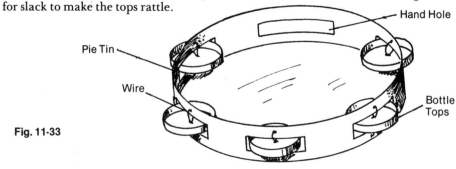

Hand Hole

Pie Tin

Wire

Bottle Tops

Fig. 11-33

34. *GOURD BANJO:* Select gourd with long stem. Cut gourd lengthwise just above stem so that the part you cut off is less than half the gourd. Use larger half (including stem) as banjo. Clean out pith and seeds and lacquer or varnish gourd. Stretch wet chamois over opening and lace around gourd with heavy string or leather thongs. Space lacing as shown to hold chamois in place. Cut a bridge, 2½ X 1¼, from thin wood and glue it to chamois near one end. Cut four notches in neck end. Stick a nail in other end of gourd about 1½" down from the edge. Tie four banjo strings or thin wires to the nail. Separate strings and securely tack to chamois. Draw strings over the bridge and through notches in neck. Tie all four strings around stem firmly. Raising strings over bridge makes them transmit vibrations to the sound box. (See #66.)

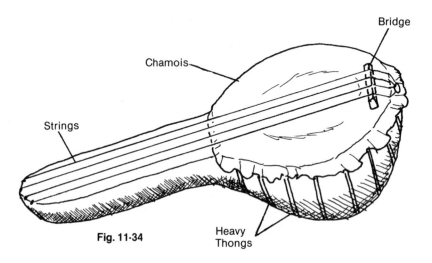

Bridge

Chamois

Strings

Heavy Thongs

Fig. 11-34

35. *MARACAS:* Made by using pop bottle caps, a stick and a nail. Remove the cork from six bottle caps. Nail three of the caps loosely to the end of a handle made from a stick. Make a pair of maracas and shake them to accentuate rhythm.

Small gourds make excellent maracas. Select a pair with natural handles. Be sure that the gourds are dry. Cut the gourds open crosswise toward the bottom and scrape out the seeds and pith. Put in some coarse gravel or tiny pebbles. Glue the two sections together and shellac.

36. *SHELL CHIME:* String six to eight clam shells (drill small hole) leaving a separation between on string. Hang four to six strings from dowel to make shell chime. Decorate or paint shells.

37. *HOOP DRUM:* Bend stiff, sturdy cardboard loops into rings and stretch heavy cloth or plastic coverings over both sides. Bend coat hangers into loops and pull a nylon 3" to 4" slices and stretch over inner tubing, canvas, leather. (Old chair covers of leatherette might be used.) Shallow round cardboard or metal boxes make hoops.

38. *DRUMS:* Make drums from hollow logs and sticks; steel drums from cans.

39. *BOTTLE MUSIC:* Arrange and fill bottles with water to levels tuned to a scale, to make xylophone.

40. *AFRICAN DRUMS AND SHAKERS:* Tribesmen create rhythmic patterns and dances. Rhythm is more important than melody in African music and these rhythms from Africa are the main basis of American jazz. Children can create dances and chants about experiences, using instruments made from natural products.

Painted pebbles knocked together	Shaking leafy branches
Bark cups filled with gravel	Shaking bunches of grass
Hitting tree trunks	Shaking sticks of various sizes
Water in pools hit with sticks	Sticks striking stones
Shaking containers of water	Stones striking sticks

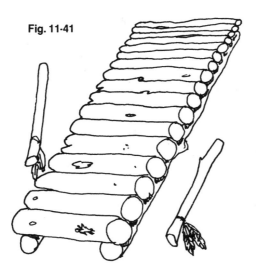

Fig. 11-41

41. *JUNGLE TELEPHONE:*

Divide into two tribes with real names. Go to different parts of a wooded area. Find talking instruments and begin to talk to the other tribe, each repeats the rhythm sent then responds with own rhythm. Some sounds will carry, others will not. Animal sounds created by children can also become part of the conversation. Each child is given a chance to explore the area to find his way of talking. Younger children can do this activity by standing on two sides of a blanket, by dividing inside and outside a tent or hut made from a big carton. A pre-selected assortment of sticks, stones, pie tins, etc. might be offered to stimulate ideas from the two's and three's.

42. *AFRICAN MARIMBA:* Nail, or tie, a row of small sticks, varying in diameter, across two supports. Lay on the ground or hang from a tree limb, over a carton, wash tub, or lean against a building. Rub with sticks to create sounds. Decorate, with feathers and streamers, the marimba and playing sticks.

43. *WILLOW WHISTLE:* Materials: small piece of green willow 3″ to 4″ long and ½″ thick, or any kind of sapling on which you can loosen bark.

Cut one end of stick on diagonal. With knife, cut around stick about an inch from diagonal end. But through *bark* only, no deeper. With handle of knife, tap bark lightly on the short end of the stick until you have loosened bark enough to slide it off stick all in one piece. Moisten stick. (This will help you work off bark without breaking it.) Cut a notch in the long end at the point where it meets the part from which you have removed bark. Slant notch away from short end. Starting at notch, slice a layer about 1/8″ thick down the length of the short end. Slide the bark back on and the whistle is ready to blow.

44. *COMMON ANIMALS:* Activities centering on animals will most naturally focus on the familiar animals living in the woods and fields around the school. To stimulate interest and find out what the children already know and can identify about animals, take an exploratory walk to find out.

What animals live here? How do you know? What signs of animal life can you discover? Where are their burrows? Nests? Tunnels? What food do they eat? Can you hear any? Keep a log of any sign of animal life your group identifies. *NOTE: Keep a special list of any misconceptions* the children have, and through stories, research and class discussion clear up and correct such ideas, i.e., "porcupines throw quills," "snakes chase you and bite," "toads cause warts." A child's interest and enjoyment can be greatly enhanced when such fears and misconceptions are corrected.

45. *UNUSUAL PLANTS, ANIMALS, INSECTS, TREES OF AFRICA:* Introduce through pictures, books and slides. Try to dispel misconceptions.

a. ANIMALS OF THE:

Bush	Desert	Plains	Jungle
Elephants	Addra	Sable Antelope	Okapi
Lions	Bustard	Cape Buffalo	Bongo
Zebras	Rock Hyrax	Impala	Gorilla
Giraffes	Sand Puppy	Giant Eland	Duilar
Rhinos	Egyptian Cobra	Grants Gazelle	Tree Hyrax
Buffalo	Fennec	Black Rhino	Monkeys
Antelope	Aoudad		Babboon
			Bush baby

b. BIRDS:

Weaver Bird
Hornbill
Flamingo
Honey Guide
Mouse Bird
Marabou Stork

Long-tailed Sunbird
Congo Peacock
Secretary Bird
Ostrich
Bee Eater

c. INSECTS:

Driver Ant
Anopheles Mosquito
Locust
Tsetse Fly
Scorpion
Termite
Rhinoestrus

d. SNAKES

Boomslang
Spitting Cobra
Black Mamba
Gaboon Viper
Rhinoceros Viper

e. TREES

Gingerbread Palm
Tree Fern
Baobab
Fever Tree
Oil Palm
Dragon Tree

Acadia
Date Palm
Traveler's Tree
Mahogany
Cocoa
Bamboo

f. FLOWERS:

Strophanthus
Clerodendron
Calla
Barleria Prionitis
Ferraria
Fragrant Falso Onion
Golden Cape Marigold

Mesembryantheum
Giant Lobelia
Yellow Flag
Neohthytis
Yellow Ififa Lily
Amaryllis
Napoleona

46. *ECOLOGY:* All things in nature are tied together, linked in an invisible chain of life. To most young children ecology has come to mean "Don't be a litterbug," "Every litter bit hurts;" good for a start but an understanding of ecology must go beyond taking walks to pick up litter. Exploring some ways the litter can be put back to use can stimulate more understanding and interest in the real meaning of ecology, the relationships of living organisms to their environment. A visit to a dump with an active recycling program is an excellent start. The ways in which waste products are recycled can lead to many interesting and valuable trips and activities. The words litter, saving, recycling, restoring, wasting, re-using, composting, polluting, conserving, re-planting, pesticide, extinct, may help to lead into a host of activities based on the Ecology theme.

47. *COMPOST:* Create a compost of leaves, small sticks, ground up food waste, shells, etc. Plant beans, pumpkin, squash, or other fast growing plants in mulch and some in regular soil. Compare difference. Dig up mulch from woods to show the differences in soils. Dig for worms in a well established mulch and in regular soil. Count. Where did you find the most life? What other things lived in the two soils? Dig sand and gravel and count living creatures.

48. *ECOLOGY TOUR:* Walk through the building and look for signs of waste: lights on, heaters running on hot days, unused towels thrown in basket, paper cups, dripping

faucets, uneaten food, dried paste.

49. *HIDDEN TREASURES:* After a little walk, use special treasures to create a large mural which has been designed with an ecology message, for example—the can rings and bottle caps become features of a smiley face or blossoms on a flower bed.

50. *MATH GAMES:* Use caps and rings to make up counting and sorting games.

51. *BLACK TOP VS. GRASS:* Set up an activity on paved area on a hot day. Set up same activity on grass. Divide into two groups. Switch places. Discuss differences. Explore both environments carefully—look for growing things, sit down, lie down, walk in bare feet, pour water, jump, roll, take temperature of both areas in shady and sunny spots. Discuss discoveries, write on chart. Relate to cities, subdivisions, parking lots and shopping centers.

52. *ROOT MILES:* In an experiment a scientist discovered that ONE wheat plant produced 9000 miles of roots in one season's growth. Try measuring the lengths of roots from a single plant. Uproot carefully; cut off each section of root, lay out and measure. Discuss the importance of roots for holding the soil in place and of decaying vegetation to enriching the soil.

53. *ROCKS, SAND AND SOIL:* The earth's crust is made up of layers of rock covered with soil. There are various ways of testing rock to determine what is in it. There are three major classifications of rock:

> Igneous: rocks formed from heat, such as volcanoes
> Metamorphic: rocks pressed together under great heat—slate
> Sedimentary: layers of sand and mud welded together under great natural pressure, made from sediments—sandstone.

Rocks and minerals have names. Some stones are sharp with broken edges. The breaking up of rocks by water, heat, cold, and pressure is important in making soil. Observe the differences in rocks.

54. *SOILS:* Weathering rocks form the products—sand and clay. Soil composed of sand and clay is called loam. The best soil contains decaying vegetation called humus. Some rocks can crumble in your hand. Sifting soil changes its appearance. Soil has many living things in it. Water goes down into some soils faster than other soils. Running water carried soil from one place to another. Sand is fun to play with. Dry sand flows more smoothly than wet. Silver sand runs more freely than coarse. Dry sand won't stick together.

55. *QUALITIES OF SOIL AND SAND:* Stir different soils into a glass of water and watch the settling process. Plant seeds in different soils and chart growth process. Put different grades of sand on scale and see the differences in weight of gravel, beach sand, pea stone, pebbles, loam (wet and dry).

56. *LIMESTONE:* Put a limestone chip in one dish and another kind of rock in a second dish. Pour a little vinegar on each stone. The limestone will fizz and bubble but the other rock will not. The limestone has lime in it which is a base and vinegar is acid. The two react to each other.

57. *STONE QUARRY:* Visit a quarry to see how granite and other stones are processed and cut into useful forms. Look for stonework in the neighborhood. (Curbstones are a common use.)

58. *ROCK COLLECTING:* During a walk on the beach and in the woods, pick up pebbles and stones. Display on table by shape, color and size. Shellac or submerge in water to enhance the colors. Number each rock; identify and label each specimen.

59. *SANDPAINTING:* Children color sand with thin tempera paint and allow to dry, then make mosaics, designs and pictures by sprinkling sand onto areas of paper coated with thinned glue.

60. *SWEET OR SOUR SOIL:* Dig a spadeful of damp soil. Press a strip of litmus paper into the soil. If the paper remains BLUE the soil is sweet, if the litmus paper turns RED there is too much acid in the soil. Work some lime into the ground and try the litmus test again. Lime sweetens the soil and prepares it with nourishment for growing.

61. *ROCK-NICS:* Construct cave people, animals, imaginary creatures by gluing rocks together, add feathers, parts of plants, paint.

62. *INSECT CAGES:* A BEETLE TRAP can be made by burying an empty tin can in the

ground so that its open rim is even with the surface. Syrup or wet sugar in the bottom will attract the beetles who will fall in and be trapped. (See Seq. 9,#84 — Ant Farm.)

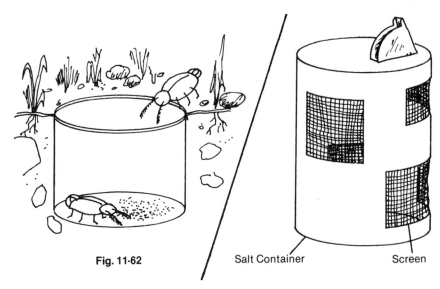

Fig. 11-62

Salt Container   Screen

An INSECT CAGE can be anything from individual plastic container with holes punched in the top to large community cages for many bugs. You can make a big insect hotel from a cardboard carton. Cut windows in the sides and top, and cover them with screening or mosquito netting. Cut a large three-sided flap door in one end which can be lifted up to admit tenants or clean the cage. Newspaper can be put on the cage bottom to make cleaning easy. Pans of moist soil should be kept in the cage, along with two or three small potted plants. Cut flowers and tender shoots should be inserted daily to provide food for the leaf eaters. A cage like this will permit you to keep grubs, the larvae of bees, wasps and beetles, in the soil so they can develop. Keep them supplied with leaves from the trees on which you find them. Caterpillars will eventually spin their cocoons for the pupa stage on the plant stalks. Cocoons that you find in the woods should be left attached to twigs or stones on which they are found. Keep the insectarium soil moist but not wet, and don't put the cage where the sun will beat on it or the pupa inside the cocoons will dry out and die. Once a moth has emerged, let it go. These delicate creatures will beat their wings apart in the cage.

63. *FEEDING LIVE INSECTS:*

Grasshopper, walking stick	Fresh grasses and weeds, clumps of sod in the cage watered occasionally will last several days. Put soil in the cage for them.
Beetles	Grubs, caterpillars, meal worms. A piece of rotten wood with soft insects in it will keep a beetle happy. Give him a tin of water, too.
Crickets	Wet bread chunks, lettuce, peanut butter. Give them water and soil to dig in.
Caterpillars, tree hoppers	Leaves from the plant on which they are found. Lettuce leaves. When they start spinning a cocoon they won't need anything.
Praying Mantis	Small live insects, gathered by shaking a bush over newspaper. Bits of raw chopped meat.

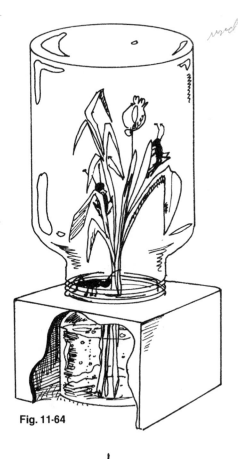

Fig. 11-64

64. *GRASSHOPPER GREENHOUSE:* Fill a small jar with water and place a 4″ deep cardboard box over it upside down. Punch a small hole in the center of the box and stick a few cut flower stems through it so the plants rise five or six inches above the box. Put the insects in a quart jar and turn it upside down over the plants so that the rim is resting on the box. This will give the hoppers a homey environment and will keep them from falling in the water and drowning. Plants should be replaced with fresh greens periodically.

65. *TRACKING:* To encourage the writing of original stories, draw tracks of animals on the blackboard, including fowl. If you wish, ask the class to identify the tracks and label the drawings as you proceed. Hold class discussion about the habits of animals—food, shelter, nesting habits, etc., enemies and prey. This will serve as incentive for the class to write stories about the adventures of the animals as suggested by their tracks. (See Seq. 8, Act. #20 and 95.)

66. *GOURD BIRDHOUSE:* Cut a round hole in the center of a gourd. Clean out pith and seeds. Varnish, paint or shellac the gourd. Fasten as a birdhouse to tree with wire or strong string. Keep supply of water nearby to attract birds.

67. *BIRDBATH:* Mix enough cement to fill a large pie tin. Press a small pie tin into the cement and brush off the excess from the sides. Remove when the cement has begun to harden. Do not remove the bottom pan. Fill with water and set in a secluded area. Place a mirror on the floor of the bath and birds will reward your effort by putting on a good show. (See Seq. 8, Act. #68.)

68. *BIRD CALL:* Drill a hole *slightly* smaller than the threads of a screw eye in a piece of close grained hardwood, such as rock maple or mountain ash, which is about 2″ long and an inch square. Put a little resin powder in the hole and screw eye back in hole. As you twist the screw, very slowly, it will make chirping sounds or trill in loud, clear, ringing notes, producing a variety of bird noises. Some birds will answer such calls.

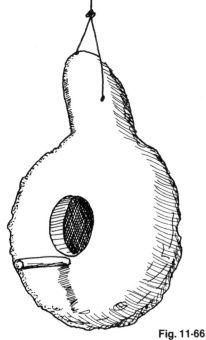

Fig. 11-66

Fig. 11-68

69. *LIFE IN THE SOIL:* Cut out a piece of untrampled soil about 2 inches thick and sift through a fine screen onto a newspaper, crumpling the clods. The first sifting should yield a collection of bugs, along with pebbles too big for the screening. Remove the pebbles and count the living things. Look through the sifted pile on the newspaper for smaller things that went through. There should be dozens of mites, some so small the children will need a magnifying glass to see them. Count as many as possible; count the little soft white insect eggs. Make the same experiment using soil from an old cellar.

70. *CATCHING FISH:* A large net is best for scooping up minnows. Tiny fish may look dull and drab from the shore as almost all fish have brownish looking backs to camouflage them from enemies, but bright colors may flash from their sides and bellies. Construct a minnow trap as shown in the diagram and leave it for a day in shallow water near the reedy shore of a pond; it should yield a surprising catch.

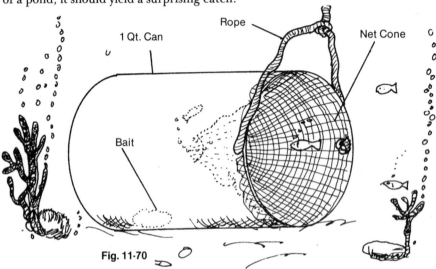

Fig. 11-70

71. *FROG EGGS:* Collect from ponds "slow" water—be sure to take green scum which the tadpoles will eat. Put eggs and scum into one to two inches of water in a tank or large container. As eggs develop, build up a rock pile and mud. Change the pond water occasionally and add water beetles, when available.

72. *WATER SCOPE:* Submerge a large mouthed jar halfway in water. The glass bottom magnifies, and many small creatures can be observed more easily.

73. *EXPLORING STREAMS AND PONDS:* Some of nature's biggest surprises are hidden along the streams, ponds and swamps. Even the smallest trickle from a tiny spring is a menagerie of unusual wildlife. Along the muddy edges of the brooklet, where it gurgles through a shady ravine, dozens of red efts and salamanders wriggle in the cool dampness. In the woods surrounding the swamp, tiny tree frogs with suction cups on their feet cling to the trunks and branches of trees. In clear pools, mud puppies and colorfully striped minnows, like dace and rainbow darters, slither or dart in and out among the rocky crevices. Lift a stone from a quiet section of silty stream bottom here or there and you'll find a delicate, semitransparent crayfish. The still waters of swamps and ponds usually furnish turtles, newts, tadpoles and an amazing variety of fresh water fish. Collecting stream and pond life, and building an aqua-terrarium to hold what you catch is a hobby that will prove endlessly rewarding. Wear sneakers to wade in the brooks to avoid slipping or cutting feet on the rocky bottom. In swamps, heavy boots are a good precaution. (See Seq. 8, Act. #72.)

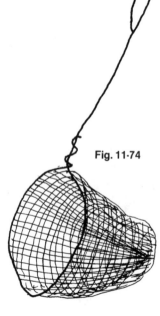

Fig. 11-74

74. *DIP NETS:* Make by unbending a wire coat hanger. Shape it into loop about 6" in diameter. Twist the ends to form a handle about 14 inches long. With waxed string, stitch a sack of plastic or cloth netting around loop ring, or cut the end of a nylon stocking about 8-10" up from foot, fold top edge over loop and stitch or staple.

75. *AQUA TERRARIUM:* Use a rectangular aquarium or build a suitable tank. A good

size is about 18 inches long, as wide as a standard 12 inch plank, and a foot high. You will need:

    a. Two pieces of glass, the same size, for side walls.
    b. One-inch redwood or cedar plank, 12 inches wide and 4 ' long.
    c. Twelve feet of ½ " quarter round molding.

    Cut piece of plank exactly as long as the glass. Cut two more pieces, each one foot long. These are the end pieces which can be nailed or screwed to the bottom plank, as shown. Cut 8 pieces of molding in one-foot lengths and nail them inside edges of end pieces as shown. Be sure to leave space between each pair of strips just the thickness of the glass so the glass will slip easily into the slot. Slide glass into place. Place strip of molding along top of each side wall and nail the strip ends to the edges of the end boards.

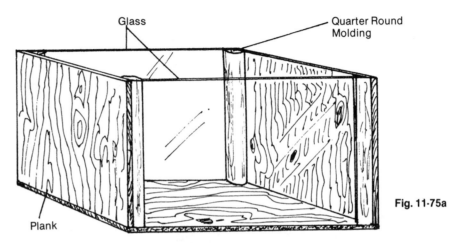

Fig. 11-75a

Fill bottom of tank with layer of sand or gravel about one inch deep. (Ocean sand will kill plants.) Then a layer of charcoal for good drainage. Then a two or three inch layer of rich loamy soil dug from the woods. Shape the soil into hulls and valleys with a high and dry area at one end of the tank. Rocks and stones can be added to build little ledges and caves to give shy creatures a dark, damp place to hide. At the low end, dig an excavation and install a pond. A shallow black enameled baking dish about 6 or 8 inches square is about the right size. Cover the bottom with dark pebbles and fill with water to a depth of about two inches. It is important for the pond to have a dark bottom so the animals can see and recognize the water. Even in a watertight aquarium tank, the pond should be a separate unit so it is easily removed for cleaning and freshening the water.

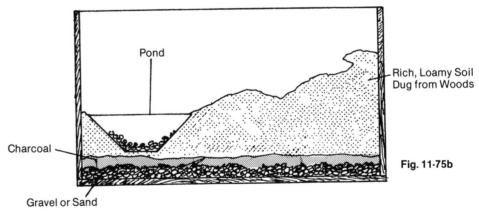

Fig. 11-75b

76. *FOOD FOR TERRARIUM TENANTS:* Newts, salamanders, baby turtles, mud puppies, tadpoles, crayfish eat: tiny bits of raw meat or fish, small worms, bits of raw oyster,

chopped up scrambled egg.

Frogs, toads, chameleons eat: live flies, mealy bugs, meal worms.

Minnows and fresh water fingerlings eat: earthworms, cooked meat, scraps, slugs, lettuce, apples, cabbage.

Snakes and lizards eat: live salamanders, toads, insects dangled on a string (don't keep small amphibians in the same cage with snakes and lizards).

Water

77. *CAPILLARY ACTION:* Stand two glasses side by side. Fill one with water. Cut a strip about an inch wide from an old bath towel. Put one end in one glass and the other in another glass. Let them stand overnight. Water will travel slowly through cloth from one glass to the other. Put a stalk of celery in water, iodine or colored water, and watch the water go up the stalk.

78. *DISSOLUTION:* Hot water dissolves things faster than cold water. To test this, put one teaspoon of sugar in one glass and stir; the sugar dissolves. Pour one glass of water in a pan. Heat the water, then pour the water back into the glass and put one teaspoon of sugar into the hot water. The sugar dissolves much faster in the hot water than the cold water. Fold paper into a cone so there is no opening at the bottom. Pour a little sugar into the cone. Touch the underside of the cone and then taste your fingers. Do you taste sugar? Dry sugar cannot pass through paper. Now pour a little water into the cone. As water soaks through, catch a few drops and taste them. Do they taste sweet? Can sugar and water pass through paper?

79. *HOW WET IS WATER?* Test wetting power of water by dipping piece of thick yarn into clear water, and another into soapy water. After a few seconds take the yarn out and pull the strands apart. Are both pieces wet through to the same extent? Now collect materials of different substances: cotton, nylon, wool, plastic, wood and metal. Using an eye dropper, place a drop of water on each. Does the drop look the same on each? Test again with soapy water. Has the addition of soap changed the shape of the drops and effectiveness of the water's ability to penetrate a material?

80. *TEMPERATURE EXPERIMENT:* Use an ordinary house thermometer. Hang it outdoors in a shady spot. An ideal place is on a post three to five feet above the ground. Daily temperature recordings should be made in the shade. To compare shade and sun temperatures set a second thermometer in a sunny spot.

81. *HOT PEPPER:* See and feel a hot pepper. It doesn't feel hot (SENSORY) or look hot. Now cut the pepper in half and ask the children to touch the cut end of the pepper with their tongues. Heat is felt in taste as well as touch.

82. *HUMIDITY:* Use a wet bulb thermometer (medical or house thermometer). Roll a piece of wet cotton cloth around the bulb and let the end of the cloth hang down into a can of water. The cloth acts as a wick (capillary). Keep the can filled. Place this wet bulb thermometer near a regular dry bulb thermometer. Record daily readings from both. When water evaporates, heat is lowered. The water in the cloth will continue to evaporate as long as the air can hold water. During dry conditions there will be a greater difference between the two readings. On humid days less difference. When the two temperatures are the same, humidity is 100%

83. *HOT—COLD—WARM:* Place three bowls on table. Place each hand in hot and cold bowls—leave for a few moments. Plunge BOTH hands into warm water—what do you feel? Our sense of touch can mislead us.

84. *COIN ON AN ICE CUBE:* Place a coin on an ice cube. It will melt its impression into the ice. It is warmer than the ice—the ice ABSORBS the heat.

85. *SPECIAL DAYS*—Special days planned around themes, such as concepts, foreign cultures and holidays, add sparkle and fun as they interrupt routine with a healthy serving of nonsense and spontaneity.

86. *BACKWARDS DAY:* Everyone wears clothing backwards, and walks backwards; the daily order of activities is done in reverse starting with a closing sing and bidding everyone 'goodbye.' Games include backwards races, meals begin with dessert, stories are read and told from end to start. A special treat would be a film shown backwards. (Public libraries often have films on loan.)

87. *TELEVISION DAY:* The school becomes a television studio with scenery, cameras, screens, props and costumes. Children take turns producing shows. This idea can be combined with a talent show. Children migh make up 'ads' to sell a favorite toy or game. Some might read favorite picture books or use them as a basis for plays. A news program tells of events past and future at the school. You might also want to contact a local television station to arrange a tour, and perhaps even a visit to the school of one of their well-known local announcers or personalities. (See Seq. 10, #9, 10, 11, 12.)

88. *ROCKET DAY:* Slides, books and pictures help to tell the story of the launchings of real rockets at Cape Canaveral. (NASA via the United States Government Printing Office has many useful materials.) Children make rockets and other space-related materials. Astronaut helmets, jump suits and hard hats serve as costumes. (See Seq. 3, Act. #86-94.)

89. *PUPPET DAY:* The children make puppets from old socks, paper bags, cardboard boxes; and finger puppets from small paper tubes, plastic bottles and painted bottle caps. Puppet shows are presented as children take turns reading or telling stories with puppets, or telling each other private stories through puppet conversations. (For puppet suggestions, see Props and Visual Aids.)

90. *PAINTING DAY:* Materials are set up in each area for every kind of painting (described in the Painting section). Children might try as many of the materials as they wish. This day might lead into an Art Show or Sale of Art, using play money, or an Art Swap or perhaps a special visiting day for parents. You might serve juice in plastic stem glasses at a 'reception' for the artists who might wish to dress 'formally' in the clothes from the dress-up collection.

91. *STORYBOOK DAY:* Children dress as characters in story books (see Instant Costumes, Seq. 3, #9) and combine talents to act out dramatic productions which are rehearsed during the morning and produced during the afternoon at a Story Book Fair. Such an event might also include a book sale for children's books arranged by a parent group as a fund raising project. In one school, an election campaign for MY FAVORITE BOOK was held during the weeks preceding the day. Children voted for their favorite books and made posters, puppets, banners, and costumes as campaign aids. The leading favorites were used as the basis for placing book orders for the sale.

92. *BOX DAY:* Children were told, in advance, to bring boxes and tubes of all sizes. This is especially appropriate during December vacation when households are overloaded with these items. Glue, staples, paste, and a good supply of elegant junk—a whole day was spent making creations of wondrous sizes and appearances, ingenious and inventive. (It should be decided, in advance, what will happen to a project worked on by several children!) (See Seq. 3, #51, and Seq. 7, #109.)

93. *SERENDIPITY DAY:* The dictionary says this means, "the faculty for making wonderful discoveries in unusual places." An aura of mystery was created in advance. Treasure hunts, scavenger hunts, hidden surprise supplies for a fun project were discovered through a series of clues.

A piñata was constructed, filled with goodies, and broken open at a party later that day.

The success will depend on the ability of the staff to build anticipation and maintain suspense throughout the day, holding back surprises for different parts of the day. "You could never possibly guess what 'serendipitous surprise' we will have when the clock strikes three." Most schools won't have a striking clock but a cymbal, triangle, alarm clock or chime will serve. The surprise for four o'clock is eating something and making something at the same time. The children make figures with tiny marshmallows, cereal and raisins.

94. *PEANUT DAY:* The children had a peanut hunt. They made peanut shell puppets, peanut men and animals. The teacher put out ads for Planters' Peanuts on a table for cutting and mounting. Some children made peanut butter using a food mill. Others made paper from peanut shells (see Seq. 9, Act. #51). Younger children used peanut shells to fill in outlined shapes on paper (animals, etc.).

95. *TOY SWAP DAY:* In one school, children brought in toys and swapped for a day. This activity needed careful supervision but was very successful and taught a valuable lesson in sharing.

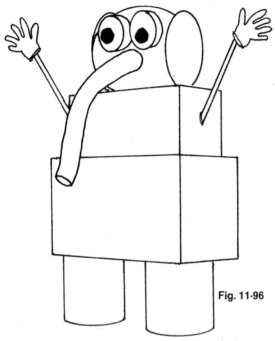

Fig. 11-96

96. *HORRIBLE CREATURES DAY:* Children work in groups to create huge dragons, "Heffalumps" (see *Winnie the Pooh*, Milne), 'Elphanuts' and miniature monsters and wiggly creatures; using boxes, large pieces of styrofoam, cloth, egg cup sections for scaly skin, wires and twisties as antennae, etc. Many of these larger creatures might be large enough to play inside.

This is a good time to hold discussions about scary things, make believe, and to talk about fears, and to clear up misconceptions which may be causing fears. (See Seq. 2, #13, Some Thoughts About Hallowe'en for the Very Young.)

97. *MUSIC AND DANCE DAY:* Invite instrumentalists to come and give simple demonstrations on their various instruments and perhaps come together to play some songs and dances for the children at a concert. Older children who can play instruments will be an excellent resource. Sing along, have folk jamborees, and creative dance sessions throughout the day.

Many local folk dance leaders give simple demonstrations and lead sessions for the very young.

Whenever practical, if children can try out some of the instruments it adds to their experiences. Use homemade instruments of all kinds in creative movement and rhythm demonstrations. Use recordings and experiment with sounds in a 'laboratory'—perhaps a glass harmonica made up of tuned bottles or glasses filled with water. Laboratories might be set up according to themes, such as MUSIC MADE WITH AIR (wind instruments), MUSIC MADE BY SHAKING THINGS (Maracas), MUSIC MADE BY STRIKING THINGS (Drums), etc.

98. *CARNIVAL DAY:* The children make popcorn, popsicles, paper hats of various styles decorated with streamers, feathers and paper flowers. They have their faces decorated as clowns or other characters. Special tents might be set up for simple games (parents might offer camping tents). Game booths can be made from large cardboard boxes and decorated. The atmosphere can be enhanced by playing records of circus or organ grinder music. (See Games, this Sequence, for ideas.) (See Seq. 10, #22—Mini-Circus; also #52, 53, 54, 55, 56 and 61.)

99. *PIRATES DAY:* Eye patches, paper swords and kerchiefs serve as simple pirate costumes. Pirate ships are large boxes with sails, seat blocks set up in rows, overturned tables with sails attached to the legs. Children love to 'walk the plank' and jump into piles of hay, sand or leaves. A treasure hunt with picture clues strung out around the playground and leading to a chest of gold-covered money candies will be a great climax. (Peter Pan recordings and story offer good background materials and extra entertainment.) Children will probably not be clear as to what real pirates really did, so stories and pictures about them will be necessary.

100. *COOKING DAY:* Use *Stone Soup* by Marcia Brown, pub. Scribner, as background for an entire day of preparing a super caldron of soup. If this can be cooked and served around an open fire, the day will be extra special. A vegetable soup from fresh vegetables, such as zucchini, celery, onions, carrots, potatoes, noodles, rice, spices, etc. will keep many hands busy chopping, paring and stirring. Another group might bake yeast breads to serve with the soup. If the children can shop for the ingredients, this will enrich their experience.

101. *PICNIC DAY:* Groups prepare picnic lunches and visit a variety of different places, either right on the school grounds or in the neighborhood or perhaps to a beach or playground. (See Field Trips.) A picnic to the home of a staff member will be a special treat and even a picnic on the floor of the block room on a blanket and much make believe about sand, surf and swimming, will be a treat. If groups go to various places on the same day, they might return and each take turns telling of their particular adventures during a

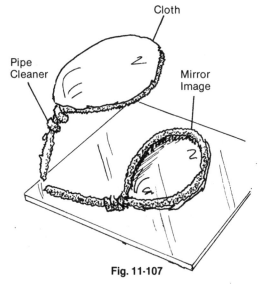

Cloth

Pipe
Cleaner

Mirror
Image

Fig. 11-107

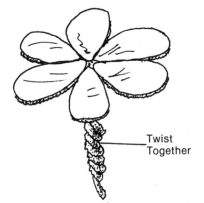

Twist
Together

closing group meeting.

102. *ARTS AND CRAFTS:* There are numerous books available on Arts and Crafts, many are listed in our bibliography which we have found to be especially useful; therefore, we have included only a few, very simple ideas which have been successful and in many cases originated within our schools. These ideas added to the many already given throughout the previous sequences should provide ample stimulation for you to offer a good program of arts and crafts to your own youngsters.

The important thing to keep in mind, in our view, is that kits and samples used to encourage carbon copies or simple, put-together-in-a-certain-way 'creations' have no place in a program for young children. We *do not* encourage samples or models of the adult's version or expectations of a project. We *do* encourage the personal expression of each child as he uses the materials in his very own way. The teacher might expect or want to get a dog from the bits of cloth, buttons and pipe cleaners offered—the child might create "a giraffe holding a blue umbrella on top of a high mountain." (!) Therein lies the FUN of art projects (indeed, in all of teaching)—the *joy of the child as he uses materials* to create a totally unexpected response.

103. *ALLIGATOR BOTTLES:* Children tear bits of masking tape and stick in overlapping pattern over the entire surface of a bottle, jar or can, then rub shoe polish to finish the surface. The result is an authentic looking "alligator" texture. The finished products will serve as candle holders, pencil containers, vases, etc.

104. *DESIGN PLAQUES:* Create 3-D designs by winding telephone wire and threads around nails driven in small boards.

105. *BOTTLE VASES AND CANDLE HOLDERS:* Use bottles and cans to create candle holders by winding yarn and string, dipped in white glue and painted on container. Shellac after drying.

106. *PLASTER PINS AND HANG-UPS:* Drop thin plaster of Paris (as drop cookies) onto waxed paper. Insert eyelet hangers or safety pin backs. When plaster hardens, decorate with acrylic paints.

107. *CLOTH FLOWERS:* Bend four to six pipe cleaners into petal shape, leaving about one inch at point to twist petals together. Glue each to bright cloth. Cut off edges. Twist petals together into flower.

108. *SCAVENGER HUNT WITH NATURAL OBJECTS:* Make up a list of eight to ten natural things known to be in the area. (Pine cones, acorns, shells, cattails, white pebbles.) Send children out to find. Return and create art plaques and designs from objects (people, animals, pictogram stories, sorting games, etc.)

109. *SHINGLE COLLAGES:* Glue natural objects to swatches of wooden shingles and varnish over. Pieces of bark (do not tear from trees) or dark corkboard can also be used.

110. *ANIMALS AND PEOPLE FROM NATURAL OBJECTS:* Create animals and people from natural objects, such as pine cones, acorns, pine spills, oak galls, grass and pebbles. (See also #116 and 12)

111. *SPATTER AND SPRAY PAINT:* Arrange ferns, flowers and leaves on paper. Spatter paint, dry, and remove objects.

112. *WOVEN MATS:* Weave mats and wall hangings with grasses.

BEANBAGS: See ideas in Games Section of this Sequence.

113. *STYROFOAM PRINTS:* Press-carve a design into the smooth bottom of a styofoam meat tray. Paint over with water soluble printer's ink. Lay paper on top and lift off prints.

114. *MIXING COLORS TO MATCH NATURAL OBJECTS:* Collect a variety of natural color samples, leaves, flowers, bark, stones, etc. Mount objects of like color range on cardboard panels. Divide into teams (reds, blues, greens, browns) and mix paints to match the natural objects.

115. *POTATO PEOPLE:* (See Seq. 7, #120)

116. *BERRY AND TWIG FIGURES:* Stick figures and tiny furniture may be made from a variety of berries and thin twigs or dried fern stems. Cranberries lend themselves especially well to this type of work. Cut the twigs the desired length and string the berries on the sticks. To hold the sticks together at the corners, use a berry to serve as a joint. The corners will be strengthened as the berries dry. Peas and toothpicks may be used instead of berries and twigs. To thread the peas, pierce them with a needle.

117. *FEATHER ART:* Fasten a collection of feathers to sheets of colored paper with transparent tape to make pictures. Make a feather album by inserting feathers in plastic envelopes and bind them in a loose leaf book, identify and label, using a bird book. The best time to look for feathers is late summer when most birds molt.

118. *QUILL PEN:* Slice the end of the quill diagonally from the underside. Sharpen the point, then make a short cut through the center of the point. Use feathers also as paint brushes.

119. *LACQUERED MÂCHÉ BOXES:* The Shakers of early America were known for their creativity and ingenuity. Lacquered mache boxes were one of the many useful items they created.

Paint newspaper with a thin layer of wallpaper paste or thinned white glue. Press paper over a form which has been rubbed with a thin coating of petroleum jelly. Use bottles, cans, plastic containers, wood blocks as forms. When first layer has dried, apply a second. Continue adding several layers, allowing to dry each time. Remove the form, paint and decorate and lacquer the mâche.

120. *BOTTLE ART:* Press designs into mud or wet sand, using the bottom of a bottle. Fill forms with paster of Paris, add feathers, pebbles and other natural materials. When dry, remove castings, paint and decorate to create 3-D plaques.

121. *ACORN PEOPLE:* From clothespins and acorns and circles or squares of cloth with a slit cut in the center which slips over the head of the doll.

122. *RAINY DAYS CAN BE THE BEST:* During training sessions for summer programs which stress outside activities, it is well to devote a special session to discussion of rainy day days, with emphasis on attitudes and a demonstration and planning of some special ideas. What activities can continue as usual? Which will be postponed? What and where will equipment be kept for use during the rain?

The success of a rainy day will depend on two factors, *attitude and preparation.* Teachers and counselors first make certain that everyone keeps dry and warm, knowing that disposition will be related to comfort and that weather has little effect upon the enthusiasm and exuberance of children.

The teacher who has been faced with innumerable yellow slickers and hats and as many pairs of unmarked rubbers, will provide marking pencils or pens with instructions for counselors to inspect each article as it is taken off, marking where necessary. A snap clothespin for every child, also with a name on it, will help to keep rubbers together. Decorating these clothespins could be an early crafts project and help the children to recognize their own. If the group moves from one building to another, the clothespin should go along in the raincoat pocket. Teachers/counselors, too, need to be reminded of the necessity for keeping warm and dry *all* day. An extra pair of socks and dungarees may be as necessary for them as for the campers. Emergency raincoats can be made from polyethylene, cut into four foot squares with a slit in the center as a neck hole.

Dry outdoor shelter can be extended by making polyethylene tents. These should be taken down when the weather clears. Using these shelters only on rainy days makes them a special treat.

Everyone is encouraged to greet a rainy day with the spirit of adventure! Suggestions follow for activities *in the rain or inside out of the rain!* (See also Seq. 8, #33-48)

123. *FROG HUNT:* (Easier to find them in the rain) Divide into teams to count the most found.

124. *WONDER BALL:* Children stand in a line, one behind the other with legs apart. First in line tries to roll the ball through their legs. Line tries to keep the ball from getting through.

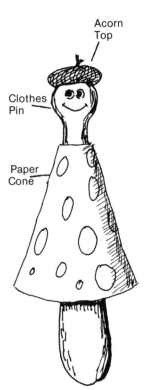

Acorn Top

Clothes Pin

Paper Cone

Fig. 11-121

125. *BLOCK TOWERS:* Children sit in a circle around a pile of blocks. Each in turn adds one block to a tower. When the tower falls everybody claps and the tower is started all over again. Older children form two teams facing each other and each team member takes a turn at adding a block. When the tower falls, opposite team takes all the blocks used. When all the blocks are on one side that team wins.

126. *STACKING STRAWS:* Plastic straws are stacked two at a time (alternating directions each time) on top of a wide mouthed jar.

127. *TOOTHPICK STACKING:* Toothpicks are stacked (as above) on top of a small mouth bottle.

128. *TIE DYEING:* Use sheets, T shirts or old dress shirts to create costumes with tie-dyed designs. (See Tie Dyeing)

129. *DRAMATIZE NURSERY RHYMES, POEMS AND SONGS:* Use puppets and props.

130. *FOLK DAYS:* Emphasize a particular culture (or theme) by showing slides, wearing costumes, sampling foods, reading stories based on the culture.

131. *FLAGS AND BANNERS:* Make a large banner to identify the group and small flags to match for each child.

132. *TRAILS:* Divide into two groups. One group makes a trail using pebbles or blocks (or other small objects) and hides at the end of the trail. Second group follows the trail to find the first.

133. *SCAVENGER HUNT:* Paste or draw five to ten pictures of familiar objects found in the building (use words for readers) onto individual cards. Child finds the object on his card. Can also work in teams of two or more.

134. *RELAY RACES:* Put two piles of magazines in front of two teams. Leader calls out the name of a familiar object. First child in each line hunts through the magazines for the object. First one to find it wins a point for the team. Vary the game for younger children by pasting the pictures onto oak tag and placing them in two boxes. Child finds the picture in the box. Lotto card sets will be a resource for these pictures.

135. *PAPER CUP SCULPTURES:* Rinse out used cups and staple or glue together into a large sculpture. Paint inside and outside of the cups. Hang as a mobile or mount on a large sheet of cardboard.

137. *DRESS UP:* This is a good time for staff to search through costumes and dress up in outlandish outfits; a derby hat and a pair of shorts; red flannel ski pajamas; or a Peter Pan hat with a rakish feather. Children, too, can spend happy hours with a few costume accessories. Crepe paper can be used to make paper costumes. (See #143)

138. *MAKE UP:* Each child is made up as a different character part and the group is challenged to make up and produce a short play.

139. *COOKING:* The very youngest children can make uncooked pudding in paper cups. They may be eaten for dessert or saved for a special party after rest. Popping corn with an old fashioned hand popper is fun or it can be done over a charcoal fire, under a shelter. Cookies or cakes can be baked utilizing and indoor or outdoor fireplace with a reflector oven.

140. *ICE CREAM:* Making ice cream with an old fashioned hand freezer and rock salt is usually a new experience for most children. (See Seq. 9, #98)

141. *PARTIES:* Planning in the morning for a special party to take place in the afternoon can provide enough ideas for a full day's program. Children are intrigued by a Halloween, Christmas or Valentine party out of season. Making invitations, decorations, favors, refreshments and entertainment all help to make the day a busy and interesting one. An "Unbirthday" party can be a traditional rainy day event.

142. *SELF PORTRAITS:* The child lies down on a large sheet of brown paper while another child or teacher draws around him. He fills in the details of hair, face and clothing with crayons or paint. They may be hung in a gallery and other groups invited to identify them.

143. *SILLY SKITS:* (See #149)

Counselors dramatize nursery rhymes—children guess which one. (Use a few props and costumes)

Blindfold two counselors and have them put makeup on each other.

One counselor hits another in face with pie made with paper plate and shaving cream.

Counselors dress as clowns, painted and dressed in any funny clothes—women for men, hobo, etc. Do a few silly actions—carrying a pail of water and chasing each other. One finally throws contents of pail on the audience, confetti has been substituted for water when audience was not aware.

Small counselors on shoulders of larger counselors, who are blindfolded. Riders armed with rolled up newspapers, guide horses and fight opponents.

MAGICIAN makes up story about making water burn and drops a concealed cake of dry ice in bucket which creates smoke-like reaction.

Counselor comes into barber shop and asks for shampoo. Barber says, "Your hair is in bad shape. Better have one of my special shampoos." Breaks egg on head, adds ketchup and powder.

144. *INDOOR CARNIVAL:* Preparing for a carnival can be as much fun as the actual event. The word suggest color, music and gaiety. A supply of flags, bunting, crepe paper streamers, pennants and other decorations will create a festive atmosphere. Roofing buttons (tin discs which can be purchased by the pound from building supply houses), may be used for money or awards which can later be redeemed for more tangible prizes. Beans, pebbles, buttons can also be used as money.

145. *GAMES OF CHANCE FOR CHILDREN:* (See also Games #155-159)

Pitching tennis balls into a large tin can set on the floor or fastened to a pole.

Ping-pong balls rolled into a muffin tin set on a slant.

Clothespins dropped into a wide mouthed bottle.

Pennies or buttons tossed onto numbered saucers floating in a tub of water.

Wet sponges thrown at the face of a child or counselor who puts his head through a hole in a sheet.

A nail pounded into a block of wood in fewest blows possible.

Jar rubbers thrown onto a board with numbered cup hooks.

A flame of candle put out with water pistol.

Shaving a balloon.

146. *INDOOR TRACK MEET:*

Shot put with balloons or blown up paper bags.

High jump from standing position with broom stick.

Broad jump from standing position.

Javelin throw with drinking straws.

Discuss throw with paper plates.

Standing broad grin—measure width of grins.

Running high whistle—time length of sustained whistle.

Feather blow relay—blow a feather 25 ft. using relay teams.

Foot race—measure combined length of both feet.

Jumping over a broomstick held in both hands.

147. *GAMES:* One of the most valuable resources a teacher/counselor can have is a variety of games suited to every occasion. Quiet games for small spaces, active games for cool days when swimming is out of the question, sit down games for hot days when active children are content to sit under a tree, games which can be used to fill in waiting periods, games which develop the senses and increase awareness, and games just for fun.

There are many excellent books of games available but when the game is needed it should be in the counselor's head, not on the library shelf. Enthusiasm will be lost if the counselor has to hunt for an idea.

During the training period a game session will help to stimulate more ideas. In playing games with children, the following simple suggestions may be kept in mind:

a. Know the play interests or abilities of your group. When deciding which game to introduce, consider temperature, space, size of group, age and skill of players, time of day, mood of group.

b. Get group into game formation. Start with few directions. Then stop and explain.

Learn by doing.

c. Know the game and the rules, song if used and the skills needed. Know an easy way to play as well as ways to make a game progressively harder, depending on ages.

d. Watch for signs of fatigue and restlessness. Rest the group by alternating active and quiet games.

e. Play game only as long as it holds interest of the group.

f. Introduce a variety of games to group so each child may succeed. For example, games which require skills a child does not have causes frustration and lack of interest.

g. Be absolutely *FAIR*.

h. Stress *cooperation not competition*. Competition limits happiness and success to a few.

i. Avoid elimination games. Slow children are always elminated first and they are the ones who need to play and develop skills.

j. Do not spoil the fun of playing games by granting special privileges, making unfair decisions, or using one person as the butt of a joke.

148. *COLLECTIONS:* Children and counselors can share their special interests. A collection of bells, dolls, miniature animals, stamps, or other items can be carried from one small group to another, or six or eight displays might be set up in one large room. Articles which can be handled will be more satisfactory to children than those which can only be viewed, but both have their place.

149. *TRAVELING SHOWS:* (See #143.) Short skits, plays, puppet shows, marionette shows, shadow box shows or flannel board stories, can travel from one group to another, providing entertainment for the performers as well as the audience. The preparations for these might start at the beginning of the summer, as a major project, or they may be planned and rehearsed in the morning for an afternoon performance. A counselor who plays a musical instrument might go about as a wandering minstrel, playing a few numbers at each stop. These traveling shows give the children a delightful feeling of suspense, since they never know what treat is in store.

150. *WALKING AND LISTENING TO THE RAIN:* Go for a walk in the rain. Return to shelter and sit in a circle. The children close their eyes and pretend they are in a forest. Each in turn describes what he saw there. Children open eyes. The leader then helps the group to recreate the sounds of rain (a storm) coming to the forest and receding. Begin by rubbing hands together and then through eye contact tells each one in turn (going around the circle), when to begin the same motion. When·all are included, the leader adds a second motion (finger snapping), when all are again included a third motion is added (foot thumping). When all are in and the storm is very noisy, the leader begins to take away the motions until all has quieted and the storm is over. (Various rhythm instruments can be added to create new sounds.)

151. *BEANBAGS:* Use scrap materials, odd mittens, old cloth napkins, etc. Cut them into different geometric shapes and in different colors (coded perhaps to match target boxes—see below). Decorate beanbags with crayon, magic marker, applique or embroidery. Cut out two identical squares of fabric, slightly larger than you want your bean bag to be. Stitch it (inside out) using tiny stitches, all the way around, leaving a small opening for filling. Turn the bag inside out and fill it two thirds full of dried beans, rice or tiny pebbles.

152. *BEANBAG SHAPE TOSS:* Make three beanbags, a square, a circle, a triangle. Cut corresponding shapes out of the bottom of a cardboard carton. Decorate the carton with paint, crayon, collage, etc. Place the target box on the floor or on a table against the wall. Put a piece of masking tape on the floor as a marker from which the child will throw the beanbags. Child tries to throw the shaped beanbag into the corresponding shaped hole. The target box should be secured to the floor or table.

153. *BEANBAG TIC TAC TOE:* Make five beanbags in each of two colors. Lay out a large tic-tac-toe board in masking tape on the floor or large sheet of cardboard or masonite. Two children stand behind a tape marker at some distance from the board. The first child to pitch three of his color in a row, wins the game.

154. *STUFFED BAG TARGETS:* Sew colorful targets on the front of two or three large cloth or paper bags. Fill them with foam rubber or fabric scraps and tie up the opeining

securely. Hang the bags at various heights. Toss beanbags at them from behind a tape marker. Score higher for targets that are hung higher or at a greater distance. Add bells of different sizes to the targets so that the chldren may distinguish between the tones.

155. *TOSS SCOOPS:* For use in tossing soft balls and beanbags. Take a shoe box and cut it in half at an angle as shown in illustration. Glue a wooden ruler or flat stick to the bottom of the box, with half of it extending for the handle. Wrap end of handle with tape to cover sharp edges. Cut two pieces of cardboard from the other half of the box to reinforce the inside and bottom of the scoop. Glue these securely, over the ruler, and reinforce with staples as close to the ruler as possible. Suspend tin pie pans and other targets which will make interesting sounds when struck by a tossed bean bag or ball, such as silverware, cardboard, wood, tin cans, milk cartons or bells.

Index

Suggested Readings

Alexander and the Terrible Horrible No Good Day, Voight; Atheneum, 1972
Angus and the Ducks, Marjorie Flack; Doubleday
Ask Mr. Bear, Flack; MacMillan
Behavior and Misbehavior, James Hymes; Prentice-Hall
Big Book of Real Trains, Zaffo; Grosset
Black Is Beautiful, Ann McGovern; Scholastic
Black Is Brown Is Tan, Arnold Adoff; Harper-Row, 1973
Block Book, Elizabeth Hirsch; National Association of Childhood Education, 1974
Blocks, a Tool of Learning, Adele Franklin; Bank St. College
Caps for Sale, Esphyr Slobodkina; Young Scott
Carrot Seed, Kraus; Gryphon
Children Discover Music and Dance, Emma D. Sheehy; Teachers College
Children Today, Dept. H.E.W.; U.S. Government Printing Office, Washington, D.C. 20402 (6 issues a year)
Conspiracy Against Childhood, Eda LaShan; Atheneum
Creative Movement for the Developing Child: School Handbook for Non-Musicians, Clare Cherry; Fearon
Curriculum Is What Happens, Laura Ditmann; N.A.E.Y.C., 1970
Day Camp Program Book, Musselman; Associated Press, N.Y.
Early Years Magazine, Monthly, September through May; P.O. Box 1223, Darien, Conn. 06820
Elephant's Child, Rudyard Kipling; Walker and Co., 1970
Eskimo's Knew, The, Levine; McGraw
Explaining Death to Children, Earl A. Grollman; Beacon Press
Finger Plays and Action Rhymes, Frances Jacobs; Lothrop
Finger Plays for Nursery and Kindergarten, Emillie Poulsson; Dover
Fireside Book of Children's Songs, Ed. By Winn and Miller; Simon & Shuster
Fun with Naturecraft, Nagle and Leeming; Lippincott
Giant Book of Things in Space, George Zaffo; Doubleday, 1969
Gilberto and the Wind, Ets; Gryphon
Goggles, Keats; MacMillan
Grownups Cry Too, Nancy Hazer; Lollipop-Power, 1973
Guidance Nursery Schook, Pticher-Amers; Harper-Row
Guide to Discipline, A, N.A.E.Y.C.
Helping Young Children Learn, Pitcher, Lasher, Feinburg, Hammond; Charles Merrill
Hospital Story, Sarah B. Stein; Walker and Co., 1974
How to Raise a Brighter Child, Joan Beck; Trident
How to Survive Parenthood, Eda LaShan; Warner Books
I'll Fix Anthony, Judith Vorst; Harper-Row, 1969
Indians Knew, The, Levine and Pine; McGraw Hill
Insects, Golden Books
Just So Stories, Rudyard Kipling; Doubleday
Katy and the Big Snow, Virginia Lee Burton; Houghton-Mifflin
Kids Are Natural Cooks, The Parents Nursery School; Houghton-Mifflin
Lap to Sit On, A, —and Much More; Assoc. Childhood Ed. Int., 1971
Magic Years, The, Selma Frailberg; Scribner
Make Way for Ducklings, Robert McCloskey; Viking
Making Music Your Own, Silver Burdett
Meet Martin Luther King; Random House
Mike Mulligan and His Steam Shovel, Virginia Lee Burton; Houghton-Mifflin
Millions of Cats, Wanda Gag; Coward, 1938
Montessori in Perspective; N.A.E.Y.C.
Mousekin's Golden House, Edna Miller; Prentice-Hall, 1964
Mummies at Work, Eve Merriam; Scholastic, 1973
Iusic and Movement Improvisations: Vol. 4, Thresholds Early Learning Library, Miriam Stecher; MacMillan

My Dog Is Lost, Ezra Keats and Cherr; T.Y. Crowell
Native N'Creative, Stinsen; Cokesbury
New Neighbors, Ray Prather; McGraw, 1974
Nine Days to Christmas, Marie Hall Ets; Viking Press, 1959
Peter's Chair, Ezra Keats; Harper-Row
Poems to Grow On, Thompson; Beacon
Poems Young Children Will Sit Still For; Citation
Quiet Noisy Book, Margaret Wise Brown; Harper-Row
Ranger Rick's Nature Magazine; National Wildlife Federation, 1412 16th St. Washington, D.C. 20036
Revolution in Learning: The Years from Birth to Six, Maya Pines; Harper-Row
Run Away Bunny, Margaret Wise Brown; Harper, 1972
Stone Soup, Marcia Brown, Scribner, 1947
Story About Ping, Marjorie Flack, Viking Press, 1933
Snowy Day, Exra Keats; Viking Press, 1962
Teacher; One Fawcett Place, Greenwich, Conn. 06830
Teacher, Sylvia Ashton-Warner; Simon-Schuster
Teaching the Child under Six, James Hymes, Jr.; Chas. Merrill
Teaching Young Children, Evelyn Beyer; Pegasus
Thinking Is Child's Play, Evelyn Sharp; Avon
Told Under the Blue Embrella, A.C.E.I.; MacMillan
Umbrella, Tara Yashima, Viking Press
Water, Sand and Mud as Play Materials; Natl Assoc. Ed. Young Child.
What Mary Jo Shared, Janice Udry; Whitman, 1966
What Mary Jo Wanted, Janice Udry; Whitman, 1968
What's Inside the Egg?, May Garelick; Scholastic
When We Were Very Young, A.A. Milne; Dutton
Will I Have a Friend?, Miriam Cohen; MacMillan, 1967
William's Doll, Charlotte Zolotow; Harper-Row, 1972
Winnie the Pooh, A.A. Milne; Dutton
Wolf and the Raven: Totem Poles of Southwestern Alaska, Garfield and Forrest; U. Of Washington, 1948
You—How Your Body Works, Leslie McGuire; Platt, 1974